GRAMMAR

FOR THE WELL-TRAINED MIND

BLUE WORKBOOK

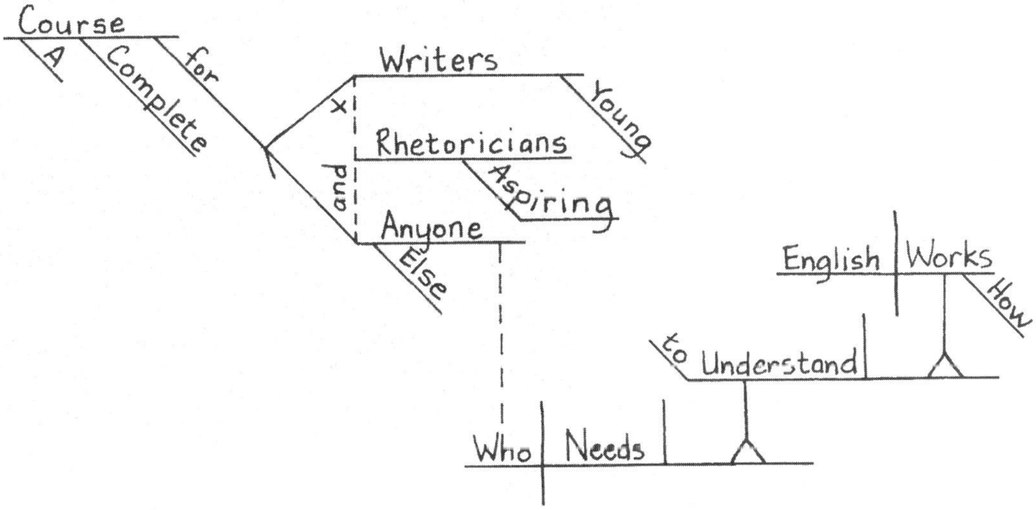

BY SUSAN WISE BAUER
WITH AMANDA SAXON DEAN AND AUDREY ANDERSON,
DIAGRAMS BY PATTY REBNE

LAYOUT AND DESIGN BY SHANNON ZADROZNY

WELL-TRAINED MIND PRESS

Photocopying and Distribution Policy
Please do not reproduce any part of this material on e-mail lists or websites.

For **families**: You may make as many photocopies from this book as you need for use WITHIN YOUR OWN FAMILY ONLY.

Schools and co-ops MAY NOT PHOTOCOPY any portion of this book without express written permission from Well-Trained Mind Press. To purchase a reprinting license, please contact Well-Trained Mind Press at support@welltrainedmind.com or at the phone number below. To purchase bulk quantities of this book, please contact Well-Trained Mind Press: e-mail order@welltrainedmind.com; phone 1.877.322.3445.

For a list of corrections, please visit **www.welltrainedmind.com/corrections**.

Address requests for permissions to make copies to support@welltrainedmind.com or call 1.877.322.3445.

TABLE OF CONTENTS

FOREWORD

Welcome to *Grammar for the Well-Trained Mind*!

This innovative grammar program will take you from basic definitions ("A noun is the name of a person, place, thing, or idea") all the way through detailed analysis of complex sentence structure. Once you complete it, you'll have all the skills needed for the study of advanced rhetoric—persuasive speech and sophisticated writing.

WHAT MAKES UP THE FULL PROGRAM

Grammar for the Well-Trained Mind is a four-year program. Once you've finished it, you will have a thorough grasp of the English language. No further grammar studies will be necessary.

The nonconsumable *Core Instructor Text* is used for each of the four years of the program. It contains scripted dialogue for the instructor, all rules and examples, and teaching notes that thoroughly explain ambiguities and difficulties.

There are four *Workbooks* with accompanying *Keys*. Each consumable workbook provides one full year of exercises and assignments. Each corresponding key gives complete, thoroughly explained answers. You should aim to complete one workbook during each of the four years of study.

All rules and definitions, with accompanying examples, have been assembled into a handy reference book, *The Grammar Guidebook*. This handbook will serve you for all four years of study—and will continue to be useful as you move through advanced high school writing, into college composition, and beyond.

HOW THE PROGRAM WORKS

Language learning has three elements.

First: You have to understand and memorize rules. We call this "prescriptive learning"—grasping the explicit principles that govern the English language and committing them to memory. *Grammar for the Well-Trained Mind* presents, explains, and drills all of the essential rules of the English language. Each year, you will review and repeat these rules.

Second: You need examples of every rule and principle ("descriptive learning"). Without examples, rules remain abstract. When you memorize the rule "Subjunctive verbs express situations that are unreal, wished for, or uncertain," you also need to memorize the example "I would not say such things if I were you!" Each year, you will review and repeat the same examples to illustrate each rule.

Third: You need *practice*. Although the four workbooks repeat the same rules and examples, each contains a completely new set of exercises and writing assignments, along with a *Key* providing complete answers.

The combination of *repetition* (the same rules and examples each year) and *innovation* (brand-new practice materials in every workbook) will lead you to complete mastery of the English language.

HOW TO USE GRAMMAR FOR THE WELL-TRAINED MIND

When you first use the program, begin with the *Core Instructor Text* and any one of the *Workbooks* with its accompanying *Key* (Purple, Red, etc). Keep *The Grammar Guidebook* on hand for reference.

During this first year, you won't necessarily grasp every principle thoroughly. Simply go through the dialogue with your instructor, complete the exercises, check the answers, and discuss any mistakes.

You may need more than one year to complete your first *Workbook*; the exercises increase in complexity and difficulty from Week 20 on. That's absolutely fine. Feel free to take as much time as necessary to finish this workbook.

When your first *Workbook* is completed, you and your instructor will go back to the beginning of the *Core Handbook* and start over, this time using a *Workbook/Key* combination of a different color. You'll go over the same dialogue, the same rules, and the same examples—with an entirely fresh set of exercises. This combination of repeated information along with new and challenging exercises will truly begin to build your competence in the English language.

Follow this same procedure for the third and fourth years of study, using workbooks of the remaining two colors, along with their matching keys.

Regular reviews are built into the program. Every three weeks, take some extra time to do the exercises reviewing what was covered in the three weeks before. After Week 27, the reviews double in scope: twelve exercises review the material all the way back to the beginning of the course. These reviews, beginning with Review 9, become one week's work each. During review weeks, try to do three exercises per day, and then go back and review the rules and principles of any exercise in which you miss two or more sentences/examples.

WHICH WORKBOOK?

Because each workbook makes use of the same rules and examples, you may use any one of the four workbooks during your first year in the program. It is highly recommended, however, that you then go back and finish the earlier workbooks as well. The program is designed to take four years, no matter where you begin.

IMPORTANT PRINCIPLES OF LEARNING

As you study, keep the following in mind.

- Language is a rich, complicated tapestry. It is occasionally logical, and sometimes irrational. Mastering its complexities takes time and patience. Don't expect to master—or even completely understand—every principle the first time through. Repetition and practice will eventually bring clarity. Be diligent—don't abandon the curriculum because of frustration! But accept occasional confusion as a natural part of learning. If you don't understand subjunctives the first time through, for example, accept it, move on, and then repeat the following year. Eventually, the concepts will come into focus.
- Always ask for help if you need it. This isn't a test. It's a learning process.

- From Week 19 (halfway through the course) on, you are encouraged to read sentences out loud. Reading out loud is an important part of evaluating your own writing. Follow the directions—don't ignore them and read silently.
- Take as long as you need to finish each lesson. As noted above, it's perfectly acceptable to take more than one year to finish a workbook (particularly the first time through). The earlier lessons are shorter and simpler; they increase in both complexity and length as the book goes on. But especially in the later lessons, don't worry if you need to divide a lesson over two days, or take more than one week to complete a week's worth of lessons. In subsequent years, you'll go much more quickly through the earlier lessons, giving you time to stop and concentrate on areas of challenge later on.

ABOUT DIAGRAMMING

Grammar for the Well-Trained Mind uses diagramming exercises throughout.

Diagramming is a learning process. Think of the diagrams as experimental projects, not tests. Attempt the diagram, look at the answer, and then try to figure out why any differences exist. Expect these assignments—particularly in the second half of the book—to be challenging. Ask for help when you need it. Always diagram with a pencil (or on a whiteboard or blackboard), and expect to erase and redo constantly.

Also remember that diagramming is not an exact science! If you can explain clearly why you've made a particular choice, the diagram might be correct even if the key differs. To quote a 1914 grammar text: "Many constructions are peculiar, idiomatic, and do not lend themselves readily to any arrangement of lines" (Alma Blount and Clark S. Northup, *An English Grammar for Use in High and Normal Schools and in Colleges*).

WEEK 1

Introduction to Nouns and Adjectives

— LESSON 1 —

Introduction to Nouns
Concrete and Abstract Nouns

A noun names a person, place, thing, or idea.
Concrete nouns can be observed with our senses. Abstract nouns cannot.

Exercise 1A: Abstract and Concrete Nouns

Decide whether the underlined nouns are abstract or concrete. Above each noun, write *A* for abstract or *C* for concrete. If you have difficulty, ask yourself: Can this noun be touched or seen, or experienced with another one of the senses? If so, it is a concrete noun. If not, it is abstract.

The sentences below are from Benjamin Franklin's *Poor Richard's Almanack*.

At the working man's house hunger looks in but dares not enter.

Trouble springs from idleness and grievous toil from needless ease.

A child and a fool imagine twenty shillings and twenty years can never be spent.

The wise man draws more advantage from his enemies than the fool from his friends.

Men and melons are hard to know.

Beware of little expenses; a small leak will sink a great ship.

There are lazy minds as well as lazy bodies.

Great beauty, great strength, and great riches are really and truly of no great use; a right heart exceeds all.

Employ thy time well, if thou meanest to gain leisure.

Exercise 1B: Using Concrete and Abstract Nouns

Identify each noun as concrete or abstract. Write a sentence that includes the given noun *and* at least one noun of the opposite type (so, if the given noun is a concrete noun, you must use it and also include an abstract noun of your choice).

Underline the additional noun in your sentence and label it as *C* for concrete or *A* for abstract. (It's fine to use more than one extra noun, but you only need to label one.)

The first is done for you.

	C or *A*?	Your Sentence
danger	A	Danger seemed to follow the lad (C) wherever he went.
hat		
melody		
reality		
anticipation		
potato		

— LESSON 2 —

Introduction to Adjectives
Descriptive Adjectives, Abstract Nouns
Formation of Abstract Nouns from Descriptive Adjectives

An adjective modifies a noun or pronoun.
Adjectives tell what kind, which one, how many, and whose.
Descriptive adjectives tell what kind.
A descriptive adjective becomes an abstract noun when you add *-ness* to it.

cheerful	cheerfulness
grumpy	grumpiness

Exercise 2A: Descriptive Adjectives, Concrete Nouns, and Abstract Nouns

Decide whether the underlined words are concrete nouns, abstract nouns, or descriptive adjectives. Above each, write *DA* for descriptive adjective, *CN* for concrete noun, or *AN* for abstract noun.

The sentences below were taken from *Mrs. Frisby and the Rats of NIMH*, by Robert C. O'Brien. Some have been slightly adapted.

A little later the last bit of wire disappeared behind them like a thin black snake, and Mrs. Frisby climbed down from the asparagus bush.

I had been in what is called a maze, a device to test intelligence and memory.

When Mrs. Frisby thought of the danger she would face in just a few more hours, she wanted to kiss her children all goodbye.

It was in the kitchen, near her cage, a small scuffling on the hard linoleum floor.

Some field mice find their way to barn lofts; some even creep into people's houses and live under the eaves or in attics, taking their chances with mousetraps.

He continued the training, with new words and new pictures every day; but the fact is, once we had grasped the idea and learned the different sounds each letter stood for, we leaped way ahead of him.

Exercise 2B: Descriptive Adjectives and Abstract Nouns

For each sentence, identify the underlined word as *DA* for descriptive adjective or *AN* for abstract noun. Then change the underlined word to the other form (adjective to noun or noun to adjective) and rewrite the sentence with the new form. You may rearrange, add, or subtract words as necessary to make a sensible sentence. Your new sentence doesn't have to match the original exactly in meaning, but it should be close.

The first is done for you.

AN

The store had a quaintness that made me smile.

The quaint store made me smile.

Amy is a lively child, isn't she?

____

I'm beginning to question the <u>usefulness</u> of this particular rule.

____

The <u>cloudiness</u> worried us on the morning of the picnic, but by noon the sky was clear.

____

Peter's <u>bashfulness</u> disappears the moment he steps on stage.

____

The manager was pleased to hear that he had such a <u>helpful</u> employee.

____

Exercise 2C: Color Names

Underline all the color words in the following sentences. Then write *A* for adjective or *N* for noun above each underlined color word.

These sentences are taken from L. Frank Baum's *The Marvelous Land of Oz*. Some have been slightly adapted.

The boy found several lines clearly written in red ink.

They soon regained the road of yellow brick.

She wore a costume that struck the boy as being remarkably brilliant: her silken waist being of emerald green and her skirt of four distinct colors—blue in front, yellow at the left side, red at the back and purple at the right side.

These flowers were almost blinding in their vivid hues of red and gold.

The powder sifted down from Jack's head and scattered over the red shirt and pink waistcoat and purple trousers Tip had dressed him in.

The front was striped with alternate bands of light brown and white, blending together at the edges.

He was clothed all in green and wore a high, peaked green hat upon his head and green spectacles over his eyes.

The tent of the Sorceress was larger than the others, and was composed of pure white silk, with scarlet banners flying above it.

— LESSON 3 —

Common and Proper Nouns
Capitalization and Punctuation of Proper Nouns

A common noun is a name common to many persons, places, things, or ideas.
A proper noun is the special, particular name for a person, place, thing, or idea.
Proper nouns always begin with capital letters.

Capitalization Rules

1. Capitalize the proper names of persons, places, things, and animals.

boy	Peter
store	Baskin-Robbins
book	*Little Women*
horse	Black Beauty

sea	Sea of Galilee
port	Port of Los Angeles
island	Isle of Skye

2. Capitalize the names of holidays.

Memorial Day
Christmas
Independence Day
Day of the Dead

3. Capitalize the names of deities.

Minerva (ancient Rome)
Hwanin (ancient Korea)
God (Christianity and Judaism)
Allah (Islam)
Gitche Manitou or Great Spirit (Native American—Algonquin)

4. Capitalize the days of the week and the months of the year, but not the seasons.

Monday	January	winter
Tuesday	April	spring
Friday	August	summer
Sunday	October	fall

5. Capitalize the first, last, and other important words in titles of books, magazines, newspapers, movies, television series, stories, poems, and songs.

book	*Alice's Adventures in Wonderland*
magazine	*National Geographic*
newspaper	*The Chicago Tribune*
movie	*A River Runs Through It*
television series	*The Waltons*

television show	"The Chicken Thief"
story	"The Visit of the Magi"
poem	"The Night Before Christmas"
song	"Joy to the World"
chapter in a book	"The End of the Story"

6. Capitalize and italicize the names of ships, trains, and planes.

ship	*Titanic*
train	*The Orient Express*
plane	*The Spirit of St. Louis*

Exercise 3A: Capitalizing Proper Nouns

Write a proper noun for each of the following common nouns. Don't forget to capitalize all of the important words of the proper noun. If the proper noun requires quotation marks, include them.

You may either write your answers below or use a computer. If you are handwriting your answers, underline any proper noun that should be italicized.

Common Noun	**Proper Noun**
television series	____________________
poem	____________________
newspaper	____________________
author	____________________
city	____________________
school	____________________

Exercise 3B: Proper Names and Titles

On your own paper, rewrite the following sentences properly. Capitalize and punctuate all names and titles correctly.

anna sewell wrote black beauty.

My favorite of robert frost's poems is stopping by woods on a snowy evening.

the miracle worker is a movie about anne sullivan, who was helen keller's teacher.

The words to take me out to the ball game were written by jack norworth.

The television show i love lucy began airing in october 1951.

Exercise 3C: Proofreading for Proper Nouns

In the following sentences, indicate which proper nouns should be capitalized by underlining the first letter of the noun three times. This is the proper proofreading mark for "capitalize." The first noun is done for you.

jackie robinson was born in cairo, georgia, in 1919.

robinson played second base for the brooklyn dodgers and was the first african american to play major league baseball in the modern era.

He was part of the team when the dodgers won the 1955 world series.

In 1962, robinson was inducted into the baseball hall of fame.

— LESSON 4 —

Proper Adjectives
Compound Adjectives (Adjective-Noun Combinations)

1. Capitalize the proper names of persons, places, things, and animals.
2. Capitalize the names of holidays.
3. Capitalize the names of deities.
4. Capitalize the days of the week and the months of the year, but not the seasons.
5. Capitalize the first, last, and other important words in titles of books, magazines, newspapers, movies, television series, stories, poems, and songs.
6. Capitalize and italicize the names of ships, trains, and planes.

A proper adjective is formed from a proper name. Proper adjectives are capitalized.

	Proper Noun	Proper Adjective
Person	Aristotle	the Aristotelian philosophy
Place	Spain	a Spanish city
Holiday	Valentine's Day	some Valentine candy
Month	March	March madness

Shakespeare wrote a number of sonnets.
I was reading some Shakespearean sonnets yesterday.

Mars is the fourth planet from the sun.
The Martian atmosphere is mostly carbon dioxide.

On Monday, I felt a little down.
I had the Monday blues.

The English enjoy a good cup of tea and a muffin.
Gerald enjoys a good English muffin.

The German-speaking tourists were lost in Central Park.
The archaeologist unearthed some pre-Columbian remains.

Words that are not usually capitalized remain lowercase even when they are attached to a proper adjective.

A compound adjective combines two words into a single adjective with a single meaning.

When the mine collapsed, it sent a plume of dust sky high.
I just had a thirty-minute study session.

N ADJ
sky high

ADJ N
thirty minute

N ADJ
user friendly

ADJ N
high speed

The sky-high plume of dust could be seen for miles.
My study session was thirty minutes.

Those directions are not user friendly!
I prefer user-friendly directions.

The connection was high speed.
He needed a high-speed connection.

Exercise 4A: Forming Proper Adjectives from Proper Nouns

Form adjectives from the following proper nouns. (Some will change form and others will not.) Write each adjective into the correct blank below. If you are not familiar with the proper nouns, you may look them up online on Encyclopaedia Britannica, Wikipedia, or some other source (this will help you complete the sentences as well). This exercise might challenge your general knowledge! (But you can always ask your instructor for help.)

April	Hungary	Aquinas	Maine	Augusta
Ptolemy	Chile	Songkran	Elizabeth	Spain

_______________________ goulash is one of my favorite comfort foods.

My sister thought it would be funny to take some ____________________ moss she found on the ground and put it on her head—until I informed her that it often has bugs in it!

The ____________________ flamingo, which is native to western and southern South America, can be distinguished from other species by its gray legs with pink joints.

In her argumentative essay, Kimberly supported an ____________________ position on lending money at interest.

Our picnic was ruined by one of those famous ____________________ showers.

For over 1500 years, astronomers used the ____________________ system, which places Earth at the center of the universe.

William Shakespeare penned his plays and poems during England's ______________ era.

The ____________________ National Golf Club, which hosts the Masters Tournament every spring, was founded by Bobby Jones and Clifford Roberts.

Held every August, the ____________________ Lobster Festival attracts visitors from around the world.

In the ____________________ Water Festival, the people of Thailand celebrate the new year with water fights.

Exercise 4B: Capitalization of Proper Adjectives

In the following sentences, correct each lowercase letter that should be capitalized by underlining it three times.

Then, underline each proper adjective. Finally, circle each proper adjective that has not changed its form from the proper noun.

hans janssen and his son zacharias were dutch spectacle makers who may have developed the first compound microscope.

esperanto, developed by a polish-jewish ophthalmologist named l. l. zamenhof, is a constructed language, but there are between 1000 and 2000 native esperanto speakers today.

a new york law in 1910 was the first north american law to require a license for driving a motor vehicle, but it only required this for professional chauffeurs.

jordan romero, an american mountain climber, is on record as the youngest person to complete a mount everest climb, having done so at the age of thirteen.

Exercise 4C: Hyphenating Attributive Compound Adjectives

Hyphens prevent misunderstanding! Explain to your instructor the differences between each pair of phrases. The first is done for you. If you're confused, ask your instructor for help.

heavy-metal detector
heavy metal detector

a heavy-metal detector detects heavy metals

a heavy metal detector detects all metal, and is heavy to carry (a heavy detector and a metal detector)

good-morning wave
good morning wave

slow-motion video
slow motion video

dog-friendly restaurant
dog friendly restaurant

grape-flavored medicine
grape flavored medicine

WEEK 2

Introduction to Personal Pronouns and Verbs

— LESSON 5 —

Noun Gender
Introduction to Personal Pronouns

Exercise 5A: Introduction to Noun Gender

How well do you know your animals? Fill in the blanks with the correct name (and don't worry too much if you don't know the answers . . . this is mostly for fun).

Animal	Male	Female	Baby	Group of Animals
bear	______	______	cub	sleuth OR sloth of bears
water buffalo	______	cow	______	______
mallard	______	______	duckling	______
ferret	______	______	kit	______
hare	______	doe	______	band OR down of hares
peafowl	______	peahen	______	______
raccoon	boar	______	cub	______
dolphin	bull	______	______	______

Nouns have gender.
Nouns can be masculine, feminine, or neuter.
We use *neuter* for nouns that have no gender, and for nouns whose gender is unknown.

Subha Datta set off for the forest, intending to come back the same evening. He began to cut down a tree, but he suddenly had a feeling that he was no longer alone. As it crashed to the ground, he looked up and saw a beautiful girl dancing around and around in a little clearing nearby. Subha Datta was astonished, and let the axe fall. The noise startled the dancer, and she stood still.

Subha Datta thought he was dreaming.

Although she did not yet know it, the fairy had not convinced Subha Datta.

A pronoun takes the place of a noun.
The antecedent is the noun that is replaced by the pronoun.
Personal pronouns replace specific nouns.

I	we
you	you (plural)
he, she, it	they

Exercise 5B: Nouns and Pronouns

Write the correct pronoun above the underlined word(s). The first is done for you.

he

After Thomas Edison invented the phonograph, Thomas Edison became known as the Wizard of Menlo Park.

Massachusetts legislators did not want Edison's invention of a device that would count their votes quickly; Massachusetts legislators wanted to be able to change their colleagues' minds before the votes were tallied.

Although Alexander Graham Bell invented the telephone, the telephone was not something Alexander Graham Bell particularly liked. Alexander Graham Bell refused to have a telephone in his study because a telephone would allow the outside world to interfere with the time Alexander Graham Bell spent thinking and working.

Mary Anderson invented the windshield wiper and was granted a patent in 1903, but Mary Anderson was unable to sell the rights to her invention. After the patent expired in 1920, automobile manufacturers began including windshield wipers; windshield wipers became standard equipment starting in 1922.

Margaret E. Knight invented a machine that would make flat-bottomed paper bags, but Margaret E. Knight had to file a lawsuit when her design was stolen and her patent was granted to the thief. Margaret E. Knight won the rights to her patent, and her patent allowed her to start up the Eastern Paper Bag Company.

Exercise 5C: Substituting Pronouns

The following passage is from a nineteenth-century translation of the Welsh myth cycle called the *Mabinogion*. The translation, made by Charlotte Guest, sounds a little bit stiff and formal to us, because it is over a hundred years old. But in this version, it sounds even odder because the pronouns *I*, *you*, *he*, *she*, *it*, *we*, and *they* have all been replaced by nouns.

Choose the nouns that can be replaced by pronouns, cross them (and any accompanying words such as "the") out, and write the appropriate pronouns above them.

You may also need to cross out and replace some verbs or helping verbs if necessary to maintain agreement.

So Gwalchmai and Peredur rode forth together joyfully towards the place where Arthur was; and when Kai saw them coming, Kai said, "I knew that Gwalchmai did not need to fight the knight. No wonder that Gwalchmai should gain fame; Gwalchmai can do more by his fair words, than Kai by the strength of my arm." And Peredur went with Gwalchmai to his tent, and Peredur and Gwalchmai took off their armour. And Peredur put on garments like those that Gwalchmai wore; and Peredur and Gwalchmai went together to Arthur, and saluted him.

"Behold, lord," said Gwalchmai, "him whom Arthur has sought so long."

"Welcome to Peredur, Peredur," said Arthur. "With me Peredur shall remain; and had Arthur known thy valour had been such, Peredur would not have left me as Peredur did. Nevertheless, this was predicted of Peredur by the dwarf and the dwarfess, whom Kai ill treated, and whom Peredur has avenged."

And hereupon, behold there came the Queen and her handmaidens, and Peredur saluted the Queen and her handmaidens. And the Queen and her handmaidens were rejoiced to see him, and bade him welcome. And Arthur did him great honour and respect, and Arthur, Peredur, Gwalchmai, Kai, and the Queen and her handmaidens returned towards Caerlleon.

Exercise 5D: Pronouns and Antecedents

Circle the personal pronouns in the following sentences, and draw an arrow from each pronoun to its antecedent. If the noun and pronoun are masculine, write *m* in the margin. If they are feminine, write *f*; if neuter, write *n*. Look carefully: Some sentences may have more than one personal pronoun, and some personal pronouns may share an antecedent! In addition, some antecedents may not actually appear in the sentences provided.

If the antecedent is the speaker or the listener, simply write "speaker" or "listener" above the pronoun. In such cases, if the gender of the noun and pronoun are unknown, write *u* in the margin.

These sentences are from *David Copperfield*, by Charles Dickens. Some have been slightly adapted.

The servant was seen along with—our poor girl—last night. He's been in hiding about here, this week or over.

Mr. Spenlow had stepped out, old Tiffey said, to get a gentleman sworn for a marriage license; but as I knew he would be back directly, our place lying close to the Surrogate's, and to the Vicar-General's office too, I told Peggoty to wait.

"Not, of course, but that Sophy is beautiful too in my eyes," said Traddles, "and would be one of the dearest girls that ever was, in anybody's eyes (I should think). But when I say the eldest is a Beauty, I mean she really is a—" he seemed to be describing clouds about himself, with both hands: "Splendid, you know," said Traddles, energetically.

This gave my aunt such unspeakable satisfaction, that I believe she took a delight in prowling up and down, with her bonnet insanely perched on the top of her head, at times when Mrs. Crupp was likely to be in the way.

"I found out an English gentleman as was in authority," said Mr. Peggotty, "and told him I was a going to see my niece. He got me them papers as I wanted fur to carry me through—I don't rightly know how they're called—and he would have given me money, but that I was thankful to have no need on."

I doubt whether two young birds could have known less about keeping house, than I and my pretty Dora did. We had a servant, of course. She kept house for us.

I made the toast on the usual infallible principles. When it was ready for my aunt, she was ready for it.

— LESSON 6 —

Review Definitions

Introduction to Verbs
Action Verbs, State-of-Being Verbs
Parts of Speech

A noun names a person, place, thing, or idea.
A common noun is a name common to many persons, places, things, or ideas.
Concrete nouns can be observed with our senses. Abstract nouns cannot.
An adjective modifies a noun or pronoun.
Adjectives tell what kind, which one, how many, and whose.
Descriptive adjectives tell what kind.
A descriptive adjective becomes an abstract noun when you add *-ness* to it.

A verb shows an action, shows a state of being, links two words together, or helps another verb.

Part of speech is a term that explains what a word does.

State-of-Being Verbs

am	were
is	be
are	being
was	been

Exercise 6A: Identifying Action Verbs

Circle the action verbs in the following passage. Underline the state-of-being verbs.

This passage has been slightly adapted from a piece written by Mary Mapes Dodge in 1873, when smallpox was still a common disease.

The last known case of smallpox was in 1975. In 1980, the World Health Organization declared that smallpox had been eradicated—completely removed from the human population.

In the days when young Edward Jenner worked and studied in a surgeon's office in the town of Sodbury, in Gloucestershire, he heard a good deal of talk about the small-pox. This disease makes great trouble in our own time, and people fear it more than any other sickness; but it is not so bad now-a-days as it was in Jenner's time. It was a frightful plague, and carried, in England alone, away 45,000 people every year! Kings died of it, queens, princes, princesses, the rich and the poor, the high and the low, the learned and the ignorant. When it appeared in an army, it often slew more than the sword, and our soldiers suffered grievously from this pestilence in the beginning of the War of Independence.

Thirty-one years before Edward Jenner's birth, a bright, witty lady, with a sharp tongue but a good heart,—Lady Mary Wortley Montague,—discovered that in Turkey, where the small-pox raged terribly every year, they treated healthy people so they caught the disease,—but in a lighter and less dangerous form than if they took it in the common way. Well persons agreed to this treatment, because they knew that smallpox very rarely comes to a person more than once. They called this treatment *inoculation*. Lady Mary, who believed in the treatment, inoculated her own son in 1718, and with perfect success.

People thought this a great discovery, but the small-pox raged on, as badly as ever.

Exercise 6B: Choosing Verbs

Provide both an appropriate action and state-of-being verb for each of the following nouns or pronouns. The first is done for you.

	State-of-Being	Action
The beginner	is (or was)	attempted
A snail		
She		
My observations		
The rules		
The jail		
His property		
Apple trees		
It		
Donkeys		

Exercise 6C: Strong Action Verbs

Good writers use descriptive and vivid verbs!

In the following sentences, replace the underlined state-of-being and action verbs, which are bland and general, with more vigorous and colorful action verbs. The first is done for you.

Write your new verbs above the underlined verbs. You may use a thesaurus if necessary.

Mary Roach, the author of these sentences, used much more interesting verbs! Your instructor will show you her original sentences when you're finished.

Shooting stars <u>move</u> past below you, and the sun rises in the middle of the night.
Shooting stars <u>streak</u> past below you, and the sun rises in the middle of the night.

Antarctica is a useful analogue for space, and people who <u>are</u> there are thought to be psychologically well equipped for the isolation and confinement of space travel.

As gravity <u>goes</u> out on the twenty-eighth parabola, I pull up my legs, <u>sit</u> on the windowpane, and then gently <u>act</u>, launching myself across the cabin of the plane.

You can't <u>run</u> the weather or gravity, but you can <u>run</u> the shoes your visitor wears and the amount of water that <u>goes</u> onto the floor from her umbrella.

Gravity ends again, and we go up off the floor like spooks from a grave.

Mary Roach, *Packing for Mars: The Curious Science of Life in Space*

The mortician took us into a large, dim, hushed room with heavy drapes and too much air-conditioning.

I say that the surgeon in charge of the symposium told me to observe.

She walks into her office and dials the phone, staring at me while she talks, like security guards in bad action movies just before Steven Seagal hits them on the head from behind.

Though the surgeons clearly do not like dissection of dead people's heads, they just as clearly like the opportunity to practice and explore on someone who isn't going to wake up and look in the mirror anytime soon.

He introduced me to Ben the cadaver, who, despite having by then been reduced to a head, lungs, and arms, had an air of purpose and dignity.

Mary Roach, *Stiff: The Curious Lives of Human Cadavers*

— LESSON 7 —

Helping Verbs

Part of speech is a term that explains what a word does.

Exercise 7A: Action and Helping Verbs

Underline the action verbs in both columns of sentences once. The sentences in the second column each contain at least one helping verb. Underline these helping verbs twice. These sentences are adapted from the *Biggle Poultry Book*, by Jacob Biggle.

COLUMN 1	COLUMN 2
A chicken rearer begins his work early.	The successful chicken rearer must begin his operations long before the advent of the chickens.
People built incubators for hatching eggs during colder months.	Mammoth incubators are now built with a capacity of as high as 20,000 eggs at a hatching.

COLUMN 1	COLUMN 2
The market for broiler chickens opens soon after the New Year but is not at its best until asparagus appears.	Broilers must all be hatched and reared during the most unfavorable season for such operations, winter.
The most successful hen farms consist mainly of houses with yards of only moderate size.	With proper care a flock will produce a fifth more eggs in confinement than when at liberty.
Farmers sometimes, though rarely, make the mistake of keeping too small a number of fowls.	Fowls, if allowed the privileges of the premises, will utilize much that would otherwise go to waste.
Persons living in towns and villages sometimes keep too many in their flock.	Attention should be paid to the variety of fowls kept, and to the yard fences.

Helping Verbs

am, is, are, was, were
be, being, been
have, has, had
do, does, did
shall, will, should, would, may, might, must
can, could

Exercise 7B: Providing Missing Helping Verbs

Fill in each blank with a helping verb. Sometimes, more than one helping verb might be appropriate. This excerpt is adapted from William Makepeace Thackeray's *The Rose and the Ring*.

The Fairy Blackstick, by whose means this young King and Queen ________________ certainly won their respective crowns back, ________________ come not unfrequently to pay them a little visit—as they ________________ riding in their triumphal progress toward Giglio's capital—change her wand into a pony, and travel by their Majesties' side, giving them the very best advice. I am not sure that King Giglio ________________ not think the Fairy and her advice rather a bore, fancying that it was his own valor and merits which ________________ put him on his throne, and conquered Padella; and, in fine, I fear he rather gave himself airs toward his best friend and patroness. She exhorted him to deal justly by his subjects, to draw mildly on the taxes, never to break his promise when he ______________ once given it—and in all respects to be a good King.

"A good King, my dear Fairy!" cries Rosalba. "Of course he will. Break his promise! ______________ you fancy my Giglio ______________ ever do anything so improper, so unlike him? No! never!" And she looked fondly toward Giglio, whom she thought a pattern of perfection.

"Why ______________ Fairy Blackstick always advising me, and telling me how to manage my government, and warning me to keep my word? ______________ she suppose that I am not a man of sense, and a man of honor?" asks Giglio, testily. "Methinks she rather presumes upon her position."

"Hush! dear Giglio," says Rosalba. "You know Blackstick ______________ been very kind to us, and we ______________ not offend her." But the Fairy ______________ not listening to Giglio's testy observations: she ______________ fallen back, and ______________ trotting on her pony now, by Master Bulbo's side—who rode a donkey, and made himself generally beloved in the army by his cheerfulness, his kindness, and good-humor to everybody. He was eager to see his darling Angelica. He thought there never was such a charming being. Blackstick ______________ not tell him it was the possession of the magic rose that made Angelica so lovely in his eyes. She brought him the very best accounts of his little wife, whose misfortunes and humiliations ______________ indeed very greatly improved her; and you see, she ______________ whisk off on her wand a hundred miles in a minute, and be back in no time, and so carry polite messages from Bulbo to Angelica, and from Angelica to Bulbo, and comfort that young man upon his journey.

When the Royal party arrived at the last stage before you reach Blombodinga, who ______________ be in waiting, in her carriage there, with her lady of honor by her side, but the Princess Angelica?

A splendid luncheon ______________ served to the Royal party, of which all our friends partook. You ______________ hear the joy-bells ringing in the capital, and the guns which the citizens were firing off in honor of their Majesties.

"What ____________ ______________ induced that hideous old Gruffanuff to dress herself up in such an absurd way? _________________ you ask her to be your bridesmaid, my dear?" says Giglio to Rosalba. "What a figure of fun Gruffy is!"

— LESSON 8 —

Personal Pronouns

First, Second, and Third Person
Capitalizing the Pronoun *I*

Personal Pronouns

	Singular	**Plural**
First person	I	we
Second person	you	you
Third person	he, she, it	they

Although they are not very hungry, I certainly am.

ich i I

As the German-built plane rose into the air, I experienced a strange loneliness.

Exercise 8A: Capitalization and Punctuation Practice

Correct the following sentences. Mark through any incorrect small letters and write the correct capitals above them. Insert quotation marks if needed. Use underlining to indicate any italics.

noah mcvicker, who worked for the soap company kutol products in cincinnati, ohio, developed a product for cleaning soot off wallpaper. after world war II, when wallpaper and heat sources had changed, there was less of a market for mcvicker's wallpaper cleaning putty.

a schoolteacher named kay zufall thought her students might enjoy playing with the putty, and she convinced mcvicker's nephew to try producing it as a toy called play-doh.

in the mid-1950s, play-doh was introduced at an educational convention, stores in new york and chicago began selling it, and advertisements for it were played during such programs as captain kangaroo and romper room.

peg solitaire is known to have existed at least since the time of louis XIV of france. the game may have been invented by a mathematician named pelisson in louis's court. a 1687 engraving of the princess of soubise, anne de rohan-chabot, includes the game on a table beside the princess.

an edition of the magazine mercure galant from the same year includes a description of the game and its rules. by 1710, it had caught the attention of gottfried wilhelm leibniz, who wrote that he preferred to play the game backwards, replacing pegs in empty holes that had been leaped over.

in 1883, heyliger de windt, who lived in chicago, filed a patent for a board to be used in a game called parlor quoits. de windt's board was angled and had a square hole, into which the players of parlor quoits would try to toss a bag filled with beans.

"in some cases," wrote de windt in his patent application, "i propose to suspend a bell" at the end of the board; a player whose bag struck the bell would lose ten points.

a version of his game sold by a toy manufacturer in massachusetts was called faba baga. faba baga had two round holes, worth different point values for the players, and one larger bag to toss each round.

today, the game is known as cornhole and is played with boards with one round hole. the american cornhole organization establishes rules and organizes tournaments for the game.

Exercise 8B: Person, Number, and Gender

Label each personal pronoun in the following selection with its person (*1*, *2*, or *3*) and number (*S* or *PL*). For third-person-singular pronouns only, indicate gender (*m*, *f*, or *n*). The first is done for you.

The selection below is adapted from Anna Sewell's *Black Beauty.*

1s

The longer I lived at Birtwick, the more proud and happy I felt at having such a place. Our master and mistress were respected and beloved by all who knew them. They were good and kind to everybody and everything; not only men and women, but horses and donkeys, dogs and cats, cattle and birds. If any of the village children were known to treat any creature cruelly, they soon heard about it from the Hall.

The Squire and Farmer Grey had worked together, as they said, for more than twenty years, to get bearing-reins on the cart-horses done away with, and in our parts you seldom saw them; but sometimes if mistress met a heavily laden horse, with his head strained up, she would stop the carriage; and get out, and reason with the driver in her sweet, serious voice, and try to show him how foolish and cruel it was.

I don't think any man could withstand our mistress. I wish all ladies were like her. Our master, too, used to come down very heavy sometimes. I remember he was riding me towards home one morning, when we saw a powerful man begin to lash his pony furiously. I knew what fearful pain it gave that delicate little creature; but master gave me the word, and we were up with him in a second.

"Do you think," said master sternly, "that treatment like this will make him fond of your will? I must say, Mr. Sawyer, that more unmanly, brutal treatment of a little pony it was never my painful lot to witness; and by giving way to such passion, you injure your own character as much, nay more, than you injure your horse; and remember, we shall all have to be judged according to our works, whether they be towards man or towards beast."

WEEK 3

Introduction to the Sentence

— LESSON 9 —

The Sentence
Parts of Speech and Parts of Sentences
Subjects and Predicates

A sentence is a group of words that contains a subject and predicate.

part of speech — noun — verb

The cat sits on the mat.

part of the sentence — subject — predicate

The subject of the sentence is the main word or term that the sentence is about.
Part of speech is a term that explains what a word does.
Part of the sentence is a term that explains how a word functions in a sentence.
The predicate of the sentence tells something about the subject.

part of speech ________ ________

The *Tyrannosaurus rex* crashes through the trees.

part of the sentence ________ ________

Exercise 9A: Parts of Speech vs. Parts of the Sentence

Label each underlined word with the correct part of speech AND the correct part of the sentence.

part of speech ________ ________

This strawberry is delicious.

part of the sentence ________ ________

part of speech ________ ________

A cardinal landed on the bird feeder.

part of the sentence ________ ________

part of speech ________ ________

She canceled our reservation.

part of the sentence ________ ________

part of speech ________ ________

They snarled at us.

part of the sentence ________ ________

Exercise 9B: Parts of Speech: Nouns, Adjectives, Pronouns, and Verbs

Label each underlined word with the correct part of speech. Use *N* for noun, *A* for adjective, *P* for pronoun, and *V* for verb.

These sentences are from *Tarzan of the Apes*, by Edgar Rice Burroughs.

Had they known that the child had seen thirteen moons before it had come into Kala's possession they would have considered its case as absolutely hopeless, for the little apes of their own tribe were as far advanced in two or three moons as was this little stranger after twenty-five.

Tublat, Kala's husband, was sorely vexed, and but for the female's careful watching would have put the child out of the way.

"He will never be a great ape," he argued. "Always will you have to carry him and protect him. What good will he be to the tribe? None; only a burden."

"Let us leave him quietly sleeping among the tall grasses, that you may bear other and stronger apes to guard us in our old age."

"Never, Broken Nose," replied Kala. "If I must carry him forever, so be it."

Exercise 9C: Parts of the Sentence: Subjects and Predicates

In each of the following sentences, underline the subject once and the predicate twice. Find the subject by asking, "Who or what is this sentence about?" Find the predicate by saying, "Subject what?"

Manatees are large mammals.

Manatees live in the water.

They eat water plants.

Sometimes people call manatees "sea cows."

That name arose due to similarities in behavior between manatees and cows.

Manatees have good memories.

Florida's Wakulla Springs State Park is a good place for manatee sightings.

— LESSON 10 —

Subjects and Predicates

Diagramming Subjects and Predicates
Sentence Capitalization and Punctuation
Sentence Fragments

A sentence is a group of words that contains a subject and predicate.
The subject of the sentence is the main word or term that the sentence is about.
The predicate of the sentence tells something about the subject.

He does.
They can.
It is.

Hurricanes form over warm tropical waters.

A sentence is a group of words that contains a subject and a predicate.
A sentence begins with a capital letter and ends with a punctuation mark.

No running in the kitchen.

> Can we measure intelligence without understanding it? Possibly so; physicists measured gravity and magnetism long before they understood them theoretically. Maybe psychologists can do the same with intelligence.
>
> **Or maybe not.**
>
> —James W. Kalat, *Introduction to Psychology* (Cengage Learning, 2007)

Because he couldn't go.
Since I thought so.

A sentence is a group of words that usually contains a subject and a predicate.
A sentence begins with a capital letter and ends with a punctuation mark.
A sentence contains a complete thought.

Exercise 10A: Sentences and Fragments

If a group of words expresses a complete thought, write *S* for sentence in the blank. If not, write *F* for fragment.

because it's raining outside __________

we ate three pieces of candy each __________

nightmares interrupting her sleep __________

the umbrella opened with a pop __________

a jealous child wants his sister's ice cream __________

the sleepy little town by the river __________

or inside the dilapidated barn __________

Exercise 10B: Proofreading for Capitalization and Punctuation

Add the correct capitalization and punctuation to the following sentences. In this exercise you will use proofreader's marks. Indicate letters which should be capitalized by underlining three times. Indicate ending punctuation by using the proofreader's mark for inserting a period: ⊙ Indicate words which should be italicized by underlining them and writing *ital* in the margin.

in 1949, george lerner invented a toy for children that involved sticking face parts into a potato or other vegetable or fruit

lerner's toy required the use of actual produce, which was seen as wasteful following the years of food rationing in world war ii finally, lerner found a food company that would include the plastic parts as prizes in cereal boxes

in 1951, lerner showed his toy to henry and merrill hassenfeld, who owned a toy company called hassenfeld brothers

the company, which has since changed its name to hasbro, decided to buy the rights to the toy, and mr potato head made his debut on may 1, 1952

mr potato head was the first toy to be advertised on television

mr potato head (and his wife, mrs potato head) appeared in disney's toy story movies

in 1998, the first and only season of the mr potato head show aired on the fox television network

Exercise 10C: Diagramming

Find the subjects and predicates in the following sentences. Diagram each subject and predicate on your own paper. You should capitalize on the diagram any words that are capitalized in the sentence, but do not put punctuation marks on the diagram. If a proper name is the subject, all parts of the proper name go onto the subject line of the diagram.

The raucous raccoons ran right into the river.

Cecily celebrated the centennial.

A heartbroken hedgehog hijacked the helicopter!

The preferred present for the precocious preschooler is a pretend prairie dog.

Dana Daniels dutifully danced to the drumbeats.

Annie's anaconda answers to Anthony.

The garrulous goose gossiped with Gloria about the gawky gatekeeper.

Jennifer jettisoned her jacket—in January!

— LESSON 11 —

Types of Sentences

A sentence is a group of words that usually contains a subject and a predicate.
A sentence begins with a capital letter and ends with a punctuation mark.
A sentence contains a complete thought.

A purple penguin is playing ping-pong.

A statement gives information. A statement always ends with a period.
Statements are declarative sentences.

An exclamation shows sudden or strong feeling.
An exclamation always ends with an exclamation point.
Exclamations are exclamatory sentences.

A command gives an order or makes a request.
A command ends with either a period or an exclamation point.
Commands are imperative sentences.

Sit!
Stand!
Learn!

The subject of a command is understood to be *you*.

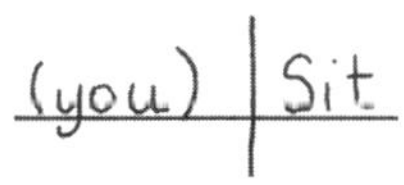

A question asks something.
A question always ends with a question mark.
Questions are known as interrogative sentences.

He is late.
Is he late?

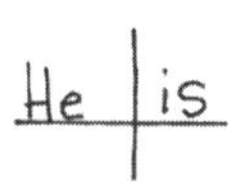

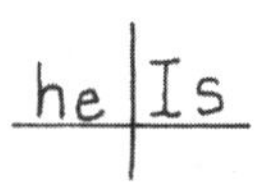

Exercise 11A: Types of Sentences: Statements, Exclamations, Commands, and Questions

Identify the following sentences as *S* for statement, *E* for exclamation, *C* for command, or *Q* for question. Add the appropriate punctuation to the end of each sentence.

	Sentence Type
Put the toys in the basket	________
Where did you get your new shirt	________

	Sentence Type
Remember to clean up your dishes after dinner	__________
Is the game tonight or tomorrow	__________
Please call me when you get this message	__________
What a beautiful day	__________
I can't wait to go ice skating	__________
We were both at the library yesterday	__________
I'd like to see that movie	__________
Would you like the last piece of bread	__________

Exercise 11B: Proofreading for Capitalization and Punctuation

Proofread the following sentences. If a lowercase letter should be capitalized, draw three lines underneath it. Add any missing punctuation by writing it into the sentence.

she has been in the hospital for a whole week

several people came to visit yesterday

did they bring these flowers

put them in a vase

add a little water

that's too much water

will you help me clean up this mess

Exercise 11C: Diagramming Subjects and Predicates

On your own paper, diagram the subjects and predicates of the following sentences. Remember that the understood subject of a command is "you," and that the predicate may come before the subject in a question.

Mail the letter.
Am I awake?
I remember this movie.
Philip ascended the stairs.
Quietly take your seat.
You look fabulous!
Are your sisters nearby?
The show begins in two minutes!

— LESSON 12 —

Subjects and Predicates
Helping Verbs

Simple and Complete Subjects and Predicates

The subject of the sentence is the main word or term that the sentence is about.
The simple subject of the sentence is *just* the main word or term that the sentence is about.

Its fleece was white as snow.

The complete subject of the sentence is the simple subject and all the words that belong to it.

The predicate of the sentence tells something about the subject.
The simple predicate of the sentence is the main verb along with any helping verbs.
The complete predicate of the sentence is the simple predicate and all the words that belong to it.

Complete Subject	**Complete Predicate**
Lambs born in the spring	must remain with their mothers until July.
Plentiful turnips	should be provided for them.

Exercise 12A: Complete Subjects and Complete Predicates
Match the complete subjects and complete predicates by drawing lines between them.

A dishonest magician	sees the sultan's daughter.
Inside the cave, the boy	rubs a magic ring, revealing a genie.
The ring genie	provides food and prosperity to Aladdin and his mother for many years.
Back at home, Aladdin's mother	eventually lives happily ever after.
The lamp genie	manages to marry the sultan's daughter.
One day, Aladdin	tricks Aladdin into going into a cave to fetch a lamp.
Determined to marry the princess, Aladdin	rubs at the lamp, revealing a more powerful genie.
With a few more tricks, Aladdin	uses wealth provided by the genie to amaze the sultan.
Although some misfortunes befall them, the couple	frees Aladdin from the cave.

Exercise 12B: Simple and Complete Subjects and Predicates

In the following sentences, underline the simple subject once and the simple predicate twice. Then, draw a vertical line between the complete subject and the complete predicate. The first is done for you.

These sentences are adapted from Norton Juster's *The Phantom Tollbooth.*

An ominous silence | dropped like a curtain around them.

Five very tall, thin gentlemen regally dressed in silks and satins, plumed hats, and buckled shoes rushed up to the car.

A slavish concern for the composition of words is the sign of a bankrupt intellect.

Most people have forgotten me entirely.

My cabinet members can do all sorts of things.

I am quite ordinary.

The hours passed.

He stood bravely at the fortress door.

Exercise 12C: Diagramming Simple Subjects and Simple Predicates

On your own paper, diagram the simple subjects and simple predicates from Exercise 12B.

— REVIEW 1 —

Weeks 1-3

Topics:
Concrete/Abstract Nouns
Descriptive Adjectives
Common/Proper Nouns
Capitalization of Proper Nouns and First Words in Sentences
Noun Gender
Pronouns and Antecedents
Action Verbs/State-of-Being Verbs
Helping Verbs
Subjects and Predicates
Complete Sentences
Types of Sentences

Review 1A: Types of Nouns

Fill in the blanks with the correct description of each noun. The first is done for you.

	Concrete / Abstract	Common / Proper	Gender (**M, F, N**)
Clara Barton	C	P	F
uncle	______	______	______
eye	______	______	______
incredulity	______	______	______
queen	______	______	______
Pythagoras	______	______	______
Lake Victoria	______	______	______
snore	______	______	______
New York Times	______	______	______
education	______	______	______
artistry	______	______	______

Review 1B: Types of Verbs

Underline the complete verbs in the following sentences. Identify any helping verbs as *HV*. Identify the main verb as *AV* for action verb or *BV* for state-of-being verb.

Magnets attract certain metals.

Every magnet has a positive pole and a negative pole.

The opposite poles are attracted to each other.

You can turn an iron object into a temporary magnet!

Rub a magnet on the item repeatedly in the same direction.

Inside the item, the poles will line up.

The item has been magnetized!

The poles do not remain that way.

The object will not be a magnet after a while.

Review 1C: Subjects and Predicates

Draw one line under the simple subject and two lines under the simple predicate in the following sentences. Remember that the predicate may be a verb phrase with more than one verb in it. If the subject is an understood "you" in a command, write "(you)" in the left margin and underline it once to indicate that it is the simple subject.

You can also make a magnetic compass.

First, magnetize a needle by rubbing a magnet on it many times.

The needle should be inserted into a thin piece of cork.

A bowl of water is the next thing needed.

Place the magnetized needle (with the cork) in the water.

The needle will point toward the north.

You can spin the needle around.

Because of the earth's magnetic poles, the needle will spin itself back toward the north.

Just keep the needle away from the sides of the bowl.

The sides can interfere with the needle's rotation.

Review 1D: Parts of Speech

Identify the underlined words as *N* for noun, *P* for pronoun, *A* for adjective, *AV* for action verb, *HV* for helping verb, or *BV* for state-of-being verb.

The following passage is from Norton Juster's *The Phantom Tollbooth.*

"He looks friendly enough," thought Milo, not sure just how friendly a friendly bumblebee should be, and tried to think of a very difficult word. "Spell 'vegetable,'" he suggested, for it was one that always troubled him at school.

"That is a difficult one," said the bee, winking at the letter man. "Let me see now . . . hmmmmmm . . ." He frowned and wiped his brow and paced slowly back and forth on top of the wagon. "How much time do I have?"

"Just ten seconds," cried Milo excitedly. "Count them off, Tock."

Review 1E: Capitalization and Punctuation

Use proofreading marks to indicate correct capitalization and punctuation in the following sentences. Be careful: Some of these may have more than one sentence, so ending punctuation will need to be inserted to split sentences correctly!

Small letter that should be capitalized: ≡ beneath the letter.

Italics: single underline | insert period: ⊙ | insert exclamation point: ↑!

insert question mark: ?̂ | insert quotation marks: ∜

ernest thayer wrote the famous baseball poem casey at the bat in 1888

have you seen the beautiful work of the paper artist yulia brodskaya

how beautiful you look today

adriana caselotti starred as the title character's voice in snow white and the seven dwarfs

after the 2000 summer olympics in sydney, australia, the international table tennis federation set a new standard size for balls at 40 millimeters these balls moved more slowly than the 38-millimeter balls used previously, making the game easier to watch on television

ray bradbury, who wrote fahrenheit 451 and many other works in a variety of genres, also wanted to be a magician the national anthem of canada is o canada, composed and written in 1880

on that famous 1492 voyage, christopher columbus captained the santa maria brothers martín alonso pinzón and vicente yáñez pinzón captained the pinta and the niña, respectively

Review 1F: Types of Sentences

Identify the following sentences as *S* for statement, *C* for command, *E* for exclamation, or *Q* for question. If the sentence is incomplete, write *I*.

The following sentences are from *The House on Mango Street*, by Sandra Cisneros. Some have been slightly adapted.

	Sentence Type
The boys and the girls live in separate worlds.	________
The boys in their universe and we in ours.	________
That does it!	________
Come here.	________
Which one is your house?	________
Okay, I'll be your friend.	________
But only till next Tuesday.	________
How do I know this is so?	________
Wait a minute.	________
Meme won.	________
And broke both arms.	________
The green metal cage, the porcelain table top, the family that spoke like guitars.	________
I like to tell stories.	________

WEEK 4

Verb Tenses

— LESSON 13 —

Nouns, Pronouns, and Verbs
Sentences
Simple Present, Simple Past, and Simple Future Tenses

A noun names a person, place, thing, or idea.
A pronoun takes the place of a noun.
A verb shows an action, shows a state of being, links two words together, or helps another verb.

State-of-Being Verbs

am	were
is	be
are	being
was	been

Helping Verbs
am, is, are, was, were
be, being, been
have, has, had
do, does, did
shall, will, should, would, may, might, must
can, could

A sentence is a group of words that usually contains a subject and a predicate. A sentence begins with a capital letter and ends with a punctuation mark. A sentence contains a complete thought.

A verb in the present tense tells about something that happens in the present.
A verb in the past tense tells about something that happened in the past.
A verb in the future tense tells about something that will happen in the future.

Exercise 13A: Simple Tenses

	Simple Past	Simple Present	Simple Future
I			will whisper
You	boasted		
She		preserves	
We	sneezed		
They		stir	

Form the simple future by adding the helping verb *will* in front of the simple present.
A suffix is one or more letters added to the end of a word to change its meaning.

Forming the Simple Past
To form the past tense, add *–ed* to the basic verb.

sharpen–sharpened
utter–uttered

If the basic verb ends in *-e* already, only add *–d*.

rumble–rumbled
shade–shaded

If the verb ends in a short vowel sound and a consonant, double the consonant and add *–ed*.

scam–scammed
thud–thudded

If the verb ends in *-y* following a consonant, change the *y* to *i* and add *-ed*.

cry–cried
try–tried

Exercise 13B: Using Consistent Tense

When you write, you should use consistent tense—if you begin a sentence in one tense, you should continue to use that same tense for any other verbs in the same sentence. The following sentences use two verb tenses. Cross out the second verb and rewrite it so that the tense of the second verb matches the tense of the first one.

The first sentence is done for you.

For a bit of fun, see if you can guess which board game each of these sentences is referring to!

will knock
The monsters will attack the castle and ~~knocked~~ down the walls. *(Castle Panic)*

On her turn, Amy built a settlement and trades wool to Kendra in exchange for ore.

Everyone visits a variety of places in Japan and kept track of his or her experiences.

This city will be hit by an epidemic soon, and then we have another outbreak!

Sean places trains on the board, and Amelie will groan at the disruption of her planned route.

I will reserve this sapphire card worth two points on this turn, and on my next turn I purchased it.

James chose fishing as his final action before the harvest and will have plenty of food for his family.

Exercise 13C: Forming the Simple Past Tense

Using the rules for forming the simple past, put each one of the verbs in parentheses into the simple past. Write the simple past form in the blank. Be sure to spell the past forms of regular verbs correctly, and to use the correct forms of irregular verbs.

These sentences are taken from *What Katy Did*, by Susan Coolidge.

Of course Katy ____________ (is) too young to understand these whispers, or the reasons why people were not disposed to think well of Mr. Spenser. The romance of the closed door and the lady whom nobody ______________ (see), ______________ (interest) her very much. She ______________ (use) to stop and stare at the windows, and wonder what was going on inside, till at last it ______________ (seem) as if she *must* know. So, one day she ______________ (take) some flowers and Victoria, her favorite doll, and boldly ______________ (march) into the Spensers' yard.

She ______________ (tap) at the front door, but nobody __________________ (answer). Then she tapped again. Still nobody answered. She ______________ (try) the door. It was locked. So shouldering Victoria, she ____________________ (trudge) round to the back of the house. As she _________________ (pass) the side-door she saw that it was open a little way. She _____________ (knock) for the third time, and as no one ______________ (come), she ______________ (go) in, and passing through the little hall ________________ (begin) to tap at all the inside doors.

There ________________ (seem) to be no people in the house. Katy ________________ (peep) into the kitchen first. It was bare and forlorn. All sorts of dishes were standing about. There was no fire in the stove. The parlor was not much better. Mr. Spenser's boots _______________ (lie) in the middle of the floor. There were dirty glasses on the table. On the mantle-piece was a platter with bones of meat upon it. Dust lay thick over everything, and the whole house ______________ (look) as if it hadn't been lived in for at least a year.

Katy _____________ (try) several other doors, all of which were locked, and then she _________________ (go) up stairs. As she ___________________ (stand) on the top step, grasping her flowers, and a little doubtful what to do next, a feeble voice from a bed-room ___________________ (call) out:

"Who is there?"

— LESSON 14 —

Simple Present, Simple Past, and Simple Future Tenses

Progressive Present, Progressive Past, and Progressive Future Tenses

A verb in the present tense tells about something that happens in the present.
A verb in the future tense tells about something that will happen in the future.
A verb in the past tense tells about something that happened in the past.

study will study studied

Forming the Simple Past:
To form the past tense, add *–ed* to the basic verb.
If the basic verb ends in *e* already, only add *–d.*
If the verb ends in a short vowel sound and a consonant, double the consonant and add *–ed.*
If the verb ends in *-y* following a consonant, change the *y* to *i* and add *-ed.*

Exercise 14A: Forming the Simple Past and Simple Future Tenses

Form the simple past and simple future of the following regular verbs.

Past	Present	Future
	stay	
	whisper	

Past	Present	Future
	scare	
	trouble	
	turn	
	sin	
	stretch	
	jam	
	hurry	

Yesterday, I cried. I was crying for a long time.
Today, I learn. I am learning my grammar.
Tomorrow, I will celebrate. I will be celebrating all afternoon.

A progressive verb describes an ongoing or continuous action.

Exercise 14B: Progressive Tenses

Circle the ending of each verb. Underline the helping verbs.

is camping

were gluing

has been interrupting

was avoiding

am reaching

will be collecting

were suggesting

was polishing

The progressive past tense uses the helping verbs *was* and *were*.
The progressive present tense uses the helping verbs *am, is,* and *are*.
The progressive future tense uses the helping verb *will be*.

Spelling Rules for Adding *-ing*
If the verb ends in a short vowel sound and a consonant, double the consonant and add *–ing*.

skip–skipping
drum–drumming

If the verb ends in a long vowel sound plus a consonant and an -*e*, drop the *e* and add *–ing*.

smile–smiling
trade–trading

Exercise 14C: Forming the Progressive Past, Present, and Future Tenses

Complete the following chart. Be sure to use the spelling rules above.

	Progressive Past	Progressive Present	Progressive Future
I stitch	I was stitching	I am stitching	I will be stitching
I mourn			
I manage			
I borrow			
You communicate	You were communicating	You are communicating	You will be communicating
You visit			
You remain			
You step			

	Progressive Past	Progressive Present	Progressive Future
We belong	We were belonging	We are belonging	We will be belonging
We serve			
We plan			
We melt			

Exercise 14D: Simple and Progressive Tenses

Fill in the blanks with the correct form of the verb in parentheses.

In 1928, Dr. Alexander Fleming ____________ (progressive past of *return*) from vacation when he ____________ (simple past of *see*) the mess in his petri dishes.

When he ____________ (simple past of *look*) at the dishes under his microscope, he ____________ (simple past of *realize*) that a mold ____________ (progressive past of *keep*) the bacteria from growing.

This discovery ____________ (simple past of *lead*) to the development of penicillin.

In 1945, Fleming ____________ (simple past of *predict*) that overusing penicillin could lead to resistant bacteria, and today, doctors ____________ (progressive present of *discover*) that Fleming ____________ (simple past of *is*) correct.

Dr. Percy Spencer ____________ (progressive past of *work*) with a magnetron, which ____________ (simple past of *generate*) microwaves.

Spencer ____________ (simple past of *discover*) that the waves from the magnetron ____________ (progressive past of *melt*) the chocolate he ____________ (simple past of *have*) in his pocket.

He also ____________________ (simple past of *learn*) that popcorn ____________________ (simple past of *pop*) when it was brought close to the magnetron.

People all over the world ________________________ (progressive present of *enjoy*) the convenience of microwave ovens today because of Spencer's affinity for chocolate.

— LESSON 15 —

Simple Present, Simple Past, and Simple Future Tenses
Progressive Present, Progressive Past, and Progressive Future Tenses
Perfect Present, Perfect Past, and Perfect Future Tenses

A progressive verb describes an ongoing or continuous action.

Yesterday, I was studying tenses.
Today, I am studying tenses.
Tomorrow, I will be studying something else!

NEWS BULLETIN!
A diamond theft occurred at the National Museum yesterday. The thief had already fled the scene when a security guard discovered that the diamond was missing.

A perfect verb describes an action which has been completed before another action takes place.

I practiced my piano.
I was practicing my piano all day yesterday.
I had practiced my piano before I went to bed.

Perfect Past	Perfect Present	Perfect Future
I had practiced yesterday.	I have practiced.	I will have practiced tomorrow.
I had eaten before bed.	I have eaten already.	I will have eaten by bedtime tomorrow.
I had seen the movie a week ago.	I have seen the movie once.	I will have seen the movie before it leaves the theater.

Perfect past verbs describe an action that was finished in the past before another action began.

Helping verb: had

Perfect present verbs describe an action that was completed before the present moment.

Helping verbs: have, has

Perfect future verbs describe an action that will be finished in the future before another action begins.

Helping verb: will have

Exercise 15A: Perfect Tenses

Fill in the blanks with the missing forms.

Simple Past	Perfect Past	Perfect Present	Perfect Future
I packed	I had packed	I have packed	I will have packed
I wailed			
I fried			
I traveled			
We reflected	We had reflected	We have reflected	We will have reflected
We offered			
We batted			
We unlocked			
He camped	He had camped	He has camped	He will have camped
He dreamed			
He haunted			
He encouraged			

Exercise 15B: Identifying Perfect Tenses

Identify the underlined verbs as perfect past, perfect present, or perfect future. The first one is done for you.

perfect present
I <u>have decided</u> to make an edible model of an animal cell.

I <u>had learned</u> about the different parts of a cell before making my decision.

I <u>have studied</u> diagrams of cells, and I <u>have looked</u> at a few different cells under a microscope.

Yesterday I needed to go to the grocery store because we <u>had run</u> out of eggs for my cake.

Now I <u>have baked</u> the cake.

Once the cake <u>has cooled</u>, I will use icing and candy to represent the parts of the cell.

In a few hours, I <u>will have created</u> a beautiful—and tasty—cell model!

Exercise 15C: Perfect, Progressive, and Simple Tenses

Each underlined verb phrase has been labeled as past, present, or future. Add the label *perfect, progressive,* or *simple* to each one. The first one has been done for you.

This passage is adapted from Robert Lawson's *Robbut: A Tale of Tails.*

simple
PAST PRESENT
"Goodness gracious, Robbut!" the Snake <u>cried</u>, "whatever<u>'s happened</u> to you, and

PRESENT PRESENT
what's wrong with your tail, or whoever's tail it <u>is</u>? It can't be yours, but it <u>seems</u> to be

PRESENT
on you. It <u>looks</u> like a Cat's, but no Cat would have that mussy a tail. What's this all about anyway?"

PAST PAST
Robbut rather sheepishly <u>explained</u> about it; how he <u>had saved</u> the Little Old Man

PAST
from the trap and how the Little Old Man <u>had given</u> him a new tail.

PAST PAST
"Well, I must say you <u>made</u> an awfully poor choice," <u>exclaimed</u> the Snake. "Of all the

PRESENT
stupid things I've ever heard, that's about the stupidest—even for a Rabbit. What would anyone, especially you, want with a long, furry nuisance like that?

PAST PRESENT
"Now there—" and he was twitching his own tail in the sunshine—"there's what I call a tail. It's clean cut, useful, no trouble, and if I do say so, quite handsome. What's more, it

FUTURE PRESENT
will never get muddy, stained, or spotted—or stuck up with burrs or pine needles. It sheds

PRESENT
water like a Duck and has real life and style to it."

PAST
His tail was flickering and quivering in the sunshine, and it really did look most

PAST
attractive and extremely lively. It certainly was neat and clean. Robbut eyed it with envy and his unfortunate tail with regret.

— LESSON 16 —

Simple Present, Simple Past, and Simple Future Tenses
Progressive Present, Progressive Past, and Progressive Future Tenses
Perfect Present, Perfect Past, and Perfect Future Tenses
Irregular Verbs

go	run	are	know	make
go-ed	run-ned	ar-ed	know-ed	mak-ed
went	ran	were	knew	made

Exercise 16A: Irregular Verb Forms: Simple Present, Simple Past, and Simple Future

Fill in the chart with the missing verb forms.

	Simple Past	Simple Present	Simple Future
I			will overtake

	Simple Past	Simple Present	Simple Future
You			will draw
She	arose		
We		kneel	
They		say	
I	left		
You		drink	
He			will bear
We		ring	
They		win	
I			will hear
You	fed		
It		sticks	
We	bent		
They			will steal
I		sting	
You	shot		
We		beat	
They		sleep	

	Simple Past	Simple Present	Simple Future	Progressive Past	Progressive Present	Progressive Future	Perfect Past	Perfect Present	Perfect Future
go	went	go	will go	was going	am going	will be going	had gone	have gone	will have gone
eat	ate	eat	will eat	was eating	am eating	will be eating	had eaten	have eaten	will have eaten

Exercise 16B: Irregular Verbs, Progressive and Perfect Tenses

Fill in the remaining blanks. The first row is done for you.

Simple Present	Progressive Past	Progressive Present	Progressive Future	Perfect Past	Perfect Present	Perfect Future
overtake	was overtaking	am overtaking	will be overtaking	had overtaken	have overtaken	will have overtaken
draw						
arise						
kneel						
say						
leave						
drink						
bear						
ring						

Simple Present	Progressive Past	Progressive Present	Progressive Future	Perfect Past	Perfect Present	Perfect Future
win						
hear						
feed						
stick						
bend						
steal						
sting						
shoot						
beat						
sleep						

WEEK 5

More About Verbs

— LESSON 17 —

Simple, Progressive, and Perfect Tenses
Subjects and Predicates
Parts of Speech and Parts of Sentences
Verb Phrases

I yawn today. Yesterday, I yawned. Tomorrow, I will yawn.
I am yawning today. Yesterday, I was yawning. Tomorrow, I will be yawning.

A progressive verb describes an ongoing or continuous action.

I have yawned today already.
Yesterday, I had yawned before I had my dinner.
Tomorrow, I will have yawned by the time the sun goes down.

A perfect verb describes an action which has been completed before another action takes place.

Exercise 17A: Simple, Progressive, and Perfect Tenses

All the bolded verbs are in the past tense. Label each bolded verb as simple (*S*), progressive (*PROG*), or perfect (*PERF*). These sentences are adapted from George MacDonald's *At the Back of the North Wind*.

I cannot tell whether Diamond **knew** what his mother **was thinking**, but I think I know. She **had heard** something at church the day before, which **came** back upon her—something like this, that she hadn't to eat for tomorrow as well as for today; and that what was not wanted couldn't be missed. So, instead of saying anything more, she **stretched** out her hand for the basket, and she and Diamond **had** their dinner.

And Diamond did enjoy it. For the drive and the fresh air **had made** him quite hungry; and he did not, like his mother, trouble himself about what they should dine off that day week. The fact was he **had lived** so long without any food at all at the back of the north wind, that he **knew** quite well that food **was** not essential to existence; that in fact, under certain circumstances, people could live without it well enough.

His mother did not speak much during their dinner. After it was over she **helped** him to walk about a little, but he was not able for much and soon got tired. He did not get fretful, though. He was too glad of having the sun and the wind again, to fret because he could not run about. He **lay** down on the dry sand, and his mother **covered** him with a shawl. Then, as she **was sitting** by his side, she **took** a bit of work from her pocket. But Diamond **felt** rather sleepy, and **turned** on his side and **gazed** sleepily over the sand. A few yards off he **saw** something; it **was fluttering**.

---

had rejoiced
will have rejoiced

A phrase is a group of words serving a single grammatical function.

have greatly rejoiced
They will have all rejoiced

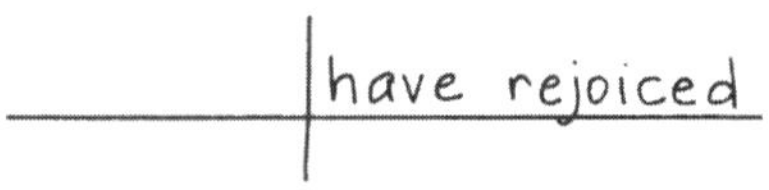

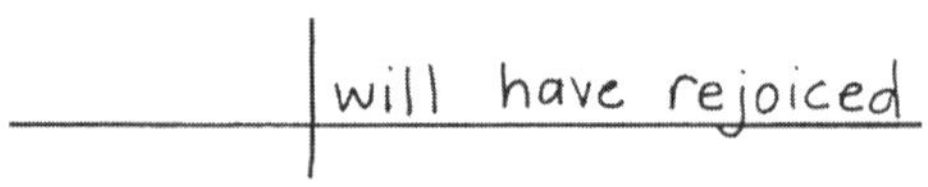

The subject of the sentence is the main word or term that the sentence is about.

The simple subject of the sentence is *just* the main word or term that the sentence is about.

The predicate of the sentence tells something about the subject.

The simple predicate of the sentence is the main verb along with any helping verbs.

Part of speech is a term that explains what a word does.

A noun names a person, place, thing, or idea.

A pronoun takes the place of a noun.

Part of the sentence is a term that explains how a word functions in a sentence.

A verb shows an action, shows a state of being, links two words together, or helps another verb.

Exercise 17B: Identifying and Diagramming Subjects and Predicates; Identifying Verb Tenses

Underline the subject once and the predicate twice in each sentence. Be sure to include both the main verb and any helping verbs when you underline the predicate. Identify the tense of each verb or verb phrase (*simple past, present,* or *future; progressive past, present,* or *future; perfect past, present,* or *future*) on the line. Then diagram each subject and predicate on your own paper.

These sentences are adapted from George MacDonald's *At the Back of the North Wind.*

His father had shut the door of his cab upon a fare. ____________________

Mr. Raymond took the little book. ____________________

That van is moving now. ____________________

I will tell my father about your goodness to me. ____________________

He carried with him one pound one shilling and sixpence. ____________________

She was thinking of her twenty-one shillings and sixpence. ____________________

With the help of the stone he scrambled out by the opening. ____________________

Why, that girl has been to the back of the north wind! ____________________

I will write it down. ____________________

Nobody has ever heard it before? ____________________

You will be sailing against me. ____________________

My older readers will have already discovered this. ____________________

They were sweeping with the speed of the wind itself towards the sea. ____________________

— LESSON 18 —

Verb Phrases
Person of the Verb
Conjugations

	Progressive Past	Progressive Present	Progressive Future
I run	I was running	I am running	I will be running
You call	You were calling	You are calling	You will be calling
He jogs	He was jogging	He is jogging	He will be jogging
We fix	We were fixing	We are fixing	We will be fixing
They call	They were calling	They are calling	They will be calling

PERSONS OF THE VERB

	Singular	Plural
First person	I	we
Second person	you	you
Third person	he, she, it	they

Simple Tenses

REGULAR VERB, SIMPLE PRESENT

	Singular	Plural
First person	I pretend	we pretend
Second person	you pretend	you pretend
Third person	he, she, it pretends	they pretend
First person	I wander	we wander
Second person	you wander	you wander
Third person	he, she, it wanders	they wander

REGULAR VERB, SIMPLE PAST

	Singular	Plural
First person	I wandered	we wandered
Second person	you wandered	you wandered
Third person	he, she, it wandered	they wandered

REGULAR VERB, SIMPLE FUTURE

	Singular	Plural
First person	I will wander	we will wander
Second person	you will wander	you will wander
Third person	he, she, it will wander	they will wander

Perfect Tenses

REGULAR VERB, PERFECT PRESENT

	Singular	Plural
First person	I have wandered	we have wandered
Second person	you have wandered	you have wandered
Third person	he, she, it has wandered	they have wandered

REGULAR VERB, PERFECT PAST

	Singular	Plural
First person	I had wandered	we had wandered
Second person	you had wandered	you had wandered
Third person	he, she, it had wandered	they had wandered

REGULAR VERB, PERFECT FUTURE

	Singular	Plural
First person	I will have wandered	we will have wandered
Second person	you will have wandered	you will have wandered
Third person	he, she, it will have wandered	they will have wandered

Exercise 18A: Third Person Singular Verbs

In the simple present conjugation, the third person singular verb changes by adding an *-s*. Read the following rules and examples for adding *-s* to verbs in order to form the third person singular. Then, rewrite the first person verbs as third person singular verbs. The first of each set is done for you.

Usually, add *-s* to form the third person singular verb.

First Person Verb	Third Person Singular Verb	
I battle	he	battles
I weigh	she	______________
I inform	it	______________

Add *-es* to verbs ending in *-s*, *-sh*, *-ch*, *-x*, or *-z*.

First Person Verb	Third Person Singular Verb	
we bless	she	blesses
we attach	it	______
we mix	he	______

If a verb ends in *-y* after a consonant, change the *y* to *i* and add *-es*.

First Person Verb	Third Person Singular Verb	
I multiply	it	multiplies
I dry	he	______
I fancy	she	______

If a verb ends in *-y* after a vowel, just add *-s*.

First Person Verb	Third Person Singular Verb	
we pay	he	pays
we annoy	she	______
we prey	it	______

If a verb ends in *-o* after a consonant, form the plural by adding *-es*.

First Person Verb	Third Person Singular Verb	
I lasso	she	lassoes
I veto	it	______
I undo	he	______

Exercise 18B: Simple Present Tenses

Choose the correct form of the simple present verb in parentheses, based on the person. Cross out the incorrect form.

Thea and her brother Nazim (want / wants) to surprise their parents.

Thea (tidy / tidies) her room while Nazim (clean / cleans) the bathroom.

They (work / works) together to clean all the floors.

Nazim (start / starts) dinner right before their parents (call / calls) to say they'll be home soon.

"I (think / thinks) we should have some flowers on the table," (say / says) Thea.

"If you (pick / picks) some from the back yard, I will get a vase ready," (reply / replies) Nazim.

Thea (get / gets) the flowers and (come / comes) back inside.

When their parents (arrive / arrives) a few minutes later, the siblings (wish / wishes) them a happy anniversary.

Exercise 18C: Perfect Present Tenses

Write the correct form of the perfect present verb in the blank. These sentences are from Jules Verne's *Around the World in Eighty Days*.

"You ________________ [forget] nothing?" asked he.

I'm off, you see; and if you will examine my passport when I get back, you will be able to judge whether I ________________ [accomplish] the journey agreed upon.

But the East India Company ________________ now ________________ [pass] away, leaving the British possessions in India directly under the control of the Crown.

You ________________ [be] serviceable and devoted. I ________________ [pay] for your service, but not for your devotion.

He ________________ not ________________ [make] his appearance since yesterday.

At least I ________________ not ________________ [miss] the steamer, which is the most important thing.

— LESSON 19 —

Person of the Verb
Conjugations
State-of-Being Verbs

English	**Latin**		
conjugate	*conjugare*	*con*	+ *jugare*
to join a verb to each person in turn	to join together	with	+ to yoke

REGULAR VERB, SIMPLE PRESENT

	Singular	Plural
First person	I conjugate	we conjugate
Second person	you conjugate	you conjugate
Third person	he, she, it conjugates	they conjugate

REGULAR VERB, SIMPLE PAST

conjugated

REGULAR VERB, SIMPLE FUTURE

will conjugate

REGULAR VERB, PERFECT PRESENT

	Singular	Plural
First person	I have conjugated	we have conjugated
Second person	you have conjugated	you have conjugated
Third person	he, she, it has conjugated	they have conjugated

REGULAR VERB, PERFECT PAST

had conjugated

REGULAR VERB, PERFECT FUTURE

will have conjugated

REGULAR VERB, PROGRESSIVE PRESENT

am conjugating

STATE-OF-BEING VERB, SIMPLE PRESENT

	Singular	Plural
First person	I am	we are
Second person	you are	you are
Third person	he, she, it is	they are

Exercise 19A: Forming Progressive Present Tenses

Fill in the blanks with the correct helping verbs.

Regular Verb, Progressive Present

	Singular	Plural
First person	I ______________ commanding	we ______________ commanding
Second person	you ______________ commanding	you ______________ commanding
Third person	he, she, it ______________ commanding	they ______________ commanding

STATE-OF-BEING VERB, SIMPLE PRESENT

	Singular	Plural
First person	I am	we are
Second person	you are	you are
Third person	he, she, it is	they are

STATE-OF-BEING VERB, SIMPLE PAST

	Singular	Plural
First person	I was	we were
Second person	you were	you were
Third person	he, she, it was	they were

STATE-OF-BEING VERB, SIMPLE FUTURE

	Singular	Plural
First person	I will be	we will be
Second person	you will be	you will be
Third person	he, she, it will be	they will be

STATE-OF-BEING VERB, PERFECT PRESENT

	Singular	Plural
First person	I have been	we have been
Second person	you have been	you have been
Third person	he, she, it has been	they have been

STATE-OF-BEING VERB, PERFECT PAST

	Singular	Plural
First person	I had been	we had been
Second person	you had been	you had been
Third person	he, she, it had been	they had been

STATE-OF-BEING VERB, PERFECT FUTURE

	Singular	Plural
First person	I will have been	we will have been
Second person	you will have been	you will have been
Third person	he, she, it will have been	they will have been

STATE-OF-BEING VERB, PROGRESSIVE PRESENT

	Singular	Plural
First person	I am being	we are being
Second person	you are being	you are being
Third person	he, she, it is being	they are being

STATE-OF-BEING VERB, PROGRESSIVE PAST

	Singular	Plural
First person	I was being	we were being
Second person	you were being	you were being
Third person	he, she, it was being	they were being

STATE-OF-BEING VERB, PROGRESSIVE FUTURE

	Singular	Plural
First person	I will be being	we will be being
Second person	you will be being	you will be being
Third person	he, she, it will be being	they will be being

Exercise 19B: Forming Progressive Past and Future Tenses

Regular Verb, Progressive Past

	Singular	Plural
First person	I ______________ commanding	we ______________ commanding
Second person	you ______________ commanding	you ______________ commanding
Third person	he, she, it ___________ commanding	they ______________ commanding

Regular Verb, Progressive Future

	Singular		Plural	
First person	I ____________	commanding	we ______________	commanding
Second person	you ____________	commanding	you ____________	commanding
Third person	he, she, it __________	commanding	they ____________	commanding

— LESSON 20 —

Irregular State-of-Being Verbs
Helping Verbs

Forms of the State-of-Being Verb *Am*

SIMPLE PRESENT

	Singular	Plural
First person	I am	we are
Second person	you are	you are
Third person	He, she, it is	they are

SIMPLE PAST

	Singular	Plural
First person	I was	we were
Second person	you were	you were
Third person	he, she, it was	they were

SIMPLE FUTURE

	Singular	Plural
First person	I will be	we will be
Second person	you will be	you will be
Third person	he, she, it will be	they will be

PERFECT PRESENT

	Singular	Plural
First person	I have been	we have been
Second person	you have been	you have been
Third person	he, she, it has been	they have been

PERFECT PAST

	Singular	Plural
First person	I had been	we had been
Second person	you had been	you had been
Third person	he, she, it had been	they had been

PERFECT FUTURE

	Singular	Plural
First person	I will have been	we will have been
Second person	you will have been	you will have been
Third person	he, she, it will have been	they will have been

PROGRESSIVE PRESENT

	Singular	Plural
First person	I am being	we are being
Second person	you are being	you are being
Third person	he, she, it is being	they are being

PROGRESSIVE PAST

	Singular	Plural
First person	I was being	we were being
Second person	You were being	you were being
Third person	he, she, it was being	they were being

PROGRESSIVE FUTURE

	Singular	Plural
First person	I will be being	we will be being
Second person	you will be being	you will be being
Third person	he, she, it will be being	they will be being

Exercise 20A: Simple Tenses of the Verb *Have*

Try to fill in the missing blanks in the chart below, using your own sense of what sounds correct as well as the hints you may have picked up from the conjugations already covered. Be sure to use pencil so that any incorrect answers can be erased and corrected!

Simple Present

	Singular	**Plural**
First person	I have	we ______
Second person	you ______	you ______
Third person	he, she, it ______	they ______

Simple Past

	Singular	**Plural**
First person	I ______	we ______
Second person	you ______	you ______
Third person	he, she, it ______	they ______

Simple Future

	Singular	**Plural**
First person	I will ______	we ______
Second person	you ______	you ______
Third person	he, she, it ______	they ______

Exercise 20B: Simple Tenses of the Verb *Do*

Try to fill in the missing blanks in the chart below, using your own sense of what sounds correct as well as the hints you may have picked up from the conjugations already covered. Be sure to use pencil so that any incorrect answers can be erased and corrected!

Simple Present

	Singular	**Plural**
First person	I do	we ______
Second person	you ______	you ______
Third person	he, she, it ______	they ______

Simple Past

	Singular	Plural
First person	I ______________	we ______________
Second person	you ______________	you ______________
Third person	he, she, it ____________	they ______________

Simple Future

	Singular	Plural
First person	I will ______________	we ______________
Second person	you ______________	you ______________
Third person	he, she, it ____________	they ______________

I will be	I shall be	I shall be!
You will run	You will run	You shall run!
He, she, it will sing	He, she, it will sing	He, she, it shall sing!
We will eat	We shall eat	We shall eat!
You will shout	You will shout	You shall shout!
They will cavort	They will cavort	They shall cavort!

I **will** go to bed early.
When I was young, I **would** always go to bed early.

I **would** like to go to bed early.
I **should** probably go to bed now.

I **would** eat the chocolate caramel truffle.
I **should** eat the chocolate caramel truffle.
I **may** eat the chocolate caramel truffle.
I **might** eat the chocolate caramel truffle.
I **must** eat the chocolate caramel truffle.
I **can** eat the chocolate caramel truffle.
I **could** eat the chocolate caramel truffle.

Am, is, are, was, were, be, being, and *been* are forms of the verb *am.*
Have, has, and *had* are forms of the verb *has.*
Do, does, and *did* are forms of the verb *do.*
Shall and *will* are different forms of the same verb.
Should, would, may, might, must, can, and *could* express hypothetical situations.

WEEK 6

Nouns and Verbs in Sentences

— LESSON 21 —

Person of the Verb
Conjugations
Noun-Verb/Subject-Predicate Agreement

SIMPLE PRESENT

	Singular	**Plural**
First person	I enjoy	we enjoy
Second person	you enjoy	you enjoy
Third person	he, she, it enjoys	they enjoy

PERFECT PAST

	Singular	**Plural**
First person	I had been	we had been
Second person	you had been	you had been
Third person	he, she, it had been	they had been

PROGRESSIVE FUTURE

	Singular	**Plural**
First person	I will be running	we will be running
Second person	you will be running	you will be running
Third person	he, she, it will be running	they will be running

Complete Conjugation of a Regular Verb

SIMPLE PRESENT

	Singular	**Plural**
First person	I grab	we grab
Second person	you grab	you grab
Third person	he, she, it grabs	they grab

SIMPLE PAST

I grabbed, etc.

SIMPLE FUTURE

I will grab, etc.

PERFECT PRESENT

	Singular	**Plural**
First person	I have grabbed	we have grabbed
Second person	you have grabbed	you have grabbed
Third person	he, she, it has grabbed	they have grabbed

PERFECT PAST

I had grabbed, etc.

PERFECT FUTURE

I will have grabbed, etc.

PROGRESSIVE PRESENT

	Singular	**Plural**
First person	I am grabbing	we are grabbing
Second person	you are grabbing	you are grabbing
Third person	he, she, it is grabbing	they are grabbing

PROGRESSIVE PAST

	Singular	**Plural**
First person	I was grabbing	we were grabbing
Second person	you were grabbing	you were grabbing
Third person	he, she, it was grabbing	they were grabbing

PROGRESSIVE FUTURE

I will be grabbing, etc.

Exercise 21A: Person and Number of Pronouns

Identify the person and number of the underlined pronouns. Cross out the incorrect verb(s) in parentheses. The first one is done for you.

These sentences are adapted from L. M. Montgomery's *Anne of the Island*.

	Person	Singular/Plural
You (remember / ~~remembers~~), Marilla, what a consuming desire I had to sleep in the spare room bed.	second	singular
They (am / is / are) all nice, kind, motherly souls.	______	______
Wherever I (go / goes),	______	______
they (confront / confronts) me.	______	______
It (am / is / are) just the end of the beginning.	______	______
She (were / was) the prettiest freshette I saw to-day.	______	______
We (am / is / are) going for a walk in the park.	______	______
He (have / has) always been crazy about you.	______	______
You all (do / does) well to remember him.	______	______

SIMPLE PRESENT

	Singular	Plural
Third person	He, she, it grabs	They grab
	The man grabs	The men grab
	The woman grabs	The women grab
	The eagle grabs	The eagles grab

PERFECT PRESENT

	Singular	Plural
Third person	He, she, it has grabbed	They have grabbed
	The boy has grabbed	The boys have grabbed
	The girl has grabbed	The girls have grabbed
	The bear has grabbed	The bears have grabbed

PROGRESSIVE PRESENT

	Singular	Plural
Third person	He, she, it is grabbing	They are grabbing
	The father is grabbing	The fathers are grabbing
	The mother is grabbing	The mothers are grabbing
	The baby is grabbing	The babies are grabbing

PROGRESSIVE PAST

	Singular	Plural
Third person	He, she, it was grabbing	They were grabbing
	The king was grabbing	The kings were grabbing
	The queen was grabbing	The queens were grabbing
	The dragon was grabbing	The dragons were grabbing

Exercise 21B: Identifying Subjects and Predicates

Draw two lines underneath each simple predicate and one line underneath each simple subject in the following sentences. If a phrase comes between the subject and the predicate, put parentheses around it to show that it does not affect the subject-predicate agreement.

The sentences below are taken or adapted from *Creatures of the Sea: Rays* by Kris Hirschmann.

About five hundred species of rays exist around the world.

The skate family, a type of ray, has about two hundred species.

A ray's flat body is called a disc.

At only four inches across, the smallest ray is the shortnose electric ray.

Because of the position of its eyes, a ray cannot see anything directly below itself.

Other senses compensate for this.

A tail with spikes and venomous barbs serves as a defense mechanism for some rays.

Exercise 21C: Subject-Verb Agreement

Cross out the incorrect verb in parentheses so that subject and predicate agree in number and person. Be careful of any confusing phrases between the subject and predicate.

Ravi and Philip (want/wants) to see what plant cells look like.

Ravi's mother, after a bit of instruction, (allow/allows) them to use her microscope.

Philip (tear/tears) a small bit of the skin off an onion and (place/places) it on a slide.

The boys (remember/remembers) that they (need/needs) to add a drop of water.

Then Ravi, working carefully, (put/puts) a cover slip on top.

Once the slide (am/is/are) under the microscope, the two boys (take/takes) turns looking at it.

Each boy (draw/draws) a picture of what he (see/sees).

— LESSON 22 —

Formation of Plural Nouns
Collective Nouns

A collective noun names a group of people, animals, or things.

Exercise 22A: Collective Nouns

Write the collective noun for each description. Then fill in an appropriate singular verb for each sentence. (Use the simple present tense!) The first one is done for you.

Description		Collective Noun	Verb	
a group of teachers working at a school	The	faculty	instructs	the students.
several dancers performing together	The	______________	______________	beautifully.
a group of listeners	The	______________	______________	loudly.
several experts	The	______________	______________	animatedly.
many sailors on a ship	The	______________	______________	well.
two shoes	This	______________	______________	too tight.
several bananas together	This	______________	______________	brown.

Exercise 22B: Plural Noun Forms

Read each rule and the example out loud. Then rewrite the singular nouns as plural nouns in the spaces provided.

Usually, add *-s* to a noun to form the plural.

Singular Noun	Plural Noun
beginner	beginners
snail	______________
airport	______________
morning	______________

Add *-es* to nouns ending in *-s*, *-sh*, *-ch*, *-x*, or *-z*.

Singular Noun	Plural Noun
kiss	kisses
crash	______________
watch	______________
mailbox	______________
klutz	______________

If a noun ends in *-y* after a consonant, change the *y* to *i* and add *-es*.

Singular Noun	Plural Noun
activity	activities
spy	__________________
tendency	__________________
memory	__________________

If a noun ends in *-y* after a vowel, just add *-s*.

Singular Noun	Plural Noun
tray	trays
boy	__________________
monkey	__________________
railway	__________________

Some words that end in *-f or -fe* form their plurals differently. You must change the *f* or *fe* to *v* and add *-es*.

Singular Noun	Plural Noun
half	halves
loaf	__________________
wolf	__________________
calf	__________________

Words that end in *-ff* form their plurals by simply adding *-s*.

Singular Noun	Plural Noun
muff	muffs
handcuff	__________________
knockoff	__________________

Some words that end in a single *-f* can form their plurals either way.

Singular Noun	Plural Noun
hoof	hoofs/hooves
wharf	__________________

If a noun ends in *-o* after a vowel, just add *-s*.

Singular Noun	Plural Noun
video	videos
embryo	__________________

(note that the "y" makes a vowel sound in this word!)

Singular Noun	Plural Noun
stereo	__________________
kazoo	__________________

If a noun ends in *-o* after a consonant, form the plural by adding *-es*.

Singular Noun	Plural Noun
torpedo	torpedoes
peccadillo	________________
volcano	________________
embargo	________________

To form the plural of foreign words ending in *-o*, just add *-s*.

Singular Noun	Plural Noun
bonobo	bonobos
taco	________________
chorizo	________________
piccolo	________________
silo	________________

Irregular plurals don't follow any of these rules!

Singular Noun	Irregular Plural Noun
cactus	cacti
vertex	vertices
shrimp	shrimp
bison	________________
datum	data
offspring	offspring
parenthesis	________________
criterion	criteria

Exercise 22C: Plural Nouns

Complete the following excerpt by filling in the plural form of each noun in parentheses. The following passage is condensed from Frances Hodgson Burnett's *The Secret Garden*.

Mary asked no more (question) ________________ but waited in the darkness of her corner, keeping her (eye) ________________ on the window. The carriage (lamp) ________________ cast (ray) ________________ of light a little distance ahead of them and she caught (glimpse) ________________ of the (thing) ________________ they passed. After they had left the station they had driven through a tiny village and she had seen whitewashed (cottage) ________________ and the (light) ________________ of a public house. Then they had passed a church and a vicarage and a little shop-window or so in a cottage with (toy) ________________ and (sweet) ________________ and odd (thing) ________________ set out for sale. Then they were on the highroad and she saw (hedge) ________________ and (tree) ________________. After that there seemed nothing different for a long time—or at least it seemed a long time to her.

At last the (horse) ________________ began to go more slowly, as if they were climbing up-hill, and presently there seemed to be no more (hedge) ________________ and no more (tree) ________________. She could see nothing, in fact, but a dense darkness on either side. She leaned forward and pressed her face against the window just as the carriage gave a big jolt.

"Eh! We're on the moor now sure enough," said Mrs. Medlock.

The carriage (lamp) ________________ shed a yellow light on a rough-looking road which seemed to be cut through (bush) ________________ and low growing (thing) ________________ which ended in the great expanse of dark apparently spread out before and around them. A wind was rising and making a singular, wild, low, rushing sound.

"It's—it's not the sea, is it?" said Mary, looking round at her companion.

"No, not it," answered Mrs. Medlock. "Nor it isn't (field) ________________ nor (mountain) ________________, it's just (mile) ________________ and (mile) ________ and (mile) ________________ of wild land that nothing grows on but heather and gorse and broom, and nothing lives on but wild (pony) ________________ and (sheep) ________________."

They drove into a clear space and stopped before an immensely long but low-built house which seemed to ramble round a stone court. At first Mary thought that there were no (light) ________________ at all in the (window) ________________, but as she got out of the carriage she saw that one room in a corner up-stairs showed a dull glow.

The entrance door was a huge one made of massive, curiously shaped (panel) ________________ of oak studded with big iron (nail) ________________ and bound with great iron (bar) ________________. It opened into an enormous hall, which was so dimly lighted that the (face) ________________ in the (portrait) ________________ on the (wall) ________________ and the (figure) ________________ in the (suit) ____________ of armor made Mary feel that she did not want to look at them.

— LESSON 23 —

Plural Nouns
Descriptive Adjectives
Possessive Adjectives
Contractions

An apostrophe is a punctuation mark that shows possession. It turns a noun into an adjective that tells whose.

Possessive adjectives tell whose.

An adjective modifies a noun or pronoun.
Adjectives tell what kind, which one, how many, and whose.
Descriptive adjectives tell what kind.
A descriptive adjective becomes an abstract noun when you add *-ness* to it.

Form the possessive of a singular noun by adding an apostrophe and the letter *-s*.

Exercise 23A: Introduction to Possessive Adjectives

Read the following nouns. Choose a person that you know to possess each of the items. Write that person's name, an apostrophe, and an *s* to form a possessive adjective.

Example: Cecily ______ Cecily's ______ encyclopedia

______ water bottle

______ ticket to *Phantom of the Opera*

______ capybara

______ calculator

______ growl

Form the possessive of a plural noun ending in *-s* by adding an apostrophe only.

Form the possessive of a plural noun that does not end in *-s* as if it were a singular noun.

Exercise 23B: Singular and Plural Possessive Adjective Forms

Fill in the chart with the correct forms. The first is done for you. Both regular and irregular nouns are included.

Noun	Singular Possessive	Plural	Plural Possessive
pencil	pencil's	pencils	pencils'
grass			
robin			
creator			
bison			
potato			
island			
motion			
knife			
fireman			
fairy			

	SINGULAR		PLURAL	
	Pronoun(s)	**Possessive Adjective**	**Pronoun(s)**	**Possessive Adjective**
First person	I	my	we	our
Second person	you	your	you	your
Third person	he, she, it	his, her, its	they	their

INCORRECT	CORRECT
I's book	my book
you's candy	your candy
he's hat	his hat
she's necklace	her necklace
it's nest	its nest
we's lesson	our lesson
they's problem	their problem

Contraction	**Meaning**
he's	he is
she's	she is
it's	it is
you're	you are
they're	they are

A contraction is a combination of two words with some of the letters dropped out.

Exercise 23C: Common Contractions

Drop the letters in grey print and write the contraction in the blank. The first one is done for you.

Full Form	Common Contraction	Full Form	Common Contraction
you had	you'd	would not	______
I will	______	we would	______
could not	______	it has	______
have not	______	I had	______
they will	______	what has	______
he had	______	does not	______
when is	______	she will	______
they would	______	should not	______

— LESSON 24 —

Possessive Adjectives
Contractions
Compound Nouns

A contraction is a combination of two words with some of the letters dropped out.

Contraction	Meaning	Not the Same as
he's	he is	his
she's	she is	her
it's	it is	its
you're	you are	your
they're	they are	their

It's hard for a hippopotamus to see its feet.
***It is** hard for a hippopotamus to see its feet.*
*It's hard for a hippopotamus to see **it is** feet.*

You're fond of your giraffe.
***You are** fond of your giraffe.*
*You're fond of **you are** giraffe.*

They're searching for their zebra.
***They are** searching for their zebra.*
*They're searching for **they are** zebra.*

Exercise 24A: Using Possessive Adjectives Correctly

Cross out the incorrect word in parentheses.

(Its / It's) very icy out there; I'm not sure if the car will be able to make (its / it's) way up the hill.

I want to put (his / he's) hat back before (his / he's) had a chance to miss it.

(Your / You're) the famous detective, right? I've read (your / you're) book!

(Their / They're) alibis prove that (their / they're) innocent.

(Hers / She's) adamant that the jacket is not (yours / your's); (its / it's) (hers / she's).

(His / He's) trying to adjust (their / they're) microphones; (their / they're) starting the conference soon.

(Its / It's) head drooping, the dog walked through the rain toward (its / it's) favorite hole.

When (your / you're) feeling sleepy, (your / you're) bed is a welcome sight.

(Its / It's) almost time; (hers / she's) going to be here any minute.

If (yours / your's) is the red car, you should know that (your / you're) lights were left on.

A compound noun is a single noun composed of two or more words.

One word	shipwreck, haircut, chalkboard
Hyphenated word	self-confidence, check-in, pinch-hitter
Two or more words	air conditioning, North Dakota, *The Prince and the Pauper*

Exercise 24B: Compound Nouns

Underline each simple subject once and each simple predicate (verb) twice. Circle each compound noun.

The restrooms are down the hallway.

I have selected new curtains for the living room.

Captain Picard is my favorite character on *Star Trek: The Next Generation.*

I enjoy our city's fireworks on Independence Day.

The queen's lady-in-waiting was standing on the other side of the drawbridge.

Monday's earthquake startled my great-aunt.

A grand jury has found sufficient evidence for the indictment of the ninety-three-year-old.

Hazel remembered her password.

If a compound noun is made up of one noun along with another word or words, pluralize the noun.

passerby passersby passerbys

If a compound noun ends in *-ful*, pluralize by putting an *-s* at the end of the entire word.

truckful trucksful truckfuls

If neither element of the compound noun is a noun, pluralize the entire word.

grown-up growns-up grown-ups

If the compound noun includes more than one noun, choose the most important to pluralize.

attorney at law attorneys at law attorney at laws

Exercise 24C: Plurals of Compound Nouns

Write the plural of each singular compound noun in parentheses in the blanks to complete the sentences.

Marie Curie was the first person to win two (Nobel Prize) ____________________.

My friend and I discovered that both our (mother-in-law) ____________________ live in (cul-de-sac) ____________________ in this neighborhood.

All the (washing machine) ____________________ are already in use.

Indoor (swimming pool) ____________________ are a great place to exercise in the winter.

Last night, I dreamed that (truckful) ____________________ of (catfish) ____________________ were being delivered to my house!

The women talking over there are not medical doctors, but (doctor of philosophy) ____________________.

How many (cupful) ____________________ of sugar did you put in these cookies?

The (lieutenant colonel) ____________________ agreed to take the issue to their (higher-up) ____________________.

— REVIEW 2 —

Weeks 4-6

Topics
Simple, Progressive, and Perfect Tenses
Conjugations
Irregular Verbs
Subject/Verb Agreement
Possessives
Compound Nouns
Contractions

Review 2A: Verb Tenses

Write the tense of each underlined verb phrase on the line in the right-hand margin: simple past, present, or future; progressive past, present, or future; or perfect past, present, or future. Watch out for words that interrupt verb phrases but are not helping verbs (such as *not*).

These sentences are adapted from Sir Walter Scott's *Ivanhoe*.

	Verb Tense
The date of our story refers to a period towards the end	__________
of the reign of Richard I, when his return from his long	
captivity had become an event rather wished than hoped for by his despairing subjects.	__________
Reginald Front-de-Boeuf is coming down to this country	__________
in person, and we shall soon see how little	__________
Cedric's trouble will avail him.	__________
The upper dress of this personage resembled that of his companion.	__________
Silk and embroidery distinguished their dresses.	__________
These were forming, at the same time, a striking contrast with the martial simplicity of his own attire.	__________
I have seen no maiden so beautiful since Pentecost was a twelve-month.	__________

Prior, your collar is in danger; ________________

I will wear it over my gorget in the lists at ________________
Ashby-de-la-Zouche.

One grisly old wolf-dog alone had planted himself close by ________________
the chair of state, and was occasionally putting his large ________________
hairy head upon his master's knee.

He had exchanged his shirt of mail for an under tunic of dark purple silk. ________________

He followed modestly the last ________________
of the train which entered the hall. ________________

My vow binds me to advance no farther upon this floor of my fathers. ________________

My steward has expounded to you the cause of my seeming discourtesy. ________________

I will have marred his archery. ________________

But our bards are no more; ________________
our deeds are lost in those of another race—our ________________
language—our very name is hastening to decay, ________________
and none mourns for it save one solitary old man. ________________

Review 2B: Verb Formations

Fill in the charts with the correct conjugations of the missing verbs. Identify the person of each group of verbs.

PERSON: ____________

	Past	Present	Future
SIMPLE	she	she	she will carry
PROGRESSIVE	she was carrying	she	she
PERFECT	she	she	she

PERSON: ___________

	Past	Present	Future
SIMPLE	I cycled	I	I
PROGRESSIVE	I	I	I
PERFECT	I	I have cycled	I

PERSON: ___________

	Past	Present	Future
SIMPLE	you	you gather	you
PROGRESSIVE	you	you	you will be gathering
PERFECT	you	you	you

PERSON: ___________

	Past	Present	Future
SIMPLE	they	they	they will walk
PROGRESSIVE	they were walking	they	they
PERFECT	they	they	they

Review 2C: Person and Subject/Verb Agreement

Cross out the incorrect verb or contraction in parentheses. The following sentences are taken or adapted from the Irish story "Deirdre and the Sons of Uisneach" as retold by Una Leavy in *Irish Fairy Tales and Legends.*

The stars never (lies / lie)!

We (has / have) looked at the stars to see this baby's future.

She (is / are) only a little baby!

When she (grows / grow) up, I will marry her myself.

Naoise, son of Uisneach, (is / are) the only such man in the world.

I only (wants / want) to be with you, Naoise.

Conor's men (is / are) just behind us!

When morning came, they (was / were) near the sea again.

King Conor (has / have) forgiven you! He (wants / want) you to come home.

You (doesn't / don't) know how I (has / have) longed for this news!

The king (has / have) asked you to his fort at once. You, Fergus, (has / have) been invited to a harvest feast.

Review 2D: Possessives and Compound Nouns

Complete the chart below, writing the singular possessive, plural, and plural possessive of each singular pronoun or compound noun. The first one has been done for you.

Noun	Possessive	Plural	Plural Possessive
nightmare	nightmare's	nightmares	nightmares'
dragonfly	__________	__________	__________
she	__________	__________	__________
has-been	__________	__________	__________
I	__________	__________	__________
grapefruit	__________	__________	__________
toothbrush	__________	__________	__________
you	__________	__________	__________
father-in-law	__________	__________	__________
congresswoman	__________	__________	__________
it	__________	__________	__________
crybaby	__________	__________	__________
he	__________	__________	__________
runner-up	__________	__________	__________

Review 2E: Plurals and Possessives

In the following sentences, provide the possessive, the plural, or the plural possessive for each noun in parentheses as indicated. These sentences are from *The Wind in the Willows*, by Kenneth Grahame.

Why can't (fellow, plural) ________________ be allowed to do what they like when they like and as they like, instead of other (fellow, plural) ________________ sitting on (bank, plural) ________________ and watching them all the time and making (remark, plural) ________________ and poetry and (thing, plural) ________________ about them?

Some ten (minute, plural possessive) ____________________ hard work, and the point of the (Rat, possessive) ____________________ cudgel struck something that sounded hollow.

In accordance with the kindly (Badger, possessive) ____________________ (injunction, plural) ________________, the two tired (animal, plural) ________________ came down to breakfast very late next morning.

The (hedgehog, plural) ________________________ dropped their (spoon, plural) ____________________, rose to their (foot, plural) ____________________, and ducked their (head, plural) ______________________ respectfully as the two entered.

The (Mole, possessive) ____________________ thoughts ran a good deal on supper.

Your own idea, those little (sleeping-bunk, plural) ____________________ in the wall? Capital!

The result was not so very depressing after all, though of course it might have been better; a tin of (sardine, plural) ____________________ —a box of (captain, possessive) ____________________ (biscuit, plural) ____________________, nearly full—and a German sausage encased in silver paper.

Mole saw his little (friend, plural possessive) ____________________ (face, plural) ____________________ brighten and beam as they fell to without delay.

Review 2F: Contractions

In the following sentences, form contractions from the words in parentheses. These sentences are adapted from Andrew Peterson's *The Warden and the Wolf King*.

I never thought ____________________ (I would) see ye again!

I guess ____________________ (that is) the downward fork.

Why ____________________ (do not) you love me?

Of course ____________________ (it is) real.

And ____________________ (we are) going to fight.

____________________ (You had) better have that dagger ready.

____________________ (You are) still a Throne Warden.

The sight made Sara's heart ache like it ____________________ (had not) in years.

She ____________________ (did not) allow herself to hope that she might see her own parents again.

____________________ (Who is) hungry?

I think ____________________ (you will) find that many of us at Clovenfast have…quirks.

And yes, ____________________ (he is) alive.

If what Cadwick said is true, ____________________ (they will) be wilder.

____________________ (There is) one just ahead.

And once ____________________ (we are) out, what then?

________________ (I have) done my best to teach the replacements the messenger posts.

"____________________ (Let us) eat," Kal said.

Janner ____________________ (could not) see his eyes.

And ____________________ (I am) proud to be your brother.

____________________ (We will) eat on the way.

WEEK 7

Compounds and Conjunctions

— LESSON 25 —

Contractions
Compound Nouns
Diagramming Compound Nouns
Compound Adjectives
Diagramming Adjectives
Articles

A contraction is a combination of two words with some of the letters dropped out.

Exercise 25A: Contractions Review

Write the two words that form each contraction on the blanks to the right. Some contractions have more than one correct answer. The first is done for you.

Contraction	Helping Verb	Other Word
we'd	would OR had	we
she'll		
I'm		
didn't		
you've		
isn't		
weren't		
it'll		
they're		

Our air conditioning is working!

Exercise 25B: Diagramming Adjectives and Compound Nouns

On your own paper, diagram every word of the following sentences.

Our solar system moves.

Louisa May Alcott wrote.

Melissa's high school instructs.

Good hearing aids assist.

The large-headed monster had twenty-seven teeth.

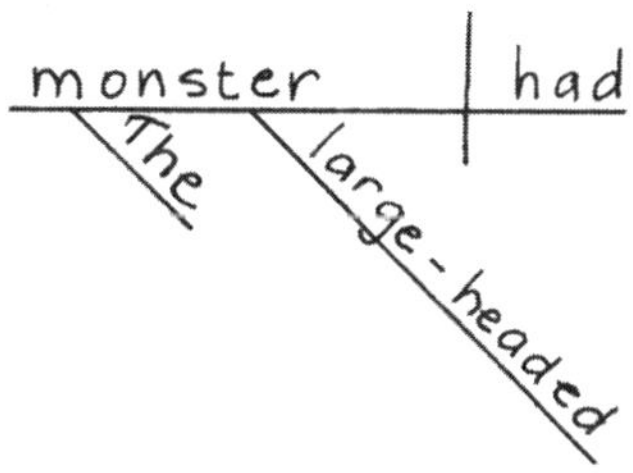

The articles are *a*, *an*, and *the*.

Exercise 25C: Compound Nouns

Using the list of words below, make as many single-word compound nouns as you can. Each word in the list can be used *at least* twice.

ball	book	case	cut	fall
foot	mark	rest	room	suit
store	snow	water	work	

______________	______________	______________
______________	______________	______________
______________	______________	______________
______________	______________	______________
______________	______________	______________
______________	______________	______________
______________	______________	______________
______________	______________	______________

Exercise 25D: Compound Adjectives

Correctly place hyphens in the following phrases.

four hundred fifty one degrees Fahrenheit

the mixed up files

the life changing magic

a fifty year friendship

twenty two high end watches

a two day old lamb

a germ destroying air purifier

Exercise 25E: Diagramming Adjectives, Compound Nouns, and Compound Adjectives

On your own paper, diagram every word in the following sentences.

The old two-story house collapsed.
Fragile eggshells can break.
An out-of-breath police officer hurried.
A sweet-smelling yellow flower had opened.
Sixty-three left-handed men responded.

— LESSON 26 —

Compound Subjects
The Conjunction *And*
Compound Predicates
Compound Subject-Predicate Agreement

The fireman hurries.
The policeman hurries.
The fireman and the policeman hurry.

SIMPLE PRESENT

	Singular	**Plural**
First person	I hurry	we hurry
Second person	you hurry	you hurry
Third person	he, she, it hurries	they hurry

Compound subjects joined by *and* are plural in number and take plural verbs.
A conjunction joins words or groups of words together.

The farmer plants.
The farmer harvests.
The farmer plants and harvests.

Exercise 26A: Identifying Subjects, Predicates, and Conjunctions

Underline the subjects once and the predicates twice in each sentence. Circle the conjunctions that join them. The first one is done for you.

These sentences are adapted from Jack London's *The Call of the Wild.*

He drank eagerly, and later bolted a generous meal of raw meat.

All passiveness and unconcern had dropped from them.

An oath from Perrault, the resounding impact of a club upon a bony frame, and a shrill yelp of pain, heralded the breaking forth of pandemonium.

Here were many men, and countless dogs.

The hair rose along his back and stood on end across his shoulders and up his neck.

He whittled and listened and gave monosyllabic replies and terse advice.

Exercise 26B: Diagramming Compound Subjects and Predicates

Draw one line under the subject[s] and two lines under the predicate[s] in the following sentences. Circle any conjunctions that connect subjects and/or predicates. When you are finished, diagram the subjects, predicates, and conjunctions ONLY of each sentence on your own paper.

These sentences are adapted from the Britannica Illustrated Science Library's *Plants, Algae, and Fungi.*

The gametes, spores, and seeds of plants can move about, especially with the help of water and wind.

Grasses grow and reproduce in the long hours of summer daylight.

Red algae can thrive at relatively high temperatures and live inside thermal water vents.

Optimal temperature and appropriate quantities of water and air are the important factors for a seed's awakening.

Orchids' flowers are large and very colorful and secrete a sugary nectar.

Water and nutrients are sufficient for the cultivation of tomatoes.

Exercise 26C: Forming Compound Subjects and Verbs

Combine each of these sets of simple sentences into one sentence with a compound subject and/or a compound predicate joined by *and*. Use your own paper.

The boy plays with the ball.
The dog plays with the ball.

The engineer studies the problem.
The engineer develops a solution.
The engineer searches for ways to improve the solution.

Paul runs up onto the stage.
Janice runs up onto the stage.
Yuan runs up onto the stage.
Paul sings.
Janice sings.
Yuan sings.

After the science fair, Josué packed up his project.
After the science fair, Josué went home.
After the science fair, I packed up my project.
After the science fair, I went home.

Exercise 26D: Subject-Verb Agreement with Compound Subjects

Choose the correct verb in parentheses to agree with the subject. Cross out the incorrect verb.

Amaya (dash/dashes) down the street and (dart/darts) into a shop.

The baker and his assistant (stop/stops) talking and (stare/stares) at Amaya.

Amaya (catch/catches) her breath and (look/looks) at the display case.

She (order/orders) a cake and (tell/tells) the baker that it will be a surprise for her sister.

The baker (prepare/prepares) and (decorate/decorates) the cake.

Amaya (pay/pays) for the cake and (thank/thanks) the baker.

— LESSON 27 —

Coordinating Conjunctions
Complications in Subject-Predicate Agreement

A conjunction joins words or groups of words together.
A coordinating conjunction joins similar or equal words or groups of words together.

and, or, nor, for, so, but, yet

Indonesia and Greater Antilles are groups of islands.
I will nap or go running.
They will not help me, nor you.
I ran after them, for I needed help.
I stubbed my toe, so now my foot hurts.
I was exhausted, but my sister was still full of energy.
He was laughing, yet he seemed sad.

Exercise 27A: Using Conjunctions

Fill the blanks in the sentences below with the appropriate conjunctions. You must use each conjunction (*and, or, nor, for, so, but, yet*) at least once. (There is more than one possible answer for many of the blanks!)

These sentences are adapted from Sir Walter Scott's *Ivanhoe.*

It becomes not one wearing this badge to answer, ________________ to whom, besides the sworn champions of the Holy Sepulchre, can the palm be assigned among the champions of the Cross?

There was a stranger at the gate, imploring admittance ________________ hospitality.

Cedric hastened to meet her, ________________ to conduct her, with respectful ceremony, to the elevated seat at his own right hand.

Replacing his javelin, he resumed his seat, bent his looks downward, ________________ appeared to be absorbed in melancholy reflection.

It was the Knight of Ivanhoe; ________________ was there one of the six that, for his years, had more renown in arms.

Pride ________________ jealousy there was in his eye, ________________ his life had been spent in asserting rights which were constantly liable to invasion.

I can guess thy want, ________________ I can supply it.

If I had a horse, I would be your guide, ______________ the way is somewhat intricate, though perfectly well known to me.

The path soon led deeper into the woodland, ______________ crossed more than one brook, the approach to which was rendered perilous by the marshes through which it flowed; ______________ the stranger seemed to know, as if by instinct, the soundest ground ______________ the safest points of passage.

In this dress I am vowed to poverty, ______________ do I change it for aught save a horse ______________ a coat of mail.

Compound subjects joined by *and* are plural in number and take plural verbs.

I am friendly.
George and I are friends.

The policeman or the fireman hurries.

The dog and the cat are sleeping on the sofa.
The dog or the cat is sleeping on the sofa.
The dogs or the cat is sleeping on the sofa.

When compound subjects are joined by *or*, the verb agrees with the number of the nearest subject.

The pies were scrumptious.
The pies on the table were scrumptious.
The box of pencils is on the top shelf.

A can of red beans sits on the table.

The young man at all of the meetings was bored.

Fractions are singular if used to indicate a single thing.
Fractions are plural if used to indicate more than one thing.

Three-fourths of the pie was missing.
Three-fourths of the socks were missing.

Expressions of money, time, and quantity (weight, units, and distance) are singular when used as a whole, but plural when used as numerous single units.

Thirty dollars is too much to pay for that shirt.
Thirty dollars are spread across the table.

Seven years is a long time to wait.
The minutes tick by.

A thousand pounds is far too heavy for that truck.
Fifty gallons of water are divided among the refugees.
Four miles is too far to walk.

Collective nouns are usually singular. Collective nouns can be plural if the members of the group are acting as independent individuals.

The herd of cattle was grazing quietly.
The herd of cattle were scattered throughout the plains.

Exercise 27B: Subject-Predicate Agreement: Troublesome Subjects

Circle the correct verb in parentheses so that it agrees with the subject noun or pronoun in number.

The mirrors on the shelf (reflect / reflects) the candlelight.

Half of the milk (has / have) spilled on the counter and (is / are) dripping onto the floor!

The kindergarten class (wreck / wrecks) the art room on a daily basis, but the teacher and the aide (clean / cleans) things up afterward.

The crew (was / were) alerted to the danger by the captain's loud cry.

The flock of birds (was / were) flying in all directions.

Two-thirds of the students (describe / describes) the visitor as a good storyteller.

Kenneth and Dawson (dislike / dislikes) pumpkin pie but (love / loves) brownies.

The staff (entertain / entertains) themselves during slow times by creating art with sticky notes.

One million gallons of water (was / were) brought onto the hurricane-battered island.

The jar of cookies (tempt / tempts) me.

My brother or sister (has / have) been experimenting with recipes again—cookies should be sweet, but four cups of sugar for two dozen cookies (is / are) just too much!

One-fourth of the fence (has / have) been painted.

One-fourth of the fences (has / have) been painted.

Five years (remain / remains) before the next election.

The panel of experts (disagree / disagrees) on how to solve this issue.

The guide or some tourists usually (spot / spots) a manatee around this part of the boat ride.

Exercise 27C: Fill In the Verb

Choose a verb in the present tense that makes sense to complete each sentence. Be sure the verb agrees in number with its subject!

The fury of the people ____________________ a riot.

My brother and I ____________________ snails and worms under those rocks all the time.

Either the bus or one of the vans ____________________ late for the retreat every year.

Your observations about the painting ____________________ very astute.

The class ____________________ elections for officers in October.

The mayor, the city council, and the police department ____________________ credit for the decrease in violent crimes over the last year.

The ink in all of my pens ____________________ too quickly!

Either the berries or the milk ____________________ me to have an allergic reaction, so I will avoid both!

Half of the pages in this book ____________________ covered with pencil marks.

— LESSON 28 —

Further Complications in Subject-Predicate Agreement

Many nouns can be plural in form but singular in use: measles, mumps, rickets, politics, mathematics, economics, news.

Mathematics is my favorite subject.

Singular literary works, works of art, newspapers, countries, and organizations can be plural in form but are still singular in use.

Little Women was written by Louisa May Alcott.
The United States is south of Canada.

Many nouns are plural in form and use but singular in meaning: pants, scissors, pliers, glasses.

Pants are too hot in the summertime.

In sentences beginning with *There is* or *There are*, the subject is found after the verb.

There is a skunk in the brush.
There are three skunks in the brush.

***Each* and *every* always indicate a singular subject.**

In Masai villages, each woman cares for her own cattle.
In Masai villages, each of the women cares for her own cattle.
In Masai villages, each cares for her own cattle.

In Masai villages, women care for their own cattle.

Every man needs friends.
Men need friends.

Compound nouns that are plural in form but singular in meaning take a singular verb.

Fish and chips is my favorite British dish.

Compound subjects joined by *and* take a singular verb when they name the same thing.

The owner and manager of the ice cream shop is also working behind the counter.

Nouns with Latin and Greek origins take the singular verb when singular in form and the plural verb when plural in form.

The data suggest otherwise.

Singular	Plural
medium	media
datum	data
criterion	criteria
phenomenon	phenomena
focus	foci
appendix	appendices

Exercise 28A: Subject-Verb Agreement: More Troublesome Subjects

Find the correct verb (agrees with the subject in number) in parentheses. Cross out the incorrect verb.

Gymnastics (is/are) Maria's favorite activity of the week.

Every part in the play (has/have) been cast.

In *The Lord of the Rings*, there (is/are) one ring more powerful than all the rest.

The vertices of a regular polygon (lies/lie) on the circle that can be drawn around the polygon.

The teacher and technology director (is/are) running late for his meeting.

Biscuits and gravy (was/were) not on the menu today.

There (is/are) only six Wonder Gadgets left—you'd better order yours now!

Each fork, knife, and spoon (was / were) placed in precisely the right spot.

"Each of the dresses (has / have) something wrong with it," complained Julia.

Green Eggs and Ham (was / were) written as the result of a bet Dr. Seuss's publisher made with him; the publisher believed Dr. Seuss could not write a book using no more than fifty unique words.

My new binoculars (allows / allow) me to observe birds all the way across the lake!

Today's news (is / are) not good.

The alumni of our campus organization (supports / support) us financially.

Jane Austen's *Pride and Prejudice* (was / were) published in 1813.

Billiards (is / are) a game with many variations.

Science and Nature (is / are) my favorite category in Trivial Pursuit.

Here on the handout (is / are) the criteria for this project.

Each of the poisons (has / have) a unique antidote.

Trinidad and Tobago (has / have) been an independent nation since 1962.

Every minute (brings / bring) us closer to the deadline.

Exercise 28B: Correct Verb Tense and Number

Complete each of these sentences by writing the correct number and tense of the verb indicated in the blank. The sentences are taken or adapted from Nathaniel Hawthorne's *The Scarlet Letter.*

Externally, the jollity of aged men (simple present of *have*) ____________________ much in common with the mirth of children.

This rose-bush, by a strange chance, (perfect present of *am*) ____________________ kept alive in history.

In some two years, or less, that the woman has been a dweller here in Boston, no tidings (simple present of *have*) ______________ come of this learned gentleman, Master Prynne.

Here, to witness the scene which we are describing, (simple past of *am*) ________________ Governor Bellingham himself.

The discipline of the family, in those days, (simple past of *am*) ____________________ of a far more rigid kind than now.

Physical compulsion or restraint (simple past of *am*) ____________________ effectual, of course, while it lasted.

The children of the settlement (progressive past of *play*) ____________________ at going to church.

All the powers of nature (simple present of *call*) ____________________ so earnestly for the confession of sin.

A knowledge of men's hearts (simple present of *am*) ____________________ needful to the completest solution of that problem.

There (simple present of *am*) ____________________ no law nor reverence for authority mixed up with that child's composition.

Here (simple present of *am*) ____________________ a child of three years old, and she cannot tell who made her!

Their wide, short trousers (simple past of *am*) ____________________ confined about the waist by belts, often clasped with a rough plate of gold.

A sluggish bond-servant or an undutiful child (simple past of *am*) ____________________ to be corrected at the whipping-post.

The Governor and gentlemen (progressive present of *come*) ____________________!

WEEK 8

Introduction to Objects

— LESSON 29 —

Action Verbs
Direct Objects

A direct object receives the action of the verb.

Cara built a bonfire.
We roasted marshmallows over the bonfire.
Tom ate the delicious cookie.
Julia, hot and thirsty, drank the fresh-squeezed lemonade.
She visited her grandfather.
He had forgotten her name.
She found peace.

We roasted marshmallows.

We roasted soft marshmallows and beefy hot dogs.

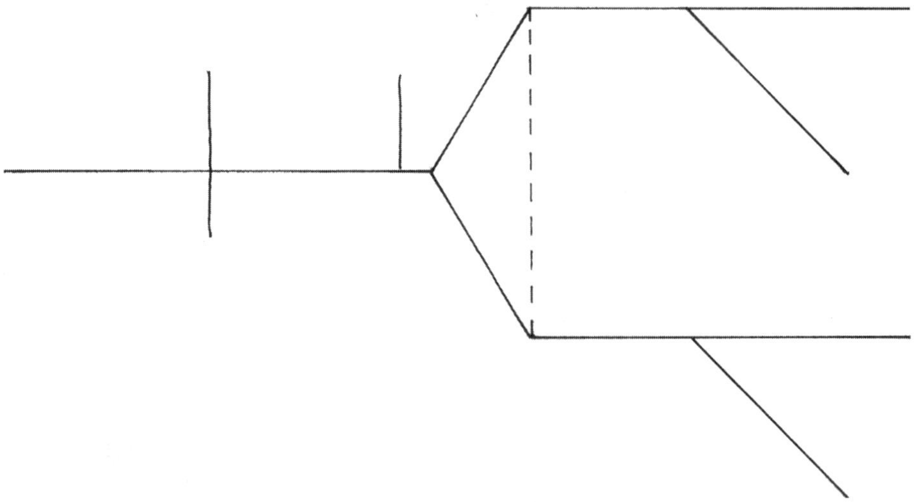

My friend and I rode roller coasters and ate popcorn and cotton candy.

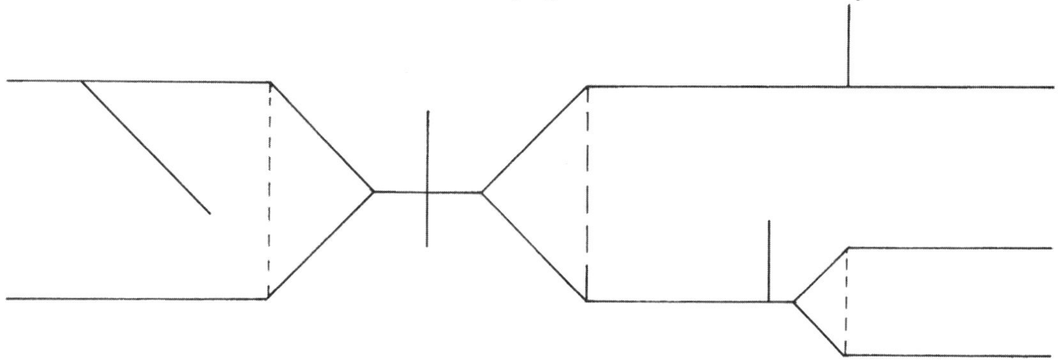

Exercise 29A: Direct Objects

In the following sentences, underline the subjects once and the predicates twice. Circle each direct object. These sentences are adapted from Daniel Defoe's *Robinson Crusoe.*

I had lived a dreadful life.

We never see the true state of our condition.

I had no powder or shot left.

I would build another *Periagua* or *Canoe.*

I had thus laid the scheme of my design.

The floor had a sort of small loose gravel upon it.

I took him up, and made much of him, and encouraged him.

In this voyage I visited my colony in the island, saw my successors, and had the whole story of their lives.

They must run out and see the battle.

However, they used some caution too.

They soon outdid their masters.

I cut the thread of his comforts and shortened his days.

We made signals of distress to the ship.

I got much money by the first adventure, and an insight into the method of getting more.

The tree effectually shaded him over the head.

Exercise 29B: Diagramming Direct Objects

On your own paper, diagram the subjects, verbs, and direct objects ONLY in the sentences from Exercise 29A.

— LESSON 30 —

Direct Objects
Prepositions

I broke my breakfast plate!
The pottery plate broke into pieces.

A preposition shows the relationship of a noun or pronoun to another word in the sentence.

Prepositions
aboard, about, above, across
after, against, along, among, around, at

before, behind, below, beneath
beside, between, beyond, by

down, during, except, for, from
in, inside, into, like

near, of, off, on, over
past, since, through, throughout

to, toward, under, underneath
until, up, upon
with, within, without

Exercise 30A: Identifying Prepositions

In the following sentences (adapted from Oscar Wilde's *The Picture of Dorian Gray*), find and circle each preposition.

In the centre of the room, clamped to an upright easel, stood the full-length portrait of a young man of extraordinary personal beauty, and in front of it, some little distance away, was sitting the artist himself, Basil Hallward, whose sudden disappearance some years ago caused, at the time, such public excitement, and gave rise to so many strange conjectures.

As the painter looked at the gracious and comely form he had so skilfully mirrored in his art, a smile of pleasure passed across his face. But he suddenly started up, and, closing his eyes, placed his fingers upon the lids, as though imprisoning within his brain some curious dream from which he feared he might awake.

Exercise 30B: Word Relationships

The following sentences all contain action verbs. Underline each subject once and each action verb twice. If the sentence has an action verb followed by a direct object, write *DO* above the direct object.

If the sentence contains a preposition, circle the preposition and draw a line to connect the two words that the preposition shows a relationship between. The first two are done for you.

Mathieu apologized (to) me (for) his mistake.

DO
Zoey collected the trash.

This new strategy will double our profit.

I burned my finger on the cookie sheet.

Three children in shabby clothes shivered pitifully in the snow.

Our cousins arrived on the early flight from Atlanta.

The computer at the end of the row works slowly.

The kingdom's borders extend beyond the mountain.

Amina laughed heartily at my joke.

The exhausted heroes stepped warily into the cave.

Someone must change the baby's diaper!

This key will unlock any door in the building.

Gleefully, the soldiers obeyed the evil queen's orders.

Harold sheepishly grinned at his sister.

Exercise 30C: Diagramming Direct Objects

On your own paper, diagram the subjects, predicates, and direct objects ONLY from the sentences above. If a sentence does not have a direct object, do not diagram it.

— LESSON 31 —

Definitions Review
Prepositional Phrases
Object of the Preposition

A noun names a person, place, thing, or idea.
An adjective modifies a noun or pronoun.
A pronoun takes the place of a noun.
A verb shows an action, shows a state of being, links two words together, or helps another verb.
A conjunction joins words or groups of words together.
A coordinating conjunction joins similar or equal words or groups of words together.
A phrase is a group of words serving a single grammatical function.
A preposition shows the relationship of a noun or pronoun to another word in the sentence.

Prepositions
aboard, about, above, across
after, against, along, among, around, at
before, behind, below, beneath
beside, between, beyond, by
down, during, except, for, from
in, inside, into, like
near, of, off, on, over
past, since, through, throughout
to, toward, under, underneath
until, up, upon
with, within, without

A brook sluggishly flows through low ground.

Dark draperies hung upon the walls.

The tunnel wound into the green hill.

A prepositional phrase begins with a preposition and ends with a noun or pronoun. That noun or pronoun is the object of the preposition.

Put your hand beneath your workbook.

Calvin ran across the floor.

I baked a pie for my mother.

Exercise 31A: Objects of Prepositional Phrases

Fill in the blanks with a noun as the object of the preposition to complete the prepositional phrases.

Somehow, a library book ended up behind the ______________________________.

You can find more pretzels in the ____________________________.

We raced down the ___________________________ to deliver the news.

Throughout the ____________________, the people rejoiced to hear about the ______________________.

Suzanne enjoyed the documentary about ___________________________.

I like my pizza with ____.

(Use as many objects as you'd like for this one!)

Exercise 31B: Identifying Prepositional Phrases

Can you find all eleven of the prepositional phrases in the following excerpt, adapted from *The Time Machine* by H. G. Wells? (Beware words that can be prepositions but can also function as other parts of speech!)

Underline each complete prepositional phrase. Circle each preposition. Draw a box around each object of a preposition. One preposition has a compound object.

I saw the sun hopping swiftly across the sky, leaping it every minute, and every minute marking a day. I supposed the laboratory had been destroyed, and I had come into the open air. I had a dim impression of scaffolding, but I was already going too fast for consciousness of any moving things. The slowest snail that ever crawled dashed by too fast for me. The twinkling succession of darkness and light was excessively painful to the eye. Then in the intermittent darkness, I saw the moon spinning swiftly through her quarters, and had a faint glimpse of the circling stars.

Exercise 31C: Remembering Prepositions

Can you remember all forty-six prepositions without looking back at your list? The first letter of each preposition has been given for you.

A	B	D	E	F	I	L
aboard	______	______	______	______	______	______
______	______	______		______	______	
______	______				______	
______	______					
______	______					
______	______					
______	______					
______	______					
______						
______						

N	O	P	S	T	U	W
______	______	______	______	______	______	______
	______			______	______	______
	______			______	______	______
	______			______	______	
					______	

— LESSON 32 —

Subjects, Predicates, and Direct Objects
Prepositions
Object of the Preposition
Prepositional Phrases

The subject of the sentence is the main word or term that the sentence is about. The simple subject of the sentence is *just* the main word or term that the sentence is about.

The complete subject of the sentence is the simple subject and all the words that belong to it.

The warrior saw on the opposite mountain two great globes of glowing fire.

The predicate of the sentence tells something about the subject.
The simple predicate of the sentence is the main verb along with any helping verbs.
The complete predicate of the sentence is the simple predicate and all the words that belong to it.
A direct object receives the action of the verb.
A preposition shows the relationship of a noun or pronoun to another word in the sentence.

Prepositions
aboard, about, above, across
after, against, along, among, around, at
before, behind, below, beneath
beside, between, beyond, by
down, during, except, for, from
in, inside, into, like
near, of, off, on, over
past, since, through, throughout
to, toward, under, underneath
until, up, upon
with, within, without

A prepositional phrase begins with a preposition and ends with a noun or pronoun. That noun or pronoun is the object of the preposition.

DO
The warrior | saw on the opposite mountain two great globes of glowing fire.

The warrior saw two great globes.

The Dragon King with his retainers accompanied the warrior to the end of the bridge, and took leave of him with many bows and good wishes.

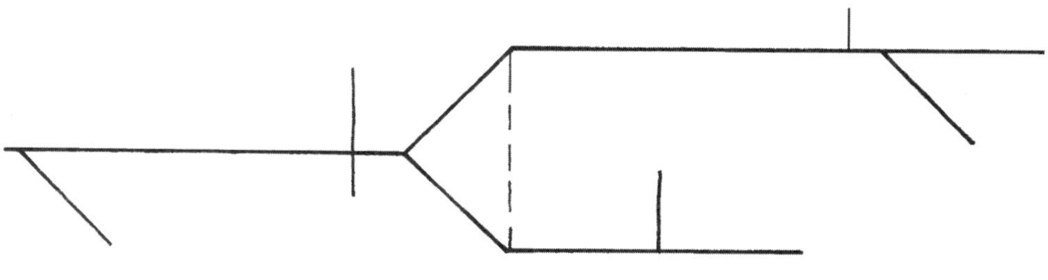

Exercise 32A: Identifying Prepositional Phrases and Parts of Sentences

In the following sentences, circle each prepositional phrase. Once you have identified the prepositional phrases, underline subjects once, underline predicates twice, and label direct objects with *DO*.

Things to watch out for:

1) Words that could be prepositions but are acting as other parts of speech instead. If it doesn't have an object, it's not a preposition!
2) In some of these sentences, subjects and predicates are inverted so that the predicate comes first. Find the verb first, then ask, "Who or what [verb]?" to find the subject. Remember that the subject will not be the object of a preposition!

These sentences are adapted from "The Padishah of the Forty Peris," from *Turkish Fairy Tales and Folk Tales*, collected by Ignácz Kunos and translated by R. Nisbet Bain.

The first is done for you.

DO

She put her ring (upon her sewing-table).

They went on and on and on, through the level plains by the flowing river.

She rose from her bed and promised a great treasure for the youth.

Then the youth went to the cupboard, opened it, and took the ring, the bracelet, and the lace handkerchief of the sultan's daughter.

He would be with her for two hours of the day.

In that same city dwelt the bald-headed son of a bed-ridden mother.

With that he flew into the room and turned into a man.

He was filled with joy at the sight of his child.

He looked to the right of him and to the left.

Exercise 32B: Diagramming

On your own paper, diagram all of the uncircled parts of the sentences from Exercise 32A. EXCEPTION: Do not diagram the *and* in the last sentence, since its only function is to connect two prepositional phrases.

WEEK 9

Adverbs

— LESSON 33 —

Adverbs That Tell How

A sneaky squirrel stole my sock slowly.
A sneaky squirrel stole my sock sleepily.
A sneaky squirrel stole my sock cheerfully.
A sneaky squirrel stole my sock rapidly.

An adverb describes a verb, an adjective, or another adverb.

An **exceptionally** sneaky squirrel stole my sock slowly.
A sneaky squirrel stole my sock **very** rapidly.

Adverbs tell how, when, where, how often, and to what extent.

Adjective	**Adverb**
serious	seriously
fierce	__________
thorough	__________
crazy	crazily
scary	__________
cheery	__________

He left hurriedly.
Hurriedly, he left.
He hurriedly left.

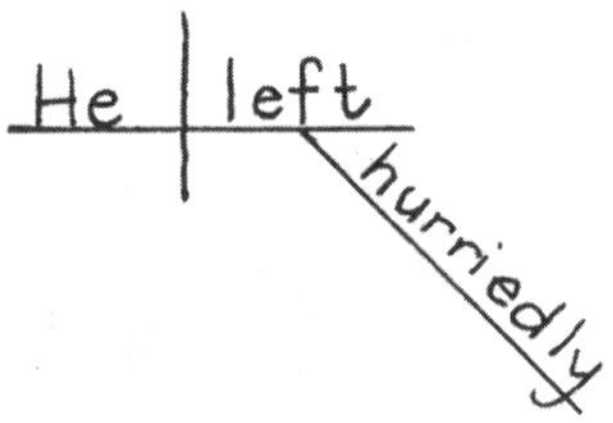

Exercise 33A: Identifying Adverbs That Tell *How*

Underline the adverbs telling *how* in the following sentences, and draw arrows to the verbs that they modify.

"May I have another cookie?" the child asked sweetly.

The captured spy glared defiantly as the enemy soldiers roughly pushed her toward the interrogation room.

Absentmindedly, Elissa stirred the soup on the stove.

Eamon spoke with us frankly about his desire to join the circus.

The coach dealt justly with the conflict between the teammates.

"If you can make a bed properly, you're hired," said the hotel manager exhaustedly.

When Akari's stage fright threatened to overcome her, the director spoke reassuringly to her.

Truly, I believe this is the best choice.

His shield and sword lying in the field behind him, the knight courageously—and rather foolishly—rode toward the monster's lair.

I called my parents to tell them I'd arrived home safely.

Exercise 33B: Forming Adverbs from Adjectives

Turn the following adjectives into adverbs.

Adjective	Adverb	Adjective	Adverb
thoughtful	______________	dizzy	______________
sore	______________	languid	______________
spotty	______________	hideous	______________
decorous	______________	bouncy	______________
flagrant	______________		

Exercise 33C: Diagramming Adverbs

Diagram the following sentences on your own paper.

I dearly love this place.

Violet thankfully accepted the gift.

My adorable new kitten mewed questioningly.

Has she answered knowledgeably?

Nervously, we entered the decrepit old house.

Toby completed the application thoroughly.

— LESSON 34 —

Adverbs That Tell When, Where, and How Often

Exercise 34A: Telling When

Tim dropped his recipe cards for chocolate chip cookies. Help him get organized by numbering the following sentences from 1 to 5 so he can make the cookies.

_______ Second, add the salt, vanilla, and applesauce.

_______ Later, chill the dough for at least an hour.

_______ First, cream together the butter and sugars.

_______ Finally, bake for about 10 minutes in a 350° oven.

_______ Next, mix in the flour and baking soda before adding the chocolate chips.

An adverb describes a verb, an adjective, or another adverb.
Adverbs tell how, when, where, how often, and to what extent.

Yesterday I washed my dog outside.

The dog ran away.

Then the dog lay down.

Now my dog is sleeping there.

My glasses are lying there.

My red book is sitting here.

There are my glasses.

Here is my red book.

Now my dog is sleeping there.

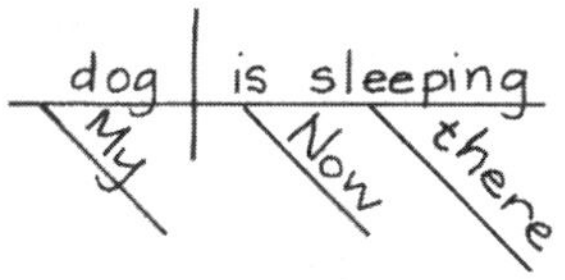

There are my glasses.

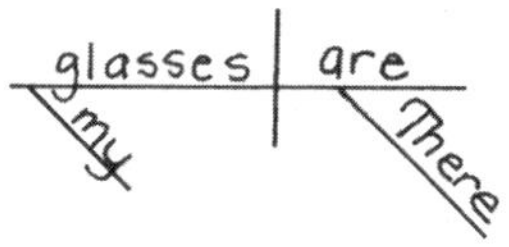

Here is my red book.

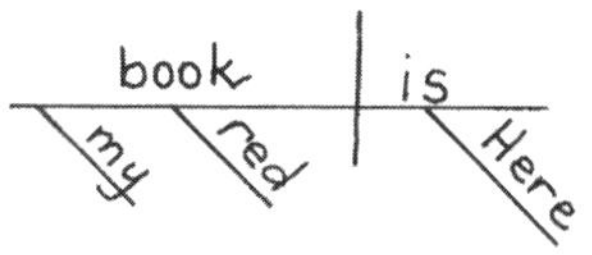

***Here* and *there* are adverbs that tell where.**

I wash my dog weekly.
Richie is always looking for adventure.
I will often be eating.

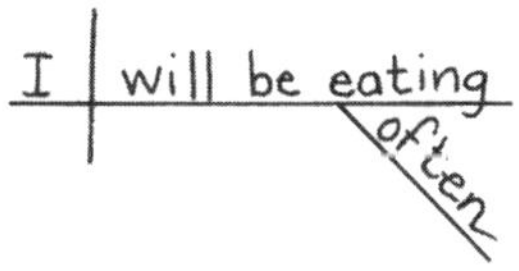

When will you arrive?
Where is my hat?
How are you doing?

you will arrive When.

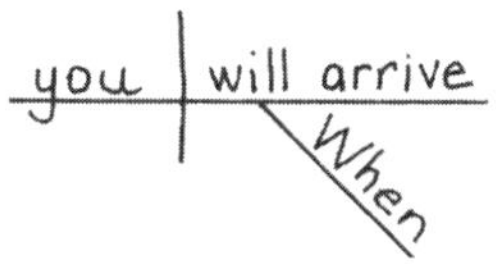

my hat is Where.

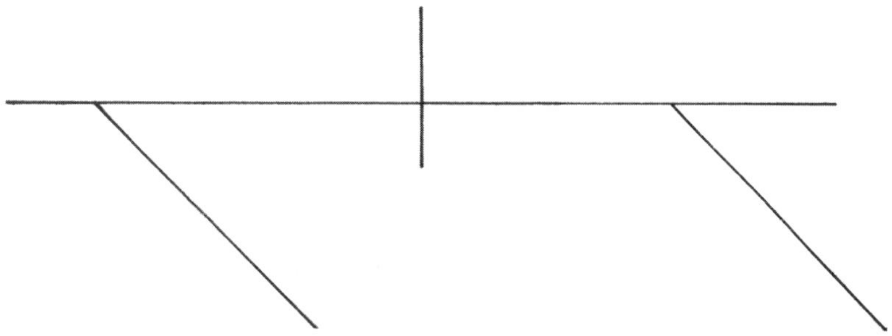

Exercise 34B: Distinguishing Among Different Types of Adverbs

Put each of the following adverbs in the correct category, according to the question each one answers.

below	greedily	then	rarely
today	kindly	outside	yearly
daily	earlier	angrily	down

When	Where	How	How Often
__________	__________	__________	__________
__________	__________	__________	__________
__________	__________	__________	__________

Exercise 34C: Identifying Adverbs of Different Types

Underline the adverbs in the following sentences that tell *when, where,* or *how often.*

I lost my way once yesterday.

Sometimes Shanika plays her saxophone outdoors.

Nikki talked incessantly during the movie.

Let's go downstairs now.

That piano key occasionally sticks.

I usually sit there.

Winston will visit his grandfather tomorrow.

Mrs. Lee always arrives early.

Unless that cough improves soon, you should see a doctor.

Where did Miguel put his keys?

Exercise 34D: Diagramming Different Types of Adverbs

Diagram the following sentences on your own paper.

Lenore will eat these leftovers later.
When is Dad going outside?
Today I breakfasted late.
Complete your exercises now.
Gloria and Caleb clapped enthusiastically and then stood.
You left your hat here yesterday.

— LESSON 35 —

Adverbs That Tell To What Extent

An adverb describes a verb, an adjective, or another adverb.
Adverbs tell how, when, where, how often, and to what extent.

The extremely humid day was unpleasant.
Sharon runs quite quickly.
Larry shrieked especially loudly.

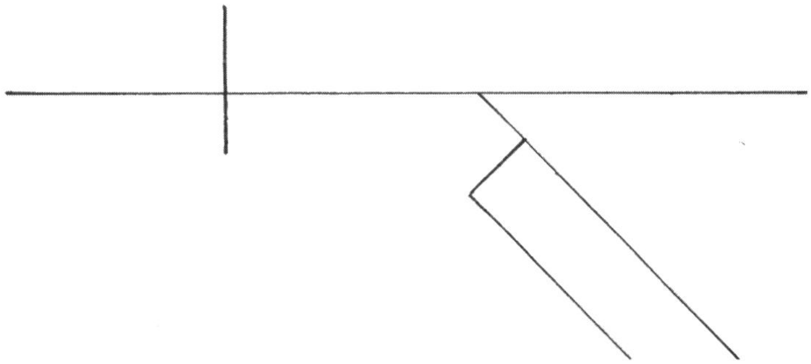

Extremely skittish Larry ran away.

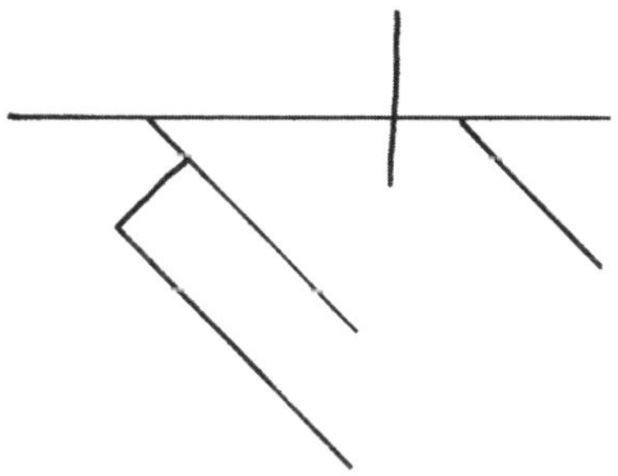

Exercise 35A: Identifying the Words Modified by Adverbs

Draw an arrow from each underlined adverb to the word it modifies. These sentences are from J. M. Barrie's *Peter Pan*.

No nursery could possibly have been conducted <u>more</u> <u>correctly</u>.

It had begun <u>so</u> <u>uneventfully</u>, <u>so</u> <u>precisely</u> like a hundred other evenings.

The little stars are not <u>really</u> friendly to Peter, who had a mischievous way of stealing up behind them and trying to blow them out; but they are <u>so</u> fond of fun that they were on his side <u>tonight</u>.

Of course I'm very sorry, but how could I know you were in the drawer?

I nipped a bit out of that eagle's mouth pretty neatly, Wendy.

Of course this was rather unsatisfactory.

Tink was not all bad; or, rather, she was all bad just now, but, on the other hand, sometimes she was all good.

Then they had to tell Peter of Tink's crime, and almost never had they seen him look so stern.

And how ardently they grew to love their home under the ground.

He often went out alone, and when he came back you were never absolutely certain whether he had had an adventure or not.

She was really glad for the sake of his reputation that no one heard him except herself.

She had to admit that she was too tired.

"It is sweet, Peter, isn't it?" Wendy said, frightfully gratified.

The awful cynicism of this made an uncomfortable impression, and most of them began to look rather doubtful.

Exercise 35B: Diagramming Different Types of Adverbs

Diagram the following sentences on your own paper.

Your new puppy is almost unbearably cute!

Zoe regarded the overly eager salesman suspiciously.

Currently, skies are partly cloudy.

Rafael will soon attempt a surprisingly difficult feat.

The freshman rather nervously addressed the senior class.

A fairy appeared quite suddenly and waved her wand mysteriously.

— LESSON 36 —

Adjectives and Adverbs
The Adverb *Not*
Diagramming Contractions
Diagramming Compound Adjectives and Compound Adverbs

An adjective modifies a noun or pronoun.
Adjectives tell what kind, which one, how many, and whose.

An adverb describes a verb, an adjective, or another adverb.
Adverbs tell how, when, where, how often, and to what extent.

It matters naught.

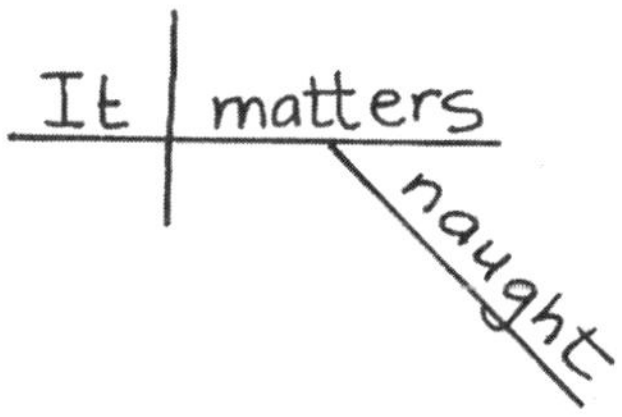

It does not matter.

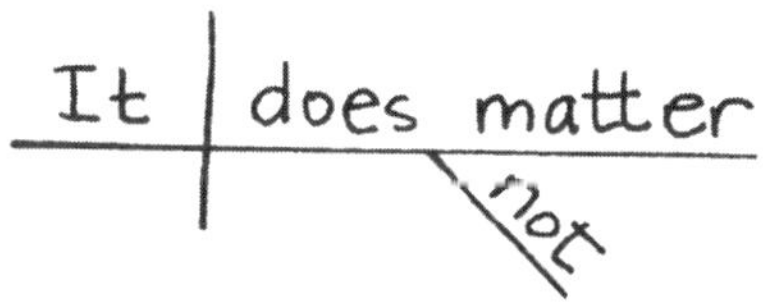

A contraction is a combination of two words with some of the letters dropped out.

It doesn't matter.

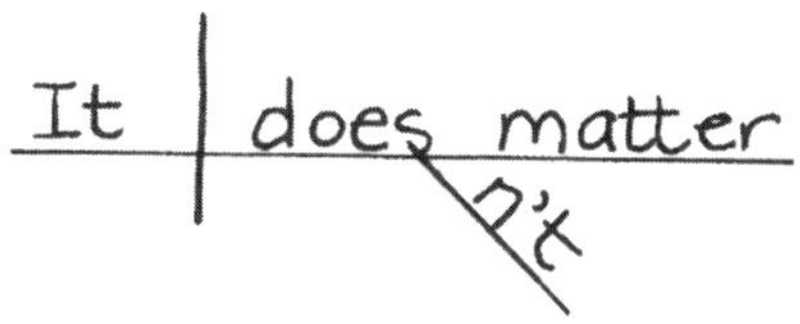

It's not there.

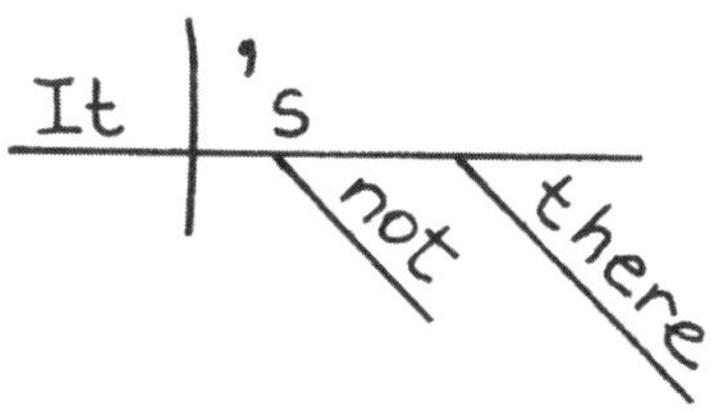

Tall and wide arches weren't often built.

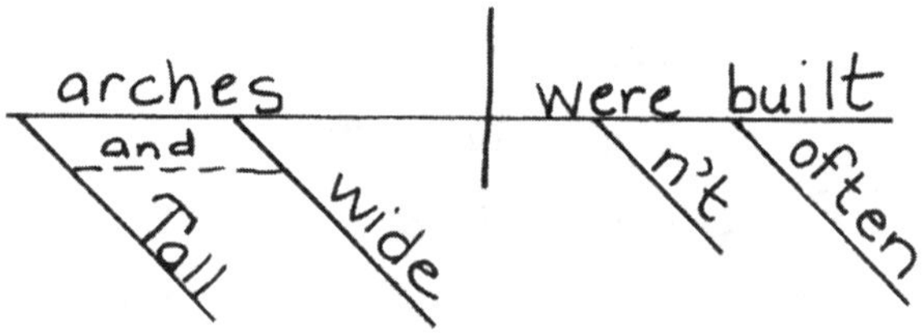

The idea was deeply and widely held.

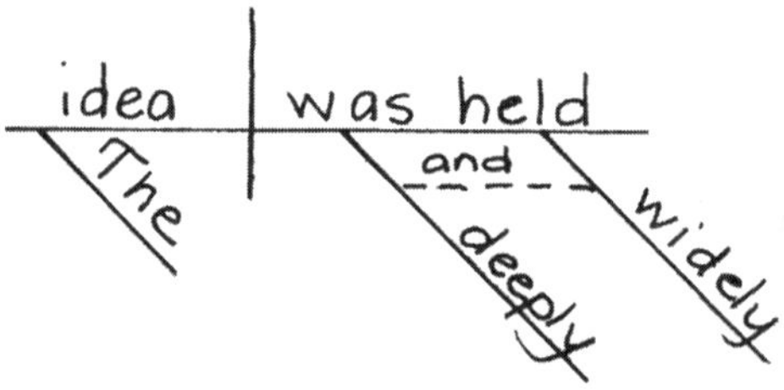

Exercise 36A: Practice in Diagramming

On your own paper, diagram every word of the following sentences. They are adapted from Johanna Spyri's *Heidi.*

If this is your first time through this course, you may skip #1, #4 and #8. If not, diagram them!

She was so hot and uncomfortable.

She ran busily to and fro.

Here a neat little bed was already prepared.

The little goat pressed close and became perfectly quiet.

Why should there be a change?

People only half believed these reports.

Get away and don't try it again.

The child does not look very terrible.

This little incident had ruffled Miss Rottenmeier's temper very much.

A large hall came next.

— REVIEW 3 —

Weeks 7-9

Topics
Parts of Speech
Compound Parts of Sentences
Prepositions
Prepositional Phrases
Objects of Prepositions
Subjects and Predicates
Subject-Verb Agreement
Verbs and Direct Objects

Review 3A: Parts of Speech

In the passage below from Orson Scott Card's *Ender's Game*, identify the underlined words as *N* for noun, *ADJ* for adjective, *ADV* for adverb, *PREP* for preposition, or *CONJ* for conjunction. The first is done for you.

N

The monitor lady smiled very nicely and tousled his hair and said, "Andrew, I suppose by now you're just absolutely sick of having that horrid monitor. Well, I have good news for you. That monitor is going to come out today. We're going to take it right out, and it won't hurt a bit."

Ender nodded. It was a lie, of course, that it wouldn't hurt a bit. But since adults always said it when it *was* going to hurt, he could count on that statement as an accurate prediction of the future. Sometimes lies were more dependable than the truth.

"So if you'll just come over here, Andrew, just sit right up here on the examining table. The doctor will be in to see you in a moment."

The monitor gone. Ender tried to imagine the little device missing from the back of his neck. I'll roll over on my back in bed and it won't be pressing there. I won't feel it tingling and taking up the heat when I shower.

Review 3B: Recognizing Prepositions

Circle the forty-six prepositions from your list in the following bank of words. Try to complete the exercise without looking back at your list of prepositions.

up among then until side

and my around you above

before through from there into

down throughout within pen much

jump they but aboard without

like between most near off

toward about of play beyond

with however along behind to

by on paper then except

sort during nor for less

eat against below air since

where underneath inside beside across

in when kind at spot

beneath after over well his

whom past upon move under

Review 3C: Subjects and Predicates

Draw one line under the simple subject and two lines under the simple predicate. Watch out for compound subjects or predicates! Also, remember that in poetry, sometimes the order of words is different than in normal speech—once you have found the verb, ask "who or what" before it to find the subject.

The following lines are from the poem "The Tyger," by William Blake.

What immortal hand or eye could frame thy fearful symmetry?

In what distant deeps or skies burnt the fire of thine eyes?

And what shoulder, and what art, could twist the sinews of thy heart?

In what furnace was thy brain?

The following lines are from the poem "Buttercups," by Wilfrid Thorley.

There must be fairy miners just underneath the mould.

They take the shining metals and beat them into shreds.

Sometimes they melt the flowers to tiny seeds like pearls and store them up in bowers for little boys and girls.

And still a tiny fan turns above a forge of gold.

The following lines are from the poem "The Ingenious Little Old Man," by John Bennett.

A little old man of the sea went out in a boat for a sail.

The water came in almost up to his chin.

But this little old man of the sea just drew out his jack-knife so stout.

And a hole with its blade in the bottom he made.

All of the water ran out.

Review 3D: Complicated Subject-Verb Agreement

Circle the correct verb form in parentheses.

My extended family (is / are) scattered around the country.

Twenty dollars (is / are) a great deal for this dress!

The pianist or the flautists (needs / need) to play louder.

Three-fourths of the employees (has / have) donated to this month's charity.

Julian's family (is / are) arriving in three hours.

The judging criteria for the art competition (is / are) available on the website.

The plants near the window (requires / require) frequent watering.

There (is / are) two buttons missing from this shirt.

Books and papers (covers / cover) a writer's desk.

A painted rocking chair (sits / sit) invitingly in the corner of the playroom.

Cristina or Isobel (times / time) each runner in the race.

Aleksandra and Madeline (counts / count) the money after the bake sale.

Newsies (is / are) a musical.

My clothes (was / were) not in the blue suitcase.

Review 3E: Objects and Prepositions

Identify the underlined words as *DO* for direct object or *OP* for object of preposition. For each direct object, find and underline twice the action verb that affects it. For each object of a preposition, find and circle the preposition to which it belongs.

These sentences are from *The Giver*, by Lois Lowry.

Now, thinking about the feeling of fear as he pedaled home along the river path, he remembered that moment of palpable, stomach-sinking terror when the aircraft had streaked above.

But his mind was still on December and the coming Ceremony.

It was effortless for Jonas, and even boring, though Asher enjoyed it.

He had held a magnifying glass to it.

They all listened carefully and discussed with Lily the warning that the dream had given.

Now Father sat beside Mother in the audience.

In each dwelling tonight they would be studying the instructions for the beginning of their training.

Jonas grinned with delight, and blew his own steamy breath into view.

He could see an odd look on The Giver's face.

In one ecstatic memory he had ridden a gleaming brown horse across a field that smelled of damp grass, and had dismounted beside a small stream from which both he and the horse drank cold, clear water.

He waved his hand in the familiar gesture.

WEEK 10

Completing the Sentence

— LESSON 37 —

Direct Objects
Indirect Objects

She gave **Odysseus** bread and sweet wine and sent him forth.

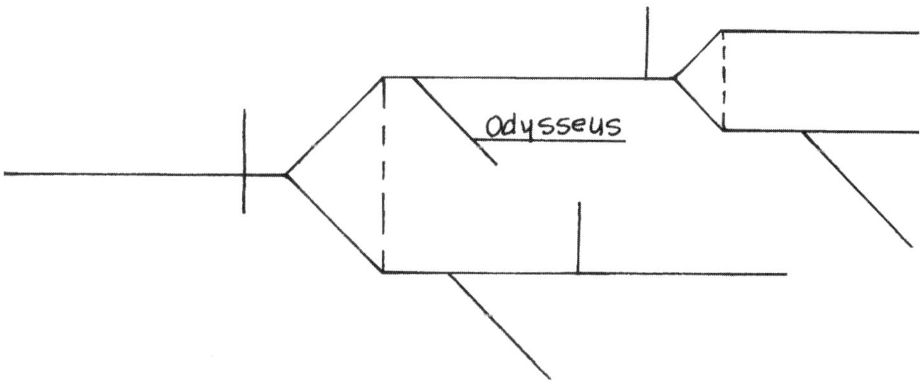

A direct object receives the action of the verb.
An indirect object is the noun or pronoun for whom or to whom an action is done.
An indirect object comes between the action verb and the direct object.

Odysseus asked the stranger a question.
Brandon sent his cousin and uncle an email.

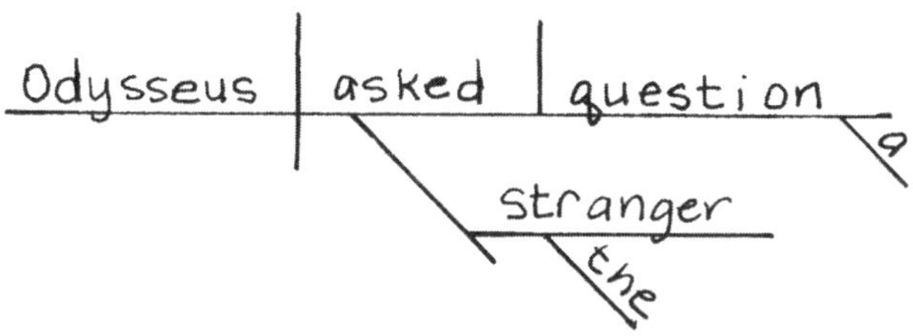

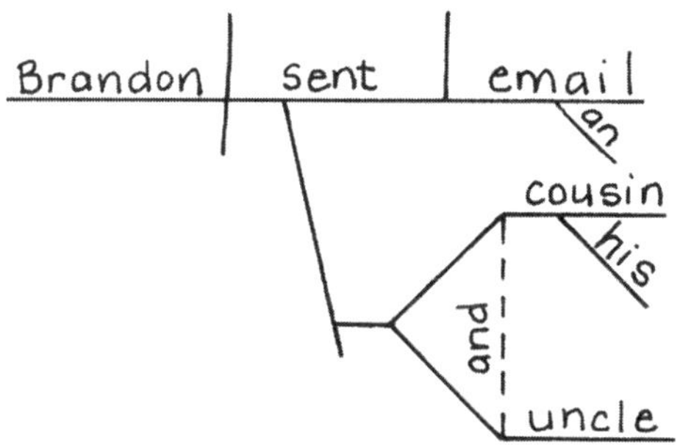

Exercise 37A: Identifying Direct Objects

Underline the action verbs and circle the direct objects in these sentences. Remember that you can always eliminate prepositional phrases first if that makes the task easier.

The sentences are adapted from May R. Berenbaum's *Bugs in the System: Insects and Their Impact on Human Affairs.*

Linnaeus described only about 2,000 species of insects.

Some insects carry metamorphosis to an extreme and undergo major anatomical modification with each and every molt.

Like most higher animals, insects perceive information about their environment through the nervous system.

These alarm pheromones can evoke different responses through the content and composition of the secretion.

With all the cooperative workers, a queen bee can raise literally thousands of offspring.

Bees have provided useful services.

Exercise 37B: Identifying Direct Objects and Indirect Objects

Underline the direct and indirect objects in the following sentences. Write *DO* for direct object and *IO* for indirect object.

Please bring me the mail.

Marcella will leave George a few cookies.

Will Nermin play us a song on her harp?

That will cost you an arm and a leg!

We are offering Shivani the job tomorrow.

After class, I can teach you the new dance.

Exercise 37C: Diagramming Direct Objects and Indirect Objects

On your own paper, diagram the following sentences.

Buy me a new toy!
I made you a quilt.
He has promised her the moon.
Asher got us some doughnuts.
You owe me a favor.
Can you tell me another story and sing me another song?
Purnama has written her father a long letter.

— LESSON 38 —

State-of-Being Verbs
Linking Verbs
Predicate Adjectives

The tiny, jewel-colored hummingbird is strong and frantically energetic.

A verb shows an action, shows a state of being, links two words together, or helps another verb.

A linking verb connects the subject to a noun, pronoun, or adjective in the complete predicate.

A predicate adjective describes the subject and is found in the complete predicate.

The subject of the sentence is the main word or term that the sentence is about.
The simple subject of the sentence is *just* the main word or term that the sentence is about.
The complete subject of the sentence is the simple subject and all the words that belong to it.

The predicate of the sentence tells something about the subject.
The simple predicate of the sentence is the main verb along with any helping verbs.
The complete predicate of the sentence is the simple predicate and all the words that belong to it.

State-of-Being Verbs

am	were
is	be
are	being
was	been

I am.

I am hungry.

They are being.

They are being loud.

The sunset was.

The sunset was spectacular.

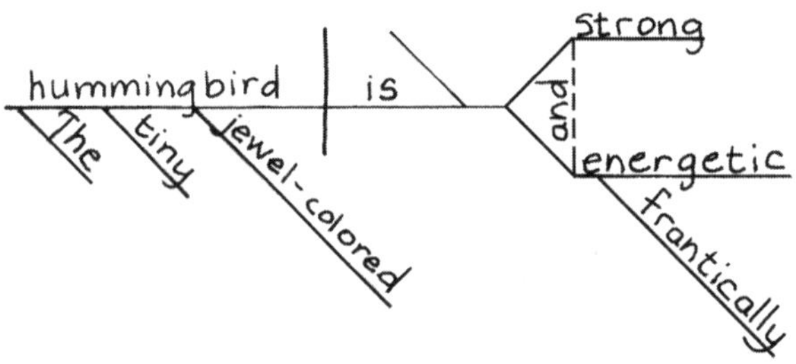

LV PA
Hummingbirds are tiny.

AV DO
Tiny hummingbirds sipped sweet nectar.

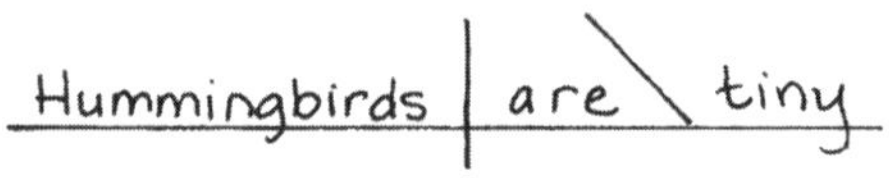

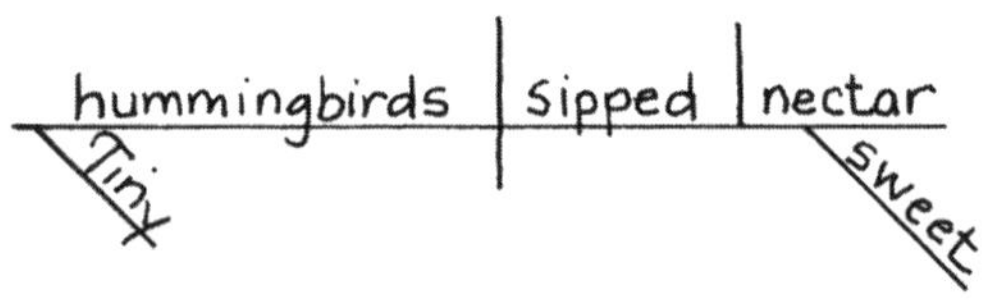

Exercise 38A: Action Verbs and Linking Verbs

In the following sentences, underline the subjects once and the predicates twice. If the predicate is a linking verb, write *LV* over it, circle the predicate adjective, and label it *PA*. If the predicate is an action verb, write *AV* over it, circle the direct object, and label it *DO*. The first is done for you.

These sentences are slightly condensed from *Flatland: A Romance of Many Dimensions*, by Edwin A. Abbott.

AV DO
I admit the truth of your critic's facts.

During my slumber I had a dream.

All our lines are EQUALLY and INFINITESIMALLY thick.

Straight Lines are in many important respects superior to the Circles.

Many-sidedness was almost essential as a pretext for the Innovators.

All, except the Isosceles, were either neutral or averse to the Bill.

I heard the sound of many voices in the street.

The sights tantalized and tempted me to outspoken treason.

BRIGHTNESS, as well as length, is necessary to the existence of a Line.

On the reply to this question I am ready to stake everything.

Once or twice I even spoke the forbidden terms "the Third and Fourth Dimensions."

A third appeal on my part was equally ineffectual.

The Working Men they spared but decimated.

Exercise 38B: Diagramming Direct Objects and Predicate Adjectives

On your own paper, diagram ONLY the subjects, predicates, and direct objects or predicate adjectives (along with any conjunctions used to connect compounds) from the sentences in Exercise 38A.

— LESSON 39 —

Linking Verbs
Predicate Adjectives
Predicate Nominatives

I am unpopular.
I am a flower.
I am a berry.

A predicate adjective describes the subject and is found in the complete predicate.
A predicate nominative renames the subject and is found in the complete predicate.

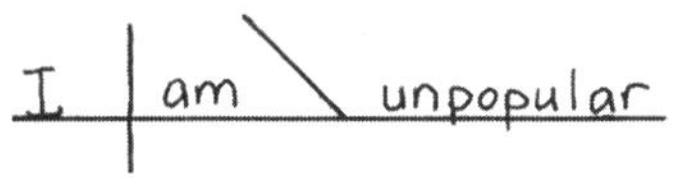

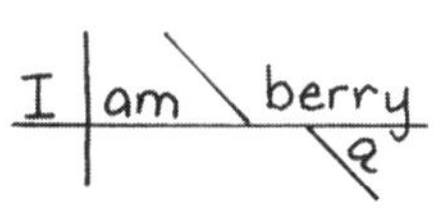

Iguanas are reptiles.
Iguanas = reptiles (predicate nominative)

Iguanas are scaly.
scaly iguanas (predicate adjective)

reptiles iguanas not a predicate adjective
iguanas ≠ scaly not a predicate nominative

Exercise 39A: Identifying Predicate Nominatives and Adjectives

In the following sentences, underline the subjects once and the predicates twice. Circle the predicate nominatives or adjectives and label each one *PN* for predicate nominative or *PA* for predicate adjective. Draw a line from the predicate nominative or adjective to the subject that it renames or describes. There may be more than one of each.

These sentences are adapted from Noel Streatfeild's *Theater Shoes*.

Her father was an actor, and her mother was and still is an actress.

Your mother was very young and perhaps a little afraid of your grandmother.

The woman was interested and asked about schools.

Mark was not fussy.

Diction and dancing aren't so usual at a boys' school.

The road will be wet.

It was a warm evening.

I am just an old mother.

Exercise 39B: Writing Predicate Nominatives and Adjectives

Finish each sentence in two ways: with a predicate nominative and with a predicate adjective. If you need to use more than one word in a blank to complete your sentence, circle the word that is the predicate nominative or predicate adjective.

The first is done for you.

Football is ______ my favorite (sport) ______. (predicate nominative)
Football is ______ entertaining ______. (predicate adjective)

My grandmother's jewels are ______________________. (predicate nominative)
My grandmother's jewels are ______________________. (predicate adjective)

The elderly passenger was ______________________________. (predicate nominative)

The elderly passenger was ______________________________. (predicate adjective)

The proposed tax is ______________________________. (predicate nominative)

The proposed tax is ______________________________. (predicate adjective)

All the girls at the party were ______________________________. (predicate nominative)

All the girls at the party were ______________________________. (predicate adjective)

That thunder was ______________________________. (predicate nominative)

That thunder was ______________________________. (predicate adjective)

Exercise 39C: Diagramming

On your own paper, diagram every word of the following sentences.

Science can be fascinating.
The speed limit is lower here.
The dark cellar was not inviting.
A golden ticket was an exciting prospect.
Is this book the right one?
Some giants may be friendly.
Be a participant!
Her errors were minor.

— LESSON 40 —

Predicate Adjectives and Predicate Nominatives
Pronouns as Predicate Nominatives
Object Complements

A linking verb connects the subject to a noun, pronoun, or adjective in the complete predicate.

A pronoun takes the place of a noun.
The antecedent is the noun that is replaced by the pronoun.

I	we
you	you (plural)
he, she, it	they

It is I.
The winner is you.
My best friend is she.

It = I
winner = you
friend =she

(plural noun) ______________________________ are we.

(singular noun) ______________________________ has been you.

(plural noun) ______________________________ were they.

We elected Marissa leader.
The explorers found the camp abandoned.
He painted the fence white.

An object complement follows the direct object and renames or describes it.

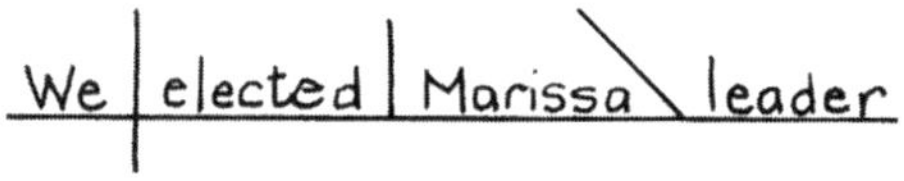

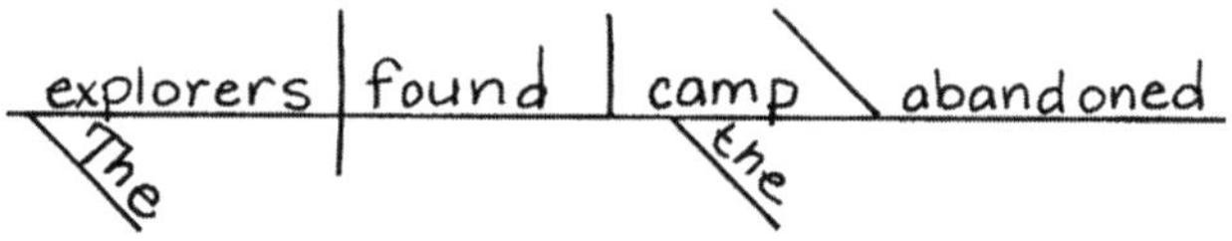

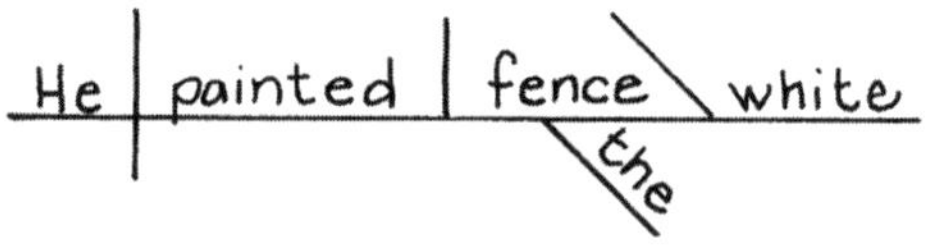

An adjective that comes right before the noun it modifies is in the *attributive position*.

They are user-friendly directions.

An adjective that follows the noun is in the *predicative position*.

Those directions are user friendly.

My friend dyed his hair purple.
My friend dyed his purple hair.
My friend dyed his purple hair orange.

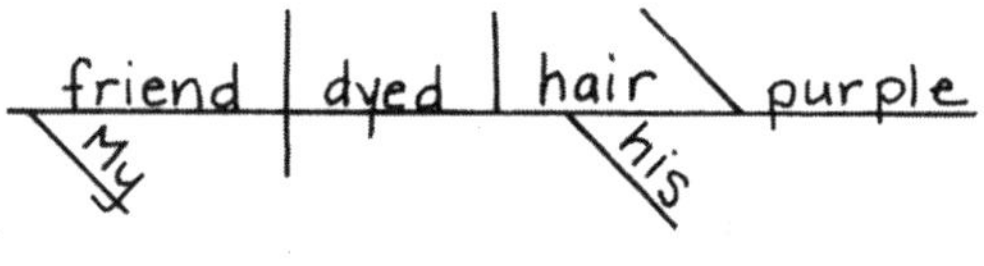

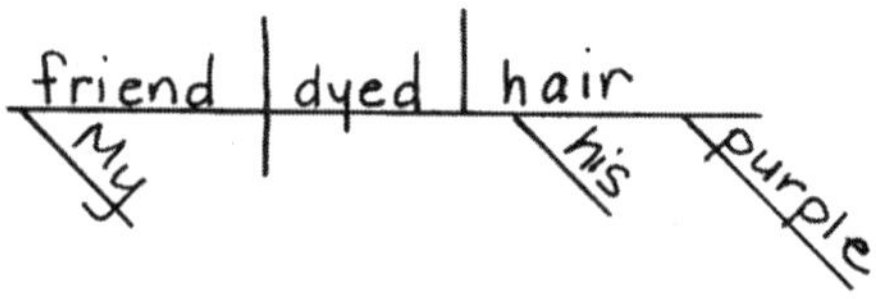

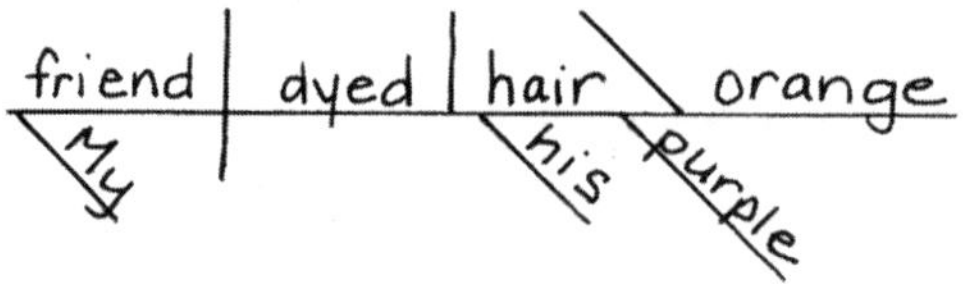

Exercise 40A: Reviewing Objects and Predicate Adjectives and Nominatives

Identify the underlined words as *DO* for direct object, *IO* for indirect object, *OP* for object of preposition, *PN* for predicate nominative, or *PA* for predicate adjective.

- For each direct object (or direct object/indirect object combination), find and underline twice the action verb that affects it.
- For each object of the preposition, find and circle the preposition to which it belongs.
- For each predicate nominative and predicate adjective, find and draw a box around the linking verb that it follows.
- When you are finished, fill in the blank in the statement at the end of the selection.

The following passage is from *Where the Red Fern Grows*, by Wilson Rawls. It has been condensed and slightly adapted.

It was always a pleasure to prowl where fishermen had camped. I usually could find things: a fish line, or a forgotten fish pole. On one occasion, I found a beautiful knife stuck in the bark of a sycamore tree, forgotten by a careless fisherman. But on that day, I found a great treasure, a sportsman's magazine, discarded by the campers. It was a real treasure for a country boy.

... The advertisement was from a kennel in Kentucky. I read it over and over. By the time I had memorized the ad, I was seeing dogs, hearing dogs, and even feeling them. The magazine was forgotten. I was lost in thought. The brain of an eleven-year-old boy can dream some fantastic dreams.

... I took the magazine from my pocket and again I read the ad. Slowly a plan began to form. I'd save the money. I could sell the fishermen stuff: crawfish, minnows, and fresh vegetables. In berry season, I could sell all the berries I could pick at my grandfather's store. I could trap in the winter. There was the way to get those pups—save my money.

I could almost feel the pups in my hands. I planned the little doghouse, and where to put it. Collars I could make myself. Somehow, some way, I was determined to have those dogs.

Find the compound adjective in this passage. Write it in the blank below and cross out the incorrect choice.

______________________________ is in the (attributive/predicative) position.

Exercise 40B: Parts of the Sentence

Label the following in each sentence: *S* (subject), *LV* (linking verb), *AV* (action verb), *DO* (direct object), *OC-A* (object complement-adjective), *OC-N* (object complement-noun), *IO* (indirect object), or *PN* (predicate nominative).

Leave me alone.

Leave me some pizza money.

Arnold pronounced the event a success.

We found the old house easily.

We found the old house empty.

The old house was empty.

Clarice prefers her tea hot.

Clarice prefers water occasionally.

Now for a challenge. A man finds a genie and gives the first order he can think of: "Make me a sandwich!" The genie smiles and replies, "Done! You're a sandwich."

Label (as above) the man's order in two ways—first, how the man intended it, and second, how the genie interpreted it.

Make me a sandwich. (intended meaning)

Make me a sandwich. (genie's interpretation)

Exercise 40C: Diagramming

On your own paper, diagram the sentences from Exercise 40B, including both versions of the final sentence.

WEEK 11

More About Prepositions

— LESSON 41 —

Prepositions and Prepositional Phrases
Adjective Phrases

Prepositions
aboard, about, above, across
after, against, along, among, around, at
before, behind, below, beneath
beside, between, beyond, by
down, during, except, for, from
in, inside, into, like
near, of, off, on, over
past, since, through, throughout
to, toward, under, underneath
until, up, upon
with, within, without

A preposition shows the relationship of a noun or pronoun to another word in the sentence.
A prepositional phrase begins with a preposition and ends with a noun or pronoun. That noun or pronoun is the object of the preposition.
A phrase is a group of words serving a single grammatical function.

I could have been running away.

Speed of Sound

Ring of Fire

Bridge Over Troubled Water

Time of Your Life

The Sound of Silence

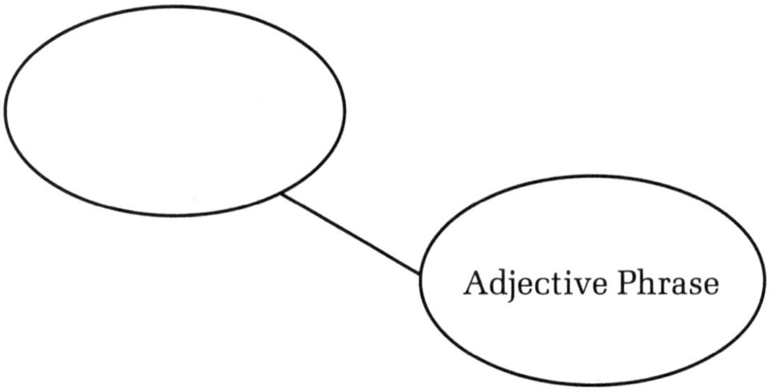

Prepositional phrases that act as adjectives are also called adjective phrases.

The boy with the freckles was whistling.
The old man on the bench hummed a tune.
Arthur borrowed a book of mine.

Adjective phrases usually come directly after the words they modify.

Caleb climbed a tree with thick branches.

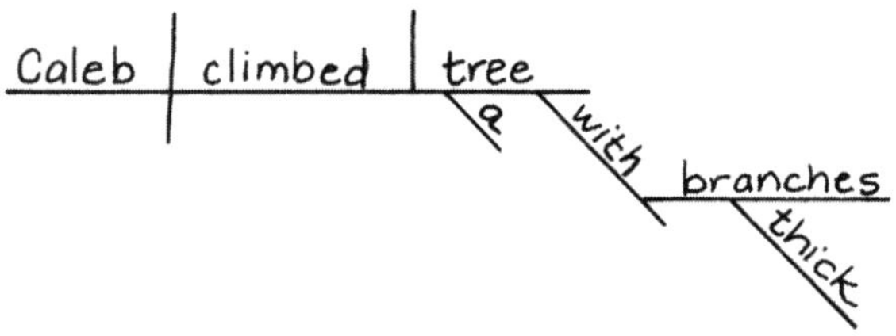

The children in the house were sleeping.

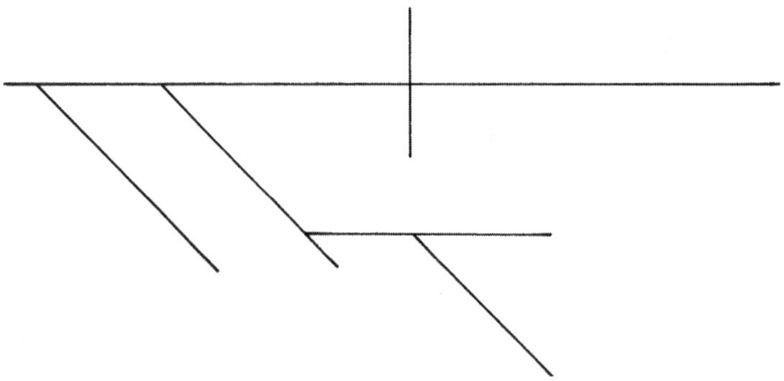

Exercise 41A: Identifying Adjective Phrases

Underline the adjective phrases in the following sentences. Draw an arrow from each phrase to the word it modifies. The first is done for you.

These sentences are adapted from *What the Robin Knows*, by Jon Young.

Her mother had a special relationship with a robin in her yard.

The feathers of the spotted towhee have little black and white patterns.

Some of it may be more desirable, high-rent terrain, with good access to food, water, and cover, and with relatively less danger from nest robbers and other predators.

You will see the mink and the fox in repose.

The current mystery was the identification of a new woodpecker.

Speed of delivery, intensity, volume, position on landscape, and body language will confirm the alarm.

Knowledge of the territories will clear up any confusion about the alarm responses.

Exercise 41B: Diagramming Adjective Phrases/Review

Diagram each sentence from Exercise 41A on your own paper. Follow this procedure, and ask yourself the suggested questions if necessary.

1. Find the subject and predicate and diagram them first.
   What is the verb?
   Who or what [verb]?
2. Ask yourself: Is the verb an action verb? If so, look for a direct object.
   Who or what receives the action of the verb?

   If there is a direct object, check for an indirect object.
   To whom or for whom is the action done?

   Remember that there may be no direct object or no indirect object—but you can't have an indirect object without a direct object. If there is an indirect object, it will always come between the verb and the direct object.
3. Ask yourself: Is the verb a state-of-being verb? If so, look for a predicate nominative or predicate adjective.
   Is there a word after the verb that renames or describes the subject?
4. Find all prepositional phrases. Ask yourself: Whom or what do they describe?
5. Place all other adjectives and adverbs on the diagram. If you have trouble, ask for help.

— LESSON 42 —

Adjective Phrases
Adverb Phrases

Prepositional phrases that act as adverbs are also called adverb phrases.
An adverb describes a verb, an adjective, or another adverb.
Adverbs tell how, when, where, how often, and to what extent.

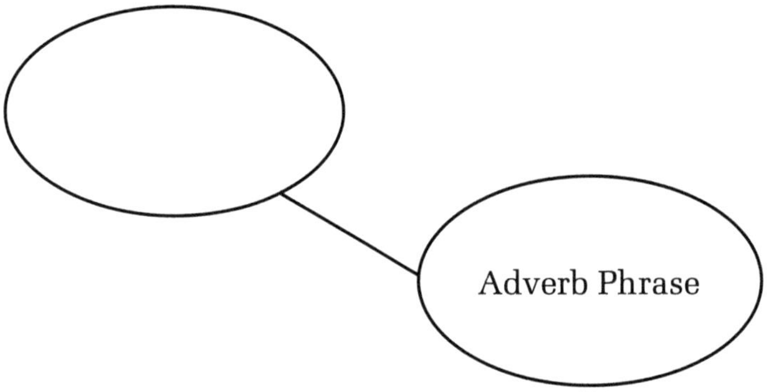

Fly Me (to) the Moon

I Fall to Pieces

Wake Me at Sunset

Sitting on the Dock of the Bay

Cameron scuba-dives in Hawaii.
At 6:00 a.m., Cameron wakes.

Adverb phrases can be anywhere in a sentence.

With great confidence, Hank Aaron swung the bat through the air.

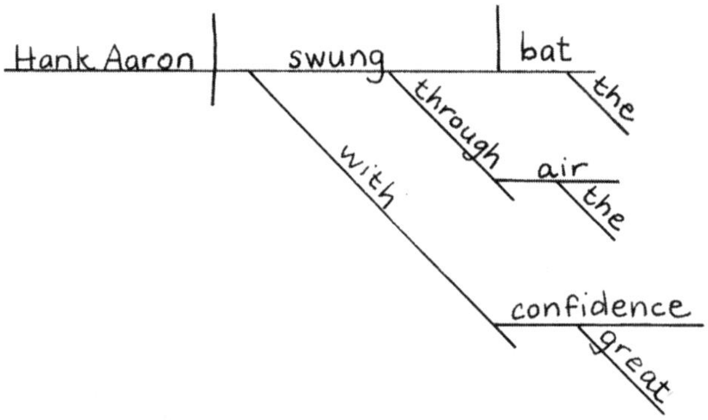

In summer, the car was hot beyond belief.

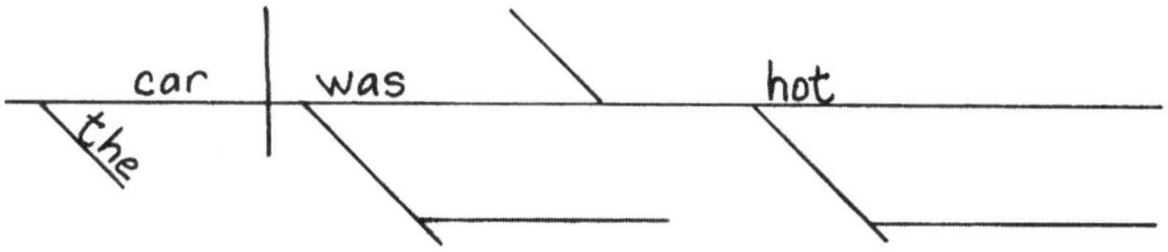

Exercise 42A: Identifying Adverb Phrases

Underline the adverb phrases in the following sentences and circle the preposition that begins each phrase. Draw an arrow from each phrase to the word it modifies. Be careful! There are three adjective phrases hiding in these sentences as well. Don't mistake them for adverbs!

These sentences are adapted from *Pompeii: The Living City,* by Alex Butterworth and Ray Laurence.

The first is done for you.

Tombs have also been found outside the Herculaneum gate.

Abroad, two new provinces had been added to the Empire through skilful diplomacy and well-weighted military pressure.

Jucundus had competitors in Pompeii.

Elite life was conducted within a shame culture.

Amongst the statues, two figures would have caught the eye.

The family gladiators would doubtless have been used in the games.

Bursts of colour exploded beside the city's thoroughfares.

Unlike Augustus's organizations, Nero's new club did not revolve around piety, obedience, conformity, and respect.

Amid the bewilderment, for hours and days there would have been little realistic sense of the eventual final death toll.

On his arrival he befriended Julius Polybius.

In the past these fish had shoaled in large numbers around the rocky headlands of Italy.

At one point, a suit was brought by the entire district against a tax-collector.

Exercise 42B: Diagramming Adverb Phrases

On your own paper, diagram the following five sentences from Exercise 42A.

Jucundus had competitors in Pompeii.

Amongst the statues, two figures would have caught the eye.

Unlike Augustus's organizations, Nero's new club did not revolve around piety, obedience, conformity, and respect.

On his arrival he befriended Julius Polybius.

At one point, a suit was brought by the entire district against a tax-collector.

— LESSON 43 —

Definitions Review
Adjective and Adverb Phrases
Misplaced Modifiers

An adjective modifies ______________________________.

Adjectives tell ______________________________.

A preposition shows ______________________________ **word in the sentence.**

A prepositional phrase ______________________________ ______________ **or pronoun.**

______________________________ **object of the preposition.**

A phrase is ______________________________ **function.**

Prepositional phrases that ______________________________ **adjective phrases.**

Adjective phrases usually ______________________________.

An adverb describes ______________________________.

Adverbs tell ______________________________ **extent.**

______________________________ **are also called adverb phrases.**

Prepositions

A ___________________, a ___________________, a ___________________, a _________________.

A __________, a _____________, a __________, a _____________, a __________, a ____________.

B ___________________, b ___________________, b ___________________, b __________________.

B ___________________, b ___________________, b ___________________, b __________________.

D ______________, d _____________, e ______________, f ______________, f _______________.

I ____________________, i ___________________, i ___________________, l __________________.

N ______________, o _______________, o _______________, o _______________, o ______________.

P ___________________, s ___________________, t ___________________, t ___________________.

T ___________________, t ___________________, u ___________________, u __________________.

U ___________________, u ___________________, u ___________________.

W ___________________, w ___________________, w ___________________.

The cat scratched Brock's sister with the striped tail.

A misplaced modifier is an adjective phrase in the wrong place.

The beautiful girl was dancing with the handsome man in the red dress.

On the pizza, Molly ate the mushrooms.

I cut my finger while I was cooking badly.

I saw that the toast was burned with a glance.

I spotted the dog chewing on the sofa leg from the stairs.

Exercise 43A: Distinguishing Between Adjective and Adverb Phrases

Underline all the prepositional phrases in the following sentences. Write *ADJ* above the adjective phrases and *ADV* above the adverb phrases. These sentences are adapted from R. G. Collingwood's *Roman Britain*.

The army was permanently distributed along the frontiers.

The Vallum ran from the Tyne above Newcastle to the Solway below Burgh-by-Sands.

For this purpose an entirely new series of forts was created at about this time along the "Saxon Shore."

The towns of Roman Britain may be conveniently divided into three classes.

Sculptural and architectural fragments of unusually fine quality give an impressive idea of the artistic development of Romanized British taste.

In 367 practically the whole of Britain was overrun by hordes of barbarian invaders.

Sharp angles in the profile of a vessel are replaced by sweeping open curves.

We find a real Romano-British art not in the civilized area of the province, but in the outlying military fringe.

The same desire was certainly at work in the mind of the carver of the tombstone of Flavinus.

The temple of Nodens at Lydney was built on the site of a prehistoric hill-fort in the fourth century.

Exercise 43B: Correcting Misplaced Modifiers

Circle the misplaced adjective and adverb phrases in the following sentences. Draw an arrow to show where the phrase should be.

For some of the sentences, the phrase may make sense where it is—but if a phrase doesn't communicate what the author wants it to, it is misplaced. Assume that each sentence contains a phrase that is misplaced (that is, a different meaning was intended), correct as instructed above, and explain to your instructor how the placement changes the meaning.

The first is done for you, with a sample explanation provided.

Inside the clock Daniel watched the huge pendulum swinging back and forth.

Inside the clock as initially placed indicates the place from which Daniel did the watching. In the corrected position, the phrase answers the question "which pendulum?"

The girl fell down on the skating rink in the yellow dress.

The bird above the trees escaped the predator by flying.

I saw six huge birds flying through my car window.

The woman with the worn keys selected the piano.

The man with the fluffy tail tossed the dog a ball.

The student on the flute played "Hot Cross Buns."

Behind the desk, the teacher knocked over the trash can.

The tiny ship beyond the horizon has sailed to a far-off land.

My friend during the test jumped out of her seat at the sound of the fire alarm.

We followed the narrow path to a quaint cottage through the woods.

— LESSON 44 —

Adjective and Adverb Phrases

Prepositional Phrases Acting as Other Parts of Speech

The ship went down into the Gulf of Guinea and, with many stops on the way, approached the mouth of the Congo.

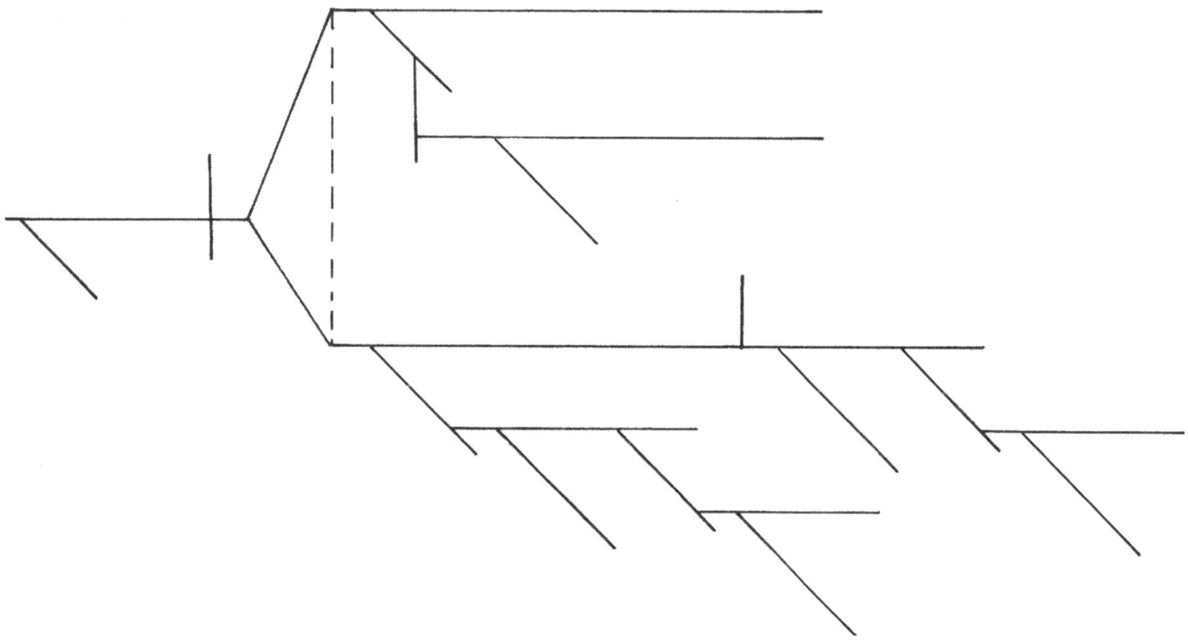

A swamp is not a safe place.

Under the bridge is not a safe place.

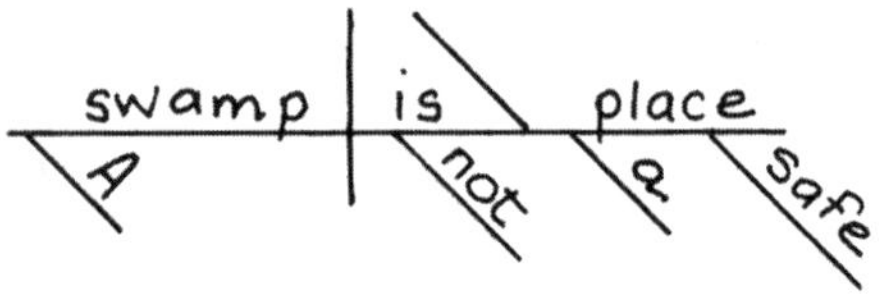

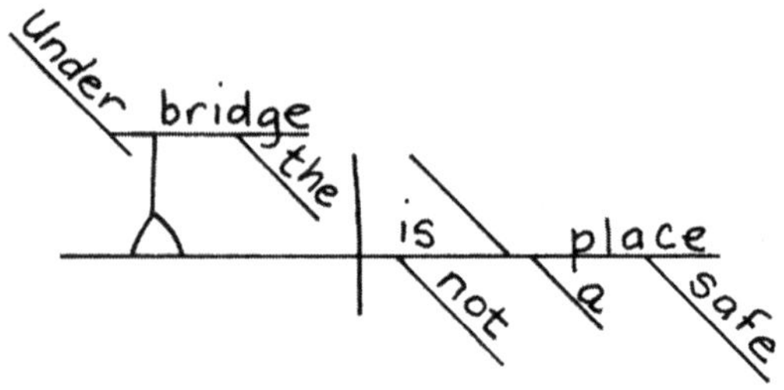

The best place for the treasure is my closet.

The best place for the treasure is under the bed.

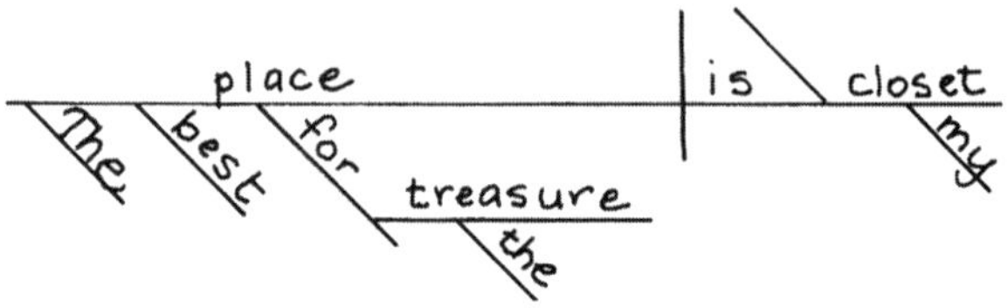

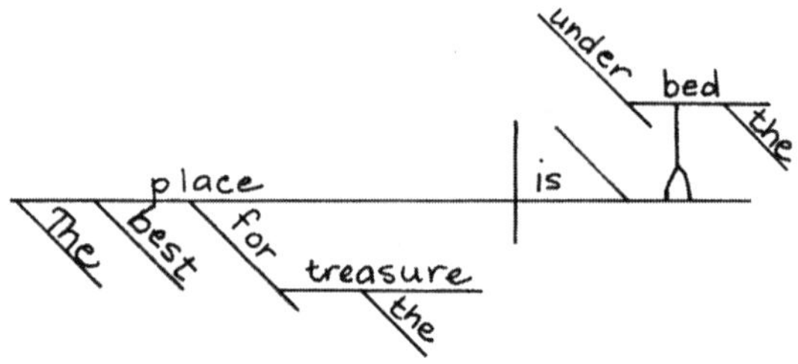

He stepped from the dark.

He stepped from behind the tree.

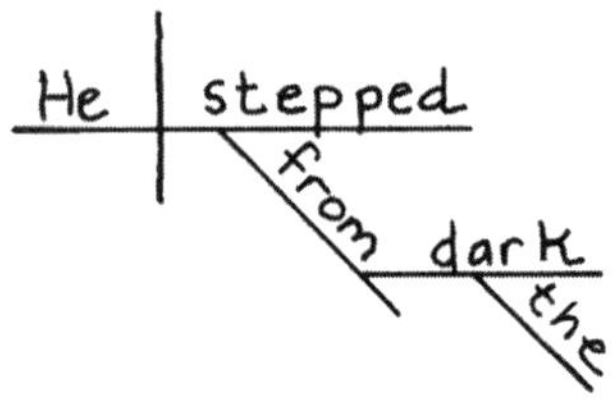

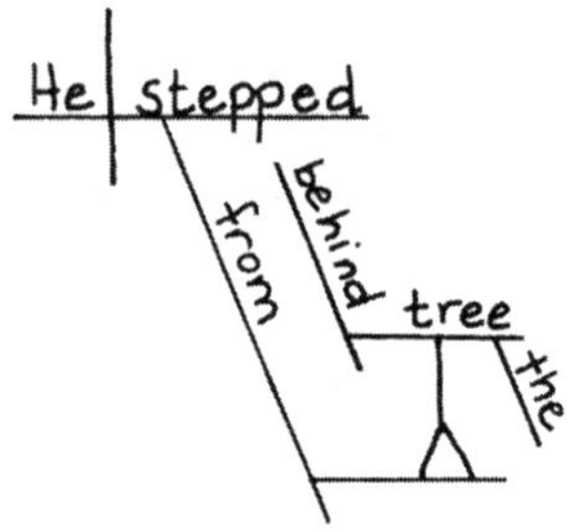

The man is happy.

The man is in love.

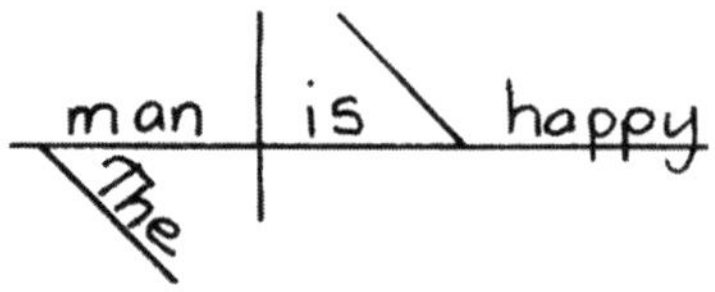

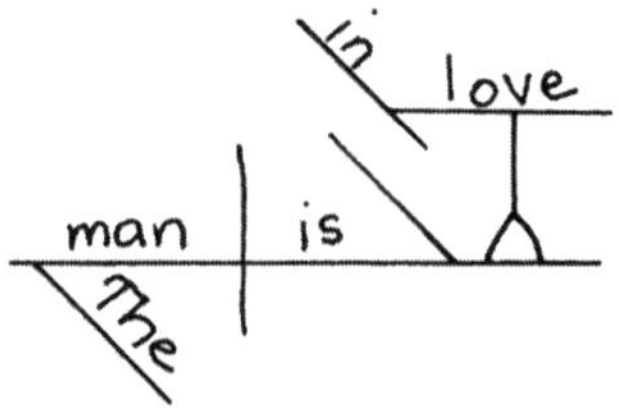

Exercise 44A: Prepositional Phrases Acting as Other Parts of Speech

In each sentence below, circle any prepositional phrases. Underline the subject of the sentence once and the predicate twice. Then label the prepositional phrases as *ADJ* (adjective phrase), *ADV* (adverb phrase), *S* (subject), *PA* (predicate adjective), *PN* (predicate nominative), or *OP* (object of a preposition).

In her mother's arms is the newborn baby's favorite place.

A book about unicorns is on order.

With a timid voice, Iris answered the question from the teacher.

Among the trees in the deepest part of the forest lives the wise old owl.

Toward those trees is your path.

The scariest place to be is in very deep dark woods.

Laura has been smiling since before the beginning of class.

The steps in the hallway seem steep to me.

Allan is in love with Rita.

I will listen to the children in a moment.

Exercise 44B: Diagramming

On your own paper, diagram these sentences from Exercise 44A.

In her mother's arms is the newborn baby's favorite place.
A book about unicorns is on order.
With a timid voice, Iris answered the question from the teacher.
Among the trees in the deepest part of the forest lives the wise old owl.
Toward those trees is your path.
Laura has been smiling since before the beginning of class.
The steps in the hallway seem steep to me.
Allan is in love with Rita.
I will listen to the children in a moment.

WEEK 12

Advanced Verbs

— LESSON 45 —

Linking Verbs
Linking/Action Verbs

State of Being/Linking Verbs
am, is, are, was, were
be, being, been

Additional Linking Verbs
taste, feel, smell, sound, look
prove, grow
remain, appear, stay
become, seem

I tasted the candy.

The candy tasted delicious.

The fried chicken tasted crispy.

The chicken tasted the birdseed.

Thomas felt the baby chick.
Thomas felt sad.

ACTION	LINKING
He proved the theory.	He proved unreliable.
The farmer grew wheat.	The farmer grew tired.
The dog remained on the porch.	The dog remained wary.
The cloud appeared in the sky.	The cloud appeared threatening.
We stayed home.	We stayed happy with our home.

The student became confused.
The grammar seemed difficult.

Exercise 45A: Distinguishing Between Action Verbs and Linking Verbs

Underline the verbs in the following sentences. Identify them as *AV* for action verb or *LV* for linking verb. If the verb is followed by a direct object (*DO*), predicate adjective (*PA*), or predicate nominative (*PN*), label it.

Remember that a verb with *no* direct object, predicate adjective, or predicate nominative will be an action verb, unless it is a state-of-being verb. Also remember that direct objects, predicate adjectives, and predicate nominatives are never found within prepositional phrases.

Do not turn another page in this book!

Your nose will turn green!

Turn around now.

Ethan looked around the room quickly.

He looked nervous.

She may become the next president of our club.

Does the dog smell bacon?

Does the dog smell bad?

Her boots were purple.

Can you prove me wrong?

Your son will prove a strong manager.

Elyse remained awake throughout the night.

Tavi grows taller with every passing week!

Tavi grows zucchini in his garden.

Exercise 45B: Distinguishing Among Different Kinds of Nouns

Underline all the nouns in the following sentences. Identify them as *S* for subject, *OP* for object of a preposition, *IO* for indirect object, *DO* for direct object, or *PN* for predicate nominative.

These sentences are adapted from *A Dog on Barkham Street*, by M. S. Stolz.

Mrs. Frost gave the mailman a sweet bun with his coffee.

Edward hadn't seen a sign of a wren.

The sun burned right through that glass and set the leaves on fire.

But Toad was a problem to all his friends.

On the afternoon of assembly day, all the classes would have a dress rehearsal.

Maybe a genie will come out and give my father the answer.

Buffalo have never been considered good pets.

Exercise 45C: Diagramming Action Verbs and Linking Verbs

Diagram the following sentences.

Sophia is a cat.
Jordan gave Sophia a treat.
Sophia tasted the treat.
The treat tasted delicious.
Sophia is sleepy.
Sophia fell asleep.
Sophia fell off the chair.

— LESSON 46 —

Conjugations
Irregular Verbs
Principal Parts of Verbs

Verbs in the simple past, simple present, and simple future describe actions that simply happen.
Verbs in the progressive past, progressive present, and progressive future describe actions that go on for a while.
Verbs in the perfect past, perfect present, and perfect future describe actions which have been completed before another action takes place.

Exercise 46A: Forming Simple, Perfect, and Progressive Tenses

Fill in the missing blanks in the chart below.

Simple Present

	Singular	Plural
First person	I blink	We ______________
Second person	You ______________	You blink
Third person	He, she, it ____________	They blink

Simple Past

	Singular	Plural
First person	I ______________	We ______________
Second person	You ______________	You ______________
Third person	He, she, it ______________	They blinked

Simple Future

	Singular	Plural
First person	I ______________	We ______________
Second person	You will blink	You ______________
Third person	He, she, it ______________	They ______________

Perfect Present

	Singular	Plural
First person	I ______________	We ______________
Second person	You ______________	You ______________
Third person	He, she, it has blinked	They ______________

Perfect Past

	Singular	Plural
First person	I ______________	We ______________
Second person	You ______________	You had blinked
Third person	He, she, it ______________	They ______________

Perfect Future

	Singular	Plural
First person	I will have blinked	We ______________
Second person	You ______________	You ______________
Third person	He, she, it ______________	They ______________

Progressive Present

	Singular	Plural
First person	I ______________	We are blinking
Second person	You ______________	You ______________
Third person	He, she, it ______________	They ______________

Progressive Past

	Singular	Plural
First person	I ______________________	We ______________________
Second person	You were blinking	You ______________________
Third person	He, she, it ______________________	They ______________ blinking

Progressive Future

	Singular	Plural
First person	I will be blinking	We ______________________
Second person	You ______________________	You ______________________
Third person	He, she, it ______________________	They ______________________

Simple Present	Simple Past	Simple Future
build	built	will build
buy	bought	will buy
choose	chose	will choose
sell	sold	will sell

Exercise 46B: Spanish and English Words

Draw lines to match each English word with its Spanish equivalent. Because English and Spanish have similar backgrounds, you should be able to complete this exercise easily, even if you've never learned any Spanish!

English	Spanish
adventure	pingüino
traffic	paciencia
giraffe	voleibol
patience	jirafa
fascinate	aventura
penguin	preparar
leader	sorpresa
prepare	tráfico
volleyball	líder
surprise	fascinar

English verbs have three principal parts.

First principal part: the simple present (present)

(I) conjugate *(I)* ______________

Second principal part: the simple past (past)

(I) conjugated *(I)* ______________

Third principal part: the perfect past, minus helping verbs (past participle)

(I have) conjugated *(I have)* ______________

Exercise 46C: Principal Parts of Verbs

Fill in the chart with the missing forms.

	First Principal Part Present	Second Principal Part Past	Third Principal Part Past Participle
I	launch	launched	launched
I	bury		buried
I			competed
I	enter		
I		corrected	
I			imagined
I	hurry		
I		tipped	
I	brake		
I			betrayed

Exercise 46D: Distinguishing Between First and Second Principal Parts

Identify each underlined verb as *1* for first principal part or *2* for second principal part. These sentences are from Steven Ujifusa's *A Man and His Ship*.

On March 28, 1918, the men of the 301st Heavy Tank Battalion joined some six thousand other troops on *Olympic* bound for Europe.

We note with great interest the suggestion made that future construction should be of steel largely in place of wood.

The liners traveled alone because they were too fast for escorts to keep up with them.

"On behalf of myself and the people of the United States," he said in closing, "I thank you from the bottom of my heart."

In stark contrast to most employers of the time, William Francis Gibbs based his hires not on background, but on ability.

— LESSON 47 —

Linking Verbs
Principal Parts
Irregular Verbs

Linking Verbs
am, is, are, was, were
be, being, been
taste, feel, smell, sound, look
prove, grow
remain, appear, stay
become, seem

Present	Past	Past Participle
(I) taste	(I) tasted	(I have) tasted
(I) become	(I) became	(I have) become
(I) feel	(I) felt	(I have) felt

COMMON IRREGULAR VERBS

SAME PRESENT, PAST & PAST PARTICIPLE:

Present	Past	Past Participle	
beat	beat	beat	(OR beat beat beaten)
burst	burst	burst	
cost	cost	cost	
cut	cut	cut	
fit	fit	fit	
let	let	let	
put	put	put	
quit	quit	quit	
hit	hit	hit	
hurt	hurt	hurt	
set	set	set	
shut	shut	shut	

SAME PAST & PAST PARTICIPLE:

Present	Past	Past Participle
bend	bent	bent
send	sent	sent
lend	lent	lent
bleed	bled	bled
feed	fed	fed
feel	felt	felt
keep	kept	kept
lead	led	led
leave	left	left
meet	met	met
read	read	read
sleep	slept	slept
bring	brought	brought
buy	bought	bought
catch	caught	caught
fight	fought	fought
seek	sought	sought
teach	taught	taught
think	thought	thought
lay	laid	laid
pay	paid	paid
say	said	said
sell	sold	sold
tell	told	told

lose	lost	lost
shoot	shot	shot
find	found	found
wind	wound	wound
dig	dug	dug
sit	sat	sat
win	won	won
stand	stood	stood
understand	understood	understood
hear	heard	heard
make	made	made
build	built	built

DIFFERENT PAST AND PAST PARTICIPLE:

awake	awoke	awoken
bite	bit	bitten
break	broke	broken
choose	chose	chosen
forget	forgot	forgotten
freeze	froze	frozen
get	got	gotten
give	gave	given
drive	drove	driven
eat	ate	eaten
fall	fell	fallen
hide	hid	hidden
rise	rose	risen
shake	shook	shaken
speak	spoke	spoken
steal	stole	stolen
take	took	taken
write	wrote	written
ride	rode	ridden
become	became	become
begin	began	begun
come	came	come
run	ran	run

drink	drank	drunk
shrink	shrank	shrunk
ring	rang	rung
sing	sang	sung
swim	swam	swum
draw	drew	drawn
fly	flew	flown
grow	grew	grown
know	knew	known
tear	tore	torn
wear	wore	worn
do	did	done
go	went	gone
lie	lay	lain
see	saw	seen

— LESSON 48 —

Linking Verbs
Principal Parts
Irregular Verbs

Linking Verbs
am, is, are, was, were
be, being, been
taste, feel, smell, sound, look
prove, grow
remain, appear, stay
become, seem

Verbs in the simple past, simple present, and simple future describe actions that simply happen.
Verbs in the progressive past, progressive present, and progressive future describe actions that go on for a while.
Verbs in the perfect past, perfect present, and perfect future describe actions which have been completed before another action takes place.

PRINCIPAL PARTS
present, past, past participle

Exercise 48A: Principal Parts

Fill in the blanks in the following chart of verbs.

Present	Past	Past Participle
bear		
breed		
	felt	
		had
	overtook	
show		
		spread
sweep		
		won
	beat	
		broadcast
forbid		
hold		
		paid
		sunk
	stood	
		swollen *or* swelled
arise		
	blew	
	ate	
		hung
spit		
swear		
		mown *or* mowed
	wept	
bend		

Present	Past	Past Participle
______	______	burst
______	______	forgiven
kneel	______	______
put	______	______
______	______	sat
______	______	stuck
swing	______	______
______	bet	______
______	______	clung
______	______	gotten
______	left	______
______	______	sawn *or* sawed
slide	______	______
sting	______	______
______	woke	______
______	______	bound

Exercise 48B: Forming Correct Past Participles

Write the correct third principal part (past participle) in each blank. The first principal part is provided for you in parentheses. The first is done for you.

I have ___drawn___ (draw) you a beautiful picture!

The bell has not ______ (ring) on time at all this week.

By the time I realized I had ______ (steal) the wrong suitcase, the right one had ______ (set) off for France.

Hattie has ______ (ride) her horse for three hours already.

Louis had ______ (show) me the plan, but I hadn't ______ (think) it would work.

Since that bad experience, Hyung has never ______ (eat) at that restaurant again.

I have ______________ (give) you too many chances already!

What has ______________ (lead) you to this conclusion?

Exercise 48C: Forming Correct Past Tenses

Write the correct second principal part (past) in each blank. The first principal part is provided for you in parentheses. The first is done for you.

The little fish ____swam____ (swim) upstream.

Yesterday, I ______________ (run) all the way from the post office to the park.

Maria's pencil ______________ (fall) off her desk, but she ______________ (catch) it before it ______________ (hit) the floor.

I ______________ (choose) the design for my new bookcase, and my father ______________ (build) it.

We ______________ (go) hiking and ______________ (lose) our way.

The squirrel ______________ (hide) ten nuts and ______________ (keep) searching for more.

Jamil ______________ (read) the contract and ______________ (pay) the membership fee.

Exercise 48D: Proofreading for Irregular Verb Usage

In the passage below, from Dorothy Canfield Fisher's *Understood Betsy*, you will find seven errors in irregular verb usage. Cross out the incorrect forms and write the correct ones above them.

But it haved a weighty, satisfying ring to it. The little girl feeled the importance of having her statement recognized. She turned back to her driving.

The slow, heavy plow horses had stopped during her talk with Uncle Henry. They standed as still now as though their feet had growed to the road. Elizabeth Ann looked up at the old man for instructions. But he beed deep in his figures. She had been teached never to interrupt people, so she sitted still and waited for him to tell her what to do.

Exercise 48E: Diagramming

On your own paper, diagram the following four sentences.

When did we elect Jim president?

Abigail and Joanna look adorable in their new dresses.

The bird looked questioningly at the little boy.

After nine is an acceptable time for a phone call.

— REVIEW 4 —

Weeks 10-12

Topics:
Direct and Indirect Objects
Linking Verbs
Predicate Adjectives
Predicate Nominatives
Articles
Adjective Phrases
Adverb Phrases
Action vs. Linking Verbs
Irregular Verbs
Principal Parts (Present, Past, Past Participle)

Review 4A: Action vs. Linking Verbs

Identify the underlined verbs as *A* for action or *L* for linking.

Zebras are not tame like horses.

A baby zebra smells its mother.

The mother smells familiar, so the foal follows her.

Lions and painted hyenas are predators of the zebra.

The spotted hyena usually scavenges for leftovers from another's meal, but it can kill zebras as well.

The stripes on a zebra protect it from predators; they make the zebra look blurry when it runs.

Mother zebras look carefully at unfamiliar animals to make sure that they pose no threat.

If the animal is a predator, the mother sounds an alarm.

Although the zebra seems gentle, it can kick and bite attackers when needed.

The zebra's whinny, or bray, sounds odd, a little like the bark of a small dog.

Mountain zebras, which live in southern Africa, are a protected species.

The quagga, a subspecies of zebra with stripes on the front half of its body and brown on the back half, has become extinct.

Scientists in the Quagga Project are trying to use DNA from a quagga to breed new animals that resemble the extinct ones.

Review 4B: Predicate Adjectives and Predicate Nominatives

Underline the linking verb in each of the following sentences. If the sentence concludes with a predicate nominative or predicate adjective, circle each and write *PA* for predicate adjective or *PN* for predicate nominative above it.

Miles is my best friend.

Rehema looked nervous but excited.

My cousin's birthday party was a sleepover.

That pizza smells wonderful, but I am not very hungry.

Glory will become a famous athlete one day.

Jacob remained a computer programmer for the university until his retirement.

Will Sora look older with her new hairstyle?

These cookies from your new recipe taste weird; macaroni is a strange ingredient for cookies!

Review 4C: Adjective and Adverb Phrases

In the following excerpt from Aldous Huxley's *Brave New World*, identify each underlined prepositional phrase as *ADJ* for adjective phrase or *ADV* for adverb phrase.

Lenina and Henry climbed into their machine and started off. At eight hundred feet Henry slowed down the helicopter screws, and they hung for a minute or two poised above the fading landscape. The forest of Burnham Beeches stretched like a great pool of darkness towards the bright shore of the western sky. Crimson at the horizon, the last of the sunset faded, through orange, upwards into yellow and a pale watery green.

Northwards, beyond and <u>above the trees</u>, the Internal and External Secretions factory glared <u>with a fierce electric brilliance</u> <u>from every window</u> <u>of its twenty stories</u>. <u>Beneath them</u> lay the buildings of the Golf Club.

Review 4D: Forming Principal Parts

Complete the following excerpt (from Anna Sewell's *Black Beauty*) by writing the correct principal part (*PP*) of the verb (first, second, or third) in parentheses.

"I am the best friend and the best riding-master those children __________ (have, 1st PP). It is not them; it is the boys. Boys," ______________ (say, 2nd PP) he, shaking his mane, "are quite different; they must be ______________ (break, 3rd PP) in, as we were ______________ (break, 3rd PP) in when we were colts, and just be ______________ (teach, 3rd PP) what's what. The other children had ______________ (ride, 3rd PP) me about for nearly two hours, and then the boys ______________ (think, 2nd PP) it was their turn; and so it was, and I was quite agreeable. They ______________ (ride, 2nd PP) me by turns, and I ______________ (gallop, 2nd PP) them about up and down the fields and all about the orchard for a good hour. They had each ______________ (cut, 3rd PP) a great hazel stick for a riding-whip, and ______________ (lay, 2nd PP) it on a little too hard, but I ______________ (take, 2nd PP) it in good part, till at last I ______________ (think, 2nd PP) we had ______________ (have, 3rd PP) enough, so I ______________ (stop, 2nd PP) two or three times by way of a hint."

Review 4E: Irregular Verbs

Find and correct the SIX errors in irregular verb usage in the following excerpt from *Five Little Peppers and How They Grew*, by Margaret Sidney. Cross out the incorrect form and write the correct form above it.

But Jasper didn't come! Thursday comed and goed; a beautiful, bright, sunny day, but with no signs of the merry boy whom all had beginned to love, nor of the big black dog. The children had maked all the needful preparations with much ostentation and bustle, and beed in a state of excited happiness, ready for any gale. But the last hope had to be gived up, as the old clock ticked away hour after hour.

Review 4F: Misplaced Modifiers

Circle the misplaced adjective and adverb phrases in the following sentences. Draw an arrow to the place where each phrase should be.

Sierra Leone with a green, white, and blue flag is the only country.

Inside the oven, Frank checked on the casserole.

Mr. Gutiérrez explained to us how his mother taught him to ride a bike in homeroom.

The book belongs to my cousin on the highest shelf.

The children in the nest watched the eggs hatching.

The gift is for the wonderful coach inside this beautifully wrapped box.

The little rabbit lives in our classroom with the floppy ears.

Annabel handed a pen to the very tall man from her purse.

Review 4G: Diagramming

Diagram the following sentences.

The children stomp their feet in unison.

Johanna told her brother a secret.

After three consecutive victories, our team is looking great!

Did Jeff and Kristen name their new baby Luna?

Dr. Gonzales looked at the students in the back of the room.

Our neighbors in the yellow house fed their pet turtle cucumbers.

Pet turtles can live for a long time!

A turtle with a flaky shell may be sick.

WEEK 13

Advanced Pronouns

— LESSON 49 —

Personal Pronouns

Antecedents

Possessive Pronouns

Lindsay woke up when Lindsay heard Lindsay's mother call Lindsay. Lindsay ate Lindsay's breakfast and brushed Lindsay's teeth and got ready for Lindsay's day.

A pronoun takes the place of a noun.
The antecedent is the noun that is replaced by the pronoun.

Personal Pronouns

	Singular	**Plural**
First person	I	we
Second person	you	you (plural)
Third person	he, she, it	they

Exercise 49A: Personal Pronouns and Antecedents

Circle the personal pronouns in the following sentences, adapted from *Parachuting into Poland, 1944: Memoir of a Secret Mission with Józef Retinger*, by Marek Celt, trans. Jan Chciuk-Celt. Draw an arrow from each pronoun to the antecedent. In the margin, write the gender (*f*, *m*, or *n*) and number (*S* or *PL*) of each pronoun.

My companion practically never left the house. He did a lot of reading, and listened to the radio often.

The men who went on these missions were an elite group of special forces called the *Cichociemni*, literally "the silent Dark Ones." They've become something of a heroic legend in Polish war lore.

The airplane landed, and the little old man ran to it in a hurry, but he only got a good look at the taillights as it flew off.

We, the passengers of the Third Air Bridge, had run a gauntlet of difficulties and dangers, and we were met and greeted joyously in Brindisi.

Personal Pronouns (Full List)
I, me, my, mine

you, your, yours

he, she, him, her, it

his, hers, its

we, us, our, ours

they, them, their, theirs

Possessive Adjectives (same as Possessive Pronouns)

my	our
your	your
his, her, its	their

Peter's sword	__________ sword
The Pevensie children's wardrobe	__________ wardrobe
The tree's silver leaves	__________ leaves
Lucy's cordial	__________ cordial

The tree's silver leaves glistened.
Its silver leaves glistened.

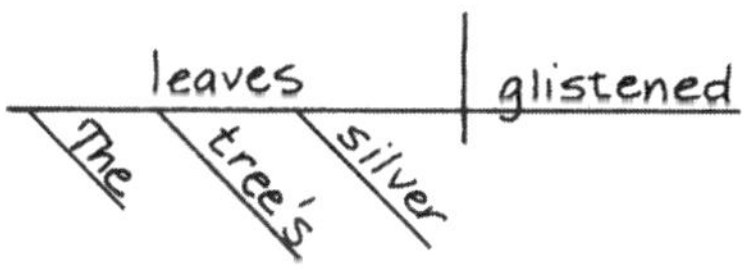

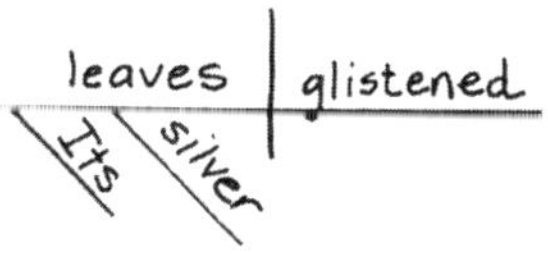

Lucy's cordial healed Edmund.

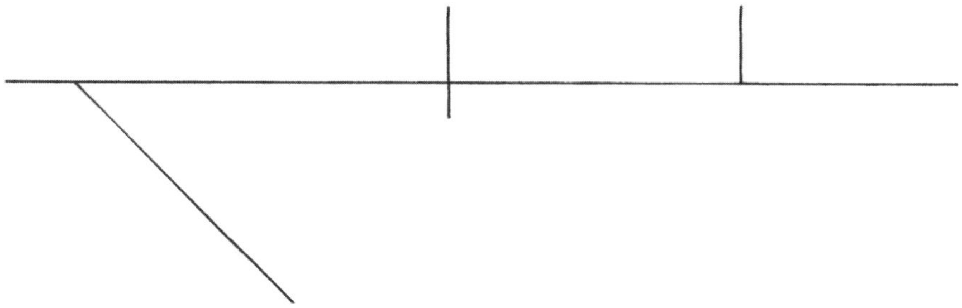

Her cordial healed Edmund.

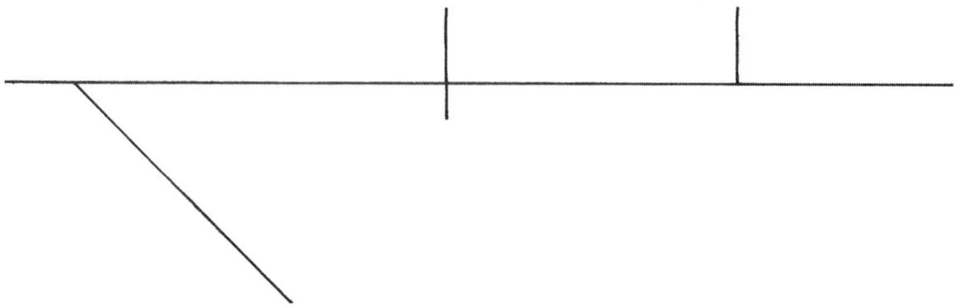

The chocolate is my candy.
The chocolate is mine candy.
The chocolate is mine!

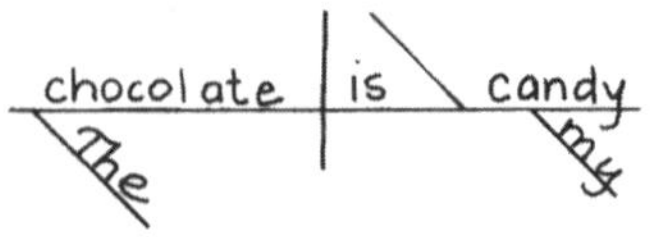

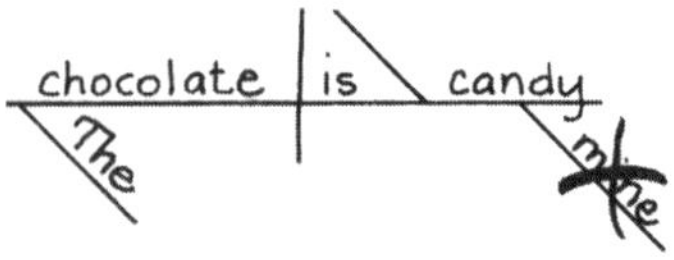

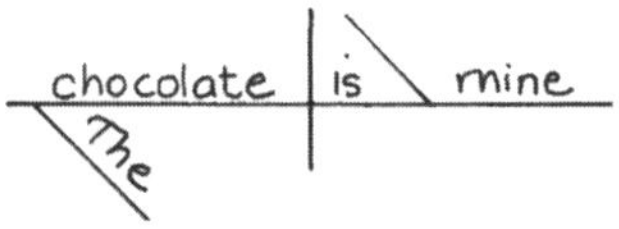

He is your baby brother.
He is yours baby brother.
The baby brother is yours!

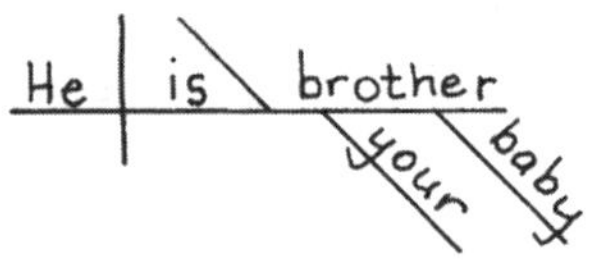

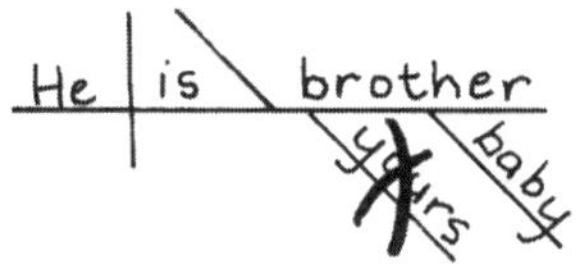

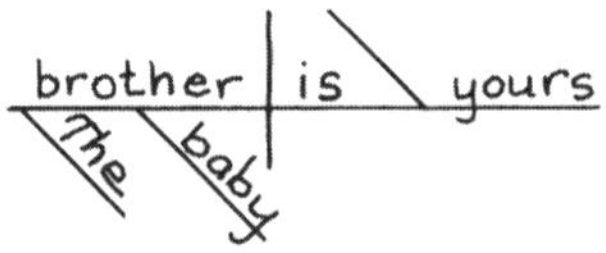

Exercise 49B: Identifying Possessive Pronouns

Underline the possessive pronouns in the following sentences from *Silk Parachute*, by John McPhee. Each possessive pronoun is acting as an adjective. Draw an arrow from the pronoun to the noun that is the pronoun's antecedent. There may be more than one pronoun in each sentence.

In the first game, an English midfielder, sprinting up his left sideline to take a pass on a clear, looked over his shoulder and saw that the ball was headed wide, low, and out of bounds.

On hulks and barges, boatmen serving the ships lived on the river with their families and with their cats, dogs, chickens, sheep, and cows.

Such river runes are not beyond the grasp of Livia Svenvold McPhee, who is six and quick to learn, but they're off the scale for her two-year-old brother, Jasper, and their father and mother.

The puffin is among the nation's emblematic birds. With its bright-white chest, its orange webbed feet, and its big orange scimitar bill, it could be an iced toucan.

Exercise 49C: Using Possessive Pronouns

In the following sentences, taken from *Bird Dream: Adventures at the Extremes of Human Flight,* by Matt Higgins, write the correct possessive pronoun above the underlined noun(s).

The 1991 movie *Point Break*...depicted a group of California surfer/skydivers who robbed banks to fuel the group's lifestyle, a story that struck a chord with males of a certain age and bent.

By 1995 this generation would get this generation's Woodstock when ESPN created a festival for radical sports in Providence, Rhode Island, called the Extreme Games, soon to be rechristened the X Games.

Finally, on Jeb's fourth jump, Jeb pitched in full flight and swung into severe line twists, requiring a nasty cutaway to Jeb's reserve.

Afterwards, the officer gave Jeb a lift back to Jeb's hotel and asked casually, "Who was Jeb's friend?"

Clinicians tell us that all humanity's brain's occipital lobe, which processes visual information, becomes highly active during sleep.

Exercise 49D: Diagramming Possessive Pronouns

On your own paper, diagram every word in the following sentences, slightly adapted from *Barbarian Days: A Surfing Life*, by William Finnegan.

The wide white board was mine.

I took my next wave far too lightly.

Our street and our lane formed a main funnel for local storm runoff.

We murmured our business with Sina Savaiinaea to her young assistant.

The waves were the object of your deepest desire and adoration.

At the same time, they were your adversary, your nemesis, your mortal enemy.

Its clear prose and subtle wit make it a must-read for all surfers.

It's the only book for all surfers.

— LESSON 50 —

Pronoun Case

Personal Pronouns (Full List)
I, me, my, mine
you, your, yours
he, she, him, her, it
his, hers, its
we, us, our, ours
they, them, their, theirs

My crown, I am; but still my griefs are mine.
—William Shakespeare, *Richard II*

Object pronouns are used as objects in sentences.
me, you, him, her, it, us, them

Mark each bolded pronoun as *DO*, *IO*, or *OP*.

For **me**, my lords, I love **him** not, nor fear **him.**
—William Shakespeare, *Henry VIII*

Give **us** notice of his inclination.
—William Shakespeare, *Richard III*

A virtuous and a Christian-like conclusion,/To pray for **them** that have done scathe to **us**.
—William Shakespeare, *Richard III*

Subject pronouns are used as subjects and predicate nominatives in sentences.
I, you, he, she, it, we, they

Mark each bolded pronoun as *S* or *PN*.

I am **he**.
—William Shakespeare, *Richard III*

Stand **we** in good array; for **they** no doubt,/Will issue out again and bid us battle.
—William Shakespeare, *Henry VI*

I blame her not, **she** could say little less;/**She** had the wrong. But what said Henry's queen?
—William Shakespeare, *Henry VI, Part III*

You need to learn grammar. I will teach you.

I met her at the park. She was wearing her jacket.

It is not very hard. I will learn it.

CORRECT	***INCORRECT***
I am he.	I am him.
The students are we.	The students are us.
The teachers are they.	The teachers are them.

The kitten licked Jim. The kitten licked _________.

The winners were Judy and Diane. The winners were _________.

OP OP
Give the prize to Madison and him. NOT: Give the prize to *he*.

S S
Dad and I made brownies. NOT: *Me* made brownies.

Exercise 50A: Subject and Object Pronouns

Underline all the personal pronouns in the following sentences. Identify them as *S* for subject, *O* for object, or *P* for possessive.

These sentences are from *Will in the World: How Shakespeare Became Shakespeare*, by Stephen Greenblatt.

If before his success with the *Henry VI* plays Shakespeare had not already met Marlowe, he would certainly have met him soon afterward, and along with Marlowe he would have met many of the other playwrights—poets, as they were then called—who were writing for the London stage.

The small revision makes a large point: the dead are completely dead. No prayers can help them; no messages can be sent to them or received from them. Hamnet was beyond reach.

Anne Hathaway represented an escape in another sense: she was in the unusual position of being her own woman. Very few young, unmarried Elizabethan women had any executive control over their own lives; the girl's watchful father and mother would make the key decisions for their daughter, ideally, though not always, with her consent. But Anne—an orphan in her midtwenties, with some resources left to her by her father's will and more due to her upon her marriage—was, in the phrase of the times, "wholly at her own government."

In his old age, a man named Willis, born the same year as Will, recalled a play...that he saw in Gloucester...when he was a child..." At such a play, Willis remembered, "my father took me with him, and made me stand between his legs, as he sat upon one of the benches, where we saw and heard very well." The experience was a remarkably intense one for Willis: "This sight took such an impression in me," he wrote, "that when I came towards man's estate, it was as fresh in my memory as if I had seen it newly acted."

Exercise 50B: Using Personal Pronouns Correctly

Choose the correct word(s) in parentheses and cross out the incorrect choice(s). Be sure to choose the grammatically correct choice for writing and not the choice that sounds the best.

My mother and sister and (me/I) planned to go on a weekend knitting retreat.
My mother helped (us/we) to choose projects for the weekend.
My mother and (her/she) chose sweaters, and I decided to tackle a fringed scarf.
Mom bought (my sister and me/my sister and I) new yarns for our new projects.
At the end of the retreat, (us/we) had gotten more than half of each project finished.
My mother gave my sister and (me/I) a huge compliment.
She said that the best company she'd ever had on a retreat were (us/we).

Exercise 50C: Diagramming Personal Pronouns

On your own paper, diagram the following sentences. Personal pronouns are diagrammed exactly like the nouns or adjectives they replace.

They threw us a life-line.
We thanked them profusely.
Where am I?
He gave me a dry towel.
I hear you!
The recipients of their help were we.

— LESSON 51 —

Indefinite Pronouns

Gollum wanted the ring. He longed for it.
Everyone hoped that Frodo would succeed.

Indefinite pronouns are pronouns without antecedents.

Indefinite Pronouns
Singular

anybody	anyone	anything
everybody	everyone	everything
nobody	no one	nothing
somebody	someone	something
another	other	one
either	neither	each

Plural
both, few, many, several

Singular or Plural
all, any, most, none, some

All of the cake was eaten.

All of the pieces were eaten.

Most of the people . . .

None of the water . . .

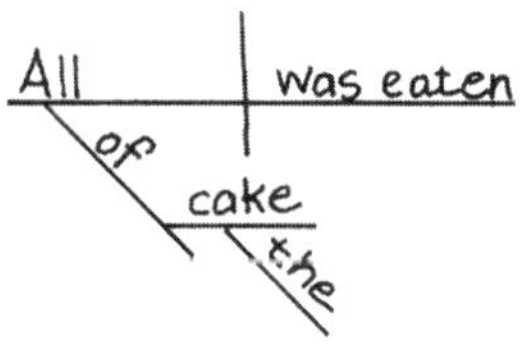

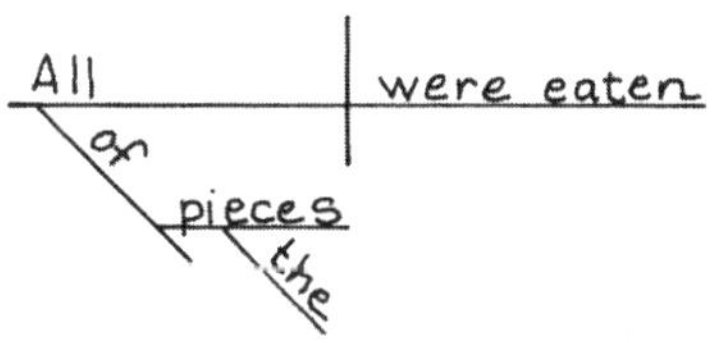

Many of the guests arrived early.

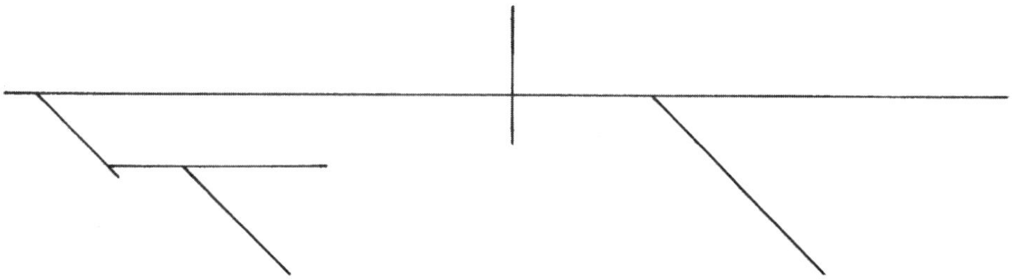

Many guests arrived early.

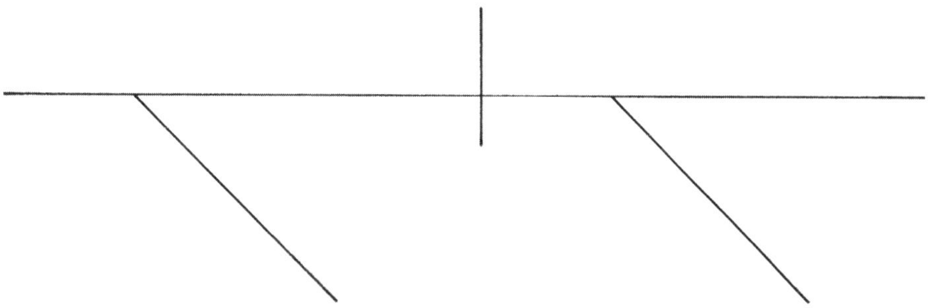

Exercise 51A: Identifying Indefinite Pronouns

Underline all of the indefinite pronouns in the following sentences. Each sentence may contain more than one pronoun.

These sentences are drawn from *Don Quixote*, by Miguel de Cervantes, trans. John Ormsby.

Don Quixote, without uttering a word or imploring aid from anyone, once more dropped his buckler and once more lifted his lance.

But there was nobody now to listen to these words of Don Quixote's.

Master Nicholas, the village barber, however, used to say that neither of them came up to the Knight of Phoebus, and that if there was any that could compare with him it was Don Galaor, the brother of Amadis of Gaul, because he had a spirit that was equal to every occasion.

Yesterday was the first day of our coming here; we have a few of what they say are called field-tents pitched among the trees on the bank of an ample brook that fertilises all of these meadows.

In the meantime Sancho had recounted to them several of the adventures and accidents that had happened to his master.

All or most of the knights-errant in days of yore were great troubadours and great musicians, for both of these accomplishments, or more properly speaking gifts, are the peculiar property of lovers-errant.

Exercise 51B: Subject-Verb Agreement: Indefinite Pronouns

Choose the correct verb in parentheses. Cross out the incorrect verb.

Everyone (has / have) agreed to go trail riding in the mountains!
All of the company (is / are) going on this exciting adventure.
All of the horses (is / are) guaranteed to be gentle and calm.
A few of the guests (has / have) ridden before, but some of them (is / are) just a little bit nervous.
Most of the horses (has / have) been saddled already.
Most of the group (is / are) mounting up.
One of the horses (was / were) named Volcano.
Nobody (want / wants) to ride Volcano!
Another of the horses (was / were) named Sleepyhead.
Everybody (asks / ask) to ride Sleepyhead.
(Does / Do) anyone know which horse is named Killer?
None of us (want / wants) to ride Killer either!

Exercise 51C: Diagramming Indefinite Pronouns

On your own paper, diagram the following sentences, slightly adapted from *The Knights Hospitaller: A Military History of the Knights of St John*, by John C. Carr.

By now, Rome and most of Italy had become insecure.

Turanshah demanded all of Outremer.

To his surprise and chagrin, everyone did not agree with him.

In 1309, the papacy had split into one in Rome and the other in Avignon.

A few refused, on the grounds of conscience.

Nothing came of the move.

— LESSON 52 —

Personal Pronouns
Indefinite Pronouns

Personal Pronouns
I, me, my, mine
you, your, yours
he, she, him, her, it
his, hers, its
we, us, our, ours
they, them, their, theirs

Subject pronouns: ____

____

______________________ am delighted to be doing grammar.

______________________ are delighted to be doing grammar.

______________________ is delighted to be doing grammar.

Object pronouns: ____

____

The walrus splattered water all over ______________________.

The rain drenched Kim and ______________________.

Possessive pronouns/possessive adjectives in attributive position: ______________________

____

I grabbed ______________________ umbrella.

The cloud began dropping ____________________ moisture.

The soaked tourists ran for ____________________ cars.

Possessive pronouns/possessive adjectives in predicate position: ____________________

____

That raincoat is ________________________________.

Those waterproof ponchos are _____________________.

Indefinite pronouns are pronouns without antecedents.

Singular Indefinite Pronouns

anybody anyone anything
everybody everyone everything

nobody no one nothing
somebody someone something

another other one
either neither each

Everyone _________ in the kitchen.

Nobody __________ in the dining room.

Neither of them __________ in the garden.

Plural Indefinite Pronouns

both, few, many, several

Both _________ cooking eggplants.

A few of the crowd _________ objecting to eggplant.

Several _________ quite happy with the prospect of eggplant.

Singular or Plural Indefinite Pronouns

all, any, most, none, some

All of the fire engines _________ there.

All of the mansion _________ destroyed in the fire.

Is everyone coming to get _________ Christmas present?

____

Are they all coming to get their Christmas presents?

Exercise 52A: Subject and Object Pronouns

In the following sentences, cross out the incorrect pronoun.

This first set of sentences is from *Number the Stars*, by Lois Lowry.

But if (they / them) are watching (we / us)—if (they / them) see all of (we / us) leave?

And (I / me) have named (he / him) Thor, for the God of Thunder.

"Soon (we / us) will have to add another blanket to your bed," Mama said one morning as (her / she) and Annemarie tidied the bedroom.

(She / Her) remembered how (she / her) had stared at the others, frightened, when (them / they) had stopped (she / her) on the street.

Annemarie called to (him / he) and (him / he) came to the side, his face worried when (him / he) recognized (she / her) on the dock.

This second set of sentences is from *The Tenant of Wildfell Hall*, by Anne Brontë.

(Me / I) am very much attached to my little friend, and so is (her / she) to (me / I).

"Oh, yes! come in," said (she / her) (for (me / I) had met (them / they) in the garden).

Millicent told (me / I) (I / me) was the life of the party.

It is (I / me) who have left (they / them).

When (us / we) did meet, it was (he / him) that sought (I / me) out.

But what is (him / he) doing—what is it that keeps (him / he) away?

(I / Me) would not believe (they / them), for (me / I) knew (she / her) better than (them / they).

Oh, it would be cruel to make (her / she) feel as (me / I) feel now, and know what (me / I) have known!

(Me / I) was annoyed at the continual injustice (her / she) had done (me / I) from the very dawn of our acquaintance.

(Him / He) and Lord Lowborough were accompanying Annabella and (I / me) in a long, delightful ride.

Exercise 52B: Possessive and Indefinite Pronouns

In these sentences, taken from *The House of Mirth,* by Edith Wharton, cross out the incorrect word in each set of parentheses.

"Do let us go and take a peep at the presents before everyone else (leaves / leave) the dining-room!" suggested Miss Farish, linking her arm in her friend's.

I always say no one (do / does) things better than cousin Grace!

Each of them (want / wants) a creature of a different race.

But at this point one or two belated passengers from the last station forced (his / their / his or her) way into the carriage, and Lily had to retreat to her seat.

The landscape outspread below her seemed an enlargement of her present mood, and she found something of herself in (its / their) calmness, (its / their) breadth, (its / their) long free reaches.

The topmost shelf of every closet (were / was) made to yield up (its / their) secret, cellar and coal-bin (were / was) probed to (its / their) darkest depths and, as a final stage in the lustral rites, the entire house (were / was) swathed in penitential white and deluged with expiatory soapsuds.

Her discretions interested him almost as much as her imprudences: he was so sure that both (were / was) part of the same carefully-elaborated plan.

Under the Georgian porch she paused again, scanning the street for a hansom. None (were / was) in sight.

And I suppose most of the owners of Americana (are / is) not historians either?

To the lady and her acquaintances there (were / was) something heroic in living as though one were much richer than one's bank-book denoted.

It (were / was) the last week in June, and none of her friends (were / was) in town.

Every one (knows / know) you're a thousand times handsomer and cleverer.

The fire, like the lamps, (were / was) never lit except when there (were / was) company.

And there (were / was) everybody talking about you.

There (were / was) something to be done before she left the house.

None of the desultory interests which she dignified with the name of tastes (were / was) pronounced enough to enable her to live contentedly in obscurity.

Some (were / was) in small fragments, the others merely torn in half.

And there (is / are) others who (is / are) afraid of me.

In the center of the table, between the melting marrons glaces and candied cherries, a pyramid of American Beauties lifted (its / their) vigorous stems.

Exercise 52C: Writing Sentences from Diagrams

Use the diagrams below to reconstruct these sentences from Simon Schama's *The Story of the Jews: Finding the Words (1000 BCE-1492).*

Write the original sentence on the blank below each diagram. Pay careful attention to each part of speech! Punctuate each sentence properly.

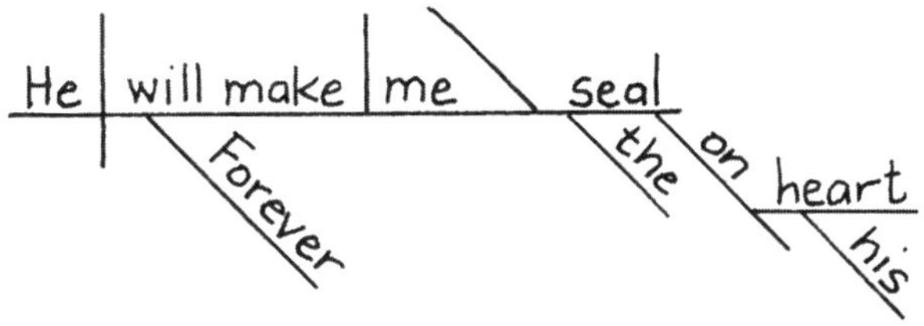

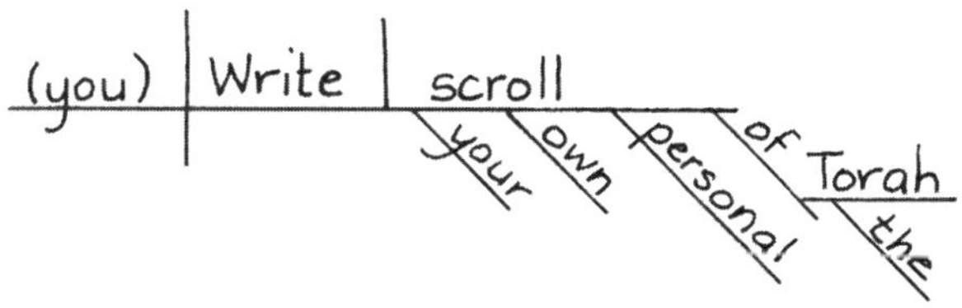

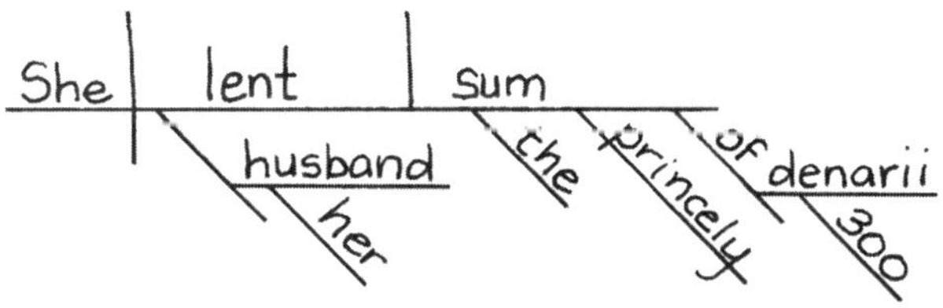

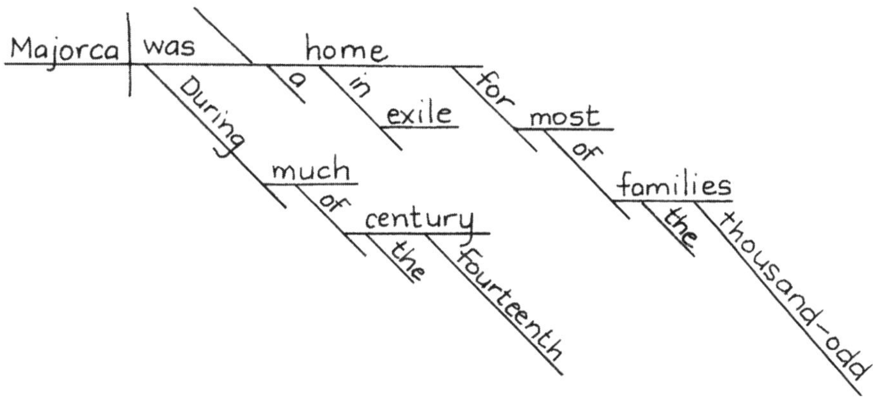

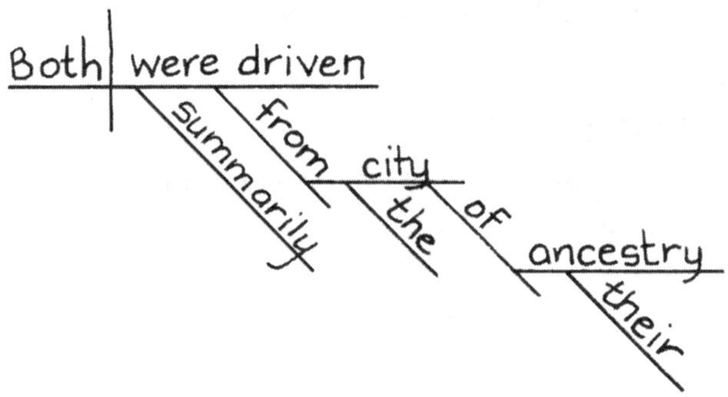
Both
were driven
summarily
from
city
the
of
ancestry
their

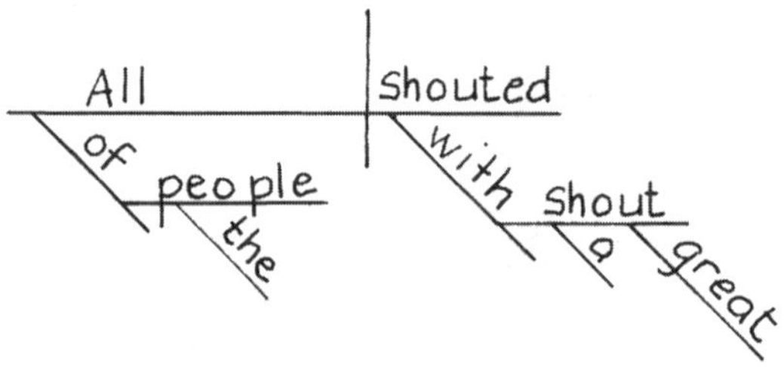
All
shouted
of
people
the
with
shout
a
great

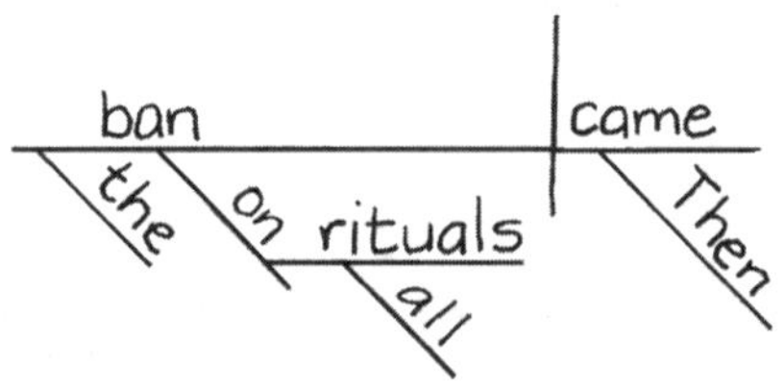
ban
came
the
on
rituals
all
Then

WEEK 14

Active and Passive Voice

— LESSON 53 —

Principal Parts
Troublesome Verbs

She set the set of sorted stuff
Beside the seat where she had sat.

English verbs have three principal parts.
The first principal part is the simple present.
The second principal part is the simple past.
The third principal part of a verb is found by dropping the helping verb from the perfect past.

Exercise 53A: Principal Parts of Verbs

Fill in the chart with the missing forms.

	First Principal Part Present	Second Principal Part Past	Third Principal Part Past Participle
I	provide		
I		split	
I		drove	
I			tried
I	watch		
I			flown
I	live		
I		played	

Troublesome Irregular Verbs

Verb	Principal Parts	Definition
sit	(sit, sat, sat)	to rest or be seated
set	(set, set, set)	to put or place something
lie	(lie, lay, lain)	to rest or recline
lay	(lay, laid, laid)	to put or place something
rise	(rise, rose, risen)	to get up or go up
raise	(raise, raised, raised)	to cause something to go up or grow up
let	(let, let, let)	to allow
leave	(leave, left, left)	to go away from or allow to remain

Exercise 53B: Using Correct Verbs

Choose the correct verb in parentheses. Cross out the incorrect verb.

First thing in the morning on July 1, Lea's father (rose / raised) the flag outside their Whistler house.

He (let / left) Lea alone until ten o'clock and (let / left) her sleep late.

Lea loves to (lay / lie) in bed a little longer on holiday mornings.

Her father (rose / raised) early to celebrate Canada Day!

Lea's father (lay / laid) out a special breakfast of beaver tails—fried dough with cinnamon and sugar.

Lea had (laid / lain) out her favorite red and white clothes the night before.

Lea and her father (set / sat) at the table, eating breakfast and listening to Leonard Cohen and Feist.

Afterwards, Lea (set / sat) out cupcakes for her friends to decorate.

Sprinkles, red and white frosting, candy maple leafs, and tiny Canadian flags all (lay / laid) ready to be used!

Exercise 53C: Correct Forms of Troublesome Verbs

Fill in the blanks with the correct form of the indicated verb.

He went to work in a foundry pouring molten iron where the work was steady and backbreaking, but he simply could not be home often and yet he still ____________________ his boys responsibly. (raise, simple past)

Bill was ________________ in the segregated South and saw strict limitations for black people there compared to when he moved to Oakland, California. (raise, past participle)

After being incarcerated, he converted to Islam through his brother's encouragement and then ________________ within the ranks of Elijah Muhammad's Nation of Islam organization called Black Muslims. (rise, simple past)

Despite his hard work, Bill _______________ the university in 1956, 16 credits shy of graduation. (leave, simple past)

But Swegle _______________ the players play and his coaching really involved merely substituting. (let, simple past)

—Murry R. Nelson, *Bill Russell: A Biography*

He wondered what Iktomi would do, thus he _______________ still where he fell. (lie, simple past)

Saying this, he _______________ a firm hand upon the muskrat's shoulder, and started off along the edge of the lake. (lay, simple past)

A man in buckskins _______________ upon the top of a little hillock. (sit, simple past)

Wordless, the avenger ate in silence the food _______________ before him on the ground. (set, past participle)

She did not wish a guest in her dwelling _______________ upon the bare hard ground. (sit, present infinitive)

—Zitkala-Sa, *Old Indian Legends: Stories from the Dakotas*

Exercise 53D: Proofreading for Correct Verb Usage

The following excerpts are from *Prairie Gothic: The Story of a West Texas Family,* by John R. Erickson. Find and correct sixteen errors in verb usage by crossing out the incorrect verbs and writing the correct forms above them. Be careful—some sentences might not have any errors at all, and others might have more than one!

The original house set on several acres of land where a windmill provided water for the house as well as for chickens and several milk cows, a big garden, and an orchard of fruit trees.

We rose ducks, rabbits, and chickens in the back yard, and from her I was learned to wring a chicken's neck and pluck the feathers after dipping the bird into boiling water, skills she had been learned from her mother and grandmother. We rose a garden, collected horned toads, and hanged out the weekly wash on the clothesline.

On thousands of nights we have unrolled our bedrolls, lying them side by side, out under the stars.

Olive had been risen on a ranch that had plenty of rattlers and she should have known what to do: set down, stay calm, grit your teeth and look the other way while a rescuer went through the gory process of trying to save your life.

Into her eighties, she writted letters that would be the envy of any college graduate: words wrote in a precise hand, lines that couldn't have been straighter if they had been lain out with a ruler, and whole pages that contained no misspellings, ink smudges, coffee stains, or cross-outs.

Neither lawman had a chance to saw what was coming, and both laid dead on the floor.

I had arrived just in time for supper and Mrs. Tennill had already sat two places at Grandmother's big rectangular dining table, which looked out on the green expanse of the back yard.

I soon realized that the death of Martha Sherman, a story that had lain half-forgotten in the memory of my family, was a major news event on the Texas frontier in the winter of 1860-1861.

But make that same drive in a drought year and you might see snowplows pushing dunes of red sand off the highways, and tumbleweed cannonballs snapping power lines and lying barbed wire fence on the ground—this my mother remembered during the drought of the 1930s.

— LESSON 54 —

Verb Tense

Active and Passive Voice

past	simple
present	progressive
future	perfect

A simple verb simply tells whether an action takes place in the past, present, or future.
A progressive verb describes an ongoing or continuous action.
A perfect verb describes an action which has been completed before another action takes place.

Exercise 54A: Reviewing Tenses

Write the tense of each underlined verb above it. These two excerpts are from the Sherlock Holmes story "A Scandal in Bohemia," by Arthur Conan Doyle. The first is done for you.

progressive past

One night—it was on the twentieth of March, 1888—I was returning from a journey to a patient (for I had now returned to civil practice), when my way led me through Baker Street. As I passed the well-remembered door, which must always be associated in my mind with my wooing, and with the dark incidents of the Study in Scarlet, I was seized with a keen desire to see Holmes again, and to know how he was employing his extraordinary powers.

I was already deeply interested in his inquiry, for, though it was surrounded by none of the grim and strange features which were associated with the two crimes which I have already recorded, still, the nature of the case and the exalted station of his client gave it a character of its own.

We both thought the best resource was flight, when pursued by so formidable an antagonist; so you will find the nest empty when you call. As to the photograph, your client may rest in peace. I love and am loved by a better man than he. The King may do what he will without hindrance from one whom he has cruelly wronged.

The door had been fastened upon the inner side, and the windows were blocked by old-fashioned shutters with broad iron bars.

He fastened the door upon the inner side.

In a sentence with an active verb, the subject performs the action.
In a sentence with a passive verb, the subject receives the action.

I punched you.
You were punched by me.

The Egyptians constructed pyramids.
Pyramids were constructed.
Pyramids were constructed by the Egyptians.

Active Verb	Passive Verb
Present	**is/are + past participle**
Freddy tricks the alligator.	The alligator is tricked by Freddy.

Past Freddy tricked the alligator.	**was/were + past participle** The alligator was tricked by Freddy.
Future Freddy will trick the alligator.	**will be + past participle** The alligator will be tricked by Freddy.
Progressive Present Freddy is tricking the alligator.	**is/are being + past participle** The alligator is being tricked by Freddy.
Progressive Past Freddy was tricking the alligator.	**was/were being + past participle** The alligator was being tricked by Freddy.
***Progressive Future** Freddy will be tricking the alligator.	***will be being + past participle** The alligator will be being tricked by Freddy.
Perfect Present Freddy has tricked the alligator.	**has/have been + past participle** The alligator has been tricked by Freddy.
Perfect Past Freddy had tricked the alligator.	**had been + past participle** The alligator had been tricked by Freddy.
Perfect Future Freddy will have tricked the alligator.	**will have been + past participle** The alligator will have been tricked by Freddy.

*The passive form of progressive future verbs is awkward and not often used.

State-of-being verbs do not have voice.

Exercise 54B: Distinguishing Between Active and Passive Voice

Identify the following sentences, from Doyle's "A Scandal in Bohemia," as *A* for active or *P* for passive. If you're not sure, ask yourself: Is the subject *doing* the verb, or is the verb *happening* to the subject?

I am loved by a better man than he. _______

Godfrey Norton came running as hard as he could towards me. _______

A blow was struck. _______

She responded beautifully. _______

Your task is confined to that. _______

We will be shown into the sitting-room. _______

I was just balancing whether I should run for it. _______

The lamps were just being lighted. _______

It widened the field of my inquiry. _______

Twice she has been waylaid. _______

Five attempts have been made. _______

I have been too busy to think of food. _______

I am following you closely. _______

The paper was made in Bohemia. ________

I was still balancing the matter in my mind. ________

I will rejoin you in ten minutes. ________

Exercise 54C: Forming the Active and Passive Voice

Fill in the chart below, rewriting each sentence so that it appears in both the active and the passive voice. Be sure to keep the tense the same. The first is done for you.

ACTIVE	PASSIVE
Modern detectives, unlike policemen, don't wear uniforms.	Uniforms aren't worn by modern detectives, unlike policemen.
	Suspects and witnesses are interviewed by detectives as part of case investigation.
Homicide units assign murder cases to detectives.	
Detectives often set aside cases that have no evidence, no witnesses, and no suspects.	
Detectives "clear" cases when they arrest a suspect and send them to trial.	
	In modern detective work, DNA is often used to help identify the perpetrators of crimes.

— LESSON 55 —

Parts of the Sentence
Active and Passive Voice

Many other advantages were enumerated.

The poorer tenants will have something valuable of their own.

The proposal is wholly new and has something solid and real.

The squire will grow popular among his tenants.

I have no personal interest in the promotion of the necessary work.

— LESSON 56 —

Active and Passive Voice

Transitive and Intransitive Verbs

Active Voice	Passive Voice
Present	**am/is/are + past participle**
The farmer grows wheat.	Wheat is grown by the farmer.
Past	**was/were + past participle**
I made a cake.	The cake was made by me.
Future	**will be + past participle**
The princess will keep the key.	The key will be kept by the princess.
Progressive Present	**is/are being + past participle**
The farmer is growing wheat.	Wheat is being grown by the farmer.
Progressive Past	**was/were being + past participle**
I was making a cake.	The cake was being made by me.
Progressive Future	**will be being + past participle**
The princess will be keeping the key.	The key will be being kept by the princess.
Perfect Present	**has/have been + past participle**
The farmer has grown wheat.	Wheat has been grown by the farmer.
Perfect Past	**had been + past participle**
I had made a cake.	The cake had been made by me.
Perfect Future	**will have been + past participle**
The princess will have kept the key.	The key will have been kept by the princess.

I laugh out loud.
The baby slept soundly.
The queen will sit in the front row.
He died.

transire (Latin for "to pass over")

Transitive verbs express action that is received by some person or thing.
Intransitive verbs express action that is not received by any person or thing.

Common Intransitive Verbs

cough	go	arrive
sit	lie	rise
shine	sneeze	am, is, are, was, were

Common Transitive Verbs

love	eat	help
set	lay	raise
cut	hug	save

I am sitting on the front porch.

I lay down on the grass.
I will have risen early in the morning.

I am setting the heavy box down.
I laid my weary head on my arms.
I will have raised my hand at least once by the end of class.

Verbs That Can Be Used As Transitive or Intransitive

turn	break	speak
fly	run	spread
taste	eat	sing

The cook turns the meat on the spit.

I will spread gochujang mayonnaise on the burger bun.

He is singing a difficult aria.

The captain turned towards the sunset.

The mist spread across the river's surface.

He's singing in the shower.

The cook turns the meat on the spit.

___

I will spread gochujang mayonnaise on the burger bun.

___

He is singing a difficult aria.

___

Exercise 56A: Transitive and Intransitive Verbs

Find each verb serving as a predicate in the following sentences and underline it twice. Underline each subject of the predicate once. Write *T* above each transitive verb and *IT* above each intransitive verb. Circle the direct object of each transitive verb.

These sentences are adapted from *Viet Nam: A History from Earliest Times to the Present*, by Ben Kiernan.

Beginning around 14,000 BCE, the Hoabinhian people ate wild cattle, water buffalo, rhinoceros, forest birds, turtles, tortoise, shellfish, and uncultivated, or "wild," rice.

In happier times, carefree, they ate and slept.

Now, robbed of water, they fear for their land.

The catfish confessed its theft, paid the frogs' cost, and submitted to exile.

Dinh Bo Linh enjoyed less success in his effort to win domestic legitimacy.

Dinh Bo Linh governed by fear.

Dinh Bo Linh's people feared him.

The scene was set for the brief emergence of a new, separate kingdom.

Its Confucian elite ran its own affairs and challenged imperial control.

The Ming invasion of 1406-7 came on the pretext of restoring the Tran dynasty.

Imperial armies overthrew and captured Ho Quy Ly.

The Ming destroyed all records of Dai Viet governance.

A flood of neo-Confucianism washed over the country.

Inland, Chinese ran mining enterprises near the northern border.

Over the ensuing centuries Jiao's population adopted more of the northern culture and system of government.

These two regimes fought wars on other fronts.

The weekly newspaper *Trung Bac Tan Van* (Central and Northern News) ran continuously from 1919 until 1945.

By early 1968, the 80,000 PAVN troops in the South were fighting alongside 160,000 NLF infantry and service troops.

Exercise 56B: Active and Passive Verbs

In the blanks below, rewrite each sentence with an active verb so that the verb is passive. Rewrite each sentence with a passive verb so that the verb is active. You may need to add or rearrange words or phrases to make the sentences grammatical!

These sentences are slightly adapted from *Vietnam: Journeys of Body, Mind, and Spirit*, by Van Huy Nguyen and Laurel Kendall.

The Kinh welcome the solar new year with people all over the globe.

____

____

Each person, each family, and Vietnamese society as a whole approach the new year as a time of fresh aspiration and hope.

____

____

If the solar new year can be considered the government's Tet, the lunar new year is considered the family's Tet.

Each family prepares offerings to worship ancestors.

According to tradition, visits are made and gifts are distributed during the week before Tet.

On New Year's Eve they will burn votive paper money.

Vendors set their wares on the pavement under red banners declaring "Tet Shop" or "Happy New Year."

Exercise 56C: Diagramming

On your own paper, diagram every word in the following sentences. They are slightly condensed from *Vietnam (Cultures of the World)*, by Audrey Seah and Charissa M. Nair.

The water level has been raised by silt deposits on the riverbeds.

Subsequent dynasties repaired and added more canals to the network and created a system of irrigation and flood control.

Vietnam's indented eastern coastline extends from the Gulf of Tonkin to the South China Sea, past the Mekong delta, and reaches the Gulf of Thailand.

At its narrowest point, the distance between its border with Laos in the west and the South China Sea in the east is only 31 miles.

WEEK 15

Specialized Pronouns

— LESSON 57 —

Parts of Speech
Parts of the Sentence
Intensive and Reflexive Pronouns

Anita made herself a huge brownie sundae!

Reflexive pronouns refer back to the subject.
Usually, reflexive pronouns act like objects.

Part of speech is a term that explains what a word does.
Part of the sentence is a term that explains how a word functions in a sentence.

He adapted himself to their knowledge.
He gave himself a task.
He praises in himself what he blames in others.

myself, himself, herself, itself, yourself, yourselves, ourselves, themselves

Intensive pronouns emphasize a noun or another pronoun.

The Queen of England herself gave the speech.
The Queen of England gave the speech herself.

DO
The Queen of England gave herself.

IO
The Queen of England gave herself the speech.

OP
The Queen of England gave the speech to herself.

Aristotle himself observed these variations.

He jumped into the sea and drowned himself.

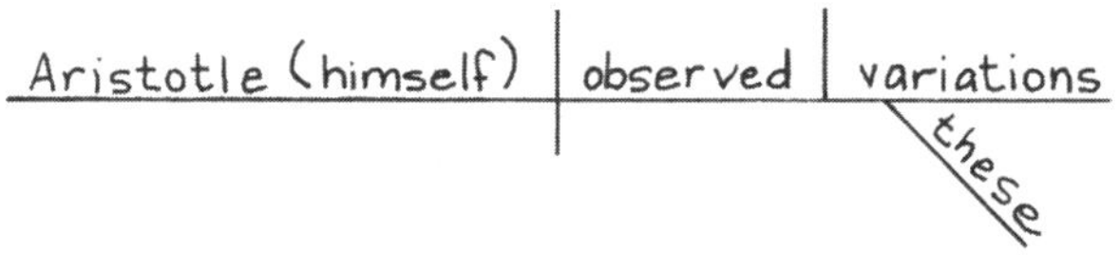

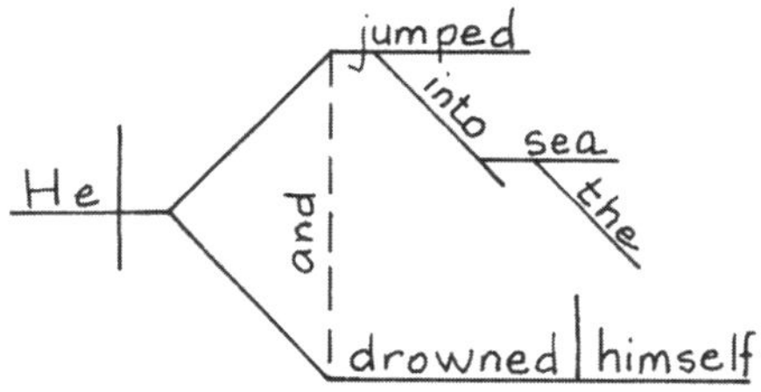

Do NOT use theirselves, hisself, or ourself.

Diana and myself cooked a casserole.
Diana and I cooked a casserole.
I myself cooked a casserole.
Take care of yourself.

Exercise 57A: Identifying Intensive and Reflexive Pronouns

Underline the intensive and reflexive pronouns in the following sentences. Above each pronoun, write *I* for intensive or *R* for reflexive. If the pronoun is reflexive, also mark it as *DO* (direct object), *IO* (indirect object), or *OP* (object of the preposition). The first is done for you.

R DO
The good woman let go with a smile, and Louise found herself alone.

But when the son received his father well, the old man was beside himself with joy.

They would also cook themselves, and wait upon each other.

Throughout the work are feeble poetic epigrams composed by the compiler himself.

The race lies between Master Schummel and yourself.

No one knows me better than I know myself.

How comes it that you have produced nothing of value yourself?

He convicted of ignorance those who had a great opinion of themselves.

I made up my mind to go myself.

Between ourselves, you owe your wife a great deal.

It would be strange indeed if I should torture myself, and make of myself something which I am not, and hide myself beneath a character foreign to me.

Exercise 57B: Using Intensive and Reflexive Pronouns Correctly

Each of the following sentences contains errors in the usage of intensive and reflexive pronouns. Cross out the incorrect word and write the correction above it.

He was quite beside hisself.

We had seated ourselfs round the table.

You yourself did myself the honor to say that you wished myself to be *fully* informed.

Then I go away for a little time and leave them to theirselves.

Our assignment of himself to the third century is based merely on the fact that he quotes writers of the second, and is hisself in turn cited by somewhat later authors.

On the contrary, himself thought the ideal and the practical life perfectly compatible, and himself strove to unite in himself the poet and the man of affairs.

Exercise 57C: Diagramming Intensive and Reflexive Pronouns

On your own paper, diagram every word in the following sentences, taken from *The Library of the World's Best Literature, Ancient and Modern*, Vol. 12, ed. Charles Dudley Warner.

I myself suffer from a different kind of education.
In the first place, I was ashamed of myself.
He prided himself on his simple manner of living, and never exacted any pay.
His love for the Northern seas shows itself in his poetry and prose.

— LESSON 58 —

Demonstrative Pronouns
Demonstrative Adjectives

Questions	Punch lines
What did the teacher say to make the student eat his quiz?	That opens up a whole new can of worms.
What did the customer in the butcher shop hear that scared him?	This will be a piece of cake!
What did the fisherman say when he dropped his bucket of bait?	These cost an arm and a leg.

Demonstrative pronouns demonstrate or point out something. They can take the place of a single word or a group of words.

this, that, these, those

"Your cousin wrote this," said Aunt Alexandra. "He was a beautiful character."

"Didn't know it was this dark. Didn't look like it'd be this dark earlier in the evening."

Demonstrative adjectives modify nouns and answer the question *which one*.

That was the only time I ever heard Atticus say it was a sin to do something . . .

"I destroyed his last shred of credibility at that trial, if he had any to begin with."

It was times like these when I thought my father, who hated guns and had never been to any wars, was the bravest man who ever lived.

I was beginning to notice a subtle change in my father these days, that came out when he talked with Aunt Alexandra.

"Dill, those were his own witnesses."

Mrs. Merriweather was one of those childless adults who find it necessary to assume a different tone of voice when speaking to children.

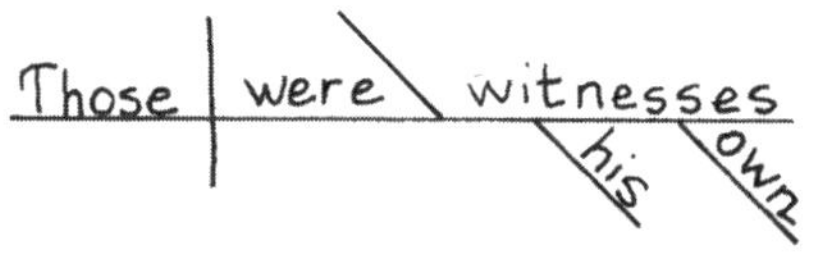

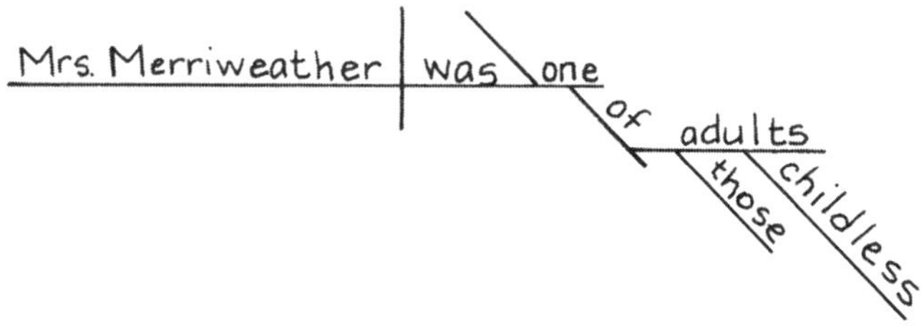

(The above sentences are from *To Kill a Mockingbird*, by Harper Lee.)

Did you see the coaster? That is one scary ride.

Raindrops on roses and whiskers on kittens, bright copper kettles and warm woolen mittens, brown paper packages tied up with strings–these are a few of my favorite things.

Exercise 58A: Demonstrative Pronouns and Demonstrative Adjectives

In the sentences below, label every occurrence of *this, that, these*, and *those* as either *DP* (demonstrative pronoun) or *DA* (demonstrative adjective). Draw an arrow from each demonstrative adjective to the noun it modifies. Label each demonstrative pronoun as *S* (subject), *DO* (direct object), *IO* (indirect object), or *OP* (object of the preposition).

These sentences are taken from *World of Warcraft and Philosophy: Wrath of the Philosopher King*, ed. Luke Cuddy and John Nordlinger.

And this is when weird things can happen.

How can we even begin to think of this?

Thus they are no longer "non-specified members of that other community," making their fights more personal than political.

Plato then proceeds to discuss what it would be like for one of these people to be freed, and roam outside of the cave.

I want to know what's on the other side of those hills.

Those occupying the hypothetical "original position" ensure fairness of society for all citizens.

However, these only function as driving licenses for the shiny siege weapons.

Boredom, he believed, was the worst of these, calling it "the root of all evil."

The story of *Warcraft II* is obviously a continuation of that.

That is guided by the game mechanics.

Since prices and goods within WoW are so similar to those seen on Earth, we should be able to measure the value generated by Blood Elves just like we measure the value generated by actual people.

Of course, this situation is unrealistic, as no reasonable entrepreneur would open a hobby store surrounded by eleven others.

But if Ner'zhul knew this, he would have no reason to trust Kil'jaeden.

These two models are very troublesome.

Exercise 58B: Demonstrative Pronouns

In the blank beneath each sentence, write a possible description of the thing or person that the underlined demonstrative pronoun stands for. Make sure to choose the correct number. (And use your imagination.)

<u>Those</u> are my least favorite ever.

____

<u>That</u> is the most spectacular thing I have ever seen.

____

<u>This</u> is truly horrifying.

____

<u>These</u> should just be thrown away immediately.

____

Exercise 58C: Diagramming

On your own paper, diagram every word in the following three sentences, taken from *What Is Your Quest?: From Adventure Games to Interactive Books*, by Anastasia Salter.

In text-only games, this is the only description available.
This take-it-or-leave-it avatar is not typical of other styles of games.
The campaign focused on the involvement of those creators and a return to the narrative.

— LESSON 59 —

Demonstrative Pronouns
Demonstrative Adjectives
Interrogative Pronouns
Interrogative Adjectives

Interrogative pronouns take the place of nouns in questions.
who, whom, whose, which, what

"Who started this?" said Uncle Jack.
"Talk like what in front of whom?" he asked.
Whose is that blanket?
Which is correct?

Whose blanket is missing?
What madness is this?
Which shoes are yours?

Interrogative adjectives modify nouns.

REMEMBER #1: Don't confuse *whose* and *who's.*

Whose orange flip-flops are those?	*Interrogative pronoun*
Who's cooking dinner?	*Contraction of* who is

I don't know whose/who's coming to dinner.

Whose/who's plate is still empty?

REMEMBER #2: Use *whom* as an object and *who* as a subject or predicate nominative.

CORRECT

Who started this?	*She started this. They started this. I started this. Jack started this.*
Talk like what in front of whom?	*In front of him? In front of her? In front of them? In front of Jack?*

Whom/Who is calling?

To whom/who did you speak?

REMEMBER #3: Diagram interrogative adjectives like any other adjective, and diagram interrogative pronouns like any other pronoun.

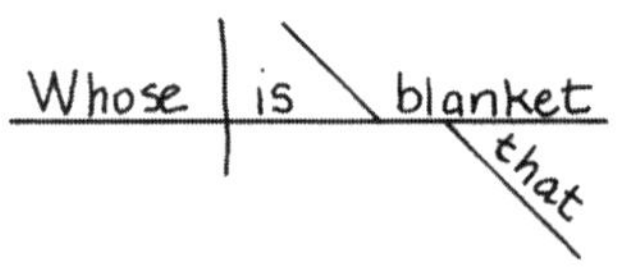

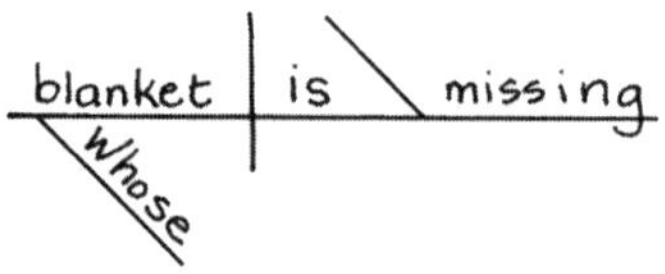

Exercise 59A: Identifying Demonstrative and Interrogative Pronouns

Underline all of the demonstrative and interrogative pronouns in the sentences. There may be more than one in each sentence.

These sentences are taken from *Japanese Fairy Tales*, compiled by Yei Theodora Ozaki.

"They have stood outside this house through the winter and the summer, often denying themselves food and sleep so they may win you. What more can you demand?"

"I shall soon take my leave if you will give me the big box—that is all I want!"

The insignia of the great Japanese Empire is composed of three treasures. These are the Yata-no-Kagami or the Mirror of Yata, the Yasakami-no-Magatama or the Jewel of Yasakami, and the Murakumo-no-Tsurugi or the Sword of Murakumo.

"This is no ordinary child. Whose can he be? I will find out before this day is done."

All the animals, those he had tamed to serve him, the bear, the deer, the monkey, and the hare, came to ask if they might attend him as usual.

But which was the way? He could not find it alone!

Slowly, very slowly, he untied the red silk cord, slowly and wonderingly he lifted the lid of the precious box. And what did he find? Strange to say only a beautiful little purple cloud rose out of the box in three soft wisps.

"That is good," said the old man. He then washed his feet in a basin of water and stepped up to the veranda.

These were placed before the old man, and the Lady Sparrow asked him to choose whichever he liked for a present, which she wished to give him.

"But next to you then, who is the strongest?"

Exercise 59B: Using Interrogative and Demonstrative Pronouns Correctly

Choose the correct word in parentheses. Cross out the incorrect word.

(These / Those) are my suitcases right here, so (these/those) must be Akari's suitcases next to the check-in counter.

(Whose / Who's) excited about flying to Tokyo tonight?

(Who's / Whose) sitting in the exit row of the plane?

(Who / Whom) is planning to take the day trip to Mount Fuji with me?

(This / These) is Akari's favorite travel pillow.

(Whose / Who's) are these blankets?

(Who / Whom) did she ask to meet us at the airport?

(Who / Whom) did you invite to dinner?

(Who / Whom) is leading the Tokyo biking tour on Thursday?

(Who / What) is the name of the guide of the walking tour of Omoide Yokocho?

With (who / whom) will you eat dinner on Friday?

(This / These) has been a very smooth plane ride.

Exercise 59C: Diagramming Interrogative and Demonstrative Pronouns

On your own paper, diagram the following sentences.

Whose are these lovely summer yukatas?

She bought what?

She carefully packed a suitcase of this and that.

Who wore this?

For whom were these shoes made?

Which is the best fish market in Tokyo?

You must try this octopus and those shrimp!

— LESSON 60 —

Pronoun Review

Sentences Beginning with Adverbs

A pronoun takes the place of a noun.
An antecedent is the noun that is replaced by the pronoun.

Personal Pronouns
I, me, my, mine,
you, your, yours
he, she, him, her, it
his, hers, its
we, us, our, ours,
they, them, their, theirs

Indefinite pronouns are pronouns without antecedents.

Singular

anybody	anyone	anything
everybody	everyone	everything
nobody	no one	nothing
somebody	someone	something
another	other	one
either	neither	each

Plural

both	few	many	several

Singular or Plural

all	any	most	none	some

Reflexive pronouns refer back to the subject.
myself, himself, herself, itself, yourself, yourselves, ourselves, themselves

She tripped and hurt herself.
She herself tripped.

Intensive pronouns emphasize a noun or another pronoun.
Demonstrative pronouns demonstrate or point out something. They can take the place of a single word or a group of words.
this, that, these, those

Interrogative pronouns take the place of nouns in questions.
who, whom, whose, which, what

Interrogative adjectives modify nouns.

What are you doing? Don't you know what direction to go?

That is she.
What is that?
Which is yours?
Where are you?
There you are.
So it is.

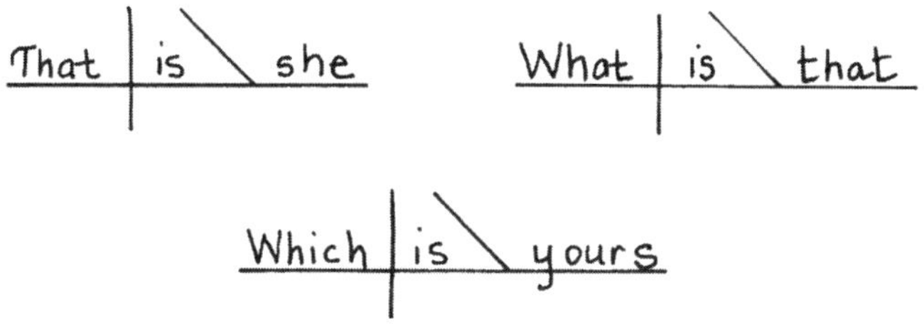

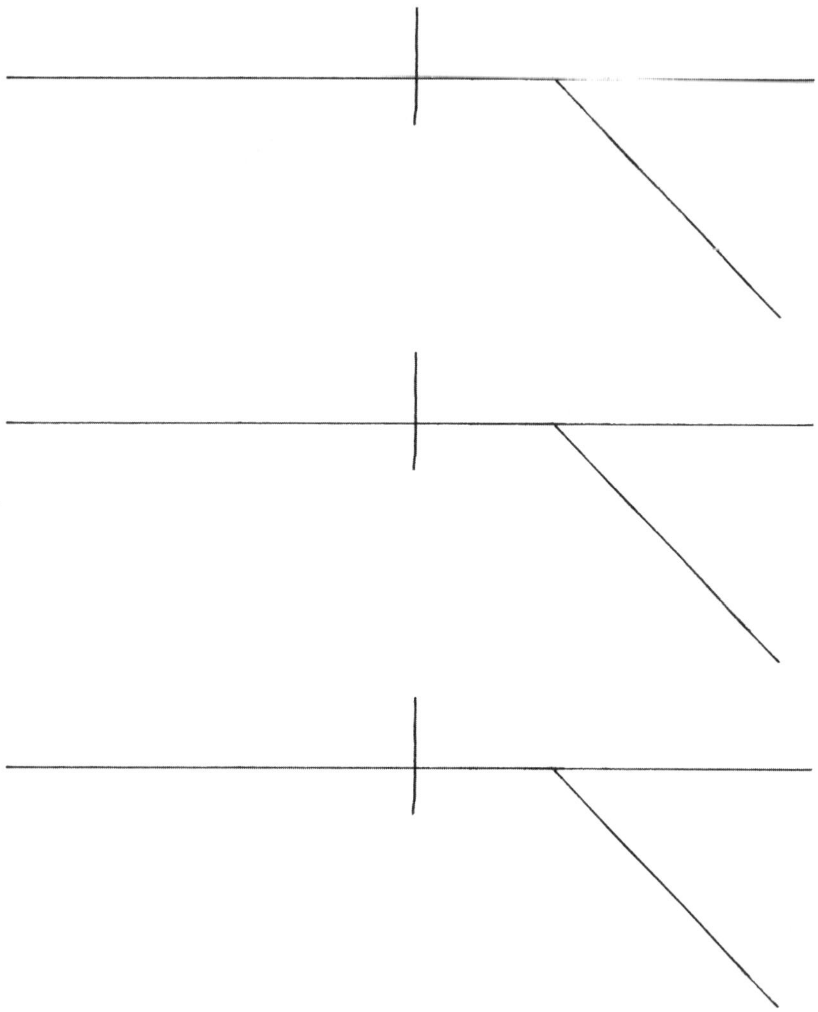

Exercise 60A: Singular/Plural Indefinite Pronouns

Cross out the incorrect verb in each sentence. These are slightly adapted from *The Autobiography of Benjamin Franklin*, which is (you'll be surprised to hear) by Benjamin Franklin.

Not all of the wagons (were / was) in serviceable condition.

None of the provisions (are / is) left.

Some of them (were / was) very unhappy.

Some of the hasty pudding (were / was) left.

Some of my faults (were / was) corrected.

I put down on paper my thoughts as they occurred. Most (are / is) now lost.

Most (were / was) men of property.

I asked for reassurance, but none (was / were) forthcoming.

Exercise 60B: Interrogatives and Demonstratives

In each of the following sentences, underline the interrogatives and demonstratives. If they are acting as adjectives, draw a line from each to the noun it modifies. If they are acting as other parts of the sentence, label them (*S* for subject, *DO* for direct object, *IO* for indirect object, or *OP* for object of the preposition).

These sentences are also from *The Autobiography of Benjamin Franklin*.

What do you intend to infer from that?

What good shall I do this day?

That amounts to nothing.

Whose shop is next door?

These were not the governor's letters!

And, perhaps, this might be one occasion of the differences we began to have about this time.

My time for these exercises and for reading was at night, after work or before it began in the morning,

I will give you what account I can of them at this distance from my papers, and if these are not lost in my absence, you will among them find many more particulars.

Exercise 60C: Diagramming Practice

On your own paper, diagram every word of the following sentences, also taken from *The Autobiography of Benjamin Franklin.*

Some of my descendants may follow this example, and reap the benefit.

Where should I look for my night's lodging?

There are no gains without pains.

Our mutual affection was revived, but there were now great objections to our union.

— REVIEW 5 —

Weeks 13-15

Topics
Pronouns and Antecedents
Possessive Pronouns
Subject and Object Pronouns
Indefinite Pronouns (and Subject-Verb Agreement)
Troublesome Verbs
Active and Passive Voice
Conjugating Passive Voice
Intensive and Reflexive Pronouns
Demonstrative and Interrogative Pronouns

Review 5A: Types of Pronouns

Put each pronoun from the word bank in the correct category. Some words may belong in more than one category.

this	my	many	who
himself	her	which	
those	myself	we	none
all	us	its	
whose	it	them	ouselves
he	these	ours	

Personal Subject _______________ _______________ _______________

Personal Object _______________ _______________ _______________

Personal Possessive _______________ _______________ _______________

Indefinite _______________ _______________ _______________

Demonstrative _______________ _______________ _______________

Interrogative _______________ _______________ _______________

Intensive/Reflexive _______________ _______________ _______________

Review 5B: Using Correct Pronouns

Cross out the incorrect pronoun in parentheses.

(Whose / Who's) going to help my mother and (I / me) shop at the farmer's market?

(Whose / Who's) basket is sitting over (there / their) with the gooseberries in it?

The first person to suggest we make gooseberry fool was (he / him).

My mother, my sister, and (he / him) were all arguing about (whose / who's) recipe for gooseberry fool is the best.

(There / their) was too much whipped cream in all of (there / their) recipes, and (their / they're) not sure how to fix (their / they're) soupy desserts.

(Who / Whom) would like to use (my / mine) recipe instead?

My father and (I / myself) would prefer to make the new gooseberry fool recipe by (ourself / ourselves).

(Who / Whom) are (they / them) cooking with tomorrow?

The last two people to finish cooking were (he / him) and (I / me).

(I / me) and (he / him) are cooking the next meal with (who / whom)?

Review 5C: Pronouns and Antecedents

Circle the nineteen personal pronouns (subject, object, and possessive) in the following excerpts from *Sideways Stories from Wayside School,* by Louis Sachar. Draw arrows to each pronoun's antecedent.

Mrs. Jewls hit her head against the wall five times. "How many times did I hit my head against the wall?" she asked.

"One, two, three, four, five, six, seven, eight, nine, ten. You hit your head against the wall ten times," said Joe.

The bell rang, and all the other children came back from recess. The fresh air had made them very excited, and they were laughing and shouting.

"Oh, darn," said Joe. "Now I missed recess."

"Hey, Joe, where were you?" asked John. "You missed a great game of kickball."

"Boy, am I hungry," said Louis. "I don't think Mrs. Gorf would mind if I ate this apple. After all, she always has so many."

He picked up the apple, which was really Mrs. Gorf, shined it up on his shirt, and ate it.

Review 5D: Agreement with Indefinite Pronouns

Choose the correct word in parentheses to agree with the indefinite pronouns. Cross out the incorrect word.

Hardly anyone can park (her or his / their) car close to the restaurant.

No one (enjoys / enjoy) a roast chicken more than I do.

(Is / Are) all of the peaches gone?

(Is / Are) all of the peach cobbler gone?

Some of these containers (hold / holds) cooking oil.

Both (was / were) silent as the meal was served.

(Is / Are) someone paying the bill?

Most of the talking (was / were) done by our host.

Most of the meal (is / are) gone by now.

(Has / Have) all of you finished eating?

(Has / Have) all of the wine been drunk as well?

Review 5E: Distinguishing Between Active and Passive Voice

Identify each underlined verb as *A* for active voice or *P* for passive voice. These sentences were taken from *Yes, Chef: A Memoir,* by Marcus Samuelsson.

I have never seen a picture of my mother. _______

The words seem meaningless, except the last is a clue because even today, in rural Ethiopia, girls are not encouraged to go to school. _______

I know this is what she fed us because this is what poor people eat in Ethiopia. _______

I have taught myself the recipes of my mother's people because those foods are for me, as a chef, the easiest connection to the mysteries of who my mother was. _______

When Mom, Dad, and Anna arrived at the customs area, they learned that our flight had been delayed for several hours. _______

In his application, my father promised to raise his adopted children in a good family, one with a dog and a cat, "both very friendly towards children." _______

Mr. Ljungqvist was shaped like a bowling ball, with thick white hair curling from under his black fisherman's cap. _______

Tram conductors who carried trolleys full of commuters were called herring packers. _______

Ljungqvist's customers bought lots and lots of herring—to poach, pickle, bake, and layer into cheesy, creamy casseroles with leeks and tomatoes. _______

Review 5F: Troublesome Verbs

Choose the correct verb form in parentheses. Cross out the incorrect forms. These sentences were taken from *Life, on the Line: A Chef's Story of Chasing Greatness, Facing Death, and Redefining the Way We Eat*, by Grant Achatz and Nick Kokonas.

Before she could agree Michael glided over to the light, (raised / rose) his arm to the bulb, and snapped his fingers.

I fired up the stove, (sat / set) my cutting board in place, and composed a couple of bains-marie with essential tools.

And of course, the ice cream had to be made, spun, (laid / lain) out in trays, frozen, and then punched out with a ring cutter and immediately refrozen.

After (setting / sitting) in Central Park for a bit we made our way to Cru.

It is the story of a man who (raised / rose) to the top of his chosen profession by working incredibly long hours and paying meticulous attention to detail to produce food in the best way he could.

He flopped his coat on the back of one of my dining room chairs and (lay / laid) out a few sheets of paper.

But the genius of the dish (lay / laid) in the use of the warmed vanilla bean as an aromatic handle.

A group of burgundy books (sat / set) on the shelf like a red siren flashing at me.

Without breaking stride he slid over to the dish machine, and again using his free hand, squeegeed the water off the rack, and starting (lying / laying) plates down.

I have been looking for about six months for a spot that would (let / leave) me produce my own food.

My overall plan for (raising / rising) the money for the restaurant was pretty simple.

He said good morning as he passed, began (sitting / setting) up his station, and then slid next to me.

WEEK 16

Imposters

— LESSON 61 —

Progressive Tenses
Principal Parts
Past Participles as Adjectives
Present Participles as Adjectives

One Sunday afternoon in 1917, cousins named Frances Griffiths and Elsie Wright, aged nine and fifteen, saw some fairies and took clear snapshots of them with their box camera . . . In 1983, sixty-six years later, Elsie Wright and Frances Griffiths decided that it was time to confess what people had suspected all along. The fairies were paper dolls . . . propped up on the grass with pins.

—Kathryn Ann Lindskoog, *Fakes, Frauds, & Other Malarkey*

	First Principal Part Present	Second Principal Part Past	Third Principal Part Past Participle
	plan	planned	planned
	burst	burst	burst
	catch	caught	caught
	fall	fell	fallen

The planned vacation did not go well.

The burst balloon fit inside the honey jar.

The caught fish wriggled on the hook.

I climbed over the fallen tree.

The past participle of a verb can act as a descriptive adjective.

The freshly picked peaches were full of flavor.

As the clock struck twelve, he heard a rustling noise in the air.

By the side of the road, he saw a fox sitting.

Her mother stirred the pot of boiling water.

The snoring guards lay at the doorstep, fast asleep.

A simple verb simply tells whether an action takes place in the past, present, or future.

I thought, I think, I will think.

A perfect verb describes an action which has been completed before another action takes place.

I had thought, I have thought, I will have thought.

A progressive verb describes an ongoing or continuous action.

I was thinking, I am thinking, I will be thinking.

First Principal Part Present	Second Principal Part Past	Third Principal Part Past Participle	Present Participle
rustle	rustled	rustled	rustling
sit	sat	sat	sitting
snore	snored	snored	snoring
am	was	been	being

The present participle of a verb can act as a descriptive adjective.

The burst balloon fit inside the honey jar.

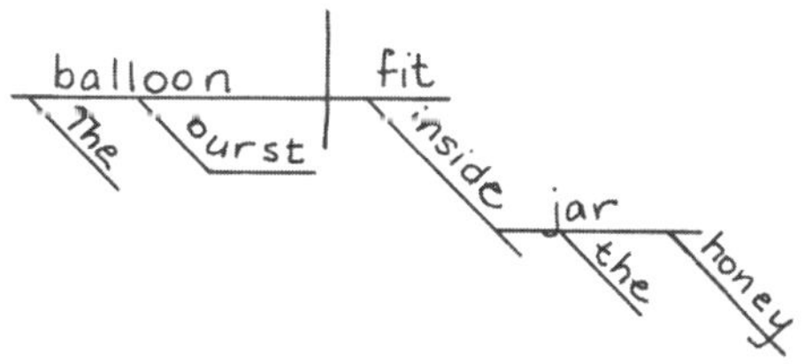

The snoring guards lay at the doorstep, fast asleep.

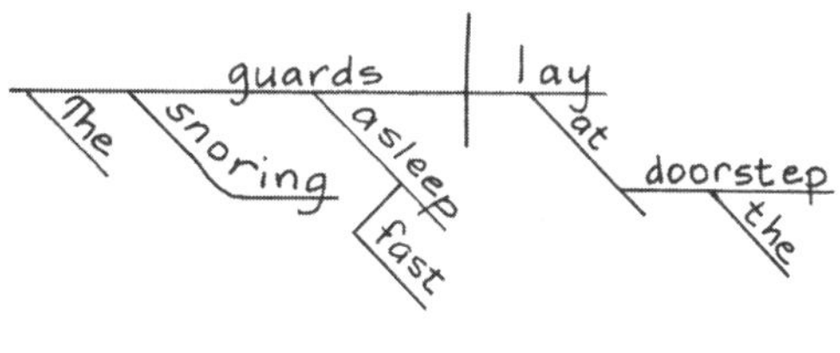

Sparkling stars shone.

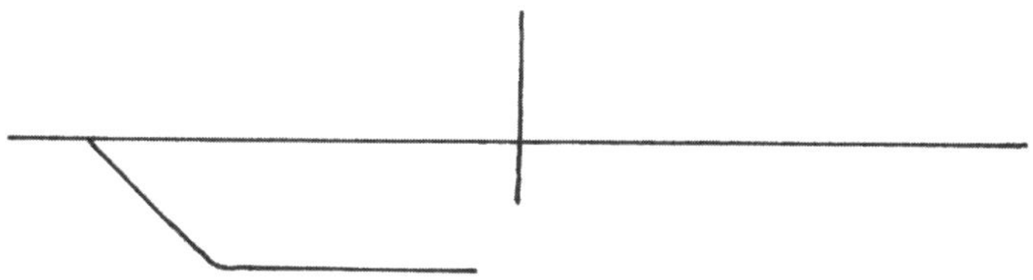

The forgotten cheese molded.

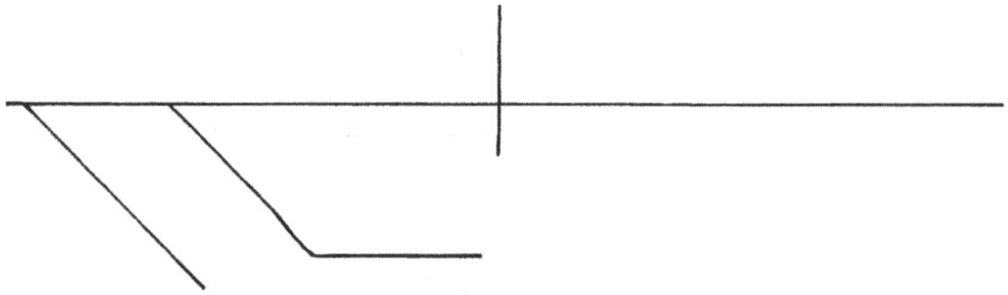

OPTIONAL:
The rustling leaves told us that the wind was rising.
The leaves, being rustled, signified the coming of fall.
Having rustled the leaves, the wind died down.
The leaves having been rustled, the wind died down.
The rustled leaves finally stilled.

Present (Active) Participle	Present (Passive) Participle	Perfect Present (Active) Participle	Perfect Present (Passive) Participle	Past Participle
add *-ing*	**being + past participle**	**having + past participle**	**having + been + past participle**	**add *-ed* (second principle part)**
rustling	being rustled	having rustled	having been rustled	rustled
eating				eaten
reading				read

Exercise 61A: Identifying Past Participles Used as Adjectives

Underline the past participles used as adjectives in the following sentences, taken from *Where the Red Fern Grows*, by Wilson Rawls. Draw a line to the noun or pronoun that each one modifies.

It was too much for him and he took off down the street, squalling like a scalded cat.

I went off to bed with my heart all torn up in little pieces, and cried myself to sleep.

However, many was the time I'd find my vegetables left in the abandoned camp.

Early the next morning, with the can jammed deep in the pocket of my overalls, I whistled and sang.

He saw the faded yellow piece of paper sticking out from the coins.

The country was new and sparsely settled.

Exercise 61B: Identifying Present Participles Used as Adjectives

Underline the present participles used as adjectives in the following sentences, taken from *Because of Winn-Dixie*, by Kate DiCamillo. Draw a line to each word modified.

There were just a lot of vegetables rolling around on the floor, tomatoes and onions and green peppers.

You are a suffering dog, so maybe he will take to you right away.

I couldn't do anything about his crooked yellow teeth because he got into a sneezing fit every time I started brushing them with my toothbrush, and I finally had to give up.

But the first time Miss Franny Block saw Winn-Dixie standing up on his hind legs like that, looking in the window, she didn't think he was a dog.

Miss Franny sat there trembling and shaking.

Exercise 61C: Diagramming Participles Used as Adjectives

On your own paper, diagram the following sentences.

Barking dogs keep us awake.
Shut windows don't keep out the sound.
My complaining father calls our neighbors.
Our embarrassed neighbors bring their dogs into the house.

— LESSON 62 —

Parts of Speech and Parts of Sentences

Present Participles as Nouns (Gerunds)

The cuckoo is one of the great con artists of the animal world. It can trick other birds into raising its children by laying their eggs in the stranger's nest. When the cuckoo chicks hatch, the youngsters continue their parents' strategy by killing any other birds in the nest before they reveal their identity. Scientists have found the imposter cuckoo even fools the foster parent into thinking its chicks are still alive by flapping yellow patches on its wings. This also creates the illusion there are more mouths to feed and tricks the foster parents into delivering more food.

—Augustus Brown, *Why Pandas Do Handstands: And Other Curious Truths About Animals*

The running rabbit was darting towards the briar patch.

Part of speech is a term that explains what a word does.

A noun names a person, place, thing, or idea.

Part of a sentence is a term that explains how a word functions in a sentence.

subject direct object indirect object object of a preposition

A gerund is a present participle acting as a noun.

Careful sailing was the duty of the captain's mate.

This day was lost from pure whim, for the pleasure of going ashore.

Providence gives the deserving their due.

With the other hand, he repressed the beatings of his heart.

Running is my favorite exercise.

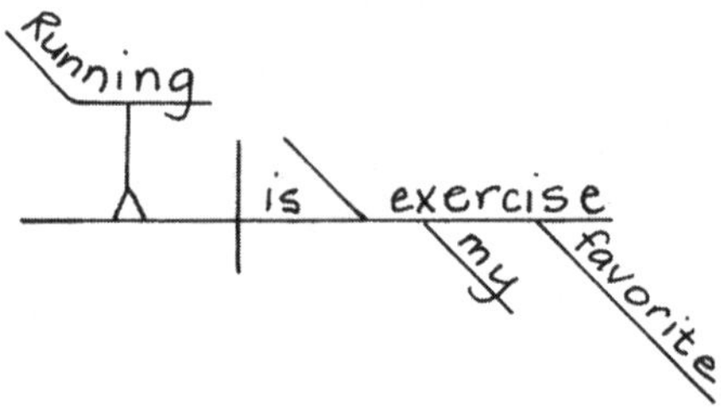

He feared falling.

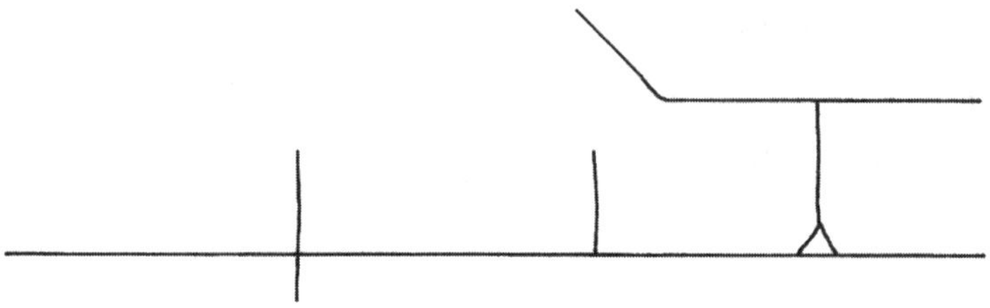

Exercise 62A: Identifying Gerunds

In the following sentences, adapted from *Thor: Viking God of Thunder*, by Graeme Davis, underline each subject once and each predicate twice. Write *DO* above any direct objects of the predicate, *IO* above any indirect objects of the predicate, *OP* above any objects of prepositions, and *PN* above any predicate nominatives. Then, circle each gerund.

Reading between the lines of the myths reveals Thor to be a model for pagan warriors.

Thor's favorite pastime is slaying giants.

Thor was known for slaughtering giants left and right.

The stories emphasize his fighting.

Protecting Asgard from encroaching giants was his primary task.

The gloves gave Thor the necessary strength for defending Asgard.

Exercise 62B: Diagramming Gerunds, Present Participles, and Progressive Verbs

On your own paper, diagram every word in the following sentences.

A giant loves eating and fighting!

They were speaking to the farmer.

Hoping propelled them forward.

I am pointing this out.

I am very tired of travelling.

Please stop shouting about the flying hammer!

— LESSON 63 —

Gerunds
Present and Past Participles as Adjectives
Infinitives
Infinitives as Nouns

The comings and goings of her acquaintances provided Mrs. Jennings great entertainment.

This circumstance was a growing attachment between her eldest girl and the brother of Mrs. John Dashwood.

The presence of the two Miss Steeles, lately arrived, gave Elinor pain.

An infinitive is formed by combining *to* and the first person singular present form of a verb.

	Present Tense		Infinitive
	Singular	**Plural**	
First person	I give	we give	
Second person	you give	you give	______________
Third person	he, she, it gives	they give	

	Present Tense		Infinitive
	Singular	**Plural**	
First person	I think	we think	
Second person	you think	you think	____________
Third person	he, she, it thinks	they think	
First person	I have	we have	
Second person	you have	you have	____________
Third person	he, she, it has	they have	

To err is human.
To forgive is divine.
—Alexander Pope

To wish was to hope.

To hope was to expect.
—Jane Austen

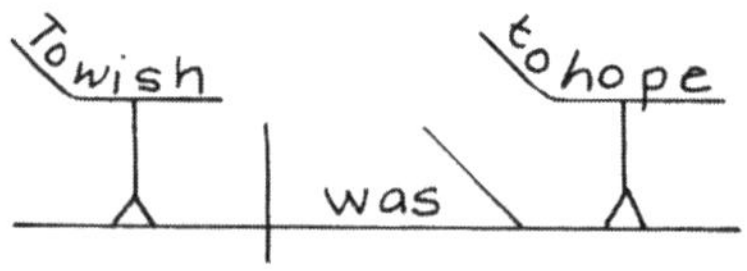

Exercise 63A: Identifying Gerunds and Infinitives

Underline the gerunds and infinitives in the following quotes about the twentieth century. Identify the imposters as *G* for gerund or *I* for infinitive. Then, identify each gerund or infinitive as a subject (*S*), predicate nominative (*PN*), direct object (*DO*), or object of a preposition (*OP*).

One of the really notable achievements of the twentieth century has been to make the young old before their time.
—Robertson Davies

. . . [M]an began to study himself as a scientific phenomenon.
—Timothy Leary

Pilots generally take pride in a good landing, not in getting out of the vehicle.
—Neil Armstrong

Avoiding danger is no safer in the long run than outright exposure. The fearful are caught as often as the bold.
—Helen Keller

The major task of the twentieth century will be to explore the unconscious, to investigate the subsoil of the mind.
—Henri Bergson

Public policy in the twentieth century was about protecting and expanding the social compact, based on recognition that effective government at the federal level provides rules and services and safety measures that contribute to a better society.
—Carl Bernstein

Twentieth-century man must . . . purposefully strive to discover the hidden secrets of our universe.
—John Young

. . . [T]he iconoclast . . . refuses to acknowledge any . . . rules or hierarchy.
—Peter Sloterdijk

. . . [P]eople . . . think they're doing a great job of hiding stuff, and it just keeps leaking out.
—Harry Shearer

I like to think of my behavior in the sixties as a learning experience.
—P. J. O'Rourke

I have a lifetime appointment and I intend to serve it.
—Thurgood Marshall

The thing the sixties did was to show us the possibilities and the responsibility that we all had.
—John Lennon

Everyone wants to be Cary Grant. Even I want to be Cary Grant.
—Cary Grant

To say "I accept," in an age like our own, is to say that you accept concentration-camps, rubber truncheons, Hitler, Stalin, bombs, aeroplanes, tinned food, machine guns, putsches, purges, slogans, Bedaux belts, gas-masks, submarines, spies, provocateurs, press-censorship, secret prisons, aspirins, Hollywood films and political murder.
—George Orwell

Exercise 63B: Diagramming Gerunds and Infinitives

On your own paper, diagram the following sentences.

We start to rock.
Stop shouting.
To live is to die.
I cannot bear to witness any longer.
Running and shrieking are very bad ideas.

— LESSON 64 —

Gerunds
Present and Past Participles
Infinitives
Gerund, Participle, and Infinitive Phrases

I love eating.

I love eating

A phrase is a group of words serving a single grammatical function.
I love eating pancakes with maple syrup, yellow cake with chocolate frosting, and grilled ribeye steaks.

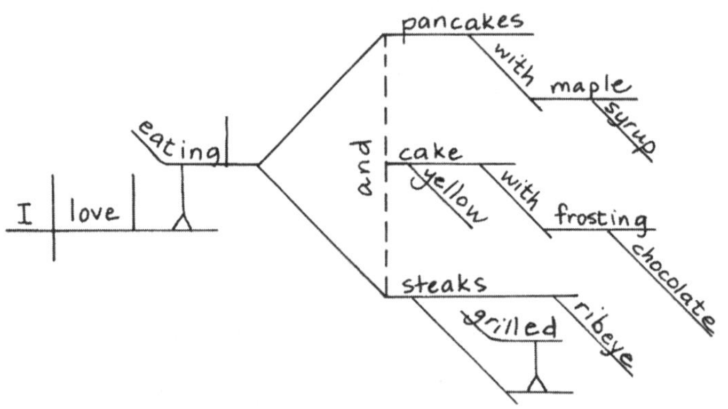

To give without expecting a reward is to receive an even greater gift.

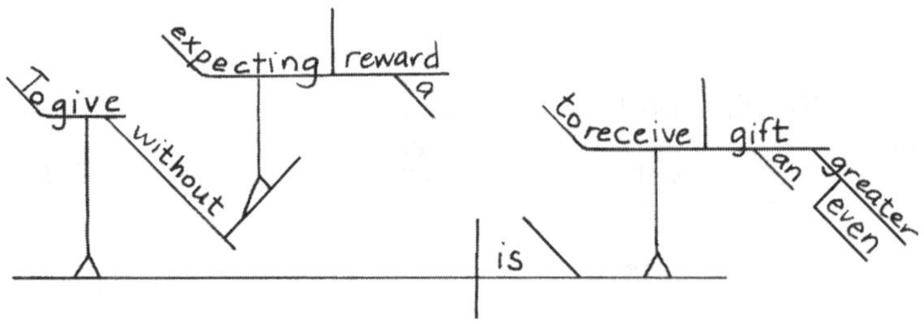

He saw the priceless antique vase shattered across the floor and scattered on the rug.

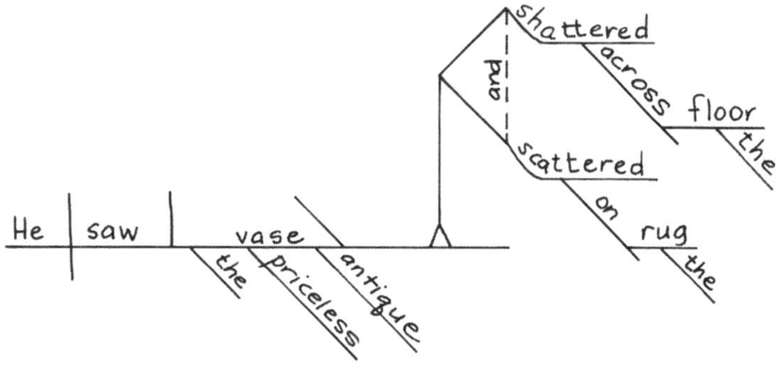

Exercise 64A: Identifying Phrases that Serve as Parts of the Sentence

In the following sentences, begin by underlining each prepositional phrase.

- Then, circle each group of words that contains a gerund, infinitive, or past participle.
- Each one serves as a part of the sentence. (Those circled phrases might include some of your prepositional phrases!) Label each circled phrase. Your options are: *ADJ* (adjective), *ADV* (adverb), S (subject), *IO* (indirect object), *DO* (direct object), *OC* (object complement), *OP* (object of the preposition), *PN* (predicate nominative), or *PA* (predicate adjective).

These sentences are taken from *Otto of the Silver Hand*, by Howard Pyle.

Why had he talked about churning butter?

No knight in those days dared to ride the roads without full armor.

He left the room to give the needful orders, bearing the babe with him.

He was to leave the happy, sunny silence of the dear White Cross, and to go out into that great world.

The light from the oriel window behind the old man shed broken rays of light upon him, and seemed to frame his thin gray hairs with a golden glory.

He was a great lover of books, and had under lock and key wonderful and beautiful volumes, bound in hog-skin and metal, and with covers inlaid with carved ivory, or studded with precious stones.

He stood intently, motionlessly, listening, listening; but all was silent except for the monotonous dripping of water in one of the nooks of the court-yard, and the distant murmur of the river borne upon the breath of the night air.

Oftentimes the good Father Abbot, coming into the garden, would find the poor, simple Brother sitting under the shade of the pear-tree, rocking the little baby in his arms, singing strange, crazy songs to it, and gazing far away into the blue, empty sky with his curious, pale eyes.

Exercise 64B: Diagramming

On your own paper, diagram all of the sentences from Exercise 64A.

WEEK 17

Comparatives and Superlatives, Subordinating Conjunctions

— LESSON 65 —

Adjectives

Comparative and Superlative Adjectives

An adjective modifies a noun or pronoun.
Adjectives tell what kind, which one, how many, and whose.

The positive degree of an adjective describes only one thing.
The comparative degree of an adjective compares two things.
The superlative degree of an adjective compares three or more things.

Most regular adjectives form the comparative by adding *-r* or *-er.*
Most regular adjectives form the superlative by adding *-st* or *-est.*

Positive	Comparative	Superlative
large	larger	largest
big	bigger	biggest
silly	sillier	silliest

Spelling Rules

If the adjective ends in *-e* already, add only *–r* or *–st.*

noble	nobler	noblest
pure	purer	purest
cute	________	________

If the adjective ends in a short vowel sound and a consonant, double the consonant and add *–er* or *–est.*

red	redder	reddest
thin	thinner	thinnest
flat	________	________

If the adjective ends in –*y*, change the *y* to *i* and add –*er* or –*est*.

hazy hazier haziest
lovely lovelier loveliest

lucky ________ ________

Many adjectives form their comparative and superlative forms by adding the word *more* or *most* before the adjective instead of using –*er* or –*est*.

unusual more unusual most unusual
fascinating more fascinating most fascinating
fun more fun most fun

She is more lovely than the dawn.
She is lovelier than the dawn.

She is the most lovely of all women.
She is the loveliest of all women.

The taller boy glanced around uneasily.

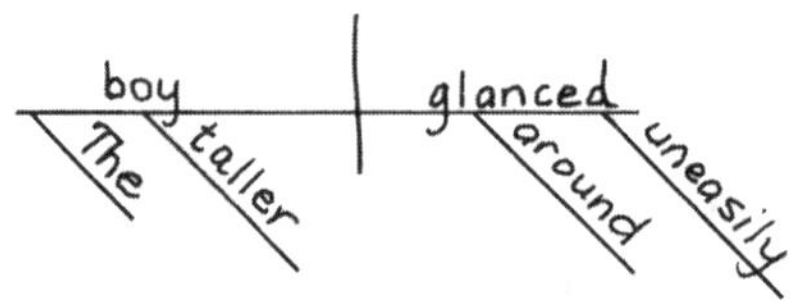

His more confident friend rang the doorbell.

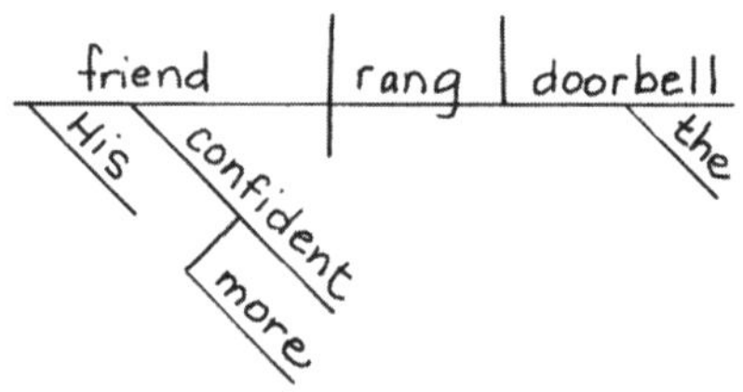

In comparative and superlative adjective forms, the words *more* and *most* are used as adverbs.

Exercise 65A: Identifying Positive, Comparative, and Superlative Adjectives

Identify the underlined adjective forms as *P* for positive, *C* for comparative, or *S* for superlative.

These sentences are from *Modern Painters,* Volume I, by John Ruskin.

If we stand for a little time before any of the more celebrated works of landscape, listening to the comments of the passers-by, we shall hear numberless expressions relating to the skill of the artist, but very few relating to the perfection of nature.

The particularization of flowers by Shakespeare and Shelley affords us the most frequent examples of the exalted use of these inferior details.

The same faults must be found with his present painting of foliage, neither the stems nor leafage being ever studied from nature; and this is the more to be regretted, because in the earlier works of the artist there was much admirable drawing.

The picture which has the nobler and more numerous ideas, however awkwardly expressed, is a greater picture than that which has the less noble and less numerous ideas, however beautifully expressed.

If this then be the definition of great art, that of a great artist naturally follows. He is the greatest artist who has embodied, in the sum of his works, the greatest number of the greatest ideas.

Leonardo's landscape has been of unfortunate effect on art, so far as it has had effect at all. In realization of detail he verges on the ornamental, in his rock outlines he has all the deficiencies and little of the feeling of the earlier men.

Exercise 65B: Forming Comparative and Superlative Adjectives

Fill in the blank with the correct form of the adjective in parentheses. These sentences are from *Women Painters of the World: From the Time of Caterina Vigri, 1413–1463, to Rosa Bonheur and the Present Day*, edited by W. S. Sparrow.

The work of Matilda Heming is interesting in a ____________________ way. (comparative of *special*)

____________________ than the authenticated history of Greek art is a tradition that connects a girl's name with the discovery of a great craft, the craft of modelling portraits in relief. (comparative of *old*)

Lavinia Fontana and Elisabetta Sirani were the ____________________ women painters whose travels did not extend beyond Italy. (superlative of *able*)

Elisabetta's health gave way, a painful disease of the stomach assailed her; and yet to the last day but one of her short life, she remained true to her colours, and was one of art's ____________________ soldiers. (superlative of *true*)

There is some work of Mary Beale's in the National Portrait Gallery, London; it is work of the quiet, genuine kind, and ________________________ than most of the painting that came for some time afterwards. (comparative of *good*)

Marianne Stokes is made of ________________________ stuff. (comparative of *stern*)

Caterina Vigri was the ____________________ of these nuns, and the picture "St. Ursula and her Maidens" was painted in the year 1456. (superlative of *early*)

The work of each has great interest, but that of Mary Cassatt is the __________________ and the _________________; it is _________________ with the emotions of the painter's own heart. (comparative of *attractive*, comparative of *enduring*, comparative of *rich*)

There are __________________ and __________________ qualities in the quiet wisdom of Julie Wolfthorn, a Berlin painter of note. (comparative of *high*, comparative of *subtle*)

Her attainments, her wit, and her eminent merits made Cornélie Lamme one of the ____________________ women of her day. (superlative of *remarkable*)

Exercise 65C: Diagramming Comparative and Superlative Adjectives

On your own paper, diagram the following four sentences from *A History of Art for Beginners and Students: Painting, Sculpture, Architecture*, by Clara Erskine Clement.

A second and even more serious fault in Egyptian architecture is a want of proportion.

Of these pyramids, the three at Giza are best known, and that of Cheops is most remarkable.

The great cathedral of Cologne is one of the largest and most famous churches in all of Europe.

This basilica had four rows of Corinthian columns; many of these pillars were taken from more ancient edifices, and were composed of very beautiful marbles.

— LESSON 66 —

Adverbs
Comparative and Superlative Adverbs
Coordinating Conjunctions
Subordinating Conjunctions

An adverb describes a verb, an adjective, or another adverb.
Adverbs tell how, when, where, how often, and to what extent.

The positive degree of an adverb describes only one verb, adjective, or adverb.
The comparative degree of an adverb compares two verbs, adjectives, or adverbs.
The superlative degree of an adverb compares three or more verbs, adjectives, or adverbs.

Most adverbs that end in *–ly* form their comparative and superlative forms by adding the word *more* or *most* before the adverb instead of using *–er* or *–est*.

thoughtfully	more thoughtfully	most thoughtfully
sadly	more sadly	most sadly
angrily	more angrily	most angrily

A few adverbs ending in *-y* change the *-y* to *i* and add *–er* or *–est*.

early	earlier	earliest

He worked more efficiently.

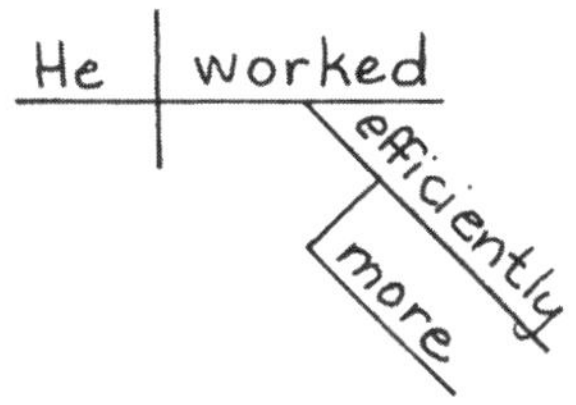

He worked more efficiently than his brother.

A conjunction joins two words or groups of words together.
and, or, nor, for, so, but, yet

A coordinating conjunction joins equal words or groups of words together.

The sun and the moon give us light.
The moon shines fitfully yet brightly.

A subordinating conjunction joins unequal words or groups of words together.

to subordinate: to place in a lower order or rank; to make secondary
sub: from *Latin preposition sub,* beneath, under
ordinate: from *Latin verb ordo,* to rank

He worked more efficiently than his brother.
He worked more efficiently than his brother [worked].

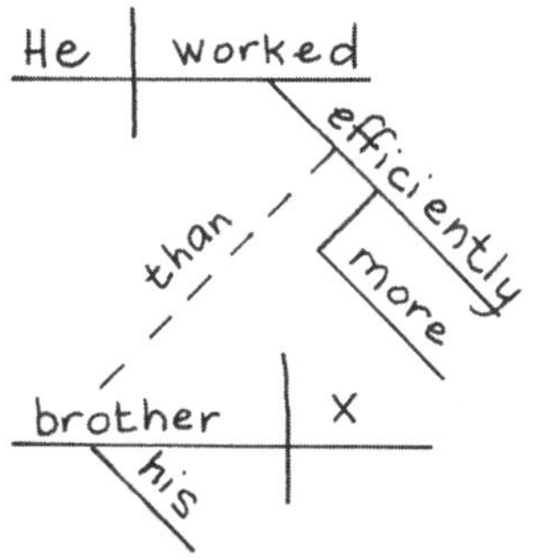

He is older than his brother.
He is older than his brother [is].

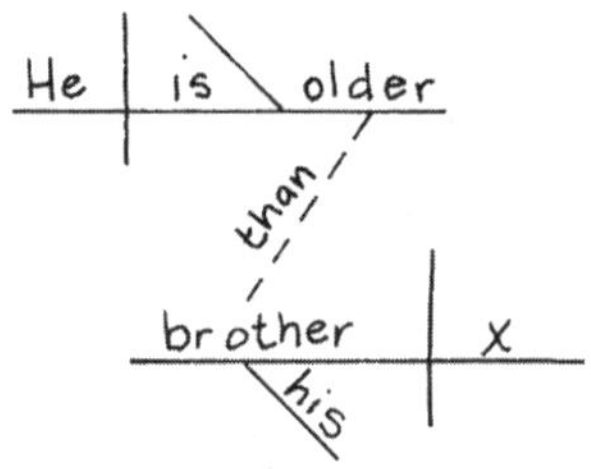

Exercise 66A: Diagramming Comparatives

Diagram the first two sentences on the frames provided. Diagram the remaining sentences on your own paper.

The sun seems brighter than the moon.

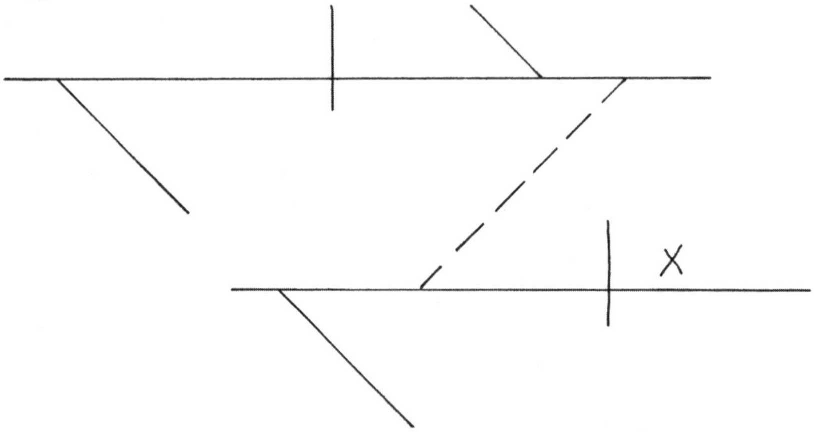

The red kettle is boiling hotter than the black cauldron.

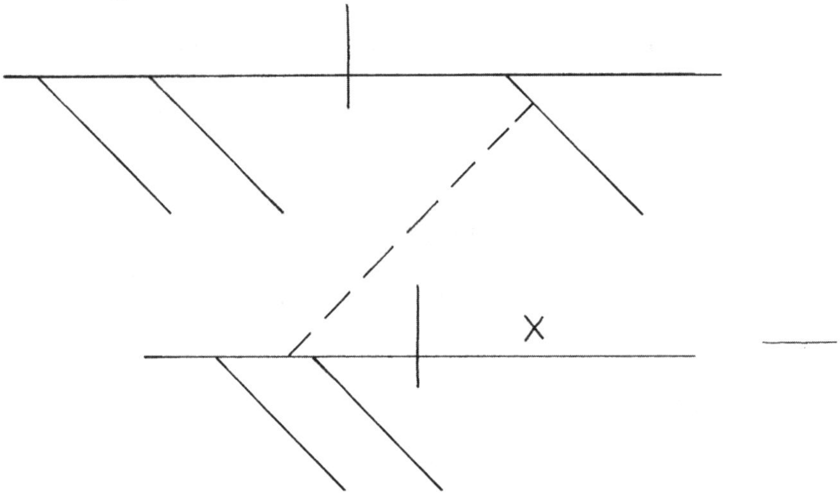

Courage is a better choice than cowardice.

You are wiser than he.

That young woman was taller and older than the others.

Exercise 66B: Identifying Positive, Comparative, and Superlative Adverbs

Identify the underlined adverb forms as *P* for positive, *C* for comparative, or *S* for superlative. These sentences are taken from *Wonder Stories*, by Carolyn Sherwin Bailey.

The waters were very heavy and took the lowest place where the earth held them safely in its hollows.

He made the daytime brighter and the gold rays of the sun shine more gloriously.

With these he chained Prometheus to a rock and sent a vulture to eat his flesh, which grew again continually so that Prometheus suffered most terrible pain as the vulture returned each day.

What a pair of shoulders they must have been, for they were, later, to uphold the sky!

"No doubt he intended it for me," Pandora said, "and most probably it contains pretty dresses for me to wear, or toys for us both, or something nice for us to eat."

Both of them had been painfully stung.

He dropped his lyre and ran after her, but she eluded him, running more swiftly than the wind.

"Pray run slower and I will follow more slowly!"

She sang to the lyre, the most beautifully of all the sisters.

Exercise 66C: Forming Comparative and Superlative Adverbs

Fill in the blank with the correct form of the adverb in parentheses.

Of all of the heroes, Hercules stood the ____________________. (tall)

Mercury could travel __________________________ than thought flies. (fast)

Daedalus loved his son Icarus __________________________ than any other being in the world. (fervent)

Of the two hammers, Thor's was by far the __________________________. (heavy)

The ram with a fleece of gold leaped __________________________ of any animal on Mount Olympus. (high)

Vulcan forged tools for the gods __________________________ than the best of earthly blacksmiths. (skillfully)

Vulcan forged tools for the gods __________________________ of all blacksmiths in the universe. (skillfully)

— LESSON 67 —

Irregular Comparative and Superlative Adjectives and Adverbs

Exercise 67A: Best and Worst Ice Cream Flavors

Put the following ice cream flavors in the columns according to your opinion. (There are no correct answers—it all depends on you.)

bacon avocado	mint chocolate chip	rum raisin
salted caramel	bubblegum	cherry cheesecake

good: ________________ **bad:** ________________

better: ________________ **worse:** ________________

best: ________________ **worst:** ________________

Irregular Comparative and Superlative Adjectives

Adjective	Comparative Form	Superlative Form
good	better	best
bad	worse	worst
little	less	least
much	more	most
many	more	most

I have more legs than a snake.
The octopus has the most legs of the three.

Irregular Comparative and Superlative Adverbs

Adverb	Comparative Form	Superlative Form
well	better	best
badly	worse	worst
little	less	least
much	more	most
far	farther	farthest

Do not use *more* with an adjective or adverb that is already in the comparative form. Do not use *most* with an adjective or adverb that is already in the superlative form.

Use an adjective form when an adjective is needed and an adverb form when an adverb is needed.

INCORRECT	CORRECT	S LV ADV PA
The team played good.	The team played well.	I am (not) well.
The tomato smells badly.	The tomato smells bad.	

Common Linking Verbs
am, is, are, was, were, be, being, been
taste, feel, smell, sound, look, prove, grow, remain, appear, stay, become, seem

The music sounds beautiful/beautifully.

Exercise 67B: Using Comparatives and Superlatives Correctly

Choose the correct form in parentheses. Cross out the incorrect form. These sentences are from *Newton's Football: The Science Behind America's Game*, by Allen St. John and Ainissa G. Ramirez.

The man who would come to be known as "Bootin' Ben" quickly discovered that with his injured foot and his modified boot, he could actually kick (farther/more far) and (accurater/more accurately) than he ever could with his toes.

No position relies (heavier/more heavily) on the applied physics of perfect technique.

This somewhat elongated ball could be cradled (easier/more easily), and even today, the rugby ball remains largely watermelon-shaped.

For example, drivers behind the wheel of large new SUVs with four-wheel drive and air bags tend to drive (faster/more fast) and (aggressiver/more aggressively) on snowy roads than they would if they were driving a tiny old economy car.

Like Hornung, Bart Starr had yet to establish himself fully, and the coach obliged by defining his role (tighter/more tightly).

Despite the NFL's ongoing efforts to make the kicker's job (harder/more hard) and thus reduce the number of field goals, there isn't a player whose success—or failure—is reflected (more direct/more directly) on the scoreboard.

Despite that, if we examine the numbers (closer/more closely), Gibson's supremacy still makes a certain kind of sense.

The player who used this strategy (more successfully/most successfully) was Patriots linebacker Mike Vrabel, who lined up at tight end in short-yardage situations and caught ten passes in his career, all for touchdowns.

When a player is feeling (well/good), rested, and ready for the next play, Wyche explains, he stands up straight in a posture with more than a little Superman-style swagger: hands on hips, fingers across his belly, thumbs pointing back.

"Losses seem to hurt (more/most) than a win feels (well/good)," explains Keith Chen, a Yale economist who has worked with Santos.

"It's an amazing thing. It feels so (easy/easily)," says Jim Breech.

In 1988, the Bengals started the season 6–0 on their way to a 12–4 regular season, the (better/best) record in football.

He considered that Miami's two (better / best) players were running backs Ronnie Brown and Ricky Williams.

Piedmont's second A-11 game was somewhat (better / best) from an execution standpoint, but the score was still lopsided.

It's not that the leather helmet was surprisingly (well / good) at protecting players from concussion. It's that the modern helmet was surprisingly (bad / badly).

The helmets currently in use don't seem to protect players particularly (well / good) from concussions.

Game theory works (well / good) in explaining actual games and especially ones that are conceptually tidy, if not actually simple.

Most of the way through the 2011 season, the Carolina Panthers were a (bad / badly) team getting (more better / better). The Tampa Bay Buccaneers were a (bad / badly) team getting (worse / more worse).

Exercise 67C: Using Correct Adverbs and Adjectives

Choose the correct word in parentheses. Cross out the incorrect word.

We ran so (good / well)! We were much faster than the other cross-country team.

The opponents did not run (slow / slowly), but we are extremely (good / well) at middle distances.

The baby doesn't feel (good / well) today. She has a cold.

The gangster looks (bad / badly). He's not a very nice man!

The gangster looks (bad / badly). He's not wearing his glasses and he has to squint.

The young thief is growing (good / well). He's getting larger by the day.

The young thief is growing (good / well). He is returning what he stole and making amends.

She remains (bad / badly); she only thinks about herself and is cruel to others.

She remains (bad / badly); she hates to stay in one spot and keeps leaving!

— LESSON 68 —

Coordinating and Subordinating Conjunctions
Correlative Conjunctions

When my mother makes *tacos al pastor*, she uses ancho chilies and pasilla chilies and cumin seed and garlic and pork roast and fresh cilantro.

A coordinating conjunction joins equal words or groups of words together.
and, but, for, nor, or, so, and yet

For dessert, I will have *tres leches* cake with fresh raspberries or caramel sandwich cookies with ice cream.
In my opinion, pork without pineapple is much better than pork with pineapple.

A subordinating conjunction joins unequal words or groups of words together.

We are cooking either pork roasts or goat chops tonight.
The patient was neither worse nor better.

Correlative conjunctions work in pairs to join words or groups of words.
Coordinating correlative conjunctions join equal words or groups of words.
both . . . and
not only . . . but/but also
either . . . or
neither . . . nor
although/though . . . yet/still
if . . . then

In the beginning, both the Sun and the Moon were dark.

Not only the town itself, but also the ranches in the neighborhood are built on hilltops.

Although he did not remember the way, still he pressed on.

If we run faster, then we will escape.

Though weary, still he presses on.

If unseated, then he will be unable to continue jousting.

Subordinating correlative conjunctions join unequal words or groups of words.
although/though . . . yet/still
if . . . then

In the beginning, the Sun and the Moon were dark.
In the beginning, both the Sun and the Moon were dark.

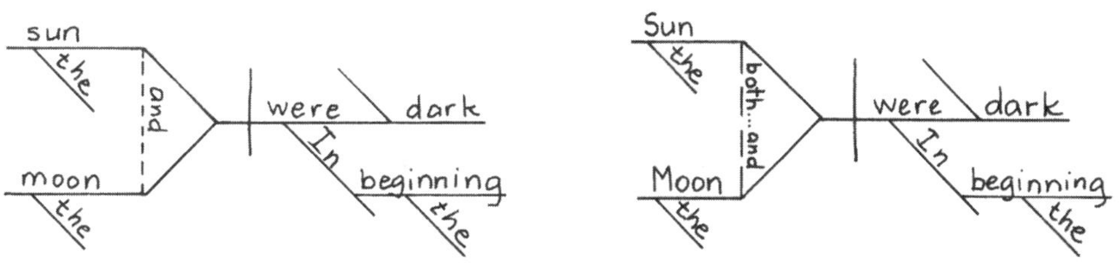

Although he did not remember, still he pressed on.

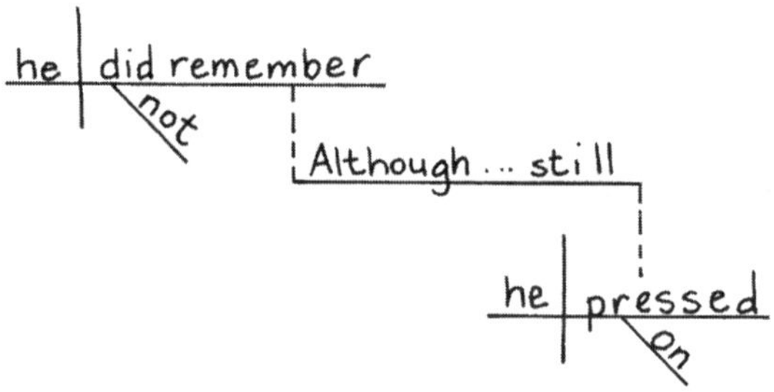

Both the grey foxes and the lion are watching for rabbits.

Not only the grey foxes but also the lion is watching for rabbits.
Either the mountain lion or the bears are growling.
Neither the butterflies nor the hummingbird was in the garden.

When compound subjects are connected by *not only . . . but/but also*, *either . . . or*, or *neither . . . nor*, the verb agrees with the subject that is closest to the verb.

Exercise 68A: Coordinating and Subordinating Correlative Conjunctions

In each of the following sentences, circle the correlative conjunctions. Underline the words or groups of words that the conjunctions connect. In the blank, write *C* for coordinating or *S* for subordinating.

These sentences have been slightly adapted from *A Brief History of Pakistan*, by James Wynbrandt.

Once they seize a plain, no one escapes, neither men nor cattle. ________

Yet the passages that breached the guarding massifs served as funnels through which invaders both hostile and friendly have poured for millennia. ________

Now old and nonthreatening, he was unable to keep either his officers or the Mongols in check. ________

Though an independent state only since 1947, yet its homeland has a history unique from the rest of the subcontinent it shares with India. ________

Though the Mughal Empire would survive for another century, yet it was increasingly subservient to Britain's agenda. ________

If I were to follow your advice, then how could I show my face? ________

Gandhi had come, he said, on a personal mission, and not as a representative of either Congress or the Hindus. ________

Though rich in minerals, including iron ore and copper, yet Baluchistan has lagged in development of these resources. __________

These new leaders not only hardened the league's stance against the British but advocated greater cooperation with Hindus through the Congress Party as well. __________

If he agreed, then Pakistan stood to gain substantial benefits. __________

Although many leading Muslims supported Great Britain during the war, still some backed the Ottoman Empire. __________

Both the loss of territory and the war with India shook the soul of Pakistanis. __________

Exercise 68B: Subject-Verb Agreement

Cross out the incorrect verb in each set of parentheses.

Either the farmer and the barber or the farmer's wife (is / are) going to win the bet.

Both the king and his two soldiers (was / were) agreed that the sound was a jackal, not a tiger.

Not only the old woman's foot but also the cords (was / were) cut by the prince's sword.

Both the parrots and the starling (was / were) hanging in cages in the apartments.

Neither scars nor sign (is / are) visible on the queen's hands.

Not only one ring, but also three precious anklets (was / were) presented to the princess.

Bracelets of emeralds and a chain of rubies (is / are) more glorious than anything the prince has ever seen.

Exercise 68C: Diagramming

On your own paper, diagram every word of the following sentences.

Neither the jackal nor the peacock was able to pass the test.

Either air or water will penetrate the cunningly carved great chest.

Both the yogi and his pupils were amazed to see the chest floating.

Not only beauty but also wisdom were hers.

The fine horse had both a skin like snow and a neigh like thunder.

WEEK 18

Clauses

— LESSON 69 —

Phrases
Sentences
Introduction to Clauses

A phrase is a group of words serving a single grammatical function.

A verb phrase is the main verb plus any helping verbs.

Four musketeers were waiting their turn.

A prepositional phrase begins with a preposition and ends with a noun or pronoun.

The center of the most animated group was a musketeer of great height.

A prepositional phrase that describes a noun or pronoun is called an adjective phrase.

He wore a long cloak of crimson velvet.

A prepositional phrase that describes a verb, adjective, or adverb is called an adverb phrase.

The young man advanced into the tumult and disorder.

(Sentences adapted from *The Three Musketeers* by Alexandre Dumas.)

A clause is a group of words that contains a subject and a predicate.

Behind the dusty wardrobe.
Lucy opened the door.
Leaping and bounding.
They did not believe her.
He tasted the delicious candy.
Because he wanted more.

An independent clause can stand by itself as a sentence.

A sentence is a group of words that usually contains a subject and a predicate. A sentence begins with a capital letter and ends with a punctuation mark. A sentence contains a complete thought.

> *Can we measure intelligence without understanding it?* Possibly so. *Physicists measured gravity and magnetism long before they understood them theoretically. Maybe psychologists can do the same with intelligence.*
>
> Or maybe not.
>
> —James W. Kalat, *Introduction to Psychology*

A dependent clause is a fragment that cannot stand by itself as a sentence.

Although Jamie didn't mean to eat the entire cake. __________

Whether they won or lost. __________

He picked up the pieces. __________

That milk is from Uncle Louie's cow. __________

Since she was already covered in mud. __________

Because my grandmother came to visit.
I cleaned up my room.

Because my grandmother came to visit, I cleaned up my room.

Dependent clauses begin with subordinating words.
Dependent clauses are also known as subordinate clauses.

Exercise 69A: Distinguishing Between Phrases and Clauses

Identify the following groups of words as *phrases* or *clauses*. The clauses may be independent or dependent, but you only need to identify them as clauses. In each clause, underline the subject once and the verb twice.

These phrases and clauses are taken from *Kingdoms of the Yoruba*, by Robert Sydney Smith.

Whose sources are largely unwritten. ____________________

However rich in primary and secondary material. ____________________

The past of the Yoruba of West Africa. ____________________

Who form the population of the Western State of Nigeria. ____________________

All having specific and complex traditions. ____________________

Although these traditions are often of a legendary and miraculous kind. ____________

They may be sifted, correlated, and cross-checked. ____________

From ceremonies recalling and re-enacting the past. ____________

All these preserve fragments. ____________

It is a platitude. ____________

Working from tradition. ____________

Reconstructing the Yoruba past. ____________

Nigeria exemplifies this contrast. ____________

Exercise 69B: Distinguishing Between Independent and Dependent Clauses

Identify the following clauses as independent (*IND*) or dependent (*DEP*). These clauses are drawn from *Yoruba Legends,* by M. I. Ogumefu.

When he returned home ____________

Who returned to his father after some time ____________

In due course they returned ____________

Wherever he went ____________

The weapon glanced off his hide ____________

A great king sent his various sons ____________

Two women quarrelled ____________

The King employed the charm ____________

As he sat gloomily on the ground ____________

The whole earth was covered with water ____________

Exercise 69C: Turning Dependent Clauses into Complete Sentences

Choose three of the dependent clauses in Exercise 69B and attach independent clauses to them to form complete thoughts. Write your three new sentences on your own paper. (The dependent clause can go before or after the independent clause.)

— LESSON 70 —

Adjective Clauses
Relative Pronouns

Intro 70: Introduction to Adjective Clauses

The following sentences describe famous ghost sightings! Complete each sentence by filling in the blank with the appropriate letter from the clauses below.

You can learn more about these haunts in *Famous Ghost Stories: Legends and Lore*, by Brian Haughton.

The village of Brill, in Buckinghamshire, boasted five different headless horsemen ______.

She fell in love with a handsome stableboy ______.

He is the ghost of a knight, killed in battle with the Scots, ______.

The deathly paleness of the faces was an omen ______.

The phantom London bus, ______, tears down the middle of the road towards startled drivers and then disappears.

A. whose horse brought his headless body home

B. which appears between the Cambridge Gardens and Chesterton Road junctions on St. Mark's Road

C. who roamed the four roads and one field track leading into the village

D. that Lincoln would not live through his last term

E. whom she then threw over for a more eligible suitor

Dependent clauses can act as adjectives, adverbs, or nouns.

An adjective clause is a dependent clause that acts as an adjective in a sentence, modifying a noun or pronoun in the independent clause.

They banded together in small groups that whispered and discussed and disputed.

A man who passed by spoke to them.

Relative pronouns introduce adjective clauses and refer back to an antecedent in the independent clause.
who, whom, whose, which, that

The men **who had been champions before Finn came** rallied the others against him.

Among the young princes was a boy **whom the High King preferred**.

The Chain of Silence was shaken by the servant **whose duty and honor it was.**

The thing **which was presented to us** is not true.

The people believed in gods **that the king did not accept**.

Use *who, whom,* and *whose* to refer to persons.
Use *which* to refer to animals, places, and things.
Use *that* and *whose* to refer to persons, animals, places, or things.

She saw him, and he saw her.

Use *P* for prepositions, *OP* for objects of prepositions, *ADJ* for adjectives, *ADV* for adverbs, *IO* for indirect objects, *DO* for direct objects, and *OC* for object complements.

I who speak to you have seen many evils.

At the door is a gentleman for whom no seat has been found.

He was the boy whom they called Little Fawn.

They are men whose happiness lies in ambition.

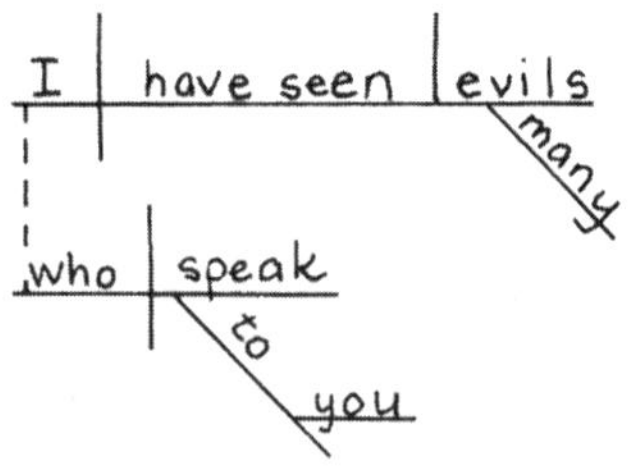

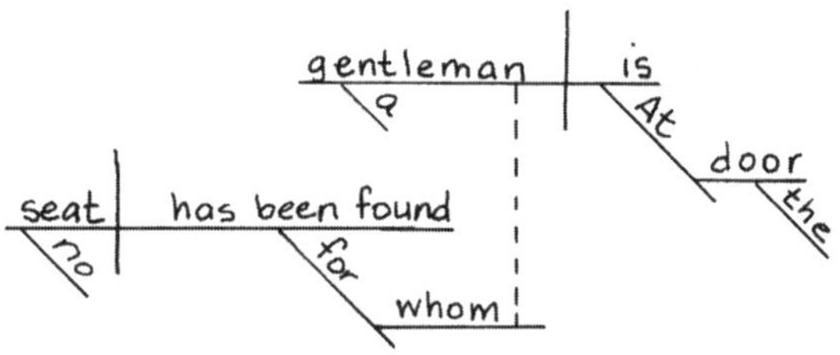

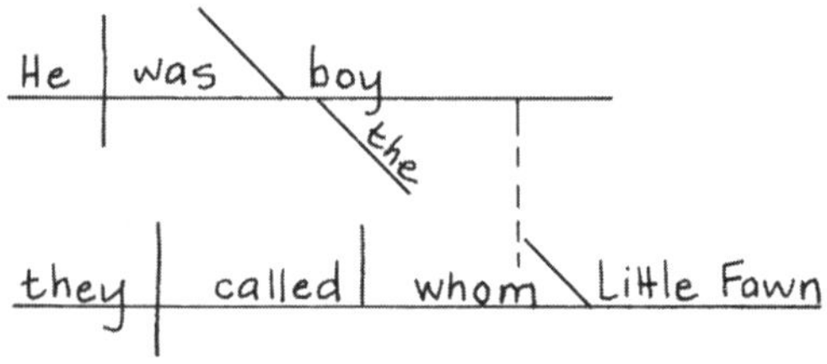

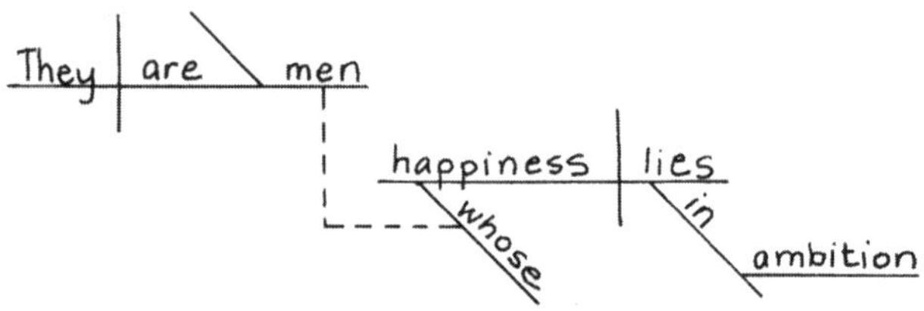

Exercise 70A: Identifying Adjective Clauses and Relative Pronouns

Underline the adjective clauses in the following sentences, and circle the relative pronouns. Draw an arrow from each relative pronoun to its antecedent.

These sentences are taken from *Ghosts: True Tales of Eerie Encounters*, by Robert C. Belyk.

The ghosts that haunt the Cherry Bank hotel are rarely seen.

One incident frightened a guest who had come with a group of friends.

As her eyes adjusted to the light, she was aware of a bearded man, whom she later described as wearing old-fashioned clothing, floating above her.

There was nothing on the tape but a noise that sounded like someone walking heavily across the floor.

The three chandeliers that lit the banquet room had been turned off and the room was in darkness.

Local children would turn the stones over to reveal the names of the children whose graves they had marked.

He was a bully whose manners were uncouth.

The best spot was near a stream which eventually tumbled over the cliff to the beach below.

When he returned, however, the person who had been sitting on the hearth was gone.

Exercise 70B: Choosing the Correct Relative Pronoun

In each sentence, cross out the incorrect relative pronoun. Above the correct pronoun, write *S* for subject, *OP* for object of the preposition, or *DO* for direct object to show how the relative pronoun is used within the dependent clause.

These sentences are adapted from *Ghost Stories of an Antiquary*, by the classic horror writer M. R. James.

"Good heavens!" said the little man, (who / whom) the suggestion threw into a state of unaccountable terror.

He had some talk upon the matter with the Vicar of his parish, with (who / whom) he travelled home.

The Templars, to (who / whom) this site had belonged, were in the habit of building round churches.

The little boy (who / whom) was the only passenger in the chaise, and (who / whom) jumped out as soon as it had stopped, looked about him with the keenest curiosity.

The picture lay face upwards on the table where the last man (who / whom) looked at it had put it.

He made tea for the friend with (who / whom) he had been playing golf.

He was a man (who / whom) liked to be on pleasant terms with those about him.

Lady Fell was with her mother, (who / whom) was dangerously ill.

Mrs. Bunch was the most comfortable and human person (who / whom) Stephen had as yet met.

Exercise 70C: Diagramming Adjective Clauses

On your own paper, diagram every word of the following sentences, adapted from M. R. James's *A Thin Ghost and Others.*

Saul, whose face expressed great anger, hastily picked the object up.

The ground rose to a field that was park-like in character.

He held several long conversations with old women whom we met.

Dr. Quinn was a plain, honest creature, and a man to whom I would have gone.

His wife, who accompanied him, was to make a series of illustrative drawings for his report.

— LESSON 71 —

Adjective Clauses
Relative Adverbs
Adjective Clauses with Understood Relatives

A phrase is a group of words serving a single grammatical function.
A clause is a group of words that contains a subject and a predicate.

An independent clause can stand by itself as a sentence.
A dependent clause is a fragment that cannot stand by itself as a sentence.

Dependent clauses begin with subordinating words.
Dependent clauses are also known as subordinate clauses.

Adjective clauses are also known as relative clauses because they relate to another word in the independent clause.

Relative pronouns introduce adjective clauses and refer back to an antecedent in the independent clause.
who, whom, whose, which, that

This was the very spot **where** a proud tyrant raised an undying monument to his own vanity.

He was going back to serve his country at a time **when** death was the usual reward for such devotion.

The reasons **why** he vented his ill humor on the soldiers were many.
—Adapted from *The Scarlet Pimpernel* by Baroness Emmuska Orczy

Relative adverbs introduce adjective clauses and refer back to a place, time, or reason in the independent clause.
where, when, why

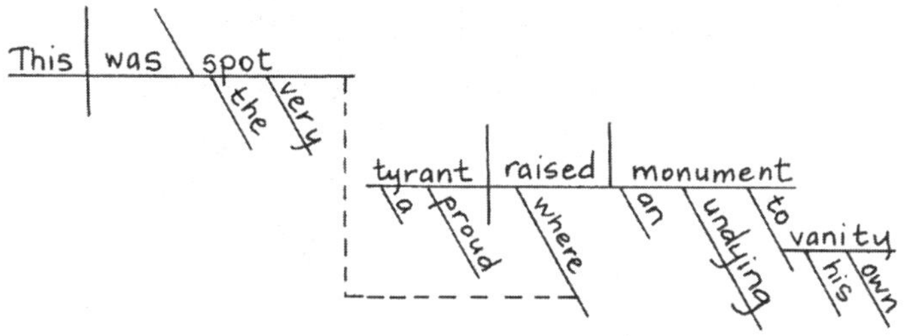

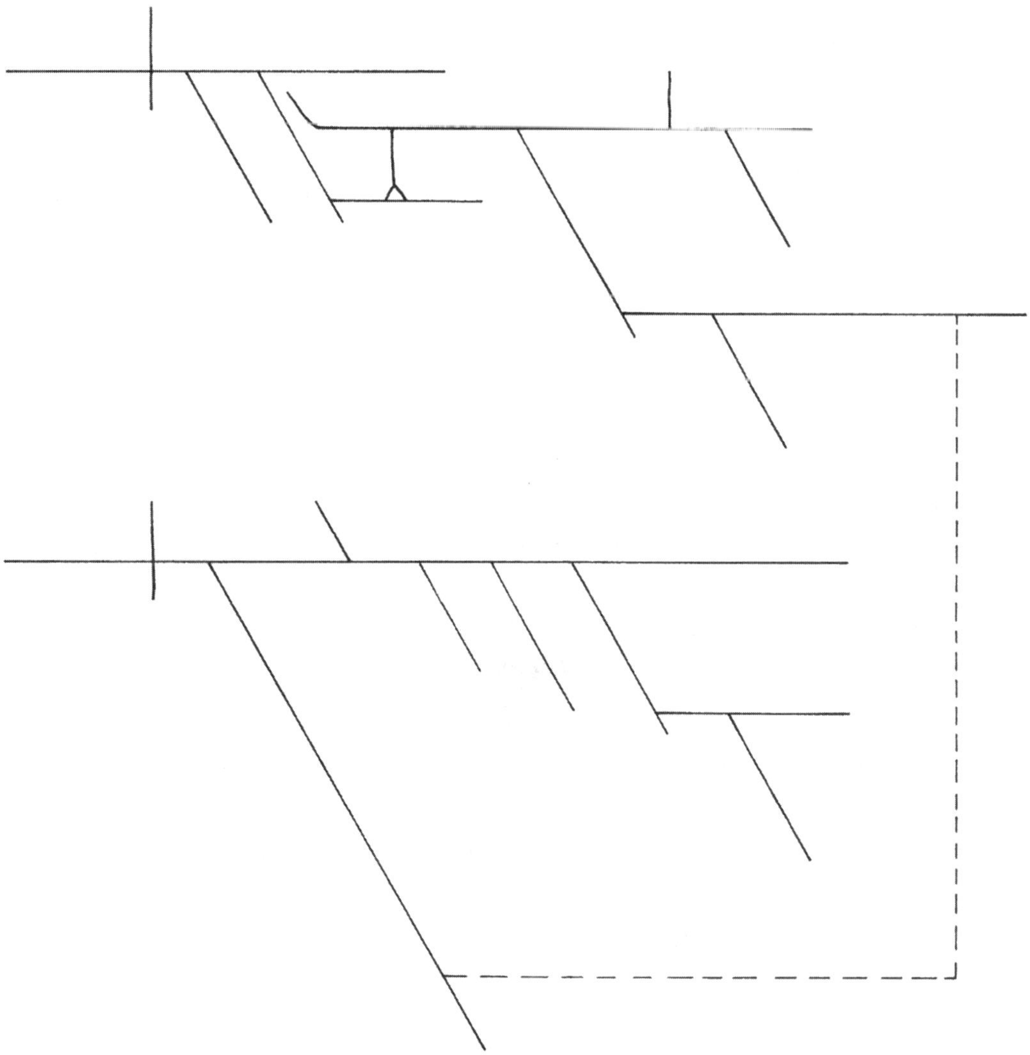

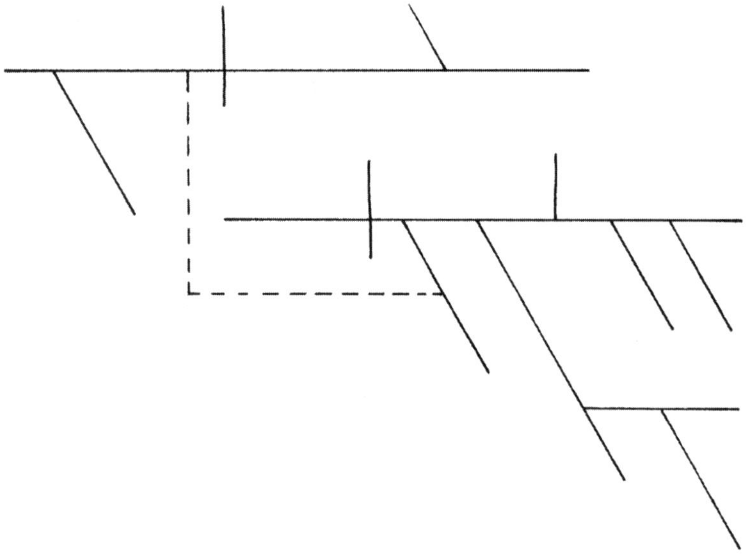

The evil men do lives after them.

I read the book you sent me.

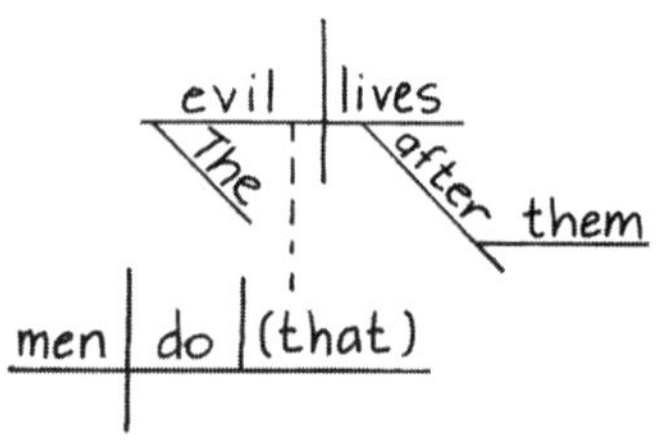

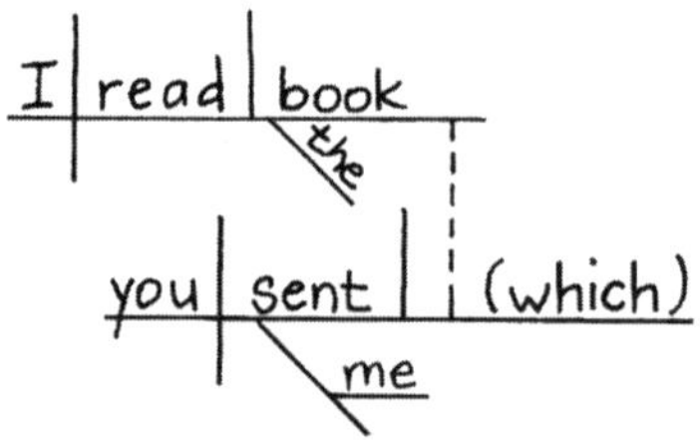

Exercise 71A: Relative Adverbs and Pronouns

In the following sentences, underline each adjective clause. Circle each relative word and label it as *RP* for relative pronoun or *RA* for relative adverb. Draw an arrow from each relative word back to its antecedent in the independent clause.

These sentences are taken from *Bartleby, The Scrivener*, a novel by Herman Melville, who also wrote *Moby Dick*. Some have been slightly adapted or condensed.

He was afflicted by a continual discontent with the height of the table where he worked.

On a cold morning when business was dull, Turkey would gobble up scores of these cakes.

What is the reason why I should do no more writing?

He is a wanderer who refuses to budge.

He received visits from certain ambiguous-looking fellows in seedy coats, whom he called his clients.

He was a man whom prosperity harmed.

What was the time when he departed?

I procured a high green folding screen, which might entirely isolate Bartleby from my sight.

There are two scriveners in the office, where they assist each other.

It was 6 PM, after which I saw no more of the proprietor.

"Then sir," said the stranger, who proved a lawyer, "you are responsible for the man you left there."

As yet, nothing that I know of has ever been written.

Simply record the fact, that I was not unemployed in my profession.

It was the time when he must unconditionally leave the office.

Exercise 71B: Missing Relative Words

Draw a caret in front of each adjective clause and insert the missing relative pronoun. (For the purposes of this exercise, *which* and *that* may be used interchangeably.) These sentences are also loosely adapted from *Bartleby, The Scrivener.*

The cake he most enjoyed was small, flat, round, and very spicy.

He carefully considered each statement I made.

The folio he copied for me cost four cents.

You are responsible for the man you left there.

One report I heard about will appear tomorrow.

It is a name he loves to repeat.

He scorned all further words I spoke.

Exercise 71C: Diagramming

On your own paper, diagram the following sentences from your first two exercises.

It was 6 PM, after which I saw no more of the proprietor.

He was afflicted by a continual discontent with the height of the table where he worked.

He received visits from certain ambiguous-looking fellows in seedy coats, whom he called his clients.

On a cold morning when business was dull, Turkey would gobble up scores of these cakes.

The cake he most enjoyed was small, flat, round, and very spicy.

— LESSON 72 —

Adverb Clauses

A clause is a group of words that contains a subject and a predicate.

A dependent clause is a fragment that cannot stand by itself as a sentence.
Dependent clauses begin with subordinating words.
Dependent clauses are also known as subordinate clauses.

Dependent clauses can act as adjective clauses, adverb clauses, or noun clauses.

Adverb clauses modify verbs, adjectives, and other adverbs in the independent clause.
They answer the questions where, when, how, how often, and to what extent.

When the supper was finished, the king expressed a wish.

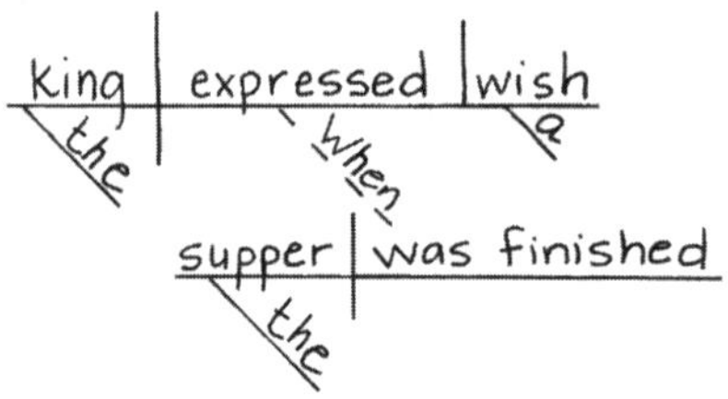

Adverb clauses can be introduced by adverbs.

Common Adverbs that Introduce Clauses
as (and its compounds: as if, as soon as, as though)
as if
how (and its compound: however)
when (and its compound: whenever)
whence
where (and its compounds: whereat, whereby, wherein, wherefore, whereon)
while
whither

A subordinating conjunction joins unequal words or groups of words together.

An honest enemy is better than an agreeable coward.

An honest enemy is better than an agreeable coward [is].

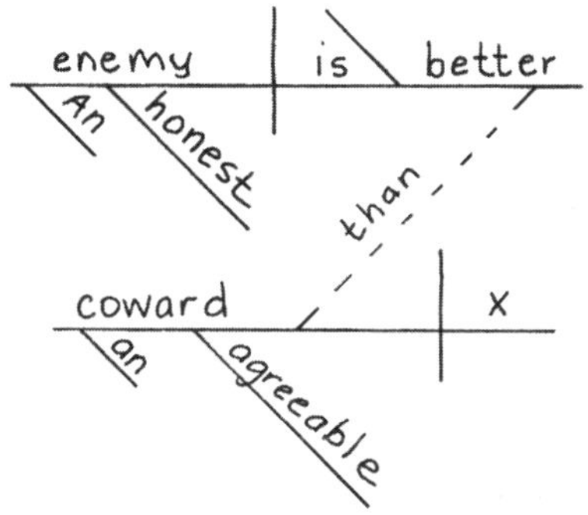

Subordinating conjunctions and subordinating correlative conjunctions often join an adverb clause to an independent clause.

Common Subordinating Conjunctions
after
although
as (as soon as)
because
before
if
in order that
lest
since
though
till
unless
until
although/though . . . yet/still
if . . . then

Because she loves Korean food, my aunt taught me to cook kimchi.

I will put six plates on the table unless our neighbors are also coming for dinner.

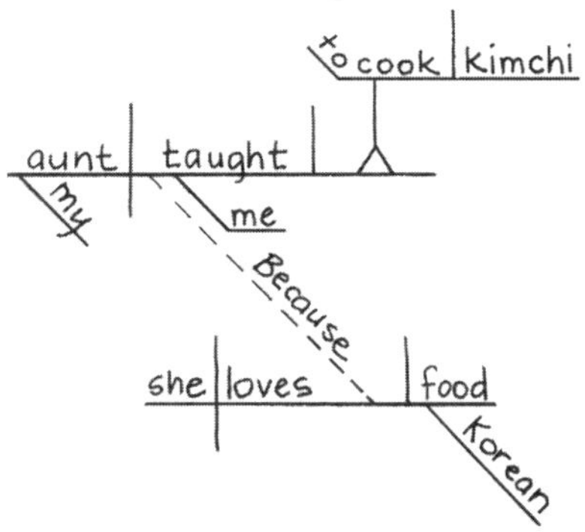

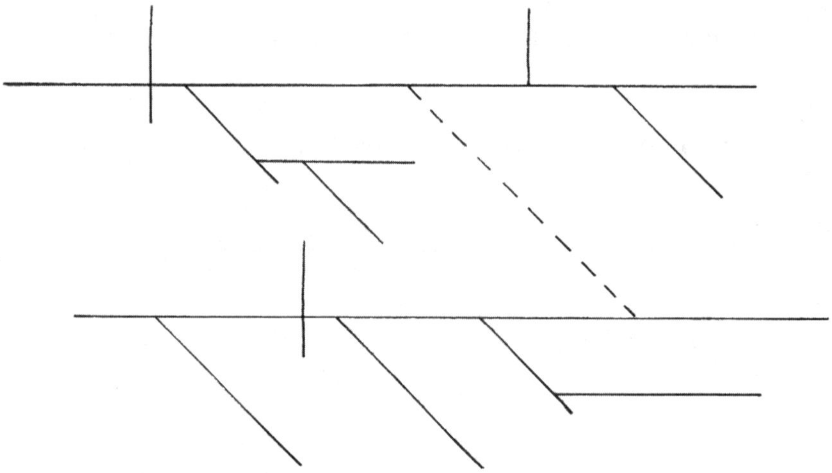

The task is difficult if you do not take care.

She was confident that she could reach the top of the mountain.

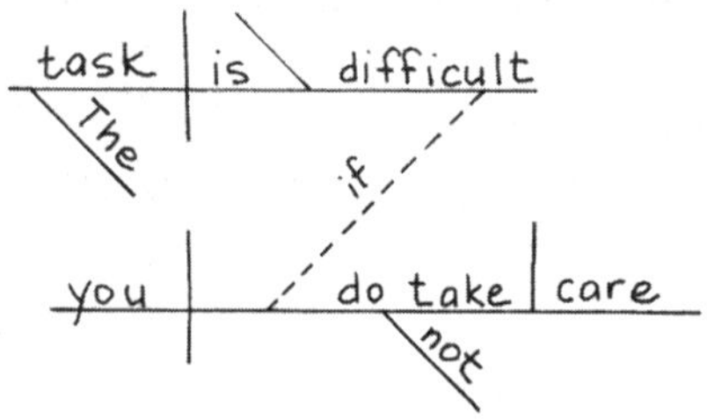

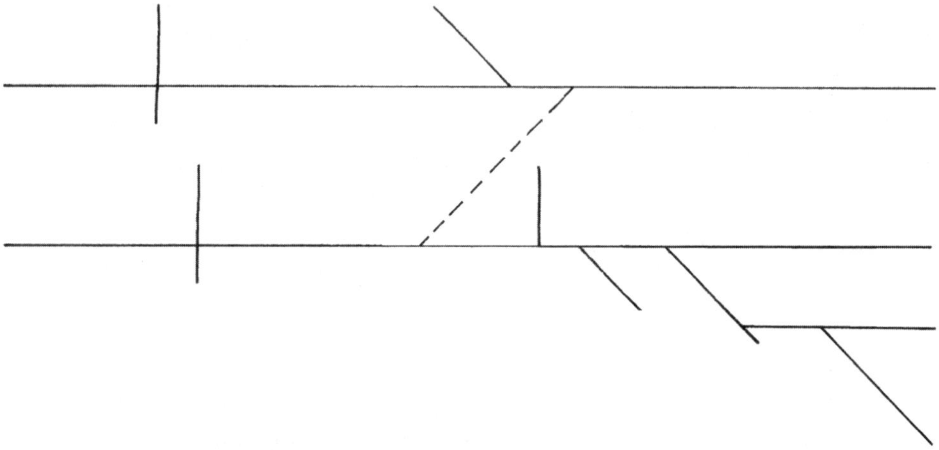

He sprinted quickly as though he were being chased by monsters.

The judge spoke severely because the attorney was not paying attention.

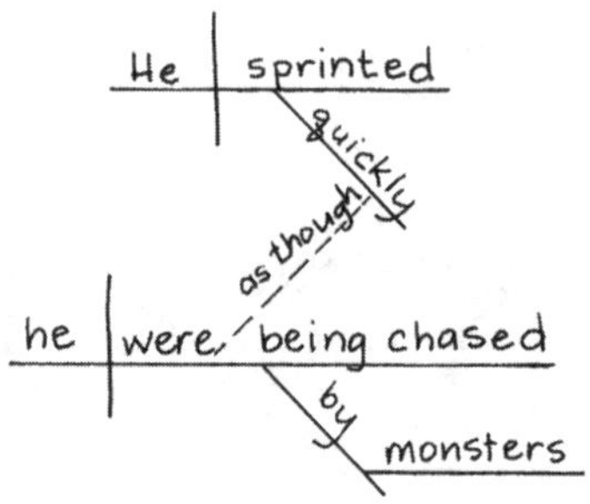

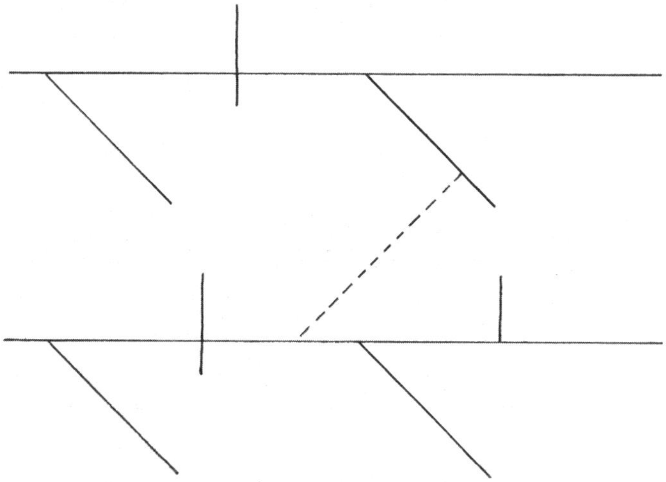

I will wait where I am.

I waited at the place where I had marked the ground.

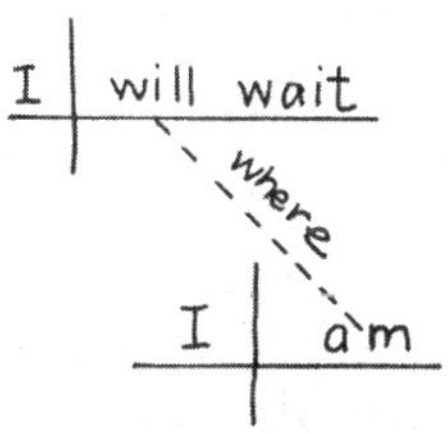

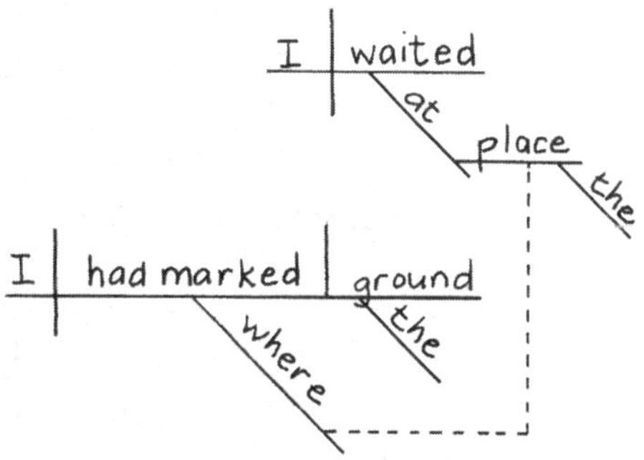

Exercise 72A: Adverb Clauses

In the following sentences, underline each adverb clause. Circle the subordinating word(s) at the beginning of each clause and label it *ADV* for adverb or *SC* for subordinating conjunction. Draw an arrow from the subordinating word(s) back to the verb, adverb, or adjective that the clause modifies.

These sentences are slightly condensed from the Chinese classic *The Art of War*, by Sun Tzu, as translated by Lionel Giles.

If I fail, I shall make myself a laughing-stock.

We can form a single united body, while the enemy must split up into fractions.

After that, you may crush him.

We are not fit to lead an army on the march unless we are familiar with the face of the country.

Although he had no practical experience of war, he was extremely fond of discussing the subject.

He speaks as a man of Wu, a state which ceased to exist as early as 473 B.C.

I fully believe he was a good soldier, but I had him beheaded because he acted without orders.

The spirit of the enemy's soldiers will be keenest when they have newly arrived on the scene.

I attacked when their spirit was gone and ours was at its height.

Throw your soldiers into positions whence there is no escape, and they will prefer death to flight.

Attack him where he is unprepared, and appear where you are not expected.

Though only eight days have passed since I threw off my allegiance, an army is already at the city-gates.

Exercise 72B: Descriptive Clauses

In the following sentences, underline each dependent clause. Above each, write *ADVC* for adverb clause or *ADJC* for adjective clause. Circle each subordinating word(s) and label it as *ADV* for adverb, *RP* for relative pronoun, or *SC* for subordinating conjunction. Draw an arrow from the subordinating word back (or forward) to the word in the independent clause that the dependent clause modifies.

These sentences are adapted from *Nonviolence: The History of a Dangerous Idea*, by Mark Kurlansky.

Nonviolence is not the same thing as pacifism, for which there are many words.

When nonviolence becomes a reality it is a powerful force.

Pacifism is harmless and therefore easier to accept than nonviolence, which is dangerous.

Interestingly, although Gandhi's teachings and techniques have had a huge impact on political activists around the world, his word for nonviolence, *satyagraha*, has never caught on.

The human being who achieved complete nonviolence, according to Gandhi, would not be a saint.

This concept of man as an imperfect being who is obligated to strive for an unattainable perfection runs through most of human thought.

Most religions and philosophies that reject violence do not encourage passiveness but activism by other means—nonviolence.

The strongest Chinese stand on nonviolence came in opposition to Confucius, from a man named Mozi, who lived from about 470 to 390 B.C.

While Confucius was a voice of the establishment, Mozi was a rebel.

Judaism, a religion that is more than 5,700 years old, has many layers of both laws and commentaries on those laws.

On Passover, which celebrates Moses leading the Hebrews out of slavery in Egypt, there is a moment of sorrow for the Egyptians, the enemy who drowned trying to pursue the Hebrews across the Red Sea.

Exercise 72C: Diagramming

On your own paper, diagram every word of the following sentences from the first two exercises.

Although he had no practical experience of war, he was extremely fond of discussing the subject.

I attacked when their spirit was gone and ours was at its height.

Throw your soldiers into positions whence there is no escape, and they will prefer death to flight.

Nonviolence is not the same thing as pacifism, for which there are many words.

When nonviolence becomes a reality it is a powerful force.

— REVIEW 6 —

Weeks 16-18

Topics
Personal Pronouns: Subject, Object, Possessive, Reflexive
Verb Voice (Active and Passive)
Verb Tense
Adjectives
Gerunds and Participles
Phrases
Clauses (Independent and Dependent)

Review 6A: Pronouns

In the following sentences, taken from Leo Tolstoy's *War and Peace* (as translated by Louise and Aylmer Maude), circle each pronoun. Label each as *S* (subject form of the personal pronoun), *O* (object form of the personal pronoun), *P* (possessive form of the personal pronoun), *R* (reflexive), *INT* (intensive), *I* (indefinite), *INTER* (interrogative), *D* (demonstrative), or *RP* (relative pronoun).

He went up to Anna Pávlovna, kissed her hand, presenting to her his bald, scented, and shining head, and complacently seated himself on the sofa.

Another time, general attention was attracted by a small brown dog, coming heaven knows whence, which trotted in a preoccupied manner in front of the ranks with tail stiffly erect till suddenly a shell fell close by, when it yelped, tucked its tail between its legs, and darted aside.

Nicholas expressed his disapproval of the postponement of the marriage for a year; but Natásha attacked her brother with exasperation, proving to him that it could not be otherwise, and that it would be a bad thing to enter a family against the father's will, and that she herself wished it so.

Most of the time, by their officers' order, the men sat on the ground. One, having taken off his shako, carefully loosened the gathers of its lining and drew them tight again; another, rubbing some dry clay between his palms, polished his bayonet; another fingered the strap and pulled the buckle of his bandolier, while another smoothed and refolded his leg bands and put his boots on again. Some built little houses of the tufts in the plowed ground, or plaited baskets from the straw in the cornfield. All seemed fully absorbed in these pursuits.

It was evident that Kutúzov despised cleverness and learning and even the patriotic feeling shown by Denísov, but despised them not because of his own intellect, feelings, or knowledge—he did not try to display any of these—but because of something else.

"Do you know," he said at last, evidently unable to check the sad current of his thoughts, "that Anatole is costing me forty thousand rubles a year? And," he went on after a pause, "what will it be in five years, if he goes on like this?" Presently he added: "That's what we fathers have to put up with. . . . Is this princess of yours rich?"

Review 6B: Using Comparative and Superlative Adjectives Correctly

Choose the correct form in parentheses. Cross out the incorrect form.

These sentences are taken from H. G. Wells's *A Short History of the World.*

In Sumeria the priest ruler was the (most great / greatest), (most splendid / splendidest) of beings.

People travelled about (more freely / most freely) than they had ever done before, and there were high roads and inns for them.

Travel is increasing and transport growing (more easy / easier) by reason of horses and roads.

Hiram established the very (most close / closest) relations both with David and with his son and successor Solomon.

Asoka made vast benefactions to the Buddhist teaching orders, and tried to stimulate them to a (more good / better) and (more energetic / energeticer) criticism of their own accumulated literature.

Sardanapalus's library has been unearthed and is perhaps the (more precious / most precious) store of historical material in the world.

The (bitterer / bitterest) rival of Athens in Greece was Sparta.

The power of the Roman republic came out of the west to subjugate one fragment after another and weld them together into a new and (more enduring / enduringer) empire.

The Trinitarian formula may be found in its (most complete / completest) expression in the Athanasian Creed.

The steamboat was, if anything, a little ahead of the steam engine in its (more early / earlier) phases.

Review 6C: Verbs

Underline the main verb (along with any helping verbs) in every clause below (both independent and dependent).

In the space above each verb, write the tense (*SIMP PAST, PRES, FUT; PROG PAST, PRES, FUT; PERF PAST, PRES, FUT*) and voice (*ACT* for active or *PASS* for passive). For state-of-being verbs, write *SB* instead of voice.

If the verb is an action verb, also note whether it is transitive (*TR*) or intransitive (*INTR*).

The first is done for you.

These sentences are taken from the official government report on the Perry Expedition. In 1853–1854, Commodore Matthew Perry of the U.S. Navy was ordered, by President Millard Fillmore, to take warships to Japan. At that time, Japan's ports were closed—the country refused to trade with the United States. Perry's Expedition was ordered to open the ports and put trade into place—either through negotiation, or through force.

In 1854, Japan agreed to the terms the U.S. was offering, and trade with America began.

SIMP FUT SB

SIR: So soon as the steam frigate Mississippi shall be in all respects ready for sea, you will proceed in her, accompanied by the steamer *Princeton*, to Macao, or Hong Kong, in China, where the vessels of your command will rendezvous. . . . It has been deemed necessary to increase the naval force of the United States in the East India and China seas, for reasons which will be found in the enclosed copy of a communication from the Secretary of State addressed to this department under date of November, 1852.

The special mission to Japan with which you have been charged by the government will require all your firmness and prudence, in respect to which the department entertains the fullest confidence that they will be adequate for any emergency.

Your attention is particularly invited to the exploration of the coasts of Japan and of the adjacent continent and islands.

The said officer shall detain him until the vessel in which he shall be serving shall return to the United States.

Taking into view, also, the present disturbed state of China, and the need of one or more ships of the squadron in that quarter, and considering that not a single vessel which had been promised by the department had yet joined my force . . . I was glad to have a good excuse for consenting to wait until the ensuing spring. . . . In the spring I shall have concentrated my whole force, and will be prepared with store and coal vessels, and all other conveniences for remaining, if it be necessary, an indefinite time, to secure such concessions as I believe they will be constrained to make.

Review 6D: Identifying Dependent Clauses

Underline each dependent clause in the following sentences. Circle the subordinating word. Label each clause as either adjective (*ADJ*) or adverb clause (*ADV*), and draw a line from each subordinating word to the word it modifies.

These sentences are taken from *Breaking Open Japan: Commodore Perry, Lord Abe, and American Imperialism in 1853*, by George Feifer.

When the bluff fizzled, the tiny number who made Japan's political decisions could think of nothing else with which to counter the foreigners' threat.

The harassed yet privileged Dutch traders who delivered the disturbing reports lived in a compound called Deshima, which can be translated as "island in front of the town."

The Dutch East India Company, which traded in spices, tea, silk, and other much-wanted commodities, was the largest of its kind and—in keeping with Holland's commercial lead over Britain at the time—more successful than the British East India Company, founded two years earlier, in 1600.

The Dutch Factory, as its Japanese post was known, was moved to Deshima in 1641, after the other Western colonies had left the country, voluntarily or otherwise.

Smaller beacon fires were already burning all along the coast, where soldiers with pikes and "rusty flintlocks" stood guard, some additionally armed with war fans bearing the emblem of the rising sun.

While officers frantically drilled green troops, seacoast inhabitants, some of whose houses had already been razed for frenzied construction of new fortifications, were pressed into service.

With the panic and chaos swelling in the heat, the "whole city" succumbed to "uproar."

Nothing had yet been reported to the Emperor in his Kyoto palace, where life continued unchanged in its detachment from political matters.

The court's big event during the week of panic was the first celebration of Boys' Day by the baby Prince who would become the Emperor Meiji.

Review 6E: Present and Past Participles

Underline each present participle and past participle in the following sentences. Some are serving as nouns; others as adjectives. Label adjective forms as *ADJ* and draw a line to the word modified. Label noun forms as *N* and write the part of the sentence that the noun is serving as.

These sentences are taken from *On the Origins of Sports: The Early History and Original Rules of Everybody's Favorite Games*, by Gary Belsky and Neil Fine.

Knowing the history and lore of our favorite sports can only enhance our experience of watching or competing in them.

We are tribal by nature—genetically programmed to define "us" by "them"—and few things make that task easier than team jerseys.

Wiffle Ball was designed for use in congested areas. Because the ball will not travel far, ball chasing and base running have been eliminated.

The minimum number of players required to play Wiffle Ball are two—the pitcher and batter—one player to a side.

A cricket match is composed of two innings, with each team running through its eleven-man lineup twice.

Choosing the pitch offered an advantage.

Strikers, or batsmen, are "out" if a bowled ball knocks the bail off the stumps, or a fielder catches a batted ball in the air.

Rules of Ancient Greek Wrestling:

No intentional hitting or kicking is permitted.

No gouging the eyes or biting is permitted.

Infractions shall be punished by immediate whipping by the referee until the undesirable behaviour is stopped.

Review 6F: Diagramming

On your own paper, diagram every word of the following sentences from *Moon Shot: The Inside Story of America's Apollo Moon Landings*, by Jay Barbree, Alan Shepard, and Deke Slayton.

It was a beautiful airfield, where pilots could come burning out of the sky and always have a place to land, where landing-speed restrictions were nonexistent.

Although the United States recruited the cream of the German rocket scientists, the Soviets captured many of those left behind and began their own missile program.

The Saturn V roared, bellowed, and shrieked, hurling out ear-stabbing sonic waves and a crackling thunder which sent birds flying and wildlife fleeing, and which slammed into people who were far away, fluttering their clothing and causing them to step back uncertainly.

WEEK 19

More Clauses

— LESSON 73 —

Adjective and Adverb Clauses
Introduction to Noun Clauses

A clause is a group of words that contains a subject and a predicate.

I know that a noun is the name of a person, place, thing, or idea.

I know an old lady who swallowed a fly while she was sitting on the front porch.

Dependent clauses can act as adjective clauses, adverb clauses, or noun clauses.

An adjective clause is a dependent clause that acts as an adjective in a sentence, modifying a noun or pronoun in the independent clause.
Relative pronouns introduce adjective clauses and refer back to an antecedent in the independent clause.

Adverb clauses modify verbs, adjectives, and other adverbs in the independent clause.
They answer the questions where, when, how, how often, and to what extent.
Adverb clauses can be introduced by adverbs.
Subordinating conjunctions and subordinating correlative conjunctions often join an adverb clause to an independent clause.

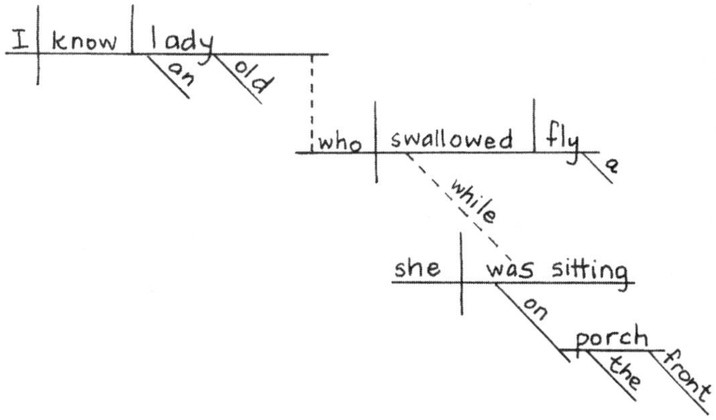

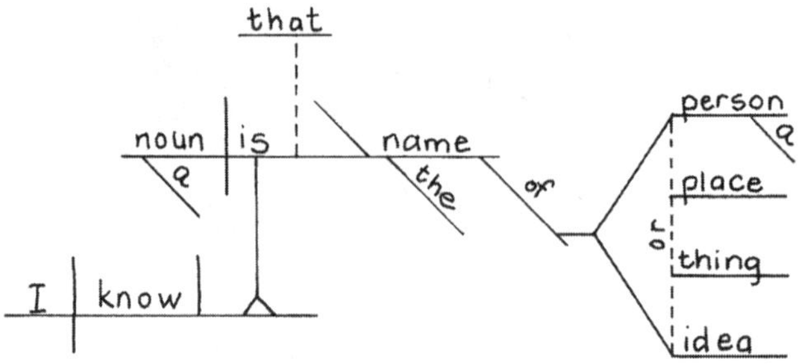

A noun clause takes the place of a noun.
Noun clauses can be introduced by relative pronouns, relative adverbs, subordinating conjunctions, or understood subordinating words.

I know where your lost keys are.

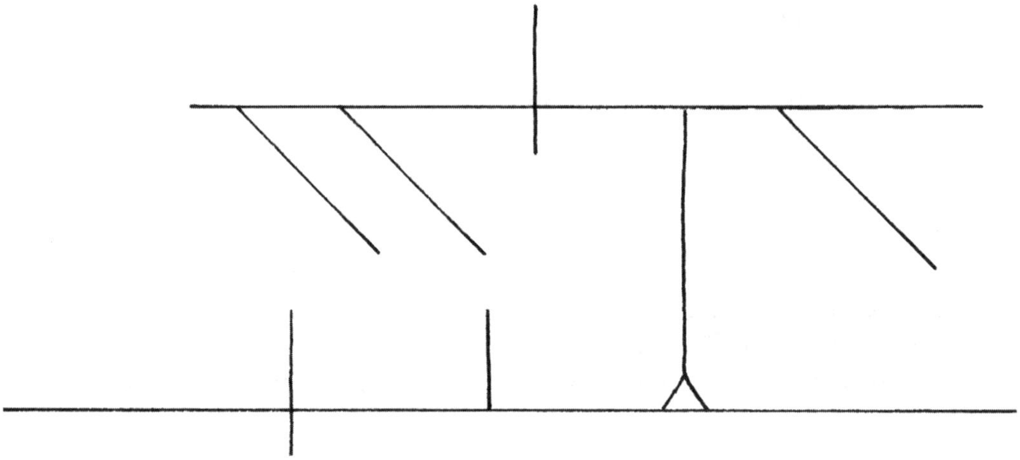

Whoever runs fastest will win the race.

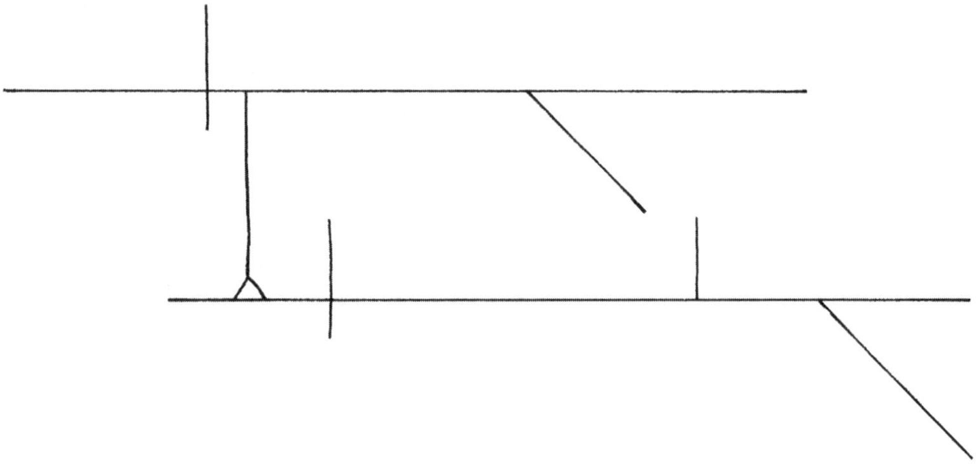

I really wish I had more chocolate.

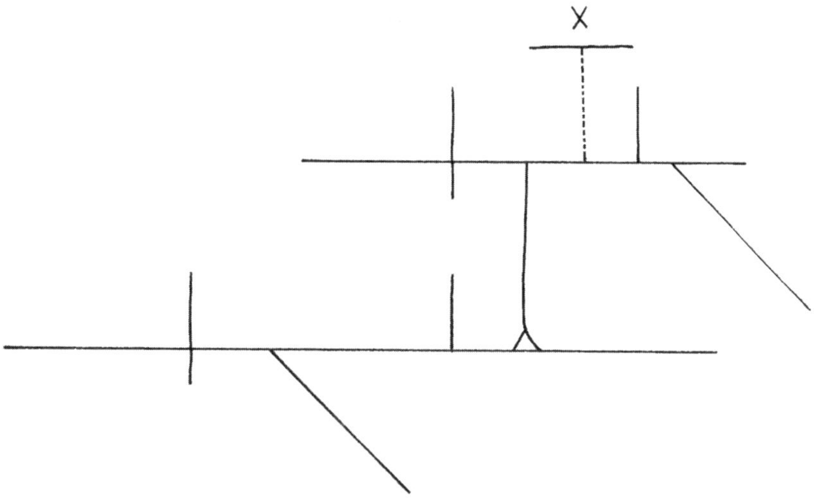

Nothing was as it should be.

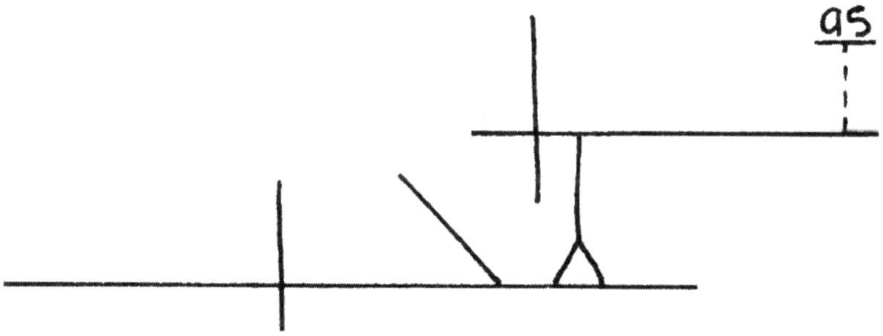

What matters most in this situation is how you feel about it.

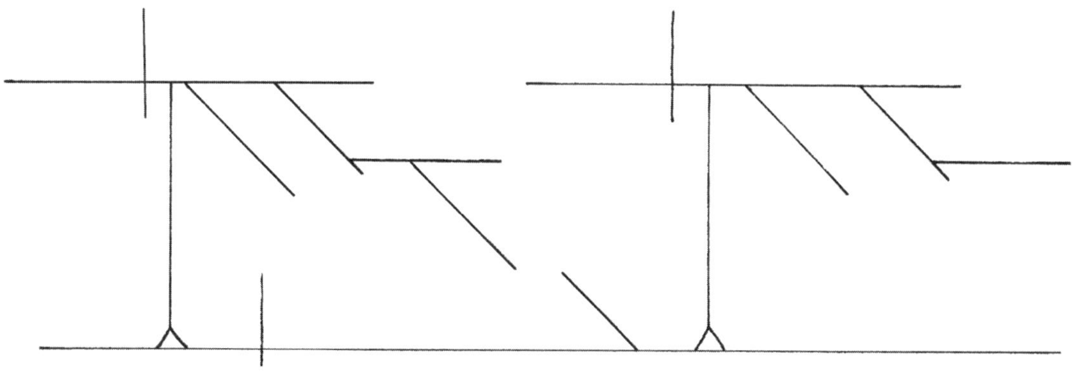

Exercise 73A: Identifying Clauses

In the following sentences, circle each dependent clause. Label each as *N* for noun, *ADJ* for adjective, or *ADV* for adverb. Also indicate the part of speech that each noun clause plays: subject (*S*), direct object (*DO*), predicate nominative (*PN*), or object of the preposition (*OP*). Draw a line from the subordinating word of each adjective and adverb clause to the word it modifies.

Some of these clauses may have another clause within them! Do your best to find both, and ask your instructor for help if needed.

These sentences are taken from *The Return of Tarzan* by Edgar Rice Burroughs—the 1913 sequel to Burroughs's 1912 best-seller *Tarzan of the Apes*.

Nikolas has been a bad man since I can remember.

But first I will remind you that you maligned me before the girl.

Tarzan could not but wonder what manner of conspiracy was on foot, or what the scheme of the two men might be.

It was difficult to imagine a world without a friend—without a living thing who spoke the new tongues which Tarzan had learned to love so well.

And so it was that before they left the amphitheater to return to their wanderings they had once more chosen him as their leader.

They were standing on deck at a point which was temporarily deserted, and as Tarzan came upon them they were in heated argument with a woman.

And then, as the men stood looking first at Tarzan and then at their superior the ape-man did the one thing which was needed to erase the last remnant of animosity which they might have felt for him.

From where I sat in that chair yonder I saw the reflection of it all in the mirror before me.

It was decided that although three of them would have to ride after practically no sleep, it would be best to make an early start in the morning, and attempt to ride all the way to Bou Saada in one day.

That she would have spurned Clayton once he had been stripped of both his title and his estates never for once occurred to Tarzan, for he credited to others the same honest loyalty that was so inherent a quality in himself.

Exercise 73B: Creating Noun Clauses

On your own paper, create five sentences by adding a noun clause into each of the blanks below.

If you have trouble coming up with a dependent clause, try starting out with one of the following subordinating words: *that, how, why, what/whatever, who/whoever* (these are always subjects within the dependent clause), *whom/whomever* (these are always objects within the dependent clause), *where, whether.* (This is not an exhaustive list of the possibilities—just a jumping-off place for you.)

I really wonder ____.

________________________________ was unusually hard to decide.

Explain to your brother ____

________________________________.

____ is not welcome in this house.

The most extraordinary development was ________________________________

________________________________.

Exercise 73C: Diagramming

On your own paper, diagram every word of the following sentences (taken from *The Return of Tarzan*).

I would not care who knew that I had killed you.

Where Tarzan stood was dark.

When one of the sailors had taken me out to him in another boat the professor became quite indignant at my suggestion that we return at once to land.

CHALLENGE SENTENCE

The last few seconds of my life have taught me that it would be hideous to attempt further to deceive myself and you, or to entertain for an instant longer the possibility of ever becoming your wife, if we should regain civilization.

— LESSON 74 —

Clauses Beginning With Prepositions

The sun itself, which makes time, is elder by a year now.

Any man's death diminishes me, because I am involved in mankind.

What we call fortune here has another name above.

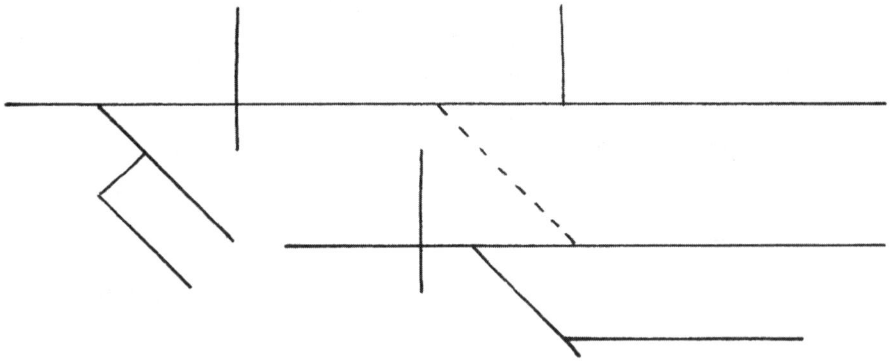

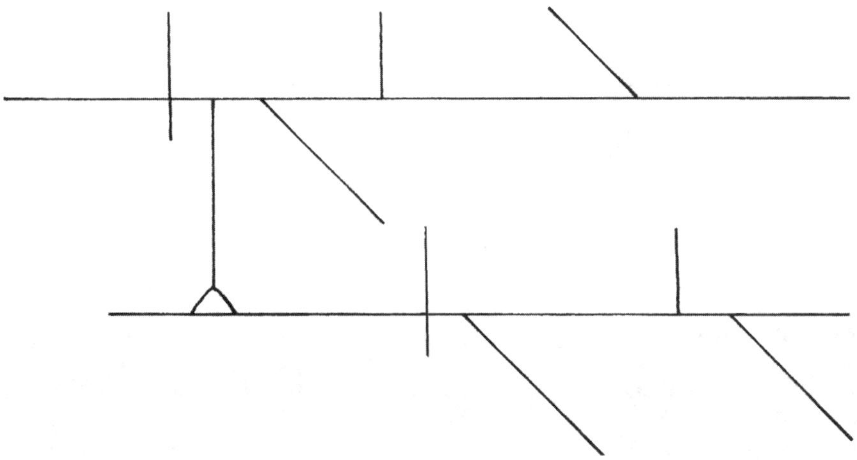

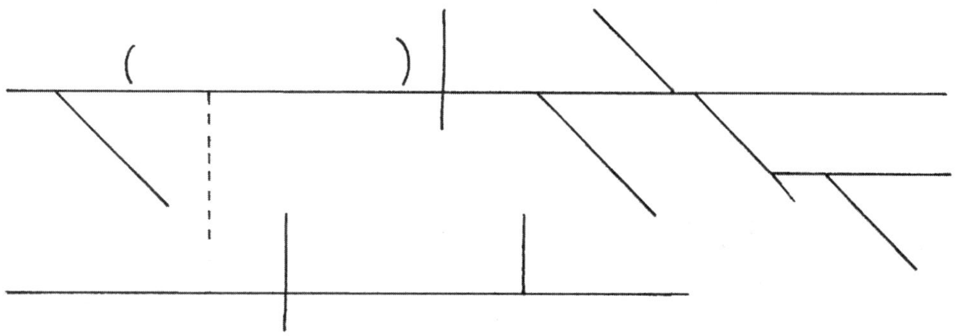

That carrack is the ship in which they are to sail.

He sent for his friends, of whom he took a solemn farewell.

Do not ask for whom the bell tolls.

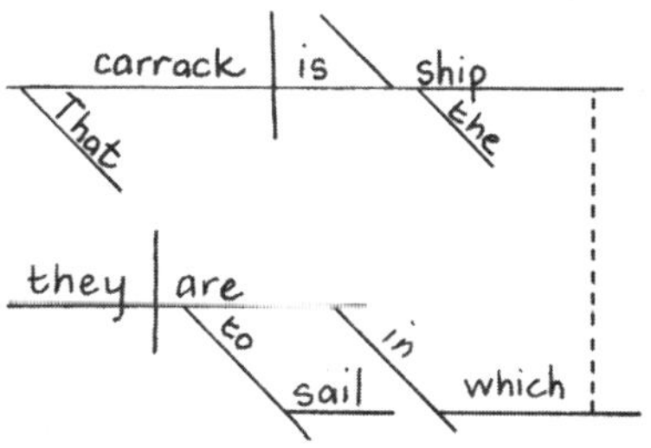

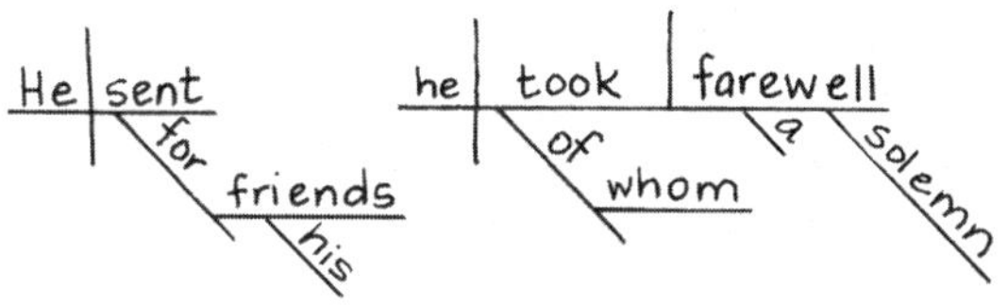

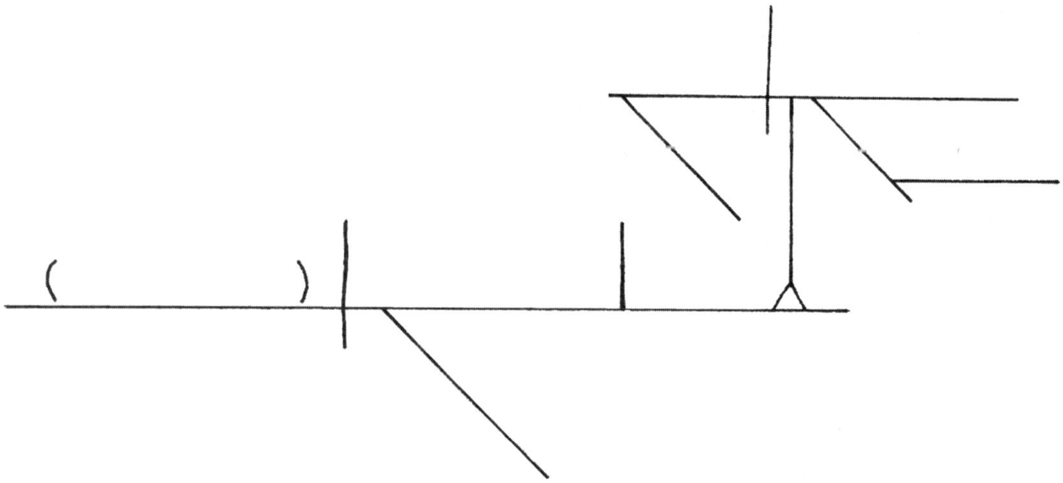

***Who* always acts as a subject or predicate nominative within a sentence. *Whom* always acts as an object.**

INCORRECT
He sent for his friends, of who he took a solemn farewell.
Do not ask for who the bell tolls.

ALSO INCORRECT (Informal)
He sent for his friends, who he took a solemn farewell of.

Do not ask who the bell tolls for.

CORRECT (Informal)
He sent for his friends, whom he took a solemn farewell of.
Do not ask whom the bell tolls for.

She is growing angry at the person who/whom she is arguing with.

____

Rude behavior is something I won't put up with!
Rude behavior is something up with which I will not put!

Exercise 74A: Adjective Clauses Beginning with Prepositions

In the following sentences, circle each adjective clause. Draw a line from the subordinating word back to the word the clause modifies. If the clause begins with a preposition, underline that preposition and label its object with *OP.*

These sentences are taken from *The Clockwork Universe: Isaac Newton, the Royal Society, and the Birth of the Modern World,* by Edward Dolnick.

It means we can talk about its slope, which is a number—a regular, run-of-the-mill number, not an infinitesimal or any other colorful beast.

They make exceptions for a tiny number of geniuses whom they treat as time travelers from the present day, thinkers just like us who somehow found themselves decked out in powdered wigs.

Something is changing, and the rate at which it is changing is changing, too.

Unlike Newton, who often slept in his clothes, Leibniz was a dandy who had a weakness for showy outfits with lace-trimmed cuffs, gleaming boots, and silk cravats.

"I have done a deed which shakes the Moon in her path, which causes the Sun to be no longer the Sun, and which alters forever the destiny of the multitudinous myriads of stars that roll and glow in the majestic presence of their Creator."

"As a blind man has no idea of colors," Newton wrote, "so have we no idea of the manner by which the all-wise God perceives and understands all things."

It was Lely whom Oliver Cromwell instructed to "paint my picture truly like me," warts and all.

By paying close attention to what others had overlooked, they could find their way to utterly unexpected conclusions.

This picture of history was completely false, but Newton and many others had boundless faith in what they called "the wisdom of the ancients."

Isaac Newton was not only the supreme genius of modern times but also a man so jealous and bad-tempered that he exploded in fury at anyone who dared question him.

Leibniz had allied himself with those scoundrels of whom it "may reasonably be suspected that they would like very well to set the king aside."

Skeptics contended that any correct results must have been due to happy accidents in which multiple errors canceled themselves out.

Exercise 74B: Correct Use of *Who* and *Whom*

Choose the correct pronoun within the parentheses; cross out the incorrect pronoun. These sentences are adapted from *Famous Men of Science*, by Sarah K. Bolton.

He returned with two gentlemen, to (who / whom) he did not introduce me.

A woman, a princess, (who / whom) knew about the bright boy, spoke of him to her brother.

(Who / Whom) do the arrow heads and hatchets belong to?

He did not know a single individual from (who / whom) he could borrow money.

Caroline, (who / whom) loved him tenderly, was desolate.

The following year, Napoleon I, (who / whom) was usually wise in his selection of men, appointed him one of the six inspectors-general of education.

He met Baron Humboldt, from (who / whom) he received a large photograph.

Especially welcome were teachers, for (who / whom) admission was free.

(Who / Whom) should you ask?

In Rome he met a fellow painter, (who / whom) showed him great attention, and to (who / whom) he wrote a sonnet.

Those (who / whom) oversee the affairs of others rarely oversee their own.

No one can be too kind to my dear wife, (who / whom) is worth her weight in gold many times over.

(Who / Whom) did he teach physiology to?

He gained inspiration from the young man (who / whom) could travel four thousand miles through the marshes of Lapland, nearly barefoot and half-starved, in his study of plants.

I think he was the only man I ever knew against (who / whom) I never heard a word said.

He brought three friends, each of (who / whom) purchased a picture.

Exercise 74C: Formal and Informal Diction

On your own paper, rewrite the following informal sentences in formal English, placing the preposition before its object. In five sentences, you will also need to insert a relative pronoun. The first has been done for you.

Read both versions of each sentence out loud, and place a star by any sentence that sounds better in informal English.

Whom should I speak to?

To whom should I speak?

Georges Cuvier's coffin was carried by the students at the universities which he had taught in.

Those students were the ones whom his books were written for.

Linnaeus discovered that the friend he had entrusted his correspondence to was hiding his letters.

Galileo asked to stand on the same level as the Aristotelian philosophers he was arguing against.

The captain had no idea of the fate of the person the treasure had originally belonged to.

The discovery of refraction was one no other scientist had laid claim to.

We are greatly influenced, for good or for evil, by those we associate with.

Exercise 74D: Diagramming

On your own paper, diagram every word of the following two sentences from Exercise 74A.

Something is changing, and the rate at which it is changing is changing, too.

Skeptics contended that any correct results must have been due to happy accidents in which multiple errors canceled themselves out.

— LESSON 75 —

Clauses and Phrases
Misplaced Adjective Phrases
Misplaced Adjective Clauses

In many East Asian countries, the day a baby is born is considered its first birthday.

The first birthday after a baby is born is considered its second birthday.

A phrase is a group of words serving a single grammatical function.

A clause is a group of words that contains a subject and a predicate.

Western birthdays are often celebrated with a cake made especially for the occasion.

The first reference to a "birthday cake" dates from 1785, when the Oxford Dictionary listed the phrase for the first time.

The young woman went to the awards ceremony with her father in a gorgeous ball gown.

She gave the cookie to the little girl made of gingerbread.

Paige gave a birthday cake to her cousin which she had baked herself.

Adjective clauses and phrases should usually go immediately before or after the noun or pronoun they modify.

Exercise 75A: Correcting Misplaced Modifiers

Circle the misplaced adjective clauses and phrases in the following sentences. Draw an arrow to the place where each modifier should be.

The comic books were eagerly seized by the children with colorful covers.

The runners aimed for the finish line tapes that were sprinting around the track.

The black-clad man rode up to the town saloon wearing a fringed cowboy hat.

The chef filled with chives and capers drizzled the sauce over the steak.

I bought a horse from my dressage coach named Whirlaway Blaze Boy.

The bridge collapsed into the gulch with the rotting wooden rails.

The cornfield was covered in crows with three varieties of corn.

The visitors stared at the massive statue eating candy bars and swigging sodas.

I gave Jeremy a golden retriever puppy who is my best friend.

The cat finally got to the doorway that was running home.

We gathered many different kinds of fruit into our baskets that were ripe.

Exercise 75B: Diagramming

Each of the following sentences contains a misplaced clause or phrase. On your own paper, diagram each sentence correctly, and then read the corrected sentence out loud to your instructor. These sentences are taken from *Grimm's Fairy Tales*!

Sprinkled with blood, the queen gazed upon the white snow.

Streaming from her shoe, the older sister tried to conceal the blood from the prince.

The straw stretched itself from one bank to the other, and the coal tripped quite boldly onto the newly-built bridge, who was of an impetuous disposition.

— LESSON 76 —

Noun, Adjective, and Adverb Clauses

Restrictive and Non-Restrictive Modifying Clauses

Type of clause	Function in the sentence	Introduced by . . .	Diagram by . . .	Also known as
Adjective clause	Modifies a noun or pronoun in the main clause. Answers the questions *Which one? What kind? How many? Whose?*	. . . a relative pronoun, relative adjective, or relative adverb that refers back to a noun or pronoun in the main clause. The most common are *who, whom, whose, that, which, where, when, why.*	. . . placing every word of the dependent clause on a separate diagram below the diagram of the main clause. Connect the relative pronoun, adjective, or adverb to the word it refers to in the main clause with a dotted line.	Relative clause, dependent clause, subordinate clause
Adverb clause	Modifies a verb, adjective, or adverb in the main clause. Answers the questions *Where? When? How? How often? To what extent?*	. . . subordinating conjunctions, such as *when, until, before, after, as, while, where, although, unless, because, since, though, so that, even though.* (NOTE: There are many other subordinating conjunctions.)	. . . placing every word of the dependent clause EXCEPT for the subordinating word on a separate diagram below the diagram of the main clause. Draw a dotted line connecting the predicate of the dependent clause to the word modified in the independent clause, and write the subordinating word on the dotted line.	Subordinate clause, dependent clause

Type of clause	Function in the sentence	Introduced by . . .	Diagram by . . .	Also known as
Noun clause	Stands in as any part of the sentence that a noun can fill: subject, direct object, indirect object, predicate nominative, object of the preposition, appositive [see Lesson 94], object complement.	. . . most commonly, *that.* Can also be introduced by *who, whom, which, what, whether, why, when, where, how,* or other subordinating words.	. . . drawing a tree in the appropriate "noun" space on the diagram and placing each word in the noun clause on a diagram that sits on top of the tree. If the subordinating word only connects the dependent clause to the rest of the sentence and doesn't have a grammatical function *within* the dependent clause, diagram it on a line that floats above the predicate of the clause and is attached to the predicate by a dotted line.	Nominal clause, subordinate clause, dependent clause

Exercise 76A: Clause Review

For each of the three sentences below, complete these steps:

1) Find and circle the dependent clauses. Label each one as adjective, adverb, or noun.
2) Identify and underline the subordinating word. (Look out for a missing subordinating word! When you find it, insert it and underline it.)
3) For the adverb and adjective clauses, draw a line from the subordinating word to the word modified. For the noun clauses, identify the part of the sentence that each clause is serving as.
4) Diagram the sentences on your own paper.

These sentences are taken from the introduction to *Women of the First Nations: Power, Wisdom, and Strength*, edited by Christine Miller and Patricia Chuchryk.

Compassion and strength are what we are, and we have translated these into every area of our existence because we have had to.

It is a fundamental right that parents determine their own children's culture and heritage, and what their own children learn.

Only those who know the true nature of despair and suffering can express compassion and understanding in all we do.

A restrictive modifying clause defines the word that it modifies. Removing the clause changes the essential meaning of the sentence.

A non-restrictive modifying clause describes the word that it modifies. Removing the clause doesn't change the essential meaning of the sentence.

In much of Asia, the day that a baby is born is considered to be its first birthday.

Wei's second birthday, which would have been considered his first in North America, was celebrated with a feast of long noodles and red-dyed eggs.

The movie, which lasted far too long, was quite boring.
I get very angry at people who talk during a movie.
My sister, who enjoys ballet and *muay thai* fighting, has gone to climb Denali.
She ran faster because there was a mountain lion behind her.

Only non-restrictive clauses should be set off by commas.

CORRECT
Hammurabi, who spent much of his life at war, created one of the first law codes.
INCORRECT
Hammurabi who spent much of his life at war created one of the first law codes.

CORRECT
The bricks that formed their city walls were made of mud.
INCORRECT
The bricks, that formed their city walls, were made of mud.

The king had no firm foundation on which to build. ____________________

The king had no firm foundation, on which to build. ____________________

Exercise 76B: Nonrestrictive Clauses and Missing Commas

In the following sentences, taken from *The Great Circle: A History of the First Nations* by Neil Philip, underline each dependent clause. Place commas around each nonrestrictive clause. Use the proofreader's mark: ^,. Leave sentences with restrictive clauses as they are.

This was the Tree of the Great Peace under which the Iroquoian peoples were to shelter and beneath which they were to cast all their weapons of war.

There was a time when our forefathers owned this great island.

When the whole tribe was united in the tribal circle the unity of the people was represented by a sacred cottonwood pole known as the Venerable Man.

The Venerable Man was kept in one of three Sacred Tents which contained all the sacred objects of the nation such as the White Buffalo Hide.

The Venerable Man had a basketwork of twigs that was filled with feathers around his middle.

Although Tenskwatawa was preaching peace his brother Tecumseh was preparing for war.

Tenskwatawa seems to have tried to obscure the fact that the Shawnee Creator was female.

But again and again his plans were disrupted by hotheads who could not wait until the agreed time before launching an attack.

While the news spread that Tecumseh was dead the Indians melted from the battlefield.

This was the end of the long struggle in which both Tecumseh's father and his beloved brother had lost their lives.

Exercise 76C: Restrictive Clauses and Unnecessary Commas

In the following sentences, taken from John Sugden's book *Tecumseh: A Life*, underline each dependent clause. Some dependent clauses may have other dependent clauses within them—double underline clauses within clauses!

Delete the incorrect commas that have been placed around restrictive clauses. Use proofreader's marks: ℓ. Leave sentences with nonrestrictive clauses as they are.

Mill Creek was a stream, that babbled into the Cumberland through pastures, in which the cows lowed.

On the upper Wabash, far from American settlements, they might make a home, where the bounty of the earth had not been degraded.

The shadows, that hung over Tecumseh's childhood, were cast by the relationships between the Shawnees and the advancing white frontier, which tried to push them aside.

There are stories, that Cheeseekau quarrelled with Watts about the propriety of the attack, but the details are hazy.

In the station the defenders fought like devils, making a defense, that deservedly entered the folklore of Tennessee.

But many Indians saw this as an issue, that went beyond land.

Tecumseh had gone to the Mid-Day, but Tenskwatawa remained at Prophetstown, where several hundred Kickapoos and Winnebagos camped to listen to him preach.

He hovered in the background, behind his brother, helping, where he could.

These Indians had no doubt that the land on the northwestern bank of the Wabash, which the Prophet had earmarked, was theirs.

The implicit obedience and respect, which the followers of Tecumseh pay to him, is really astonishing.

In later years he took the name Tenskwatawa, which meant the Open Door.

WEEK 20

Constructing Sentences

— LESSON 77 —

Constructing Sentences

Exercise 77A: Making Sentences out of Clauses and Phrases

The independent clauses below are listed in order and make up a story—but they're missing all their supporting pieces.

On your own paper, rewrite the story by attaching the dependent clauses and phrases in Lists 2 and 3 to the independent clauses in List 1 to make complete sentences. You may insert dependent clauses that act as adjectives or adverbs into the beginning, middle, or end of independent clauses (usually by putting them right before or after the word they modify), and you may change any capitalization or punctuation necessary. But do not add or delete words.

The first sentence has been constructed for you.

Crossing out each clause or phrase as you use it will help you not to repeat yourself!

List 1. Independent Clauses

~~They grew tired~~
They thought
So they all met, and with much noise prayed
Jove and all the gods laughed
Jove threw them a log and told them
The loud fall made a great splash and frightened the Frogs
It was a long time
Some finally swam
They jumped upon it, and saw
So they asked Jove
Jove sent a Stork
The Frogs did not like this new King either
They prayed again
They told him
But Jove would not grant their prayer
He told them
They had to pay the cost
Moral: Bear the ills

List 2. Dependent Clauses

when they saw
that you have
that you do not know
that it was no King but a log
that they would like a change
that they would like
as fast as he could
before they dared
that it would be their new King
that it had been their own wish
~~when the Frogs swam at ease~~
that it did not move but lay quite still
who had some life and would move
which started to eat the Frogs
because the Frogs had been vain and foolish
rather than wishing

List 3. Phrases

to have no King at all
for new misfortunes
of course
~~through the ponds and lakes~~
to Jove
~~in old times~~
to send a King
at their new King
of the log
of the bravest
to the log
this time
to take away the Stork
to Jove, king of the gods
to send them a king
to take a peep
at the Frogs
to keep them happy
in the lake
~~of their tame mode of life~~

FIRST SENTENCE

In old times, when the Frogs swam at ease through the ponds and lakes, they grew tired of their tame mode of life.

— LESSON 78 —

Simple Sentences
Complex Sentences

A sentence is a group of words that usually contains a subject and a predicate.
A sentence begins with a capital letter and ends with a punctuation mark.
A sentence contains a complete thought.

(The following sentences are from *The Cricket in Times Square* by George Selden.)

A mouse was looking at Mario.

Gradually the dirt that had collected on the insect fell away.

A complex sentence contains at least one subordinate clause.
A simple sentence contains one independent clause and no subordinate clauses.

But in all his days, and on all his journeys through the greatest city in the world, Tucker had never heard a sound quite like this one.

No matter what else is in a simple sentence, it will only have *one* subject-predicate set in it.

Then he folded a sheet of Kleenex, tucked it in the box, and put the cricket in it.

The thrumming of the rubber tires of automobiles, and the hooting of their horns, and the howling of their brakes made a great din.

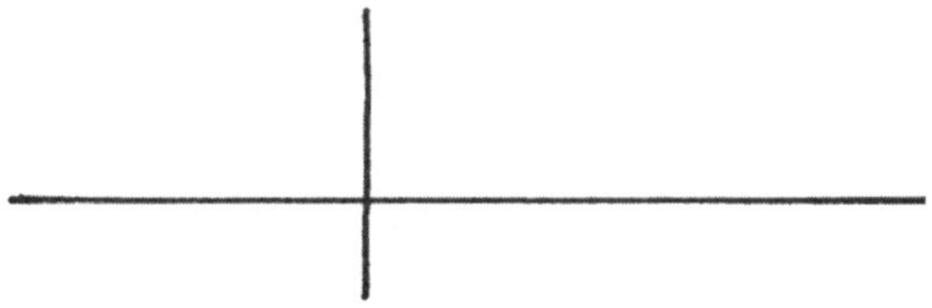

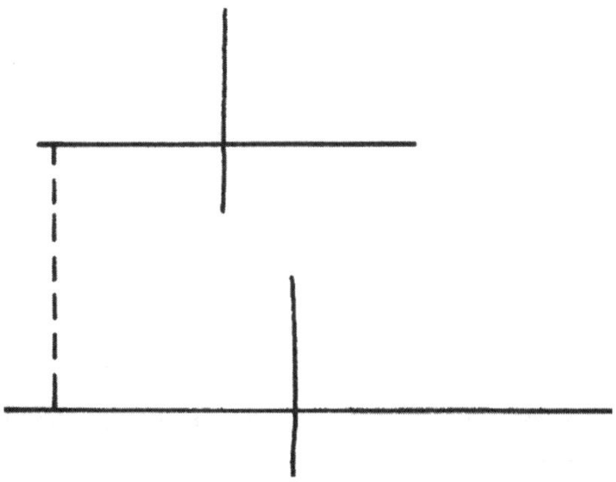

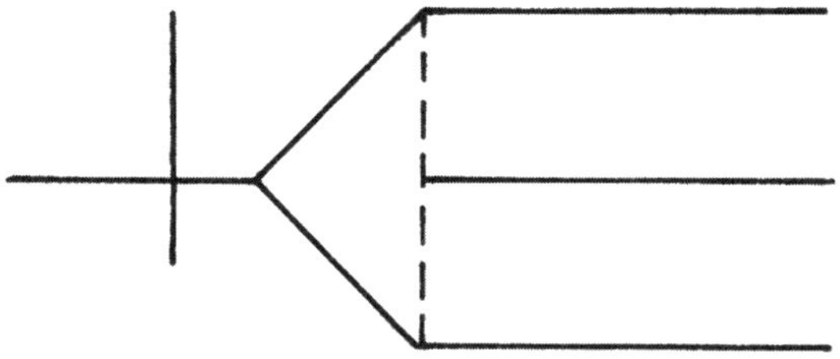

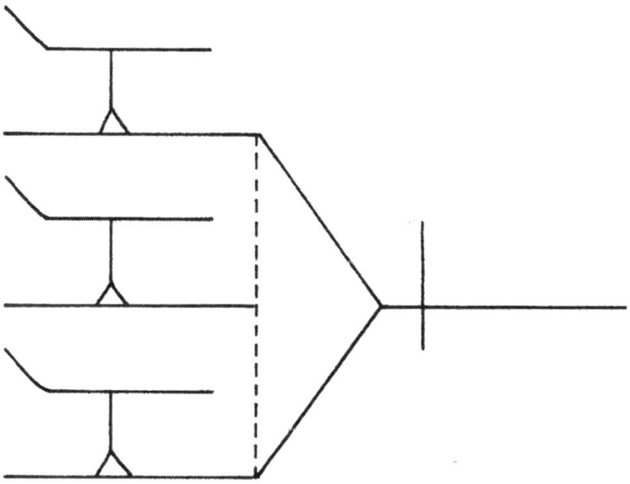

My closest friend and my greatest enemy met on the battlefield and fought bitterly.

Exercise 78A: Identifying Simple and Complex Sentences

In the sentences below, underline each subject once and each predicate twice. (Find the subjects and predicates in both independent and dependent clauses.) In the blank at the end of each sentence, write *S* for simple or *C* for complex.

These sentences are taken from *A World History of Art*, by Hugh Honour and John Fleming.

The word *style* is derived from *stylus*, the writing instrument of the ancient Romans, and was first used metaphorically for the various ways of public speaking appropriate for different occasions. __________

The style of a group, from which that of an individual initially derives, is a visual language with a vocabulary of forms and motifs. __________

Styles were the creation of painters, sculptors, architects, weavers, potters, and so on. __________

The categorization of styles has, however, been the work not of artists, but of writers who have tried to impose a semblance of order on infinitely diverse expressions of creative activity. __________

From the earliest times, artists used colored pigments to define images by outline. __________

Flesh tones look pale against a red background but reddish against yellow. __________

Painters in the West, from the fifteenth to the mid-nineteenth century, aimed for verisimilitude, an appearance of visual truth. __________

The French Impressionists did their best to forget what they knew of the local color of objects and record only their optical perceptions. __________

The development of systems of perspective coincided with the emergence of the peculiarly Western concept of a painting as a window onto a real or imaginary world. __________

Naturalism is usually contrasted with Idealism, which characterized the Neoclassical style of the late eighteenth century. __________

Exercise 78B: Forming Complex Sentences

On your own paper, rewrite each pair of simple sentences as a single complex sentence. The first is done for you.

- You will need to add a subordinating word to one of the sentences to turn it into a dependent clause.
- There may be more than one way to rewrite each sentence, as you can see in the example.
- In the last set of sentences, try to combine all three simple sentences into one complex sentence.

These are adapted from *Byzantine Art,* by Robin Cormack.

Icons were at the center of Byzantine art. They were seen and venerated by thousands.

Icons, which were at the center of Byzantine art, were seen and venerated by thousands.

Icons, which were seen and venerated by thousands, were at the center of Byzantine art.

Icons were at the center of a burning dispute. The dispute was over imagery and the Second Commandment.

Byzantine icons have a timeless quality. The timeless quality is a distinctive feature of icons.

The Byzantines called themselves Romans. The Byzantines kept the trappings and institutions of empire.

There are hundreds of icons in the Monastery of St. Catherine's. Some of the icons originally belonged to hermits and other chapels.

The period around 730 marks a significant time in the history of art. Around 730, three religions held the Old Testament in common. Around 730, those three religions rejected icons as graven images.

Exercise 78C: Diagramming

On your own paper, diagram the following four sentences. Beside each diagram, write the number of vertical lines dividing subjects from predicates, along with the label *S* for simple or *C* for complex.

The cat and her kittens put on their mittens to eat a Christmas pie.

When the pie was open, the birds began to sing.

The maid was in the garden, hanging out the clothes, when down came a blackbird and pecked off her nose.

Wynken, Blynken, and Nod sailed off in a wooden shoe, sailed on a river of crystal light, into a sea of dew.

— LESSON 79 —

Compound Sentences
Run-on Sentences
Comma Splice

(The sentences in this lesson are taken from *Pride and Prejudice* by Jane Austen.)

Bingley had never met with more pleasant people or prettier girls in his life; everybody had been most kind and attentive to him; there had been no formality, no stiffness; he had soon felt acquainted with all the room.

A compound sentence is a sentence with two or more independent clauses.

Everybody was surprised.
Darcy, after looking at her for a moment, turned silently away.

Everybody was surprised, and Darcy, after looking at her for a moment, turned silently away.

A coordinating conjunction joins similar or equal words or groups of words together.
and, or, nor, for, so, but, yet

Run-on sentence

INCORRECT (run-on sentences)

I ran quickly down the road, it was a very long way to the end.
The rabbit leaped out of the bushes, the children watched with eager interest.

CORRECT

I ran quickly down the road**, but** it was a very long way to the end.
The rabbit leaped out of the bushes, **and** the children watched with eager interest.

Comma Splice

Mr. Bennet, you are wanted immediately.

We are all in an uproar.

Mr. Bennet, you are wanted immediately; we are all in an uproar.

colon :

semicolon ;

The envelope contained a sheet of elegant, little, hot-pressed paper, well covered with a lady's fair, flowing hand.

Elizabeth saw her sister's countenance change as she read it.

The envelope contained a sheet of elegant, little, hot-pressed paper, well covered with a lady's fair, flowing hand; and Elizabeth saw her sister's countenance change as she read it.

The independent clauses of a compound sentence must be joined by a comma and a coordinating conjunction, a semicolon, or a semicolon and a coordinating conjunction. They cannot be joined by a comma alone.

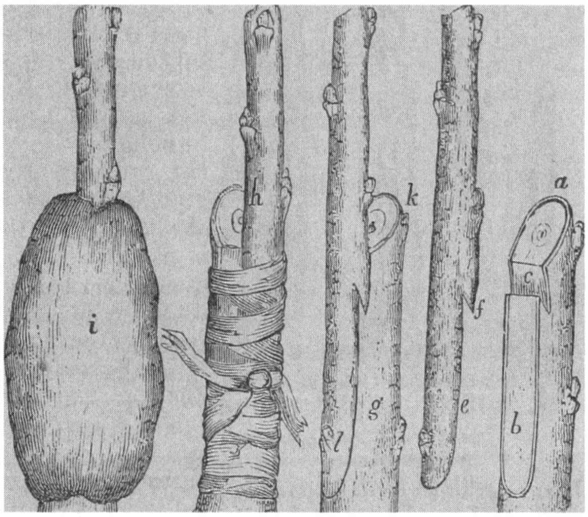

An illustration of splicing from A. J. Downing's 1889 manual *The Fruits and Fruit Trees of America*

Mr. Collins was not agreeable; his society was irksome, and his attachment to her must be imaginary.

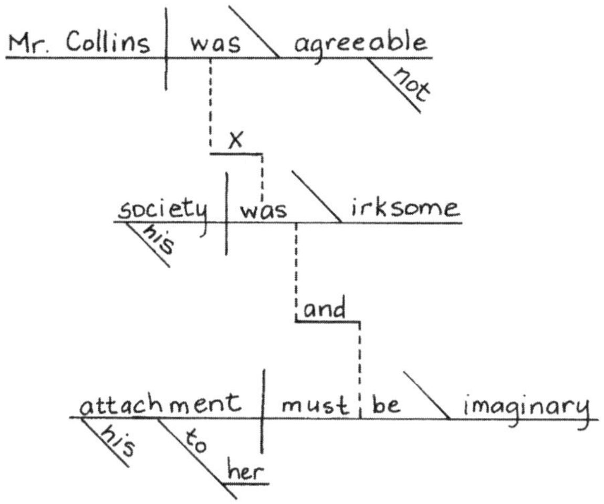

Mr. Collins is a conceited, pompous, narrow-minded, silly man; you know it, and you shall not defend Charlotte Lucas.

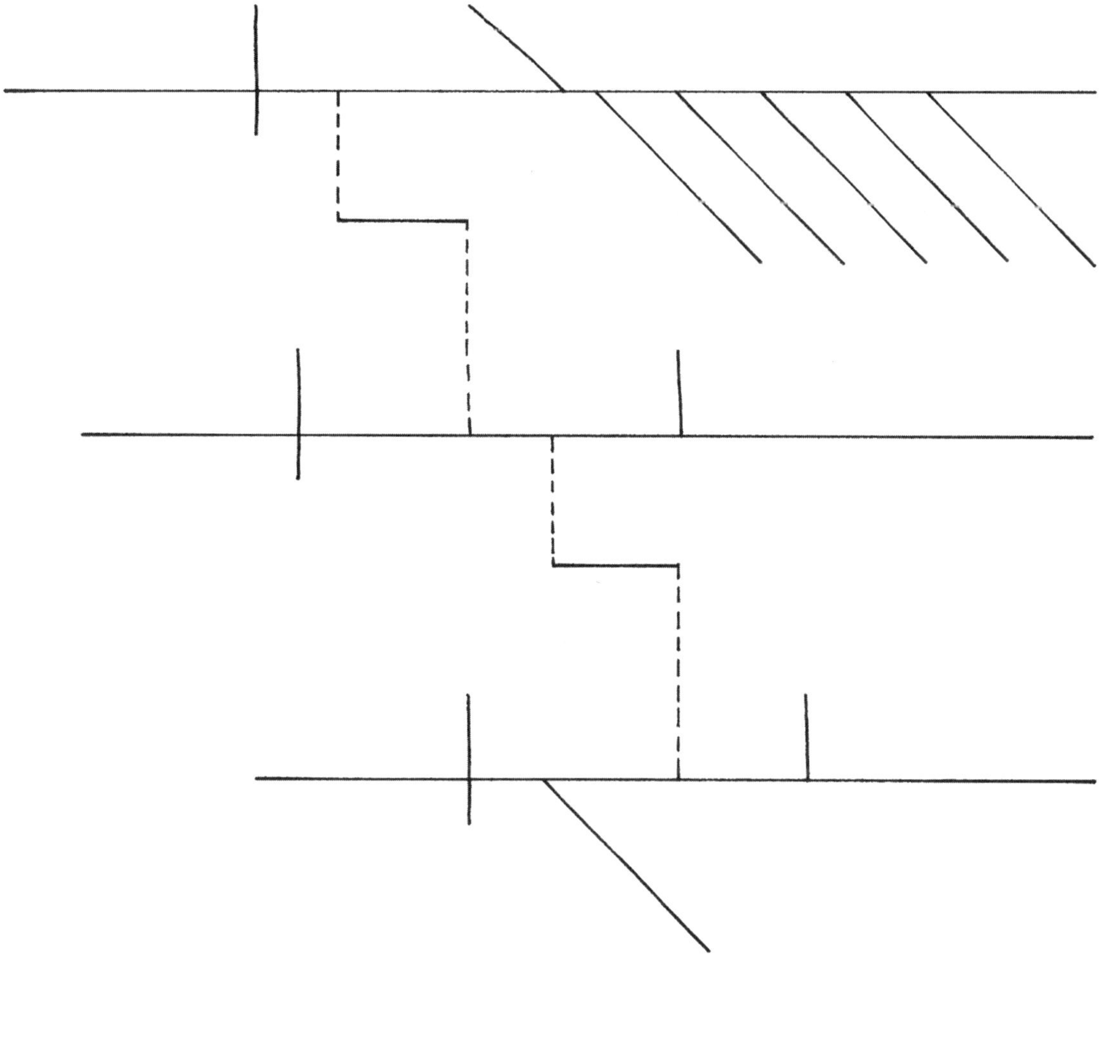

Coordinating Conjunction	Meaning/Function	Example
and	simply *in addition to*	I ran and he ran.
or	presents alternatives	He can teach or his assistant can teach.
nor	presents negative alternatives	He did not work, nor did he sleep.
for	*because*	I sang loudly, for I was happy.
so	showing results	He ate too much, so his stomach hurt.
but	*despite that*	I ran ten miles, but I wasn't tired.
yet	*nevertheless*	I had little money, yet I was content.

Exercise 79A: Forming Compound Sentences

Choose at least one independent clause from Column 1 and at least one independent clause from Column 2. Using correct punctuation and adding coordinating conjunctions as needed, combine the clauses into a compound sentence. (You may use more than two clauses, as long as your sentence makes sense!) Write your new compound sentences on your own paper. Use every clause at least once.

These clauses are taken from compound sentences written by A. A. Milne about Winnie-the-Pooh!

Column 1	**Column 2**
He climbed.	That will deceive them.
He put his head between his paws.	I have come to a very important decision.
I shall try to look like a small black cloud.	You missed the balloon.
Winnie-the-Pooh went to a very muddy place.	Winnie-the-Pooh floated down to the ground.
I have just been thinking.	Rabbit pulled and pulled and pulled.
You didn't exactly miss.	He climbed.
The air came slowly out of the balloon.	He thought very carefully.
Pooh Bear stretched out a paw.	He rolled until he was black all over.
	He sang a little song to himself.

Exercise 79B: Correcting Run-on Sentences (Comma Splices)

Using proofreader's marks (^ to insert a coordinating conjunction, ^, to insert a comma, ^; to insert a semicolon), correct each of the run-on sentences below.

These are taken from *The Enchanted Places: A Childhood Memoir*, by Christopher Milne (the son of Winnie-the-Pooh creator A. A. Milne).

Organ grinders always made me feel sad, I used to throw them a penny.

There was a large chest by the window, this was opened for me I climbed inside while my father finished his marmalade and my mother ate her apple.

We sat next to each other in class while Miss Walters did her best to teach us this and that mostly we got it wrong.

She and I inevitably drifted apart as we grew older, she and my parents remained devoted to each other, until I was twenty-five my mother cherished fond hopes that one day we would marry.

The Christopher Robin who appears in so many of the poems is not always me this is where my name came into its own it was a wonderful name for writing poetry around.

Sometimes my father is using my name to describe something I did sometimes he is borrowing it to describe something he did as a child sometimes he is using it to describe something that any child might have done.

On the whole it doesn't greatly matter which of the two of us did what I'm happy to accept responsibility.

Exercise 79C: Diagramming

On your own paper, diagram every word of the following sentences from A. A. Milne's stories about Winnie-the-Pooh.

The wind was behind them now, so they didn't have to shout.

There are twelve pots of honey in my cupboard, and they've been calling to me for hours.

They walked off together; and for a long time Piglet said nothing, and then suddenly he made a squeaky noise.

Pooh hasn't much Brain, but he never comes to any harm; he does silly things and they turn out right.

— LESSON 80 —

Compound Sentences

Compound-Complex Sentences

Clauses with Understood Elements

The rabbit jumped, and the lion roared, and the giraffe ambled.

The boy **who had the tickets** boarded the train, but his brother decided to hail a taxi instead; their mother knew **that they would both arrive home by bedtime**.

A compound-complex sentence is made up of two or more independent clauses, at least one of which is a complex sentence.

He was the proudest, most disagreeable man in the world, and everybody hoped that he would never come there again.

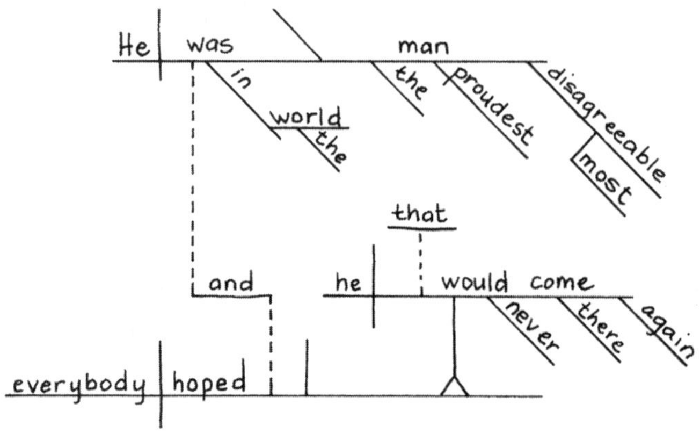

She could not recover from the surprise of what had happened; it was impossible to think of anything else; and, totally indisposed for employment, she resolved, soon after breakfast, to indulge herself in air and exercise.

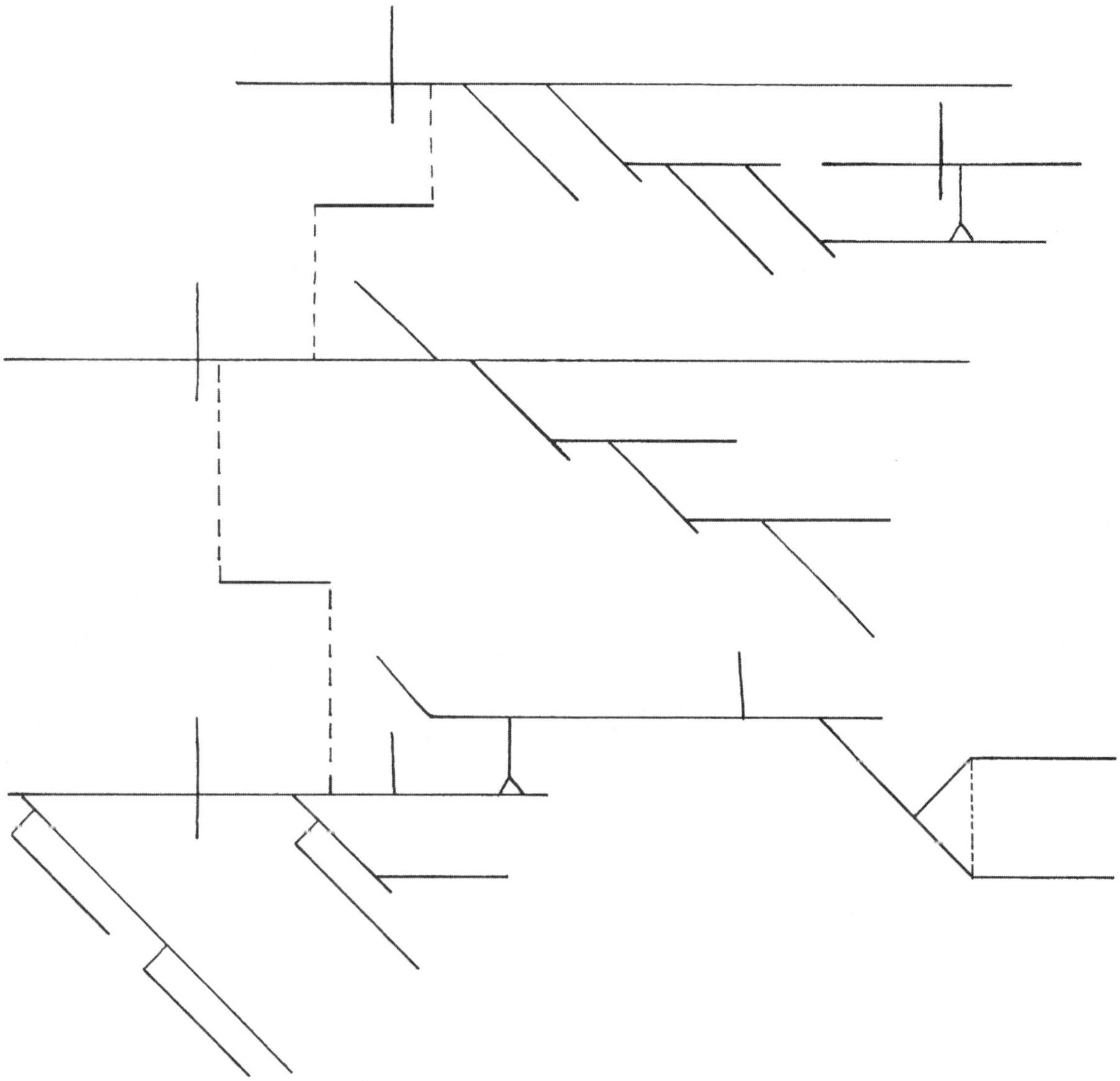

That was the weirdest thing I have ever seen.

The apples I bought yesterday had just been picked.

The speech he made was short and powerful.

He is vain, and you know he is not a sensible man.

He was at the same time haughty, reserved, and fastidious, and his manners, although well-bred, were not inviting.

The situation that troubled her remained the same, her peace equally disturbed by the circumstances.

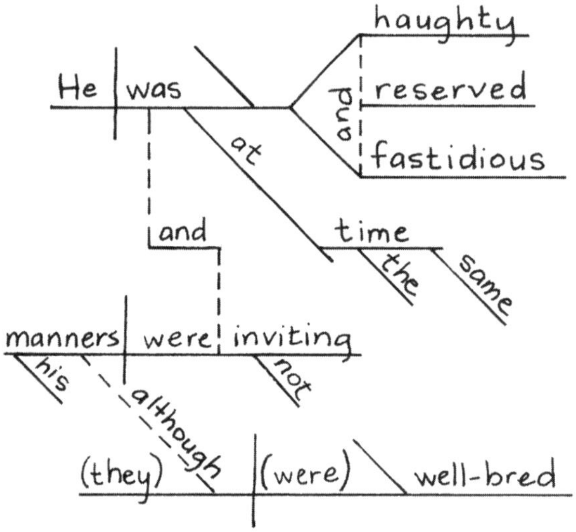

Exercise 80A: Analyzing Complex-Compound Sentences

The sentences below are all complex-compound sentences. For each sentence, carry out the following steps:

a) Cross out each prepositional phrase.
b) Circle any dependent clauses. Label them as *ADJ*, *ADV*, or *NOUN*. Draw a line from adjective and adverb clauses to the word modified. Label noun clauses with the part of the sentence that they function as.
c) Underline the subject of each independent clause once and the predicate twice.
d) Draw a vertical line between each simple and/or complex sentence.
e) Insert missing words (if any).

The first sentence has been done for you. Be careful—some dependent clauses may be within other dependent clauses!

These sentences are taken from a novel called *The Enchanted April*, by Elizabeth von Arnim. She was a well-known English writer, married to a Prussian nobleman, who lived in the late nineteenth and early twentieth centuries. Her books were extremely popular during her lifetime, but although they are still studied by critics, they are less read now by the general public.

<u>She</u> <u>had slept</u> ~~like a baby~~, and <u>had woken</u> up confident; | <u>she</u> <u>had found</u> (that) [there was nothing she wished to say ~~in her morning prayer~~, ~~except Thank you~~.] NOUN DO

Down the stone steps on either side were periwinkles in full flower, and she could now see what it was that had caught at her the night before and brushed, wet and scented, across her face.

No sounds were to be heard in the house, so she supposed it was very early, yet she felt as if she had slept a long while—so completely rested, so perfectly content.

Peering out they could see they were still in the village street, with small dark houses each side; and Beppo, throwing the reins over the horse's back as if completely confident this time that he would not go any farther, got down off his box.

Mrs. Wilkins had never yet spoken to Mrs. Arbuthnot, who belonged to one of the various church sets, and who analysed, classified, divided and registered the poor; she and Mr. Wilkins, when they did go out, went to the parties of impressionist painters, of whom in Hampstead there were many.

Across the bay the lovely mountains, exquisitely different in colour, were asleep too in the light; and underneath her window, at the bottom of the flower-starred grass slope from which the wall of the castle rose up, was a great cypress, cutting through the delicate blues and violets and rose-colours of the mountains and the sea like a great black sword.

Exercise 80B: Constructing Complex-Compound Sentences

From each set of independent clauses, construct a single complex-compound sentence. You may turn any of the clauses into dependent clauses by adding subordinating words, inserting any other words necessary, omitting unnecessary words, and making any other needed changes, but try to keep the original meaning of each clause. You must use every clause in the set!

You may turn a clause into a prepositional phrase or another form, as long as your resulting sentence has at least two independent clauses and one dependent clause and contains all of the information in the listed clauses.

Write your new sentences on your own paper. The first has been done for you.

The Iguana Research and Breeding Station and Visitors' Center was founded in 1997.

It is on the island of Utila.

Utila is one of the Bay Islands in Honduras.

The Station helps preserve the black iguana.

The black iguana lives in mangrove forests.

It is the only iguana native to mangrove forests.

The Iguana Research and Breeding Station and Visitors' Center, founded in 1997 on the Honduran Bay Island known as Utila, helps preserve the black iguana; the black iguana, which lives in mangrove forests, is the only iguana native to mangroves.

Columbus claimed Honduras for Spain in 1504.

Before 1504, the islands near Honduras were occupied by Native American groups.

Honduras did not have very much gold or other valuable minerals.

Because of the lack of minerals, the Spanish didn't pay very much attention to the islands at first.

The Spanish conquistador Cristóbal de Olid claimed Honduras for himself in 1523.

The Spanish conquistador Hernán Cortés fought against de Olid between 1524 and 1526.

In September of 1821, the people of Mexico declared independence from the Spanish Empire.

The islands of Honduras joined with the new Mexican Empire.

The emperor of this new Mexican Empire was an army officer named Augustín de Iturbide.

He became Emperor Augustín I of Mexico.

He also became the emperor of Honduras.

His empire only lasted until 1823.

In 1969, El Salvador and Honduras fought a five-day war.
It became known as the Football War.
The two countries had disagreed about the border between them.
The president of Honduras had also objected to immigrants coming from El Salvador into Honduras.
Football (soccer) teams from the two countries played preliminary matches to qualify for the World Cup.
Fans rioted.
Then El Salvador invaded Honduras.

In 1998, Hurricane Mitch caused over 11,000 deaths in Central America.
7,000 of those deaths were in Honduras.
Hurricane Mitch was a Category 5 storm with winds of up to 180 mph.
Some areas of Honduras received 75 inches of rain.
A million Hondurans were left homeless.
According to the president of Honduras, Carlos Flores, the hurricane wiped out fifty years of progress in his country.

Exercise 80C: Diagramming

On your own paper, diagram the following epigrams. (Epigram: a short, clever saying)

Next to your diagram, label each sentence as compound (*C*), complex (*CX*), or compound-complex (*CCX*).

You cannot do a kindness too soon, for you never know how soon it will be too late.

—Ralph Waldo Emerson

It's a recession when your neighbor loses his job; it's a depression when you lose yours.

—Harry S. Truman

When a true genius appears, you can know him by this sign: that all the dunces are in a confederacy against him.

—Jonathan Swift

Love is the strongest force the world possesses, and yet it is the humblest imaginable.

—Mahatma Gandhi

WEEK 21

Conditions

— LESSON 81 —

Helping Verbs
Tense and Voice
Modal Verbs

Helping Verbs
am, is, are, was, were
be, being, been
have, has, had
do, does, did
shall, will, should, would, may, might, must
can, could

In a sentence with an active verb, the subject performs the action.
In a sentence with a passive verb, the subject receives the action.

The progressive past tense uses the helping verbs *was* and *were*.
The progressive past passive voice uses the helping verbs *was/were being.*
The progressive present tense uses the helping verbs *am, is,* and *are*.
The progressive present passive voice uses the helping verbs *is/are being.*
The progressive future tense uses the helping verbs *will* and *be*.
The progressive future passive voice uses the helping verbs *will be being.*

Perfect past verbs describe an action that was finished in the past before another action began.
The active voice uses the helping verb *had.*
The passive voice uses the helping verbs *had been.*
Perfect present verbs describe an action that was completed before the present moment.
The active voice uses the helping verb *have.*
The passive voice uses the helping verbs *has/have been.*
Perfect future verbs describe an action that will be finished in the future before another action begins.
The active voice uses the helping verb *will have.*
The passive voice uses the helping verbs *will have been.*

NOTE: Shall and will are different forms of the same verb.

I do not believe in aliens.

He does not believe in aliens.

We did not believe in aliens (until they landed).

Do you believe in aliens?
Does he believe in aliens?
Did we believe in aliens (after they landed)?

I do too believe in aliens!
He does believe in aliens!
We did believe in aliens (once they had landed)!

Use the helping verbs *do, does,* and *did* to form negatives, ask questions, and provide emphasis.

	SIMPLE PRESENT		**SIMPLE PRESENT EMPHATIC**	
First person	I believe	we believe	I do believe	we do believe
Second person	you believe	you believe	you do believe	you do believe
Third person	he, she, it believes	they believe	he, she, it does believe	they do believe

	SIMPLE PAST		**SIMPLE PAST EMPHATIC**	
First person	I believed	we believed	I did believe	we did believe
Second person	you believed	you believed	you did believe	you did believe
Third person	he, she, it believed	they believed	he, she, it did believe	they did believe

We should be prepared for the arrival of alien spacecraft.
On earth, a Martian would weigh three times more than on Mars.
Strange creatures may visit Earth in our lifetime.
Alien invaders might want to conquer us.
The arrival of aliens must change our world.
We can scarcely imagine what that change will be.
We could find out that the aliens are friendly.

Modal verbs express situations that have not actually happened.
would, can, could, may, might: **possibility**
must, should: **obligation**
may: **permission**
can: **ability**

I would love to go eat a huge cheeseburger.
I can either sleep or eat.
I could probably finish my work by supper.
I may go down to the hamburger stand on the boardwalk.

I might get a burger with onions and Swiss cheese.

I must stop eating this cheeseburger!
I really should eat more vegetables.

Yes, you may eat that burger!

I can exercise self-control!

SIMPLE PRESENT MODAL		
First person	I could eat	We could eat
Second person	You could eat	You could eat
Third person	He could eat	They could eat

PERFECT PRESENT MODAL		
First person	I should have eaten	We should have eaten
Second person	You should have eaten	You should have eaten
Third person	She should have eaten	They should have eaten

I should've finished my work early; I could've finished it, if I'd had peace and quiet; I would've finished it, if everyone hadn't kept interrupting me.

Exercise 81A: Using *Do, Does,* and *Did*

On your own paper, rewrite each sentence, putting it into the form described in brackets. Use the appropriate form of the helping verb along with any interrogatives or negatives necessary. Don't forget that you may have to change the form of the verb! The first one is done for you.

These sentences are taken from the alien invasion novel *The Forge of God,* by Greg Bear.

You think of the President's statement that aliens have landed and are intent on destroying earth. [Change into a question.]

What do you think of the President's statement that aliens have landed and are intent on destroying earth?

The Guest's three golden-yellow eyes stared at him without blinking. [Provide emphasis.]

They told you why your world was being destroyed. [Change into a question.]

You had to call the Air Force. [Change into a question.]

I object. [Turn into a negative statement.]

We knew what was happening. [Turn into a negative statement.]

You had children. [Change into a question.]

The spiders got through airport security. [Change into a question.]

You have a way with words. [Provide emphasis.]

Exercise 81B: Modal Verbs

Fill in the blanks below with an appropriate helping verb (*should, would, may, might, must, can, could*) to form a modal verb. There may be more than one correct answer for each sentence. Use each helping verb at least once.

These sentences are taken from John Wyndham's 1957 novel *The Midwich Cuckoos*—the story of a different sort of alien invasion! After you finish the exercise, be sure to read the original sentences in the Answer Key.

And why Midwich ________________ have been singled out in preference to any one of a thousand other villages for the curious event of the 26th of September seems likely to remain a mystery for ever.

But we ________________ not simply be silent and secretive, as if we were concealing something. We ________________ make it seem that there is nothing unusual in Midwich at all.

Babies ________________ be joy and fun.

I ________________ feel my scalp prickling, and my hair beginning to rise.

Therefore you ________________ take her away without the baby. If you ____________ persuade her to that, we ______________ arrange to have it excellently looked after here.

Do your utmost to make her forget this changeling in order that she ________________ have a normal life.

That's the subconscious for you—trying to pass off the uncomfortable by telling me that the peculiarities ________________ diminish as the Children grew older.

After all, if we were to discover dangerous wild animals in our midst our duty ________ be clear.

However interesting, scientifically, the Children ________________ have been during the first year of their lives there was little about them during that time to cause further misgiving.

The only possible compromise ________________ be for you to surrender to the baby's challenge, and come to live here, too.

I think he ________________ be able to help us, if he's willing.

We ___________________ get this thing out in the open, and relieve the tension.

The only thing that ___________________ beat us is something with a still better brain.

I told the Children I ___________________ see very little hope of getting anyone to listen to me seriously.

No one there ___________________ have been warned without the Children getting to know of it.

Exercise 81C: Verb Tense and Voice

For each sentence below, underline each verb phrase (in both dependent and independent clauses) and identify the tense and voice of the verb. For state-of-being verbs which are neither active nor passive in voice, identify the tense and write *state-of-being.* Mark modal verbs as *perfect past modal* or *simple present modal.* The first sentence is done for you.

These sentences are taken from H. G. Wells's classic science fiction novel *The First Men in the Moon.*

Perfect past, active
Why had we come to the moon?

But curiously enough he seemed to be labouring under a conviction that I was either dead in the moon crater or lost in the deep of space.

Immediately the train of thought that our conversation had suggested must have resumed its sway.

Where there are minds they will have something similar—even though they have been evolved on different planets.

I tried to imagine what could have happened to him.

I have already brought you farther than I should have done.

He had had a fever, but it had left no bad effects.

I infer rather than learn from his narrative that he was captured by the mooncalf herds under the direction of these other Selenites who "have larger brain cases (heads?) and very much shorter legs."

A wind was blowing down the shaft, and far above I fancy I heard, growing fainter and fainter, the bellowing of the mooncalves that were being driven down again from their evening pasturage on the exterior.

It was quite clear to me that what I had to do was to get back to earth, but as far as I could see I was drifting away from it.

Our attention was taken up by the movements and attitudes of the Selenites immediately about us, and by the necessity of controlling our motion, lest we should startle and alarm them and ourselves by some excessive stride.

— LESSON 82 —

Conditional Sentences
The Condition Clause
The Consequence Clause

(The following sentences are from *The Phantom Tollbooth* by Norton Juster.)

If you have any more questions, please ask the giant.

If one is right, then ten are ten times as right.

If you are not perfectly satisfied, your wasted time will be refunded.

A condition is a circumstance that restricts, limits, or modifies.

Snow only falls when three conditions are met: the temperature up high is freezing, the temperature at ground level is freezing, and there are water droplets in the air.

A condition clause describes a circumstance that has not yet happened.

A consequence clause describes the results that will take place if the condition clause happens.

Unless it gets warmer, I will stay inside.

I will not go for a walk if it remains this cold.

When the temperature reaches 70 degrees, I will go outside.

Should it rain, I will not come.

Had he been fired, he could have left immediately.

Refuse my conditions, and I will become your enemy!

A conditional sentence expresses the conditions under which an action may take place. It contains a condition clause and a consequence clause.

CONDITION CONSEQUENCE
If you have any more questions, please ask the giant. ____________________

CONDITION CONSEQUENCE
If one is right, then ten are ten times as right. ____________________

CONDITION CONSEQUENCE
If you are not perfectly satisfied, your wasted time will be refunded. ____________________

First conditional sentences express circumstances that might actually happen.

The predicate of the condition clause is in a ________________________ tense.

The predicate of the consequence clause is an ________________________ or is in a

________________________ or ________________________ tense.

If only Rhyme and Reason were here, things would improve.

If you walked as fast as possible and looked at nothing but your shoes, you would arrive at your destination more quickly.

Second conditional sentences express circumstances that are contrary to reality.

The predicate of the condition clause is in a ________________________ tense.

The predicate of the consequence clause is in the __________________________ tense.

Modal verbs express situations that have not actually happened.

Simple Present

I would improve	We would improve
You would improve	You would improve
He would improve	They would improve

Perfect Past

I could have arrived	We could have arrived
You could have arrived	You could have arrived
She could have arrived	They could have arrived

If we had told you then, you might not have gone.

If the kingdom had been divided equally, both sons would now rule as kings.

Third conditional sentences express past circumstances that never happened.

The predicate of the condition clause is in the __________________________ tense.

The predicate of the consequence clause is in the __________________________ or

__________________________ tense.

Exercise 82A: Identifying Conditional Sentences

Some of the sentences in this exercise are conditional sentences—and others are not! Identify each conditional sentence by writing a *C* in the margin. For each conditional sentence, label the clauses as *condition* or *consequence*.

I promise you all you wish, if you will but bring my ball back again.

The dress pleased the Bride so well that she thought it might do for her wedding-dress, and asked if it was for sale.

The little brother did not drink, although he was so thirsty.

Unless he could point out the thief, he himself should be looked upon as guilty and should be executed.

Although she was many thousand times better off here than at home, still she had a longing to be there.

As soon as the mother heard how she had come by such great riches, she was anxious for the same good fortune.

Every one wanted to have a new coat made by the little tailor, whose importance increased daily.

Nothing can save you, unless you will promise to give me for mine own what first meets you on your return home.

She remained with them while the wedding-feast lasted, and then went back again to the forest.

If you forget to throw down the nut, he will let you fall into the sea.

Exercise 82B: Tense in Conditional Sentences

Fill in each blank below with the correct tense and form of the verb in brackets. Some sentences may have more than one possible correct answer.

First conditional sentences

If I ____________________ [negative form of *study*] a little harder for this test, I __________ [get] a very bad grade.

If you ____________________ [negative form of *manage*] to buy a ticket at the box office, __________________ [go] on home and I ____________________ [meet] you there.

Unless he ____________________ [run] faster, he ____________________ [miss] his flight to Antarctica.

If you ____________________ [tell] me where to turn, we ____________________ [find] the haunted corn maze much faster!

There ______________________ [state-of-being] no point in the chef putting all that chocolate frosting on the cake, unless he ______________________ [intend] to serve it to chocolate fanatics.

Second conditional sentences

If the barn ________________ [burn] down, the zombies ________________ [state-of-being] in flames.

If the elephant ____________ [see] the mouse run across the floor, we ________________ [know] it.

If I ____________________ [know] the answer, I ____________________ [write] it down.

If the sun ______________ [explode], we ______________ [state-of-being] very, very cold.

Third conditional sentences

If Alice ____________________ [ate] more of the mushroom, she ____________________ [disappear] altogether.

If the space lasers ____________________ [destroy] the asteroid headed for earth, we ____________________ [negative form of *prepare*] for the end of the world.

If the zombies ____________________ [negative of *overrun*] Atlanta, the CDC ___________ [negative of *explode*] into a giant fireball.

If Gollum ____________________ [decide] to give up the ring willingly, Frodo __________ [have] ten fingers.

Exercise 82C: Diagramming

On your own paper, diagram these sentences, taken from J. R. R. Tolkien's *The Return of the King*. A conditional clause should be diagrammed like any other dependent clause.

He'd spot me, pretty quick, if I put the Ring on now, in Mordor.

> **Note to Student:** because Sam, the speaker, is using colloquial language, *quick* is serving as an adverb. If you were writing formally, it would need to be *quickly*.

But if I should return, think better of me!

If you had waited at Orthanc, you would have seen him, and he would have shown you wisdom and mercy.

The Company halted, and there was not a heart among them that did not quail, unless it were the heart of Legolas of the Elves, for whom the ghosts of Men have no terror.

— LESSON 83 —

Conditional Sentences

The Subjunctive

First conditional sentences express circumstances that might actually happen.
The predicate of the condition clause is in a present tense.
The predicate of the consequence clause is in an imperative, present or future tense.

If we surrender and I return with you, will you promise not to hurt this man?

So bow down to her if you want, bow to her.

If she is otherwise when I find her, I shall be very put out.

Unless I am wrong (and I am never wrong), they are headed dead into the fire swamp.

Second conditional sentences express circumstances that are contrary to reality.
The predicate of the condition clause is in a past tense.
The predicate of the consequence clause is in the simple present modal tense.

I would not say such things if I were you!

If I had a month to plan, maybe I could come up with something.

If we only had a wheelbarrow, that would be something.

Third conditional sentences express past circumstances that never happened.
The predicate of the condition clause is in the perfect past tense.
The predicate of the consequence clause is in the perfect present modal or simple present modal tense.

But they would have killed Westley, if I hadn't done it.

CONTRARY TO FACT	FACT
If we surrender	We surrender.
If you want	We want.
If she is	She is.
If I were	I was.
If we had	We had.

Subjunctive verbs express situations that are unreal, wished for, or uncertain.
Indicative verbs affirm or declare what actually is.

I eat gingerbread men.

If I eat too many gingerbread men, I will not want any dinner.

The three little pigs build houses.

If the three little pigs build straw houses, the wolf will blow them all down.

INDICATIVE SIMPLE PAST		
First person	I was	we were
Second person	you were	you were

Third person	he, she, it was	they were

SUBJUNCTIVE SIMPLE PAST		
First person	I were	we were
Second person	you were	you were
Third person	he, she, it were	they were

CORRECT I would not say such things if I were you!
INCORRECT I would not say such things if I was you!

CORRECT I was cold.
CORRECT If I were cold, I would put on a hat.
INCORRECT If I was cold, I would put on a hat.

He was smart.

If he _________ smart, he would go immediately.

I insist that she leave the door open.

I recommend that he arrive early.

The professor asked that the student read out loud.

	INDICATIVE SIMPLE PRESENT		**SUBJUNCTIVE SIMPLE PRESENT**	
First person	I leave	we leave	I leave	we leave
Second person	you leave	you leave	you leave	you leave
Third person	he, she, it leaves	they leave	he, she, it leave	they leave

It is vital that a life guard ____________ the children swim. [subjunctive present of *watch*]

The life guard ____________________ the children swim. [indicative present of *watch*]

The woman demanded that the mechanic __________ her car. [subjunctive present of *fix*]

The mechanic _________________ her car. [indicative present of *fix*]

My mother suggested that my sister ____________ to bed early. [subjunctive present of *go*]

My sister _______________ to bed early. [indicative present of *go*]

Exercise 83A: Subjunctive Forms in Lines of Poetry

Fill in each blank with the correct state-of-being verb.

But O that I ______________ young again
And held her in my arms.
—William Butler Yeats, "Politics"

She bid me take life easy,
as the grass grows on the weirs;
But I ______________ young and foolish,
and now ______________ full of tears.
—William Butler Yeats, "Down By the Salley Gardens"

I would I ______________ alive again
To kiss the fingers of the rain,
—Edna St. Vincent Millay, "Renascence"

If I ______________ a shepherd, I would bring a lamb;
If I ______________ a Wise Man, I would do my part;
—Christina Rossetti, "In the Bleak Midwinter"

So I went on softly from the glade,
And left her behind me throwing her shade,
As if she ______________ indeed an apparition—
—Thomas Hardy, "The Shadow on the Stone"

That's my last Duchess painted on the wall,
Looking as if she ______________ alive.
—Robert Browning, "My Last Duchess"

So then he asked me if I knew the Viceroy.
I said I did. And I asked the Captain,
"If he ______________ Captain Drake himself and no other?"
—Ernesto Cardenal, "Drake in the Southern Sea," trans. Thomas Merton

Exercise 83B: Correct Verb Forms in Complex Sentences

In each pair of verb forms, cross out the incorrect form. These sentences are from *All Creatures Great and Small,* by James Herriot.

Boardman's features seemed to soften and a light came into his eyes as though he (was / were) talking more to himself than to me.

She (wasn't / weren't) getting to her feet in the normal way of dogs, it was as though she (was / were) being lifted up by strings somewhere in the ceiling, the legs straightening almost imperceptibly, the body rigid, every hair bristling.

One thing (was / were) sure—she (was / were) going to come at me any second, and I blessed the luck that had made me stand right by the door.

The others followed suit immediately and though we danced about and waved our arms they ran past us as if we (wasn't / weren't) there.

Siegfried had fallen back and (was / were) staring at the ceiling with feverish eyes. His lips moved feebly as though he (was / were) praying.

When he (was / were) caught in bed he usually scored a few points by being half way through his breakfast before his brother came in.

It (was / were) old-fashioned treatment but effective. By the time I (was / were) half way down the pint pot I felt as though I (was / were) being consumed by fire.

The farmer lifted it as if it (was / were) a whippet dog and (lay / laid) it by its mother's head.

It hadn't been a happy episode but at least I did (feel / felt) a certain peace in the knowledge that there (was / were) no more doubts. I knew what (was / were) wrong, I knew that there (was / were) no hope.

As I came into the operating room I saw that Siegfried (has / had) a patient on the table. He (was / were) thoughtfully stroking the head of an elderly and rather woebegone border terrier.

— LESSON 84 —

Conditional Sentences
The Subjunctive
Moods of Verbs
Subjunctive Forms Using *Be*

Tense
A simple verb simply tells whether an action takes place in the past, present, or future.
A progressive verb describes an ongoing or continuous action.

A perfect verb describes an action which has been completed before another action takes place.

The air was bracing, yet with a cold edge which made the travelers grateful for the cloaks

Medwyn had given them.

Voice
In a sentence with an active verb, the subject performs the action.
In a sentence with a passive verb, the subject receives the action.

It is not given to men to know the ends of their journeys.

Mood
Indicative verbs express real actions.
Subjunctive verbs express unreal actions.
Imperative verbs express intended actions.
Modal verbs express possible actions.

"Drink," the stranger said again, while Taran took the flask dubiously. "You look as

though I were trying to poison you."

There can be no victory over the Cauldron-Born, but with luck, we can hold.

First conditional sentences express circumstances that might actually happen.
The predicate of the condition clause is in a present tense.
The predicate of the consequence clause is an imperative, present or future tense.

Unless I am wrong (and I am never wrong), they are headed dead into the fire swamp.

Second conditional sentences express circumstances that are contrary to reality.
The predicate of the condition clause is in a past tense.
The predicate of the consequence clause is in the simple present modal tense.

If we only had a wheelbarrow, that would be something.

Third conditional sentences express past circumstances that never happened.
The predicate of the condition clause is in the perfect past tense.
The predicate of the consequence clause is in the perfect present modal or simple present modal tense.

But they would have killed Westley, if I hadn't done it.

SIMPLE PAST INDICATIVE
He left me behind.

SIMPLE PAST SUBJUNCTIVE SIMPLE PRESENT MODAL
If he left me behind, I would feel quite upset.

	INDICATIVE PRESENT (SIMPLE)		**SUBJUNCTIVE PRESENT (SIMPLE)**	
First person	I leave	we leave	I leave	we leave
Second person	you leave	you leave	you leave	you leave
Third person	he, she, it leaves	they leave	he, she, it **leave**	they leave

INDICATIVE He leaves at noon.
SUBJUNCTIVE It's important that he leave at noon.

	INDICATIVE PAST (SIMPLE)		**SUBJUNCTIVE PAST (SIMPLE)**	
First person	I was	we were	I were	we were
Second person	you were	you were	you were	you were
Third person	he, she, it was	they were	he, she, it were	they were

SIMPLE PRESENT MODAL PAST SUBJUNCTIVE
I <u>would</u> not <u>say</u> such things if I <u>were</u> you!

SIMPLE PRESENT INDICATIVE SIMPLE PAST SUBJUNCTIVE
CORRECT You look as though I were trying to poison you.

SIMPLE PRESENT INDICATIVE SIMPLE PAST INDICATIVE
INCORRECT You look as though I was trying to poison you.

I wish he were here.

A trace of a smile appeared on his face, as though he were savoring something pleasant.

	INDICATIVE PRESENT (SIMPLE)		SUBJUNCTIVE PRESENT (SIMPLE)	
First person	I am	we are	I be	we be
Second person	you are	you are	you be	you be
Third person	he, she, it is	they are	he, she, it be	they be

INDICATIVE	I am well-organized.
SUBJUNCTIVE	My job requires that I be well-organized.
INDICATIVE	You are on time.
SUBJUNCTIVE	I strongly suggest that you be on time.
SUBJUNCTIVE/MODAL	Tomorrow, you should be on time.

He suggested that she be given a new task.

The captain ordered that the anchor be lifted.

It is vital that we all be properly prepared.

The present passive subjunctive is formed by pairing *be* with the *past participle* of a verb.

enjoy ____________________

juggle ____________________

plan ____________________

roast ____________________

Exercise 84A: Parsing Verbs

In the following sentences from *Virtuous Women: Three Classic Korean Novels* (translated by Richard Rutt and Kim Chong-un), underline each predicate, in both main clauses and dependent clauses. Above each, write the tense, voice, and mood of the verb:

Tenses: Simple past, present, future; progressive past, present, future; perfect past, present, future

Voice: Active, passive (or state-of-being)

Mood: Indicative, subjunctive, imperative, modal, subjunctive/modal

A son should not go against his father's wishes. Never speak of this again.

He opened his eyes and stared at her as though he could not see her, mumbling every now and then as though he were still half asleep.

Hsing-chen stood for a long while on the bridge looking in all directions, but he could not see where they had gone, and soon the shimmering mists had dispersed and the fragrance had faded away.

The love of father and son is deep, but the difference between immortals and men is such that even though I should like to help you I cannot.

While we have frequented this shrine where your coffin lies in state, you have seemed to be with us still; when the funeral is over your coffin will have left the palace for ever.

I have long been as fond of you as if you were my own offspring. How do you dare do this to me now?

My flesh and bones have been cremated on the Lotus Peak, where I left them. I was too young to have any disciples and so there will have been nobody to collect up my relics.

Recently I am strangely troubled by a nameless fatigue, and I feel as though I were in the midst of a thick fog.

Exercise 84B: Forming Subjunctives

William Shakespeare was a fan of subjunctives!

Fill in the blanks in the following sentences from Shakespeare's plays with the correct verb form indicated in brackets. All tenses are simple.

If you ________________ [present active subjunctive of *say*] so, I ________________ [present active indicative of *hope*] you will not kill me.

If she ______________ [present subjunctive, state-of-being] false, O, then heaven ________ [present active indicative of *mock*] itself!

By heaven, he __________________. [present active indicative of *echo*]

As if there ___________ [present subjunctive, state-of-being] some monster in his thought,
Too hideous to be shown.

Othello

She speaks, yet she __________________ [present active indicative of *say*] nothing.

Romeo and Juliet

You __________________ [present indicative, state-of-being] plebians, if they ___________ [present subjunctive, state-of-being] senators.

Coriolanus

If I ________________ [past subjunctive, state-of-being] Brutus now, and he ____________ [past subjunctive, state-of-being] Cassius, he should not humour me.

Julius Caesar

I will not rise, unless your highness ___________ [present active subjunctive of *hear*] me.

Richard III

Unless my study and my books ______________ [present subjunctive, state-of-being] false,

The argument you held, _________________ [past indicative, state-of-being] wrong in you.

Henry VI, Part I

Unless I _______________ [present active subjunctive of *find*] him guilty, he shall not die.

We __________________ [present active indicative of *intend*] to try his grace to-day, if he

__________________ [present subjunctive, state-of-being] guilty.

Henry VI, Part II

And, when the king comes, ____________________ [present active imperative of *offer*] him no violence,

Unless he ________________ [present active subjunctive of *seek*] to put us out by force.

Is this the alliance that he ____________ [present active indicative of *seek*] with France?

Henry VI, Part III

If it ________________ [present subjunctive, state-of-being] now, 'tis not to come; if it ________________ [present subjunctive, state-of-being] not to come, it ______________ [future indicative, state-of-being] now; if it ________________ [present subjunctive, state-of-being] not now, yet it will come; the readiness ________________ [present indicative, state-of-being] all.

Hamlet

Exercise 84C: Diagramming

On your own paper, diagram the following sentences, from Frank Herbert's classic science fiction novel *Dune*.

And if I die here, they'll say I sacrificed myself that my spirit might lead them.

He realized that he was semi-delirious, that he should dig himself into the sand, find the relatively cool underlayer and cover himself with it.

Whether a thought is spoken or not it is a real thing and it has power.

— REVIEW 7 —

Weeks 19-21

Topics
Phrases and Clauses
Adjective, Adverb, and Noun Clauses
Pronouns
Mood: Modal, Subjective, Imperative, Indicative
Conditional Sentences

Review 7A: Improving Sentences with Phrases

In the blanks below, supply phrases that meet the descriptions in brackets. You may supply more than one phrase in any blank, as long as at least one phrase fulfills the requirements (often, additional prepositional phrases may be needed). The first is done for you, with explanation provided.

The original sentences are taken from James Herriot's memoir *All Things Bright and Beautiful*, about his years as a Yorkshire veterinarian.

This is a challenging assignment—prepare to spend some time on it!

When you are finished, compare your sentences with the originals in the Answer Key.

[adverbial prepositional phrase describing the location of the archway] [adjectival participle phrase saying which archway]

Just beyond the kitchen door was a stone archway ______________________ and through this black opening there whistled a Siberian draught which cut

[adverbial prepositional phrase describing where the draught cut]

effortlessly ______________________.

EXPLANATION: The phrase "beyond the kitchen door" modifies the state-of-being verb *was* and answers the question *where.*

[adverbial prepositional phrase describing where the lamb huddled]

______________________, a tiny lamb huddled close to her flank.

They don't give vets medals for bravery, but as I pulled off my overcoat and jacket and

[adverbial present participle phrase that begins with the present participle and includes two adverbial prepositional phrases, both of them describing the present participle]

stood ______________________ I felt I deserved one.

[adjectival present participle phrase describing the ewe]

The ewe, clearly ______________________ without her uncomfortable

[adverbial prepositional phrase describing *trotted* and answering the question *where*]

burden, trotted ______________________.

[adverbial prepositional phrase answering the question *where*]

We pushed the ewe and lambs ________________ which was piled high

[adverbial prepositional phrase answering the question *when*. Can you use a present participle as the object of a preposition?]

with hay, and ________________ I struck a match and looked down at the

[past participle phrase acting as an adjective, describing the sheep and her family, containing a prepositional phrase acting as an adverb and answering the question *where*]

little sheep and her new family ________________.

[past participle phrase acting as an adjective, describing the pens]

At the top of the grassy slope the pens, ________________, formed a long row

[present participle phrase acting as an adjective, describing *each*]

of square cubicles each ________________ with her lambs and I could see

[present participle phrase acting as an adjective, describing *Rob Benson*] [another present participle phrase acting as an adjective, also describing *Rob Benson*]

Rob Benson ________________, ________________.

Turning, I kneeled again and began the same procedure and as I once more groped forward

[another present participle phrase acting as an adjective, describing *dodged*]

a tiny lamb dodged ________________ and began to suck at my patient's udder.

[present participle phrase acting as an adjective, describing *tail*]

He was clearly enjoying it, too, if the little tail, ________________, meant anything.

[infinitive phrase acting as the object of the verb *began*]

The ewe bent over him and began ________________ with little quick

[adjectival prepositional phrase describing *chuckle*]

darts of her tongue; and she gave the deep chuckle ________________

[adverbial prepositional phrase answering the question *when*]

that you hear from a sheep only ________________.

Review 7B: Improving Sentences with Clauses

Rewrite each sentence on your own paper, adding a dependent clause that meets the description in brackets. The first is done for you, with explanation provided.

The original sentences are taken from *All Things Wise and Wonderful*, by James Herriot. When you are finished, compare your sentences with the originals in the Answer Key.

That kitten grew rapidly into a sleek handsome cat with a boisterous nature

[adjective clause describing *nature*]

which earned him the name of Buster.

EXPLANATION: The adjective clause answers the question *what kind* about the cat's nature; *which*, the subject of the clause, is a relative pronoun referring back to *nature*, and *earned* is the predicate.

[noun clause serving as the direct object of the verb]

That was very clever—I don't know ______________________________.

[noun clause serving as the direct object of *can remember*]

I can't remember ______________________________ because the animals have never got round to recognising it as a holiday; but with the passage of the years the

[adjective clause describing *resentment*]

vague resentment ______________________________ has been replaced by philosophical acceptance.

The long moist furrows of the new-turned soil glittered under the pale February sun,

[adjective clause describing *pastures*]

contrasting with the gold stubble fields and the grassy pastures ______________________________.

[adverb clause describing *stood*]

We stood, ______________________________, eyeball to eyeball, in mutual

[noun clause acting as the object of the preposition *till* (a form of *until*)]

disagreement till ______________________________.

[adverb clause describing *found*]

______________________________ I found the cow comfortably ensconced in a field, in the middle of a rolling yellow ocean of buttercups.

[noun clause acting as the object of the preposition *of*, containing a second adverb clause modifying a verb or verb form within the noun clause]

Firstly, there was usually an anxious-faced farmer to greet me with news of ______________________________, but today I was like an unwelcome stranger.

Suddenly his teeth shone as the brown face broke into an ever-widening grin

[adjective clause describing *grin*]

______________________________. He was still laughing

[adverb clause describing was *laughing*]

helplessly ______________________________ and

[adverb clause describing *leaned* and *wiped*]

______________________________ he leaned against the wall and wiped his eyes.

Review 7C: Conditional Clauses

Label the following sentences as first, second, or third conditional by writing *1*, *2*, or *3* in the blank next to each one. Underline each conditional clause. Circle each consequence clause.

These sentences are taken from *Wonder Tales from Many Lands*, by Katharine Pyle.

If you should disobey me and do this thing, you will suffer the greatest dangers, and may even pay for it with your life. ________

With the first rays of the sun, the treasure would crumble away, unless the life of a human being had been sacrificed. ________

She scarcely breathed, lest he should hear her. ________

Misfortune would come upon you if ever you entered that room. ________

If at any time I think I am going in the wrong direction, it is easy to right myself. ________

If each morning I return and find her still with you, then you shall have her for a bride after the third morning. ________

Had I known yesterday what I know to-day, I would have taken the heart of flesh out of your bosom and put in a heart of clay. ________

If no good comes of it, no harm can either. ________

If ever again you venture into my country, you shall be thrown into a dungeon and remain there as long as you live. ________

If they found anyone in the house at that time, they would surely tear him to pieces. ________

If you like, I will take you on my back and carry you down to the bottom of the sea. ________

They would have been very contented there if it had not been for a herd of buffaloes that lived on the other side of the forest. ________

If they told the ogre of the strange warrior who had come to live in their lodge, he would without doubt challenge the stranger to race with him. ________

Review 7D: Pronoun Review

The following sentences are taken from James Herriot's *The Lord God Made Them All*, the last in his four-volume memoir series.

Circle every pronoun. Label each as personal (*PER*), possessive (*POSS*), reflexive (*REF*), intensive (*INT*), demonstrative (*DEM*), interrogative (*INTER*), relative (*REL*), or indefinite (*IND*). Beside this label, add the abbreviation for the part of the sentence (or clause) that the pronoun serves as: adjective (*ADJ*), subject (*SUBJ*), predicate adjective (*PA*), direct object (*DO*), indirect object (*IO*), or object of the preposition (*OP*). (Intensive pronouns will not have one of these parts of speech—they act as appositives, which you'll cover in Lesson 94 if this is your first time through this course.)

The first has been done for you.

PER
SUBJ
She was throwing chips from a bag in her lap to her dog, Puppy, sitting opposite.

"But Mr. Ripley, that's exactly what you said last time when you saw the blood running down my knee. Those were your very words."

It was difficult since neither of us spoke a word of the other's language, but I managed to get over to her that most of the sheep were of the Romney Marsh breed.

Farmers are notoriously bad gardeners but Mr. Ripley was in a class by himself.

Neither Siegfried nor I suffered from insomnia, but on the rare occasions when sleep would not come we had recourse to our particular books. Mine was *The Brothers Karamazov*, a great novel, but to me, soporific in its names.

I had never prescribed the stuff myself, but it was supposed to be beneficial in horses with colic and dogs with digestive troubles.

I tipped the driving mirror down and had a look at myself.

There were eight strapping yearlings in there, some of them returning my stare with mild interest, others cavorting and kicking up their heels among the straw.

"Who is this?" I asked a little breathlessly. "What on earth is the trouble?"

And that was a funny thing. Where was the anxious farmer? I had expected to find him pacing up and down the yard, wringing his hands, but the place seemed deserted.

The farmer's voice thundered in my ear. He was one of the many who still thought you had to bawl lustily to cover the miles between.

Review 7E: Parsing

In the sentences below, underline every verb or verb phrase that acts as the predicate of a clause (dependent or independent). Label each verb with the correct tense, voice, and mood.

Tenses: Simple past, present, future; progressive past, present, future; perfect past, present, future

Voice: Active, passive (or state-of-being)

Mood: Indicative, subjunctive, imperative, modal, subjunctive/modal

The first is done for you.

These sentences are taken from *Seabiscuit: An American Legend*, by Laura Hillenbrand.

progressive past, active, indicative

It was raining again.

In 1918 he had plunked down $5,000 at an auction and walked away with the most extraordinary creature the sport had ever seen, Man o'War.

If two track vets could confirm that the horse was really injured, Smith could scratch him.

During his sojourn in the East in 1937, Smith had been caught working Seabiscuit at night four times.

Hot pursuit would be Seabiscuit's downfall, but holding back might hand the race to Special Agent.

Asked to run, he would drop low over the track and fall into a comical version of what horsemen call an eggbeater gait, making a spastic sideways flailing motion with his left foreleg as he swung it forward, as if he were swatting at flies.

Swope must have swallowed hard.

I will never forget his eloquence, his wit, and his magnanimity.

A spontaneous call was echoing over the sea of heads: "Bring on Rosemont!"

Everyone was wondering what Smith possibly could have been thinking.

Exhibit was promptly disqualified, and the stewards scheduled a meeting to determine if Pollard would have to serve a suspension for the incident.

His jaw had a recalcitrant jut to it that implied a run-in with something—an errant hoof or an ill-placed fence post—but maybe it was the only shape in which it could have been drawn.

Review 7F: Diagramming

On your own paper, diagram every word of the following two sentences from J. R. R. Tolkien's *The Two Towers*.

Unless our enemies rest also, they will leave us far behind, if we stay to sleep.

The hobbits could see that Bregalad was now listening intently, although to them, down in the dell of his ent-house, the sound of the Moot was faint.

WEEK 22

Parenthetical Elements

— LESSON 85 —

Verb Review

INDICATIVE TENSES

SIMPLE		Active	Passive
	Past	he followed he was	he was followed
	Present	he follows he is	he is followed
	Future	he will follow he will be	he will be followed
PROGRESSIVE			
	Past	he was following he was being	he was being followed
	Present	he is following he is being	he is being followed
	Future	he will be following he will be being	he will be being followed
PERFECT			
	Past	he had followed he had been	he had been followed
	Present	he has followed he has been	he has been followed
	Future	he will have followed he will have been	he will have been followed

MODAL TENSES
(would OR should, may, might, must, can, could)

SIMPLE		Active	Passive
	Present	he would follow he would be	
PERFECT			
	Past	he would have followed he would have been	

SUBJUNCTIVE TENSES

SIMPLE		Active	Passive
	Past	he followed he were	
	Present	he follow he be	

Complete the following chart with the third-person-singular form of the verb indicated in the left-hand column. If you need help, ask your instructor.

INDICATIVE TENSES

		Active	Passive
SIMPLE			
betray	Past	[he, she, it]	[he, she, it]
decorate	Present	[he, she, it]	[he, she, it]
loan	Future	[he, she, it]	[he, she, it]
PROGRESSIVE			
gobble	Past	[he, she, it]	[he, she, it]
sketch	Present	[he, she, it]	[he, she, it]
prepare	Future	[he, she, it]	[he, she, it]
PERFECT			
crush	Past	[he, she, it]	[he, she, it]
stop	Present	[he, she, it]	[he, she, it]
taunt	Future	[he, she, it]	[he, she, it]

MODAL TENSES
(would OR should, may, might, must, can, could)

		Active	Passive
SIMPLE			
jump	Present	[he, she, it]	
PERFECT			
yawn	Past	[he, she, it]	

SUBJUNCTIVE TENSES

		Active	Passive
SIMPLE			
plunge	Past	[he, she, it]	
terrify	Present	[he, she, it]	

On your own paper, write sentences that use each of the forms above as the predicate of an independent or dependent clause. If you need help (or ideas), ask your instructor.

— LESSON 86 —

Restrictive and Non-Restrictive Modifying Clauses
Parenthetical Expressions

In after-years Piglet liked to think that he had been in Very Great Danger during the Terrible Flood, but the only danger he had really been in was in the last half-hour of his imprisonment, when Owl, who had just flown up, sat on a branch of his tree to comfort him, and told him a very long story about an aunt who had once laid a seagull's egg by mistake, and the story went on and on, rather like this sentence, until Piglet, who was listening out of his window without much hope, went to sleep quietly and naturally, slipping slowly out of the window towards the water until he was only hanging on by his toes, at which moment luckily a sudden loud squawk from Owl, which was really part of the story, woke Piglet up and just gave him time to jerk himself back into safety and say, "How interesting, and did she?" when—well, you can imagine his joy when at last he saw the good ship *The Brain of Pooh* (Captain, C. Robin; 1st Mate, P. Bear) coming over the sea to rescue him.

—From *Winnie-the-Pooh* by A. A. Milne

A restrictive modifying clause defines the word that it modifies. Removing the clause changes the essential meaning of the sentence.

A non-restrictive modifying clause describes the word that it modifies. Removing the clause doesn't change the essential meaning of the sentence.

Only non-restrictive clauses should be set off by commas.

Parentheses ( ) can enclose words that are not essential to the sentence.
singular: parenthesis
plural: parentheses

when Owl who had just flown up sat on a branch of his tree to comfort him

until Piglet who was listening out of his window without much hope went to sleep quietly

a sudden loud squawk from Owl which was really part of the story woke Piglet up

Parenthetical expressions often interrupt or are irrelevant to the rest of the sentence.

Punctuation goes inside the parentheses if it applies to the parenthetical material; all other punctuation goes outside the parentheses.

Parenthetical material only begins with a capital letter if it is a complete sentence with ending punctuation.

As soon as he saw his companion fall, the other soldier, with a loud cry, jumped out of the boat on the far side, and he also floundered through the water (which was apparently just in his depth) and disappeared into the woods of the mainland.

If you can swim (as Jill could) a giant bath is a lovely thing.

He had only once been in a ship (and then only as far as the Isle of Wight) and had been horribly seasick.

The cabin was very tiny but bright with painted panels (all birds and beasts and crimson dragons and vines) and spotlessly clean.

From the waist upward he was like a man, but his legs were shaped like a goat's (the hair on them was glossy black) and instead of feet he had goat's hoofs.

Get me a score of men-at-arms, all well mounted, and a score of Talking Dogs, and ten Dwarfs (let them all be fell archers), and a Leopard or so, and Stonefoot the Giant.

Edmund had had no gift, because he was not with them at the time. (This was his own fault, and you can read about it in the other book.)

Because it was such an important occasion they took a candle each (Polly had a good store of these in her cave).

I read the *Chronicles of Narnia* (all seven of them!) in three days.
Did you know that C. S. Lewis wrote the *Chronicles of Narnia* (all seven of them)?
C. S. Lewis and J. R. R. Tolkien were good friends (amazing, isn't it?).

Exercise 86A: Restrictive and Non-Restrictive Modifying Clauses

In the following sentences, mark each bolded clause as either *ADV* for adverb or *ADJ* for adjective, and draw an arrow from the clause back to the word modified. Some sentences contain more than one modifying clause.

Then, identify each adjective clause as either restrictive (*R*) or nonrestrictive (*NR*).

Finally, set off all of the nonrestrictive adjective clauses with commas. Use the proofreader's mark (^) for comma insertion. When you are finished, compare your punctuation with the original.

These sentences are slightly condensed from *African Myths and Folk Tales*, by Carter Godwin Woodson. The original commas around the nonrestrictive clauses have been removed.

One of the brothers had a glass **into which he could look and find out each day everything that had happened**.

While he was trying to cut through the stems a black fly began to buzz round him.

He lifted his hand to drive it away and **as he did so** he dropped the knife.

The place **where the rat had stopped** was near a plantain-eater's nest.

This startled a monkey **which rushed forth ready for a fight**.

The ripe fruit fell from its stalk onto the back of an elephant **which was passing beneath**.

The elephant rushed away in terror and carried off a flowering creeper **which caught round his neck**.

The creeper in turn pulled over an ant hill **which fell on the bush fowl's nest and broke its eggs**.

Then the bush fowl stood forth and answered, "My eggs were broken by the ant hill **which was pulled over by the creeper which was dragged down by the elephant which was knocked over by the Ntun fruit which was plucked by the monkey which was frightened by the plantain-eater which was startled by the rat which was scared by the serpent which had been jumped over by a sick woman who had been made to run by the fall of a knife which had been dropped by her husband who had been bitten by a black fly**."

At that time, the Fangs were living on the bank of a large river, so large **that one could not see the other side.**

The crocodiles **that you see today** are not crocodiles any more!

I shall send the storm **which falls from the clouds and sweeps everything in front of him**.

I shall send the lightning **which flashes through the sky**.

Exercise 86B: Identifying Parenthetical Expressions

Identify each parenthetical expression as phrase, dependent clause, or sentence. These sentences are taken from John Ormsby's translation of Miguel de Cervantes Saavedra's 1605 novel *Don Quixote* (often described as the first Western novel!).

CHALLENGE EXERCISE

Provide a fuller description of each expression. What kind of phrase, clause, or sentence is it? What does it do or modify?

When you are finished, ask your instructor for the fuller explanations. Compare your descriptions to these explanations.

They will have it his surname was Quixada or Quesada (for here there is some difference of opinion among the authors who write on the subject), although from reasonable conjectures it seems plain that he was called Quexana.

You must know, then, that the above-named gentleman whenever he was at leisure (which was mostly all the year round) gave himself up to reading books of chivalry with such ardour and avidity that he almost entirely neglected the pursuit of his field-sport.

Many an argument did he have with the curate of his village (a learned man, and a graduate of Siguenza) as to which had been the better knight, Palmerin of England or Amadis of Gaul.

So, without giving notice of his intention to anyone, and without anybody seeing him, one morning before the dawning of the day (which was one of the hottest of the month of July) he donned his suit of armour, mounted Rocinante with his patched-up helmet on, braced his buckler, took his lance, and by the back door of the yard sallied forth upon the plain.

Meanwhile Don Quixote worked upon a farm labourer, a neighbour of his, an honest man (if indeed that title can be given to him who is poor), but with very little wit in his pate.

This strange spectacle at such an hour and in such a solitary place was quite enough to strike terror into Sancho's heart, and even into his master's; and (save in Don Quixote's case) did so, for all Sancho's resolution had now broken down.

All anger and gloom removed, they mounted and, without taking any fixed road (not to fix upon any being the proper thing for true knights-errant), they set out, guided by Rocinante's will.

Therefore it seems to me it would be better (saving your worship's better judgment) if we were to go and serve some emperor or other great prince who may have some war on hand, in whose service your worship may prove the worth of your person, your great might, and greater understanding.

Exercise 86C: Punctuating Sentences with Parenthetical Expressions

Correct each of the following sentences, using the proofreader's marks listed below.

delete:
insert comma:
insert period: ⊙
insert exclamation point:
insert question mark:
move punctuation mark:

If the sentence is correct, write *C* in the margin next to it.

These sentences are taken from the British best-seller *Eats, Shoots & Leaves: The Zero Tolerance Approach to Punctuation*, by Lynne Truss.

I remember, at the start of the *Two Weeks Notice* publicity campaign in the spring of 2003, emerging cheerfully from Victoria Station (was I whistling) and stopping dead in my tracks with my fingers in my mouth.

If it were "one month's notice" there would be an apostrophe (I reasoned;) yes, and if it were "one week's notice" there would be an apostrophe.

A sign has gone up in a local charity-shop window which says, baldly, "Can you spare any old records" (no question mark) and I dither daily outside on the pavement.

It is no accident that the word "punctilious" "(attentive to formality or etiquette)" comes from the same original root word as "punctuation".

A child sitting a County Schools exam in 1937 would be asked to punctuate the following puzzler: "Charles the First walked and talked half an hour after his head was cut off" (answer: "Charles the First walked and talked. Half an hour after, his head was cut off")

Well, taking just the initial capital letters and the terminating full stop (the rest will come later,) they have not always been there.

Every time the sentence ends, there is a full stop (or a full-stop substitute such as the exclamation mark or the question mark.)

There will be those, for example, who insist that the Oxford comma is an abomination (the second comma in "ham, eggs, and chips)," whereas others are unmoved by the Oxford comma but incensed by the trend towards under-hyphenation—which the Oxford comma people have quite possibly never even noticed.

I heard from people whose work colleagues used commas instead of apostrophes; from someone rather thoughtfully recommending a restaurant called l'Apostrophe in Reims (address on request;); and from a Somerset man who had cringed regularly at a sign on a market garden until he discovered that its proprietor's name was—you couldn't make it up—R. Carrott.

— LESSON 87 —

Parenthetical Expressions

Dashes

(The sentences in this lesson are from Lewis Carroll's novel *Through the Looking-glass.)*

A little provoked, she drew back, and after looking everywhere for the queen (whom she spied out at last, a long way off), she thought she would try the plan, this time, of walking in the opposite direction.

There was a Beetle sitting next to the Goat (it was a very queer carriage-full of passengers altogether).

Or—let me see—suppose each punishment was to be going without a dinner; then, when the miserable day came, I should have to go without fifty dinners at once!

I can see all of it when I get upon a chair—all but the bit behind the fireplace.
I can see all of it when I get upon a chair, all but the bit behind the fireplace.

But the beard seemed to melt away as she touched it, and she found herself sitting quietly under a tree—while the Gnat (for that was the insect she had been talking to) was balancing itself on a twig just over her head, and fanning her with its wings.

Parentheses ( ) can enclose words that are not essential to the sentence.
Parenthetical expressions often interrupt or are irrelevant to the rest of the sentence.
Punctuation goes inside the parentheses if it applies to the parenthetical material; all other punctuation goes outside the parentheses.
Parenthetical material only begins with a capital letter if it is a complete sentence with ending punctuation.

Dashes — — can enclose words that are not essential to the sentence.
Dashes can also be used singly to separate parts of a sentence.

I read Lewis Carroll's poem "Jabberwocky" which, I thought, was very weird.
I read Lewis Carroll's poem "Jabberwocky" which—I thought—was very weird.
I read Lewis Carroll's poem "Jabberwocky" which (I thought) was very weird.

Commas make a parenthetical element a part of the sentence.
Dashes emphasize a parenthetical element.
Parentheses minimize a parenthetical element.

1. You can set off parenthetical elements in three different ways.
2. You can turn a dependent clause into a parenthetical element just by putting it inside dashes or parentheses.
3. You can use a dash in place of a comma to emphasize the part of the sentence that follows.

The independent clauses of a compound sentence must be joined by a comma and a coordinating conjunction, a semicolon, or a semicolon and a coordinating conjunction. They cannot be joined by a comma alone.

CORRECT
Alice ventured to taste it, and finding it very nice (it had, in fact, a sort of mixed flavour of cherry tart, custard, pineapple, roast turkey, toffee, and hot buttered toast) she very soon finished it off.

INCORRECT
Alice ventured to taste it, and finding it very nice, it had, in fact, a sort of mixed flavour of cherry tart, custard, pineapple, roast turkey, toffee, and hot buttered toast, she very soon finished it off.

Exercise 87A: Types of Parenthetical Expressions

Identify each parenthetical expression as phrase, dependent clause, or sentence.

CHALLENGE EXERCISE

- Provide a fuller description of each expression. What kind of phrase, clause, or sentence is it? What does it do or modify?
- When you are finished, ask your instructor for the fuller explanations. Compare your descriptions to these explanations.

These sentences are taken from *The Devil's Doctor: Paracelsus and the World of Renaissance Magic and Science*, by Philip Ball.

The hardy miners of the Harz and Saxony, known as Bergleute (mountain people), became famed throughout Europe for their skills and found employment as far afield as Serbia and Sardinia.

The Lutheran pastor Andreas Osiander explained in a sermon after an outbreak of the plague in Nuremberg in 1533 (shortly after Paracelsus passed through the city) that "such a scourge comes perchance from the influence of the stars, from the effects of comets, from extraordinary weather conditions and changes of the air, from southerly winds, from stinking waters, or from rotten vapours of the earth." From everything that anyone could think of, in other words—everything except the actual cause, a bacterium carried by fleas on the back of black rats.

Aristotle wrote very widely and was happy enough to draw analogies between disparate phenomena, but he was conspicuously silent on some topics (such as what we would now call chemistry) and gives little impression of the need for congruence and continuity.

The central distinction between the mystical magus like Paracelsus and the academics at the universities was that, while the latter tended to believe that these rules had already been deduced by the ancients through the power of pure thought and logic, the magical adepts thought that they could be found only by studying nature—crudely speaking (and I shall be more precise later), by experiment.

But much of contemporary science is itself occult in the Renaissance sense, insofar as it is "hidden" from our senses—that, of course, being the literal meaning of the word.

Hohenheim Castle stood near Stuttgart in Swabia, and it was the seat (the name means "mountain home") of Conrad Bombast, who died in 1299.

Paracelsus is often credited with coining the name himself (he was fond of naming things), an amalgam of the two metals (zinne and kupfer; tin and copper) that zinc somewhat resembles.

This scholastic tradition allowed that one might mine the "scientific" aspects of the Greek and Roman world—so that Ptolemy's astronomy, Galen's medicine, and Aristotle's physics and logic were all standard components of the curriculum—but insisted that the poetry, moral philosophy, and literature of these pagans was best left untouched.

Paracelsus takes the nickname Alpenus—a man from the Alpine slopes—which becomes corrupted to Arpenus or Arpinas, from which it is a short step to Orpinas and then to legendary Orpheus, a central character in the great tradition of natural magic, who gained victory over death.

Exercise 87B: Punctuating Parenthetical Expressions

On either side of each bolded parenthetical expression, place parentheses, dashes, or commas. There are not necessarily correct answers for these, but compare them to the originals when you have finished.

These sentences are taken from a collection of short stories by Robert Louis Stevenson.

"Will O'the Mill"

And then the river goes out into the lowlands, and waters the great corn country, and runs through a sight of fine cities **so they say** where kings live all alone in great palaces, with a sentry walking up and down before the door.

It seemed like a great conspiracy of things animate and inanimate; they all went downward, fleetly and gaily downward, and only he **it seemed** remained behind, like a stock upon the wayside.

It scarcely seemed to have been the girl's doing **it seemed as if things had merely so fallen out** that she and her father took their departure that same afternoon in a farm-cart.

He hoped **on the whole** she would refuse him.

"The Treasure of Franchard"

We have now arrived at some idea of the composition of the gang **for I incline to the hypothesis of more than one** and we now leave this room, which can disclose no more, and turn our attention to the court and garden.

Besides **and this is an argument exactly suited to your intellectual level** many of them are English and American. Where else should we expect to find a thief?

And yet **you will bear me out** I supported the emotion nobly.

You have your usual flow of spirits **I perceive** but even less than your usual deliberation.

Some of the turtle is still left **the most wholesome of delicacies** and we are not a penny the worse.

"Olalla"

If they knew you were the handsomest and the most pleasant man that ever came from England **where I am told that handsome men are common, but pleasant ones not so much so** they would doubtless make you welcome with a better grace.

To me **indeed** it seems discourteous.

Now she would speak of the warmth in which **like her son** she greatly delighted.

Here was a solution; and yet when I called to mind the cries **which I never did without a shuddering chill** it seemed altogether insufficient.

I told her you had done so **I remembered that** and she was pleased.

I dwell, or I think I dwell **if I exist at all** somewhere apart **an impotent prisoner** carried about and deafened by a mob that I disown.

When she was young **God help me, I fear I neglected that wild lamb** she was surely sane.

Exercise 87C: Using Dashes for Emphasis

On your own paper, rewrite the next five sentences, substituting dashes for the underlined punctuation marks and making any other capitalization or punctuation changes needed.

These sentences are taken from the classic early-twentieth-century novella (short novel, halfway between a short story and a full-length novel) *Typhoon*, by Joseph Conrad.

They are seas full of every-day, eloquent facts, such as islands, sand-banks, reefs, swift and changeable currents (tangled facts that nevertheless speak to a seaman in clear and definite language).

There were matters of duty, of course. Directions, orders, and so on; but the past being to his mind done with, and the future not there yet, the more general actualities of the day required no comment, because facts can speak for themselves with overwhelming precision.

But he had never been given a glimpse of immeasurable strength and of immoderate wrath, the wrath that passes exhausted but never appeased: the wrath and fury of the passionate sea.

There are on sea and land such men thus fortunate, or thus disdained by destiny or by the sea.

The old people ultimately became acquainted with a good many names of ships, and with the names of the skippers who commanded them; with the names of Scots and English shipowners; with the names of seas, oceans, straits, promontories; with outlandish names of lumber-ports, of rice-ports, of cotton-ports; with the names of islands; with the name of their son's young woman.

— LESSON 88 —

Parenthetical Expressions
Dashes
Diagramming Parenthetical Expressions

We met the new neighbors today, who, we think, are very pleasant people.
It was a glorious morning—a cool, sunny, sweet-scented morning.
The chef decided to put liver, which was one of his favorites, on the dinner menu.
The liver (which most diners didn't order) was cooked with onions and red wine.

Recognizing Parenthetical Elements

Dashes and parentheses always turn a clause or phrase into a parenthetical element—even if there's actually a grammatical relationship between the clause or phrase and the rest of the sentence.

If a clause or phrase is set off by commas, but doesn't have a clear grammatical relationship to the rest of the sentence, it is parenthetical.

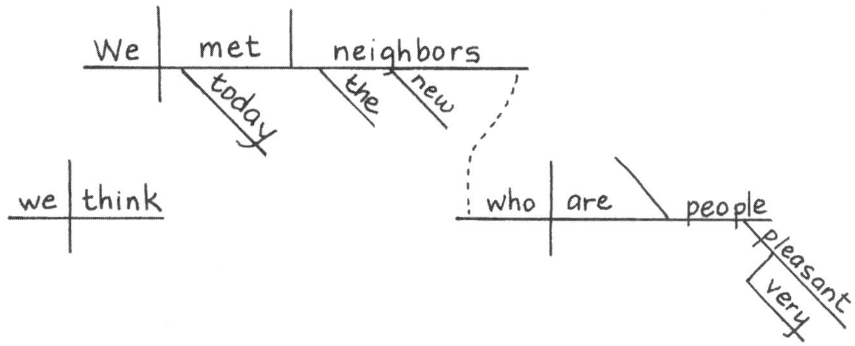

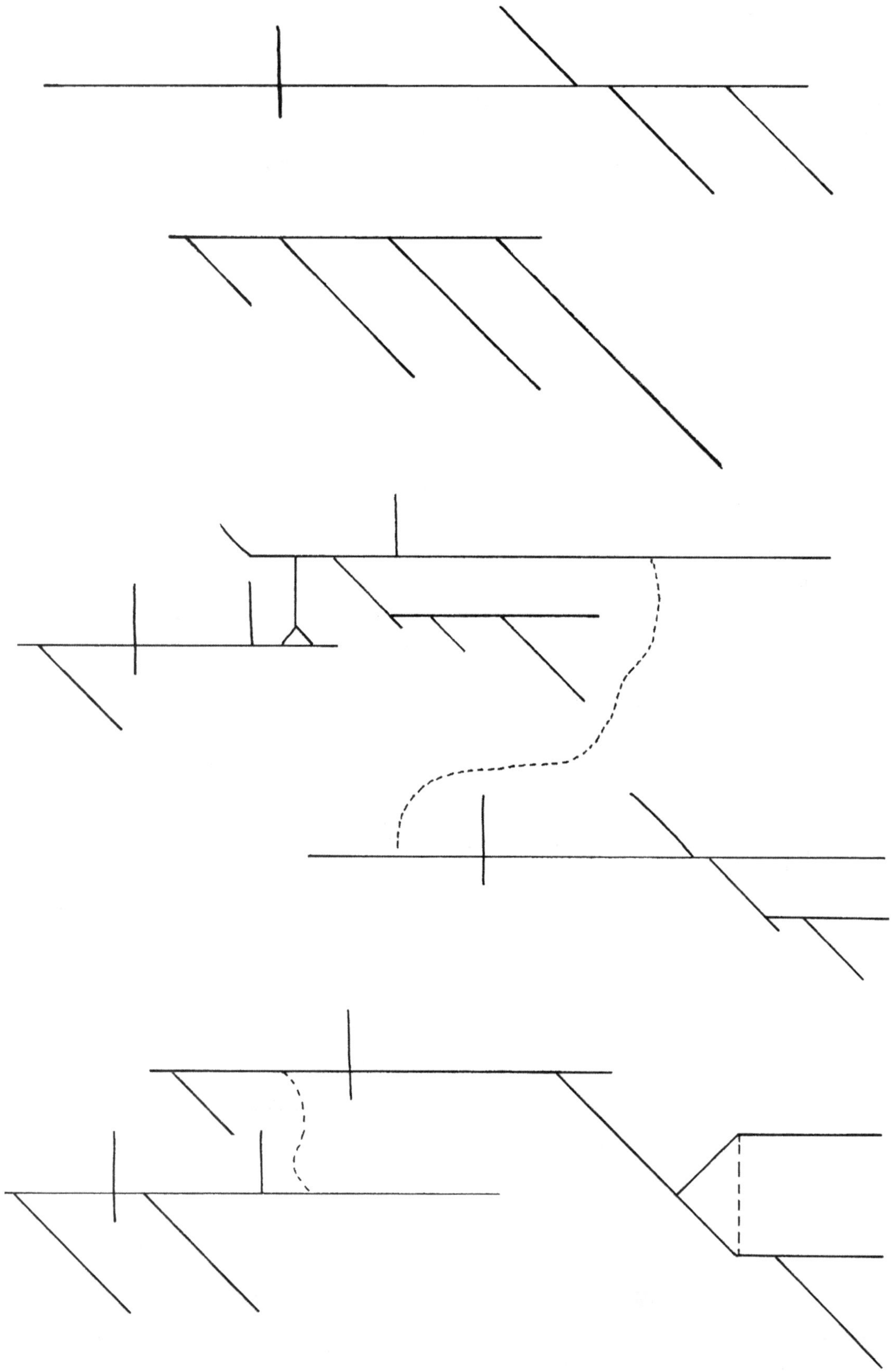

The train—can you believe it?—was on time (a rare and happy occurrence!).

Exercise 88A: Diagramming Parenthetical Expressions

On your own paper, diagram each of the following sentences.

These sentences are taken from short stories written by O. Henry (the pen name of the writer William Sidney Porter). These are meant to be challenging! Do your best, and ask your instructor for help if you get frustrated. When you are finished, compare your answers to the Key. There may be more than one way to diagram these elements!

"The Skylight Room"
Your hand crept to your throat, you gasped, you looked up as from a well—and breathed once more.

In the next morning's paper I saw a little news item, and the last sentence of it may help you (as it helped me) to weld the incidents together.

"The Cop and the Anthem"
Soapy, with disgust in his heart, loafed along, twice unsuccessful.

Through one violet-stained window a soft light glowed, where, no doubt, the organist loitered over the keys, making sure of his mastery of the coming Sabbath anthem.

"An Adjustment of Nature"
In Cypher's she belonged—in the bacon smoke, the cabbage perfume, the grand, Wagnerian chorus of hurled ironstone china and rattling casters.

And then Milly loomed up with a thousand dishes on her bare arm—loomed up big and white and pink and awful as Mount Saint Elias—with a smile like day breaking in a gulch.

"A Ramble in Aphasia"
She laughed softly, with a strange quality in the sound—it was a laugh of happiness— and of content—and of misery.

"A Municipal Report"
At nine o'clock on the next morning, after my chicken livers en brochette (try them if you can find that hotel), I strayed out into the drizzle, which was still on for an unlimited run.

WEEK 23

Dialogue and Quotations

— LESSON 89 —

Dialogue

"I'm sorry, Ender," Valentine whispered. She was looking at the band-aid on his neck.

Ender touched the wall and the door closed behind him. "I don't care. I'm glad it's gone."

"What's gone?" Peter walked into the parlor, chewing on a mouthful of bread and peanut butter.

Ender did not see Peter as the beautiful ten-year-old boy that grown-ups saw, with dark, thick, tousled hair and a face that could have belonged to Alexander the Great. Ender looked at Peter only to detect anger or boredom, the dangerous moods that almost always led to pain. Now as Peter's eyes discovered the band-aid on his neck, the telltale flicker of anger appeared.

Valentine saw it too. "Now he's like us," she said, trying to soothe him before he had time to strike.

—From *Ender's Game* by Orson Scott Card

Dialogue: the actual words characters speak
Narrative: the rest of the story

Dialogue is set off by quotation marks.

A dialogue tag identifies the person making the speech.
When a dialogue tag comes after a speech, place a comma, exclamation point, or question mark inside the closing quotation marks.

"I ate the cookie," my brother said.
"I ate seventeen cookies!" my brother exclaimed.
"Do you think I'll be sick?" my brother asked.

INCORRECT:
"I ate the cookie." My brother said.

When a dialogue tag comes before a speech, place a comma after the tag. Put the dialogue's final punctuation mark inside the closing quotation marks.

My brother said, "I ate the cookie."

My brother exclaimed, "I ate seventeen cookies!"

My brother asked, "Do you think I'll be sick?"

Speeches do not need to be attached to a dialogue tag as long as the text clearly indicates the speaker.

"I've watched through his eyes, I've listened through his ears, and I tell you he's the one. Or at least as close as we're going to get."

"That's what you said about the brother."

"The brother tested out impossible. For other reasons. Nothing to do with his ability."

"Same with the sister. And there are doubts about him. He's too malleable. Too willing to submerge himself in someone else's will."

"Not if the other person is his enemy."

"So what do we do? Surround him with enemies all the time?"

"If we have to."

—From *Ender's Game* by Orson Scott Card

Usually, a new paragraph begins with each new speaker.

CORRECT:
"I'm not afraid to say what I think," George retorted. "I wish you could be honest too."
"I'm not afraid to say what I think," George retorted, "whether or not you like it."

INCORRECT: (Run-on sentence):
"I'm not afraid to say what I think," George retorted, "I wish you could be honest too."

INCORRECT: (Ends with a sentence fragment):
"I'm not afraid to say what I think," George retorted. "Whether or not you like it."

When a dialogue tag comes in the middle of a speech, follow it with a comma if the following dialogue is an incomplete sentence. Follow it with a period if the following dialogue is a complete sentence.

Exercise 89A: Punctuating Dialogue

The excerpt below is from the mystery novel *The Murder of Roger Ackroyd*, by Agatha Christie. All of the dialogue is missing quotation marks, and some of it is missing ending punctuation as well. Do your best to supply the missing punctuation marks. (Don't use proofreader's marks—just write the punctuation directly into the sentences.)

When you are finished, compare your version with the original.

Mrs. Ferrars' husband died just over a year ago, and Caroline has constantly asserted, without the least foundation for the assertion, that his wife poisoned him.

She scorns my invariable rejoinder that Mr. Ferrars died of acute gastritis, helped on by habitual overindulgence in alcoholic beverages. The symptoms of gastritis and arsenical poisoning are not, I agree, unlike, but Caroline bases her accusation on quite different lines.

You've only got to look at her, I have heard her say.

Mrs. Ferrars, though not in her first youth, was a very attractive woman, and her clothes, though simple, always seemed to fit her very well, but all the same, lots of women buy their clothes in Paris, and have not, on that account, necessarily poisoned their husbands.

As I stood hesitating in the hall, with all this passing through my mind, Caroline's voice came again, with a sharper note in it.

What on earth are you doing out there, James? Why don't you come and get your breakfast

Just coming, my dear I said hastily. I've been hanging up my overcoat.

You could have hung up half a dozen overcoats in this time.

She was quite right. I could have.

I walked into the dining-room, gave Caroline the accustomed peck on the cheek, and sat down to eggs and bacon. The bacon was rather cold.

You've had an early call remarked Caroline.

Yes I said. King's Paddock. Mrs. Ferrars.

I know said my sister.

How did you know

Annie told me.

Annie is the house parlourmaid. A nice girl, but an inveterate talker.

There was a pause. I continued to eat eggs and bacon. My sister's nose, which is long and thin, quivered a little at the tip, as it always does when she is interested or excited over anything.

Well? she demanded.

A sad business. Nothing to be done. Must have died in her sleep.

I know said my sister again.

This time I was annoyed.

You can't know I snapped. I didn't know myself until I got there, and haven't mentioned it to a soul yet. If that girl Annie knows, she must be a clairvoyant.

It wasn't Annie who told me. It was the milkman. He had it from the Ferrarses' cook.

As I say, there is no need for Caroline to go out to get information. She sits at home and it comes to her.

My sister continued:

What did she die of? Heart failure?

Didn't the milkman tell you that I inquired sarcastically.

Sarcasm is wasted on Caroline. She takes it seriously and answers accordingly.

He didn't know she explained.

After all, Caroline was bound to hear sooner or later. She might as well hear from me.

She died of an overdose of veronal. She's been taking it lately for sleeplessness. Must have taken too much.

Nonsense said Caroline immediately She took it on purpose. Don't tell me!

Exercise 89B: Writing Dialogue Correctly

On your own paper, rewrite the following sentences as dialogue, using the past tense for the dialogue tags. Use the notations in parentheses to help you.

You may choose to place dialogue tags before, in the middle of, or after dialogue, or to leave the tags out completely. But you must have at least one sentence with a dialogue tag that comes before, at least one sentence with a dialogue tag that comes after, at least one speech with the dialogue tag in the middle, and at least one speech with no dialogue tag at all.

When you are finished, compare your answers with the original. The first is done for you.

This passage was taken from *Emily of New Moon*, by L. M. Montgomery. In this scene, Emily, a high school student who lives with her stern Aunt Elizabeth, her mild Aunt Laura, and her Cousin Jimmy, has offended her teacher, Miss Brownell. Miss Brownell is a vindictive teacher who doesn't like Emily, and she has come to Emily's home to tell Elizabeth, Laura, and Jimmy the worst possible version of what happened at school during the day. The farmhand, Perry, is also in high school; he saw what happened, and he's listening to the conversation from the loft above the kitchen, where he sleeps.

The text in italics is part of the scene and should be included in your final version, but it isn't dialogue.

(Aunt Elizabeth says) You have been behaving disgracefully in school. I am ashamed of you.

(Emily says, steadily) It was not as bad as that, Aunt Elizabeth. You see it was this way—

(Aunt Elizabeth says) I don't want to hear anything more about it.

(Emily cries) But you must. It isn't fair to listen only to HER side. I was a little bad—but not so bad as she says—

(Aunt Elizabeth says, grimly) Not another word! I have heard the whole story.

(Suddenly sticking his head down through the black hole, Perry says) You heard a pack of lies.

Everybody jumped—even Aunt Elizabeth, who at once became angrier than ever because she HAD jumped.

(Aunt Elizabeth commands) Perry Miller, come down out of that loft instantly!

(Perry says laconically) Can't.

(Aunt Elizabeth says) At once, I say!

(Perry repeats, winking audaciously at Miss Brownell) Can't.

(Aunt Elizabeth says) Perry Miller, come down! I WILL be obeyed. I am mistress here YET.

(Perry says cheerfully) Oh, all right. If I must.

He swung himself down until his toes touched the ladder. Aunt Laura gave a little shriek. Everybody also seemed to be stricken dumb.

(Perry is saying cheerfully, waving his legs about to get a foothold on the ladder while he hangs on to the sides of the black hole with his elbows) I've just got my wet duds off. Fell into the brook when I was watering the cows. Was going to put on dry ones—but just as you say—

(Aunt Elizabeth implores, not able to cope with the situation) Jimmy.

(Cousin Jimmy orders) Perry, get back into that loft and get your clothes on this minute!

First answer:

"You have been behaving disgracefully in school," said Aunt Elizabeth. "I am ashamed of you."

Exercise 89C: Proofreading

Using the following proofreader's marks, correct these incorrect sentences. The originals are from *The Hunger Games*, by Suzanne Collins.

Insert quotation marks: ∨̈

insert comma: ^,

insert period: ⊙

insert question mark: ^?

insert exclamation point: ↑

delete: ℓ

move punctuation mark: ↷

"Prim"! The strangled cry comes out of my throat, and my muscles begin to move again "Prim"!

"I volunteer! I gasp "I volunteer as tribute!

Prim is screaming hysterically behind me. She's wrapped her skinny arms around me like a vise "No, Katniss! No! You can't go"!

"Prim, let go" I say harshly, because this is upsetting me and I don't want to cry.

"Well, bravo! gushes Effie Trinket, "That's the spirit of the Games!" She's pleased to finally have a district with a little action going on in it "What's your name"?

I swallow hard, "Katniss Everdeen I say.

"What an exciting day" she warbles as she attempts to straighten her wig, which has listed severely to the right "But more excitement to come! It's time to choose our boy tribute"!

— LESSON 90 —

Dialogue
Direct Quotations

The stranger said, "I have come far seeking Mali and have found great wealth here. But I must tell your king that great wealth that the world has not seen is worth less to your children's children than a rumor of water to a people dying of thirst."

The elders wondered silently about this stranger who presumed to lecture the king of Mali, but they were much too polite to say anything that might make a guest feel less than welcome.

"You will have to go to Niani, the capital city, to speak with the *mansa*—that is, the king—of Mali," said Musa Weree, with a smile that seemed to mask a secret.

But the stranger showed no interest in Niani. "The king has heard me!" he said.

—From *Mansa Musa: The Lion of Mali* by Khephra Burns

During the two months he remained in Mali, Ibn Battuta paid grudging respect to the safety and justice of the kingdom: "A traveler may proceed alone among them, without the least fear of a thief or robber," he noted.

In Sulayman's twenty-four years on the throne, Mali remained firmly under his authority. Sulayman surrounded himself with the trappings of an emperor: gold arms and armor; ranks of courtiers and Turkish mamluks, warrior slaves bought from Egypt, surrounding him. They were required to keep solemn and attentive in his presence: "Whoever sneezes while the king is holding court," al-'Umari explains, "is severely beaten."

—From *The History of the Renaissance World* by Susan Wise Bauer

Dialogue: the exact words of a speaker
Direct quotation: the exact words of a writer

Dialogue tags attach dialogue to a speaker.
Attribution tags attach direct quotations to a writer.

When an attribution tag comes after a direct quote, place a comma, exclamation point, or question mark inside the closing quotation marks.

"Many ships sank that day," the chronicler wrote.
"Seventeen ships sank that day!" the chronicler lamented.
"Who can say how many lives were lost?" the chronicler mourned.

INCORRECT:
"Many ships sank that day." The chronicler wrote.

When an attribution tag comes before a direct quote, place a comma after the tag. Put the dialogue's final punctuation mark inside the closing quotation marks.

According to the chronicler, "Many ships sank that day."
The chronicler tells us, "Seventeen ships sank that day!"
One witness asked, "Who can say how many lives were lost?"

When an attribution tag comes in the middle of a direct quotation, follow it with a comma if the remaining quote is an incomplete sentence. Follow it with a period if the remaining quote is a complete sentence.

"Many ships," the chronicler tells us, "sank that day."
"Seventeen ships sank that day," the chronicler tells us. "Who can say how many lives were lost?"

Speeches do not need to be attached to a dialogue tag as long as the text clearly indicates the speaker.

Every direct quote must have an attribution tag.

CORRECT:

The soldiers chased Yazdegerd north into the province of Kirman, but the Arab army was caught in a blizzard and froze. "The snow reached the height of a lance," al-Tabari says. Only the commander, one soldier, and a slave girl survived, the latter because her owner slit open the stomach of a camel and packed her inside it to keep her warm.

—*The History of the Medieval World* by Susan Wise Bauer

INCORRECT:

The soldiers chased Yazdegerd north into the province of Kirman, but the Arab army was caught in a blizzard and froze. "The snow reached the height of a lance." Only the commander, one soldier, and a slave girl survived, the latter because her owner slit open the stomach of a camel and packed her inside it to keep her warm.

Exercise 90A: Punctuating Dialogue

The passages of dialogue below, from Suzanne Collins's *Catching Fire,* are missing punctuation. Write in all of the missing punctuation marks (insert them directly rather than using proofreader's marks). When you are finished, compare your answers to the original.

Why would he paint a picture of me, Effie I ask somehow annoyed.

To show that he's going to do everything he can to defend you. That's what everyone in the Capitol's expecting, anyway Didn't he volunteer to go in with you Effie says, as if it's the most obvious thing in the world.

Actually, I painted a picture of Rue Peeta says How she looked after Katniss had covered her in flowers

There's a long pause at the table while everyone absorbs this. And what exactly were you trying to accomplish Haymitch asks in a very measured voice.

I'm not sure. I just wanted to hold them accountable, if only for a moment says Peeta…

"This is dreadful Effie sounds like she's about to cry. That sort of thinking…it's forbidden, Peeta. Absolutely. You'll only bring down more trouble on yourself and Katniss.

I have to agree with Effie on this one says Haymitch. Portia and Cinna remain silent, but their faces are very serious…

I guess this is a bad time to mention I hung a dummy and painted Seneca Crane's name on it I say.

Exercise 90B: Punctuating Direct Quotations

Write in all of the missing punctuation marks (insert them directly rather than using proofreader's marks). When you are finished, compare your answers to the original sentences.

These sentences have been slightly condensed from the classic study *The Common People of Ancient Rome,* by Frank Frost Abbott.

Now and then, too, a serious writer has occasion to use a bit of popular Latin, but he conveniently labels it for us with an apologetic phrase. Thus even St. Jerome, in his commentary on the Epistle to the Ephesians, says Don't look a gift horse in the mouth, as the vulgar proverb has it.

Sometimes a dramatic, lifelike touch is given by putting the inscription into the form of a dialogue between the dead and those who are left behind. Upon a stone found near Rome runs the inscription Hail, dear Stephanus, Moschis and Diodorus salute thee. To which the dead man replies Hail, chaste wife, hail Diodorus, my friend, my brother.

One tombstone reads Into nothing from nothing how quickly we go and another Once we were not, now we are as we were.

It was in these circumstances that the consul Marcellus cried out If I am prevented by the vote of the senate from taking steps for the public safety, I will take such steps on my own responsibility as consul. After saying this he darted out of the senate and presented a sword to Pompey, and said I command you to march against Cæsar in behalf of your country.

To this ill-fated campaign Cæsar devotes the latter half of the second book of his *Civil War*. In the beginning of his account of it he remarks Showing at the outset a total contempt for the military strength of his opponent, Curio crossed over from Sicily, accompanied by only two of the four legions originally given him by Cæsar, and by only five hundred cavalry.

As he himself puts it in his letter to Cicero I did not follow a Cæsar, but a friend.

Exercise 90C: Attribution Tags

In the following paragraphs, slightly condensed from *The Story of Prague*, by Count Francis Lützow, find and underline the direct quotes that are missing their attribution tags. Some sentences are not missing any attribution tags. When you are finished, ask your instructor to check your work.

Then, compare the paragraphs with the originals found in the answer key. Circle each attribution tag in the Answer Key.

Libussa, though the youngest, succeeded her father as ruler of Bohemia, "a wonderful woman among women, chaste in body, righteous in her morals, second to none as judge over the people."

The successor of St. Wenceslas, Boleslav I, whom František Palacký calls "one of the most powerful monarchs that ever occupied the Bohemian throne," greatly extended the frontiers of his country.

Many monks, priests and Germans who had left Prague during the recent disturbances returned, believing that the hour of their triumph had come. "The Germans laughed and joyfully clapped their hands, saying, 'now these heretical Hussites and Wycliffites will perish, and there will be an end of them.'"

The old chronicler Benes of Weitmil tells us that "Charles, King of the Romans and of Bohemia, laid the first stone, and founded the new city of Prague."

The new foundation seems to have been very successful from the first. "The University became so great that nothing equal to it existed in all Germany; and students came there from all parts."

The burning of Wycliffe's works met with almost universal disapproval at Prague. "Instantly a great sedition and discord began. Some said that many other books besides those of Wycliffe had been burnt; therefore the people began to riot."

Sigismund had remained in the rear with part of his army, and returned to his camp as soon as he saw the defeat of his troops. The King "smiled—it is said—over the fate of the brave Christians who had succumbed to the heretics, who had triumphed over them."

— LESSON 91 —

Direct Quotations
Ellipses
Partial Quotations

> A few clouds of dust moving to and fro signify that the army is encamping. Humble words and increased preparations are signs that the enemy is about to advance. Violent language and driving forward as if to the attack are signs that he will retreat. When the light chariots come out first and take up a position on the wings, it is a sign that the enemy is forming for battle. Peace proposals

unaccompanied by a sworn covenant indicate a plot. When there is much running about and the soldiers fall into rank, it means that the critical moment has come. When some are seen advancing and some retreating, it is a lure.
—Sun Tzu, *The Art of War,* trans. Lionel Giles

The good general not only deceives the enemy himself, but assumes that his enemy is always deceiving him: "Humble words and increased preparations are signs that the enemy is about to advance," Sun Tzu explains. "Violent language and driving forward as if to the attack are signs that he will retreat . . . Peace proposals unaccompanied by a sworn covenant indicate a plot." Both Confucius and Sun-Tzu, roughly contemporary as they are, offer a philosophy of order, a way of dealing with a disunified country; stability through the proper performance of social duties, or stability through intimidation.
—Susan Wise Bauer, *The History of the Ancient World*

Ellipses show where something has been cut out of a sentence.

élleipsis Greek for "omission"
ellipsis (singular), ellipses (plural)

The Roman historian Varro mentions an early division of Rome's people into three "tribes" of some kind.

The attackers were thoroughly thrashed, since the army of debtors that came

charging out to meet them was, as Livy puts it, "spoiling for a fight."

The present participle of a verb can act as a descriptive adjective.

The city needed laws "which every individual citizen could feel that he had . . .

consented to accept."

Every direct quote must have an attribution tag.
A second or third quote from the same source does not need another attribution tag, as long as context makes the source of the quote clear.

A clause is a group of words that contains a subject and a predicate.
A dependent clause is a fragment that cannot stand by itself as a sentence.
Dependent clauses begin with subordinating words.
Dependent clauses are also known as subordinate clauses.

Adjective clauses are also known as relative clauses because they relate to another word in the independent clause.
Relative pronouns introduce adjective clauses and refer back to an antecedent in the independent clause.
A noun clause takes the place of a noun.

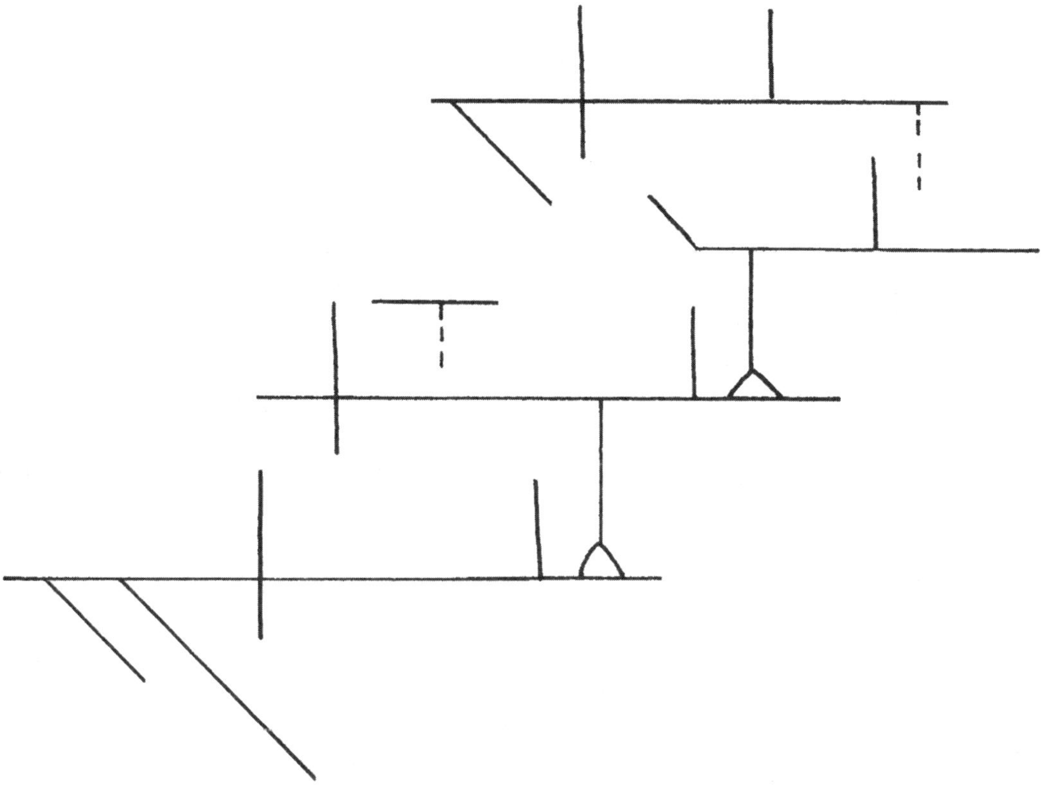

The city of Veii, Livy writes, had "inflicted worse losses than she suffered," which means that the siege had significantly weakened the Roman army.

Such was the fall of Veii, the wealthiest city of Etruria. Even her final destruction witnessed to her greatness, for after a siege of ten summers and ten winters, during which she inflicted worse losses than she suffered, even when her destined hour had come she fell by a stratagem and not by direct assault.

—Livy, *The Early History of Rome*

He had heard, "in the silence of the night," an inhuman voice saying, "Tell the magistrates that the Gauls are coming."

Direct quotes can be words, phrases, clauses, or sentences, as long as they are set off by quotation marks and form part of a grammatically correct original sentence.

Exercise 91A: Using Ellipses

The following six paragraphs are taken from the official Army account of the bombing of the Japanese city of Hiroshima, on August 6, 1945. It was published a year later, in the summer of 1946. The preface reads, "This report describes the effects of the atomic bombs which were dropped on the Japanese cities of Hiroshima and Nagasaki on August 6 and 9, 1945, respectively. It summarizes all the authentic information that is available on damage to structures, injuries to personnel, morale effect, etc., which can be released at this time without prejudicing the security of the United States."

The total word count is 538. Using a word processing program, retype the passage but condense it so that it has no more than 350 words. Do not cut the opening or closing words of any paragraph. Make sure that you don't end up with run-on sentences or fragments!

When you are finished, compare your version with the condensed version found in the Answer Key.

Hiroshima was the primary target of the first atomic bomb mission. The mission went smoothly in every respect. The weather was good, and the crew and equipment functioned perfectly. In every detail, the attack was carried out exactly as planned, and the bomb performed exactly as expected.

The bomb exploded over Hiroshima at 8:15 on the morning of August 6, 1945. About an hour previously, the Japanese early warning radar net had detected the approach of some American aircraft headed for the southern part of Japan. The alert had been given and radio broadcasting stopped in many cities, among them Hiroshima. The planes approached the coast at a very high altitude. At nearly 8:00 A.M., the radar operator in Hiroshima determined that the number of planes coming in was very small—probably not more than three—and the air raid alert was lifted. The normal radio broadcast warning was given to the people that it might be advisable to go to shelter if B-29's were actually sighted, but no raid was expected beyond some sort of reconnaissance. At 8:15 A.M., the bomb exploded with a blinding flash in the sky, and a great rush of air and a loud rumble of noise extended for many miles around the city; the first blast was soon followed by the sounds of falling buildings and of growing fires, and a great cloud of dust and smoke began to cast a pall of darkness over the city.

At 8:16 A.M., the Tokyo control operator of the Japanese Broadcasting Corporation noticed that the Hiroshima station had gone off the air. He tried to use another telephone line to reestablish his program, but it too had failed. About twenty minutes later the Tokyo railroad telegraph center realized that the main line telegraph had stopped working just north of Hiroshima. From some small railway stops within ten miles of the city there came unofficial and confused reports of a terrible explosion in Hiroshima. All these reports were transmitted to the Headquarters of the Japanese General Staff.

Military headquarters repeatedly tried to call the Army Control Station in Hiroshima. The complete silence from that city puzzled the men at Headquarters; they knew that no large enemy raid could have occurred, and they knew that no sizeable store of explosives was in Hiroshima at that time. A young officer of the Japanese General Staff was instructed to fly immediately to Hiroshima, to land, survey the damage, and return to Tokyo with reliable information for the staff. It was generally felt at Headquarters that nothing serious had taken place, that it was all a terrible rumor starting from a few sparks of truth.

The staff officer went to the airport and took off for the southwest. After flying for about three hours, while still nearly 100 miles from Hiroshima, he and his pilot saw a great cloud of smoke from the bomb. In the bright afternoon, the remains of Hiroshima were burning.

Their plane soon reached the city, around which they circled in disbelief. A great scar on the land, still burning, and covered by a heavy cloud of smoke, was all that was left of a great city.

Exercise 91B: Partial Quotations

On your own paper, rewrite the five statements below so that each one contains a partial quotation. Draw the partial quotation from the bolded sentences that follow each statement. The authors of the bolded sentences are provided for you—be sure to include an attribution tag for each direct quote!

You may change and adapt the statements freely.

One of your sentences should contain a very short one- to three-word quote; one should contain a preposition phrase, gerund phrase, participle phrase, or infinitive phrase; and one should quote a dependent clause.

If you need help, ask your instructor to show you sample answers.

Henry David Thoreau experimented with simple living.

For more than five years I maintained myself thus solely by the labor of my hands, and I found, that by working about six weeks in a year, I could meet all the expenses of living. The whole of my winters, as well as most of my summers, I had free and clear for study.

—Henry David Thoreau, nineteenth-century philosopher

St. Francis of Assisi was small and active.

Francis of Assisi was slight in figure with that sort of slightness which, combined with so much vivacity, gives the impression of smallness. He was probably taller than he looked; middle-sized, his biographers say; he was certainly very active and, considering what he went through, must have been tolerably tough.

—G. K. Chesterton, essayist and biographer

Japanese samurai were skilled swordsmen.

The essence of a samurai's worth lay in his mastery of swordsmanship. The sword was not just a weapon but a vehicle for *seishin tanren*, a spiritual forging that enabled the user to wipe out moral stains and to achieve *satori*, spiritual perfection.

—Richard Cohen, historian

Nuclear war between the U.S. and the Soviet Union could have destroyed the entire world.

It is the smoke, after all (not the fallout, which would remain mostly limited to the northern hemisphere), that would do it worldwide: smoke and soot lofted by fierce firestorms in hundreds of burning cities into the stratosphere, where it would not rain out and would remain for a decade or more, enveloping the globe and blocking most sunlight, lowering annual global temperatures to the level of the last Ice Age, and killing all harvests worldwide, causing near-universal starvation within a year or two.

—Daniel Ellsberg, military strategist

Cows, sheep, and goats are ruminants.

The word "ruminant" comes from the Latin word *ruminare*, which means "to rechew." Food is regurgitated, rechewed, and sent to the rumen, one of the animal's stomachs, to be decomposed by fermentation before passing on to the other compartments.

—Mark Kurlansky, science writer

Exercise 91C: Diagramming

On your own paper, diagram every word of the following sentences. These are slightly adapted from *Pale Rider: The Spanish Flu of 1918 and How It Changed the World*, by Laura Spinney.

These are difficult! Do your best, and then compare your answers with the Key.

The Spanish flu infected one in three people on earth, or 500 million human beings.

There are very few cemeteries in the world that, assuming they are older than a century, don't contain a cluster of graves from the autumn of 1918—when the second and worst wave of the pandemic struck—and people's memories reflect that.

In 1918, if you heard a neighbour or a relation coughing or saw them fall down in front of you, you knew there was a good chance that you were already sick yourself.

There was, in other words, no warning system in place.

— LESSON 92 —

Partial Quotations

Ellipses

Block Quotes

Colons

Brackets

If a direct quotation is longer than three lines, indent the entire quote one inch from the margin in a separate block of text and omit quotation marks.

If you change or make additions to a direct quotation, use brackets.

> And I doubt not but posterity will find many things, that are now but Rumors, verified into practical Realities. It may be some ages hence, a voyage to the Southern unknown Tracts, yea possibly the Moon, will not be more strange than one to America. To them, that come after us, it may be as ordinary to buy a pair of wings to fly into remotest Regions; as now a pair of Boots to ride a Journey. And to confer at the distance of the Indies by Sympathetick conveyances, may be as usual to future times, as to us in a litterary correspondence. The restauration of gray hairs to Juvenility, and renewing the exhausted marrow, may at length be effected without a miracle: And the turning of the now comparative desert world into a Paradise, may not improbably be expected from late Agriculture.
>
> Now those, that judge by the narrowness of former Principles, will smile at these Paradoxical expectations: But questionless those great Inventions, that have in these later Ages altered the face of all things; in their naked proposals, and meer suppositions, were to former times as *ridiculous.* To have talk'd of a *new Earth* to have been discovered, had been a Romance to Antiquity. And to sayl without sight of Stars or shoars by the guidance of a Mineral, a story more absurd, than the flight of Daedalus.
>
> —Joseph Glanvill, *Scepsis Scientifica: Or, Confest Ignorance, The Way to Science; In an Essay of the Vanity of Dogmatizing and Confident Opinion*

In 1661, the English philosopher Joseph Glanvill predicted the invention of "many things, that are now but Rumors." Among them were space travel, airplanes, and conversation over long distances. In his essay *Scepsis Scientifica,* Glanvill admits that these inventions seem farfetched, but he argues that the discovery of a new continent must have seemed just as unlikely:

> It may be some ages hence, a voyage to the Southern unknown Tracts, yea possibly the Moon, will not be more strange than one to America. To them, that come after us, it may be as ordinary to buy a pair of wings to fly into remotest Regions; as now a pair of Boots to ride a Journey. And to confer at the distance of the Indies by Sympathetick conveyances, may be as usual to future times, as to us in a litterary correspondence . . . [T]hose great Inventions, that have in these later Ages altered the face of all things . . . were to former times as *ridiculous.* To have talk'd of a *new Earth* [the North and South American continents] to have been discovered, had been a Romance [Glanvill means a "fairy tale"] to Antiquity.

Glanvill goes on to point out that navigating a ship by compass ("the guidance of a Mineral," as he puts it) instead of by the stars must have seemed just as impossible to ancient sailors as moon travel does to people of his own day.

When using a word processing program, leave an additional line space before and after a block quote.

Block quotes should be introduced by a colon (if preceded by a complete sentence) or a comma (if preceded by a partial sentence).

As the English philosopher Joseph Glanvill predicted in 1661,

> It may be some ages hence, a voyage to the Southern unknown Tracts, yea possibly the Moon, will not be more strange than one to America. To them, that come after us, it may be as ordinary to buy a pair of wings to fly into remotest Regions; as now a pair of Boots to ride a Journey.

If you change or make additions to a direct quotation, use brackets.

Exercise 92A: Writing Dialogue Correctly

The following speeches, from *Bambi: A Life in the Woods* by Felix Salten, are listed in the correct order, but are missing their dialogue tags. On your own paper, rewrite the speeches as dialogue, making use of the dialogue tags below. You must place at least one dialogue tag before a speech, one in the middle of a speech, and one following a speech.

A list of the rules governing dialogue follows, for your reference.

When you are finished, compare your dialogue to the original passage in the Answer Key.

List 1. Dialogue (in Correct Order)

Who are they, Mother?

Those are ants

Look, see that piece of grass jumping. Look how high it can jump!

That's not grass. That's a nice grasshopper

Why does he jump that way?

Because we're walking here; he's afraid we'll step on him

Oh; oh, you don't have to be afraid; we won't hurt you

I'm not afraid; I was only frightened for a moment when I was talking to my wife

Excuse us for disturbing you

Not at all. Since it's you, it's perfectly all right. But you never know who's coming and you have to be careful

This is the first time in my life that I've ever been on the meadow. My mother brought me

List 2. Dialogue Tags (Not in Correct Order)

said Bambi shyly
he said again politely
his mother explained
his mother answered
the grasshopper replied in a quavering voice
the grasshopper quavered
Bambi asked
he asked
cried Bambi
his mother answered
said Bambi, turning to the grasshopper, who was sitting on a daisy
Bambi explained

List 3. For Reference: Rules for Writing Dialogue

A dialogue tag identifies the person making the speech.

When a dialogue tag comes after a speech, place a comma, exclamation point, or question mark inside the closing quotation marks.

When a dialogue tag comes before a speech, place a comma after the tag. Put the dialogue's final punctuation mark inside the closing quotation marks.

Speeches do not need to be attached to a dialogue tag as long as the text clearly indicates the speaker.

Usually, a new paragraph begins with each new speaker.

When a dialogue tag comes in the middle of a speech, follow it with a comma if the following dialogue is an incomplete sentence. Follow it with a period if the following dialogue is a complete sentence.

Exercise 92B: Using Direct Quotations Correctly

On your own paper, rewrite the following three paragraphs, inserting at least one quote from each of the following three sources into the paragraph. Use the following guidelines:

a) At least one quote must be a block quote.
b) At least one quote must be a complete sentence.
c) At least one quote must be a partial sentence incorporated into your own sentence.
d) Each quote must have an attribution tag.
e) At least one quote must be condensed, using ellipses.
f) You must make at least one change or addition that needs to be put in brackets.

A list of the rules governing direct quotations follows, for your reference.

You may make whatever changes are needed to the paragraphs. When you are finished, compare your paragraphs to the sample answer in the Answer Key.

These paragraphs are adapted from Chapter Ten of *The History of the Renaissance World*, by Susan Wise Bauer.

List 1. Paragraphs

When Injong died in 1146, his oldest son Uijong was crowned in his place: the eighteenth king of his line, heir to an uneasy kingdom. Tact and wisdom were required, but Uijong had neither. His father and mother had preferred their second son, Uijong's younger brother Kyong; they thought Uijong to be a trifler, with no skill for governing.

Once on the throne, Uijong turned out to be more interested in building gorgeous gardens and writing poetry than in ruling the country. Ignoring military campaigns, he built Buddhist temples and gave them names like "Tranquillity" and "Joyful Pleasure." He wrote poetry and got drunk with his friends; he dug lily ponds, traveled from one beauty spot to another, and gave alms to the poor.

Meanwhile, he ordered soldiers to dig ditches and build walls for public projects and forced officers to act as ceremonial bodyguards to civil officials. Enlisted men found their salaries unexpectedly docked, or promised land tracts suddenly reassigned. On royal expeditions, military men were allowed to wait, cold and hungry, until civilians were well fed. Disrespect of Goryeo's military officers and scorn for their men grew more extreme.

List 2. Sources

In Uijong's twenty-fourth year [1170] the king was attending a memorial service, and again he partied with his favorite civilian officials, exchanging poems and forgetting the time. The military escorts became especially hungry.

—The contemporary history *Goryeosa*

When Uijong was still crown prince, both his father Injong and his mother Lady Im questioned his right to succeed to the throne. Injong harbored serious misgivings about Uijong's talent and ability to govern; his mother openly favored her second son, Uijong's brother Prince Kyong. Uijong won the throne only because of the staunch support of the royal tutor, Chong Supmyong, who assured the royal parents that he would personally guide and instruct Uijong once he became king. Inheriting the throne under this cloud of opposition, Uijong found his effectiveness as a monarch curbed and his ability to exercise royal prerogatives curtailed.

—Historian Edward J. Shultz, *Generals and Scholars: Military Rule in Medieval Korea*

However, it was the neglect and abuses of the military by King Uijong (1146-1170) that inspired the military revolt of 1170. An aesthetic who scorned the warrior class, he was enchanted by such peaceful arts as gardening, building a number of pavilions with names like "Tranquillity," "Joyful Pleasure," and "Beauty Attained." Around these he fashioned lily ponds and mock hillsides for his enjoyment. King Uijong's contempt for the military was blatantly exhibited by such practices as requiring distinguished commanders to serve as lowly military escorts. During this period other insults were recorded. Without suffering any consequences, Kim Ton-jung, the son of Kim Pu-sik, maliciously pulled and set fire with a candle the beard of Chong Chung-bue, a military officer.

—Author R. Barry Harmon, *5,000 Years of Korean Martial Arts: The Heritage of the Hermit Kingdom Warriors*

List 3. For Reference: Rules For Using Direct Quotations

When an attribution tag comes after a direct quote, place a comma, exclamation point, or question mark inside the closing quotation marks.

When an attribution tag comes before a direct quote, place a comma after the tag. Put the dialogue's final punctuation mark inside the closing quotation marks.

When an attribution tag comes in the middle of a direct quotation, follow it with a comma if the remaining quote is an incomplete sentence. Follow it with a period if the remaining quote is a complete sentence.

Direct quotes can be words, phrases, clauses, or sentences, as long as they are set off by quotation marks and form part of a grammatically correct original sentence.

An ellipsis shows where something has been cut out of a sentence.

Every direct quote must have an attribution tag.

If a direct quotation is longer than three lines, indent the entire quote one inch from the margin in a separate block of text and omit quotation marks.

If you change or make additions to a direct quotation, use brackets.

WEEK 24

Floating Elements

— LESSON 93 —

Interjections
Nouns of Direct Address
Parenthetical Expressions

Oh dear, I've dropped my keys.
Oops! The keys fell through the grate into the sewer.
Alas, I will not be able to unlock my door.
Whew! That was a close one.
Whoa, let's just slow down here for a minute.
Hush, I'm on the phone.

inter between
jacere to throw

Interjections express sudden feeling or emotion. They are set off with commas or stand alone with a closing punctuation mark.

Friends, Romans, countrymen, lend me your ears!
Stars, hide your fire!
I am afraid, my dear, that you are too late.
Run, baby, run.
Get down, dog!

Nouns of direct address name a person or thing who is being spoken to. They are set off with commas. They are capitalized only if they are proper names or titles.

Parentheses ( ) can enclose words that are not essential to the sentence.
Parenthetical expressions often interrupt or are irrelevant to the rest of the sentence.
Punctuation goes inside the parentheses if it applies to the parenthetical material; all other punctuation goes outside the parentheses.
Parenthetical material only begins with a capital letter if it is a complete sentence with ending punctuation.
Parenthetical expressions can also be set off by commas.

The doctor was so late, in fact, that the baby was born before he arrived.

To be sure, she will tell a very plausible story.

When Marco Polo travelled to China he crossed, as it were, the horizon of European knowledge.

Fear was, no doubt, the greatest enemy the army had.

In a word, he supported the other candidate.

These things are always difficult, you know.

Short parenthetical expressions such as the following are usually set off by commas: *in short, in fact, in reality, as it were, as it happens, no doubt, in a word, to be sure, to be brief, after all, you know, of course.*

Whew! That was a close one.

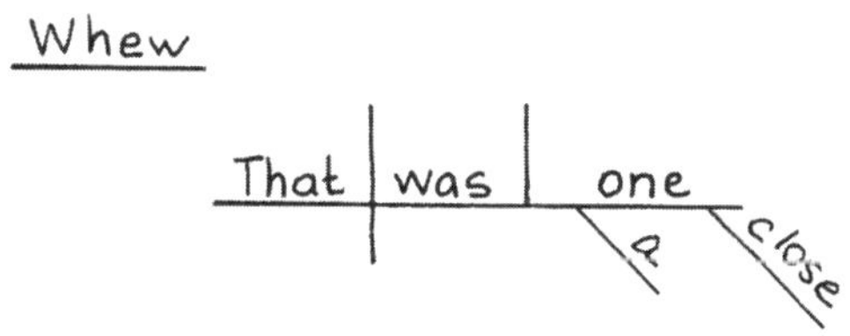

Friends, Romans, countrymen, lend me your ears!

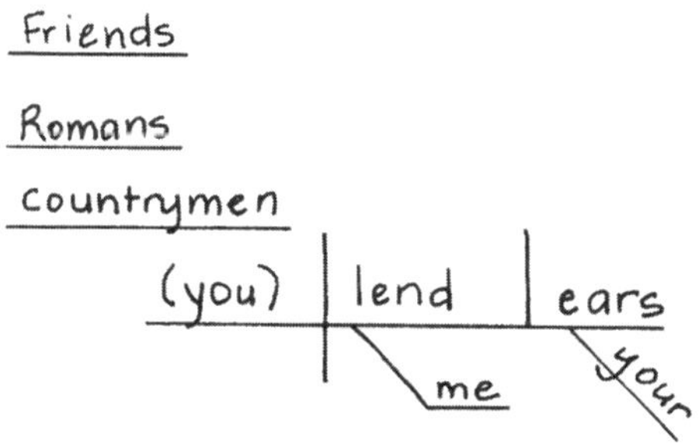

In a word, he supported the other candidate.

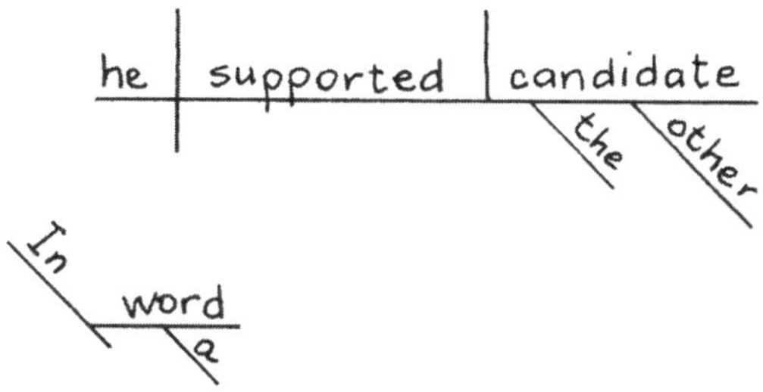

The following sentences are taken from *The Scarlet Pimpernel* by Baroness Emmuska Orczy.

Your heroism, your devotion, which I, alas, so little deserved, have atoned for that unfortunate episode of the ball.

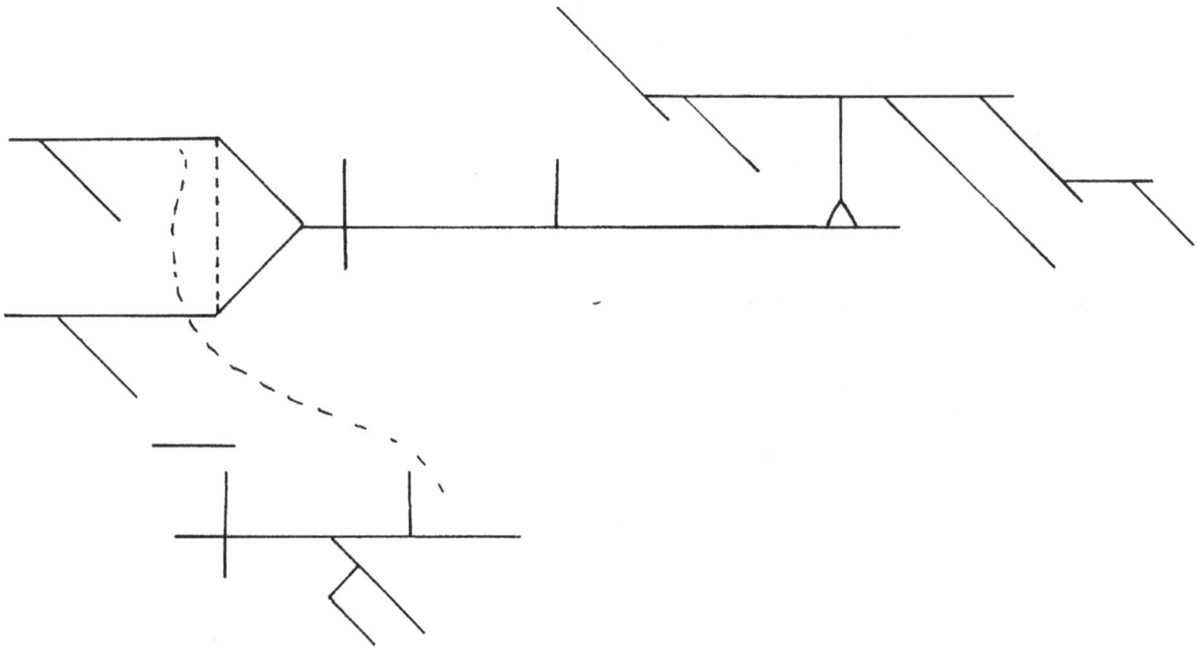

Do you impugn my bravery, Madame?

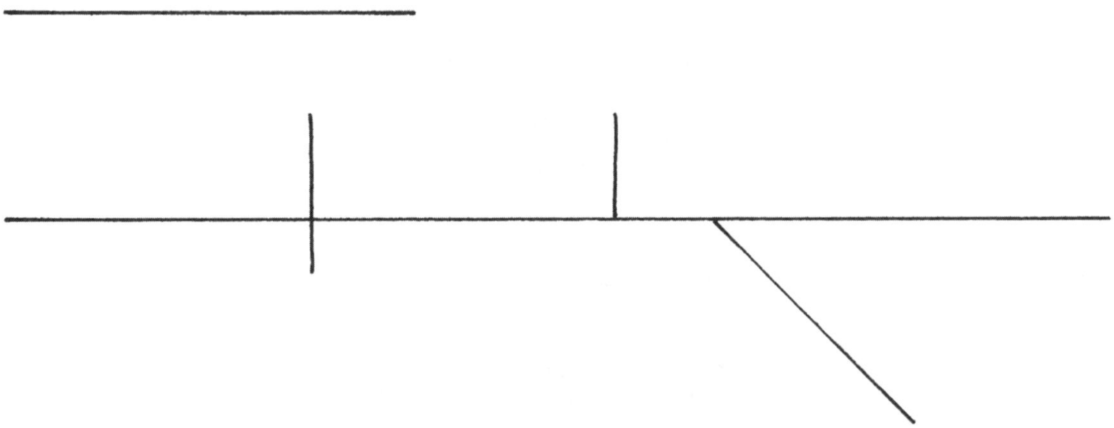

This restriction, of course, did not apply to her, and Frank would, of course, not dare to oppose her.

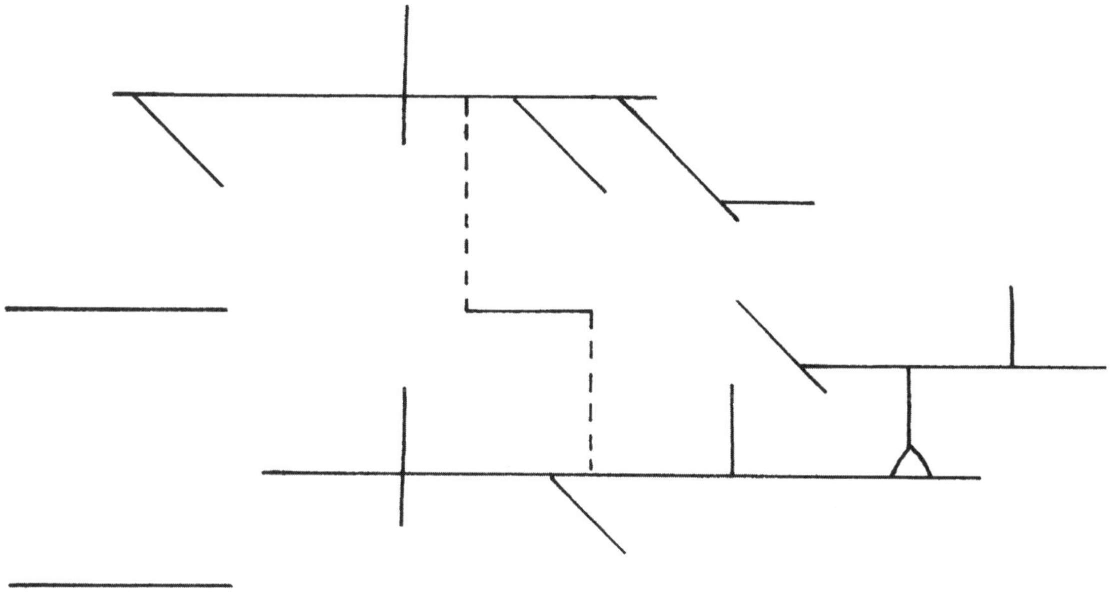

The storm will, no doubt, snarl the traffic.

There is no doubt that the storm is coming.

We aren't ready yet, you know.

You know that we aren't ready yet.

The snow caused school to be cancelled, of course.

In case of snow, school is cancelled as a matter of course.

Exercise 93A: Using Floating Elements Correctly

On your own paper, rewrite the following sentences in List 1, inserting interjections, nouns of direct address, and parenthetical expressions from List 2. You must use every item in List 2 at least once. Every sentence in List 1 must have at least one insertion.

Interjections may either come before or after sentences on their own, or may be incorporated directly into the sentence.

List 1. Sentences

I just stubbed my toe on the threshold!
Will you show me how to make your picadillo?
That piece of meat is spoiled.
Settle down or we won't be finished before recess!
I will have to leave the party early to finish my research paper.

It is so delightful to share this meal together.
Your silk scarf is exquisite.
That is the most boring movie ever made.
You sang that solo with great panache!
Climbing Mount Everest is a very stupid thing to do.
Being lazy can be a good thing.

List 2. Interjections, Nouns of Direct Address, Parenthetical Expressions

in my opinion
class
it seems to me
dear friends
Abuela
bravo
ouch
Shira
alas
after all
by the way

Exercise 93B: Parenthetical Expressions

In the following pairs of sentences, underline each subject once and each predicate twice. In each pair, cross out the parenthetical expression that is not essential to the sentences. If the expression is used as an essential part of the sentence, circle it and label it with the correct part of the sentence (e.g., *prep phrase acting as adj.*, etc.). If it acts as a modifier, draw an arrow back to the word it modifies.

The first pair is done for you.

subject and predicate
I think that I will say no more on this subject.

This subject is, ~~I think~~, one of the hardest to talk about honestly.

The knight carried, to be sure, all the weapons he needed to slay the dragon.

The knight knew it was vital to be sure of his strength.

I have heard of a great and vicious monster that haunts these woods.

The monster, I have heard, keeps the bones of its victims in a deep cave.

By the way, fifteen knights have been eaten by the monster already.

A rusty suit of armor lay by the way.

The narrator of the musical cannot sing, and so he says the words instead.

The music, so he says, is too difficult for amateurs to sing.

Exercise 93C: Diagramming

On your own paper, diagram every word of the following sentences. Several of them can be diagrammed in more than one way—when you're finished, compare your answers with the Key and look at the instructor's notes to understand the difference!

These are taken from the classic novel of the American Civil War *Gone with the Wind*, by Margaret Mitchell.

And anyway, the Yankees are too scared of us to fight.

Why, honey, of course there's going to be a war.

And here she had practically promised them the whole of tomorrow—seats by her at the barbecue, all the waltzes (and they'd see to it that the dances were all waltzes!) and the supper intermission.

Oh, Ashley, I love you so much that I'd walk every step of the way to Virginia just to be near you!

Peachtree Creek was crimson, so they say, after the Yankees crossed it.

— LESSON 94 —

Appositives

Rome, the Eternal City, is built on seven hills that lie on both sides of the Tiber River.

Dubrovnik, the Pearl of the Adriatic, is a walled seaside fortress in Croatia.

Helsinki, the White City of the North, gets no sunshine at all for about fifty days every winter.

In Mumbai, the City of Dreams, almost seven million people ride the trains every day.

Chinese tin miners founded the Malaysian city Kuala Lumpur, the Golden Triangle, in 1857.

The people of Sydney, the Harbour City, celebrate Harbour Day, a commemoration of the first convict ships landing in Sydney Cove, on January 26.

An appositive is a noun, pronoun, or noun phrase that usually follows another noun and renames or explains it.

Rome's first ruler, Romulus, killed his brother and seized power.
In the Middle Ages, many Spanish Jews, *Conversos*, migrated to Dubrovnik.
A 1981 movie about the USSR, *Reds,* was actually filmed in Helsinki.

Rome is built on seven hills that lie on both sides of the Tiber River.
Dubrovnik is a walled seaside fortress in Croatia.
Helsinki gets no sunshine at all for about fifty days every winter.

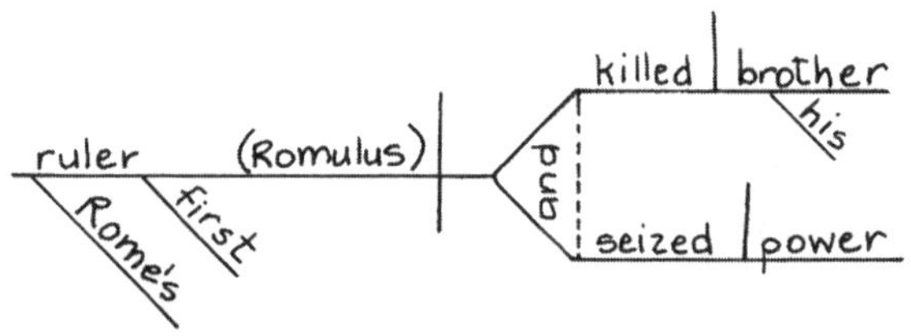

In Mumbai, the City of Dreams, almost seven million people ride the trains every day.

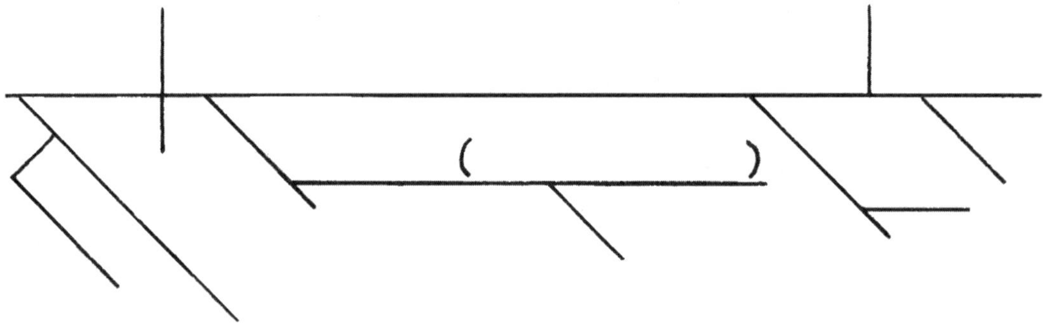

Chinese tin miners founded the Malaysian city Kuala Lumpur, the Golden Triangle, in 1857.

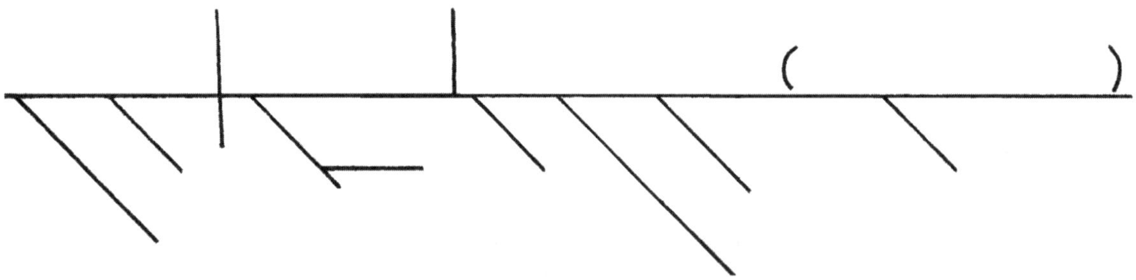

An appositive is a noun, pronoun, or noun phrase that usually follows another noun and renames or explains it.

The wisest philosopher of the ancients, Socrates wrote nothing.

A better-known destination, Marseilles is less picturesque than the surrounding villages.

An ancient breed, the Kuvasz protects helpless livestock.

Appositives are set off by commas.

The wisest philosopher of the ancients, Socrates, wrote nothing.

A better-known destination, Marseilles, is less picturesque than the surrounding villages.

An ancient breed, the Kuvasz, protects helpless livestock.

An appositive that occurs within a sentence has commas both before and after it. An appositive at the beginning of a sentence has one comma that follows it. An appositive at the end of a sentence has one comma that precedes it.

My grandfather, Aquilino Ramos, makes the best pork adobo I've ever eaten.

The best supper ever, pineapple chicken adobo waited for us on the table.

My grandfather prepared a fantastic meal, squid adobo with tomatoes.

An appositive is a noun, pronoun, or noun phrase that usually follows another noun and renames or explains it. Appositives are set off by commas.

Exercise 94A: Using Appositives

Rewrite the following sentences on your own paper, inserting at least one appositive or appositive phrase from List 1 into each of the sentences in List 2, and using correct punctuation. You may insert more than one appositive into each sentence, but you must use each appositive or phrase in List 1 at least once.

List 1. Appositives

a time of unique difficulty for England and its allies

the highest mountain peak in North America

an attack that killed between 25,000 and 40,000 German civilians

a difficult target for an amateur skygazer

Sir Winston Leonard Spencer Churchill

a Class II (mid-sized) railroad bringing in over 37.4 but less than 433.2 million dollars yearly

a period of heavy bombing raids against Britain

the Red Planet

the prime minister of Britain

a century after the first attempt to reach its peak

the German military air force

two groups of Native American peoples

List 2. Sentences

The surface of Mars shows signs of water erosion.

Mars is easiest to see during the three months that it is closest to Earth.

Winston Churchill exhorted the British people to "keep on" during World War II.

The Luftwaffe mounted the Blitz between 1940 and 1941; over 40,000 British civilians were killed.

Winston Churchill authorized the firebombing of Dresden.

The Inupiat and the Yup'ik held lands in the territory now known as Alaska.

The Alaska Railroad runs through Denali National Park.

Denali is also known as Mount McKinley.

By 2003, Denali had killed nearly a hundred mountaineers.

Exercise 94B: Identifying Appositives

In each of the following sentences, underline the subject once and the predicate twice. Circle each appositive or appositive phrase.

These sentences are taken from *If I Stay,* by Gayle Forman.

Adam's band, Shooting Star, is on an upward spiral, which is a great thing—mostly.

I sniff the coffee, the rich, black, oily French roast we all prefer.

We pile into the car, a rusting Buick that was already old when Gran gave it to us after Teddy was born.

Mom gives me a sidelong glance with her eyebrow arched, her version of a soul-searching stare.

I lean my head against the car window, watching the scenery zip by, a tableau of dark green fir trees dotted with snow, wispy strands of white fog, and heavy gray storm clouds up above.

The police politely offer alternate routes, back roads that will take people where they need to be.

They must have places to go, the people in these cars, but a lot of them don't turn back.

My middle school didn't have much of a music program, so Mom found me a private teacher, a college student who came over once a week.

It was at a hall in town, a place that usually showcased local bands, so the acoustics were terrible for unamplified classical.

I've never been in a hospital before. My best friend, Kim, has.

Adam played me snippets of bands he liked, a Swedish pop trio that sounded monotonous but then some Icelandic art band that was quite beautiful.

Gran tells her about the various people who are en route right now, aunts, uncles.

But eyelids are not like elbows or knees or shoulders, parts of the body accustomed to being jostled.

Exercise 94C: Diagramming (Challenge!)

On your own paper, diagram every word of the following five sentences from Exercise 94B.

> **NOTE**: Each one of these sentences contains a slightly ambiguous element that could, possibly, be diagrammed in more than one way! Try to come up with solutions on your own—how can you make the sentence structure clear? If you get frustrated, ask your instructor for help. And when you're finished, compare your diagrams to those in the Answer Key.

Adam's band, Shooting Star, is on an upward spiral, which is a great thing—mostly.

We pile into the car, a rusting Buick that was already old when Gran gave it to us after Teddy was born.

I lean my head against the car window, watching the scenery zip by, a tableau of dark green fir trees dotted with snow, wispy strands of white fog, and heavy gray storm clouds up above.

Adam played me snippets of bands he liked, a Swedish pop trio that sounded monotonous but then some Icelandic art band that was quite beautiful.

Gran tells her about the various people who are en route right now, aunts, uncles.

— LESSON 95 —

Appositives
Intensive and Reflexive Pronouns
Noun Clauses in Apposition
Object Complements

myself, himself, herself, itself, yourself, yourselves, ourselves, themselves

Reflexive pronouns refer back to the subject.
Intensive pronouns emphasize a noun or another pronoun.

I may have expressed myself badly.

I myself was never top in anything!

An appositive is a noun, pronoun, or noun phrase that usually follows another noun and renames or explains it. Appositives are set off by commas.

I may have expressed myself badly.

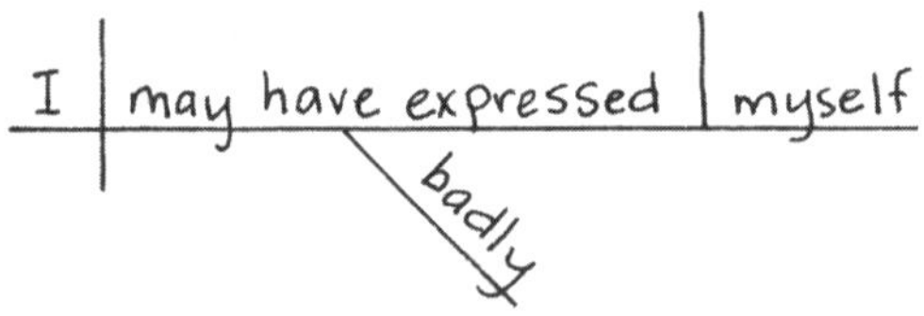

I myself was never top in anything!

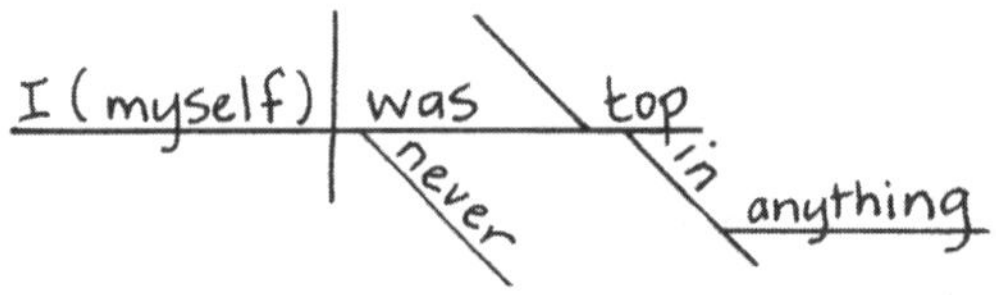

The author, Fyodor Dostoyevsky, was born in Moscow in 1821.

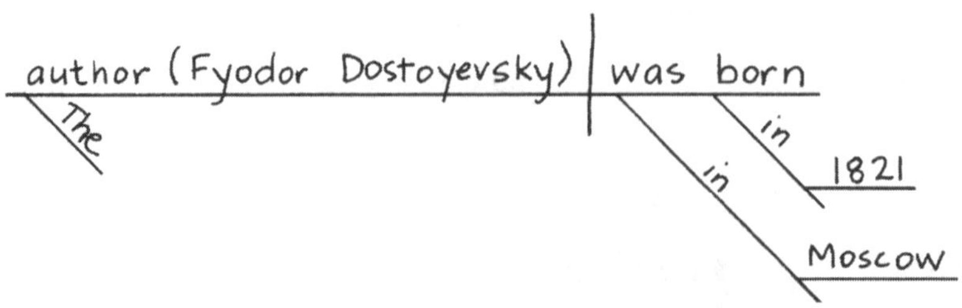

Exercise 95A: Reflexive and Intensive Pronoun Review

In the following sentences from *Inkheart*, by Cornelia Funke, underline each reflexive or intensive pronoun. Put parentheses around each intensive pronoun. Label each reflexive pronoun with one of the following labels: *DO* (direct object of a verb form), *IO* (indirect object of a verb form), or *OP* (object of a preposition).

For *DO* pronouns ONLY, draw an arrow from the label back to the verb or verb form that is affecting it.

Had he ever read the name on the cover of *Inkheart* just below the title itself?

Suppose we're next to find ourselves on a pyre?

Perhaps I ought to catch myself one, thought Dustfinger.

She wasn't sure herself why she had asked the question.

And I don't suppose you think you can just help yourself to anything you want, never mind what or where.

Your innocence always amazed me—after all, you lie very cleverly to yourself.

Let's try to make ourselves comfortable together.

Farid had run so fast he was gasping for breath as he flung himself down on the grass beside Dustfinger.

He himself had never got the knack of it.

We both know what fun it can be to get right into a book and live there for a while, but falling out of a story and suddenly finding yourself in this world doesn't seem to be much fun at all.

Sometimes Dustfinger thought Basta's constant fear of curses and sudden disaster probably arose from his terror of the darkness within himself, which made him assume that the rest of the world must be exactly the same.

I think we'd better make sure of that for ourselves, don't you?

The dog kennels lay beyond the wall, too, but when Dustfinger swung himself up and over they were empty.

They had seen for themselves that their allies knew as much about killing as their enemies.

When day dawned, she persuaded Mortimer to get a little rest himself while she kept watch.

Meggie bit her lip to stop herself from shaking, but she knew the fear showed in her eyes, and she knew that Capricorn saw it.

The world was as quiet as if it had spun itself into a cocoon like a moth preparing itself to slip out in the morning, young again and good as new.

The magic comes out of the books themselves, and I have no more idea than you or any of your men how it works.

Have I made myself clear?

A dependent clause can act as an appositive if it renames the noun that it follows.

The article's argument, that studying grammar is good for your brain, didn't convince me.

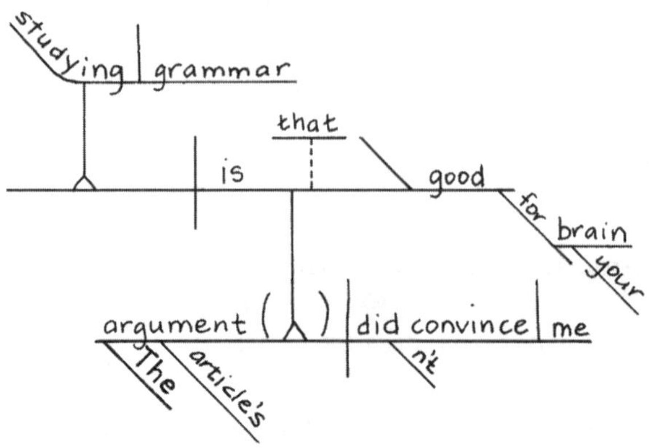

Don't forget our story, that we left early and didn't stop on the way.

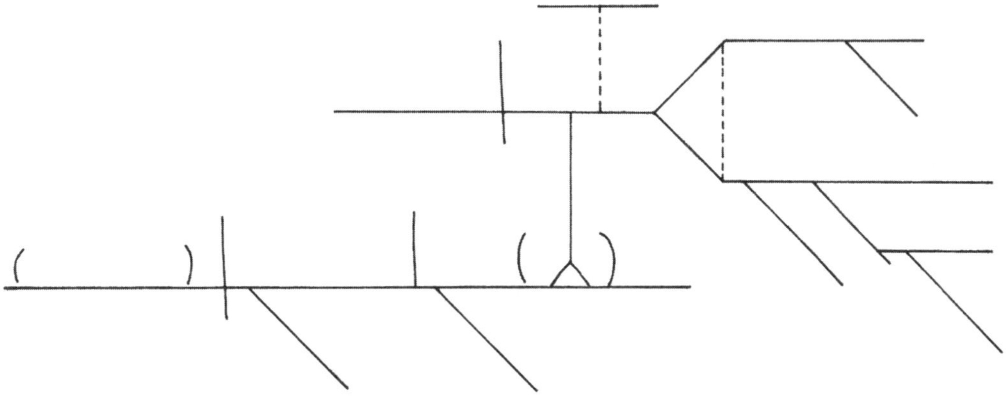

Dependent clauses can act as adjective clauses, adverb clauses, or noun clauses.

An adjective clause is a dependent clause that acts as an adjective in a sentence, modifying a noun or pronoun in the independent clause. Relative pronouns introduce adjective clauses and refer back to an antecedent in the independent clause.

A noun clause takes the place of a noun. Noun clauses can be introduced by relative pronouns, relative adverbs, or subordinating conjunctions.

Reread the story that made you happy.

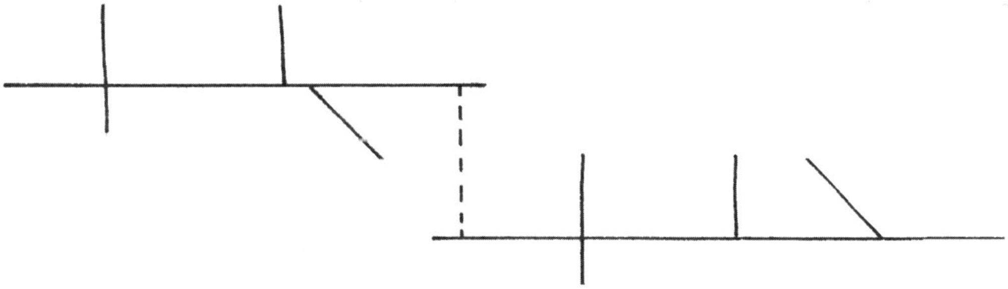

An object complement follows the direct object and renames or describes it.

The story, a long boring tale that seemed to go on forever, took up most of the evening.

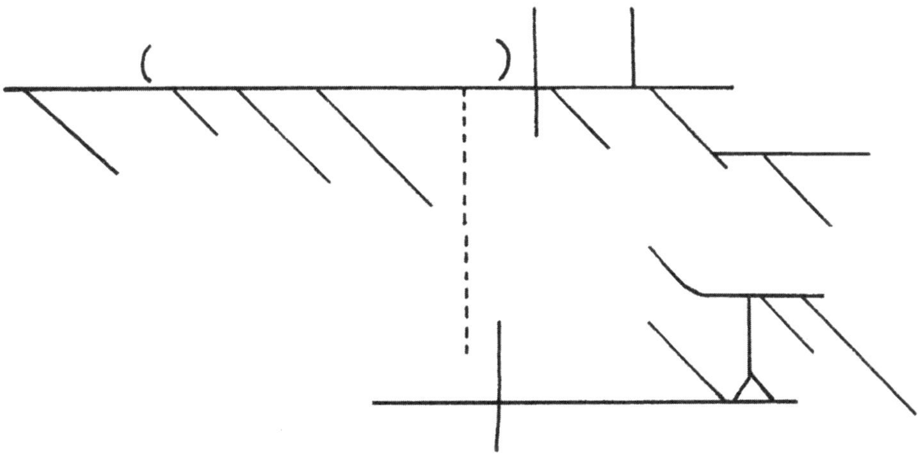

Exercise 95B: Clauses and Appositives

For each of the following sentences, carry out the following steps:

1) Underline every dependent clause. If a clause occurs within another clause, double underline it.
2) Label each clause as *N* for noun, *ADJ* for adjective, or *ADV* for adverb.
3) For each noun clause, identify the part of the sentence that it functions as (*S* for subject, *DO* for direct object, *IO* for indirect object, *OP* for object of the preposition, *PN* for predicate nominative, *APP* for appositive).
4) For each *ADJ* and *ADV* clause, draw an arrow from the label back to the word modified.
5) Find and circle any other noun or phrase serving as an appositive. Write *APP* above the circle. Place an *X* above every word renamed by an appositive.

These sentences have been taken (and in some cases slightly adapted) from *The Milky Way and Beyond: Stars, Nebulae, and Other Galaxies*, edited by Erik Gregersen.

The Milky Way is actually a large spiral system, a galaxy, that consists of several billion stars.

Astronomers can determine its large-scale structure only with the aid of radio and infrared telescopes, which can detect the forms of radiation that penetrate the obscuring matter.

The Galaxy is immense, with the Sun, our own star, nearer the edge than the center.

One of the largest-known planetary nebulae, the Helix Nebula in the constellation Aquarius, subtends an angle of about 20 minutes of arc—two-thirds the angular size of the Moon.

Surrounding the nucleus is an extended bulge of stars that is nearly spherical in shape.

Astronomers did not know that the galaxy had a spiral structure until 1953, when the distances to stellar associations were first obtained reliably.

A general spiral pattern will result simply from this fact: the rotation speed is different at different distances from the galactic centre.

Scientists do not understand how turbulence, chaotic motions of gas, affects the behavior of nebulae.

Dark matter, undetected material out there that is completely unexpected, is dark at virtually all wavelengths.

Until the dark matter is identified and its distribution determined, all that can be said is that the mass of the Milky Way is several times larger than thought earlier.

Low-luminosity stars, what we call brown dwarfs, are so faint that only a few have been detected directly.

The most commonly accepted theoretical representation of spiral structure, that of the density-wave theory, suggests that the ratio of star densities in the spiral arms is on the order of 0.6.

The white dwarfs represent the final stage in the life of a typical star, when most available sources of energy have been exhausted and the star has become relatively dim.

The differences between stars—how they formed, how dense they are, how big they are—change the ways that stars die.

The next closest star to Earth is Proxima Centauri, which is the smallest of three stars making up the triple star Alpha Centauri.

Many models of galaxy formation have been constructed on a single basis, what we know about conditions in the early universe.

Exercise 95C: Diagramming

On your own paper, diagram every word of these two sentences from C. S. Forester's classic sea novel *Mr. Midshipman Hornblower.* Do your best to place each word on the diagram, but ask your instructor if you need help—these should be challenging!

There was an occasion when Mr. Bowles, the master, was holding a class in navigation for his mates and for the midshipmen, and the captain by bad luck happened by and glanced through the results of the problem the class had individually been set to solve.

Before and below him a British seaman was fighting a furious cutlass duel with a French officer, and he realized with vague astonishment that the kettle-mending noise he had heard was the sound of cutlass against cutlass—that clash of steel against steel that poets wrote about.

— LESSON 96 —

Appositives
Noun Clauses in Apposition
Absolute Constructions

I am absolutely serious, my friend.

The whole story is absolutely untrue.

There is absolutely no question as to the alibi!

He appeared to be in an absolute frenzy.

Her face and voice were absolutely cold and expressionless.

Having no near relations or friends, I was trying to make up my mind what to do, when I ran across John Cavendish. (Adjective)

Our efforts having been in vain, we had abandoned the matter. **(Absolute construction)**

Semantic: having to do with meaning

(Greek *sēmantikós*, "having meaning")

An absolute construction has a strong semantic relationship but no grammatical connection to the rest of the sentence.

To tell the truth, an idea, wild and extravagant in itself, had once or twice that morning flashed through my brain.

Dr. Bauerstein remained in the background, his grave bearded face unchanged.

He has lived by his wits, as the saying goes.

> To tell the truth, an idea, wild and extravagant in itself, had once or twice that morning flashed through my brain.

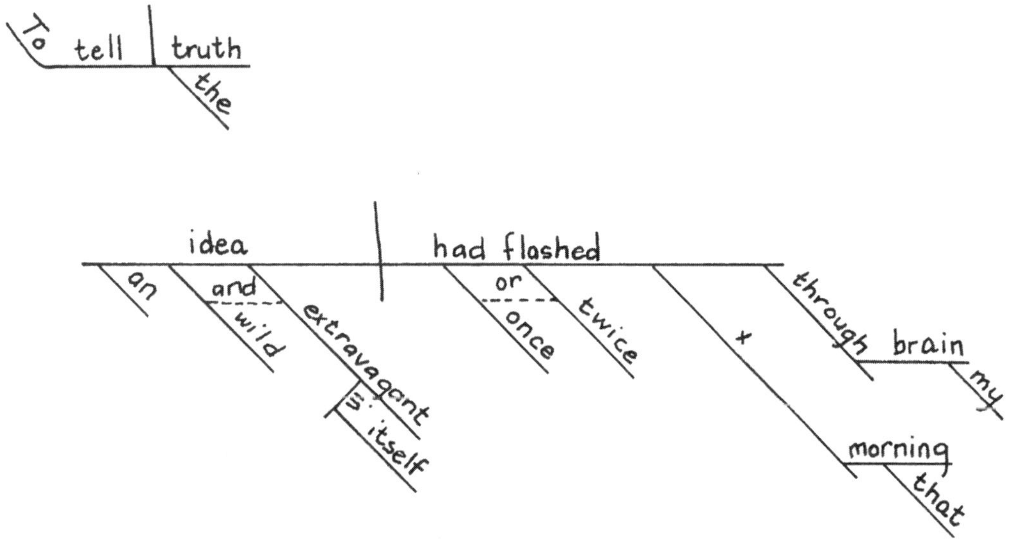

> Dr. Bauerstein remained in the background, his grave bearded face unchanged.

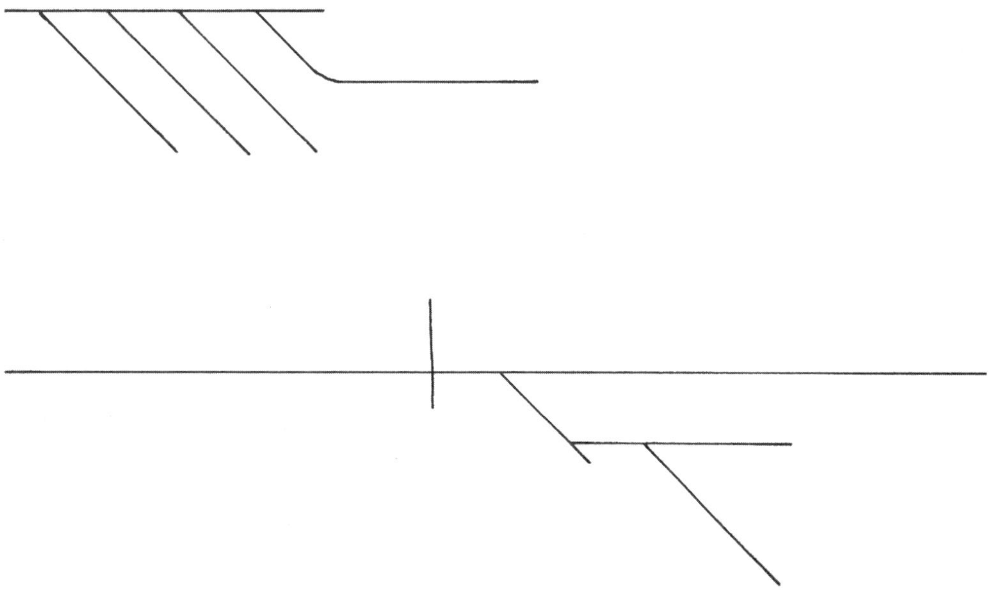

He has lived by his wits, as the saying goes.

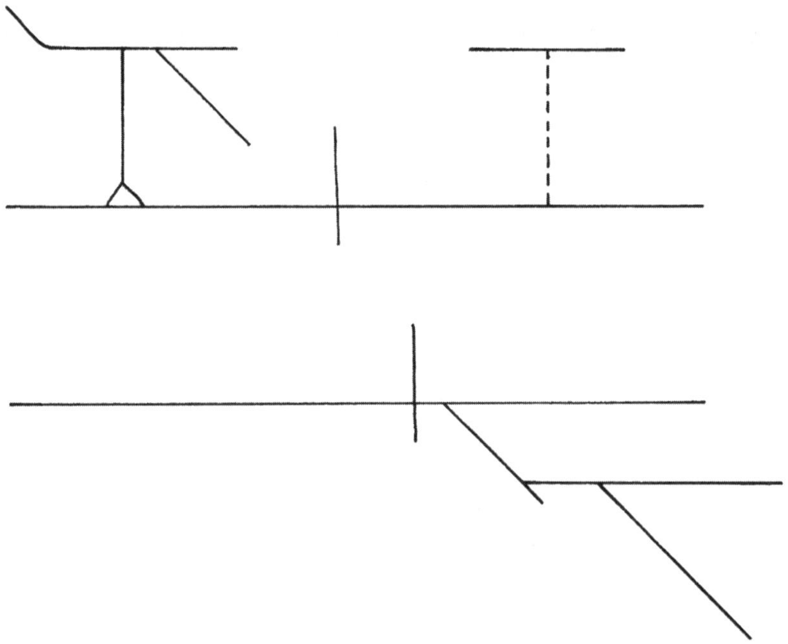

Exercise 96A: Identifying Absolute Constructions

In the following sentences, drawn from a whole range of novels and stories, circle the absolute constructions. Label each absolute construction as *CL* for clause or *PHR* for phrase. For clauses, underline the subject of each clause once and the predicate twice.

There was no bus in sight and Julian, his hands still jammed in his pockets and his head thrust forward, scowled down the empty street.

—Flannery O'Connor, "Everything That Rises Must Converge"

It was sitting as still as a statue, its eyes fixed unblinkingly on the far corner of Privet Drive.

—J. K. Rowling, *Harry Potter and the Sorcerer's Stone*

Six boys came over the hill half an hour early that afternoon, running hard, their heads down, their forearms working, their breath whistling.

—John Steinbeck, *The Red Pony*

Anthony jumped out of bed and, the night being cold, put on his dressing-gown and slippers; then, noiselessly, stepped on to his chair and from the chair (pushing aside the long baize curtain) to the window-ledge.

—Aldous Huxley, *Eyeless in Gaza*

I glared up at the sun, eyes narrowed, and my eyes were drawn to the moon hanging in the sky next to the sun.

—Maggie Stiefvater, *Lament: The Faerie Queen's Deception*

It was wretched weather; stormy and wet, stormy and wet; and mud, mud, mud, deep in all the streets.

—Charles Dickens, *Great Expectations*

To be fair to Patrick, he let us talk about dying, too.

—John Green, *The Fault in Our Stars*

They weren't making much sense; she decided they were having an argument as old and comfortable as an armchair, the kind of argument that no one ever really wins or loses, but which can go on for ever, if both parties are willing.

—Neil Gaiman, *Coraline*

Immediately upon it came the thunder: a high, tearing noise, as though some huge thing were being ripped to pieces close above, which deepened and turned to enormous blows of dissolution.

—Richard Adams, *Watership Down*

Exercise 96B: Appositives, Modifiers, and Absolute Constructions

The sentences below, taken from *Whose Body?* by the British mystery novelist Dorothy Sayers, each contain phrases or clauses set off by dashes. Some are appositives, some are modifiers, and some are absolute constructions. Identify them by writing *APP*, *MOD*, or *AC* above each one. For appositives and modifiers, draw an arrow back to the word being renamed or modified.

I believe that's his lordship just coming in again—if your Grace would kindly hold the line a moment.

But it's been a terrible shock to me, sir—my lord, I should say, but there! my nerves are all to pieces.

But the police-inspector—Inspector Sugg, they called him, from the Yard—he was very sharp with her, poor girl.

His manner as he led the way along the passage convinced Lord Peter of two things—first, that, gruesome as his exhibit was, he rejoiced in the importance it reflected upon himself and his flat, and secondly, that Inspector Sugg had forbidden him to exhibit it to anyone.

I haven't yet been able to trace the appointment, but anyhow, he returned home to his house—9 Park Lane—at twelve o'clock.

No clean clothes were missing, no suit, no boots—nothing.

An important city man, on the eve of an important transaction, without a word of warning to anybody, slips off in the middle of the night, disguised down to his skin, leaving behind his watch, purse, cheque-book, and—most mysterious and important of all—his spectacles, without which he can't see a step, as he is extremely short-sighted.

My client—an upright and honourable gentleman—is being tried for his life—for his life, gentlemen—and it is the business of the prosecution to show his guilt—if they can—without a shadow of doubt.

He might have got stuck in the suburbs one night, perhaps—last train gone and no taxi—and had to walk home.

Still—old bad habits die hard.

We can hardly suppose that; I'm afraid this man possessed what most criminals lack—a sense of humour.

It's not an old chain—hardly worn at all.

They are very distinct on the boots—surprisingly so for gloved hands—and I deduce that the gloves were rubber ones and had recently been in water.

Assigning a motive for the murder of a person without relations or antecedents or even clothes is like trying to visualize the fourth dimension—admirable exercise for the imagination, but arduous and inconclusive.

Exercise 96C: Diagramming

On your own paper, diagram every word of the following sentences, taken from the mystery novel *Gaudy Night* by Dorothy Sayers.

Her own eyes looked back at her—rather tired, rather defiant—eyes that had looked upon fear and were still wary.

She would remain detatched, a unit in an official crowd.

Richard—that's the eldest—is thrilled by the burial-places.

That feels much better—a marvelous sense of security.

The lines swayed and lurched in her clumsy hands, uncontrollable.

— REVIEW 8 —

Weeks 22-24

Topics

Parenthetical Expressions
Dashes, Colons, and Brackets
Dialogue and Dialogue Tags
Direct Quotations and Attribution Tags
Ellipses and Partial Quotations
Block Quotes
Interjections
Nouns of Direct Address
Appositives
Noun Clauses in Apposition
Absolute Constructions

Review 8A: Definition Fill-in-the-Blank

You learned many definitions in the past three weeks! Fill in the blanks in the definitions below with one of the terms from the list. Many of the terms will be used more than once.

commas	comma	parentheses
line space	dashes	coordinating conjunction
semicolon	colon	paragraph
appositive	appositives	absolute construction
period	attribution tag	exclamation point
parenthetical expression	interjections	dialogue tag
question mark	brackets	ellipses
restrictive modifying clause	nouns of direct address	quotation marks
nonrestrictive modifying clause	closing quotation marks	short parenthetical expressions

The independent clauses of a compound sentence must be joined by a ______________ and a ______________, a ______________, or a ______________ and a ______________. They cannot be joined by a ______________ alone.

____________________________ can enclose words that are not essential to the sentence.

A ____________________________ often interrupts or is irrelevant to the rest of the sentence.

Punctuation goes inside the ____________________________ if it applies to the ____________________________; all other punctuation goes outside the ____________________________.

A ____________________________ only begins with a capital letter if it is a complete sentence with ending punctuation.

A ____________________________ can also be set off by commas.

____________________________ such as the following are usually set off by commas: *in short, in fact, in reality, as it were, as it happens, no doubt, in a word, to be sure, to be brief, after all, you know, of course.*

A ____________________________ defines the word that it modifies. Removing the clause changes the essential meaning of the sentence.

A ____________________________ describes the word that it modifies. Removing the clause doesn't change the essential meaning of the sentence.

Only a____________________________ should be set off by commas.

____________________________ can enclose words that are not essential to the sentence.

____________________________ can also be used singly to separate parts of a sentence.

____________________________ make a parenthetical element a part of the sentence.

____________________________ emphasize a parenthetical element.

____________________________ minimize a parenthetical element.

An ____________________________ is a noun, pronoun, or noun phrase that usually follows another noun and renames or explains it.

_______________________________ are set off by _______________________________.

A dependent clause can act as an _______________________________ if it renames the noun that it follows.

When a _______________________________ comes before a speech, place a _______________________________ after the tag. Put the dialogue's final punctuation mark inside the _______________________________.

Speeches do not need to be attached to a _______________________________ as long as the text clearly indicates the speaker.

Usually, a new _______________________________ begins with each new speaker.

When a _______________________________ comes in the middle of a speech, follow it with a _______________________________ if the following dialogue is an incomplete sentence. Follow it with a _______________________________ if the following dialogue is a complete sentence.

When an _______________________________ comes after a direct quote, place a _______________________________, _______________________________, or _______________________________ inside the closing quotation marks.

When an _______________________________ comes before a direct quote, place a _______________________________ after the tag. Put the dialogue's final punctuation mark inside the _______________________________.

When an _______________________________ comes in the middle of a direct quotation, follow it with a _______________________________ if the remaining quote is an incomplete sentence. Follow it with a _______________________________ if the remaining quote is a complete sentence.

Every direct quote must have an ________________________________.

________________________________ show where something has been cut out of a sentence.

A second or third quote from the same source does not need another ________________, as long as context makes the source of the quote clear. Direct quotes can be words, phrases, clauses, or sentences, as long as they are set off by ________________________ ________________________ and form part of a grammatically correct original sentence.

If a direct quotation is longer than three lines, indent the entire quote one inch from the margin in a separate block of text and omit ________________________.

If you change or make additions to a direct quotation, use ________________________.

When using word processing software, leave an additional ________________________ before and after a block quote.

Block quotes should be introduced by a ________________________ (if preceded by a complete sentence) or a ________________________ (if preceded by a partial sentence).

________________________________ express sudden feeling or emotion. They are set off with ________________________ or stand alone with a closing punctuation mark.

________________________________ name a person or thing who is being spoken to. They are set off with ________________________. They are capitalized only if they are proper names or titles.

An ________________________________ has a strong semantic relationship but no grammatical connection to the rest of the sentence.

Review 8B: Punctuating Restrictive and Non-Restrictive Clauses, Compound Sentences, Interjections, Parenthetical Expressions, and Nouns of Direct Address

The sentences below contain restrictive clauses, nonrestrictive clauses, interjections, parenthetical expressions, and nouns of direct address. Some are compound sentences. But all of them have lost their punctuation! Insert all necessary punctuation directly into the sentences (use the actual punctuation marks rather than proofreader's marks).

These sentences are taken from Frederick Douglass's 1845 autobiography, *Narrative of the Life of Frederick Douglass, An American Slave: Written by Himself.*

I do not remember to have ever met a slave who could tell of his birthday

He that ate fastest got most he that was strongest secured the best place and few left the trough satisfied

Fred go get a fresh can of water

He was generally called Captain Anthony a title which I presume he acquired by sailing a craft on the Chesapeake Bay

They gave tongue to interesting thoughts of my own soul which had frequently flashed through my mind and died away for want of utterance

O that I were on one of your gallant decks, and under your protecting wing

Colonel Lloyd kept a large and finely cultivated garden, which afforded almost constant employment for four men

I sought my own employment made my own contracts and collected the money which I earned

Besides she was going to give me a pair of trousers which I should not put on unless I got all the dirt off me

The fact that he gave me any part of my wages was proof to my mind that he believed me entitled to the whole of them

In this way I got a good many lessons in writing which it is quite possible I should never have gotten in any other way

They told a tale of woe which was then altogether beyond my feeble comprehension they were tones loud long and deep they breathed the prayer and complaint of souls boiling over with the bitterest anguish

She was hired by a Mr Stewart who lived about twelve miles from my home

This bread I used to bestow upon the hungry little urchins who in return would give me that more valuable bread of knowledge

He who proclaims it a religious duty to read the Bible denies me the right of learning to read the name of the God who made me

Well that thought has this moment struck me

Review 8C: Dialogue

In the following two passages of dialogue from *Little Women* by Louisa May Alcott, all of the punctuation around, before, and after the lines of dialogue is missing. Insert all necessary punctuation directly into the sentences (use the actual punctuation marks rather than proofreader's marks).

There is a special challenge in the second excerpt! If you can't find it, your instructor will point it out to you.

By her next speech, Jo deprived herself of several years of pleasure, and received a timely lesson in the art of holding her tongue.

I don't like favors, they oppress and make me feel like a slave. I'd rather do everything for myself, and be perfectly independent

Ahem coughed Aunt Carrol softly, with a look at Aunt March.

I told you so said Aunt March, with a decided nod to Aunt Carrol.

Mercifully unconscious of what she had done, Jo sat with her nose in the air, and a revolutionary aspect which was anything but inviting.

Do you speak French, dear asked Mrs. Carrol, laying a hand on Amy's.

Pretty well, thanks to Aunt March, who lets Esther talk to me as often as I like replied Amy, with a grateful look, which caused the old lady to smile affably.

How are you about languages asked Mrs. Carrol of Jo.

Don't know a word. I'm very stupid about studying anything, can't bear French, it's such a slippery, silly sort of language was the brusque reply.

Another look passed between the ladies, and Aunt March said to Amy You are quite strong and well now, dear, I believe? Eyes don't trouble you any more, do they

Not at all, thank you, ma'am. I'm very well, and mean to do great things next winter, so that I may be ready for Rome, whenever that joyful time arrives

Good girl! You deserve to go, and I'm sure you will some day said Aunt March, with an approving pat on the head, as Amy picked up her ball for her.

*

A letter came from Aunt Carrol, and Mrs. March's face was illuminated to such a degree when she read it that Jo and Beth, who were with her, demanded what the glad tidings were.

Aunt Carrol is going abroad next month, and wants...

Me to go with her burst in Jo, flying out of her chair in an uncontrollable rapture.

No, dear, not you. It's Amy

Oh, Mother! She's too young, it's my turn first. I've wanted it so long. It would do me so much good, and be so altogether splendid. I must go

I'm afraid it's impossible, Jo. Aunt says Amy, decidedly, and it is not for us to dictate when she offers such a favor

It's always so. Amy has all the fun and I have all the work. It isn't fair, oh, it isn't fair cried Jo passionately.

I'm afraid it's partly your own fault, dear. When Aunt spoke to me the other day, she regretted your blunt manners and too independent spirit, and here she writes, as if quoting something you had said—I planned at first to ask Jo, but as favors burden her, and she hates French, I think I won't venture to invite her. Amy is more docile, will make a good companion for Flo, and receive gratefully any help the trip may give her

Oh, my tongue, my abominable tongue! Why can't I learn to keep it quiet groaned Jo, remembering words which had been her undoing.

Review 8D: Parenthetical Expressions, Appositives, Absolute Constructions

Each one of the sentences below contains an element not closely connected to the rest of the sentence: parenthetical, appositive, or absolute.

In each sentence, find and circle the unconnected element (word, phrase, or clause). Above it, write *PAR* for parenthetical, *APP* for appositive, or *AB* for absolute.

In the blank at the end of the sentence, note whether the element is set apart with commas (*C*), parentheses (*P*), dashes (*D*), or some other mark (*O*).

These are taken from *My First Summer in the Sierra*, by the great nineteenth-century nature writer John Muir.

In the great Central Valley of California there are only two seasons—spring and summer. ________

The flock, he explained, would be moved gradually higher through the successive forest belts as the snow melted, stopping for a few weeks at the best places we came to. ________

His master, a hunter with whom I was slightly acquainted, came to me as soon as he heard that I was going to spend the summer in the Sierra and begged me to take his favorite dog, Carlo, with me, for he feared that if he were compelled to stay all summer on the plains the fierce heat might be the death of him. ________

____

This morning provisions, camp-kettles, blankets, plant-press, etc., were packed on two horses, the flock headed for the tawny foothills, and away we sauntered in a cloud of dust: Mr. Delaney, bony and tall, with sharply hacked profile like Don Quixote, leading the pack-horses, Billy, the proud shepherd, and myself with notebook tied to my belt. ________

____

After the danger is past they call one another together with a loud piping note—Nature's beautiful mountain chickens. ________

Soon the whole flock seemed to be hopefully excited, the mothers calling their lambs, the lambs replying in tones wonderfully human, their fondly quavering calls interrupted now and then by hastily snatched mouthfuls of withered grass. ________

In case a tired lamb, half asleep in the smothering dust, should fail to answer, its mother would come running back through the flock toward the spot whence its last response was heard, and refused to be comforted until she found it, the one of a thousand, though to our eyes and ears all seemed alike. ________

The meal finished, the dogs were fed, the smokers smoked by the fire, and under the influences of fullness and tobacco the calm that settled on their faces seemed almost divine, something like the mellow meditative glow portrayed on the countenances of saints. ________

The mountain quail (*Oreortyx ricta*) I often meet in my walks—a small brown partridge with a very long, slender, ornamental crest worn jauntily like a feather in a boy's cap, giving it a very marked appearance. ________

____

Review 8E: Direct Quotations

The following paragraphs have been condensed slightly from a biography of John Muir, *A Passion for Nature: The Life of John Muir*, by Donald Worster. The paragraphs contain three different direct quotations from Muir's journals and essays.

Those quotations are bolded, but they are not properly punctuated. Rewrite the paragraphs on your own paper or with your own word processor. Punctuate and space the quotations properly.

When you are finished, circle any places where words have been left out of the direct quotations. Underline any places where words have been added to the direct quotations. Then compare your answers with the original.

John Muir's last essay for the Overland Monthly magazine poked at the **soft hypocrisies** of those who congratulated themselves on having vanquished nature and all its dangers. **Man's control** he wrote **is being steadily extended over the forces of nature, but it is well, at least for the present, that storms can still make themselves heard through the thickest walls.**

No amount of magazine writing, no amount of urban planning could remedy the most serious flaw in the city—its lack of wild mountain beauty. On one dreary January day, he showed how unreconciled he was to the aesthetically impoverished cityscape. T**he streets here are barren & beeless & ineffably mud[d]y & mean looking...A eucalyptus bush on every other corner, standing tied to a painted stick, & a geranium sprout in a pot on every tenth window sill may help heavenward a little, but how little amid so muckle downdragging mud.** Each winter he sweated over his writing, but always he dreamed of the summer day when the mountains would be free of snow and he could be among them again.

Review 8F: Diagramming

On your own paper, diagram every word of the following sentences from John Muir's *Steep Trails*.

Each sentence contains a challenge! Do your best, and ask your instructor for help if you need it!

Three fleeces were obtained—one that belonged to a large ram about four years old, another to a ewe about the same age, and another to a yearling lamb.

Five or six species of pines are found in the state, the most important of which, both as to lumber and as to the part they play in the general wealth and beauty of the forests, are the yellow and sugar pines (Pinus ponderosa and P. Lambertiana).

Wild wool is too fine to stand by itself, the fibers being as frail and invisible as the floating threads of spiders, while the hairs against which they lean stand erect like hazel wands; but, notwithstanding their great dissimilarity in size and appearance, the wool and hair are forms of the same thing, modified in just that way and to just that degree that renders them most perfectly subservient to the well-being of the sheep.

WEEK 25

Complex Verb Tenses

— LESSON 97 —

Verb Tense, Voice, and Mood
Tense Review (Indicative)
Progressive Perfect Tenses (Indicative)

Moods

- Indicative
- Subjunctive
- Imperative
- Modal

(The following sentences are from Beverly Cleary's novel *Fifteen*.)

He spoke rapidly, as if he were anxious to get the words out of the way.

Mood: ______________________

And be home by ten thirty.

Mood: ______________________

To hide her discomfort she took small bites of ice cream.

Mood: ______________________

Should they talk awhile, or should she suggest that they leave, or should she wait for him to suggest it?

Mood: ______________________

Indicative verbs express real actions.
Subjunctive verbs express unreal actions.
Imperative verbs express intended actions.
Modal verbs express possible actions.

Here everything looked brand-new, as if the furniture had been delivered only the day before.

Mood: ______________________

Voice: ______________________

Now the fat pug dog rose and shook himself, scattering his hair over the carpet.

Mood: ______________________

Voice: ______________________

Voice
In a sentence with an active verb, the subject performs the action.
In a sentence with a passive verb, the subject receives the action.

Tense
A simple verb simply tells whether an action takes place in the past, present, or future.
A progressive verb describes an ongoing or continuous action.
A perfect verb describes an action which has been completed before another action takes place.

Exercise 97A: Review of Indicative Tenses

The following partially completed chart shows the active and passive tenses of the regular verb *announce* (in the third-person singular), the irregular verb *fight* (in the third-person plural), and the irregular verb *feed* (in the first-person singular). Review your indicative tenses by completing the chart now.

		Active	Passive
SIMPLE TENSES			
announce *fight* *feed*	Past	he announced they I	he they were I
announce *fight* *feed*	Present	he they I feed	he is they I
announce *fight* *feed*	Future	he they will fight I	he will be they I

		Active	Passive
PROGRESSIVE TENSES			
announce *fight* *feed*	Past	he they I was	he was being announced they I
announce *fight* *feed*	Present	he they I am feeding	he is they I
announce *fight* *feed*	Future	he they will be I	he they I will be being
PERFECT TENSES			
announce *fight* *feed*	Past	he they had fought I	he had been they I
announce *fight* *feed*	Present	he has they I	he they I have been fed
announce *fight* *feed*	Future	he they I will have fed	he they I

A progressive perfect verb describes an ongoing or continuous action that has a definite end.

progressive perfect past

I had been running for half an hour before I decided to stop.

progressive perfect present

I have been running all morning.

progressive perfect future

I will have been running for an hour by the time you arrive.

PAST	
Simple	I rejoiced over my grammar!
Progressive	I was rejoicing over my grammar.
Perfect	I had rejoiced over my grammar.
Progressive Perfect	I had been rejoicing over my grammar, until I realized I had done the wrong exercises.

PRESENT	
Simple	I enjoy this schoolwork!
Progressive	I am enjoying this schoolwork.
Perfect	I have enjoyed this schoolwork.
Progressive Perfect	I have been enjoying this schoolwork, but unfortunately I have to stop now and go play Minecraft.

FUTURE

Simple	I will expect to receive a prize!
Progressive	All afternoon, I will be expecting to receive a prize.
Perfect	By dinner time, I will have expected to receive my prize.
Progressive Perfect	By dinner time, I will have been expecting to receive a prize for at least four hours.

PROGRESSIVE PERFECT PAST

Active The house had been showing signs of wear.

Passive The house had been being shown to prospective buyers for months.

PROGRESSIVE PERFECT PRESENT

Active I have been sending letters out every day.

Passive I have been being sent to the post office by my mother every day.

PROGRESSIVE PERFECT FUTURE

Active Come June, the professors will have been teaching Latin for two years.

Passive Come June, the students will have been being taught Latin for two years.

PROGRESSIVE PERFECT TENSES

Past	**Active**	**Passive**
Active: helping verb had + *helping verb* been + *present participle* *Passive: helping verb* had + *helping verb phrase* been being + *past participle*	I had been amusing you had been amusing he, she, it had been amusing we had been amusing you had been amusing they had been amusing	I had been being amused you had been being amused he, she, it had been being amused we had been being amused you had been being amused they had been being amused
Present	**Active**	**Passive**
Active: helping verb have *or* has + *helping verb* been + *present participle* *Passive: helping verb* have *or* has + *helping verb phrase* been being + *past participle*	I have been amusing you have been amusing he, she, it has been amusing we have been amusing you have been amusing they have been amusing	I have been being amused you have been being amused he, she, it has been being amused we have been being amused you have been being amused they have been being amused

PROGRESSIVE PERFECT TENSES

Future	Active	Passive
Active: helping verb phrase will have been *+ present participle*	I will have been amusing you will have been amusing he, she, it will have been amusing	I will have been being amused you will have been being amused he, she, it will have been being amused
Passive: helping verb phrase will have been being *+ past participle*	we will have been amusing you will have been amusing they will have been amusing	we will have been being amused you will have been being amused they will have been being amused

Perfect Future Passive	The students will have been taught Latin very thoroughly.
Progressive Perfect Future Passive	Come June, the students will have been being taught Latin for two years.
Progressive Perfect Future Passive (Understood)	Come June, the students will have been taught Latin for two years

Exercise 97B: Parsing Verbs

In the following sentences, underline the main verb of every clause (both independent and dependent). Above each verb, write the tense and voice. (All verbs are in the indicative mood.) You may abbreviate: *PROG, PERF, SIMP, PAST, PRES, FUT, ACT, PASS.*

These sentences are from *Hard Times*, by Charles Dickens; some have been slightly condensed.

He had been put through an immense variety of paces, and had answered volumes of head-breaking questions.

He had virtually retired from the wholesale hardware trade before he built Stone Lodge, and was now looking about for a suitable opportunity.

Sissy, who all this time had been faintly excusing herself with tears in her eyes, was now waved over by the master of the house to Mr. Gradgrind.

I had had the key that was found, made long before.

Here, for example, I have been speaking to you this morning about tumblers.

He had reached the neutral ground upon the outskirts of the town, when his ears were invaded by the sound of music.

I'll recompense myself for the way in which I have been brought up.

But since I have been looking at it, I have been wondering about you and me, grown up.

When she had said this, though nothing of her had been seen but her pleasant eyes, she replaced her hood again, and they went on together.

I have been rather troubled with shortness of breath.

The emphasis was helped by the speaker's hair, which bristled on the skirts of his bald head, a plantation of firs to keep the wind from its shining surface, all covered with knobs, like the crust of a plum pie, as if the head had scarcely warehouse-room for the hard facts stored inside.

Exercise 97C: Completing Sentences

Complete the following sentences by providing an appropriate verb in the tense and voice indicated beneath each blank. (All verbs are in the indicative mood.)

This book ______________________ for readers who are passionately curious
perfect present, passive
about medieval French history.

Very gradually, the balance of power between the two countries ______________________
progressive perfect present, active
to the smaller one.

For the last twenty-four hours, the butterfly ______________________ slowly from
progressive perfect present, active
its chrysalis.

In ten years, huge strides ______________________ in outer space exploration.
perfect future, passive

By the year 2020, I ______________________________ medieval French history for over two decades.
progressive perfect future, active

If my opponent concedes defeat in the debate, an important point ____________________.
perfect future, passive

I reassured him that his lifetime of research ____________not ____________________
perfect future, passive

in vain, even if his theories __________________________ to be false.
simple present, passive

For a number of years before the revolution, the peasants __________________________ at every turn.
progressive perfect past, passive

The pass through the mountains __________________________ for years, and it still isn't ready.
progressive perfect present, passive

The skater ______________________________ with huge confidence, since she
progressive present, active

__________________________ with a new coach.
progressive perfect, present, active

— LESSON 98 —

Simple Present and Perfect Present Modal Verbs

Progressive Present and Progressive Perfect Present Modal Verbs

Modal verbs express situations that have not actually happened.
Should, would, may, might, must, can, could

Would, may, might, can, could: **possibility**

He was afraid that, in a little while, death ______________ meet him.

I fear that we ______________ never see him in this life again.

Oh, that I ______________ strike a blow for him before I die!

Only a knight of true valor ______________ hope to win.

Madam, how then ______________ I help you?

Must, should: **obligation**

I _______________ find a man whom I can truly love.

You _______________ do homage to King Arthur for your kingdom.

May: **permission**

_______________ I go to Camelot, to see the jousting?

Can: **ability**

Nothing _______________ heal his wound on this side of the water.

	Simple Present Modal (Active)	
First person	I could help	we could help
Second person	you could help	you could help
Third person	he, she, it could help	they could help

	Perfect Present Modal (Active)	
First person	I should have helped	we should have helped
Second person	you should have helped	you should have helped
Third person	he, she, it should have helped	they should have helped

MODAL TENSES

	Simple Present	**Simple Past**	**Simple Future**
Active	I should help	none	none
Passive	I should be helped	none	none
	Progressive Present	**Progressive Past**	**Progressive Future**
Active	I could be helping	none	none
Passive	I could be being helped	none	none
	Perfect Present	**Perfect Past**	**Perfect Future**
Active	I would have helped	none	none
Passive	I would have been helped	none	none
	Progressive Perfect Present	**Prog Perfect Past**	**Prog Perfect Future**
Active	I might have been helping	none	none
Passive	I might have been being helped	none	none

Use the simple present or progressive present when the situation isn't happening in the present.

Since I slept badly last night, I might go take a nap.

mood	indicative	modal
tense	_____	_____
voice	_____	_____

People are being left in the hospital when they could be being nursed at home.

mood	indicative	_____
tense	_____	_____
voice	_____	_____

Use the perfect present or the progressive perfect present when the situation didn't happen in the past.

I was eating cheese and crackers when I could have been sitting down to a big juicy steak.

mood	indicative	_____
tense	progressive past	_____
voice	active	_____

While the floors were being scrubbed, I could have vacuumed the rugs.

mood	indicative	_____
tense	progressive past	_____
voice	passive	_____

Modal Present: Simple or Progressive
Modal Past: Perfect or Progressive Perfect

MODAL TENSE FORMATION

Simple Present

Active	I can help	modal helping verb + first person singular
Passive	I should be helped	modal helping verb + be + past participle

Progressive Present

Active	I might be helping	modal helping verb + be + present participle
Passive	I could be being helped	modal helping verb + be + being + past participle

Perfect Present

Active	I would have helped	modal helping verb + have + past participle
Passive	I may have been helped	modal helping verb + have + been + past participle

Progressive Perfect Present

Active	I must have been helping	modal helping verb + have + been + present participle
Passive	I could have been being	modal helping verb + have + been + being + past participle

Exercise 98A: Parsing Verbs

In the following sentences from *The Legend of Sleepy Hollow* by Washington Irving, find and underline each modal verb. Write the tense and voice of each verb above it. (For state-of-being verbs, the voice is simply state-of-being.) The first is done for you.

He was tall, but exceedingly lank, with narrow shoulders, long arms and legs, hands that dangled a mile out of his sleeves, feet that [perfect present, active] might have served for shovels, and his whole frame most loosely hung together.

The revenue arising from his school was small, and would have been scarcely sufficient to furnish him with daily bread, for he was a huge feeder, and, though lank, had the dilating powers of an anaconda; but to help out his maintenance, he was, according to country custom in those parts, boarded and lodged at the houses of the farmers whose children he instructed.

From hence the low murmur of his pupils' voices, conning over their lessons, might be heard in a drowsy summer's day, like the hum of a beehive; interrupted now and then by the authoritative voice of the master, in the tone of menace or command, or, peradventure, by the appalling sound of the birch, as he urged some tardy loiterer along the flowery path of knowledge.

He would delight them equally by his anecdotes of witchcraft, and of the direful omens and portentous sights and sounds in the air, which prevailed in the earlier times of Connecticut; and would frighten them woefully with speculations upon comets and shooting stars; and with the alarming fact that the world did absolutely turn round, and that they were half the time topsy-turvy!

Still he must have had fire and mettle in his day, if we may judge from the name he bore of Gunpowder.

He affirmed that on returning one night from the neighboring village of Sing Sing, he had been overtaken by this midnight trooper; that he had offered to race with him for a bowl of punch, and should have won it too, for Daredevil beat the goblin horse all hollow, but just as they came to the church bridge, the Hessian bolted, and vanished in a flash of fire.

She was withal a little of a coquette, as might be perceived even in her dress, which was a mixture of ancient and modern fashions, as most suited to set off her charms.

Could that girl have been playing off any of her coquettish tricks?

His notable little wife, too, had enough to do to attend to her housekeeping and manage her poultry; for, as she sagely observed, ducks and geese are foolish things, and must be looked after, but girls can take care of themselves.

Though the night was dark and dismal, yet the form of the unknown might now in some degree be ascertained.

"If I can but reach that bridge," thought Ichabod, "I am safe."

On mounting a rising ground, which brought the figure of his fellow-traveller in relief against the sky, gigantic in height, and muffled in a cloak, Ichabod was horror-struck on perceiving that he was headless!—but his horror was still more increased on observing that the head, which should have rested on his shoulders, was carried before him on the pommel of his saddle!

The bridge became more than ever an object of superstitious awe; and that may be the reason why the road has been altered of late years, so as to approach the church by the border of the millpond.

Exercise 98B: Forming Modal Verbs

Fill in the blanks with the missing modal verbs. Using the helping verbs indicated, put each action verb provided into the correct modal tense.

These sentences have been adapted from *Volcanoes of the World*, written by Lee Siebert, Tom Simkin, and Paul Kimberly.

Pyroclastic flows ______________________________ down slopes at hurricane speeds, devastating all living things in their paths.

helping verb: can
simple present active of *move*

During World War II, the scientists who otherwise ________________________ volcanic activity were preoccupied with other problems.

helping verb: could
progressive perfect present active of *report*

Fatalities ______________________________ from as many as 400 eruptions, with the most deadly being roughly 60,000 deaths from the 1815 Tambora eruption.

helping verb: may
perfect present passive of *record*

After a dramatic eruption, during which Tambora threw up a 33-kilometer cloud, a reasonable person ______________________________ that the volcano was finished; but this conclusion ______________________________ wrong.

helping verb: might
perfect present active of *think*

helping verb: would
perfect present, state-of-being

Within the week, Tambora ______________________________ with more force than had been seen in modern history.

helping verb: would
progressive present active of *erupt*

The eruption ______________________________ up for over three years.

helping verb: must
progressive perfect present passive of *build*

The sound of the explosion ______________________________ in Sumatra, over 1500 miles away.

helping verb: could
simple present passive of *hear*

Before the month was over, the effects of the eruption ______________________________ all around the world; global temperatures ______________________________, causing significant crop failures internationally.

helping verb: would
progressive present passive of *feel*

helping verb: would
simple present active of *drop*

— LESSON 99 —

Modal Verb Tenses
The Imperative Mood
The Subjunctive Mood
More Subjunctive Tenses

Indicative verbs express real actions.
Subjunctive verbs express unreal actions.
Imperative verbs express intended actions.
Modal verbs express possible actions.

Turn to the end of your book.
Eat more vegetables!

Go away.

Be checked by a doctor before you come back to work.

The present passive imperative is formed by adding the helping verb *be* to the past participle of the verb.

Subjunctive verbs express situations that are unreal, wished for, or uncertain.

If we kept our ponies up in the winter time, we gave them fodder to eat.

We kept our ponies up in the winter time, and we gave them fodder to eat.

	Simple Present Subjunctive State-of-Being Verb		**Simple Past Subjunctive State-of-Being Verb**	
First person	I be	we be	I were	we were
Second person	you be	you be	you were	you were
Third person	he, she, it be	they be	he, she, it were	they were

Should you be in town, come by and see me.

If I were a bird, I would fly across the water.

	Simple Present Subjunctive Action Verb: Active		**Simple Present Subjunctive Action Verb: Passive**	
First person	I leave	we leave	I be left	we be left
Second person	you leave	you leave	you be left	you be left
Third person	he, she, it leave	they leave	he, she, it be left	they be left

He leaves early to avoid traffic.
I suggest that he leave early to avoid traffic.

The present passive subjunctive is formed by pairing *be* with the past participle of a verb.

The tent was left behind.
The guide recommended that the tent be left behind.

	Simple Past Subjunctive Action Verb: Active		**Simple Present Subjunctive Action Verb: Passive**	
First person	I left	we left	I were left	we were left
Second person	you left	you left	you were left	you were left
Third person	he, she, it left	they left	he, she, it were left	they were left

If I left early, I might be able to pick up the milk.
I left early to pick up the milk.

If I were left behind, I would be upset.
I was left behind, which made me very upset.

Simple Future Subjunctive Action Verb: Active	Simple Future Subjunctive Action Verb: Passive
None	None

Use the simple past subjunctive state-of-being verb, plus an infinitive, to express a future unreal action.

If I were to die tomorrow, I would have no regrets.

PROGRESSIVE TENSES

	Progressive Present Subjunctive Action Verb: Active	
First person	I am leaving	we are leaving
Second person	you are leaving	you are leaving
Third person	he, she, it is leaving	they are leaving

	Progressive Present Subjunctive Action Verb: Passive	
First person	I am being left	we are being left
Second person	you are being left	you are being left
Third person	he, she, it is being left	they are being left

If I be running late, I must throw myself upon your kind mercies.

If I am running late, I will call you.

It is unlikely that I am being penalized.

	Progressive Past Subjunctive Action Verb: Active	
First person	I **were** leaving	we were leaving
Second person	you were leaving	you were leaving
Third person	he, she, it **were** leaving	they were leaving

	Progressive Past Subjunctive Action Verb: Passive	
First person	I **were** being left	we were being left
Second person	you were being left	you were being left
Third person	he, she, it **were** being left	they were being left

If I were running in the race, I would certainly win.

I was running in the race.

If I were being left behind, I would make a huge fuss.

I was being left behind.

	Progressive Future Subjunctive Action Verb: Active
	None

	Progressive Future Subjunctive Action Verb: Passive
	None

PERFECT TENSES

	Perfect Present Subjunctive **Action Verb: Active**	
First person	I have left	we have left
Second person	you have left	you have left
Third person	he, she, it has left	they have left

	Perfect Present Subjunctive **Action Verb: Passive**	
First person	I have been left	we have been left
Second person	you have been left	you have been left
Third person	he, she, it has been left	they have been left

	Perfect Present Subjunctive **Action Verb: Active**	
First person	I had left	we had left
Second person	you had left	you had left
Third person	he, she, it had left	they had left

	Perfect Past Subjunctive **Action Verb: Passive**	
First person	I had been left	we had been left
Second person	you had been left	you had been left
Third person	he, she, it had been left	they had been left

Perfect Future Subjunctive
Action Verb: Active

None

Perfect Future Subjunctive
Action Verb: Passive

None

PROGRESSIVE PERFECT TENSES

Progressive Perfect Present Subjunctive
Action Verb: Active

First person	I have been leaving	we have been leaving
Second person	you have been leaving	you have been leaving
Third person	he, she, it has been leaving	they have been leaving

Progressive Perfect Present Subjunctive
Action Verb: Passive

First person	I have been being left	we have been being left
Second person	you have been being left	you have been being left
Third person	he, she, it has been being left	they have been being left

Progressive Perfect Past Subjunctive
Action Verb: Active

First person	I had been leaving	we had been leaving
Second person	you had been leaving	you had been leaving
Third person	he, she, it had been leaving	they had been leaving

Progressive Perfect Past Subjunctive
Action Verb: Passive

First person	I had been being left	we had been being left
Second person	you had been being left	you had been being left
Third person	he, she, it had been being left	they had been being left

Progressive Perfect Future Subjunctive
Action Verb: Active

None

Progressive Perfect Future Subjunctive
Action Verb: Passive
None

Exercise 99A: Complete the Chart

Fill in the missing forms on the following chart. Use the verbs indicated above each chart, in order. The first form on each chart is done for you.

INDICATIVE

(abandon, catch, ignite, pat, vex, wrangle, measure, extricate, describe, bite, need, swirl)

Indicative Tense	Active Formation	Examples	Passive Formation	Examples
Simple present	Add *-s* in third- person singular	I abandon he, she, it ______	am/is/are + past participle	I am abandoned you ______ he, she, it ______
Simple past	Add *-d* or *-ed*, or change form	I ______	was/were + past participle	I ______ you ______
Simple future	+ will OR shall	they ______	will be + past participle	it ______
Progressive present	am/is/are + present participle	I ______ you ______ he, she, it ______	am/is/are being + past participle	I ______ you ______ he, she, it ______
Progressive past	was/were + present participle	I ______ you ______ he, she, it ______	was/were being + past participle	I ______ you ______ he, she, it ______

Indicative Tense	Active Formation	Examples	Passive Formation	Examples
Progressive future	will be + present participle	I __________	will be being + past participle	it __________
Perfect present	has/have + past participle	I __________ you __________ he, she, it __________	has/have been + past participle	I __________ you __________ he, she, it __________
Perfect past	had + past participle	they __________	had been + past participle	you __________
Perfect future	will have + past participle	we __________	will have been + past participle	they __________
Progressive perfect present	have/has been + present participle	I __________ he, she, it __________	have/has been being + past participle	I __________ he, she, it __________
Progressive perfect past	had been + present participle	you __________	had been being + past participle	you __________
Progressive perfect future	will have been + present participle	you __________	will have been being + past participle	they __________

MODAL
(puff, promulgate, hurl, throttle)

Modal Tense	Active Formation	Examples	Passive Formation	Examples
Simple present	modal helping verb + simple present main verb	I could puff you ______ he, she, it ______	modal helping verb + be + past participle	I ______ they ______
Progressive present	modal helping verb + be + present participle	I ______	modal helping verb + be + being + past participle	it ______
Perfect present	modal helping verb + have + past participle	you ______	modal helping verb + have + been + past participle	it ______
Progressive perfect present	modal helping verb + have been + present participle	I ______	modal helping verb + have been being + past participle	we ______

IMPERATIVE

(command, fluff)

Imperative Tense	Active Formation	Examples	Passive Formation	Examples
Present	Simple present form without subject	Command ! ____________!	be + past participle	____________! ____________!

SUBJUNCTIVE

(pummel, yell, congratulate, relax, raise, collapse, punish, wash)

Subjunctive Tense	Active Formation	Examples	Passive Formation	Examples
Simple present	No change in any person	I pummel you ____________ he, she, it ____________ we ____________ you ____________ they ____________	be + past participle	I ____________ they ____________
Simple past	**Same as indicative:** Add *-d* or *-ed*, or change form	I ____________ you ____________ he, she, it ____________	were + past participle	it ____________
Progressive present	**Same as indicative:** am/is/are + present participle	I ____________ you ____________ he, she, it ____________	**Same as indicative:** am/is/are being + past participle	I ____________ you ____________ he, she, it ____________

Subjunctive Tense	Active Formation	Examples	Passive Formation	Examples
Progressive past	were + present participle	I ____ you ____ he, she, it ____	were being + past participle	I ____ you ____ he, she, it ____
Perfect present	**Same as indicative:** has/have + past participle	I ____ he, she, it ____ they ____	**Same as indicative:** has/have been + past participle	I ____ he, she, it ____ they ____
Perfect past	**Same as indicative:** had + past participle	we ____	**Same as indicative:** had been + past participle	we ____
Progressive perfect present	**Same as indicative:** have/has been + present participle	I ____ you ____ he, she, it ____	**Same as indicative:** have/has been being + past participle	I ____ you ____ he, she, it ____
Progressive perfect past	**Same as indicative:** had been + present participle	you ____	**Same as indicative:** had been being + past participle	you ____

Exercise 99B: Parsing

Write the mood, tense, and voice of each underlined verb above it. The first is done for you.

These sentences are taken from Robert Louis Stevenson's classic novel *Dr. Jekyll and Mr. Hyde*. The first is done for you.

imperative
present
active
Mark my words, he will never more be heard of.

I have been wanting to speak to you, Jekyll.

Be seated, if you please.

If he could but once set eyes on him, he thought the mystery would lighten and perhaps roll altogether away, as was the habit of mysterious things when well examined.

He cannot have been disposed of in so short a space; he must be still alive, he must have fled!

Think before you answer, for it shall be done as you decide.

It did not seem as if the subject of his address were of great importance; indeed, from his pointing, it sometimes appeared as if he were only inquiring his way; but the moon shone on his face as he spoke, and the girl was pleased to watch it.

I began to spy a danger that, if this were much prolonged, the balance of my nature might be permanently overthrown, the power of voluntary change be forfeited, and the character of Edward Hyde become irrevocably mine.

A purse and gold watch were found upon the victim: but no cards or papers, except a sealed and stamped envelope, which he had been probably carrying to the post, and which bore the name and address of Mr. Utterson.

Had I approached my discovery in a more noble spirit, had I risked the experiment while under the empire of generous or pious aspirations, all must have been otherwise, and from these agonies of death and birth, I had come forth an angel instead of a fiend.

—LESSON 100—

Review of Moods and Tenses
Conditional Sentences

First conditional sentences express circumstances that might actually happen.
The predicate of the condition clause is in a present tense.
The predicate of the consequence clause is an imperative or is in a present or future tense.

If we surrender and I return with you, will you promise not to hurt this man?
So bow down to her if you want, bow to her.
If she is otherwise when I find her, I shall be very put out.
Unless I am wrong (and I am never wrong), they are headed dead into the fire swamp.

Second conditional sentences express circumstances that are contrary to reality.
The predicate of the condition clause is in a past tense.
The predicate of the consequence clause is in the simple present modal tense.

I would not say such things if I were you!
If I had a month to plan, maybe I could come up with something.
If we only had a wheelbarrow, that would be something.

Third conditional sentences express past circumstances that never happened.
The predicate of the condition clause is in the perfect past tense.
The predicate of the consequence clause is in the perfect present modal or simple present modal tense.

But they would have killed Westley, if I hadn't done it.

If I were you, I would go home.

If I were you, I would be dancing with joy.

If I had been wrong, I would say so now.

If I had been wrong, I would be apologizing with sincerity.

If I had been wrong, I would have said so.

If I had been wrong, I would have been running for my life.

(The examples below are adapted from Mary Shelley's *Frankenstein*.)

First conditional sentences express circumstances that might actually happen.
The predicate of the condition clause is in a present tense.
The predicate of the consequence clause is an imperative or is in a present or future tense.

If I fail, you will see me again soon, or never.

If you believe that she is innocent, rely on the justice of our laws.

If I could bestow animation upon lifeless matter, I might renew life.

Second conditional sentences express circumstances that are contrary to reality.
The predicate of the condition clause is in a past tense.
The predicate of the consequence clause is in the simple or progressive present modal tense.

Unless such symptoms had been shown early, a sister or brother could never suspect the other of fraud.

If you cherished a desire of revenge against me, you would be rejoicing in my destruction.

Third conditional sentences express past circumstances that never happened.
The predicate of the condition clause is in the perfect past tense.
The predicate of the consequence clause is in any modal tense.

If she <u>had</u> earnestly <u>desired</u> it, I <u>should have</u> willingly <u>given</u> it to her,

If you <u>had known</u> me as I once was, you <u>would</u> not <u>recognize</u> me in this state of degradation.

If the voice of conscience <u>had been heeded</u>, Frankenstein <u>would</u> yet <u>have lived</u>.

Exercise 100A: Conditional Sentences

Identify the following sentences (taken from *Tales of Tears and Laughter: Short Fiction of Medieval Japan*, translated by Virginia Skord) as first, second, or third conditional by writing a *1*, *2*, or *3* in the margin next to each.

If only I could have some boar, chicken, rabbit, raccoon, or badger—I'd eat it stewed. ________

I want to say my prayers, but if you don't give me something to eat, I might not be able to go on! ________

If I had asked you to spend morning and night at my side, I would indeed be hateful. ________

I may not be a dappled pony, but if I were, the more I ate, the more my limbs would grow strong. ________

Why, I'd sing a song if someone asked me to! ________

If I weren't worried about what people might say, I'd even walk around on stilts! ________

If you win, I will divide my domain in two and award you half, to rule just as you like. ________

He could never respond to those lines, even if he knew what they were! ________

If you learn the tales now, you will never forget them. ________

If you see your beloved too repeatedly, the blossom will wither. ________

Therefore, if your servings are too small and you want for anything, just complain bitterly and tell them that you are not used to such conditions. ________

Exercise 100B: Parsing

Write the correct mood, tense, and voice above each underlined verb. These sentences are taken from *Norse Mythology: Tales of the Gods, Sagas and Heroes*, by James Shepherd.

One day Odin and his brothers were walking near the sea, when they came upon two trees, an ash and an elm.

Were it not for your keen ears that hear the grass growing and the wool thickening on the backs of the sheep, our enemies might, ere this, have crossed the abyss, and have stormed Asgard.

Here and there were groves in whose quiet depths a less rapid traveller might have heard the trickling of fountains.

She told Odin that a place was being made ready for his son in the lower world.

I must go through the dark land of our enemies, the frost giants of the lower world; and then far beyond, to regions that few have visited.

I fear you do not know what a mighty enemy has come to fight you.

Man had not learned how to control the forces of nature, and he was continually warring against them.

She had no need of a guide to the place where her brothers had lain; for the path to the wood had been well worn by the feet of the messenger.

Thorstein said, "Herein alone Gunnlaug pleases me not, that I find him an unsettled man; but if he were of a mind like thine, little would I hang back."

The castle was apparently made of the same material as the bridge, and, as it rose toward the sky, might have been taken for a structure of cloud bathed in moonlight.

But you still have time to escape; for you have come sooner than you were expected.

The approach to the bridge was in this way made so clearly visible that it would have been impossible for anyone to get near without Heimdall's knowledge, even had his hearing been less keen.

I have been watching for you ever since I heard Sleipnir's eight hoofs strike the bridge.

Exercise 100C: Diagramming

On your own paper, diagram every word of the following sentences from *South African Folk Tales*, by James A. Honey.

Little Jackal wanted to attend, but there was a law made that no one should be present unless he had horns.

Jackal's hind feet being still free, he threatened to smash Tortoise with them if he did not release him.

Once on a time Jackal, who lived on the borders of the colony, saw a wagon returning from the seaside laden with fish; he tried to get into the wagon from behind, but he could not; he then ran on before and lay in the road as if dead.

WEEK 26

More Modifiers

—LESSON 101—

Adjective Review
Adjectives in the Appositive Position
Correct Comma Usage

It was a dark and stormy night; the rain fell in torrents, except at occasional intervals, when it was checked by a violent gust of wind which swept up the streets (for it is in London that our scene lies), rattling along the house-tops, and fiercely agitating the scanty flame of the lamps that struggled against the darkness.

—From *Paul Clifford* by Edward Bulwer-Lytton

An adjective modifies a noun or pronoun.
Adjectives tell what kind, which one, how many, and whose.
Descriptive adjectives tell what kind.
A descriptive adjective becomes an abstract noun when you add *-ness* to it.
Possessive adjectives tell whose.

Hastings kissed the duke's hand in silence.

Nouns become adjectives when they are made possessive.
Form the possessive of a singular noun by adding an apostrophe and the letter *s*.

duchess ____________________

Form the possessive of a plural noun ending in *-s* by adding an apostrophe only.

emperors ____________________

Form the possessive of a plural noun that does not end in *-s* as if it were a singular noun.

noblemen ____________________

Since choice was mine, I chose the man love could not choose, and took this sad comfort to my heart.

—From *The Last of the Barons,* by Edward Bulwer-Lytton

An adjective that comes right before the noun it modifies is in the attributive position. An adjective that follows the noun it modifies is in the predicative position.

On the floor is the image of a dog in mosaic, with the well-known motto "Cave canem" upon it.

My name is well known, methinks, in Pompeii.
—From *The Last Days of Pompeii,* by Edward Bulwer-Lytton

Possessive Pronouns (Adjectives)

Attributive	**Predicative**
my	mine
your	yours
his, her, its	his, hers, its
our	ours
your	yours
their	theirs

The eyes were soft, dark, and brilliant, but dreamlike and vague; the features in youth must have been regular and beautiful, but their contour was now sharpened by the hollowness of the cheeks and temples.

His face was far less handsome than Marmaduke Nevile's, but infinitely more expressive, both of intelligence and command,—the features straight and sharp, the complexion clear and pale, and under the bright grey eyes a dark shade spoke either of dissipation or of thought.
— From *The Last of the Barons,* by Edward Bulwer-Lytton

Appositive adjectives directly follow the word they modify.

The sea, blue and tranquil, bounded the view.

To add to the attractions of his house, his wife, simple and good-tempered, could talk with anybody, take off the bores, and leave people to be comfortable in their own way.

It was a spot remote, sequestered, cloistered from the business and pleasures of the world.

The latter was a fine dark-eyed girl, tall, self-possessed, and dressed plainly indeed, but after the approved fashion.
—From *Alice: or, The Mysteries,* by Edward Bulwer-Lytton

When three or more nouns, adjectives, verbs, or adverbs appear in a series, they should be separated by commas.

"Wrinkles" in the comma rule:

1. **When three or more items are in a list, a coordinating conjunction before the last term is usual but not necessary.**

   The horse spun, bucked, kicked with abandon.
   The horse spun, bucked, and kicked with abandon.

   Chickens, roosters, ducks filled the yard.
   Chickens, roosters, and ducks filled the yard.

   I ran quickly, efficiently, easily.
   I ran quickly, efficiently, and easily.

   It was a spot remote, sequestered, cloistered.
   It was a spot remote, sequestered, and cloistered.

   It was a dark, stormy, frightening night.
   It was a dark, stormy, and frightening night.

2. **When three or more items are in a list and a coordinating conjunction is used, a comma should still follow the next-to-last item in the list.**

   The fourteen-year-old loved her sisters, Taylor Swift, and Jennifer Lawrence.
   The fourteen-year-old loved her sisters, Taylor Swift and Jennifer Lawrence.

   Oranges, apples, and plums filled the fruit bowl.
   Oranges, apples and plums filled the fruit bowl.

3. **When two or more adjectives are in the attributive position, they are only separated by commas if they are equally important in meaning.**

   Monday was a tiring, difficult day.
   Monday was a tiring and difficult day.
   Monday was a difficult, tiring day.

   The old man was wearing a grey wool overcoat.
   The old man was wearing a grey and wool overcoat.
   The old man was wearing a wool grey overcoat.

   INCORRECT: Monday was a tiring difficult day.
   INCORRECT: The old man was wearing a grey, wool overcoat.

Exercise 101A: Identifying Adjectives

Underline every adjective (including verb forms used as adjectives) in the following paragraph of description. Draw an arrow from each adjective to the word it modifies. Above each adjective, write *DESC* for descriptive or *POSS* for possessive. Then, label each as in the attributive (*ATT*), appositive (*APP*), or predicative (*PRED*) position. (Do not underline articles! There are just too many of them.)

This paragraph is from *Pelham*, by Edward Bulwer-Lytton. This is a very old-fashioned style of description—generally, writers today try to avoid using this many adjectives!

She was apparently about twenty; her hair was of the richest chestnut, and a golden light played through its darkness, as if a sunbeam had been caught in the luxuriant tresses, and was striving in vain to escape. Her eyes, large, deep, and shaded into softness by long and very dark lashes, were of a light hazel. Her complexion alone would have rendered her beautiful, it was so clear—so pure; like roses under a clear stream, if, in order to justify my simile, roses would have the complacency to grow in such a situation. Her nose was of a fine and accurate mould that one seldom sees, except in the Grecian statues, which unites the clearest and most decided outline with the most feminine delicacy and softness; and the short curved arch which descended from thence to her mouth, was so fine—so airily and exquisitely formed, that it seemed as if Love himself had modelled the bridge. On the right side of the mouth was one dimple, which corresponded so exactly with the smiles and movements of the rosy lips, that you might have sworn the shadow of each passed there; it was like the rapid changes of an April heaven reflected upon a valley. Over her was a light, a glow, a pervading spirit, of which it is impossible to convey the faintest idea. You should have seen her by the side of a shaded fountain on a summer's day.

Exercise 101B: Punctuation Practice

The sentences below are missing all of their punctuation marks! Using everything you have learned about punctuation, insert correct punctuation. You may simply write the punctuation marks in, rather than using proofreader's marks.

These sentences are taken from the gothic short stories of Edgar Allan Poe.

They are persevering ingenious cunning and thoroughly versed in the knowledge which their duties seem chiefly to demand

My brother was at the stern holding on to a small empty water-cask

Its discovery depends upon the mere care patience and determination of the seekers

He had singular wild full liquid eyes whose shadows varied from pure hazel to intense and brilliant jet

Through two small holes that served for nostrils the monster puffed out its thick breath with prodigious violence and with a shrieking disagreeable noise

He presently addressed us in loud harsh and disagreeable accents

The ancient time worn desks and benches were piled desperately with much bethumbed books

Boats yachts and ships have been carried away by not guarding against it before they were within its reach

Looking astern we saw the whole horizon covered with a singular copper colored cloud that rose with the most amazing velocity

They blind deafen and strangle you and take away all power of action or reflection

Never shall I forget the sensations of awe horror and admiration with which I gazed about me

Here the vast bed of the waters seamed and scarred into a thousand conflicting channels burst suddenly into frenzied convulsion heaving boiling hissing gyrating in gigantic and innumerable vortices and all whirling and plunging on to the eastward with a rapidity which water never elsewhere assumes except in precipitous descents

Exercise 101C: Diagramming

On your own paper, diagram the following sentences from *Rebecca*, a modern gothic novel by Daphne du Maurier.

Each sentence has a different variation of items in a series, separated by commas. When you're finished diagramming, try to tell your instructor what they are. (They may not be exactly parallel—look at the sense of the sentences, not just the parts of speech.)

I can feel again the wind on my face, and hear my laugh, and his that echoed it.

There was Manderley, our Manderley, secretive and silent as it had always been, the gray stone shining in the moonlight of my dreams, the mullioned windows reflecting the green lawns and the terrace.

Color and scent and sound, rain and the lapping of water, even the mists of autumn and the smell of the flood tide, these are memories of Manderley that will not be denied.

—LESSON 102—

Adjective Review
Pronoun Review
Limiting Adjectives

(All sentences in this lesson are taken from *The Two Towers* by J. R. R. Tolkien.)

They had come to the desolation that lay before Mordor: the lasting monument to the dark labour of its slaves that should endure when all their purposes were made void; a land defiled, diseased beyond all healing—unless the Great Sea should enter in and wash it with oblivion.

brown curling hair	old tired horse
long black hair	white horse
snowy hair	running horse
his hair	king's horse

Descriptive adjectives *describe* by giving additional details.
Limiting adjectives *define* by setting limits.

Descriptive Adjectives	**Limiting Adjectives**
Regular	Possessives
Present participles	Articles
Past participles	Demonstratives
	Indefinites
	Interrogatives
	Numbers

The articles are *a, an*, and *the*.

Demonstrative pronouns demonstrate or point out something. They take the place of a single word or a group of words.

this, that, these, those

Demonstrative adjectives modify nouns and answer the question *which one*.

If those unhappy hobbits are astray in the woods, it might draw them hither.

The prisoners are NOT to be searched or plundered; those are my orders.

Indefinite pronouns are pronouns without antecedents.

Singular

anybody	anyone	anything
everybody	everyone	everything
nobody	no one	nothing
somebody	someone	something
another	other	one
either	neither	each

Plural

both few many several

Singular or Plural

all any most none some

I do not understand all that goes on myself, so I cannot explain it to you. Some of us are still true Ents, and lively enough in our fashion, but many are growing sleepy, going tree-ish, as you might say.

Indefinite adjectives modify nouns and answer the questions *which one* and *how many*.

We will ride for a few hours, gently, until we come to the end of the valley.

The cord hurts us, yes it does, it hurts us, and we've done nothing.

Some are quite wide awake, and a few are, well, ah, well, getting Entish.

Each Palantir replied to each, but all those in Gondor were ever open to the view of Osgiliath.

Interrogative pronouns take the place of nouns in questions.

who, whom, whose, what, which

Interrogative adjectives modify nouns.

Then if not yours, whose is the wizardry?

At whose command do you hunt Orcs in our land?

Which way do we go from here?

How far back his treachery goes, who can guess?

Cardinal numbers represent quantities (one, two, three, four . . .).
Ordinal numbers represent order (first, second, third, fourth . . .).

Treebeard was at their head, and some fifty followers were behind him.

Fifteen of my men I lost, and twelve horses, alas!

"Not Elves," said the fourth, the tallest, and as it appeared, the chief among them.

Gollum was the first to get up.

It was his turn to sleep first, and he was soon deep in a dream.

Exercise 102A: Identifying Adjectives

The following excerpt is taken from a ghost story called *Green Tea*, by the nineteenth-century gothic master Sheridan Le Fanu.

Underline every word that acts as an adjective.

Do not include phrases or clauses acting as adjectives. Also, do not include articles. (There are just too many!)

Label each one using the following abbreviations:

Descriptive Adjectives		**Limiting Adjectives**	
Regular	*DA-R*	Possessives	*LA-P*
Present participles	*DA-PresP*	~~Articles~~	~~*LA-A*~~
Past participles	*DA-PastP*	Demonstratives	*LA-D*
		Indefinites	*LA-IND*
		Interrogatives	*LA-INT*
		Numbers	*LA-N*

He would have been much better in a lodging-house, or hotel, I thought, as I drove up through a short double row of sombre elms to a very old-fashioned brick house, darkened by the foliage of these trees, which over-topped, and nearly surrounded it. It was a perverse choice, for nothing could be imagined more triste and more silent. The house, I found, belonged to him. He had stayed for a day or two in town, and, finding it for some cause insupportable, had come out here, probably because being furnished and his, he was relieved of the thought and delay of selection, by coming here.

The sun had already set, and the red reflected light of the western sky illuminated the scene with the peculiar effect with which we are all familiar. The hall seemed very dark, but, getting to the back drawing-room, whose windows command the west, I was again in the same dusky light.

I sat down, looking out upon the richly-wooded landscape that glowed in the grand and melancholy light which was every moment fading. The corners of the room were already dark; all was growing dim, and the gloom was insensibly toning my mind, already prepared for what was sinister. I was waiting alone for his arrival, which soon took place. The door communicating with the front room opened, and the tall figure of Mr. Jennings, faintly seen in the ruddy twilight, came, with quiet stealthy steps, into the room.

We shook hands, and, taking a chair to the window, where there was still light enough to enable us to see our faces, he sat down beside me, and, placing his hand upon my arm, with scarcely a word of preface began his narrative.

The faint glow of the west, the pomp of the lonely woods of Richmond, were before us, behind and about us the darkening room, and on the stony face of the sufferer—for the character of his face, though still gentle and sweet, was changed—rested that dim, odd glow which seems to descend and produce, where it touches, lights, sudden though faint, which are lost, almost without gradation, in darkness. The silence, too, was utter; not a distant wheel, or bark, or whistle from without; and within the depressing stillness of an invalid's house.

Exercise 102B: Analysis

The passage above shows you how a good writer uses adjectives: a mix of colorful descriptive adjectives and sparer, simpler limiting adjectives.

The total word count of the excerpt is 384 words. Now count each type of adjective and fill out the following chart:

Descriptive Adjectives		**Limiting Adjectives**	
Regular	_________	Possessives	_________
Present participles	_________	~~Articles~~	_________
Past participles	_________	Demonstratives	_________
		Indefinites	_________
		Interrogatives	_________
		Numbers	_________

Total Descriptive Adjectives _________ Total Limiting Adjectives _________

Total Adjectives Used _________

Good prose can't be reduced to *just* formulas—but formulas can give you some extra help in writing well. The total word count of the excerpt is 384 words. You can figure out what fraction of the total word count is taken up by adjectives by dividing the total word count by the total number of adjectives used. Determine that quotient, and ask your instructor for help if necessary.

$\overline{)384}$

The quotient above tells you that 1 out of every ____________ [insert answer to division problem!] words in this passage is an adjective. In other words, adjectives do not make up more than about 1/_____ of this descriptive writing.

Now let's look at the relationship between limiting and descriptive adjectives. Complete the following division problem:

[number of limiting adjectives] ________ $\overline{)\quad\quad\quad}$ __________ [number of descriptive adjectives]

The calculation above tells you that 1 out of every ____________ [insert answer to second division problem!] adjectives used is a limiting adjective.

Ask your instructor to share the last part of this exercise with you.

Exercise 102C: Using Adjectives

On your own paper, rewrite the passage below. It is taken from Sheridan Le Fanu's short story "The Watcher"—but all of the adjectives (except for articles) have been removed.

- Where adjectives could be removed without making the sentence ungrammatical, they have simply been deleted without a trace. Where removing an adjective made the sentence unreasonable, a blank has been inserted instead. So you know that adjectives go in the blanks—but you'll have to find a lot of other places to put them as well!
- You can also insert adverbs, additional articles, and conjunctions as necessary to make your insertions work.
- Aim to use the same proportions as the passage in Exercise 102B. This excerpt originally had 375 words, so use 60 to 62 total adjectives, not including articles.
- Use no more than 17 limiting adjectives. Use at least 3 different kinds of limiting adjectives (your choice!).
- The remainder should be descriptive adjectives. Use at least 3 participles (present or past) as adjectives.

When you are finished, compare your work with the original passage in the Answer Key.

The stranger stopped at the door of the room, and displayed ____________ form and face completely. He wore a cloak, which was ____________ and ____________, not ____________ quite to the knees; ____________ legs were cased in stockings, and ____________ shoes were adorned with roses of the ____________ colour. The opening of the cloak in front showed the under-suit to consist of ____________ very ____________, perhaps ____________ material, and ____________ hands were enclosed in a pair of gloves which ran up considerably above the wrist, in the manner of a gauntlet. In ____________ hand he carried ____________ walking-stick and ____________ hat, which he had removed, and the other hung heavily by ____________ side. A quantity of hair descended in tresses from ____________ head, and ____________ folds rested upon the plaits of a ruff, which effectually concealed ____________ neck.

So far all was ____________; but the face!—all the flesh of the face was coloured with the hue which is sometimes produced by the operation of medicines administered in quantities; the eyes were ____________, and the white appeared both above and below the iris, which gave to them an expression of insanity, which was heightened by _______________ fixedness; the mouth was writhed considerably to _______________ side, where it opened in order to give egress to fangs, which projected from the jaw, far below the lip; the hue of the lips themselves bore the _______________ relation to that of the face, and was consequently nearly _______________. The character of the face was _______________ to the _______________ degree; and, indeed, such a combination of horror could hardly be accounted for.

There was something indescribably _______________, even _______________ about _______________ motions, something _______________, something _______________ —it was as if the limbs were guided and directed by a spirit _______________ to the management of _______________ machinery. During _______________ stay he did not once suffer _______________ eyelids to close, nor even to move in the _______________ degree; and further, there was a stillness in _______________ person, owing to the absence of the motion of the chest _______________ by the process of respiration.

—LESSON 103—

Misplaced Modifiers
Squinting Modifiers
Dangling Modifiers

The party organizer passed around stuffed mushrooms to the guests on tiny bamboo mats.

Churning inexorably towards the coast, we breathlessly watched the weather reports about the hurricane.

Miranda spotted a blue heron on the way home.

The movie star rode through the crowds of fans in a limousine.

The inconsiderate child was kicking the back of the airplane seat.
The child was kicking the inconsiderate back of the airplane seat.

Mari upset almost every colleague she worked with.
Mari almost upset every colleague she worked with.

I slept for barely an hour.
I barely slept for an hour.

A misplaced modifier is an adjective, adjective phrase, adverb, or adverb phrase in the wrong place.

The chocolate fudge cake that I baked recently fell off the table onto the dirty floor.

Doing fifty chin-ups quickly strengthens your biceps.

My friend said on Monday we would go camping.

A squinting modifier can belong either to the sentence element preceding or the element following.

After reading more on the subject, the article turned out to be incorrect.
The experiment failed, not having procured the correct ingredients.
Exhausted by long days at work, the secretary's joy was unbounded when the office closed because of snow.

A dangling modifier has no noun or verb to modify.

How to Fix a Dangling Modifier

1. Provide the missing word in the main clause.

   After reading more on the subject, I discovered that the article was incorrect.

2. Turn the dangling phrase into a clause by putting the missing word(s) into the phrase itself.

   After I read more on the subject, the article turned out to be incorrect.

INCORRECT: Having been delayed by traffic, the bride's frustration was easily understood.

1. Provide the missing noun or verb in the main clause.

   ____

   ____

2. Turn the dangling phrase into a clause by putting the missing noun or verb into the phrase itself.

   ____

   ____

Exercise 103A: Correcting Misplaced Modifiers

Circle each misplaced modifier and draw an arrow to the place in the sentence that it should occupy.

He stood in the doorway with a startled expression.

The sun on the bright water shone pleasantly.

The chef handed out after-dinner treats to all his guests in paper bags.

Nell sat in the fishing boat with a smile.

Without getting permission, the chocolate frosted brownie was consumed by the hungry boy.

I decided to go home for Thanksgiving in July.

The golden brown turkey sat on the china platter steaming gently.

Running through the haunted countryside, scared and afraid, I watched the scary movie about the fleeing woman.

One morning, I spotted an elephant in my pajamas.

Exercise 103B: Clarifying Squinting Modifiers

Circle each squinting modifier. On your own paper, rewrite each sentence twice, eliminating the ambiguity by moving the squinting modifier to produce sentences with two different meanings. Insert commas and change capitalization/punctuation as needed. (And be aware—you might be able to eliminate the ambiguity by simply changing punctuation!)

The first is done for you.

The cow that was in the back pasture (recently) had twin calves.

> The cow that was recently in the back pasture had twin calves.
> The cow that was in the back pasture had twin calves recently.

The calves only seemed interested in eating more hay.
I told the farmer when the storm ended we should put all the cows back outside.
Farmers who move their cows from pasture to pasture often have healthier livestock.
The farm manager decided after two weeks to sell the belligerent bull.
When cows calve often they will give enough milk for more than two calves.
We agreed at the eight month mark to wean the calves onto grass and grain.
Feeding calf pellets rapidly produces very strong, hearty calves.
The farmer decided during calving season to spend nights at the barn.

Exercise 103C: Rewriting Dangling Modifiers

On your own paper, rewrite each of these sentences twice, using each of the strategies described in the lesson. You should feel free to change verbs and other words, as long as the sentence remains grammatical and has the same meaning as the original.

These have been adapted from *Chasing New Horizons: Inside the Epic First Mission to Pluto,* by Alan Stern and David Grinspoon. When you've finished rewriting your sentences, your instructor will show you the originals!

Reading everything he could find in the local library relating to astronomy and planets, the debate about the controversial "canals" on Mars "discovered" and promoted by the wealthy and charismatic Boston astronomer Percival Lowell absorbed him.

Meanwhile, out there on its own, deep in the Pluto system, the team was watching New Horizons do what it had been designed and built to do a dozen years before.

As it flashed past Pluto and its five moons that day, a library of data was being gathered, so vast that it would take sixteen months to send it all back to Earth.

Having traveled four hours at the speed of light from Pluto 3 billion miles away, Alice Bowman beamed and gave a thumbs-up at the expected time, when the signal reached Earth.

—LESSON 104—

Degrees of Adjectives

Comparisons Using *More, Fewer,* and *Less*

Good, better, best,
Never let it rest,
Till your good is better,
And your better, best.
—Julia Richman, *School Work 3,* No. 2 (June, 1904)

And summer days were sad and long,
And sad the uncompanioned eyes,
And sadder sunset-tinted leaves.
Of all sad words of tongue or pen,
The saddest are these: "It might have been!"
—John Greenleaf Whittier

The positive degree of an adjective describes only one thing.
The comparative degree of an adjective compares two things.
The superlative degree of an adjective compares three or more things.

Most regular adjectives form the comparative by adding *-r* or *-er*.
Most regular adjectives form the superlative by adding *-st* or *-est*.

positive	comparative	superlative
____________	____________	____________

Irregular adjectives may change form completely.

positive	comparative	superlative
____________	____________	____________

For a moment the general did not reply; he was smiling his curious red-lipped smile. Then he said slowly, "No. You are wrong, sir. The Cape buffalo is not the most dangerous game." He sipped his wine. "Here in my preserve on this island," he said in the same slow tone, "I hunt more dangerous game."

—Richard Connell, "The Most Dangerous Game" (1924)

Many adjectives form their comparative and superlative forms by adding the word *more* or *most* before the adjective instead of using *–er* or *–est*. In comparative and superlative adjective forms, the words *more* and *most* are used as adverbs.

positive	comparative	superlative
____________	____________	____________

So long as people will drink, drink will be made; and so long as drink is made, there will be those to sell it. Well, the more the restrictions, the fewer to sell; the fewer to sell, the less sold; the less sold, the less made; the less made, the less drunk; the less drunk, the fewer the inebriates—and that's what the temperance people are after.

—*The Grip,* Vol. 20, 1882

The more thoroughly we searched, the fewer treasures we found.
The more love I offered, the less enthusiasm he showed.

Use *fewer* for concrete items and *less* for abstractions.

He would do very well if he had fewer cakes and sweetmeats sent him from home.
I wanted to tease you a little to make you less sad.

—Charlotte Bronte, *Jane Eyre*

In comparisons using *more . . . fewer* and *more . . . less, more* and *less* can act as either adverbs or adjectives and *the* can act as an adverb.

We searched (the) more thoroughly. We found (the) fewer treasures.
I offered (the) more love. He showed (the) less enthusiasm.

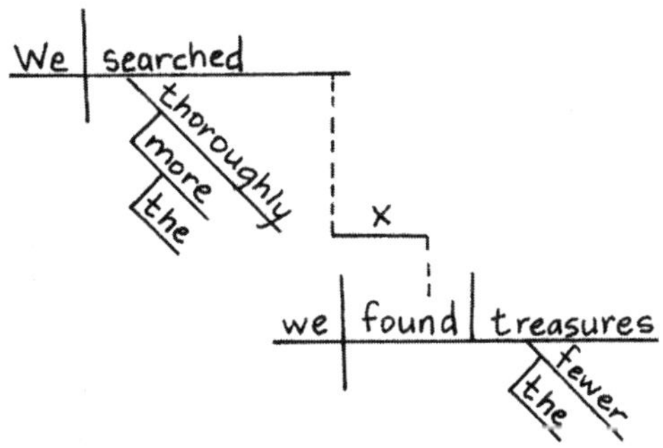

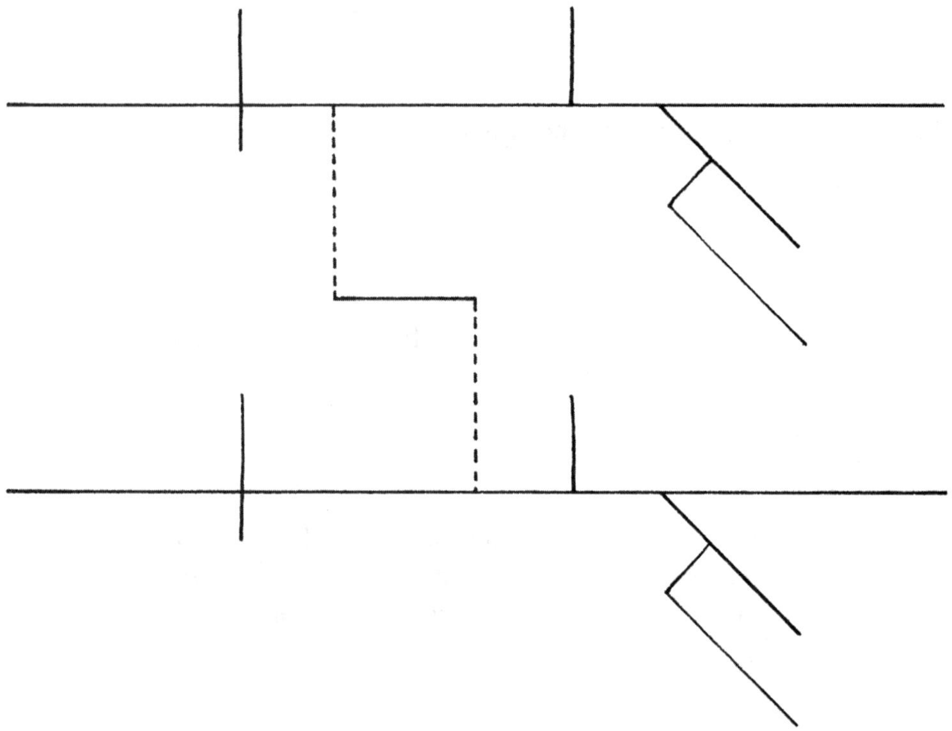

The more the building shook, the less he wanted to be there.

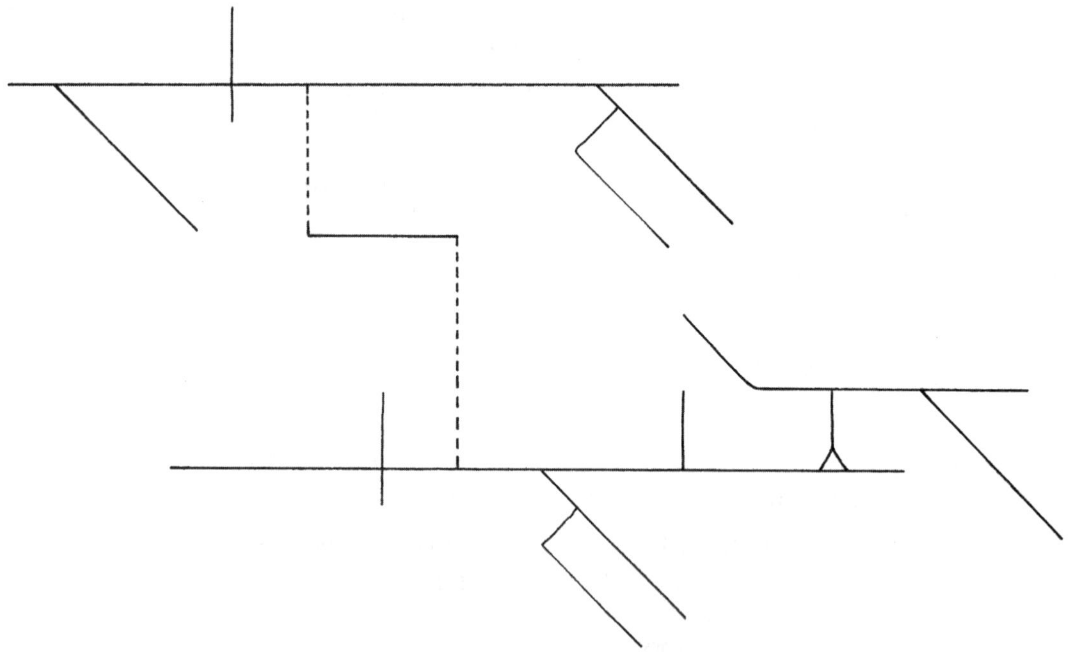

The more the building shook, the more we held on.
The less we saw, the less we knew.

The more the wave rose, the faster we ran.
The less we worried, the better we felt.
The happier we were, the more we rejoiced.
The louder the wind, the fewer words we were able to exchange.

The better we felt, the longer we stayed.
The longer the tail grew, the better the horse could swat flies.

The better we felt, the longer we stayed.

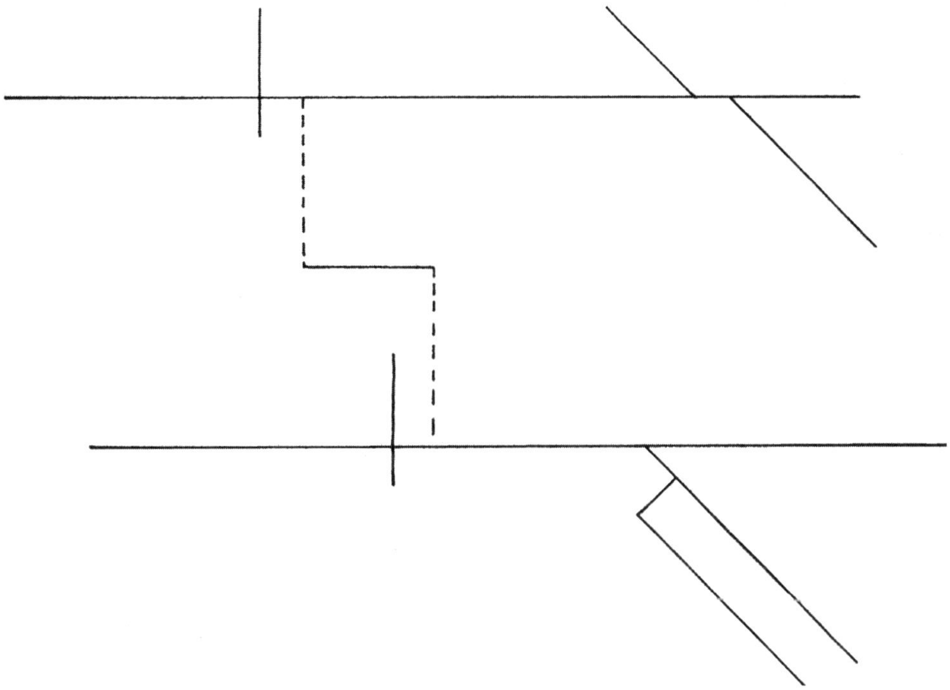

The longer the tail grew, the better the horse could swat flies.

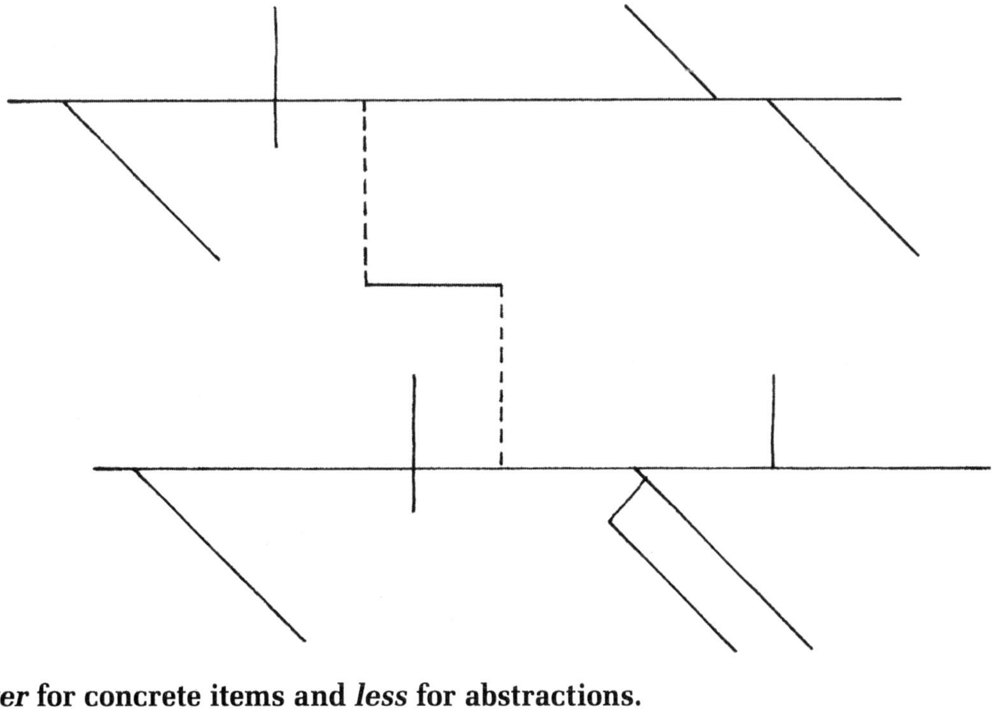

Use *fewer* for concrete items and *less* for abstractions.

Comparisons can be formed using a combination of *more* and *fewer* or *less;* a combination of *more* and *more* or *fewer/less* and *fewer/less*; a combination of *more* or *fewer/less* with a comparative form; or simply two comparative forms.

In comparisons using *more, fewer,* and *less, more* and *less* can act as either adverbs or adjectives, and *the* can act as an adverb.

In comparisons using two comparative forms, the forms may act as either adverbs or adjectives, and *the* can act as an adverb.

Exercise 104A: Positive, Comparative, and Superlative Adjectives

Use the following chart to review spelling rules for forming degrees of adjectives. Fill in the missing forms. Then, fill in the blank in each sentence with each adjective indicated in brackets (properly spelled!).

The sentences are all drawn from Charlotte Brontë's classic novel *Villette.*

Spelling Rules:

If the adjective ends in e already, add only *–r* or *–st.*

noble	nobler	noblest
pure	purer	purest
true	________	________

If the adjective ends in a short vowel sound and a consonant, double the consonant and add *–er* or *–est.*

red	redder	reddest
thin	thinner	thinnest
hot	________	________

If the adjective ends in *–y,* change the *y* to *i* and add *–er* or *–est.*

hazy	hazier	haziest
tiny	________	________

And Graham once more snatched her aloft, and she again punished him; and while she pulled his lion's locks, termed him—"The ________________, ________________, ________________, ________________ person that ever was." [in order, the superlatives of *naughty, rude, bad, untrue*]

Mr. Jones, a dried-in man of business, stood behind his desk: he seemed one of the ________________, and I one of the ________________ of beings. [in order, the superlatives of *great* and *happy*]

I took off my pink dress and lace mantle with ________________ feelings than I had experienced in putting them on. [the comparative of *happy*]

He did not grow _______________—no raillery, no levity sparkled across his aspect—but his position seemed to become one of more pleasure to himself, and he spoke his augmented comfort in _______________ language, in tones more suave. [in order, the comparatives of *gay* and *ready*]

The afternoon hours were over, and the _______________ time of evening shaded the quiet faubourg. [the comparative of *still*]

I believe, if some of you were thrown into Nebuchadnezzar's _______________ furnace you would issue forth untraversed by the smell of fire. [the superlative of *hot*]

A handsome middle-aged lady in dark velvet; a gentleman who might be her son—the _______________ face, the _______________ figure, I thought, I had ever seen; a third person in a pink dress and black lace mantle. [in order, the superlatives of *good* and *fine*]

Those eyes had looked on the visits of a certain ghost—had long waited the comings and goings of that _______________ spectre, Hypochondria. [the superlative of *strange*]

I think I should have declined had I been _______________ than I was, and with _______________ fund of resource, more stinted narrowness of future prospect. [in order, the comparatives of *poor* and *scanty*]

The Queen's eye, however, was her own; and pity, goodness, sweet sympathy, blessed it with _______________ light. [the superlative of *divine*]

The _______________ room was _______________ furnished and more habitable than the _______________; thither he introduced me. [in order, the comparatives of *small*, *good*, and *large*]

As she passed me to-night, triumphant in beauty, my emotions did her homage; but for one luckless sneer, I should yet be the _______________ of her servants. [the superlative of *humble*]

There is the wonderful Great Wall of China; here is a Chinese lady, with a foot _________ than mine. [the comparative of *little*]

Exercise 104B: Forming Comparisons

Rewrite each set of independent clauses so that they form a comparative sentence making use of *more*, *less*, *fewer*, and/or comparative forms of the adjectives indicated. The first is done for you.

When you are finished, ask your instructor to show you the original sentences, which are taken from the novel *Anna Karenina*, by Leo Tolstoy, translated by Constance Garnett.

One lives longer.
One learns.

The longer one lives the more one learns.

He tried to compose himself.
He found himself breathless.

He told her.
He did nothing.
He had less time to do anything.

He listened to the fantasia of King Lear.
He felt further from forming any definite opinion of it.

His behavior was externally obedient and respectful.
In his heart, he respected and loved her less.

He read and thought.
He read more.
He thought more.
He felt further from the aim he was pursuing.

Exercise 104C: Using *Fewer* and *Less*

Complete the sentences by filling in each blank with either *fewer* or *less*.

The original sentences are taken from Jane Austen's novel *Emma*.

As she thought ______________ of his inebriety, she thought more of his inconstancy and presumption; and with ______________ struggles for politeness, replied, "It is impossible for me to doubt any longer."

When first sounded on the subject, he was so miserable, that they were almost hopeless—a second allusion, indeed, gave ______________ pain.

A woman with ______________ resources than I have need not have been at a loss.

But Harriet was ______________ humble, had ______________ scruples than formerly.

Nothing should tempt her to go, if they did; and she regretted that her father's known habits would be giving her refusal ______________ meaning than she could wish.

She saw that with all the deep blush of consciousness, there had been a smile of secret delight, she had ______________ scruple in the amusement, and much ________ compunction with respect to her.

Exercise 104D: Diagramming

On your own paper, diagram every word of the following sentences from *Watership Down*, by Richard Adams.

Each sentence has at least one understood element! If you can't find it, ask your instructor to show you the sentences with the understood elements spelled out.

The slower the journey, the more dangerous it would be, and stragglers would attract elil and discourage the rest.

She knew what to do, and the less they were seen together the better.

CHALLENGE SENTENCE

Try to figure out the understood elements and diagram them yourself (but if you get stuck, ask for help!).

But the more he thought about it—as well as he could for hunger and fear and the trance that comes upon rabbits face to face with death—the more it seemed to him that there was at least a chance of success.

WEEK 27

Double Identities

—LESSON 105—

Clauses with Understood Elements
***Than* as Conjunction, Preposition, and Adverb**
Quasi-Coordinators

I like chocolate better than vanilla.
Other than pistachio, I'll eat any flavor of ice cream.
I am more than satisfied with chocolate, but less than happy with pistachio.
I will starve rather than eat pistachio.

A coordinating conjunction joins equal words or groups of words together.
A subordinating conjunction joins unequal words or groups of words together.

He worked more efficiently than his brother.
He worked more efficiently than his brother [worked].

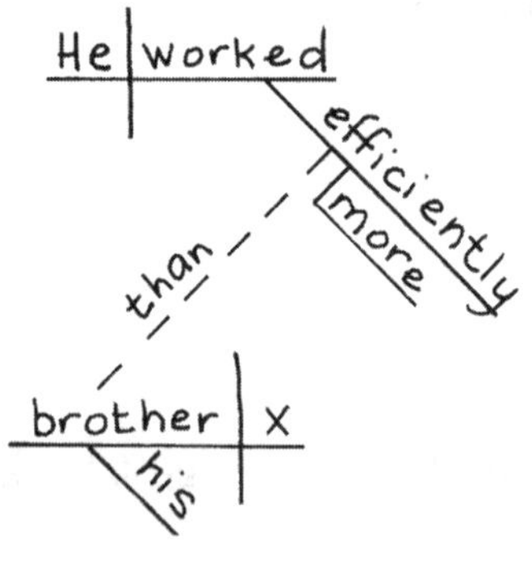

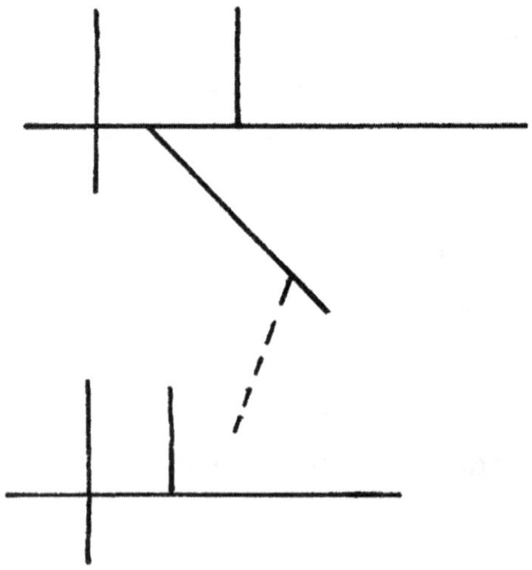

Tomorrow should be sunnier than today.
A new broom sweeps better than an old one.
The cook added more salt than he should have.

I love him more than you.

He is stronger than I.

INCORRECT: He is stronger than me.

He is stronger than I am.

not He is stronger than me.

When *than* is used in a comparison and introduces a clause with understood elements, it is acting as a subordinating conjunction.

Other than pistachio, I'll eat any flavor of ice cream.

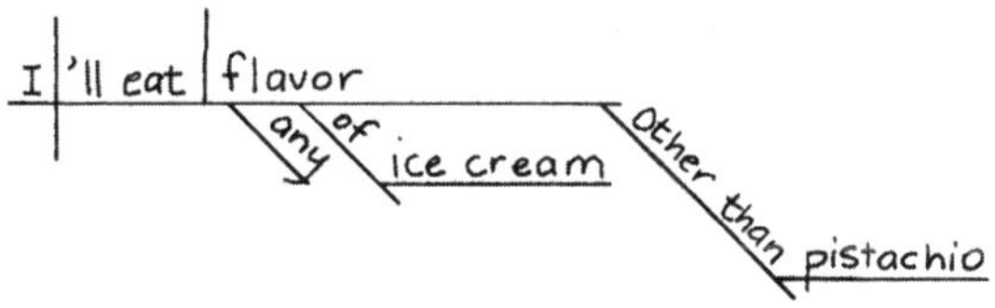

***Other than* is a compound preposition that means "besides" or "except."**

I am more than satisfied with chocolate, but less than happy with pistachio.

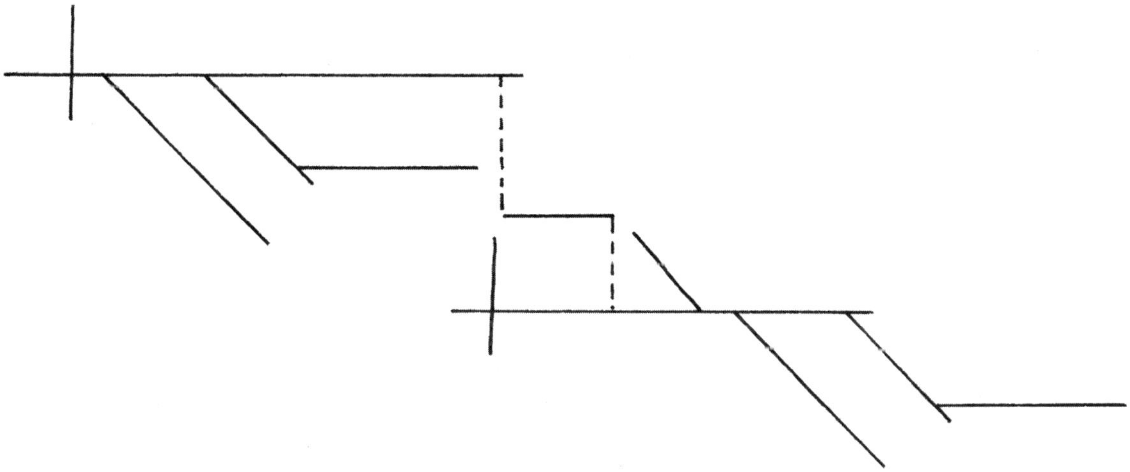

***More than* and *less than* are compound modifiers.**

I will starve rather than eat pistachio.

I will starve *and* eat pistachio.

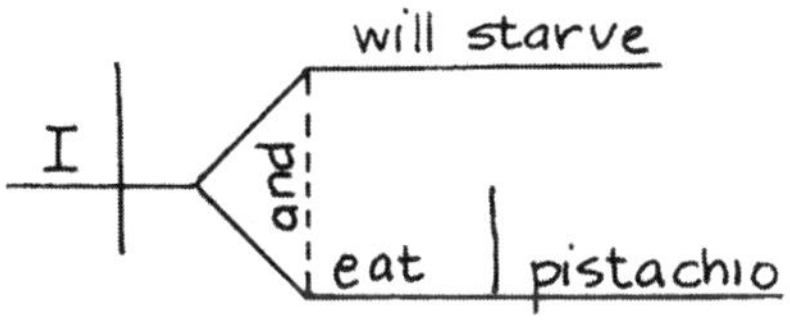

Quasi-coordinators link compound parts of a sentence that are unequal. Quasi-coordinators include *rather than, sooner than, let alone,* and *not to mention.*

I will starve rather than eat pistachio.

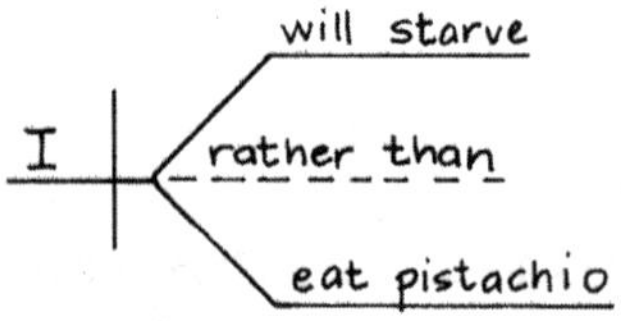

Rather than going home, she drove back up to the lake.

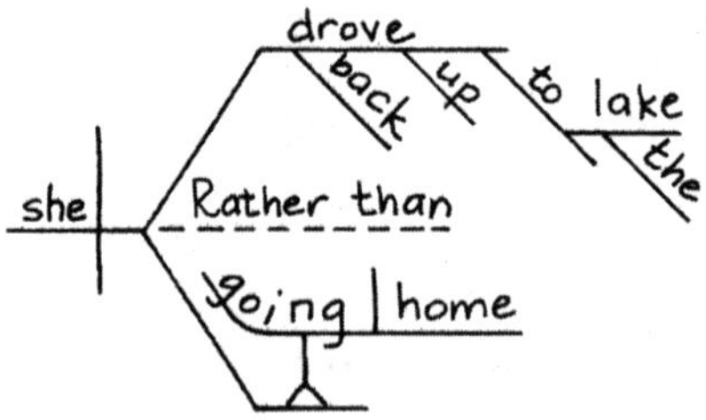

He could not keep up with Patel, let alone Krishna.

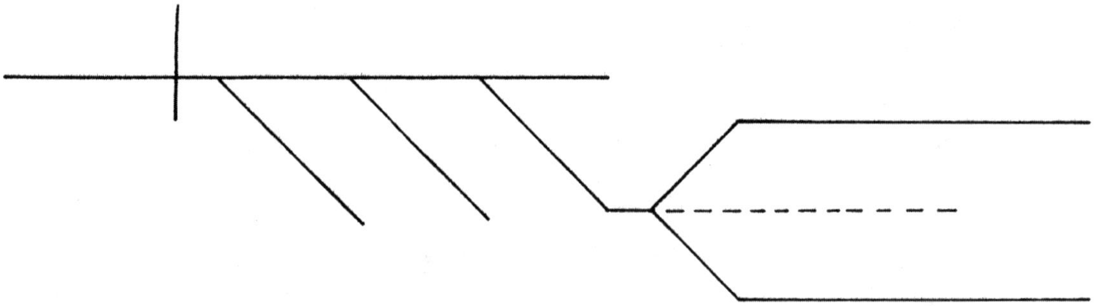

The expense, not to mention the risk, was simply too great.

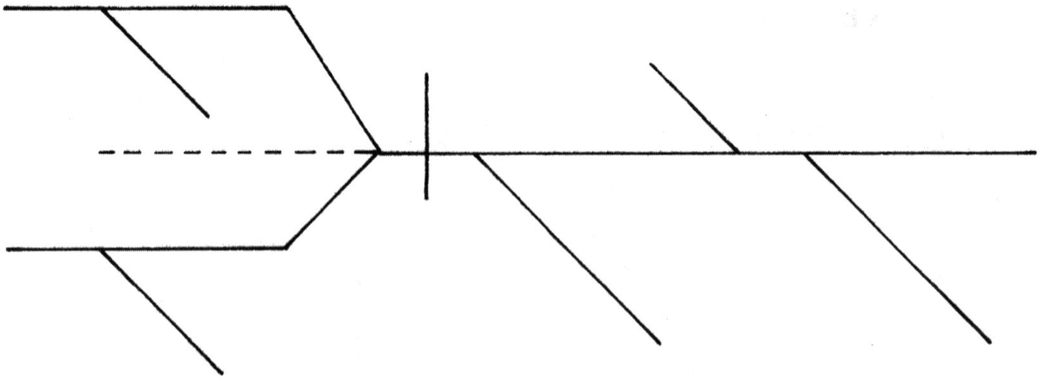

He would walk in a hailstorm sooner than pay ten dollars for a cab.

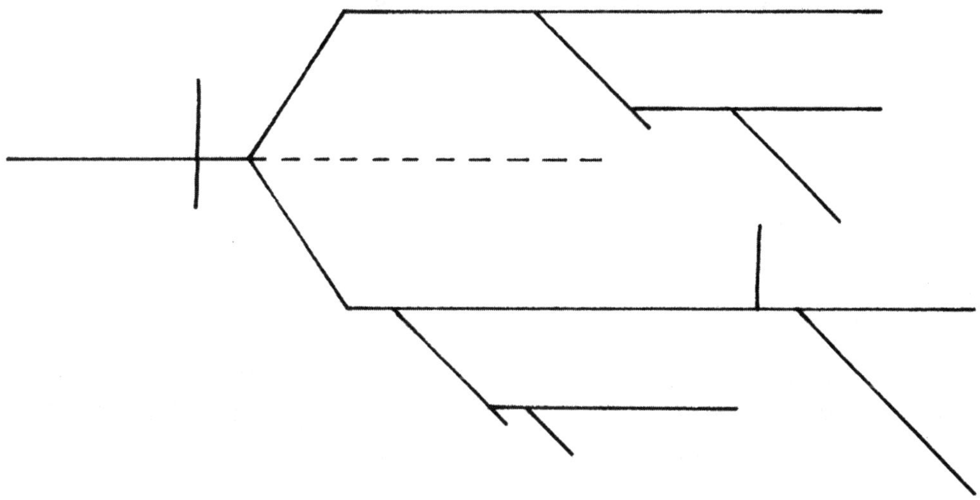

When *than* is used in a comparison and introduces a clause with understood elements, it is acting as a subordinating conjunction.
***Other than* is a compound preposition that means *besides* or *except*.**
***More than* and *less than* are compound modifiers.**

Quasi-coordinators link compound parts of a sentence that are unequal. Quasi-coordinators include *rather than, sooner than, let alone,* and *not to mention*.

Exercise 105A: Comparisons Using *Than*

Each of the following sentences, taken from *The History of the Peloponnesian War* by the ancient Greek historian Thucydides, contains a comparison clause introduced by *than* and missing some of its words. Using carets, do your best to insert the missing words.

Thucydides, an Athenian, wrote the history of the war between the Peloponnesians and the Athenians, beginning at the moment that it broke out, and believing that it would be a great war and more worthy of relation than any that had preceded it.

And so the power of the descendants of Pelops came to be greater than that of the descendants of Perseus.

He had also a navy far stronger than his contemporaries.

An examination of the facts will show that it was much greater than the wars which preceded it.

To them, laborious occupation is less of a misfortune than the peace of a quiet life.

Thus it happens that the vast experience of Athens has carried her further than you on the path of innovation.

And none care to inquire why this reproach is not brought against other imperial powers, who treat their subjects with less moderation than we do.

Exercise 105B: Identifying Parts of the Sentence

In the following sentences, also drawn from *The History of the Peloponnesian War*, identify each bolded word or phrase as *SC* for subordinating conjunction, *QC* for quasi-coordinator, *PREP* for preposition, *ADJ* for adjective, or *ADV* for adverb.

What enabled Agamemnon to raise the armament was more, in my opinion, his superiority in strength, **than** the oaths of Tyndareus, which bound the suitors to follow him.

It has possessed the same form of government for **more than** four hundred years, reckoning to the end of the late war, and has thus been in a position to arrange the affairs of the other states.

Accordingly they suddenly attacked and took Iasus, whose inhabitants never imagined that the ships could be **other than** Athenian.

For kindness opportunely shown has a greater power of removing old grievances **than** the facts of the case may warrant.

They chose to prosecute their complaints by war, **rather than** prosecuting them by a fair trial.

The Corinthians had been victorious in the sea-fight until night; and having thus been enabled to carry off most wrecks and dead, they were in possession of no **fewer than** a thousand prisoners of war.

And yet the world used to say that you were to be depended upon; but in your case, we fear, it said **more than** the truth.

Against Athens you prefer to act on the defensive instead of on the offensive, and to make it an affair of chances by deferring the struggle till she has grown far stronger **than** at first.

And indeed, in spite of the time occupied with the necessary arrangements, **less than** a year elapsed before Attica was invaded, and the war openly began.

Exercise 105C: Diagramming

On your own paper, diagram every word of the following three sentences, also taken from *The History of the Peloponnesian War.*

Less than a year elapsed before Attica was invaded, and the war openly began.
Farmers are a class of men that are always more ready to serve in person than in purse.
Accordingly they suddenly attacked and took Iasus, whose inhabitants never imagined that the ships could be other than Athenian.

—LESSON 106—

The Word *As*

Quasi-Coordinators

Middle English *alswa* "similarly" *as*

> The twenty-fourth object would be as big as a sugar cube, the twenty-seventh would be about the size of a large mammal, the fifty-fourth would be the size of the planet Jupiter and the fifty-seventh would be about as big as the Sun, where even atoms are destroyed by gravity, leaving a mixture of nuclei and free electrons called a plasma.
>
> — John R. Gribbin, *The Scientists: A History of Science Told through the Lives of Its Greatest Inventors*

is big
The twenty-fourth object would be as big as a sugar cube ^.

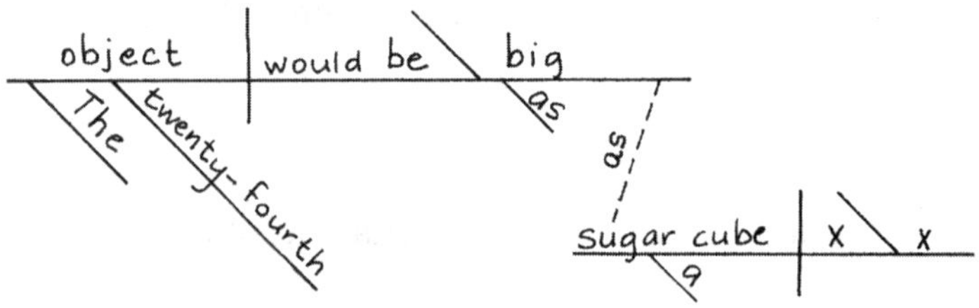

(The following sentences are all from Gribbin's *The Scientists* as well.)

. . . [A]n equally important factor, as many people have argued, was the depopulation of Europe by the Black Death . . .

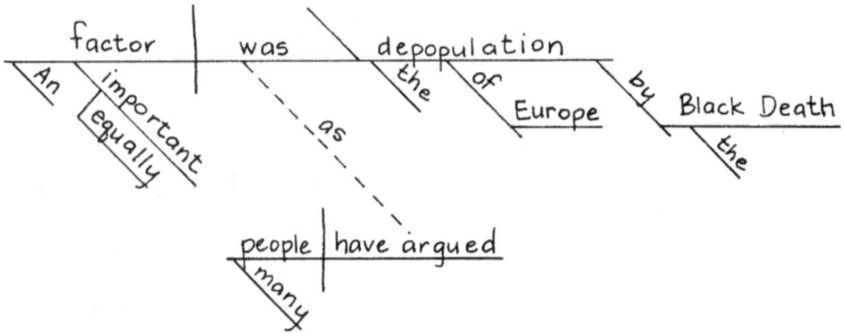

As long as Frederick remained on the throne, Tycho was able to enjoy an unprecedented amount of freedom to run his observatory just as he liked.

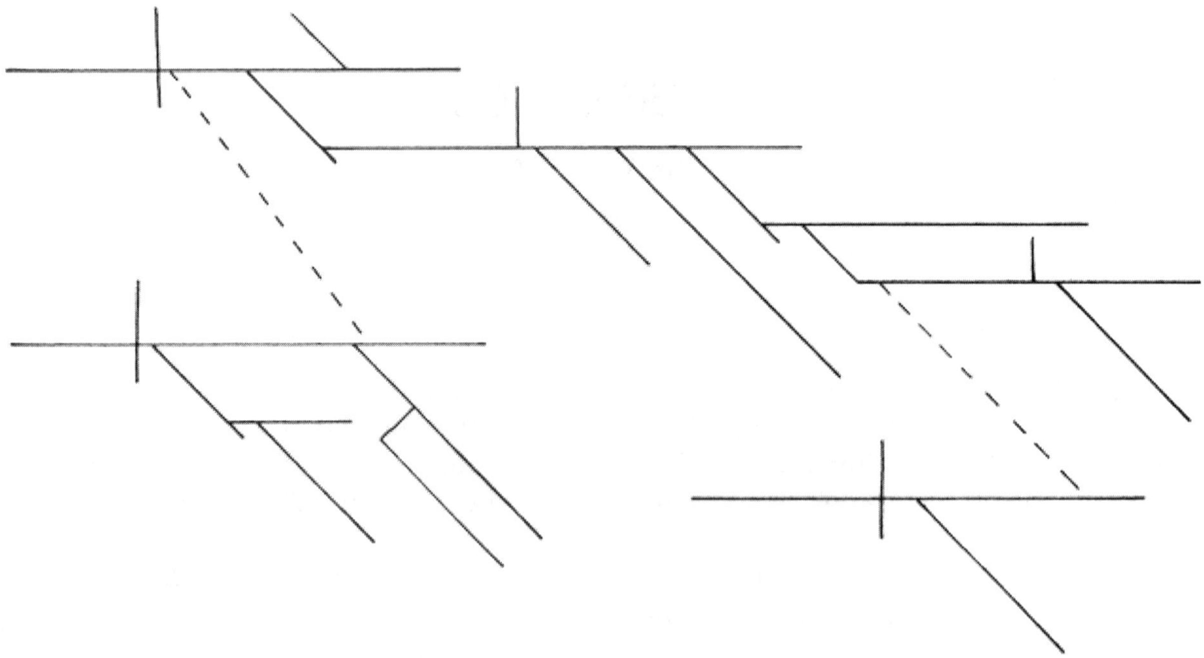

There were many translations and new editions of the book, which laid the foundations for chemistry as a genuinely scientific discipline.

Lavoisier . . . played a full part in the activities of the Academy, and during his time as a member worked on very many reports covering topics as diverse as . . . meteorites, cultivation of cabbages, the mineralogy of the Pyrenees and the nature of the gas arising from cesspools.

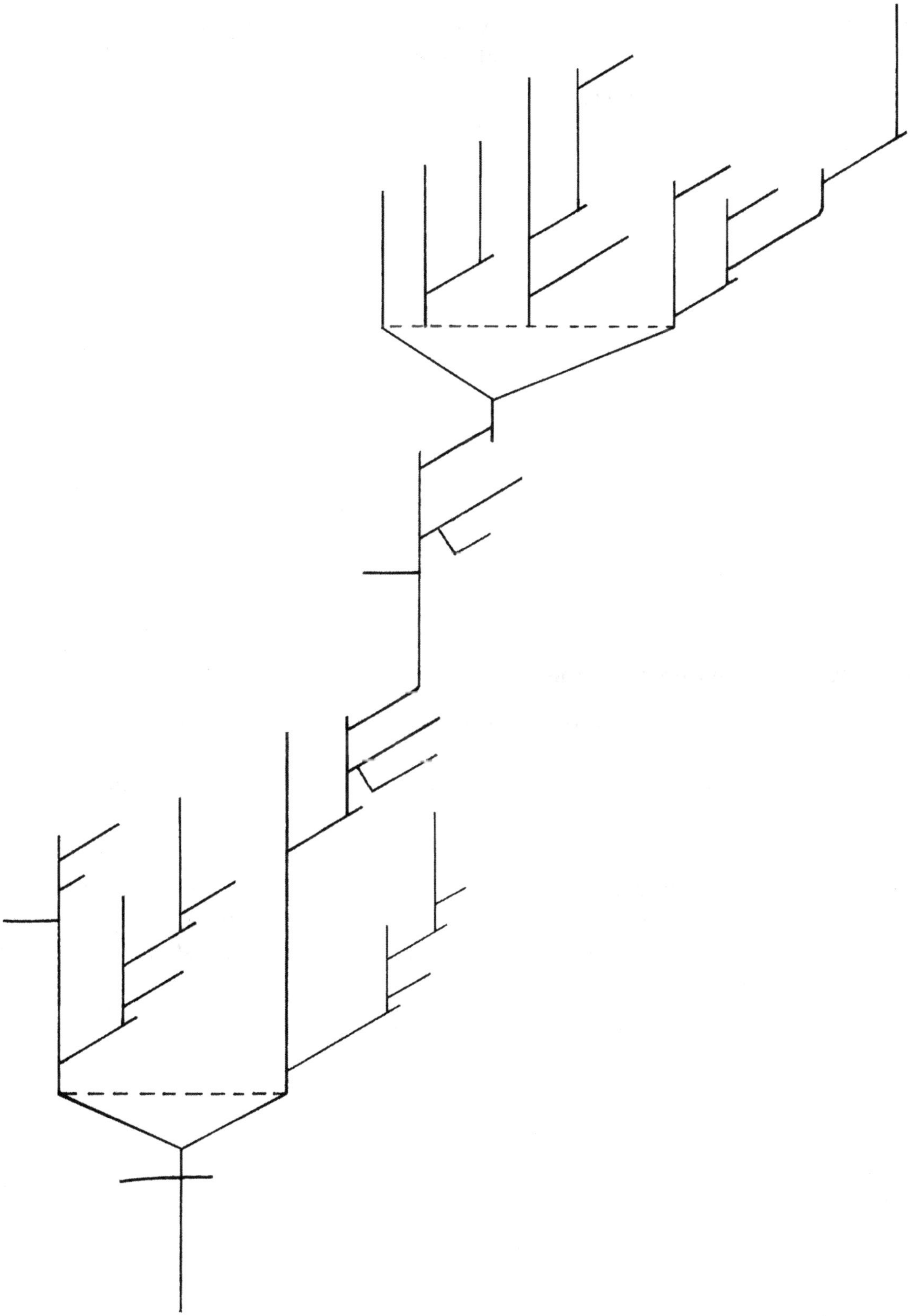

At the time of his marriage, as well as considerable property, Charles Cavendish had a disposable annual income of at least £2000, which grew as time passed.

Quasi-coordinators link compound parts of a sentence that are unequal. Quasi-coordinators include *rather than, sooner than, let alone, as well as,* and *not to mention.*

As well as his fame as a geologist, Darwin also received acclaim as a writer, in the mould of Lyell.

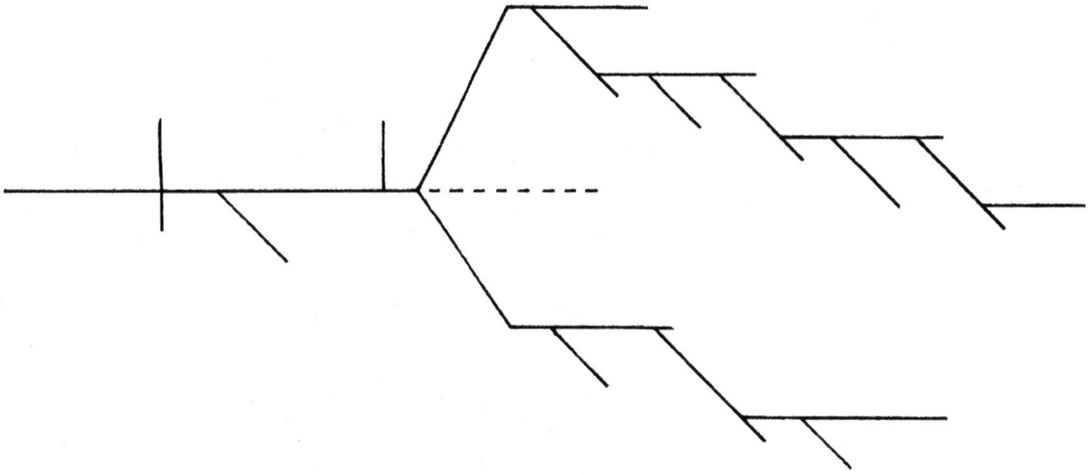

Exercise 106A: Identifying Parts of the Sentence

In the following sentences, find and underline every adverb, preposition, conjunction, and quasi-coordinator. Then label each as *ADV* for adverb, *PREP* for preposition, *CC* for coordinating conjunction, *SC* for subordinating conjunction, and *QC* for quasi-coordinator. Remember that a quasi-coordinator can be a short phrase as well as a single word.

These sentences are taken from *The Poison Squad: One Chemist's Single-Minded Crusade for Food Safety at the Turn of the Twentieth Century,* by Deborah Blum, an account of food chemist Harvey Wiley's fight for laws that would regulate how food and drink are sold to the public.

Some of these are tricky—be careful, and ask your instructor for help if you need it!

Faced with hostility, he became more rigid in his stance, often refusing to compromise even on small details.

"The cry 'Poisoned Milk'" rings through the land, he wrote, as it had over decades of government inaction and corruption.

He estimated that corn-derived glucose had about two-thirds the sweetening power of cane sugar; it was also far cheaper, produced for less than half the cost.

He urged that copper be banned as an additive from American food products as soon as possible.

In the year 1904, Dodge noted, more than twenty thousand children under the age of two had died in New York City and that milk was considered a major contributor to those fatalities.

La Follette conveniently overlooked the fact that butter itself, when produced in the winter from cows fed on hay rather than pasture grass, turns out more white than yellow.

Those with a healthy stomach, as he put it, were unlikely to be harmed by an occasional exposure to copper or zinc.

If risks were clearly and methodically identified, then those compounds should be removed from all food and drink.

Exercise 106B: Diagramming

On your own paper, diagram every word of the following sentences, very slightly adapted from *Swindled: The Dark History of Food Fraud, from Poisoned Candy to Counterfeit Coffee*, by Bee Wilson. Ask for help if you need it!

White bread was always more expensive than brown bread, because the bran was wasted and because the bread was made from wheat rather than the cheaper barley and rye.

Given the poor, sour grain, bakers used more alum than usual, which resulted in a "harsh" crumb and acrid taste.

But shouldn't all food be as safe and as pure and as fresh as possible?

The swindlers still have roughly the same kind of expertise to draw on—legal and scientific—as the antiswindlers.

Just as false and exaggerated dangers swarm everywhere, real dangers may become invisible.

—LESSON 107—

Words That Can Be Multiple Parts of Speech

(The sentences from this lesson have been slightly adapted and condensed from *Bleak House* by Charles Dickens.)

But ______________________ ______________________

I had an illness, but it was not a long one.

He has never hurt anybody but himself.

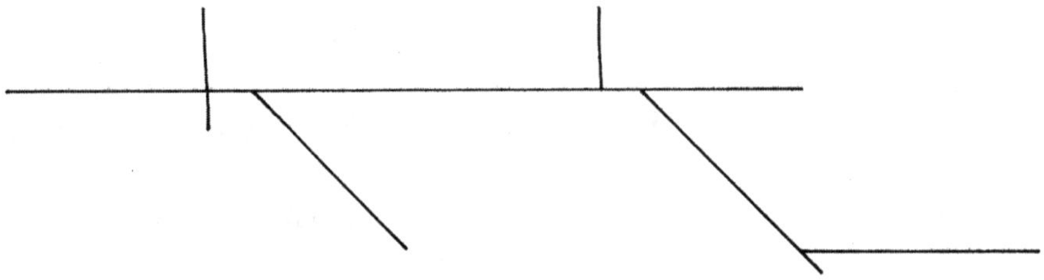

For ______________________ ______________________

I can answer for him as little as for you.

I should have been ashamed to come here to-day, for I know what a figure I must seem to you two.

About ______________________ ______________________

You could hear the horses being rubbed down outside the stable and being told to "Hold up!" and "Get over," as they slipped about very much on the uneven stones.

What with making notes on a slate about jams, and pickles, and preserves, and bottles, and glass, and china, and a great many other things; and what with being generally a methodical, old-maidish sort of foolish little person, I was so busy that I could not believe it was breakfast-time when I heard the bell ring.

Yet ______________________ ______________________

Is he here yet?
At this time, Jo has not yet died.
It is good, yet it could be improved.

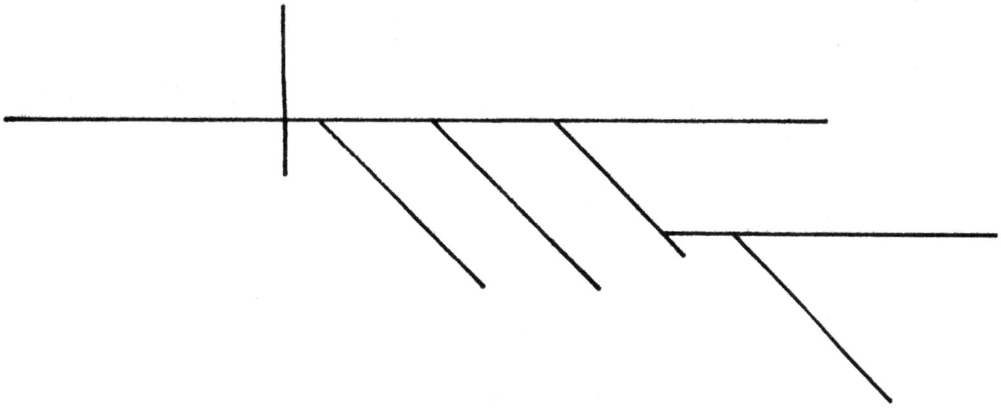

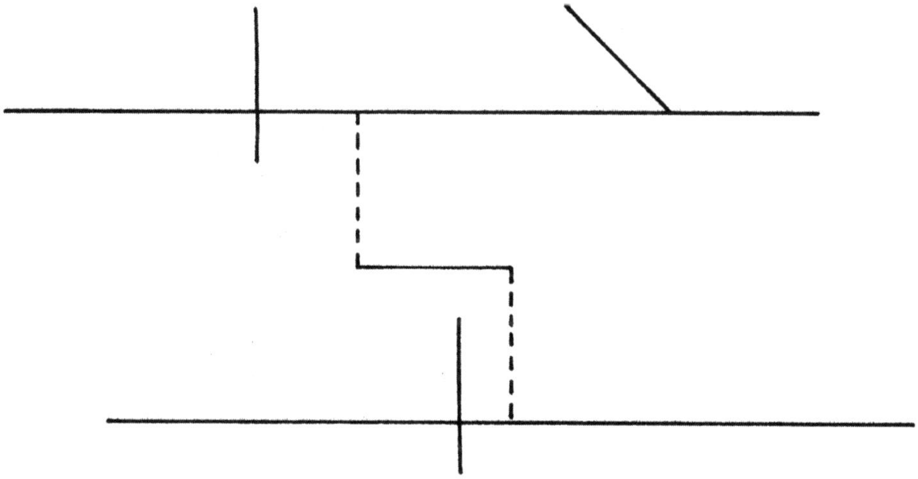

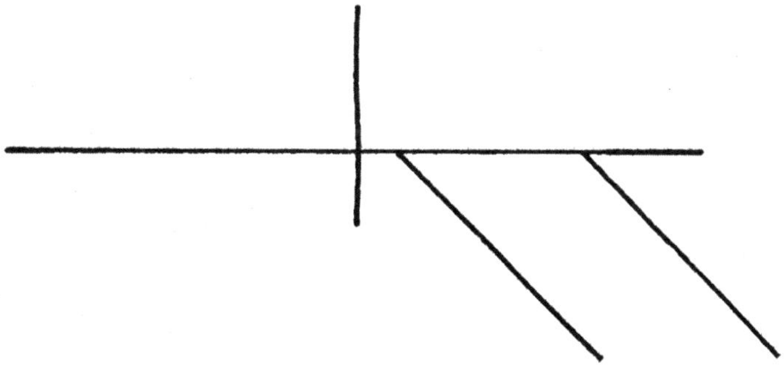

Any pronoun adjective adverb

I could not reproach myself any less.

It would be an insult to the discernment of any man with half an eye to tell him so.

I wonder whether any of the gentlemen remembered him.

I then asked Richard whether he had thought of any more congenial pursuit.

I thought it was impossible that you could have loved me any better.

Before ______________ ______________ ______________

Weariness of soul lies before her, as it lies behind.

It was past twelve before he took his candle and his radiant face out of the room.

He seemed to have been completely exhausted long before.

Above preposition ______________ ______________

The flame of gas was burning so sullenly above the iron gate.

His eyes were fixed high above.

But it is all blank, blank as the darkness above.

After preposition adverb ______________

In half an hour after our arrival, Mrs. Jellyby appeared.

I once more saw him looking at me after he had passed the door.

He presented himself soon after.

Otherwise ______________ ______________ ______________

We are not so prejudiced as to suppose that in private life you are otherwise than a very estimable man.

How could you do otherwise?

Love her and all will go well; otherwise, all will go ill.

Still

It is quite still and silent. ______________

She remained perfectly still until the carriage turned into the drive. ______________

The cause was hopeless; still, they fought. ______________

Still yourself, my dear, and wait in patience. ______________

In the still, the woods seemed massively hushed in sleep. ______________

Exercise 107A: Identifying Parts of Speech

Identify the part of speech of each underlined word (adapted from *The Old Curiosity Shop*, by Charles Dickens) by writing the correct abbreviation above it: *N* (noun), *PRO* (pronoun), *V* (verb), *ADJ* (adjective), *ADV* (adverb), *PREP* (preposition), *CC* (coordinating conjunction), or *SC* (subordinating conjunction).

Although I am an old man, night is generally my time for walking.

"I know that, sir," she replied timidly. "I am afraid it is a very long way, for I came from there to-night."

She walked on as before, growing more familiar with me as we proceeded and talking cheerfully by the way, but she said no more about her home, beyond remarking that we were going quite a new road and asking if it were a short one.

There's a friend of mine waiting outside, and as it seems that I may have to wait some time, I'll call him in, with your leave.

Now, just as Mr Quilp laid his hand upon the lock, and saw with great astonishment that the fastenings were undone, the knocking came again with the most irritating violence, and the daylight which had been shining through the key-hole was intercepted on the outside by a human eye.

There were none to see the frail, perishable figure, as it glided from the fire and leaned pensively at the open casement; none but the stars, to look into the upturned face and read its history.

Full of these meditations, she reached the church.

I called up all the strange tales I had ever heard of dark and secret deeds committed in great towns and escaping detection for a long series of years; wild as many of these stories were, I could not find one adapted to this mystery, which only became the more impenetrable, in proportion as I sought to solve it.

"It's as well not to say more than one can help before our worthy friend," said Quilp, making a grimace towards the slumbering Dick.

As it grew dusk, the wind fell; its distant moanings were more low and mournful; and, as it came creeping up the road, and rattling covertly among the dry brambles on either hand, it seemed like some great phantom for whom the way was narrow, whose garments rustled as it stalked along.

In a small dull yard below his window, there was a tree—green and flourishing enough, for such a place—and as the air stirred among its leaves, it threw a rippling shadow on the white wall.

He was soon calmed and fell asleep, singing to himself in a low voice, like a little child.

My boat is on the shore and my bark is on the sea, but before I pass this door I will say farewell to thee.

But these fears vanished before a well-trimmed lamp and the familiar aspect of her own room.

Exercise 107B: Diagramming

On your own paper, diagram every word of the following sentences from *The Old Curiosity Shop*.

If you need help, ask your instructor!

Man wants but little here below, nor wants that little long!

Of these Mr Quilp delivered himself with the utmost animation and rapidity, and with so many distortions of limb and feature, that even his wife, although tolerably well accustomed to his proficiency in these respects, was well-nigh beside herself with alarm.

There was but one lady who seemed to understand the child, and she was one who sat alone in a handsome carriage, while two young men in dashing clothes, who had just dismounted from it, talked and laughed loudly at a little distance.

—LESSON 108—

Nouns Acting as Other Parts of Speech
Adverbial Noun Phrases

Exercise 108A: Nouns

These sentences are all taken from the three volumes of the *Hunger Games* trilogy, by Suzanne Collins. Identify the part of the sentence that each underlined noun plays by labeling it as *S* for subject, *PN* for predicate nominative, *APP* for appositive, *DO* for direct object, or *OP* for object of the preposition.

We're on a flat, open <u>stretch</u> of ground.

If the Gamemakers want us in the <u>open</u>, then in the <u>open</u> we will be.

The red blinking <u>light</u> on one of the cameras catches my eye.

I can see her tallying the <u>cost</u> of my ultimatum, weighing it against my possible <u>worth</u>.

Prim was one <u>slip</u> of paper in thousands!

And whatever Peeta wants, it's his <u>turn</u> to be saved.

After days of inactivity, the <u>hunt</u> has taken its toll.

Whatever the opposite of <u>fine</u> is, that's what I am.

Prim is in my first reaping outfit, a <u>skirt</u> and ruffled blouse.

But my mind seems foggy and forming a <u>plan</u> is hard.

He got a knife in the <u>back</u> at the Cornucopia.

Exercise 108B: Nouns as Other Parts of Speech

Each of the following sentences is missing one of the nouns from the exercise above—but the noun is functioning as another part of speech!

Your task: figure out which noun can fill every blank.

These sentences are also from the *Hunger Games* trilogy.

________________________ bread like this is for special occasions.

Most of the Peacekeepers ____________________ a blind eye to the few of us who ____________________ because they're as hungry for fresh meat as anybody is.

It's this detail, the untucked blouse forming a ducktail, that brings me ________________ to myself.

Then his eyes ________________, unmistakably blue in the brown mud and green leaves.

He's got Peeta's nose blocked off but his mouth tilted ________________________, and he's blowing air into his lungs.

"Don't ____________________ a fire," he says.

But there are other people who'd make your life ____________________________ living.

I put the cheese carefully in my pocket as I ____________________________ outside.

We're on a flat, _______________________ stretch of ground.

My fingers _______________________ out, seeking Prim's warmth but finding only the rough canvas cover of the mattress.

I chop them very _____________________ and add them to the pot, switch out the rocks again, put on the lid, and let the whole thing stew.

Each tessera is _________________ a meager year's supply of grain and oil for one person.

I ___________________________ for us to ____________________________ around the corner and then detonate the Meat Grinder, but another unmarked pod lies in wait.

I ___________________________ away, panting, turn on my heel, and take off again.

Effie's having a _____________________ time ordering everybody around, keeping us all on schedule.

"What did you ___________________ me again?" I ask.

Mary and her lamb went into the school.

Mary and her lamb went home.

He followed her to school on Monday.

He followed her to school one day.

An adverbial noun tells the time or place of an action, or explains how long, how far, how deep, how thick, or how much. It can modify a verb, adjective, or adverb. An adverbial noun plus its modifiers is an adverbial noun phrase.

Before the lamb had travelled a mile, Mary turned around.

The road to school was two miles long.

The mud puddle in the road was three inches deep.

The lamb splashed in the puddle until he was covered with inch-thick mud.

The lamb splashed in the puddle until he was covered with mud an inch thick.

The storm continued all night.

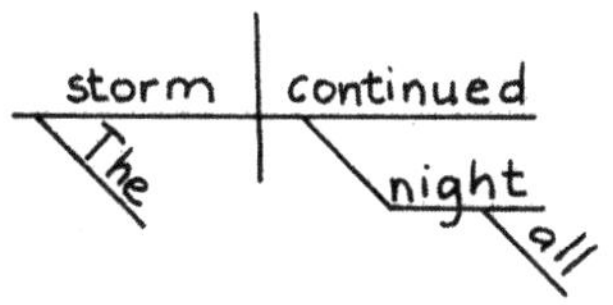

The earth's mantle is roughly 1,800 miles thick.

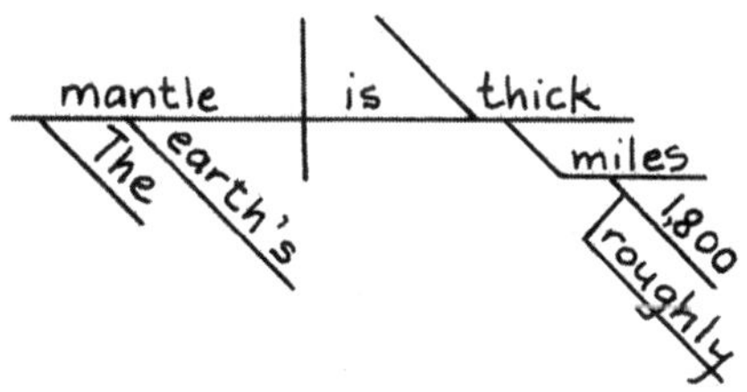

He slept eight hours and then woke up early the next morning.

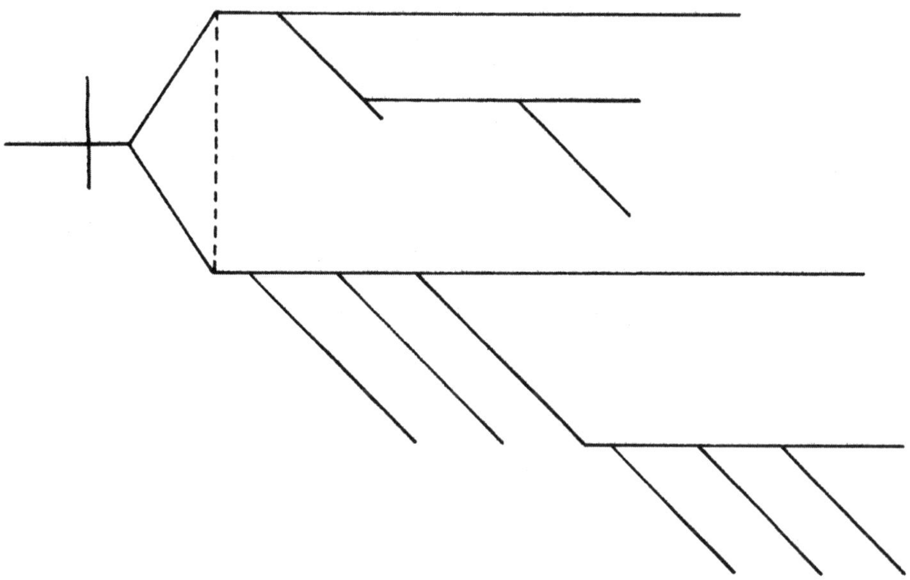

After our delicious picnic lunch, we walked the two miles to the battlefield.

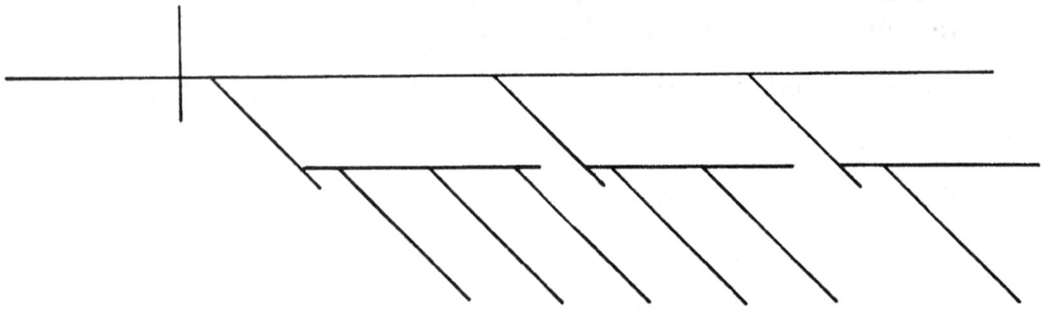

Exercise 108C: Identifying Parts of Speech

Identify the part of speech of each underlined word by writing the correct abbreviation above it: *N* (noun), *ADV-N* (adverbial noun), *PRO* (pronoun), *V* (verb), *ADJ* (adjective), *ADV* (adverb), *PREP* (preposition), *CC* (coordinating conjunction), *CorrC* (correlative conjunctions), *SC* (subordinating conjunction), or *QC* (quasi-coordinator).

These sentences are taken from *The Devil's Doctor: Paracelsus and the World of Renaissance Magic and Science*, by Philip Ball.

Some of these are very difficult—ask for help if you need it!

The Black Death swept out of Asia in late 1347, and in the following two years it killed as much as a third of the population.

As for the third item in your diagnosis, I cannot understand it, but it seems likely to me.

Agricola died a year before *De re Metallica* was published, to the dismay of learned men of every persuasion.

This was fortunate, for a student was expected to travel a lot, and the roads were seldom safe.

It would be wrong to imagine that the surgeon's lot was, in comparison to the physician's, necessarily humble.

Forty of Paracelsus's theological monographs still survive, as well as sixteen Bible commentaries, twenty sermons, twenty works on the Eucharist, and seven on the Virgin Mary.

Luther and Paracelsus never met, and it is probably just as well.

The students gather round to watch the dissection.

For Thales, there was but a single element—water—but his successors postulated a variety of elemental schemes.

"I am neither the author nor the executor of that Philosopher's Stone, which is differently described by others," he wrote in 1526, even as he worked alongside Kilian in their alchemical laboratory.

"I do not take my medicines from the apothecaries," he once insisted, "their shops are just foul sculleries which produce nothing but foul broths."

But in prescientific times there was no clear division between the inorganic and the vital worlds, for even metals were thought to have a kind of sluggish, unresponsive "life."

They bleed their patients in more ways than one, while confining them to a bleak and joyless life.

Perhaps it was hard for him to imagine that anyone could find his way to the heart of medicine by a path other than the one he himself had taken.

Exercise 108D: Adverbial Noun Phrases

Circle each adverbial noun or noun phrase, and draw an arrow from the circle to the word modified.

These sentences are taken from *The Devil's Doctor: Paracelsus and the World of Renaissance Magic and Science*, by Philip Ball.

At the University of Paris, work began at six in the morning in winter and an hour earlier in summer.

As if that were not bad enough, the student found himself confronted by such gnomic questions as "Is the loud voice warm?" and "Is it healthy to get drunk once a month?"

CHALLENGE ASSIGNMENT! Can you deduce from context what *gnomic* means? Tell your instructor and see how close you are!

Citizens of almost any town could consider themselves highly fortunate if they experienced no outbreak for two decades, and sometimes the plague returned every year.

When I returned home my first care was to procure the whole works of this author, and afterwards of Paracelsus and Albertus Magnus.

Agrippa met Faust, probably in Paris in 1528, when Francis I sent for him and saw him conjure the royal princes out of thin air even though they were many miles away.

One moment he exhibits robust skepticism and contempt for superstition; the next, he comes across as the most credulous dupe.

Becher saw many strange things on his restless travels—geese that lived in trees, stones of invisibility, bottles that captured spoken words so that they sounded again when the vessel was opened hours later.

He became abbot of the Benedictine monastery at Sponheim aged only twenty-two, barely a year after entering the order and before he had even been ordained.

The following day, the patients who had received this soothing balm were in far better shape than those cauterized with hot oil.

Exercise 108E: Diagramming

On your own paper, diagram every word of the following sentences, taken from a collection of Paracelsus's writings selected and translated (and with an introduction by) Nicholas Goodrick-Clarke.

The work was an immediate success and was reprinted a year later.

All things are created as far as we know them, but not as far as they should be.

If nature enables one to hear a voice a hundred paces away, this species enables one to hear it a hundred German miles off.

So it was that after the Creation he gave its own proper name to everything, to animals, trees, roots, stones, minerals, metals, waters, and the like, as well as to other fruits of the earth, of the water, of the air, and of the fire.

WEEK 28

— REVIEW 9 —

Weeks 25-27

Topics

Progressive Perfect Indicative Tenses
Progressive Present and Progressive Perfect Present Modal Verbs
Conditional Sentences
Adjectives in the Appositive Position
Correct Comma Usage
Limiting Adjectives
Misplaced, Squinting, and Dangling Modifier Comparisons
Using "More," "Fewer," and "Less" Quasi-Coordinators
Words That Can Be Multiple Parts of Speech
Nouns Acting as Other Parts of Speech
Adverbial Nouns

Review 9A: Definition Fill-in-the-Blank

In the last three weeks, you learned (and reviewed) even *more* definitions than in Weeks 22, 23, and 24! Fill in the blanks in the definitions below with one of the terms from the list. Many of the terms will be used more than once.

abstract noun	active	adjective
adjectives	adverb	adverbial noun
adverbs	apostrophe	appositive
attributive	cardinal numbers	clause
comma	commas	comparative
compound modifiers	compound preposition	coordinating conjunction
dangling modifier	demonstrative adjectives	demonstrative pronouns
descriptive adjective	fewer	first conditional
imperative	indefinite adjectives	indefinite pronouns
indicative	interrogative adjectives	interrogative pronouns
less	misplaced modifier	modal
noun	ordinal numbers	passive
past	past participle	perfect
perfect past	perfect present	plural
positive	possessive adjective	predicative
present	progressive	progressive perfect
progressive present	quasi-coordinators	second conditional
simple	simple present	singular
squinting modifier	state-of-being	subjunctive
subordinating conjunction	superlative	third conditional

In a sentence with an ______________________ verb, the subject performs the action. In a sentence with a ______________________ verb, the subject receives the action.

A ______________________ verb simply tells whether an action takes place in the past, present, or future.

A ______________________ verb describes an ongoing or continuous action.

A ______________________ verb describes an action which has been completed before another action takes place.

A ______________________ verb describes an ongoing or continuous action that has a definite end.

______________________ represent quantities (one, two, three, four . . .).

______________________ represent order (first, second, third, fourth . . .).

The present passive imperative is formed by adding the helping verb *be* to the ______________________ of the verb.

The present passive subjunctive is formed by pairing *be* with the ______________________ of a verb.

Use the simple past subjunctive ______________________ verb, plus an infinitive, to express a future unreal action.

______________________ sentences express circumstances that might actually happen. The predicate of the condition clause is in a ______________________ tense. The predicate of the consequence clause is an ______________________ or is in a ______________________ or ______________________ tense.

______________________ sentences express circumstances that are contrary to reality. The predicate of the condition clause is in a ______________________ tense. The predicate of the consequence clause is in the ______________________ or ______________________ modal tense.

____________________ sentences express past circumstances that never happened. The predicate of the condition clause is in the ____________________ tense. The predicate of the consequence clause is in the ____________________ modal or ____________________ modal tense.

____________________ demonstrate or point out something. They take the place of a single word or a group of words.

____________________ modify nouns and answer the question *which one.*

____________________ are pronouns without antecedents.

____________________ modify nouns and answer the questions *which one* and *how many.*

A ____________________ tells what kind.

A ____________________ becomes an ____________________ when you add *-ness* to it.

A ____ tells whose.

A ____________________ becomes an ____________________ when it is made possessive.

Form the possessive of a ____________________ noun by adding an ____________________ and the letter *s.*

Form the possessive of a ____________________ noun ending in *-s* by adding an ____________________ only.

Form the possessive of a ____________________ noun that does not end in *-s* as if it were a ____________________ noun.

____________________ verbs express real actions.

____________________ verbs express situations that are unreal, wished for, or uncertain.

____________________ verbs express intended actions.

____________________ verbs express possible actions and situations that have not actually happened.

An ____________________ that comes right before the noun it modifies is in the ____________________ position.

An ____________________ that follows the noun it modifies is in the ____________________ position.

____________________ adjectives directly follow the word they modify.

When three or more nouns, adjectives, verbs, or adverbs appear in a series, they should be separated by ____________________.

____________________ link compound parts of a sentence that are unequal.

____________________ include *rather than, sooner than, let alone, as well as,* and *not to mention.*

When three or more items are in a list, a ____________________ before the last term is usual but not necessary.

When three or more items are in a list and a ____________________ is used, a ____________________ should still follow the next to last item in the list.

When two or more adjectives are in the ____________________ position, they are only separated by ____________________ if they are equally important in meaning.

____________________ take the place of nouns in questions.

____________________ modify nouns.

The ____________________ degree of an adjective describes only one thing. The ____________________ degree of an adjective compares two things.

The ____________________ degree of an adjective compares three or more things. Most regular adjectives form the ____________________ by adding *-r* or *-er.*

Most regular adjectives form the ____________________ by adding *-st* or *-est*

Many adjectives form their ______________________ and ______________________ forms by adding the word *more* or *most* before the adjective instead of using *–er* or *–est.*

In ______________________ and ______________________ adjective forms, the words *more* and *most* are used as ______________________.

Use ______________________ for concrete items and ______________________ for abstractions. In comparisons using *more . . . fewer* and *more . . . less, more* and *less* can act as either ______________________ or ______________________ and *the* can act as an ______________________.

In comparisons using two comparative forms, the forms may act as either ______________________ or ______________________ , and *the* can act as an ______________________. A ______________________ joins equal words or groups of words together.

A ______________________ joins unequal words or groups of words together.

When *than* is used in a comparison and introduces a ______________________ with understood elements, it is acting as a ______________________.

Other than is a ______________________ that means "besides" or "except."

More than and *less than* are ______________________.

An ______________________ tells the time or place of an action, or explains how long, how far, how deep, how thick, or how much. It can modify a verb, ______________________, or ______________________.

An ______________________ plus its modifiers is an ______________________ phrase.

A ______________________ is an adjective, adjective phrase, adverb, or adverb phrase in the wrong place.

A ______________________ can belong either to the sentence element preceding or the element following.

A ______________________ has no noun or verb to modify.

Review 9B: Parsing

Above each underlined verb, write the complete tense, the voice (or note state-of-being), and the mood. The first verb is done for you.

These sentences are from *The Jamestown Project*, by Karen Ordahl Kupperman.

progressive past, active, indicative

What they were experiencing was the difference between a maritime climate, seen in countries lying to the east of great oceans, and the continental regime that prevails in lands to their west.

The Roanoke colonists had been cut loose, and their successors in Jamestown never doubted that the same could happen to them through the vagaries of ocean travel or changes in European politics.

It would have been extremely difficult to predict in 1617 that the colony would grow so dramatically in the coming years.

But without the hope of riches or access to the eastern trades, it is doubtful that colonies would have been undertaken in this period.

In 1621 the company complained about the poor quality of the tobacco they were being sent.

She refused the presents Smith offered her; with "teares running downe her cheekes, shee said shee durst not be seene to have any: for if Powhatan should know it, she were but dead."

Thomas Harriot, deeply troubled by the diseases that had struck so many coastal Carolina Algonquians while he was there with the first Roanoke colony in 1585-86, wrote that some of the English had pointed to a comet that had appeared just a few days before "the said sicknesse" broke out, and they also thought that a solar eclipse the previous year might have played a role.

They claimed that as he was dying, he begged to be buried in an English graveyard so his people would not know he had been killed by a bullet.

But Pory attested that they did not dare to "call Poole to account" because of the damage he could do to their relationship with Opechancanough.

Had the ships not fired their ordnance, the colony would have been overwhelmed.

He brought an Indian man home to Cape Cod from England; Smith identified him as Tantum, and some have speculated that he might have been the Squanto (or Squantum) who lived with the later Pilgrim colony.

Setting the beginning and end of the Little Ice Age is difficult because even a generally colder period will be interrupted by warmer decades.

Many had emigrated to the Netherlands, but now that Protestant country was threatened by the European war, and they were willing to consider the possibility of recreating English society in a completely new setting.

It spoke of the company's "great griefe" in learning of the deaths of "hundreds, and almost the utter destruction of some particular Plantations," and acknowledged that such catastrophe must be seen as the "chastisement" of God to draw people on both sides of the Atlantic away from sin.

Nemattanew said that his men would carry the Englishmen's armor and weapons for them and they would be furnished with moccasins for the march.

Review 9C: Provide the Verb

Complete each poem stanza by providing an appropriate verb in the tense indicated. You may want to use the chart in Lesson 99 for reference.

If there are two blanks for a single verb, the helping verb is divided from the main verb by another part of the sentence.

If you can't think of a verb, ask your instructor for help.

When you are finished, compare your answers to the original lines.

The sun is warm, the sky is clear,
(progressive present, active, indicative)
The waves ____________________ fast and bright,
(simple present, active, indicative)
Blue isles and snowy mountains ____________________
The purple noon's transparent light.

Percy Bysshe Shelley, "Stanzas Written in Dejection Near Naples"

(perfect present progressive, active, indicative) (perfect present progressive, active, indicative)
I ______________________, I ______________________,
Drinking late, sitting late, with my bosom cronies;
(simple present, passive, indicative)
All, all ______________________, the old familiar faces.

Charles Lamb, "The Old Familiar Faces"

"My days, my friend, are almost gone,
(perfect present, passive, indicative)
My life ______________________,
And many love me; but by none
Am I enough beloved."

William Wordsworth, "The Fountain"

So when the last and dreadful hour
(simple future, active, indicative)
This crumbling pageant ______________________,
(simple future, passive, indicative)
The trumpet ______________________ on high,
The dead shall live, the living die,
(simple future, active, indicative)
And Music ______________________ the sky.

John Dryden, "Song for St. Cecelia's Day"

simple present, active, imperative
____________________ ye rose-buds while ye may,
Old Time is still a-flying:
And this same flower that smiles to-day,
progressive future, active, indicative
To-morrow ____________________.
Robert Herrick, "Counsel to Girls"

simple present, active, modal
And I ____________________ when I think
simple present, state-of-being, modal subjunctive
Heigh ho, ____________________ she ____________________ mine!
Thomas Lodge, "Rosaline"

simple present, state-of-being, subjunctive
____________________ I as high as heaven above the plain,
And you, my Love, as humble and as low
As are the deepest bottoms of the main,
simple present, active, modal
Whereso'er you were, with you my love ____________________.
Joshua Sylvester, "Love's Omnipresence"

The vernal leaves—she loved them still,
Nor ever tax'd them with the ill
perfect past, passive, indicative
Which ____________________ to her.
William Wordsworth, "Ruth: Or the Influences of Nature"

simple past, passive, indicative
Those are Grecian ghosts, that in battle ____________________
And unburied remain
Inglorious on the plain.
John Dryden, "Alexander's Feast, or, The Power of Music"

simple present, passive, subjunctive
My Son, if thou ____________________, poor,
Hopeless of honour and of gain,
O! do not dread thy mother's door,
simple present, active, imperative
____________________ not of me with grief and pain:
William Wordsworth, "The Affliction of Margaret"

simple present, active, modal

For ________________ he ______________ us in the glen,

simple present, active, modal

My blood ________________________ the heather.

Thomas Campbell, "Lord Ullin's Daughter"

"The morn is merry June, I trow,

progressive present, active, indicative

The rose ____________________ fain;

simple future, active, indicative

But she ____________________ in winter snow

Ere we two meet again."

Sir Walter Scott, "The Rover"

Review 9D: Identifying Adjectives and Punctuating Items in a Series

In the following description, from *Ivanhoe,* by Sir Walter Scott, carry out the following three steps:

a) Underline once and label all adjectives (except for articles), using the following abbreviations:

Descriptive Adjectives		Limiting Adjectives	
Regular	DA-R	Possessives	LA-P
Present participles	DA-PresP	~~Articles~~	~~LA-A~~
Past participles	DA-PastP	Demonstratives	LA-D
		Indefinites	LA-IND
		Interrogatives	LA-INT
		Numbers	LA-N

b) Circle all adjectives that are in the predicate or in the predicative position and draw an arrow from each back to the noun it modifies.

c) The passage contains five indefinite pronouns. Find each, underline them twice, and identify them as part of the sentence (*SUBJ* for subject, *DO* for direct object, *IO* for indirect object, *OP* for object of the preposition).

d) Draw a star in the margin next to any items of three or more in a series.

The companion of the church dignitary was a man past forty, thin, strong, tall, and muscular; an athletic figure, which long fatigue and constant exercise seemed to have left none of the softer part of the human form, having reduced the whole to brawn, bones, and sinews, which had sustained a thousand toils, and were ready to dare a thousand more. His head was covered with a scarlet cap, faced with fur... His countenance was therefore fully displayed, and its expression was calculated to impress a degree of awe, if not of fear, upon strangers... His keen, piercing, dark eyes... seemed to challenge opposition to his wishes...a deep scar on his brow gave additional sternness to his countenance, and a sinister expression to one of his eyes, which had been slightly injured on the same occasion, and of which the vision, though perfect, was in a slight and partial degree distorted.

The upper dress of this personage resembled that of his companion in shape...but the colour, being scarlet, showed that he did not belong to any of the four regular orders of monks. On the right shoulder of the mantle there was cut, in white cloth, a cross of a peculiar form....He rode, not a mule, like his companion, but a strong hackney for the road, to save his gallant war-horse, which a squire led behind, fully accoutred for battle, with a chamfron or plaited head-piece upon his head, having a short spike projecting from the front. On one side of the saddle hung a short battle-axe, richly inlaid with Damascene carving; on the other the rider's plumed head-piece and hood of mail, with a long two-handed sword.

Review 9E: Correcting Modifiers

The following sentences all have modifier problems!

Rewrite each sentence correctly on your own paper, and be ready to explain the solution out loud to your instructor. You may need to add or delete words or phrases—as long as the sentence makes sense, that's fine. There may be more than one way to fix each sentence.

The first is done for you.

Exploring the maze of cobblestone streets, the farmers were setting up their booths for the farmer's market.

> While I was exploring the maze of cobblestone streets, the farmers were setting up their booths for the farmer's market.
>
> Exploring the maze of cobblestone streets, I saw the farmers setting up their booths for the farmer's market.

> **Explanation:** The present participle phrase *Exploring the maze of cobblestone streets* is dangling because it doesn't modify anything in the independent clause that follows. It needs either a subject and predicate of its own (the first answer), or it needs to relate to the subject of the independent clause (the second answer).

Eggplants, artichokes, tomatoes, and zucchini waited for buyers picked that very morning to gather them up.

I bought the amazingest tarte tatin I have ever tasted.

I find that organic elephant garlic is deliciouser than any other variety.

Getting to the cheese merchant's stall, the Camembert de Normandie and the fromage blanc were all gone, but there was plenty of Brie de Melun and Roquefort left.

Cheeses are rich, creamy, and lend a unique taste to carefully prepared dinners that are not refrigerated.

Seeing that the jam merchant had a long line at his table, checking out the olive oil table instead seemed like a good idea.

My favorite fruits to eat that I bought at the market with the Muscat wine are peaches, plums, cherries, and melon.

The artichoke salad and the celeri remoulade look much temptinger than the chickpea salad.

Surveying all of the market stalls, my favorite was the one selling spices: persillade, herbes de Provence, fines herbes, nutmeg, saffron, chervil, and chives.

Before preparing for dinner, a farmer's market might offer fresh vegetables and local meats.

If you shop at a market in the middle of the week, you'll get more low prices and find less tourists.

The Christmas markets not only sell food, hot wine, chocolates, and cheese, but also offer entertainments that are held in the north of France!

There are 246 varieties of French cheese, and fifty six kinds are protected by French law.

A yard sale, where everyone cleans out their attic and sells the random things they find there in France, is known as a vide-grenier.

Review 9F: Identifying Adverbs

In the following sentences, taken from *Mars: Our Future on the Red Planet,* by Leonard David (a companion book to the National Geographic TV series *Mars*), carry out the following steps:

a) Underline each word, phrase, or clause that is acting as an adverb.
b) Draw a line from the word/phrase/clause to the verb, adjective, or adverb modified.
c) Above the word or phrase, note whether it is a regular adverb (*ADV*), an adverbial noun or noun phrase (*AN*), a prepositional phrase (*PrepP*), an infinitive phrase (*INF*), a present participle phrase (*PresP*), a past participle phrase (*PastP*), or an adverbial clause (*C*).

Remember: within a phrase or clause acting as an adverb, there might also be an adverb modifying an adjective or verb form within the phrase or clause. Underline these adverbs a second time.

Buzz Aldrin was adamant when he told me that the next dream to work toward was putting humans on Mars.

In 2010 President Barack Obama declared that the United States was going to Mars.

Four decades have now passed since the touchdown on Mars of America's Viking 1 and Viking 2 landers, sent to probe the prospect of Martian life, extinct or extant.

Decades later and billions of dollars in Mars spacecraft costs borne by several nations, the inquiry about past or present life on the planet remains alive and well—even if life on Mars is long gone or never even existed.

The now orbiting International Space Station is acknowledged as the most complex scientific and technological endeavor ever undertaken to date.

While the International Space Station is seen as a starting point for undertaking 21st-century deep space travel, a number of analog sites on Earth are also prompting advisory notes before humans congregate in the harsh climes of Mars.

If you want mortal danger go to Antarctica.

Other Mars Society findings are that small, nimble field mobility systems like all-terrain vehicles are much more useful for a Mars crew than large pressurized rovers.

The pattern continues even as spacecraft bring human cargo as well.

Will humans on Mars, by their very presence, introduce Earth life into places on the Red Planet where it could potentially prosper, and perhaps taint the very signs of life we are looking for?

Review 9G: Comma Use

The following sentences have lost all of their commas. Insert commas directly into the text (no need to use proofreader's marks) wherever needed.

These sentences were taken from the 1934 science fiction adventure *A Martian Odyssey*, by Stanley G. Weinbaum.

The other three stared at him sympathetically—Putz the engineer Leroy the biologist and Harrison the astronomer and captain of the expedition.

There was a racket like a flock of crows eating a bunch of canaries—whistles cackles caws trills and what have you.

It had four-toed feet and four-fingered things—hands you'd have to call them—and a little roundish body and a long neck ending in a tiny head—and that beak.

There was a flurry of tentacles and a spurt of black corruption and then the thing with a disgusting sucking noise pulled itself and its arms into a hole in the ground.

The Martian wasn't a bird really.

It had a beak all right and a few feathery appendages but the beak wasn't really a beak.

The top tiers of bricks were heaving shaking and suddenly slid down the sides with a thin crash.

Well we stared at the fire a while and I decided to attempt some sort of communication with the Martian.

Then I sketched in Mercury and Venus and Mother Earth and Mars and finally pointing to Mars I swept my hand around in a sort of inclusive gesture to indicate that Mars was our current environment.

It was just before twilight that I reached the edge of Thyle and looked down over the gray Mare Chronium. And I knew there was seventy-five miles of that to be walked over and then a couple of hundred miles of that Xanthus desert and about as much more Mare Cimmerium.

"In the morning" resumed Jarvis "we started off again."

A long silvery-grey arm appeared dragging after it an armored body. Armored I mean with scales silver-grey and dull-shining.

It didn't look like a flame or torch you understand but more like a civilized light and I thought that I might get some clue as to the creatures' development.

There was something beyond the wheel something shining on a sort of low pedestal.

Review 9H: Conjunctions

In the following sentences from H. G. Wells's *The War of the Worlds*, find and circle every conjunction. Label each as coordinating (*C*), subordinating (*SUB*), coordinating correlative (*CC*), subordinating correlative (*SC*), or quasi-coordinator (*QC*).

My brother, very luckily for him as it chanced, preferred to push on at once to the coast rather than wait for food, although all three of them were very hungry.

I defied him, although I felt no assurance that he might not do this thing.

At that time it was quite clear in my own mind that the Thing had come from the planet Mars, but I judged it improbable that it contained any living creature.

Then I saw through a sort of glass plate near the edge of the body the face, as we may call it, and the large dark eyes of a Martian, peering, and then a long metallic snake of tentacle came feeling slowly through the hole.

In the darkness I could just see the thing—like an elephant's trunk more than anything else—waving towards me and touching and examining the wall, coals, wood and ceiling.

In Sunbury, and at intervals along the road, were dead bodies lying in contorted attitudes, horses as well as men, overturned carts and luggage, all covered thickly with black dust.

But he was one of those weak creatures, void of pride, timorous, anæmic, hateful souls, full of shifty cunning, who face neither God nor man, who face not even themselves.

Certainly, unless death had overtaken them suddenly, my cousins and she would have fled thence; but it seemed to me I might find or learn there whither the Surrey people had fled.

I knew I wanted to find my wife, that my heart ached for her and the world of men, but I had no clear idea how the finding might be done.

Review 91: Identifying Independent Elements

The following sentences, taken from two novels by Shannon Hale, all contain independent elements: absolutes (*ABS*), parenthetical expressions (*PE*), interjections (*INT*), nouns of direct address (*NDA*), appositives (*APP*), and/or noun clauses in apposition (*NCA*).

Locate, underline, and label each one.

From *The Goose Girl*

She was born Anidori-Kiladra Talianna Isilee, Crown Princess of Kildenree, and she did not open her eyes for three days.

The baby in her crib dreamed of milk, her round, perfect lips nursing in sleep.

In cold weather or spring rain, the aunt sat on the nursery floor and told Ani stories of fantastic and faraway things: a land where mares pawed gold nuggets from the earth and chewed them in order to breathe out music; a baker who baked birds from dough and sent them out the window in search of a treasured pot of apricot preserves; a mother who loved her baby so fiercely, she put him in a tight locket around her neck so that he might never grow up.

The aunt sang songs again and again until Ani learned the words, her toddler's voice as dry and delicate as a sparrow's call.

The key-mistress and her daughter, Seliak, passed by the pond on the walk to the garden.

The view from the window tugged at her attention, teasing her with indistinct movements in the direction of the stables, brown spots that might have been horses running.

You have grown as tall as your mother, save her, though not quite as pretty, and I wonder, since you seem to always be quite busy, if you have yet learned what duties are most important to your station?

From *Book of a Thousand Days*

These past meals have been as hearty as I ever had, and if being a lady's maid means I get to eat the same food as my lady — with spices even! — then you'll never hear me complain.

It isn't allowed for a commoner, of course, to speak to gentry first.

"Swear you'll serve me, Dashti. Swear you won't abandon me."

I led her back to the bed and had her sit while I combed the muddle of her hair and bound it in a braid, every hair criscrossing so the smarts wouldn't wander out of her head.

Qadan taught me the names of other cloths — brocade, satin, damask, silk.

And now that her hair was fixed and her face washed, I saw just how lovely she was, the glory of the Ancestors shining through her.

Surely she had a wise and profound reason for her stubbornness, one blessed by the Ancestors.

Review 9J: Words with Multiple Identities

In the following sentences, taken from *T. Rex and the Crater of Doom,* by Walter Alvarez, identify each bolded word as a noun (*N*), verb (*V*), adverb (*ADV*), adjective (*ADJ*), pronoun (*PRO*), preposition (*PREP*), subordinating conjunction (*SC*), or coordinating conjunction (*CC*).

Canadian geologist Richard Grieve had compiled a list of authenticated impact craters, and **many** of us studied the list with great **care**, looking for **one** that might be the KT **impact** site.

Dating ancient **impact** craters is difficult, and the ages of **many** craters on the list were very uncertain.

You might ask why anyone would **care** about concentrations that low, but geochemists have found that rare **trace** elements, like rare fingerprints at a crime scene, can reveal the most interesting things about events in the **past**.

Volcanism has always been of **prime** interest to geologists.

Meteors are **so** frequent that **almost** anyone who lives away from bright lights can see **one** every few minutes in the dark night sky.

Maybe the extraterrestrial event responsible for the iridium and the extinction had been a giant **impact**.

We had been wrong in thinking there was no **trace** of the crater at the surface.

Scholars of human history have two ways of identifying times **past**.

Iridium was **one** such element, **so** maybe our anomalous iridium came from a supernova.

Chuck Officer disagreed intensely and often—**not only** with me, but with **almost** everyone **else** who favored **impact**.

Although a microscope was required for studying them, microfossils became the dating material of choice by the middle of the twentieth century.

But Nature seemed to be showing us something **quite** different.

Only places which happened to be shielded by thick storm clouds would have avoided this lethal heat.

What **else** might have caused the KT extinction?

Review 9K: Phrases, Clauses, and Absolutes

The following paragraph—the first in Zane Grey's classic western *The U. P. Trail*—is made up of one single sentence!

First, read the sentence as it was written, in paragraph form. (You might want to read it out loud.)

> In the early sixties a trail led from the broad Missouri, swirling yellow and turgid between its green-groved borders, for miles and miles out upon the grassy Nebraska plains, turning westward over the undulating prairie, with its swales and billows and long, winding lines of cottonwoods, to a slow, vast heave of rising ground—Wyoming—where the herds of buffalo grazed and the wolf was lord and the camp-fire of the trapper sent up its curling blue smoke from beside some lonely stream; on and on over the barren lands of eternal monotony, all so gray and wide and solemn and silent under the endless sky; on, ever on, up to the bleak, black hills and into the waterless gullies and through the rocky gorges where the deer browsed; then slowly rising to the pass between the great bold peaks, and across the windy uplands into Utah, with its verdant valleys, green as emeralds, and its haze-filled cañons and wonderful wind-worn cliffs and walls, and its pale salt lakes, veiled in the shadows of stark and lofty rocks, dim, lilac-colored, austere, and isolated; ever onward across Nevada, and ever westward, up from desert to mountain, up into California, where the white streams rushed and roared and the stately pines towered, and seen from craggy heights, deep down, the little blue lakes gleamed like gems; finally sloping to the great descent, where the mountain world ceased and where, out beyond the golden land, asleep and peaceful, stretched the illimitable Pacific, vague and grand beneath the setting sun.

Then, look at the version of the sentence that follows. Each part of the sentence has been placed on a separate line. For each part, point out the following:

- Identity: Is it a phrase, clause, independent element (*ind*)—or other?
- Type: If it's a phrase, is it prepositional (*prep*), present participle (*pres part*), or past participle (*past part*)? If it's a clause, is it independent (*ind*) or subordinate (*sub*)? And if it's "other," how would you describe it?
- Part of speech: Then, identify whether the part serves as an adjective (*adj*), adverb (*adv*), appositive (*app*), noun—or something else.
- Finally, in the last blank, if the part modifies, renames, or otherwise relates to another word in the sentence, list that word.

The first two are done for you.

Take some time over this. Ask your instructor for help if necessary. And if you get frustrated, just remember—we could have asked you to diagram this sentence!

This exercise should give you a sense of just how an accomplished writer can string together MANY different sentence elements to create a vivid scene.

	Identity	Type	Part of Speech	Related to (if any) (modifies or renames)
In the early sixties	phrase	prep	adv	led
a trail led	clause	ind	main	none
from the broad Missouri,				
swirling yellow and turgid between its green-groved borders,				
for miles and miles out upon the grassy Nebraska plains,				
turning westward over the undulating prairie,				
with its swales and billows and long, winding lines of cottonwoods,				
to a slow, vast heave of rising ground—				
Wyoming—				
where the herds of buffalo grazed and the wolf was lord and the campfire of the trapper sent up its curling blue smoke				
from beside some lonely stream;				
on and on				
over the barren lands of eternal monotony,				
all so gray and wide and solemn and silent under the endless sky;				
on, ever on,				
up to the bleak, black hills				
and into the waterless gullies				
and through the rocky gorges				
where the deer browsed;				

	Identity	Type	Part of Speech	Related to (if any) (modifies or renames)
then slowly rising to the pass between the great bold peaks,				
and across the windy uplands into Utah,				
with its verdant valleys, green as emeralds, and its haze-filled cañons and wonderful wind-worn cliffs and walls, and its pale salt lakes,				
veiled in the shadows of stark and lofty rocks, dim, lilac-colored, austere, and isolated;				
ever onward across Nevada, and ever westward,				
up from desert to mountain,				
up into California,				
where the white streams rushed and roared and the stately pines towered,				
and seen from craggy heights, deep down,				
the little blue lakes gleamed like gems;				
finally sloping to the great descent,				
where the mountain world ceased				
and where, out beyond the golden land, asleep and peaceful, stretched the illimitable Pacific, vague and grand				
beneath the setting sun.				

WEEK 29

Still More Verbs

—LESSON 109—

Hortative Verbs

Subjunctive Verbs

A hortative verb encourages or recommends an action.

Latin *hortari*: to encourage or urge

English derivatives:
to exhort (verb): to urge, or to give urgent recommendations
I exhorted him to keep running despite his weariness.
hortative (adjective): encouraging or urging on
Patience, Charity, and Praise-God are all hortative names.

Let's be more careful next time.

Let's run faster.

Let's be finished now.

In first person plural hortative verbs, the helping verb *let* is used.
The state-of-being verb takes the form *be*.
The active verb is the same form as the present active indicative.
The passive verb combines *be* with the past participle.

May you be happy.

May you walk in joy.

May you be saved from your own foolishness.

In second person hortative verbs, the helping verb *may* is used.
The state-of-being verb takes the form *be*.
The active verb is the same form as the present active indicative.
The passive verb combines *be* with the past participle.

Let the trumpets be sounded.

May no creature on earth be silent.

Let the Lord of the Black Lands come forth.

Third person hortative verbs use the helping verbs *let* or *may*.
The state-of-being verb takes the form *be*.
The active verb is the same form as the present active subjunctive.
The passive verb combines *be* with the past participle.

Active indicative, first person	We **sing** with happiness.
second person	You **sing** with happiness.
Active hortative, first person	Let us **sing** with happiness.
second person	May you **sing** with happiness.
Active indicative, third person	He **sings** with happiness.
Active subjunctive, third person	Should he **sing**, he will be happy.
Active hortative, third person	Let him **sing** with happiness.

May you travel safely.
Let us travel safely.

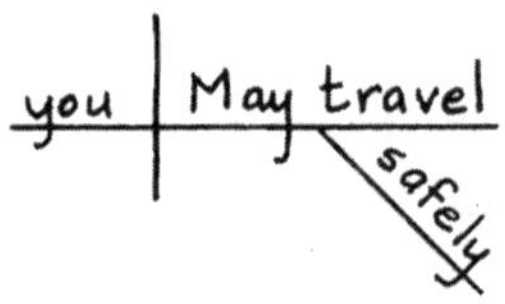

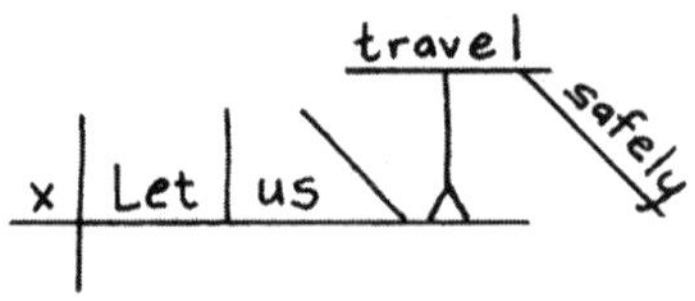

An object complement follows the direct object and renames or describes it.

DO OC
We elected Marissa leader.

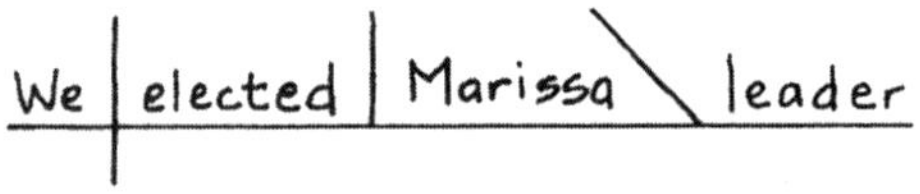

May the evildoers come forth.
Let the Lord of the Black Lands come forth.

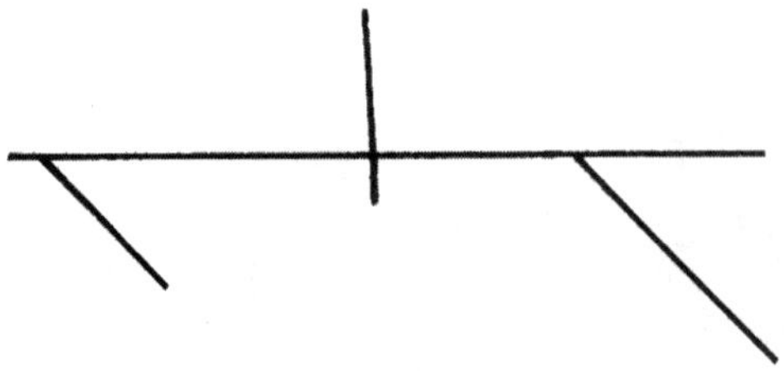

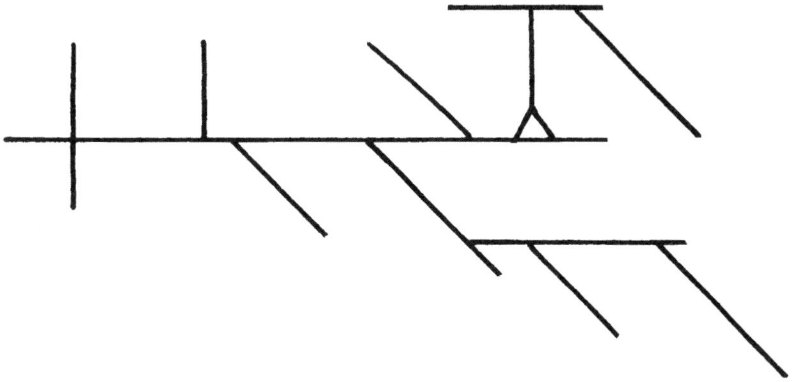

Exercise 109A: Identifying Hortative Verbs

Speechmakers are often exhorting their readers—so they tend to use many hortative verbs! In the following sentences, underline twice every element of each hortative verb (*let* or *may*, any other helping verbs, and the main verb). Above the verb, identify it as state-of-being (*SB*), active (*A*), or passive (*P*). If the person or thing being exhorted is present in the sentence, circle the noun or pronoun that identifies him/her/it, and identify it as *S* for subject or *O* for object.

Be careful—some sentences may not include any hortative verbs!

The first is done for you.

O A
Let him set to work to procure a better assemblyman or better alderman before he tries his hand at making a mayor, a governor, or a president.

Let him make up his mind to do his duty in politics without regard to holding office at all, and let him know that often the men in this country who have done the best work for our public life have not been the men in office. If, on the other hand, he attains public position, let him not strive to plan out for himself a career.

Do not let him think about the matter at all.

—"Duties of American Citizenship," by Theodore Roosevelt

Do not let him wrong any one, and do not let him be wronged.

—"Speech Given at the Grand Canyon," by Theodore Roosevelt

May it not also be that the cause of civilization itself will be defended by the skill and devotion of a few thousand airmen?

Even though large tracts of Europe and many old and famous States have fallen or may fall into the grip of the Gestapo and all the odious apparatus of Nazi rule, we shall not flag or fail.

—"We Shall Fight on the Beaches," by Winston Churchill

May you never find yourselves, men of Athens, in such a position!

And I pray to all the gods that whatever be the decision that you are about to make, it may be for your good.

And I beg you, men of Athens, if I tell you certain truths outspokenly, to let no resentment on your part fall upon me on this account.

And let no one ask, What do these things amount to?

And when we have made all these preparations ourselves, then let us call upon the other states for aid, and send envoys to carry our message in all directions, to the Peloponnese, to Rhodes, to Chios, to the king.

But if any one has a better proposal to make, let him make it, and give us his advice.

—"The Third Philippic," by Demosthenes

May all the competition between the two countries be the competition of industry, civilization, and peace! May the foolish sentiments of individual hostility entertained by some in both countries, gradually vanish before the influence of good sense and right feeling; and, as both nations possess a common language, and are derived from a common source, may they be united in lasting relations of good will and amity!

— "Address on the King's Speech," by Sir Robert Peel

So, first of all, let me assert my firm belief that the only thing we have to fear is fear itself—nameless, unreasoning, unjustified terror which paralyzes needed efforts to convert retreat into advance.

We may now restore that temple to the ancient truths.

May He protect each and every one of us.

—"First Inaugural Address," by Franklin D. Roosevelt

Let us not deceive ourselves, sir.

The war is inevitable–and let it come!

Gentlemen may cry, Peace, Peace—but there is no peace.

—"Give Me Liberty or Give Me Death," by Patrick Henry

Exercise 109B: Rewriting Indicative Verbs as Hortative Verbs

Hortative verbs also appear frequently in poetry! In the lines below, the statements and commands in bold type originally contained hortative verbs. On your own paper, rewrite each bolded clause so that the main verbs are hortative. Then, compare your answers with the original.

If you need help, ask your instructor.

The rhymes and meters of the poems might give you a hint or two!

We will go then, you and I,

When the evening is spread out against the sky.

—T. S. Eliot, "The Love Song of J. Alfred Prufrock"

Come, said my soul,

Write such verses for my Body (for we are one).

—Walt Whitman, "Leaves of Grass"

Turn the bed-clothes toward the foot of the bed,

Physician and priest, go home.

Walt Whitman, "Song of Myself"

And I say to any man or woman,

Your soul stands cool and composed

before a million universes.

—Walt Whitman, "Song of Myself"

Here's to the Dove of Peace!

She will find a mate some day,

And her tribe will increase

As fast as she can lay!

—Oliver Herford, "The Dove of Peace"

Exercise 109C: Diagramming

On your own paper, diagram every word of each sentence. These come from the collected writings and speeches of the nineteenth-century writer and speaker Robert G. Ingersoll.

Give us good money—the life-blood of business—and let it flow through the veins and arteries of commerce.

May you live long in the land you helped to save; may the winter of your age be as green as spring, as full of blossoms as summer, as generous as autumn, and may you, surrounded by plenty, with your wives at your sides and your grandchildren on your knees, live long.

—LESSON 110—

Transitive Verbs
Intransitive Verbs
Sit/Set, Lie/Lay, Rise/Raise
Ambitransitive Verbs

The reindeer broke the first house apart.

The ice between the two floes broke apart.

Transitive verbs express action that is received by some person or thing.
Intransitive verbs express action that is not received by any person or thing.

ambi- from the Latin: prefix meaning "both"

ambidextrous ______________________________

ambiguous ______________________________

ambitransitive both transitive and intransitive

When I hear my voice on a record I absolutely loathe my voice. I cannot stand my voice.
—Roger Daltrey

Music in the soul can be heard by the universe.
—Laozi

Transitive verbs can be active or passive.
Intransitive verbs can only be active.

I hate thunderstorms.
The goat bleated.

***Sit*, *lie*, and *rise* are intransitive.**
***Set*, *lay*, and *raise* are transitive.**

(simple present) Strong women ____________ above adverse circumstances.

(simple present) The waiter ____________ the coffee carefully on the table.

(progressive past) The hen ____________ four or five eggs every week.

(simple present) She ____________ primly on the elaborate throne.

(simple past) The farmer ____________ corn, wheat, and rye.

(progressive present) The horse ____________ peacefully on its side in the pasture.

The cook tied on his apron and set to work.
The travelers set off first thing in the morning.
As we reached the ocean, the sun was setting.

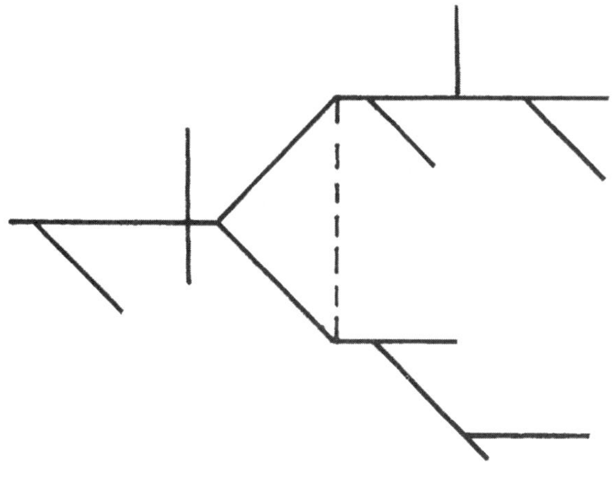

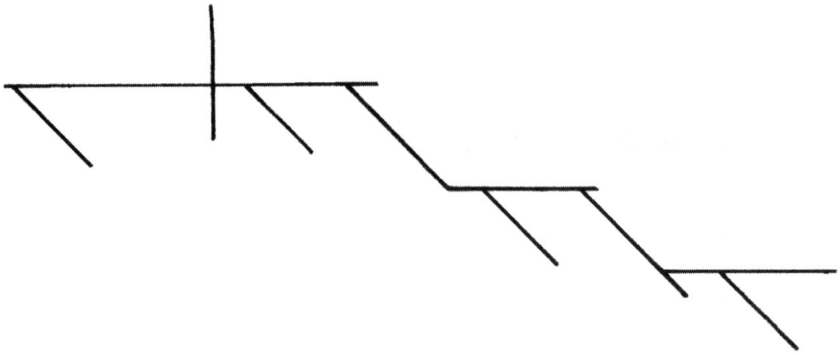

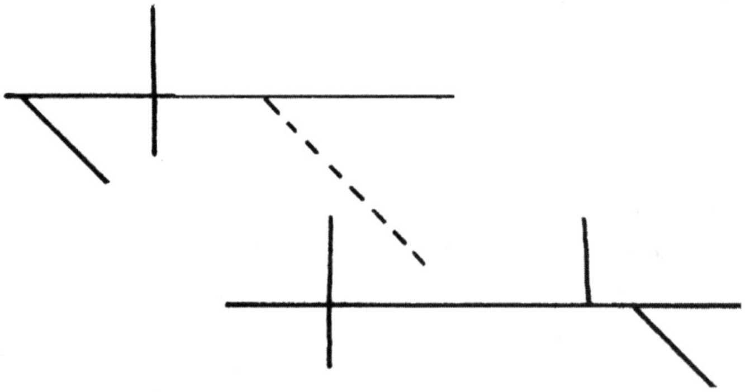

Transitive verbs can be active or passive.
Intransitive verbs can only be active.
Ambitransitive verbs can be either transitive or intransitive.
Transitive verbs express action that is received by some person or thing.
Intransitive verbs express action that is not received by any person or thing.

Exercise 110A: Ambitransitive Verbs

Each one of the sentences below (adapted from traditional Mexican folk tales) contains at least one ambitransitive verb. For each sentence, carry out the following steps:

a) Underline the action verbs that are acting as predicates (in both independent and subordinate clauses), and label each one as *TR* for transitive or *INTR* for intransitive.
b) Label each transitive verb as *A* for active or *P* for passive.
c) Circle the direct object of each active transitive verb and label it as *DO* (*TR*). Circle the subject of each passive transitive verb and label it as *S* (*TR*).
d) Choose two sentences with active transitive verbs. On your own paper, rewrite them so that the verb becomes passive.

Whenever Pedro got into trouble, he managed to get out again.

Pedro got a drum that would not stop beating.

The unfortunate sister managed her sheep-brothers with care.

She never beat them.

At the very idea, the young man's heart melted.

The sun shouted, "Mama! Mama! There is a man! I will melt him!"

The old woman stood at the window, weeping and crying to be let in.

Pedro stood the statue back up again and pretended that it had never fallen down.

He pretended very convincingly!

The old witch broke a horn of each of the oxen.

As the waves broke against the shore, the young woman began to walk into the deepening water.

The poor boy breathed in and out, in and out.

The Devil breathed fire and brimstone at the unfortunate tailor.

The tailor threaded his needle with a short thread and sewed so fast that the Devil was amazed.

The Devil sewed his cloth with a long thread that tangled constantly.

The tailor's daughters threaded between the pillars to reach him where he sat.

The sheep ate and drank in peace.

The oldest sheep ate the finest grass and drank the clearest water.

Exercise 110B: The Prefix *Ambi-*

Using a dictionary or thesaurus, find two more words using the prefix *ambi-* where the prefix carries the meaning of "both." On your own paper, write the words and their definitions, and then use each correctly in a sentence. If the word is too technical for you to write an original sentence, you may locate a sentence using an Internet search and write it down.

Exercise 110C: Diagramming

On your own paper, diagram every word of the following quotations.

When you forgive, you in no way change the past—but you change the future.
—Bernard Meltzer

Only the wisest and stupidest of men never change.
—Confucius

Not everything that is faced can be changed, but nothing can be changed until it is faced.
—James Baldwin

If you cannot forgive and forget, pick one.
–Robert Brault

The mind, once stretched by a new idea, never returns to its original dimensions.
—Ralph Waldo Emerson

And yet, when I look up at the sky, I somehow feel that everything will change for the better, that this cruelty too shall end, that peace and tranquility will return once more.
—Anne Frank

Beware of the man who does not return your blow: he neither forgives you nor allows you to forgive yourself.
—George Bernard Shaw

— LESSON 111 —

Ambitransitive Verbs
Gerunds and Infinitives
Infinitive Phrases as Direct Objects
Infinitive Phrases With Understood *To*

I may not succeed, but I will try.

Try the chocolate cake.

The concert-goers tried arriving early.

Every night, he tries to go to bed by ten.

A gerund is a present participle acting as a noun.
An infinitive is formed by combining *to* and the first person singular present form of a verb.

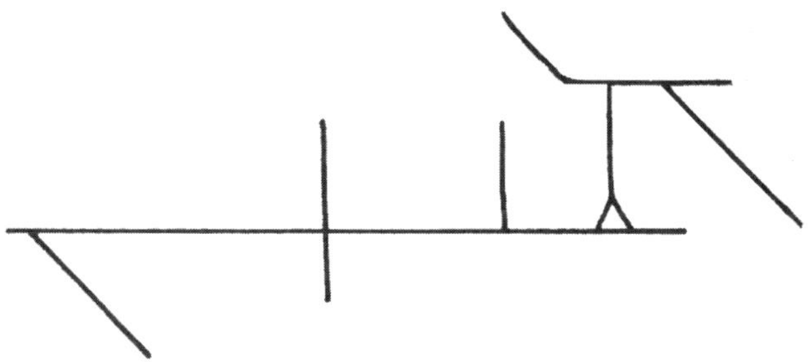

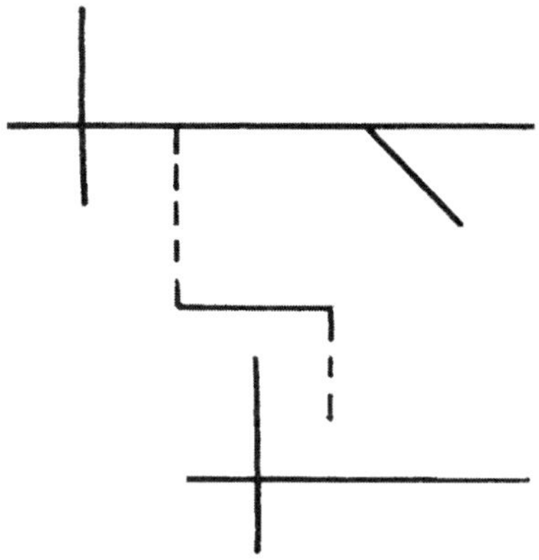

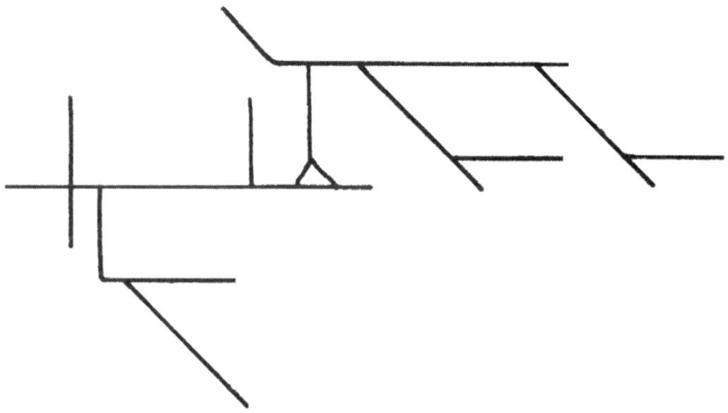

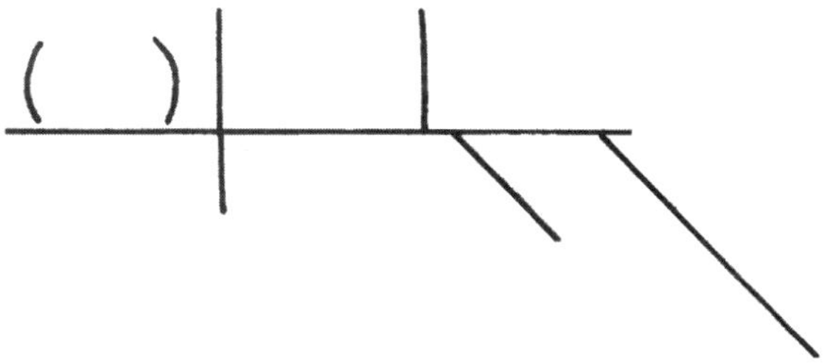

Mother told me to clean my room.

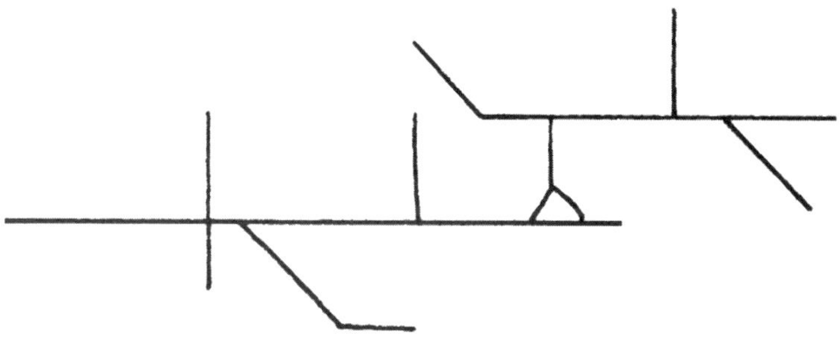

The duchess ordered the maid to arrange the flowers.

His mistake made me lose money.

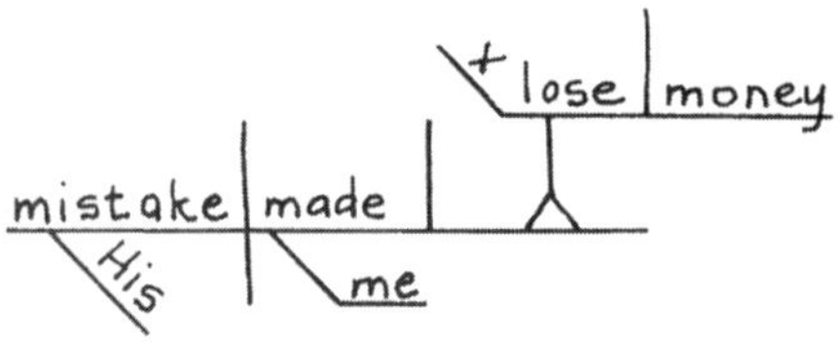

You must come and make Lizzy marry Mr. Collins, for she vows she will not have him.
—*Pride and Prejudice*

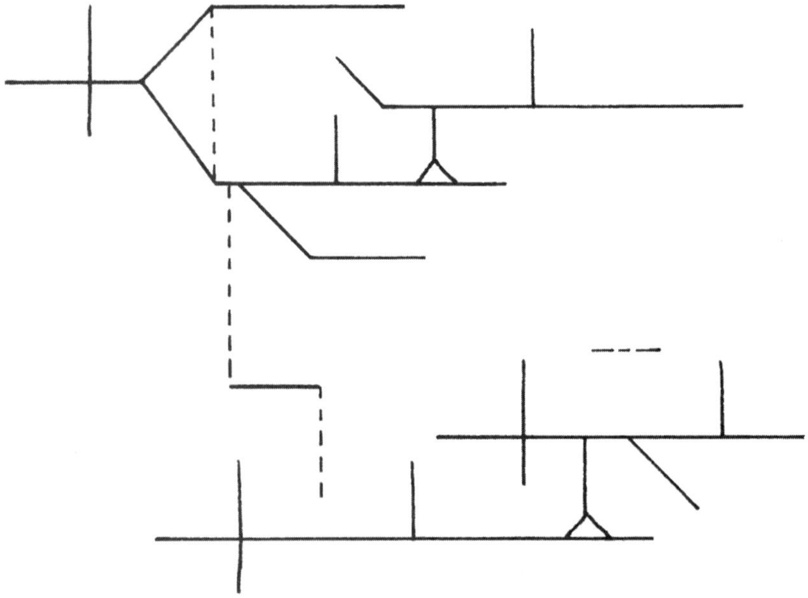

I was made to love you.

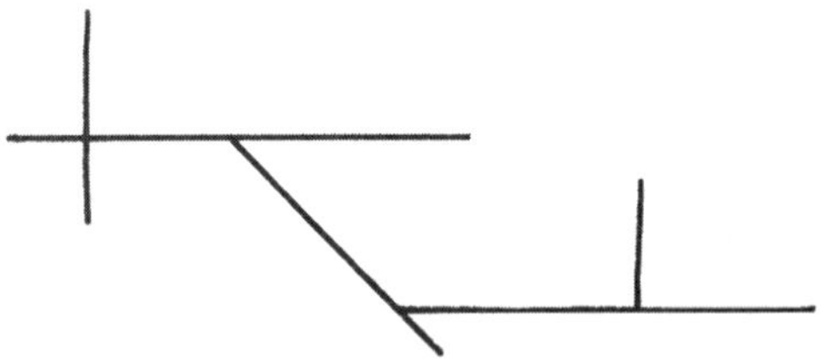

He was good enough to sing.

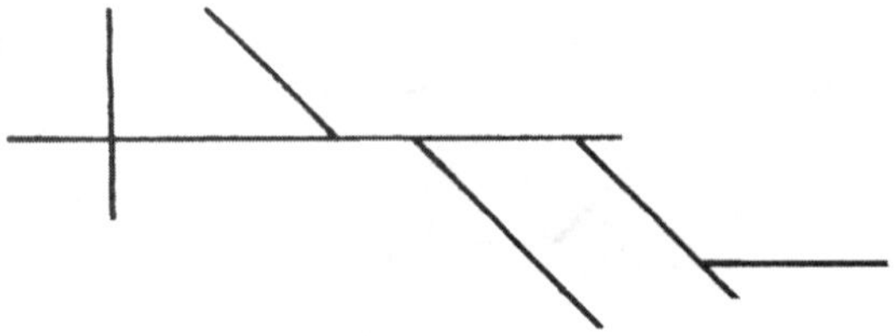

You ought to go home.

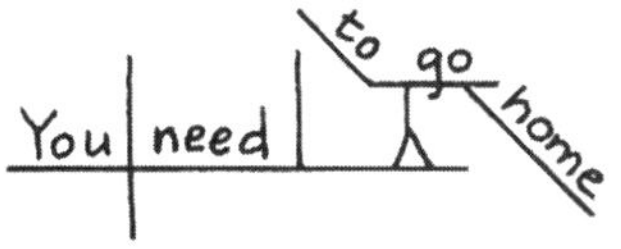

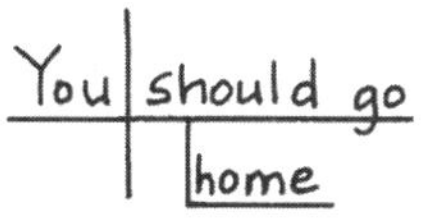

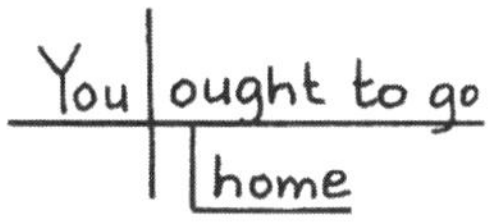

The politician ought to have been thrown in jail.

The politician should have been thrown in jail.

Exercise 111A: Infinitives and Other Uses of *To*

In the following sentences from Thomas Hardy's classic novel *The Return of the Native*, underline every phrase that incorporates the word *to*. For infinitives, underline just the infinitive itself; for prepositional phrases, underline just the preposition and its object (and any words that come between); for verb phrases, underline the entire verb.

- Label each phrase as *INF* for infinitive, *PREP* for prepositional, or *V* for verb.
- For infinitives, further identify the phrase as *S* for subject, *DO* for direct object, *PA* for predicate adjective, *PN* for predicate nominative, *ADJ* for adjective, or *ADV* for adverb.
- For prepositional phrases, label the object of the preposition as *OP*. For verb phrases, parse the verb, giving tense, voice, and mood.
- For infinitive adjective and adverb phrases, draw an arrow back to the word modified.

The first is done for you. Some of these are tricky—ask for help if you need it!

INF PA

The distant rims of the world and of the firmament seemed to be a division in time no less than a division in matter.

He wished to marry me, and I wish to marry him.

The face of the heath by its mere complexion added half an hour to evening; it could in like manner retard the dawn, sadden noon, anticipate the frowning of storms scarcely generated, and intensify the opacity of a moonless midnight to a cause of shaking and dread.

After replying to the old man's greeting he showed no inclination to continue in talk, although they still walked side by side, for the elder traveller seemed to desire company.

Now, sir, I am sorry to say that my ponies are tired, and I have further to go.

I don't know if I ought to complain to you about this, but I am not quite sure what to do.

Moreover to light a fire is the instinctive and resistant act of man when, at the winter ingress, the curfew is sounded throughout Nature.

The beaming sight, and the penetrating warmth, seemed to breed in him a cumulative cheerfulness, which soon amounted to delight.

The audience cleared their throats and tossed a few stalks into the fire, not because these deeds were urgent, but to give themselves time to weigh the moral of the story.

When Mrs. Yeobright had drawn near to the inn, and was about to enter, she saw a horse and vehicle some two hundred yards beyond it, coming towards her, a man walking alongside with a lantern in his hand.

Yeobright went down the back staircase and into the heath by another path than that in front, intending to walk in the open air till the party was over, when he would return to wish Thomasin and her husband good-bye as they departed.

Red suns and tufts of fire one by one began to arise, flecking the whole country round.

To recline on a stump of thorn in the central valley of Egdon, between afternoon and night, as now, where the eye could reach nothing of the world outside the summits and shoulders of heathland which filled the whole circumference of its glance, and to know that everything around and underneath had been from prehistoric times as unaltered as the stars overhead, gave ballast to the mind adrift on change, and harassed by the irrepressible New.

Exercise 111B: Diagramming

On your own paper, diagram every word of the following sentences from *The Return of the Native.*

I tried to get her to eat something, but she couldn't; and she fell asleep.

On the Sunday after this wedding an unusual sight was to be seen on Rainbarrow.

I have thought of your sufferings that morning on which I parted from you; I know they were genuine, and they are as much as you ought to bear.

The commanding elevation of Rainbarrow had been chosen for two reasons: first, that it occupied a central position among the remote cottages around; secondly, that the preacher thereon could be seen from all adjacent points as soon as he arrived at his post, the view of him being thus a convenient signal to those stragglers who wished to draw near.

— LESSON 112 —

Principal Parts

Yet More Troublesome Verbs

Exercise 112A: Verb Definitions

Match the terms on the left with the definitions on the right by drawing lines between them.

progressive verb	the perfect past verb form, minus helping verbs
imperative	expresses possible actions
transitive verb	describes an ongoing or continuous action
indicative	present participle acting as a noun
gerund	describes an action which has been completed before another action takes place
subjunctive	expresses action that is received by some person or thing
present participle	the simple present (first-person singular)
ambitransitive verb	formed by combining *to* and the first-person-singular present form of a verb
first principal part	the same as the simple past verb form
modal	encourages or recommends an action
perfect verb	expresses situations that are unreal, wished for, or uncertain
second principal part	simply tells whether an action takes place in the past, present, or future
hortative	can be either transitive or intransitive
intransitive verb	expresses intended actions
infinitive	affirms or declares what actually is
simple verb	expresses action that is not received by any person or thing
third principal part	a verb form ending in *-ing*

English verbs have three principal parts.

First principal part: The Simple Present (Present)

(I) pontificate	(I) sing	(I) cut	(I) become

Second principal part: The Simple Past (Past)

(I) pontificated	(I) sang	(I have) cut	(I) became

Third principal part: The Perfect Past, Minus Helping Verbs (Past Participle)

(I have) pontificated	(I have) sung	(I have) cut	(I have) become

pontificate, pontificated, pontificated
sing, sang, sung
cut, cut, cut
become, became, become

***Sit*, *lie*, and *rise* are intransitive.**
***Set*, *lay*, and *raise* are transitive.**

lie		**lay**		**lay**	
Simple Past		**Simple Present**		**Simple Past**	
I lay	we lay	I lay	we lay	I laid	we laid
you lay	you lay	you lay	you lay	you laid	you laid
he, she, it lay	they lay	he, she, it lays	they lay	he, she, it laid	they laid

(simple past) The child ____________ out her clothes for the birthday party the night before.

(simple past) She got sunburned because she ______________ out in the sun too long.

(simple present) ______________ down and go to sleep now.

(simple present) ______________ your head down and close your eyes.

	First Principal Part Present	Second Principal Part Past	Third Principal Part Past Participle
I	lie	lay	lain
	lay	laid	laid
	sit	sat	sat
	set	set	set
	rise	rose	risen
	raise	raised	raised

Exercise 112B: Using Troublesome Verbs Correctly

In the following sentences from *Korean Folk Tales: Imps, Ghosts and Fairies*, by Im Bang and Yi Ryuk, translated by James S. Gale, fill in the blanks.

The first blank (above the sentence) should be filled in with the first principal part of the correct verb: *lie* or *lay* in the first set of sentences, *sit* or *set* in the second set, and *rise* or *raise* in the third set of sentences.

You will be able to tell from the context of the sentence whether you should use the transitive verbs *lay*, set, and *raise* (if the verb is passive, or has a direct object), or the intransitive verbs *lie*, *sit*, and *rise* (if the action of the verb is not passed on to any other word in the sentence).

The second blank (in the sentence itself) should be filled in with the correct form of that verb.

The first sentence in each section is done for you.

active indicative of lay

I have something very important to say, a private matter to lay before your Excellency.

simple past active indicative of ______________

They arrived at the gate, and the spirits who had him in hand led him in, and when they entered the inner courtyard they ______________ him down on his face.

simple past active indicative of ______________

The dogs ______________ as they were all day long, and neither ate nor moved.

simple past active indicative of __________

Thus he ____________ aside his weather-beaten clothes and donned the vestments of the genii.

simple present active indicative of ______________

They followed the road that leads toward the mountains that ______________ between Yang-tok and Maing-san counties.

simple past active indicative of ______________

When he took to sea the waters ______________ quiet before him, and all his path was peace.

simple past active modal of ______________

He would awake at first cock-crow of the morning, wash, dress, and never ______________ aside his book.

After drinking it he uttered the most gruesome and awful noises; his face grew very red

simple past active indicative of ____________

and he ____________ down and slept.

perfect past active indicative of ____________

A few days later, at night, I ____________ down, when suddenly there was a sound of crackling paper overhead from above the ceiling.

simple past active indicative of ____________

I ____________ motionless at the foot of the terrace till the following morning, when my father found me and had me taken in hand and cared for, so that I came to, and we all left the haunted house, never to go back.

simple past active indicative of __sit__

The Minister __sat__ down, comforted him, and then sent him away.

Here I found the master himself, an old gentleman, who put me through my humble

active infinitive of ____________

exercises, and then ordered me gently to come up and ____________ beside him.

simple past active indicative of ____________

In the night he studied by candle-light, while she ____________ by his side and did silk-spinning.

simple past passive indicative of ____________

The pair of worn shoes ____________ aside.

simple past active indicative of ____________

The stranger and the people with him ____________ the day through without any harm overtaking them, even though they were in the midst of the enemy's camp, as it were.

simple past passive indicative of ____________

After this he brought an armful of wood, which was ____________ in the middle of the courtyard.

simple past active indicative of ____________

A little later he came and ____________ on the bank and roared his threatenings at us.

progressive past active indicative of ____________

One day he ______________ with a friend playing chess, when they agreed that the loser in each case was to pay a fine in drink.

simple past active indicative of ____________

He ______________ them all aside and fixed his affections on this one only.

His cap was made of metal, which he used to cook his food in, and which he then washed

simple past active indicative of ____________

and ______________ back on his head again.

The priest, however, beat him with his stick, and when others went to help, he beat

active infinitive of rise

them also, so that they were completely worsted and unable to rise or walk.

simple past active indicative of ____________

Kim ______________ his eyes to see, and there was the exact duplicate of his wife, with a basket in her hand and roasted chestnuts.

simple past active indicative of ____________

Vile fumes ______________ up and filled the house.

simple past active indicative of ____________

In a little the quilt began to move, and she in alarm ______________ it to see what had happened, when lo! beneath it the child was gone and there lay coiled a huge snake instead.

simple past active indicative of ____________

I ______________ to take her by the hand, when she began walking backwards, so that my hand never reached her.

simple past passive indicative of ____________

He ______________ to the rank of Prince and became, later, Prime Minister.

simple past active indicative of ____________

Then both ______________, came down to the entrance, and vaulted off into mid-air, where they disappeared from sight.

simple past active indicative of ____________

But the host smiled upon him, ______________ his hands and asked, "Do you not know me? Look now."

simple past active indicative of ____________

They ______________ him up in order to prepare him for burial, when suddenly he came to life, looked at them in anger, and asked what they meant.

	First Principal Part Present	**Second Principal Part Past**	**Third Principal Part Past Participle**
I	give	gave	given
	come	came	come
	write	wrote	written
	go	went	gone
	eat	ate	eaten

She had gave her outgrown shoes to her sister.

Has she came home from the movies yet?

The policeman had wrote her a speeding ticket.

When Mom got home, I had already went to bed.

He has ate his dinner too fast.

Exercise 112C: More Irregular Principal Parts

Fill in the chart below with the missing principal parts of each verb. (You may use a dictionary if necessary.) Then, in the sentences (from Samuel Butler's classic translation of Homer's *Odyssey*), fill in the blanks with the correct verb, in the tense, mood, and voice indicated in brackets at the end of each sentence. Each verb is used one time.

	First Principal Part **Present**	Second Principal Part **Past**	Third Principal Part **Past Participle**
I	overtake		
	bind		

	First Principal Part **Present**	Second Principal Part **Past**	Third Principal Part **Past Participle**
	pay		
	drive		
	lie		
	give		
	hear		
	leap		
	spill		
	say		
	light		
	weep		
	mean		
	show		
	go		
	strike		
	bid		

She had been nurse to Nausicaa, and ______________ now ______________ the fire for her, and brought her supper for her into her own room. [perfect past active indicative]

"Vulcan," said Neptune, "if Mars _______________ away without paying his damages, I _______________ you myself." [simple present active subjunctive] [simple future active indicative]

Mars and Minerva made me doughty in war; when I had picked my men to surprise the enemy with an ambush I never _______________ death so much as a thought, but was the first _______________ forward and spear all whom I _______________. [simple past active indicative] [active infinitive] [simple present active modal]

There it was that I _______________ news of Ulysses, for the king told me he had entertained him, and _______________ him much hospitality while he was on his homeward journey. [simple past active indicative] [perfect past active indicative]

In the end, however, he escaped with his life, _______________ the cattle from Phylace to Pylos, avenged the wrong that had been done him, and gave the daughter of Neleus to his brother. [simple past active indicative]

The chief men among the suitors _______________ in wait for you in the Strait between Ithaca and Samos, and they _______________ to kill you before you can reach home. [progressive present active indicative] [simple present active indicative]

Here was a bard also to sing to them and play his lyre, while two tumblers went about performing in the midst of them when the man _______________ up with his tune. [simple past active indicative]

The bath was overturned, so that all the water _______________ on the ground. [simple past passive indicative]

The sons of Autolycus busied themselves with the carcass of the boar, and _______________ Ulysses' wound; then, after _______________ a spell to stop the bleeding, they went home as fast as they could. [simple past active indicative] [present participle]

As she spoke, she told Eumaeus to set the bow and the pieces of iron before the suitors, and Eumaeus _______________ as he took them to do as she _______________ him. [simple past active indicative] [perfect past active indicative]

WEEK 30

Still More About Clauses

— LESSON 113 —

Clauses and Phrases

The sentences in this lesson are taken from *Redwall* by Brian Jacques.

> All eyes were on the Father Abbot. He took a dainty fork loaded precariously with steaming fish. Carefully he transferred it from plate to mouth. Chewing delicately, he turned his eyes upwards then closed them, whiskers atwitch, jaws working steadily, munching away, his tail curled up holding a napkin which neatly wiped his mouth.
>
> —Brian Jacques, *Redwall*

A clause is a group of words that contains a subject and a predicate.

An independent clause can stand by itself as a sentence.

A sentence is a group of words that usually contains a subject and a predicate. A sentence begins with a capital letter and ends with a punctuation mark. A sentence contains a complete thought.

A phrase is a group of words serving a single grammatical function.

A dependent clause is a fragment that cannot stand by itself as a sentence.

Dependent clauses can act as adjective clauses, adverb clauses, or noun clauses.

An adjective clause is a dependent clause that acts as an adjective in a sentence, modifying a noun or pronoun in the independent clause.

Relative pronouns (*who*, *whom*, *whose*, *which*, *that*) introduce adjective clauses and refer back to an antecedent in the independent clause.

Relative adverbs (*where*, *when*, *why*) introduce adjective clauses when they refer back to a place, time, or reason in the independent clause.

Matthias started to slide down the rope on the Mossflower side of the wall, where the woods came close up to the Abbey.

The Father Abbot halted in front of the wall on which hung a long tapestry.

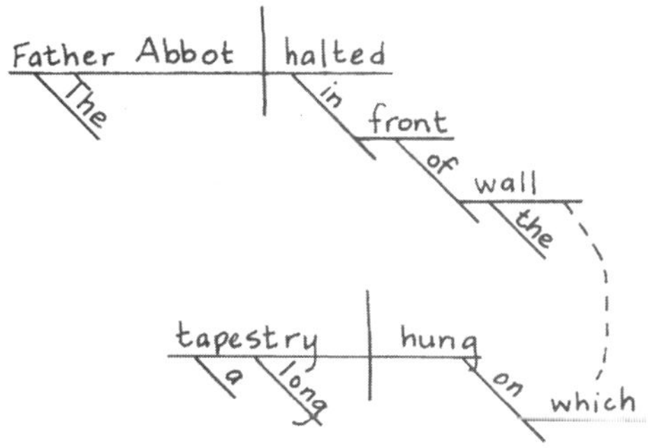

He arrived here in the deep winter when the Founders were under attack from many foxes, vermin, and a great wildcat.

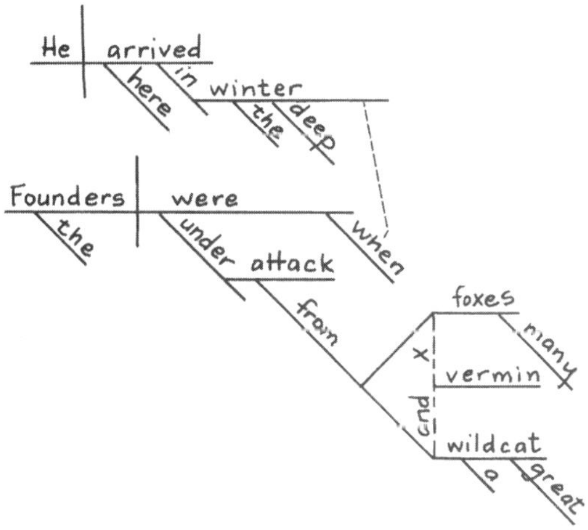

Adverb clauses can be introduced by adverbs.

Common adverbs that introduce adverbial clauses are:

as and its compounds (as if, as soon as, as though)
how and its compound (however)
when and its compound (whenever)
whence
where and its compounds (whereat, whereby, wherein, wherefore, whereon)
while
whither

Her blunt claws churned the roadside soil as she propelled the cart through a gap in the hawthorn hedge, down to the slope of the ditch where she dug her paws in, holding the cart still and secure while John Churchmouse and Cornflower's father jumped out and wedged the wheels firmly with stones.

A subordinating conjunction joins unequal words or groups of words together.

Subordinating conjunctions and subordinating correlative conjunctions often join an adverb clause to an independent clause.

Common subordinating conjunctions are:

after
although
as (as soon as)
because
before
if
in order that
lest
since
though
till
unless
until
although/though . . . yet/still
if . . . then

All the mice took a solemn vow never to harm another living creature, unless it was an enemy that sought to harm our Order by violence.

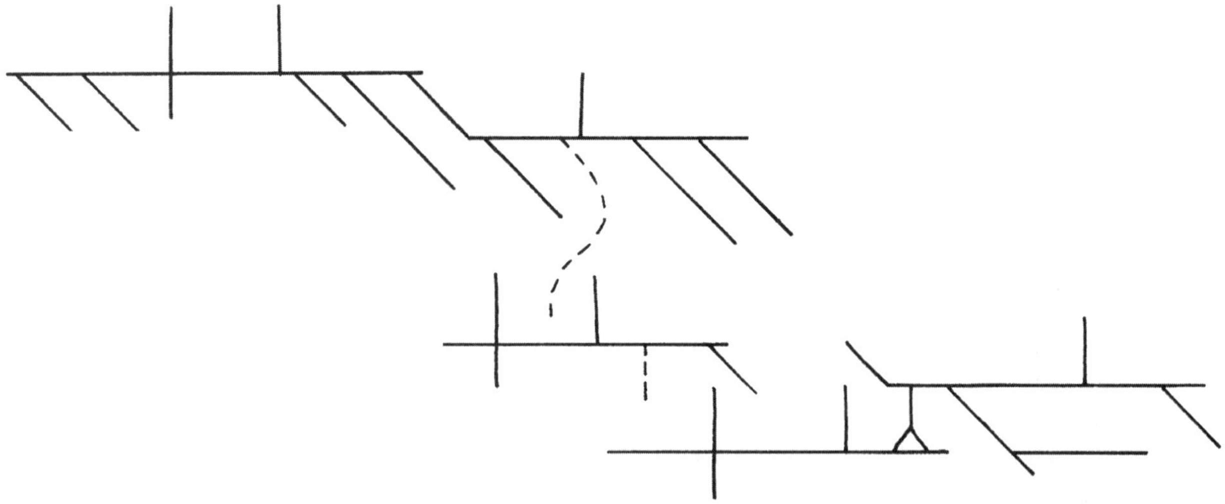

A noun clause takes the place of a noun. Noun clauses can be introduced by relative pronouns, relative adverbs, or subordinating conjunctions.

Somewhere there had to be a clue, a single lead that might tell him where the resting place of Martin the Warrior could be found, or where he could regain possession of the ancient sword for his Abbey.

The defenders stood and cheered in the depression above what had once been Killconey's tunnel.

It is because you are kind and good.

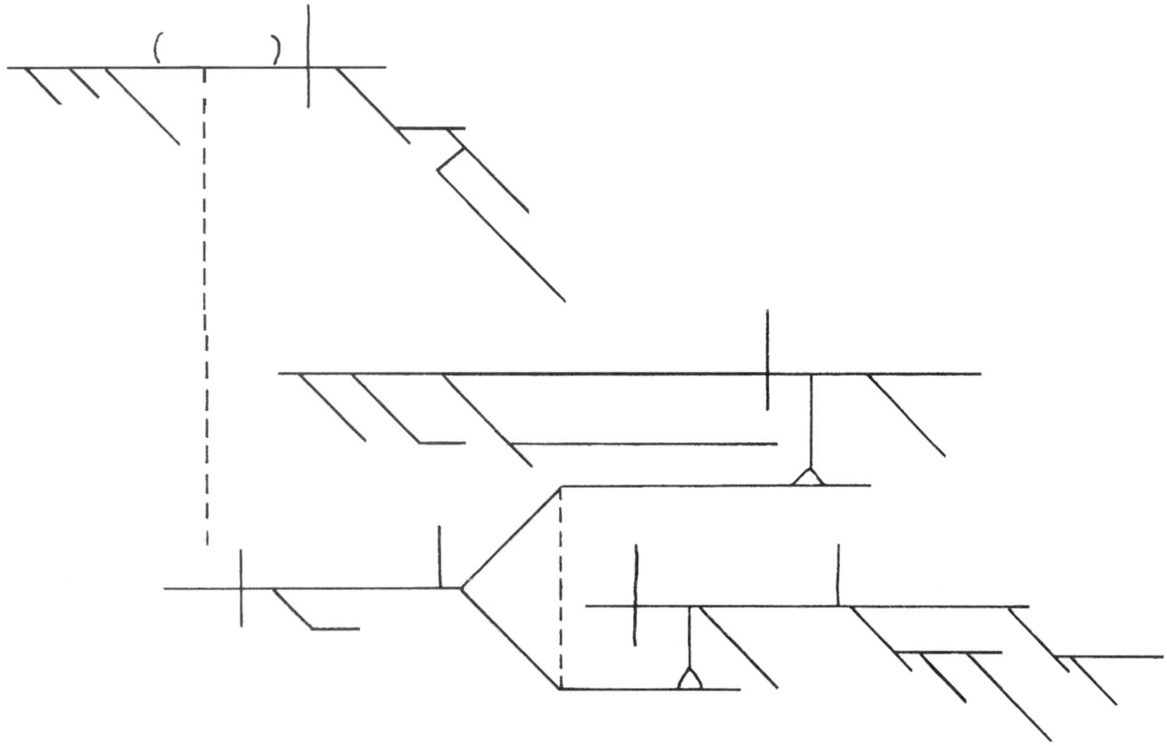

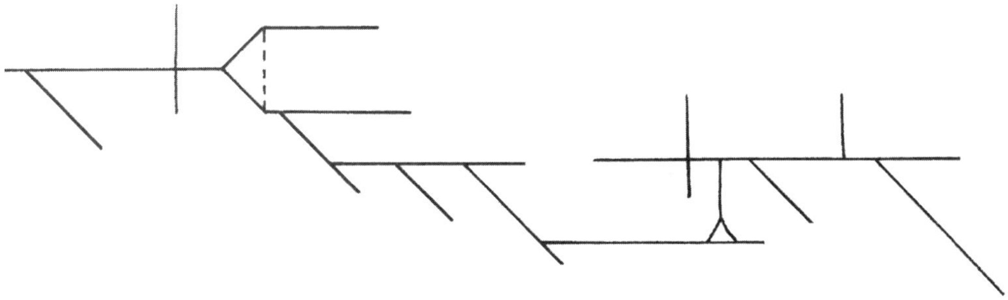

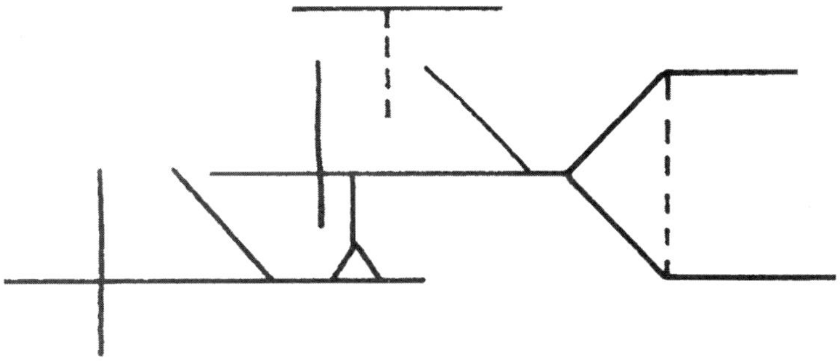

Exercise 113A: Phrases and Clauses

Identify each underlined set of words as *PH* for phrase or *CL* for clause.

- Then, identify the part of the sentence (*S, DO, IO, OP, PN, PA, ADV, ADJ*) that each set of words functions as.
- For phrases, further identify the phrase as *PREP* (prepositional), *INF* (infinitive), *PresP* (present participle), or *PP* (past participle).
- For clauses, write *S* above the subject of the clause and *P* above the predicate.
- For adjective and adverb phrases and clauses, draw an arrow to the word modified.
- If words are double-underlined, be careful—a phrase or clause is within another phrase or clause! Be sure to carry out the instructions above for both the larger phrase/clause and the phrase/clause within it.

The first is done for you. All of these sentences are taken from *Mariel of Redwall* by Brian Jacques.

CL ADV
S P PH ADV PREP
As sleep descended upon her weary body, strange thoughts flooded her mind.

He was back in a while, splashing water over his sleeping friend.

They sat around the bright flames, which provided an island of golden light against the gloomy vault of the forest in front of them.

The two mice made their way between the flowerbeds which dotted the dark greensward.

When she looked down, the lizard had gone.

With a careless shrug she pushed on, the soft swish of her paws through grass and occasional birdsong the only sound that fell upon her ears.

The prophecies carved on Salamandastron's walls tell of a time coming soon when trouble will become a byword.

Throwing herself flat, the little mousemaid shoved her head into the hole and drank greedily, disregarding the gritty sand and ooze, as life-giving water flowed down her throat.

With eye-blurring speed she belted the knotted rope twice into the bird's face.

The little mousemaid felt the blood thrumming in her veins.

To restore her confidence, in the enveloping silence Storm tried to hum odd snatches of songs, but she could not remember any.

In the silence that followed before the applause, Storm Gullwhacker gave vent to a hoarse strangled sob, which echoed amid the startled revelers.

Mariel thought of her father, wondering where he could be and how his health was.

All around them, searats squatted, cooking whatever they had found during the day.

Exercise 113B: Diagramming

On your own paper, diagram every word of the following sentences, taken from *Doomwyte* by Brian Jacques.

There were creatures inside, young mice, moles, squirrels, and hedgehogs.

Back at the dormitory, the pillow fight was at its height, as was the noise.

Brother Torilis, the Herbalist and Infirmary Keeper, did not bother to knock.

Flinging the door open, he strode straight into the scene of chaos.

A hush fell over the entire chamber, broken only by a volebabe falling from the top of a wardrobe onto a bed, where he lay at rigid attention.

Tossed about on the dark skies, like a scrap of black-and-white rag, the magpie caught sight of the imposing building as she was swept high over the swaying green of Mossflower woodlands.

—LESSON 114—

Restrictive and Non-Restrictive Modifying Clauses
Punctuating Modifying Clauses
Which and *That*

Why does the mechanism of the p-value, which seems so reasonable, work so very badly in this setting?

If the first throw is tails and the second is heads, an event which happens 1/4 of the time, Paul gets two ducats.

—From *How Not to Be Wrong: The Power of Mathematical Thinking* by Jordan Ellenberg

A non-restrictive modifying clause describes the word that it modifies. Removing the clause doesn't change the essential meaning of the sentence. Only non-restrictive clauses should be set off by commas.

A restrictive modifying clause defines the word that it modifies. Removing the clause changes the essential meaning of the sentence.

I especially like the "Methods" section, which starts "One mature Atlantic Salmon (*Salmo salar*) participated in the fMRI study."

I especially like the "Methods" section which starts "One mature Atlantic Salmon (*Salmo salar*) participated in the fMRI study."

A noun clause takes the place of a noun. Noun clauses can be introduced by relative pronouns, relative adverbs, or subordinating conjunctions.

In principle, if you carry out a powerful enough study, you can find out, which it is.

The reason the 0.999 . . . problem is difficult is, that it brings our intuitions into conflict.

An appositive is a noun, noun phrase, or noun clause that usually follows another noun and renames or explains it. Appositives are set off by commas.

The Goldbach conjecture, that every even number greater than 2 is the sum of two primes, is another one that would have to be true if primes behaved like random numbers.

The chocolate brownies that
The chocolate brownies which

The chocolate brownies that were on the counter are gone now.

The chocolate brownies, which were made with olive oil instead of butter, have been sitting on the counter since lunch time.

When the relative pronoun introducing a modifying clause refers to a thing rather than a person, *which* introduces non-restrictive clauses and *that* introduces restrictive clauses.

"These are but shadows of the things that have been," said the Ghost.

It was shrouded in a deep black garment, which concealed its head, its face, its form, and left nothing of it visible save one outstretched hand.

He lived in chambers which had once belonged to his deceased partner.

At last she said, and in a steady, cheerful voice, that only faltered once, "I have known him walk with—I have known him walk with Tiny Tim upon his shoulder, very fast indeed."

—From *A Christmas Carol* by Charles Dickens

That's certainly an impressive figure, but one which clearly indicates that the percentage doesn't mean quite what you're used to it meaning.

—From *How Not to Be Wrong* by Jordan Ellenberg

He lived in chambers that had once belonged to his deceased partner.
At last she said, and in a steady, cheerful voice, which only faltered once, "I have known him walk with—I have known him walk with Tiny Tim upon his shoulder, very fast indeed."
That's certainly an impressive figure, but one that clearly indicates that the percentage doesn't mean quite what you're used to it meaning.

Exercise 114A: Restrictive and Non-Restrictive Adjective Clauses

Find every adjective clause in the following sentences, taken from *A Little History of Science* by William Bynum, and then follow these steps:

a) Underline each adjective clause.
b) Circle the relative pronoun that introduces each clause.
c) Draw an arrow from the pronoun back to the word modified.
d) Label each clause as *R* for restrictive or *NR* for nonrestrictive.
e) Draw an asterisk or star next to each sentence that does not follow the *which/that* rule.

Ancient astronomers thought that there were seven planets: Mercury, Venus, Mars, Jupiter, and Saturn, plus the sun and the moon, which they also called planets.

He was also very interested in eclipses, which occur when the sun, moon, or one of the planets gets in the way of another planet and becomes partly or wholly covered from our sight.

Another planet, Saturn, had two big blobs which didn't look like moons and which we now call its "rings."

When most things burn, the products are gases that are difficult to collect and weigh.

He burnt a stick of fresh wood and showed that the smoke that came off it was not air.

He knew air played a part in burning, and he also knew that there was a kind of "air" (a gas) that made things burn even more vigorously than the "ordinary" air that surrounds us.

His telescope revealed that the Milky Way, which appears as a wonderful, fuzzy blur of light when looking with the naked eye on a clear night, was actually composed of thousands and thousands of individual stars, very far away from the earth.

In fact, Galileo didn't use the tower, but he did other experiments that showed him what the result would be, and he found that a ten-pound ball and a one-pound ball would hit the ground at the same time.

Second, Aristotle insisted on the central role that the heart and blood play in our lives, after observing the tiny beating heart which was the first sign of life in the speck of a chick in an egg.

The heart, which has long been associated with blood, was also fascinating to Harvey.

Anaesthesia was a triumph for chemistry in the service of medicine, since the compounds that were shown to put people to sleep—ether and chloroform—were chemicals made in the laboratory.

Exercise 114B: Dependent Clauses within Dependent Clauses

The following sentences all contain dependent clauses that have other dependent clauses within them.

Underline the whole of each one of these dependent clauses (including additional dependent clauses that act as nouns or modifiers within it). Draw a box around the subject of the main dependent clause, and underline its predicate twice. In the right-hand margin, write the abbreviation for the part of the sentence that the main dependent clause is fulfilling: *N-SUB* for a noun clause acting as subject, *N-PN* for predicate nominative, *N-DO* for direct object, *N-OP* for object of the preposition, *N-APP* for appositive, and then *ADJ* for adjective and *ADV* for adverb. For adjective and adverb clauses, draw a line from the label back to the word in the main dependent clause modified.

Then, circle any additional clauses that fall within the main dependent clause. Label each clause, above the circle, in the same way: *N-SUB* for a noun clause acting as subject, *N-PN* for predicate nominative, *N-DO* for direct object, *N-OP* for object of the preposition, *N-APP* for appositive, and then *ADJ* for adjective and *ADV* for adverb. For adjective and adverb clauses, draw a line from the label back to the word in the main dependent clause modified.

The first sentence is done for you.

These are all taken from *Science and Modern India: An Institutional History, c. 1784–1947*, edited by Uma Das Gupta.

When we deal with such small or such large objects we must expect that their behaviour will be very different from that of the objects of medium size to which we are used on the surface of this earth. N-DO

ADJ

Note to Student: The first dependent clause, *When we deal with such small or such large objects*, is not underlined because it does not contain another clause within it. It acts as an adverb modifying the modal verb *must expect*.

In the world of the atom, however, we meet with the principle of complementarity, which expresses, as Bohr has said, "the fundamental limitations, met with in atomic physics, of our ingrained idea of phenomena as existing independently of the means by which they are observed."

This equation holds for all arithmetical numbers and we can express all such statements in the general equation a x b=b x a, which forms the foundation of the mathematics which is taught at school.

During the 33 years which have elapsed since the instruments now in use in the observatory were ordered, astronomy has advanced so rapidly along certain lines that the instrumental equipment is again found very defective.

Note to Student: Don't forget—only underline the dependent clause that contains another dependent clause!

One might wonder why, of all places, Roorkee was chosen by the colonial rulers when it came to opening an engineering college.

These observations consisted of the computed elements for the comets of 1843 and 1845 and of the solar eclipse of 21 December 1843, which he observed near the source of the Mah River, where the eclipse fell just short of totality but offered a beautiful view of Baily's beads.

Note to Student: For extra credit, find out what Baily's beads are!

He also believed that the clause which made it mandatory for an alumnus to return the sum of money spent on him by the university if he refused to join the College of Science was downright unjust.

Note to Student: Be careful—the sentence above has a clause within a clause within a clause!

Exercise 114C: Diagramming

On your own paper, diagram every word of the following sentence(s). If you need help, ask your instructor. You'll need a very large piece of paper!

These are from *A Short History of Science*, by W. T. Sedgwick and H. W. Tyler.

The following sentence has seven separate clauses!

Hicetas of Syracuse, according to Theophrastus, believes that the heavens, the sun, moon, stars, and all heavenly bodies are standing still, and that nothing in the universe is moving except the earth, which, while it turns and twists itself with the greatest velocity round its axis, produces all the same phenomena as if the heavens were moved and the earth were standing still.

The following sentence has one main and three subordinate clauses—but they're hiding in plain view. Can you find them?

Pliny the Elder, sometimes called Pliny the Naturalist, is another Roman of scientific attainments, whose work entitled *Natural History*, although more an encyclopedia of miscellaneous information than a scientific treatise, is nevertheless, like the works of Herodotus, a landmark in the history of civilization.

—LESSON 115—

Conditional Sentences

Conditional Sentences as Dependent Clauses
Conditional Sentences with Missing Words
Formal *If* Clauses

The sentences in this lesson are from *Pride & Prejudice & Zombies*, by Jane Austen and Seth Grahame-Smith.

simple past, active, subjunctive

I have nothing to say against him; he has felled many a zombie; and if he had the fortune he

simple present, active modal

ought to have, I should think you could not do better. SECOND

Active verbs are active or passive in voice.
State-of-being verbs do not have voice.
Subjunctive verbs express situations that are unreal, wished for, or uncertain.

If my children are silly, I must hope to be always sensible of it. _______________

If I had known as much this morning I certainly would not have called him. ____________

If I were not afraid of judging harshly, I should be almost tempted to demand satisfaction.

____

First conditional sentences express circumstances that might actually happen.
The predicate of the condition clause is in a present tense.
The predicate of the consequence clause is an imperative or is in a present or future tense.

Second conditional sentences express circumstances that are contrary to reality.
The predicate of the condition clause is in a past tense.
The predicate of the consequence clause is in the simple or progressive present modal tense.

Third conditional sentences express past circumstances that never happened.
The predicate of the condition clause is in the perfect past tense.
The predicate of the consequence clause is in any modal tense.

In her postscript it was added that if Mr. Bingley and his sister pressed them to stay

longer, she could spare them.

However, I recollected afterwards that if he had been prevented going, the wedding need

not be put off.

If he fears me, why come hither?

If he no longer cares for me, why silent?

Should you wish to, meet me in the drawing room.

Formal conditional sentences drop *if* from the condition clause and reverse the order of the subject and helping verb.

Were you not otherwise agreeable, I should be forced to remove your tongue with my saber.

If he fears me, why come hither?

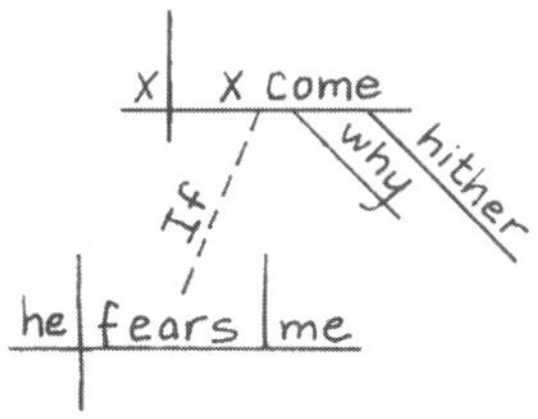

If he no longer cares for me, why silent?

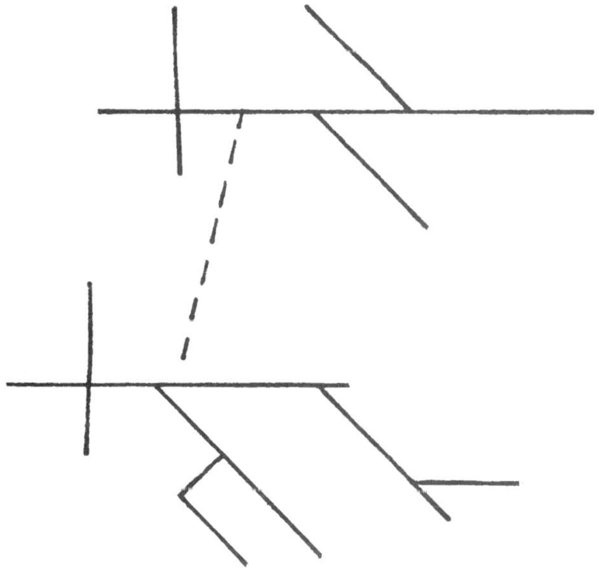

Should you wish, meet me in the drawing room.

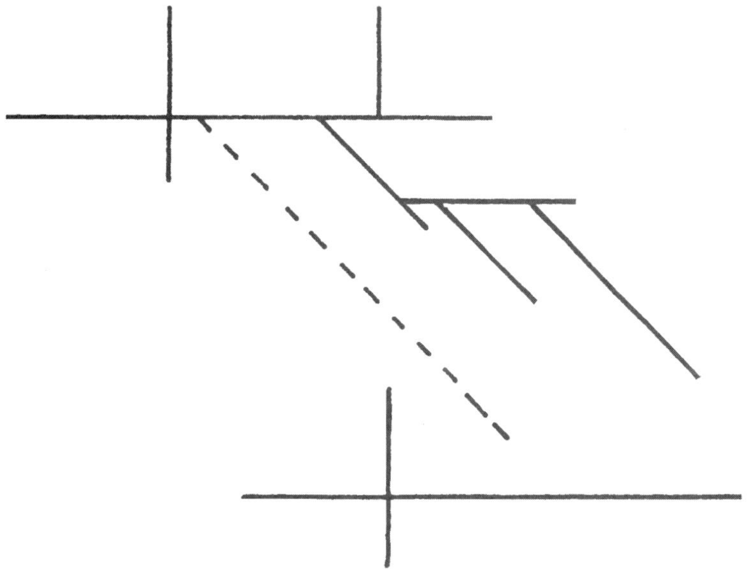

Were you not otherwise agreeable, I should be forced to remove your tongue with my saber.

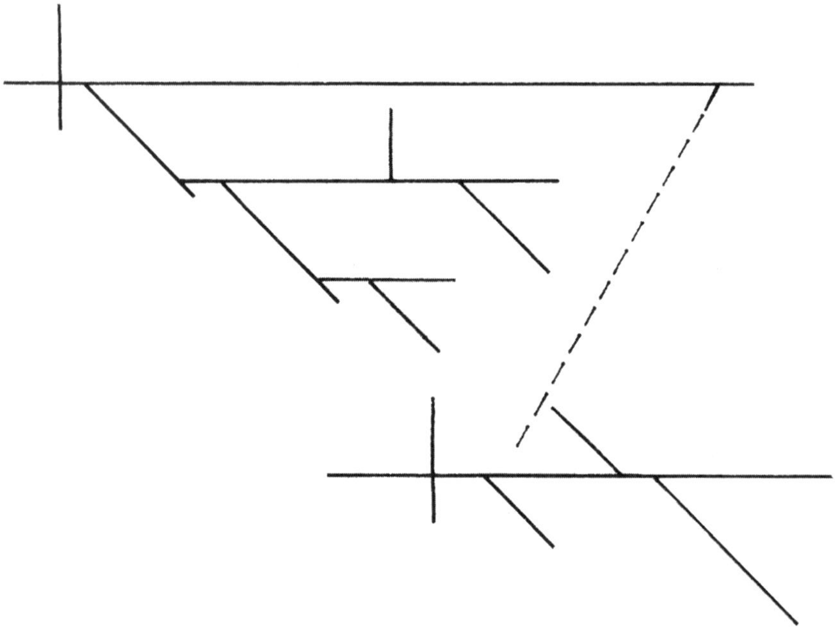

Exercise 115A: Conditional Clauses

In the following sentences from *Persuasion*, by Jane Austen (no zombies in *Persuasion*, alas!), circle every conditional sentence. This may mean circling the entire sentence, or circling simply the part of it that makes up the conditional-consequence clause set, or circling the conditional and consequence clauses separately if they are divided by other words.

After you have circled the conditional sentences, underline twice and then parse the predicate in each conditional and consequence clause.

Finally, write a *1*, *2*, or *3* in the blank to indicate first, second, or third conditional.

The first is done for you.

simple present, state-of-being, modal subjunctive

If Louisa Musgrove would be beautiful and happy in her November of life,

simple future, active, indicative

she will cherish all her present powers of mind. 1

Should he ever propose to me (which I have very little reason to imagine he has any thought of doing), I shall not accept him. _______

These valuable pictures of yours, Sir Walter, if you chose to leave them, would be perfectly safe. _______

It would have been strange if I had not gone. _______

I do believe if Charles were to see me dying, he would not think there was anything the matter with me. _______

If Louisa recovered, it would all be well again. _______

Anne will send for me if anything is the matter. _______

If there is anything disagreeable going on men are always sure to get out of it, and Charles is as bad as any of them. _______

Charles, if you see Captain Harville anywhere, remember to give Miss Anne's message. _______

I should not go, you may be sure, if I did not feel quite at ease about my dear child. _______

If a man has not a wife, he soon wants to be afloat again. _______

Everybody is always supposing that I am not a good walker; and yet they would not have been pleased, if we had refused to join them. _______

If you value her conduct or happiness, infuse as much of your own spirit into her as you can. ________

I have no scruple of observing to you, how nonsensical some persons are about their place, because all the world knows how easy and indifferent you are about it; but I wish anybody could give Mary a hint that it would be a great deal better if she were not so very tenacious. ________

Note to Student: The last sentence in this exercise does not completely follow the rules! Try to identify the type of conditional it contains, and then check with your instructor.

Anne talked of being perfectly ready, and tried to look it; but she felt that could Henrietta have known the regret and reluctance of her heart in quitting that chair, in preparing to quit the room, she would have found, in all her own sensations for her cousin, in the very security of his affection, wherewith to pity her. ________

Exercise 115B: Diagramming

On your own paper, diagram every word of the following two sentences from Exercise 115A.

Both of these sentences have challenging elements! Do your best, and ask your instructor for help if you need it. (You might want to use some scratch paper as well.)

Should he ever propose to me (which I have very little reason to imagine he has any thought of doing), I shall not accept him.

Anne talked of being perfectly ready, and tried to look it; but she felt that could Henrietta have known the regret and reluctance of her heart in quitting that chair, in preparing to quit the room, she would have found, in all her own sensations for her cousin, in the very security of his affection, wherewith to pity her.

—LESSON 116—

Words That Can Be Multiple Parts of Speech
Interrogatives
Demonstratives
Relative Adverbs and Subordinating Conjunctions

Exercise 116A: Words Acting as Multiple Parts of Speech

Use these sentences, taken from Zane Grey's classic western novel *The Light of Western Stars*, to identify the parts of speech that the bolded words can serve as. The first blank is filled in for you. Fill in the blanks with the correct labels from the following list:

conjunction	interjection	preposition	adverb
adjective	noun	pronoun	verb

Which pronoun (twice) ________________

As she sat down to wait she reviewed the causes which accounted for the remarkable situation in which she found herself.

Well, if your memory for faces is so good, maybe you can tell me which one of these cowboys wasn't clean-shaven.

One ________________ ________________ (twice)

One afternoon, however, Edith appeared prone to talk seriously.

Then, gradually, one by one they tired and went to bed.

Along ________________ ________________

A huge cloud of dust went along over our heads.

Upon the drive in to the ranch, as she was passing the lower lake, she saw Stewart walking listlessly along the shore.

Forever ________________ ________________

He was somewhat wild and sudden and—sentimental in his demand to protect me—and it was not clear whether he meant his protection for last night or forever; but I am happy to say he offered me no word that was not honorable.

I cannot stay out here forever.

Clear ______________ ______________ ______________ ______________

But Madeline detected a merry twinkle in her clear eyes.

Lastly, the fact standing clear of all others in its relation to her interest was that he had been almost ruined, almost lost, and she had saved him.

Ten thousand dollars would clear me and give me another start.

One look at him at close range in the clear was enough for Madeline to award him a blue ribbon over all horses, even her prize-winner, White Stockings.

Warm ____________________ ____________________

When she did slip her bare feet out upon the stone floor she very quickly put them back under the warm blankets.

It'll warm up directly.

Unless ____________________ ____________________

But don't yell in his ear unless you want Florence and me to see you disappear on the horizon.

Human life is not for any man to sacrifice unless in self-defense or in protecting those dependent upon him.

Even ________________ ________________ ________________

Madeline did not faint or even shut her eyes, but she felt as if she were fast in a cold vise.

Still, even had he not replied at all she would have gone on with him.

Majesty heaved upward with a snort, the wet saddle creaked, and an even motion told Madeline she was on level ground.

For ____________________ ____________________

Perhaps the station agent will return soon, or Alfred will come for me.

We'll have to go, whether we want to or not, for when Bill learns you are here he'll just pack us all off.

Since __________________ __________________ __________________

Madeline's personal opinion of Stewart had not changed in the least since the night it had been formed.

I have never had a day's worry since I bought the ranch.

I long since separated from love.

Back __________________ __________________ __________________

From the back of the house sounded the tramp of boots and voices of men, and from outside came a dull thump of hoofs, the rattle of harness, and creak of wheels.

Alfred bundled her up into the back seat, and Florence after her, and wrapped them with robes.

Nothing could have turned her back then.

---

who, whom, whose, what, which

Interrogative pronouns take the place of nouns in questions.
Interrogative adjectives modify nouns.

Interrogative Pronouns	**Interrogative Adjectives**
Who was Dragging Canoe?	Whose side was Dragging Canoe on?

With whom did Dragging Canoe fight?

What war did he fight?

What did Dragging Canoe do?

Which tribe did Dragging Canoe belong to?

Which of his countrymen followed him?

In the American Revolution, Dragging Canoe fought against the colonists who were rebelling against the British.

Dragging Canoe and his brother chiefs, whom he had known for many years, joined together and allied with the British.

Dragging Canoe told his tribesmen to consider the case of the Delaware, whose land had been swallowed by the American colonies.

At first, the American colonists did not know what Dragging Canoe was planning.

Dragging Canoe led attacks on the settlements which were in southeast North America.

The interrogative words *who, whom, whosc, what*, and *which* can also serve as relative pronouns in adjective clauses or introductory words in noun clauses.

What was the name of Dragging Canoe's father? ______________________________

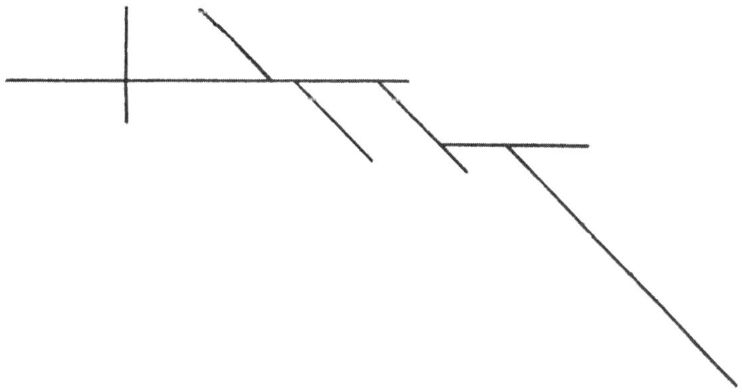

What five towns did Dragging Canoe build? ______________________________

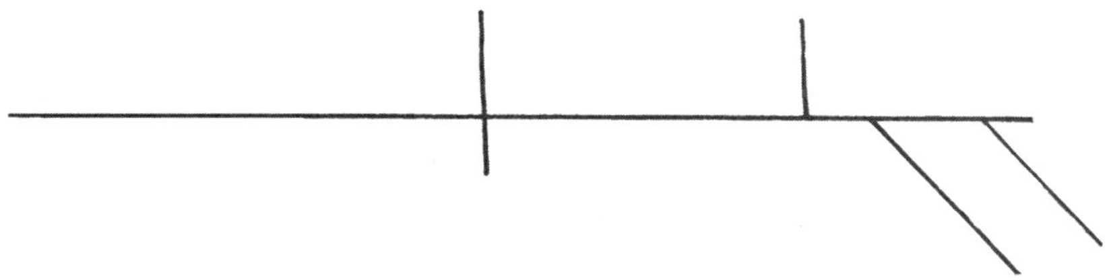

Dragging Canoe did not believe what the governor of North Carolina told him. ______________________

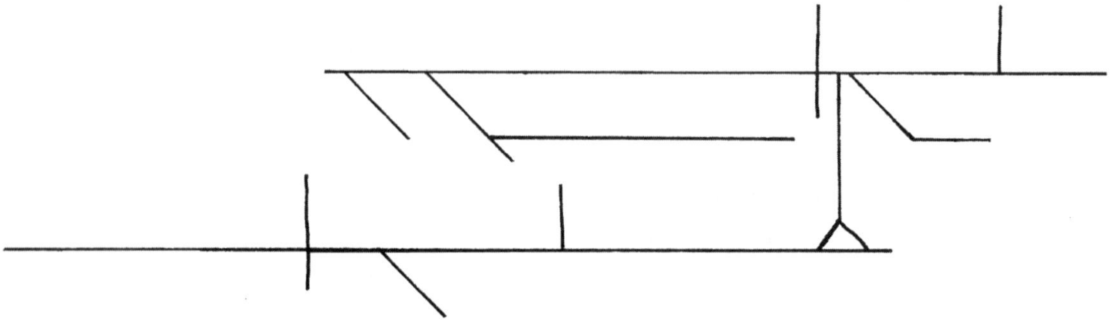

Dragging Canoe led the Cherokees who refused to stay neutral. ______________________

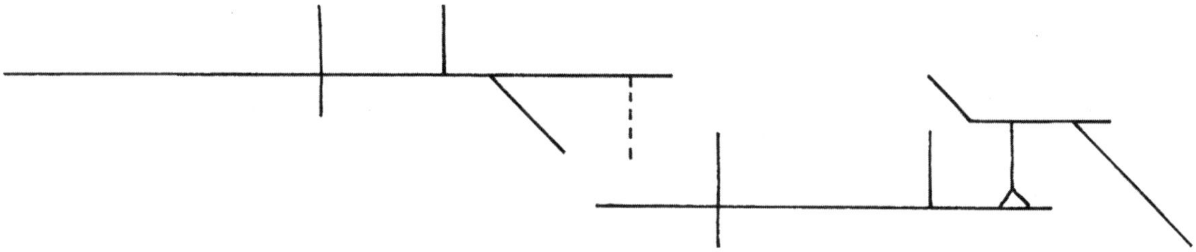

this, that, these, those

Demonstrative pronouns demonstrate or point out something. They take the place of a single word or a group of words.

Demonstrative adjectives modify nouns and answer the question *which one.*

Those were the first Spanish ships to touch American shores.

While a young boy, this future chief wanted to accompany his father, Attakullakulla, and a Cherokee war party going to battle the Shawnee.

During one of these council sessions, a young chief named Dragging Canoe exploded into prominence.

Now that hope is gone.

This was the first invasion of the Middle Towns by an enemy force on record.
—From Pat Alderman, *Nancy Ward: Cherokee Chieftainess, Dragging Canoe: Cherokee-Chickamauga War Chief*

He had come to the council because of his admiration for that great chief.

They set off at a rapid pace, little guessing that a silent scout followed them.

That would be a catastrophe for the Cherokee and their allies.

An adverb describes a verb, an adjective, or another adverb.
Adverbs tell how, when, where, how often, and to what extent.

Relative adverbs introduce adjective clauses and refer back to a place, time, or reason in the independent clause.

where, when, why

(The remaining sentences in the lesson are slightly adapted from *Trail of Tears: The Rise and Fall of the Cherokee Nation* by John Ehle.)

It was the orderly village to which he was heir, and where his mother was the pivot of the world.

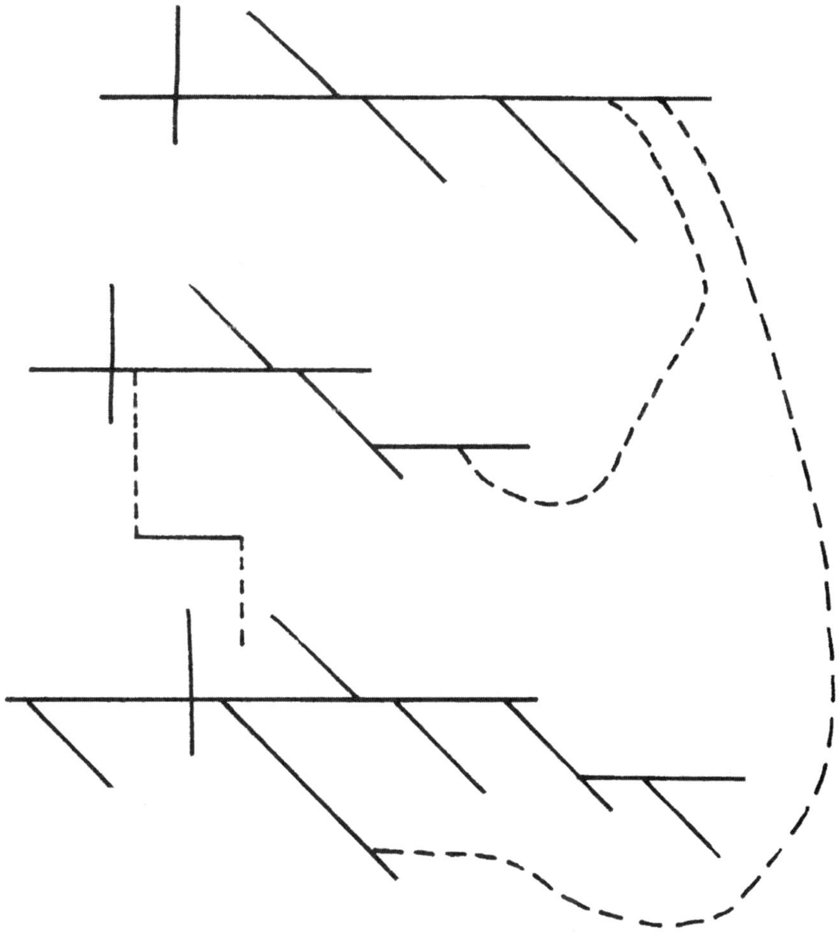

My heart rejoices when I look upon you.

Adverbs can act as subordinating conjunctions when they connect adverb clauses to a verb, adjective, or adverb in the main clause.

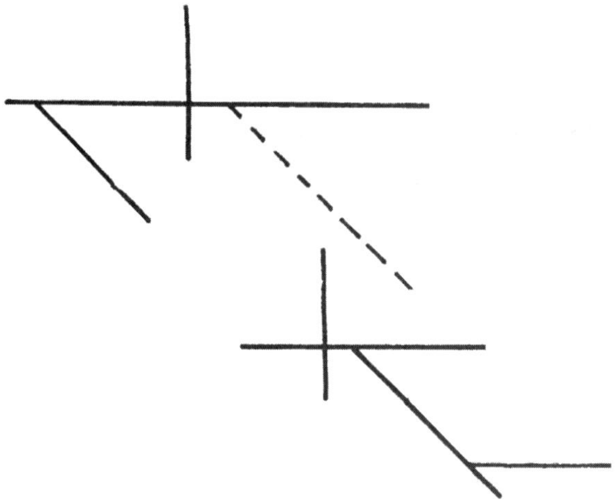

Their land was taken away because they fought for the British.

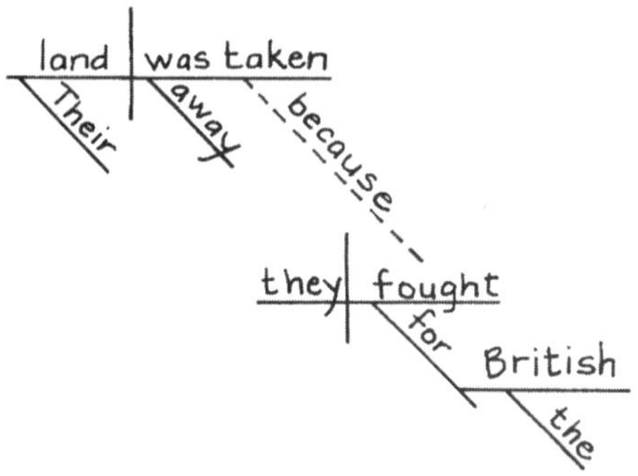

Exercise 116B: Words Introducing Clauses

In the following sentences, taken from *American Indian Stories* by the nineteenth-century Sioux writer Zitkala-Sa, underline every subordinate clause. Then, carry out the following steps:

a) Circle the introductory word of the clause. (NOTE: When the introductory word is the object of a preposition, circle the word itself, not the preposition that precedes it. See the sample sentence.) If the introductory word is understood, insert it with a caret and then circle it.

b) Label the clause as *N* (for noun), *ADJ* (for adjective), or *ADV* (for adverb).

c) For noun clauses, further identify them as *S* for subject, *O* for object, or *PN* for predicate nominative.

d) For adjective or adverb clauses, draw an arrow to the word modified.

e) Finally, label the introductory word as one of the following: *RP* for relative pronoun, *P* for a pronoun introducing a noun clause that does not refer back to a word in the main clause, *RAdj* for relative adjective (a relative pronoun functioning as an adjective and introducing an adjective clause), *RAdv* for relative adverb, *SC* for subordinating conjunction, or *A-SC* for adverb functioning as a subordinating conjunction.

The first is done for you.

ADJ
RP
An invisible power passed from her outstretched fingers to the evil at (which) she aimed.

Always, when my mother started for the river, I stopped my play to run along with her.

Then I clung to her hand and begged to know what made the tears fall.

Loosely clad in a slip of brown buckskin, and light-footed with a pair of soft moccasins on my feet, I was as free as the wind that blew my hair.

Having gone many paces ahead I stopped, panting for breath, and laughing with glee as my mother watched my every movement.

It was as if I were the activity, and my hands and feet were only experiments for my spirit to work upon.

Returning from the river, I tugged beside my mother, with my hand upon the bucket she was carrying.

Setting the pail of water on the ground, my mother stooped, and stretching her left hand out on the level with my eyes, she placed her other arm about me; she pointed to the hill where my uncle and my only sister lay buried.

My poor child, how I cried with her because the Great Spirit had forgotten us!

At last, when we reached this western country, on the first weary night your sister died.

The morning meal was our quiet hour, when we two were entirely alone.

My uncle, whose death my mother ever lamented, was one of our nation's bravest warriors.

Though I heard many strange experiences related by these wayfarers, I loved best the evening meal, for that was the time old legends were told.

I ate my supper in quiet, listening patiently to the talk of the old people, wishing all the time that they would begin the stories.

As each in turn began to tell a legend, I pillowed my head in my mother's lap.

The glare of the fire shone on a tattooed star upon the brow of the old warrior who was telling a story.

Then followed a long silence in which he clasped tighter and unclasped again his interlocked fingers.

After the warrior's story was finished, I asked the old woman the meaning of the blue lines on her chin, looking all the while out of the corners of my eyes at the warrior with the star on his forehead.

I was a little afraid that he would rebuke me for my boldness.

It was a long story of a woman whose magic power lay hidden behind the marks upon her face.

It took many trials before I learned how to knot my sinew thread on the point of my finger.

Exercise 116C: Diagramming

(You didn't think you'd escape diagramming, did you?)

On your own paper, diagram every word of the following sentences from *North American Legends*, as retold by Zitkala-Sa.

If you need help, ask your instructor.

The fat ducks waddled in through a small opening, which was the only entrance way.

They were talking of a strange young man whom they spied while out upon a hunt for deer beyond the bluffs.

He who dares to open his eyes, forever red eyes shall have.

They poked their noses at him trying to know who he was.

As the badger stood there unrecognized, he saw that the bear had brought with him his whole family.

Then it was that the people, terror-stricken, ran screaming into their lodges.

When you see the black coals rise to the surface of the water, clap your hands and shout aloud, for soon after that sign I shall return to you with some tender meat.

WEEK 31

Filling Up the Corners

After the feast (more or less) came the Speech. Most of the company were, however, now in a tolerant mood, at that delightful stage which they called "filling up the corners." They were sipping their favourite drinks, and nibbling at their favourite dainties, and their fears were forgotten. They were prepared to listen to anything, and to cheer at every full stop.

—J. R. R. Tolkien, *The Fellowship of the Ring*

— LESSON 117 —

Interrogative Adverbs
Noun Clauses
Forming Questions
Affirmations and Negations
Double Negatives

An adverb describes a verb, an adjective, or another adverb.
Adverbs tell how, when, where, how often, and to what extent.

Relative adverbs introduce adjective clauses and refer back to a place, time, or reason in the independent clause.

where, when, why

I found a shop where I could buy cheese and chocolate.

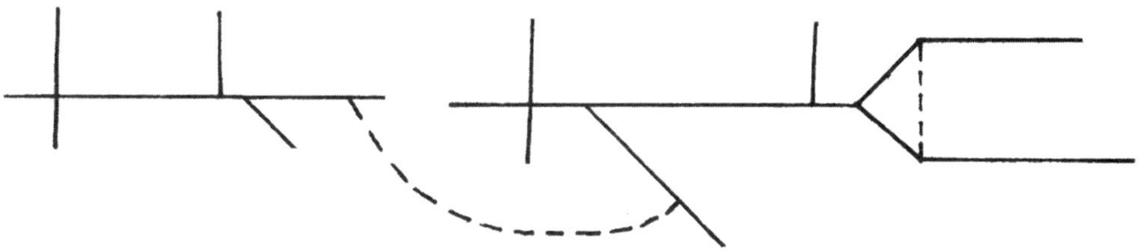

Where did you get the cheese and chocolate?

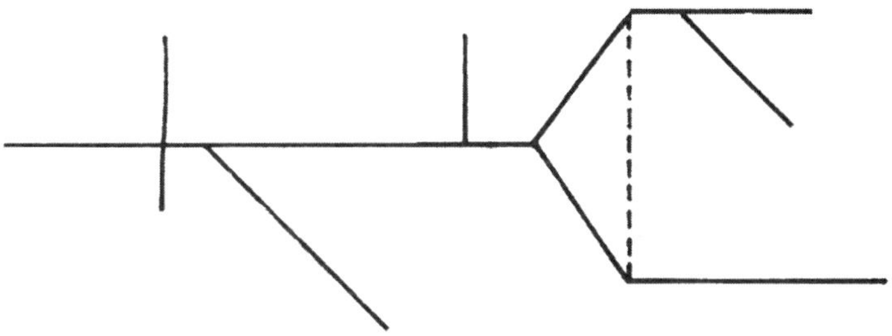

He asked me where I got the cheese and chocolate.

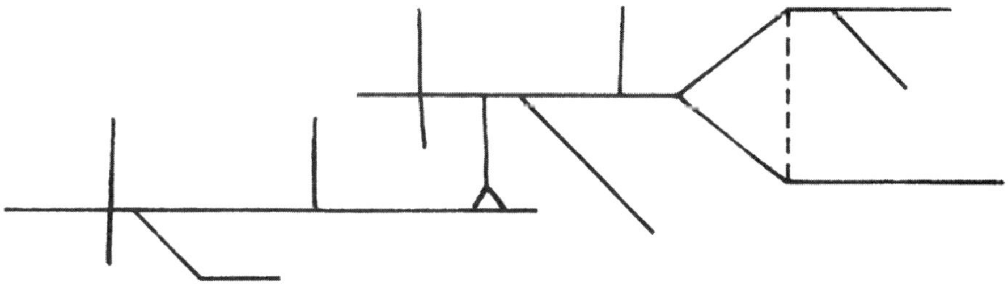

An interrogative adverb asks a question.

where, when, why, how

The interrogative adverbs can also introduce noun clauses.

I desired to know how this thing came to Gollum, and how long he had possessed it.

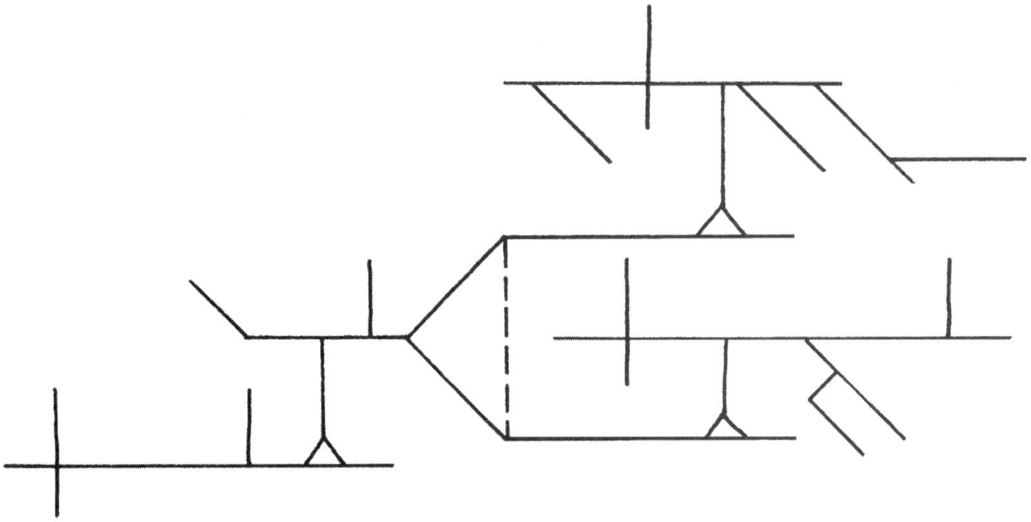

How do the Wise know that this ring is his?

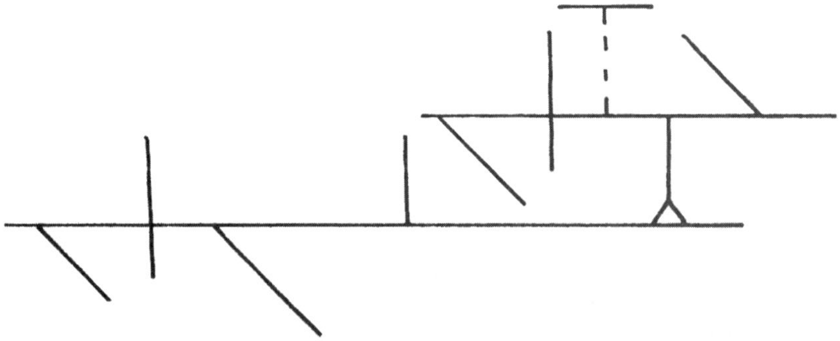

You are hungry.
Are you hungry?

You would like a big bowl of pozole.
Would you like a big bowl of pozole?

Use the helping verbs *do, does,* and *did* to form negatives, ask questions, and provide emphasis.

He fixed green pozole with sliced avocados.
Did he fix green pozole with sliced avocados?

Simple Present		**Simple Past**	
I do	we do	I did	we did
you do	you do	you did	you did
he, she it, does	they do	he, she it did	they did

They love to nibble on chalupas.

Do they love to nibble on chalupas?

Who is bringing the bread pudding with flaming brandy?

What kind of frosting are you using for the cake?

When will the mangos be ripe enough to make mango cake?

Which limes did you use in the lime pudding?

Whom have you invited to the party?

How many loaves of challah did you bake?

Whose presents are those?

An affirmation states what is true or what exists.
A negation states what is not true or does not exist.

Adverbs of affirmation
yes, surely, definitely, certainly, absolutely, very

Did he invite her in?
And he invited her in; yes, he did.

Were they merry?
Surely they were very merry.

Was the roast chicken ready?
The roast chicken was definitely ready to eat.

Were the mushrooms good?
The mushrooms were absolutely delicious.

Adverbs of negation	**Adjective of negation**
no, not, never	no

Did anyone go hungry?
No man, woman or child went hungry.

When did they stop feasting?
They did not stop feasting until well after sundown.

How much merriment was there?
Never was there so much merriment.

There is not no doubt.

I haven't heard no good of such folk.

I don't know nothing about jewels.

Do not use two adverbs or adjectives of negation together.

Exercise 117A: Identifying Adverbs, Interrogative and Demonstrative Pronouns and Adjectives, and Relatives

In the following sentences from Mort Rosenblum's *Chocolate: A Bittersweet Saga of Dark and Light*, follow these steps:

a) Label each bolded word as one of the following:

ADV for adverb

Draw an arrow from the adverb to the word modified.

If the adverb also introduces a clause, underline the clause.

PRO for pronoun

If the pronoun has an antecedent, label the antecedent as *ANT.* If the pronoun introduces a clause, underline the clause.

Label each pronoun as *S* for subject, *PN* for predicate nominative, *DO* for direct object, *IO* for indirect object, *OP* for object of the preposition, or *ADJ* (see below).

ADJ for adjective

Draw an arrow from the adjective to the word modified. If the adjective introduces a clause, underline the clause.

b) Label each underlined clause as *ADV-C* for adverb clause, *ADJ-C* for adjective clause, or *N-C* for noun clause.

c) Draw an arrow from each *ADV-C* and *ADJ-C* clause back to the word modified. Label each *N-C* noun clause as *S* for subject, *APP* for appositive, *PN* for predicate nominative, *DO* for direct object, *IO* for indirect object, or *OP* for object of the preposition.

The first is done for you. Notice that *whose* has two labels because it is both an adjective and a relative pronoun.

ANT PRO ADJ ADJ-C

She also brought her own Viennese chocolatier, **whose** specialty was a brew mixed with orchid powder, orange blossoms, and almond milk.

Marie-Antoinette, she of let-them-eat-cake fame, was yet another Austrian **who** came to France with chocolate in her baggage train.

From my first day on the chocolate trail, I was obsessed by **this** obvious and overriding question: **Who** does make the best chocolate?

This is **how** you heat water for chocolate.

I could see **why** marauding monkeys and bush rats could be a worse scourge to cacao growers than armed rebels.

This seemingly simple step is **what** marshals the molecules so the finished chocolate ends up creamy-smooth and shining.

By 2002, **when** the great chocolate tremor shook central Pennsylvania, Hershey had spent thirteen years as the largest candy-maker in the United States.

The Kiss, **which** dates back generations, is a major seller, as are Hershey's chocolate morsels, its baking chocolate, and **those** same cans of Hershey's Syrup **that** our grandparents used.

Together they introduced the aging, stately Hershey Chocolate Corp. to the cut-throat world of candy **that** Forrest Mars had created, **where** Willy Wonka is motivated by greed, rivalry, secrecy and paranoia.

This last step—the addition of sugary chocolate—is crucial for the right balance.

Someone is obviously enjoying all the Hershey bars and Kisses **that** after all these years continue to sell in the millions.

Why would you depend on someone else?

Mexico's army is great, Flores explained, because it has so many Oaxacan soldiers **whose** diet is corn and chocolate.

Exercise 117B: Forming Questions

On your own paper, rewrite the following statements as questions.

Use each of the three methods for forming questions (adding an interrogative pronoun, reversing the subject and helping verb, adding the helping verb *do, does*, or *did* in front of the subject and adjusting the tense of the main verb) at least once. You may change tenses, add or subtract words, or alter the statements in any other necessary ways, as long as the meaning remains the same.

These statements are all adapted from famous questions in books and movies. When you have transformed your statements into questions, compare them with the originals.

My super suit is somewhere.

Your king is this.

You are not entertained.

You judge me by my size.

Your damage is something.

The net amount of entropy of the universe can somehow be massively decreased.

A raven is like a writing desk.

We three shall meet again.

You're here to finish me off, sweetheart.

I am too late for Alexander's panic attack.

This corn is hand shucked.

Andy might get another dinosaur, a mean one.

Exercise 117C: Affirmations and Negations

On your own paper,

- Rewrite each of the following affirmative statements as a negation, using one adverb or adjective of negation. You may add or subtract words or change tenses as necessary.
- Rewrite each of the following negative statements as an affirmative, using at least one adverb of affirmation.
- Rewrite any double negation as an affirmative, also using at least one adverb of affirmation.

When you are finished, compare your answers with the original sentences, slightly adapted from *The Captain of the Polestar and Other Tales*, by Sir Arthur Conan Doyle (the author of the Sherlock Holmes stories—but these are all tales of adventure and seafaring!).

Talk to me more, please.

It wasn't a strange coincidence.

The night wasn't not dark.

I thought of it often before.

At last it occurred to him that by a daring and original experiment the question might never be decided.

There were many people for many miles in each direction.

The man's memory of his whole life before the fatal blow was not erased.

It was long before I discovered that her suspicions were not well founded.

Kick me under the table, Flannigan.

You will surely desert me.

—LESSON 118—

Diagramming Affirmations and Negations
Yet More Words That Can Be Multiple Parts of Speech
Comparisons Using *Than*
Comparisons Using *As*

Are you ready for your lesson?
Absolutely.
Do you remember the definition of a noun?
Definitely.
How sure are you?
Very.
Have you forgotten it?
No.
Will you ever forget it?
Never.

Affirmative and negative adverbs can also act as interjections.

Never
Absolutely

I can be **very** deaf when I need.

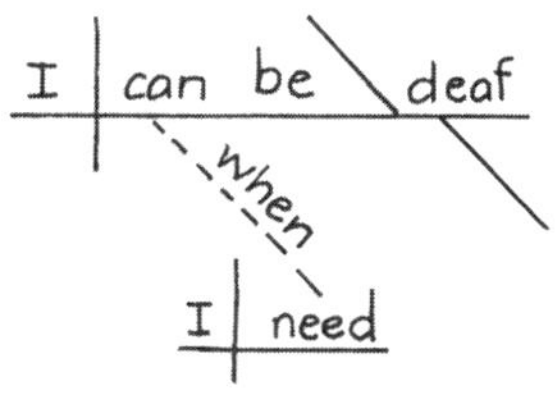

Yes, I will paint you, Juanico.

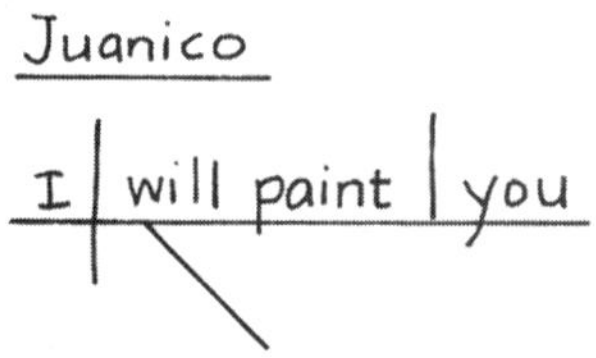

You will **never** be beaten again.

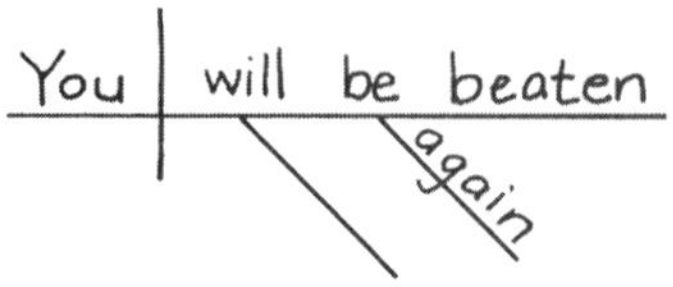

I am **no** longer a slave.

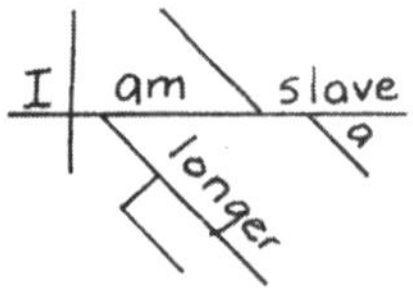

(From *I, Juan de Pareja* by Elizabeth Borton de Treviño)

Yes, I said.

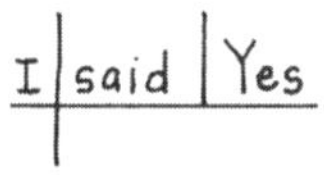

He's unbeatable and drops the dehuller with a fat Yes.

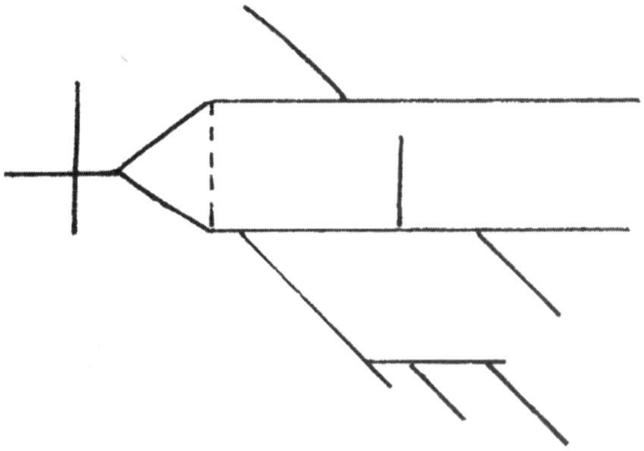

(From *Drown* by Junot Diaz)

Father might say no.

It has no shoestrings.

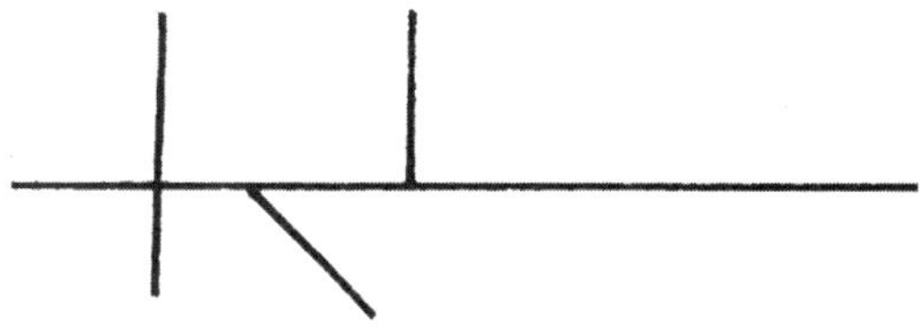

(From *The Dreamer* by Pam Muñoz Ryan)

QC: quasi-coordinator PREP: preposition ADV: adverb SC: subordinating conjunction

The stone was black and shiny, so you could see your reflection as well as the blooming trees and the clouds in the sky.
—From *Return to Sender* by Julia Alvarez

Mamadre nodded and smiled as she left the room.

As my partner, how do you think we should proceed?
—From *The Dreamer* by Pam Muñoz Ryan

When we arrived, nothing was as promised.
—From *Esperanza Rising* by Pam Muñoz Ryan

His affections became poems, as warm and supple as the wool of a well-loved sheep.
—From *The Dreamer* by Pam Muñoz Ryan

When *than* is used in a comparison and introduces a clause with understood elements, it is acting as a subordinating conjunction.

That wool is warmer than my wool.

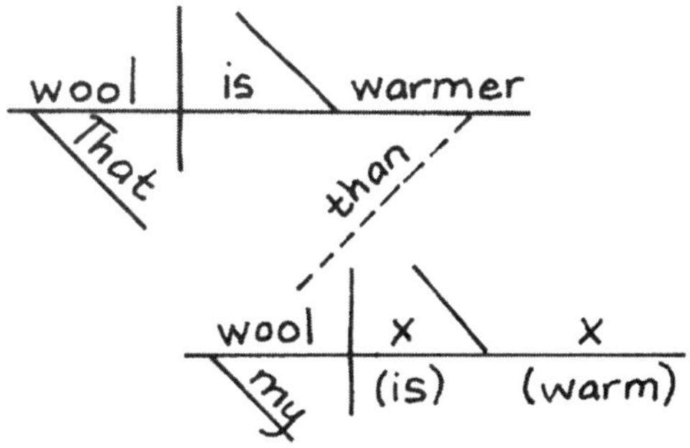

His affections became poems, as warm and supple as the wool of a well-loved sheep.
—From *The Dreamer* by Pam Muñoz Ryan

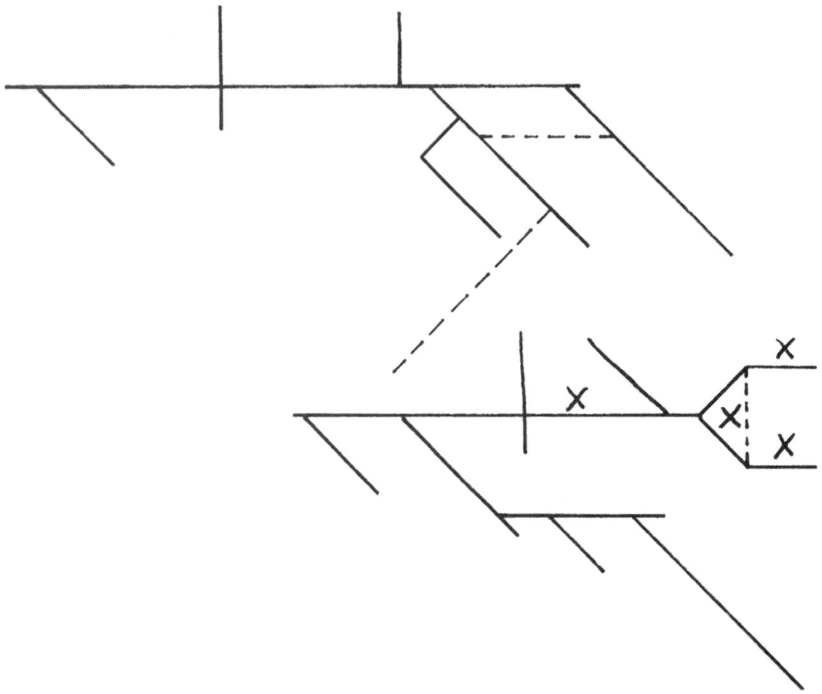

I did as he asked.

He had the same concerns as you have had.

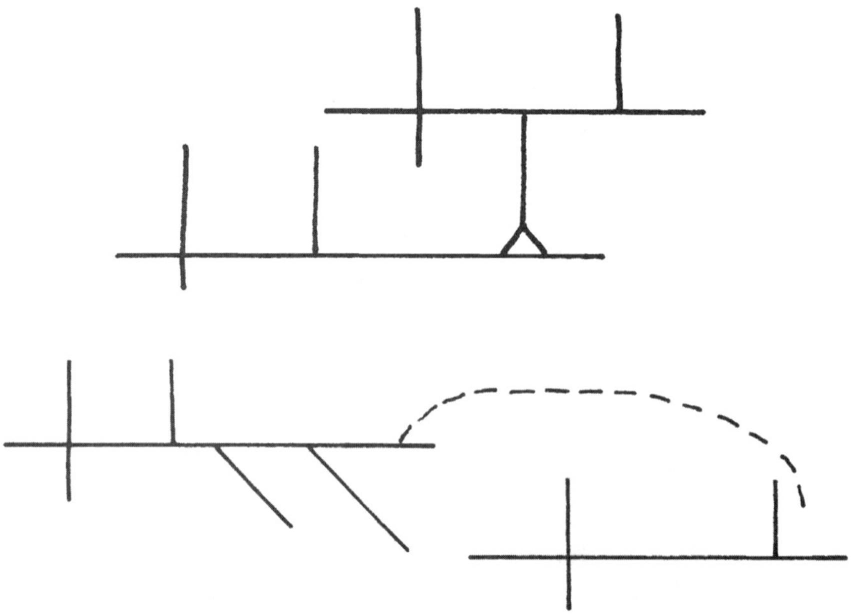

The farmer struggled with the same difficulties as you.

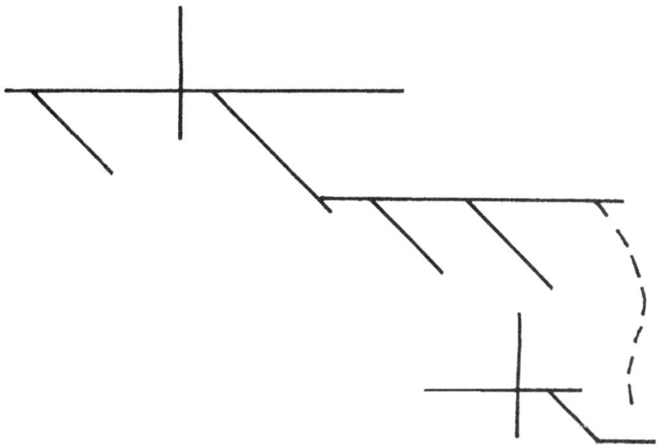

Exercise 118A: Identifying Parts of Speech

Label each of the bolded words in these sentences (from *Jewish Fairy Tales and Legends*, by Gertrude Landa) with one of the following abbreviations.

ADJ: adjective	ADV: adverb
ADV-N: adverb of negation	ADV-A: adverb of affirmation
ADV-R: relative adverb	SC: subordinating conjunction
PREP: preposition	RP: relative pronoun
DP: demonstrative pronoun	IP: indefinite pronoun
N: noun	P: plain ol' pronoun

Where a subordinating conjunction introduces a comparison clause with missing words, draw a caret and insert the missing words.

Scarcely a word was spoken **as** the king and his hunters made their way **back to** the land East of the Rising Sun.

"**No**, **no**, I know **not**," she repeated **again** and **again**, and **at length** the man departed.

With trembling hands the high priest placed it **before** his majesty.

Before King Hagag could recover **from** his surprise the youth ran **back to** the river and swam **across**.

Across the desolate plain and **through** the forest the chase continued.

Noting the direction of the sun, he bored a tiny hole in the wall, and a thin sunbeam gleamed **through**.

In their **midst** stood the princess, a dazzling vision, radiant **as** the dawn.

Hanina and his wife followed the giant frog to the woods **very early one** morning, and a comical figure it presented **as** it hobbled **along**.

There they spent **quite** an hour.

The king regarded the task of governing his subjects **as** a big nuisance.

Deal **with** affairs **as** you think best.

One of them, **indeed**, was **unduly** interested in him.

He endured agonies, **especially when** the friend invited Ben Maslia to dine **with** him, and Ben Maslia, **after** a few moments' hesitation, **firmly** declined.

He clapped his hands, and **immediately**, in **quite** startling fashion, a dozen servants stepped **from behind** the hangings **which** had hidden them and bowed **before** their master.

As well as the hunters could make **out, no** foot had **ever** trodden the region **before**.

Exercise 118B: Diagramming

On your own paper, diagram every word of the following sentences from *A Book of Giants: Tales of Very Tall Men of Myth, Legend, History, and Science*, by Henry Wysham Lanier. Ask your instructor for help if you need it.

Heave and strain as he might, Thor could only get one paw off the floor.

Nurse Elli was in fact old age—and never yet has man wrestled with her as have you.

So lofty were its walls and buildings that their heads bent back on their necks as they gazed up to the pinnacles of the towers.

Yes, the Giant was ready to do that, and he turned the six brothers into king's sons again, and their brides into king's daughters.

Yet amid this charming serenity Kronos could never forget the curse of his father Uranus whom he had overthrown, and the prophecy that he himself should in his turn be cast down by his own children.

—LESSON 119—

Idioms

I'm confused because I don't know what you are **driving at**.

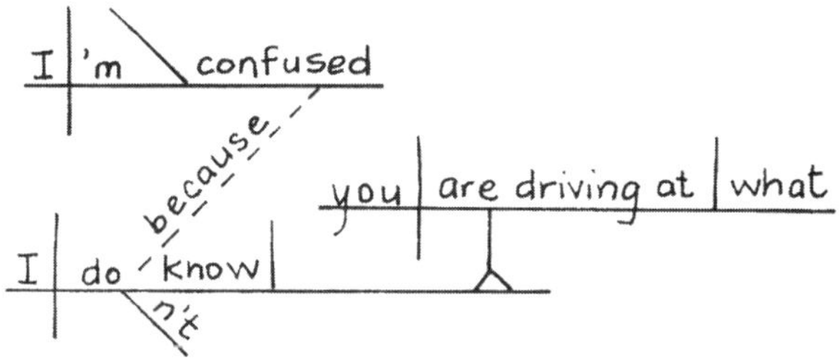

We did our best, but we failed, and now it is **back to the drawing board**.

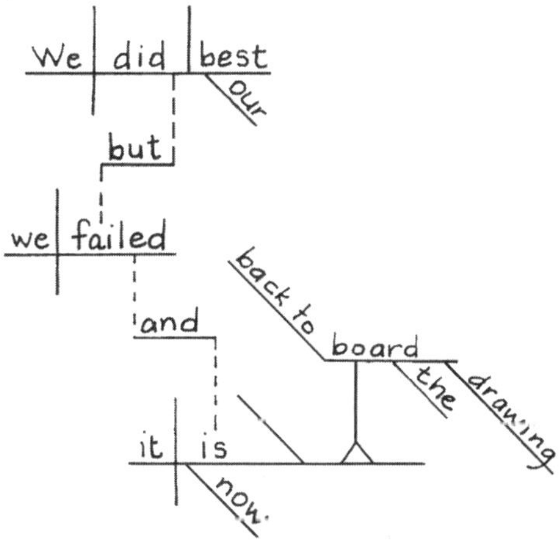

I have been burning the candle at both ends!

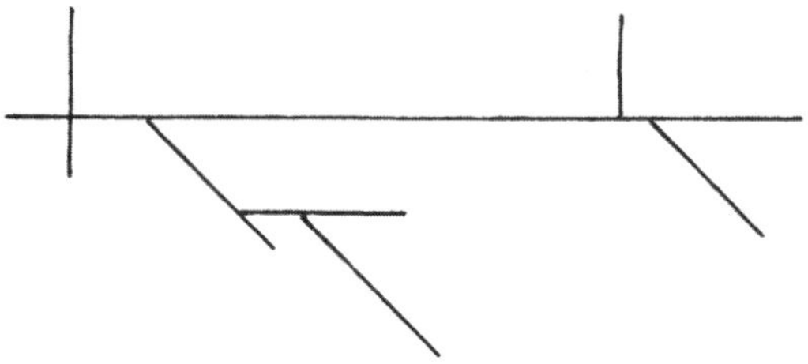

I have been overworking myself for many days!

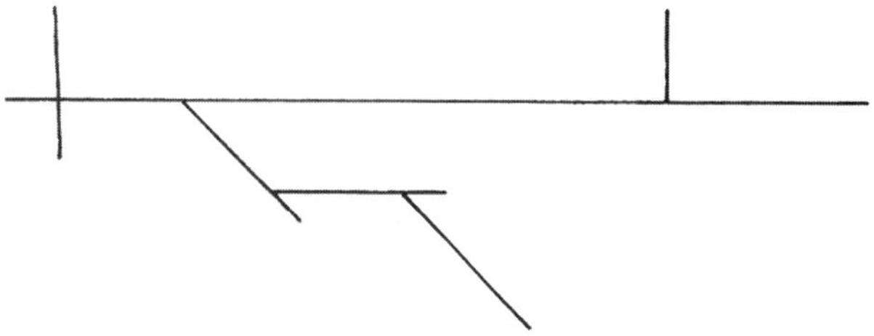

Alas, our Labor Day party plans are dead in the water.

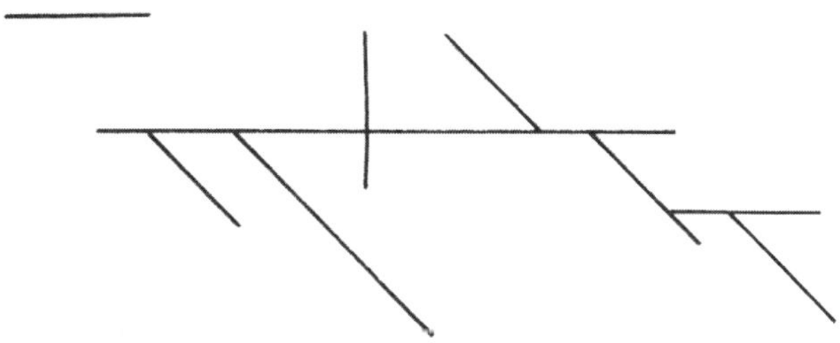

The little girl will be taken care of while her mother is sleeping.

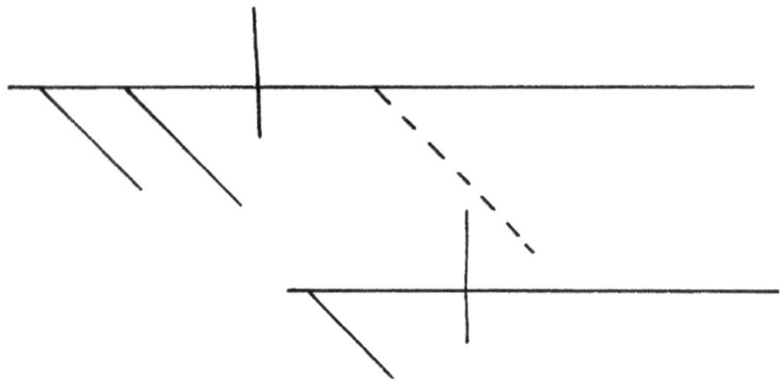

I'm all ears.

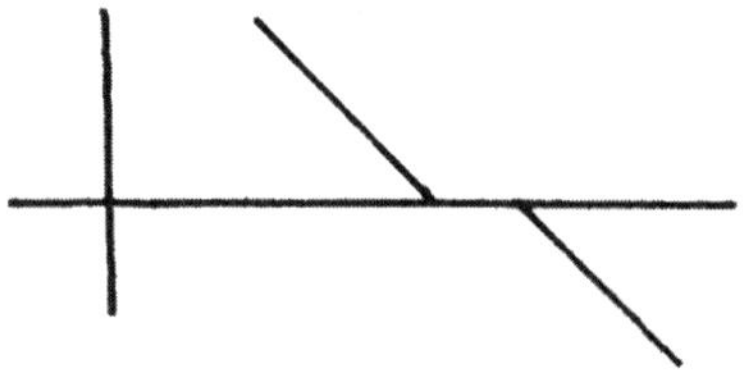

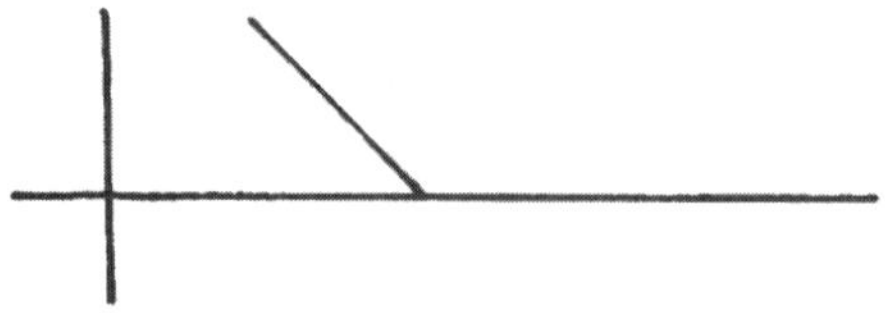

The following sentences are from *Pirates: The Complete History from 1300 BC to the Present Day*, by Angus Konstam.

By 1585, the rivalry between England and Spain was heating up.

Carleille's troops were sent ashore under cover of darkness.

The die was now cast.

They waged a low-key war that lasted well into the fourteenth century.

The Barbary beys had to make sure that reports of such attacks did not reach the ears of the sultan in Constantinople.

When the governor came aboard to pay his respects, he was kidnapped.

He was not pleased by the compliment, though he put up with it for the present.

As he stood beside the executioner's block he reputedly struck a deal—pardons would be granted to all of the crewmen whom he could walk past after his head was cut off.

Exercise 119A: Explaining Idioms

The following direct quotes are all by James Cameron, the film director of *Terminator*, *Titanic*, *Avatar*, and many other movies.

Mr. Cameron likes idioms! Circle each complete idiom. Write its meaning above it in your own words. (You can use more than one word—in fact, you may need several sentences!)

These are taken from the biography *The Futurist: The Life and Films of James Cameron*, by Rebecca Keegan.

"We have taken from nature without giving back, and the time to pay the piper is coming."

"I began to think that the message of the film might be better served by not letting the audience off the hook so easily."

"We decided not to tie it all up with a bow, but to suggest that the struggle was ongoing, and in fact might even be an unending one for us flawed creatures trying to come to terms with technology and our own violent demons."

"You roll up your sleeves and you get to work."

"I still need to bunker completely to get anything good written."

"It forces you to really have your narrative ducks in a row."

"It wasn't full stop, just leave Hollywood like J. D. Salinger or something."

"Stan and I clicked early on because we both respect the artist."

"There were a few bright lights amongst the younger art-department people, but for the most part, we despised them and they despised us."

Exercise 119B: Diagramming

On your own paper, diagram every word of the following sentences, taken from Charles Dickens's classic novel *The Old Curiosity Shop.*

When you are finished, tell your instructor what each idiom means! Several sentences have more than one idiom—and almost all of them can be diagrammed in more than one way. Do your best, and ask for help when you need it.

The old man and I will remain at daggers drawn to the end of our lives.

You mark me, sir?

Beyond that, I don't know him from Adam.

You shall not be permitted to fly in the face of your superiors in this exceedingly gross manner.

Nell felt as if her heart would break when she saw them meet.

Take my word for it, the feller that came back to work out that shilling will show himself one of these days in his true colours.

Exercise 119C: Finding Idioms

On your own paper, rewrite the following four sentences, replacing the bolded words in each with an idiom that means the same thing.

If you need help, ask your instructor.

I was just tired of being **the one who was unlike everyone else**.

You've worked very hard this year, but don't **stop trying because you've already worked hard**!

The hiker escaped from the mountain lion **but only just barely**.

When the fraud was discovered, the embezzler **confessed** his wrongdoings.

—LESSON 120—

Troublesome Sentences

Grammar is the art of speaking or writing a language correctly.
—William Greatheed Lewis, *A Grammar of the English Language* (1821)

Perfect grammar—persistent, continuous, sustained—is the fourth dimension, so to speak: many have sought it, but none has found it.
—Mark Twain, *Autobiography* (posthumous edition, 1925)

Grammar is to literary composition what a linch-pin is to a waggon. It is a poor pitiful thing in itself; it bears no part of the weight; communicates nothing to the force; adds not in the least to the celerity; but, still the waggon cannot very well and safely go on without it; she is constantly liable to reel and be compelled to stop, which, at the least, exposes the driver to be laughed at, and that, too, by those who are wholly unable to drive themselves.
—William Cobbett, *Grammar of the English Language* (1818)

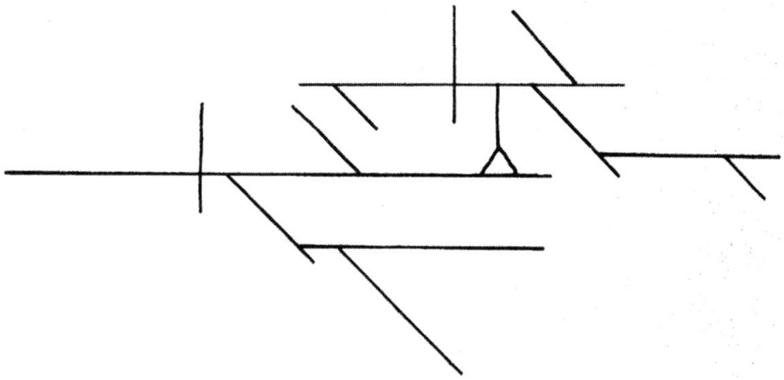

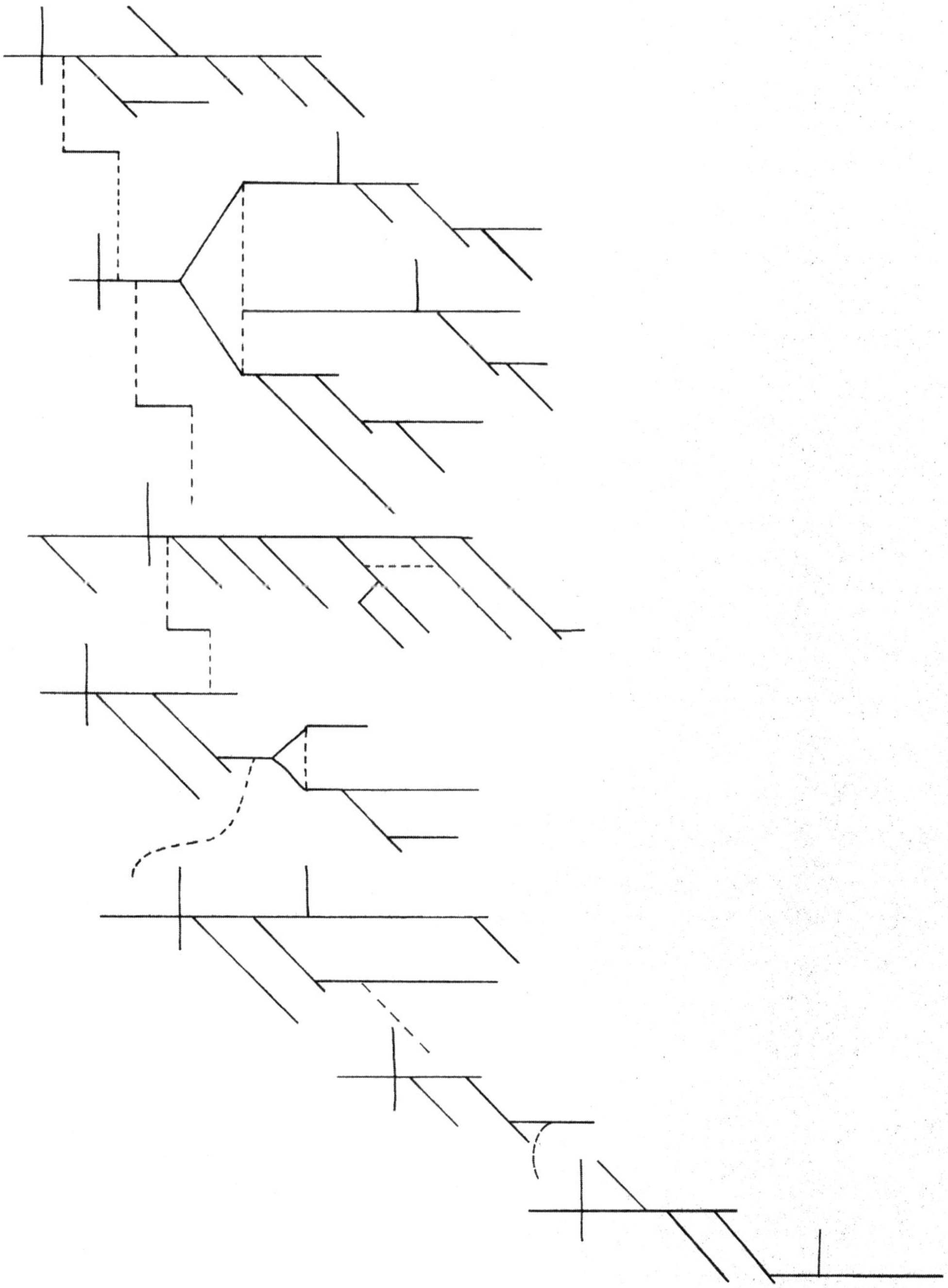

Exercise 120A: A Selection of Oddly Constructed Sentences

After your instructor discusses each sentence with you, diagram it on your own paper.

These sentences are taken from the novel *Passing*, by Nella Larsen. Larsen, who was born in Chicago in 1891, was the child of an Afro-Caribbean father and a Danish mother. Because of her African blood, she was considered to be black by early twentieth-century American culture, and so was unable to enter white-only areas or take part in white-only privileges as she was growing up. *Passing* is the story of an early twentieth-century woman who has African blood but, because of her light skin, has concealed the fact—and knows that if her husband and social circles find out that she is "black," she will lose everything.

She got out, and thanking him smilingly as well as in a more substantial manner for his kind helpfulness and understanding, went in through the Drayton's wide doors.

Did that woman, could that woman, somehow know that here before her very eyes on the roof of the Drayton sat a Negro?

Suppose the woman did know or suspect her race.

It was the idea of being ejected from any place, even in the polite and tactful way in which the Drayton would probably do it, that disturbed her.

It was as if, in a house long dim, a match had been struck, showing ghastly shapes where had been only blurred shadows.

It was that very thing which, in a way, finally decided me not to go out and see you one last time before I went away to stay.

WEEK 32

—REVIEW 10—

Weeks 29-31

Topics
Hortative Verbs
Ambitransitive Verbs
Infinitive Phrases as Objects
Infinitive Phrases With Understood "To"
Principal Parts of Irregular Verbs
Noun Clauses as Appositives
Which/That in Restrictive and Non-Restrictive Clauses
Formal Conditionals
Words Acting as Multiple Parts of Speech
Affirmations and Negations
Idioms

Review 10A: The Missing Words Game

Fill in each blank below with the exact form described—but choose your own words!

Show your answers to your instructor, who will insert them into the matching blanks in the short essay in the Answer Key.

Your instructor will then show you the original essay—and your version.

Here's the only information I'm going to give you before you fill in your forms—everything in this review has to do with *food* and *farming*.

modal active simple passive verb (third-person singular) ____________________

adjective ____________________

indicative past perfect passive verb (third-person singular) ____________________

three-word prepositional phrase ____________________

comparative form of an adjective ____________________

indicative active simple past verb (third-person singular) ____________________

adverb ____________________

adjective ____________________

compound concrete noun ______________________
adverb ______________________
present active participle ______________________
adjective that can also be an adverb ______________________
concrete noun ______________________
adjective that can also be a noun ______________________
past active participle ______________________
adjective ______________________
subordinating conjunction ______________________
adverb ______________________
adjective ______________________
subordinating adverb ______________________
indicative simple past passive verb plus adverb (third-person singular) ______________
adverb of time ______________________
active infinitive verb ______________________
concrete noun ______________________
adverb of place ______________________
demonstrative adjective ______________________
active present imperative verb ______________________
compound adjective ______________________
plural concrete noun ______________________
proper adjective ______________________
adjective ______________________
indicative present perfect active verb (third-person plural) ______________________
compound adjective that includes a past participle ______________________
modal simple present active verb (third-person singular) ______________________
adverb of negation ______________________
adverb ______________________
adverbial noun ______________________
indicative perfect present active verb (first-person plural) ______________________

indicative simple future state-of-being verb ____________________

concrete plural noun ____________________

conjunction ____________________

adjective of negation ____________________

indicative simple past active verb (third-person singular) ____________________

predicate adjective ____________________

adverb of affirmation ____________________

adverb of affirmation ____________________

indicative perfect present active verb (first-person plural) ____________________

abstract singular noun ____________________

subordinating conjunction ____________________

possessive pronoun ____________________

possessive plural noun acting as an adjective ____________________

demonstrative adjective ____________________

adverb of time ____________________

adverb of negation ____________________

adjective ____________________

indicative simple present passive verb (third-person singular) ____________________

adjective ____________________

comparison using as...as... ____________________

demonstrative pronoun ____________________

concrete singular noun ____________________

adjective ____________________

adverb ____________________

indicative simple future active verb (first-person singular) ____________________

adverb ____________________

present active participle ____________________

adjective that can also be a noun ____________________

hyphenated compound adjective ____________________

past active participle ____________________

indicative simple future passive verb (second-person singular) ____________

singular abstract noun ____________

active infinitive ____________

color adjective ____________

concrete plural noun ____________

Review 10B: Identifying Infinitive Phrases, Noun Clauses, and Modifying Clauses

In the following sets of sentences, follow these four steps:

a) Identify every set of underlined words as *INF* for infinitive phrase, *PREP* for prepositional phrase, or *CL* for clause.

b) Label each phrase or clause as *ADV* for adverb, *ADJ* for adjective, or *N* for noun.

c) For adjective and adverb phrases and clauses, draw an arrow from the label to the word modified.

d) For noun phrases and clauses, add the appropriate part of the sentence label: *S* for subject, *DO* for direct object, *IO* for indirect object, *OP* for object of a preposition, *PN* for predicate nominative, *APP* for appositive.

Notice: Some sets of words are within other sets of words, so you'll see some double underlining! If you see double underlining, be sure to follow the instructions for both sets of underlined words.

The first sentence is done for you.

Another sentence has an unexpected twist—look out for it!

INF N S

CL N DO

To say Hamilton Brothers is old school would be a serious understatement.

Note: The entire infinitive phrase is the subject. Within that phrase, the clause (introduced by an understood "that") is the direct object of the infinitive verb *To say*.

Our farm is proof that small-scale, sustainable farming is a viable alternative.

We wanted to raise our own food, to have animals and a big garden, but we didn't really know what we were doing.

The salient point when it comes to coop construction is that varmints will find and exploit any weakness, no matter how small.

The New Farm: Our Ten Years on the Front Lines of the Good Food Revolution, by Brent Preston

To have the two of them there, at opposite corners of the table, with their long endurance in their faces, and their present affection and pleasure, was a blessing of another kind.

Perhaps the most urgent task for all of us who want to eat well and to keep eating is to encourage farm-raised children to take up farming.

The goal of intelligent farmers, who desire the long-term success of farming, is to adapt their work to their places.

Bringing It to the Table: On Farming and Food, by Wendell Berry

We have the right to convenient food that is healthy. We want healthy options in corner stores while empowering the community to make better food choices.

To acknowledge that we as humans are not the most powerful force in nature and to act accordingly is not always roses and sunshine.

In Haiti the farmers say, "*Sonje lapli ki level mayi ou,*" which means, "Remember the rain that made your corn grow."

Farming While Black: Soul Fire Farm's Practical Guide to Liberation on the Land, by Leah Penniman

Until a few years ago I wouldn't say I was a particularly enlightened consumer.

I knew potato chips contained an artery-clogging dose of partially hydrogenated oil and that eating steak every day would give me a heart attack.

I was utterly disconnected from who made my food and how it ended up in my grocery store.

Local: The New Face of Food and Farming in America, by Douglas Gayeton

Review 10C: Parsing

Parse every bolded verb in the following sentences.

Provide the following information:

Person: First, second, or third
Number: Sing. or pl.
Tense: Simple past, present, or future; perfect past, present, or future; progressive past, present, or future; or progressive perfect present
Voice: Active, passive, or state-of-being
Mood: Indicative, subjunctive, imperative, hortatory, or modal
If the verb is also emphatic, add this label to the mood.

The first is done for you.

3rd sing., simple past, active, indicative

Gillian **planted** another tray of broccoli that afternoon to replace the plants that **had been lost**.

Consumers **would feel** good about themselves because they **would be helping** increase access to organic food, as well as supporting local farmers.

I **do**n't **know** if I **have** ever **seen** an animal run so fast.

They **would delight** in running back to the house to tell us what kind of animals we **had caught** that day.

The New Farm: Our Ten Years on the Front Lines of the Good Food Revolution, by Brent Preston

Even the levee, only a man-made mound, **will be breached** one day so the river **can reclaim** what **was** once naturally hers.

The inside walls **were planked** with pine 1x8s.

A life-long bachelor, Howard the Dairyman, as I called him, **worked** December 25 as if it **were** June 25.

Uncle Honey **must have had** a hand in that, too.

The Land of Milk and Uncle Honey: Memories from the Farm of My Youth, by Alan Guebert with Mary Grace Foxwell

It is fork-tender and **has been transformed** from the tough cut that it was this morning to an easily enjoyed piece of beef later this afternoon.

Each week the cucumber plants are a bit larger, the winter squash vines **are beginning** to hit the edges of the raised beds, but everything is far from robust.

If we **were** to serve a squash soup, then the squash **should be** visible as a piece of squash.

On this winter day it is hard to believe that the eventual milk of this young calf Alice **will be used** in the dinner.

The yeast **has** slowly **been expanding** and growing, puffing out the rolls.

If they **had dried** too much on the surface and crusted over, the rising **would have been hindered**.

Growing a Feast: The Chronicle of a Farm-to-Table Meal, by Kurt Timmermeister

Those carefully stacked pyramids of fruit in the produce aisle **have been placed** there just for you. If your allegiance **is** elsewhere, if the miles your food travels **matter** and you'**d prefer** instead to buy your food from a local farmer, the entire distribution apparatus **will change**.

Local: The New Face of Food and Farming in America, by Douglas Gayeton

He's certainly well on his way, **should** he **choose** to put down the whisk and pick up a pen.

Most of our waiters **have been working** with us for at least five years, many of them for ten, and some for fifteen.

Away from the Kitchen: Untold Stories, Private Menus, Guarded Recipes, and Insider Tips, by Dawn Blume Hawkes

Review 10D: *Which* and *That* Clauses

In the following sentences, underline each clause introduced by *which* or *that.* If *that* is understood, use a caret to insert it. If a *which* or *that* clause falls within another clause, underline the entire larger clause once, and the clause-within-a-clause a second time.

- Label each clause as *ADJ* for adjective, *ADV* for adverb, or *N* for noun.
- For adjective and adverb clauses, draw an arrow back to the word modified.
- For noun clauses, label the part of the sentence that the clause fulfills (*S, PN, DO, IO, APP*).
- Finally, label each adjective clause as *R* for restrictive or *NON-R* for nonrestrictive.

The first sentence is done for you.

The sheep is one of the most efficient machines for converting sun and water and nutrients

ADJ NON-R

into protein and energy, which we use in the form of meat, milk, leather, and wool.

That four ewes all decide to give birth at the same time seems like a really bad idea.

Sometimes it's a lamb that has been born overnight and is too weak or cold to stand up and nurse.

She knows which lambs are hers and she takes good care of them.

Sheepish: Two Women, Fifty Sheep, and Enough Wool to Save the Planet, by Catherine Friend

This struggle of animal against nature was a yearly childhood event, one that connected me, even as a young boy, to the mysterious natural world around me.

Local: The New Face of Food and Farming in America, by Douglas Gayeton

Urban farming is a new term for growing a kitchen garden (or, to use the French term, *potager*), which has been practiced since the advent of cities.

Your Farm in the City: An Urban Dweller's Guide to Growing Food and Raising Animals, by Lisa Taylor and the Gardeners of Seattle Tilth

I had that feeling I sometimes get when I'm up by myself in the early morning, that I'm lucky to be in this place, at this moment.

We even tried something called forage radishes, which grew enormous tubers that burrowed six feet down into the subsoil, bringing copious nutrients up to the surface.

Rather than being grumpy, they were grateful that we had come out in such terrible weather.

I had built a sturdy door that locked with heavy slide bolts, leaving a gap at the bottom of less than a quarter of an inch. Nothing could get in there that didn't have opposable thumbs.

The New Farm: Our Ten Years on the Front Lines of the Good Food Revolution, by Brent Preston

I cut a cedar tree that filled a corner of the parlor, reached to the ceiling, and gave its fragrance to the whole room.

Bringing It to the Table: On Farming and Food, by Wendell Berry

I thought this place would be mine for years, that I could live here until I was ready to move on to the next big thing and plan my life around that.

As I clicked through, I saw that the man had litters available a few times a year.

Inside it was an old dog crate, which I'd lined with fresh straw.

Barnheart: The Incurable Longing for a Farm of One's Own, by Jenna Woginrich

The bulky stockpot straddles two of the burners on the gas range, which I turn up to high, the flames hitting two sides of the heavy-bottomed stainless steel pot.

By six in the morning I was relieved that I could get out of bed and head over to the kitchen to begin the day's work.

The goal is a thick, almost sticky paste that, once cooled, will set into a jelly—rigid, and with the ability to be cut.

Growing a Feast: The Chronicle of a Farm-to-Table Meal, by Kurt Timmermeister

Review 10E: Words Acting as Multiple Parts of Speech

In each set of sentences below, underline the repeated word. Label each occurrence as *N* for noun, *V* for verb, *PRO* for pronoun, *ADV* for adverb, *ADJ* for adjective, *PREP* for preposition, *CC* for coordinating conjunction, or *SC* for subordinating conjunction.

Do not mark repeated articles or common pronouns such as *it*—all of the words you're looking for are 4 letters or longer!

Besides, the selling season was pretty nearly over.

When the grass had all been once mowed over, we resorted to the clover.

Long before I had gone over it once, the portion first mowed was up high enough to be mowed again.

This is more than one-third of the quantity estimated as above.

I cut off the canes six inches above the root.

That moisture exists not only in the skies above, but in the earth beneath our plants.

I prefer removing the old wood in the autumn, for the reasons above given.

The green and fertile tracts that lay beyond were unseen.

Over the run of four years there has been no profit beyond the manure.

Ten Acres Enough: How a Very Small Farm May Be Made to Keep a Very Large Family, by Edmund Morris

Still others, such as lettuce and onions, produce seeds after they flower.

If the seedlings are still too young to go out into the garden, you will need to throw these in the garbage and start over.

Start with good soil and keep improving on it.

It can be more economical, especially if you have a large garden, and it gives you a head start.

The Everything Grow Your Own Vegetables Book: Your Complete Guide to Planting, Tending, and Harvesting Vegetables, by Catherine Abbott

The barns protect the babies from the snow, wind, and ice, and can be warm inside from all the body heat that the sheep give off.

Mary caught the lamb and tucked it inside her jacket to warm it up.

I like patting their heads and scratching behind their ears.

Do you know what a Blue-faced Leicester looks like?

Merinos are so wrinkly they look like huge Shar Pei dogs with a seven-inch-long fleece.

Sheepish: Two Women, Fifty Sheep, and Enough Wool to Save the Planet, by Catherine Friend

The juice ran down my face and chin.

Here was Eduardo, the representation of two centuries' worth of free-ranging fowl, face to face with the insult.

Others argue that Haber's science has saturated the planet with excess nitrogen, creating a profound chemical dependence in agriculture and, in the process, precipitating many of the most vexing environmental problems we face today.

The Third Plate: Field Notes on the Future of Food, by Dan Barber

Humans are good at making our dreams manifest and we do, historically speaking, get what we wish for.

We had all shared this wish, in some way or another: that it wouldn't rain on our day off.

Animal, Vegetable, Miracle: A Year of Food Life, by Barbara Kingsolver

Review 10F: Idioms

Circle each idiom in the following sentences. Above each one, write its meaning within the sentence. The first is done for you.

carefully examined

These farmers paid close attention to things like germination percentages, and they were especially vigilant about disease, weeds, and any contamination possibilities.

You don't wear the high ideals of sustainability on your sleeve—you don't gloat about saving old, forgotten seeds of lettuce—and then serve a plate of bluefin.

The Third Plate: Field Notes on the Future of Food, by Dan Barber

With farming in my blood, I have traveled back and forth across the country for the past 17 years, helping people create the outdoor spaces of their dreams.

Many of us (me included) have been feeling a pull toward becoming more self-sufficient in sourcing our own food and are looking at how we can use our own spaces to grow that food.

Whatever the reason, if you're keen to jump on board, my advice can help you ease into this way of life as smoothly as possible.

Here is my rule of thumb for what works best.

Vegetables, Chickens & Bees: An Honest Guide to Growing Your Own Food Anywhere, by Carson Arthur

What are the just deserts for a species too selfish or preoccupied to hope for rain when the land outside is dying?

Returning now would allow my kids more than just a hit-and-run, holiday acquaintance with grandparents and cousins.

Tucson had opened my eyes to the world and given me a writing career, legions of friends, and a taste for the sensory extravagance of red hot chiles and five-alarm sunsets.

Animal, Vegetable, Miracle: A Year of Food Life, by Barbara Kingsolver

Review 10G: Ambitransitive Verbs

In the following sentences, underline each action verb that acts as a predicate. Mark each of these verbs as *T* for transitive or *IT* for intransitive. For transitive verbs, draw an arrow from the label *T* to the word that receives the action of the verb.

The first is done for you.

Goats have a curiosity that is often misunderstood.

They eat a little here and a little there, acquiring a variety of plants to meet their dietary needs.

Bring goats into your life, and you will quickly learn many lessons both about goats and yourself.

Learn by assisting your goat mentor with a few births before tackling this on your own.

The Dairy Goat Handbook: For Backyard, Homestead, and Small Farm, by Ann Starbard

When I grew up and moved away from the apple trees and into the city, growing things stayed with me.

We ate what we grew and put away for the winter so that we'd have our own supply all year long.

Hanging baskets can be moved and rotated if one side of the plant is getting all the sunlight.

Vegetables, Chickens & Bees: An Honest Guide to Growing Your Own Food Anywhere, by Carson Arthur

But you could argue it really began a few years earlier, when my brother David and I began to notice the forest encroaching on Blue Hill's pastureland.

It was two decades after my grandmother Ann had passed away.

Laws were passed to protect the grazing areas.

They are large enough to allow smaller tuna, the ones that haven't reached maturity, to escape and forge on to the Mediterranean, where they continue the cycle.

As he turned to walk back to his car, he stopped and reached into his pocket for his cell phone.

It went on so long that it stopped conversations in the dining room.

He turned over another infected leaf, and then another.

The Third Plate: Field Notes on the Future of Food, by Dan Barber

The work of adaptation must go on because the world changes; our places change and we change; we change our places and our places change us.

And his words fell upon the table like a blessing.

Unlike cow manure, which is heavy and chunky, horse manure is light and breaks up well coming out of the spreader.

Reading a few lines at random will often do the trick, break the knot.

Wendell Berry, Bringing It to the Table: On Farming and Food

Review 10H: Hunt and Find

In the following essay, find, underline, and label each of the following:

Infinitive phrase acting as a noun	Noun clause in apposition
Noun clause acting as a predicate nominative	Adverbial noun
Infinitive phrase acting as an adjective	Indirect object
Infinitive phrase acting as an adverb	Clause with an understood *that*
To as a preposition	Comparison
Hortative verb	Participle or participle phrase acting as a noun
That acting as a demonstrative pronoun	Compound subordinating conjunction
Restrictive clause introduced by *which*	*Which* acting as a demonstrative pronoun
Nonrestrictive clause introduced by *which*	Noun clause acting as a direct object

A couple of years ago, when we started growing cut flowers from seed inside, we decided to try to grow our own tomatoes from seed. Not only did this give us a greater selection of tomato varieties from which to choose, but it also allowed us to control exactly what contributed to our seedling's growth… Now we grow all of our own starts and take the extras to the farmer's market.

The Joy of Hobby Farming: Grow Food, Raise Animals, and Enjoy a Sustainable Life, by Michael Levatino and Audrey Levatino

Iowa leads the United States in pork production, and for many years raising hogs has been one of the main ways Iowa's farmers have sought to do something more profitable with their grain than selling it to the local elevator as a raw commodity.

The country is home, we fantasize, our real home, our natural home. It is what we go back to, and it is supposed to be still there when we return, even if, as the historian Bill Malone has observed, we know it really isn't.

Farming for Us All: Practical Agriculture and the Cultivation of Sustainability, by Michael Mayerfeld Bell

The feeling that it is not quite respectable to go into debt has grown out of the old habit of borrowing to pay living expenses. That was regarded, perhaps rightly, as a sign of incompetency… But to borrow for a genuinely productive purpose, for a purpose which will bring you in more than enough to pay off your debt, principal and interest, is a profitable enterprise.

Farm Knowledge: A Complete Manual of Successful Farming, ed. by Edward Loomis Davenport Seymour

Partially wilted cherry leaves produce cyanide, which can cause breathing difficulty, spasms,

coma, and death in humans and livestock.

Let us combine hunting with farming for our world to be better.

Farming While Black: Soul Fire Farm's Practical Guide to Liberation on the Land, by Leah Penniman

Review 10I: Conditionals and Formal Conditionals

In each of the following conditional sentences, parse the underlined verbs, giving tense, voice (*active, passive,* or *state-of-being*), and mood. Then, classify the sentences as first, second, or third conditional by placing a *1, 2,* or *3* in the blank at the end.

The first verb is parsed for you.

If your llama is foaming at the mouth, it's overheating and you should take steps to cool it off, including running fans on it and shearing it immediately. ________

The Joy of Hobby Farming: Grow Food, Raise Animals, and Enjoy a Sustainable Life, by Michael Levatino and Audrey Levatino

I suspected that if we'd met at a different time in our lives we would have run as fast as possible away from each other. ________

The Dirty Life: A Memoir of Farming, Food, and and Love, by Kristin Kimball

If we mean to reclaim it, asparagus seems like a place to start. ________

If the spears are allowed to proceed beyond their first exploratory six inches, they'll green out and grow tall and feathery like the houseplant known as asparagus fern, which is the next of kin. ________

If the Europeans could make a big deal of its arrival, we could too: we were waiting for asparagus. ________

For most of us, if we see asparagus in any month far removed from April,

we're looking at some hard traveling. ________

Animal, Vegetable, Miracle: A Year of Food Life, by Barbara Kingsolver

Land is the only real wealth in this country, and if we don't have any of it,

we'll be out of the picture. ________

Farming While Black: Soul Fire Farm's Practical Guide to Liberation on the Land, by Leah Penniman

If it had only been a matter of moving myself and the dogs, it wouldn't even be cause to blink. ________

Barnheart: The Incurable Longing for a Farm of One's Own, by Jenna Woginrich

If a chicken's coop is too small, the chicken will be pecked and harassed by its coop-mates. ________

The New Farm: Our Ten Years on the Front Lines of the Good Food Revolution, by Brent Preston

Thus, if we choose, we may sandwich in the poetry with the prose of life. ________

Should the milker be too impetuous; should he swear, speak loud and sharp, scold

or kick, or otherwise abuse or frighten the cow, she will probably prove refractory

as a mule, and may give the uncouth and unfeeling milker the benefit of her heels,—

a very pertinent reward, to which he, the uncouth milker, is justly entitled. ________

Ten Acres Enough: How a Very Small Farm May Be Made to Keep a Very Large Family, by Edmund Morris

So even if we wanted to go back to hunting and gathering wild species, it cannot be an option: There are far too many of us and not nearly enough of them. ________

The Omnivore's Dilemma: A Natural History of Four Meals, by Michael Pollan (sentence slightly adapted)

Review 10J: Affirmations and Negations

The following sentences all contain adverbs of affirmation and negation. Circle each one, and label them as *AFF* or *NEG*.

Then, choose three sentences and rewrite them on your own paper, turning affirmatives into negatives and vice versa. Show your sentences to your instructor.

Farmers are not us even as they are us.

Well, I don't put on any more spray, or anything like that, than I feel I absolutely have to.

Farming for Us All: Practical Agriculture and the Cultivation of Sustainability, by Michael Mayerfeld Bell

I never set out to become a gardener; it was on my list of skills to learn because growing my own food was important to me.

I told her I absolutely wanted them but I needed to get permission from my landlady first and set up a shed and pen for them.

For some, this is surely the only cure.

The animals were not concerned.

Barnheart: The Incurable Longing for a Farm of One's Own, by Jenna Woginrich

It wasn't supposed to be nearly this big, or this remote. And it was definitely not supposed to be swampy.

I had never in my life been so dirty.

There is no better lesson in commitment than the cow. Her udder knows no exceptions or excuses.

I'd forgotten how very clean my mother's world is until we walked in with those boxes, which were smudged with field dirt, a few limp leaves clinging to their bottoms.

The Dirty Life: A Memoir of Farming, Food, and Love, by Kristin Kimball

The fungi surely have a syntax of their own, but we don't know all its rules, especially the ones that govern the creation of a mushroom, which can take three years or thirty, depending.

The Omnivore's Dilemma: A Natural History of Four Meals, by Michael Pollan

Review 10K: Diagramming

On your own paper, diagram every word of the following sentences.

Greens (spinach, lettuce, kale, etc.), cucumbers, and squash also germinate and grow well when direct seeded.

The Joy of Hobby Farming: Grow Food, Raise Animals, and Enjoy a Sustainable Life, by Michael Levatino and Audrey Levatino

Eighty dollars an acre, they told me, was the current average price in the county, with some land fetching up to double that in recent months.

Farming for Us All: Practical Agriculture and the Cultivation of Sustainability, by Michael Mayerfeld Bell

The small family farm is one of the last places—they are getting rarer every day—where men and women (and girls and boys, too) can answer that call to be an artist, to learn to give love to the work of their hands.

Bringing It to the Table: On Farming and Food, by Wendell Berry

The more questions this new knowledge forces us to ask, the more we start understanding that every purchase we make is a vote to support one system over another.

Local: The New Face of Food and Farming in America, by Douglas Gayeton

We had been living on the farm for almost a year, and I was suddenly struck by the wondrous realization that we actually owned this place, that all this land was ours—a realization that struck me on a regular basis back then, and sometimes still does.

The New Farm: Our Ten Years on the Front Lines of the Good Food Revolution, by Brent Preston

Review 10L: Explaining Sentences

Tell your instructor every possible piece of grammatical information about the following sentences. Follow these steps:

a) Underline each clause. Describe the identity and function of each clause and give any other useful information (introductory word, relationship to the rest of the sentence, etc.)

b) Circle each phrase. Describe the identity and function of each phrase and give any other useful information.

c) Parse all verbs acting as predicates.

d) Describe the identity and function of each individual remaining word.

If you need help, ask your instructor.

I retreated to the house, not sure what I should do and completely mystified as to what had happened.

The New Farm: Our Ten Years on the Front Lines of the Good Food Revolution, by Brent Preston

Feeling the heartbeat of a warm young animal as he sits in your lap, stroking his head, and giggling as his tail tickles your legs...it was like living in a storybook.

Barnheart: The Incurable Longing for a Farm of One's Own, by Jenna Woginrich

As we walked, I fell into a dark mood, which I tried to blame on the weather and the fact that I hadn't yet had any coffee, but the truth was I'd gotten my hopes up, and the farm, under the filtered morning light, was disappointing.

The Dirty Life: A Memoir of Farming, Food, and Love, by Kristin Kimball

WEEK 33

Mechanics

—LESSON 121—

Capitalization Review
Additional Capitalization Rules
Formal and Informal Letter Format
Ending Punctuation

what an amazing place london was to me when i saw it in the distance and how i believed all the adventures of all my favourite heroes to be constantly enacting and re-enacting there and how i vaguely made it out in my own mind to be fuller of wonders and wickedness than all the cities of the earth i need not stop here to relate

What an amazing place London was to me when I saw it in the distance, and how I believed all the adventures of all my favourite heroes to be constantly enacting and re-enacting there, and how I vaguely made it out in my own mind to be fuller of wonders and wickedness than all the cities of the earth, I need not stop here to relate.
—Charles Dickens, *David Copperfield*

A proper noun is the special, particular name for a person, place, thing, or idea. Proper nouns always begin with capital letters.

1. Capitalize the proper names of persons, places, things, and animals.

boy	manuel
store	macy's
car	ford
horse	secretariat

2. Capitalize the names of holidays.

lent

ramadan

new year's day

3. Capitalize the names of deities.

zeus

buddha

holy spirit

god

4. Capitalize the days of the week and the months of the year, but not the seasons.

wednesday	february	spring
thursday	april	fall
saturday	september	winter

5. Capitalize the first, last, and other important words in titles of books, magazines, newspapers, stories, poems, and songs.

book	*green eggs and ham*
magazine	*the new yorker*
newspaper	*the philadelphia inquirer*
movie	*the hunger games: catching fire*
television show	*agents of s.h.i.e.l.d.*
story	"the lottery"
poem	"stopping by woods on a snowy evening"
song	"happy birthday to you"
chapter in a book	"an unexpected party"

6. Capitalize and italicize the names of ships, trains, and planes.

ship	*santa maria*
train	*hogwarts express*
plane	*air force one*

The titles *mister*, *madame*, and *miss* are capitalized and abbreviated Mr., Mrs., and Miss when placed in front of a proper name.

Miss Snevellicci made a graceful obeisance, and hoped Mrs. Curdle was well, as also Mr. Curdle, who at the same time appeared.
—Charles Dickens, *The Life and Adventures of Nicholas Nickleby*

A proper adjective is formed from a proper name. Proper adjectives are capitalized. Words that are not usually capitalized remain lowercase even when they are attached to a proper adjective.

	Proper Noun	**Proper Adjective**
Person	shakespeare	the shakespearean play
	kafka	a kafkaesque dilemna
Place	italy	an italian city
	korea	a non-korean tradition
Holiday	labor day	the labor day picnic
	christmas	an anti-christmas sentiment
Month	september	september storms
	december	the post-december blues

Capitalize the personal pronoun I.

Interjections express sudden feeling or emotion. They are set off with commas or stand alone with a closing punctuation mark.

I have prayed over them, oh, I have prayed so much.
Ahem! That is my name.
Ha, ha! The liars that these traders are!
—Charles Dickens, *David Copperfield*

Capitalize the interjection *O*. It is usually preceded by, but not followed by, a comma.

For a few weeks it was all well enough, but afterwards, O the weary length of the nights!

But, O dear, O dear, this is a hard world!
—Kenneth Grahame, *The Wind in the Willows*

After an interjection followed by an exclamation point, the next word may be lowercase.

Oh! let me see it once again before I die!
Alas! how often and how long may those patient angels hover above us!
—Charles Dickens, *The Life and Adventures of Nicholas Nickleby*

Capitalize the address, date, greeting, closing, and signature of a letter.

Your Street Address
Your City, State, and ZIP Code

June 14, 2018

Well-Trained Mind Press
18021 The Glebe Lane
Charles City, Virginia 23030

Dear Editors:

Thank you for *Grammar for the Well-Trained Mind.* It is the most exciting grammar book I have ever read. I only wish I could spend more time doing grammar.

Please publish more grammar books immediately.

Sincerely,

SIGNATURE

Your Greatest Fan

Your Street Address
Your City, State, and ZIP Code

June 14, 2018

Well-Trained Mind Press
18021 The Glebe Lane
Charles City, Virginia 23030

Dear Editors:

Thank you for *Grammar for the Well-Trained Mind.* It is the most exciting grammar book I have ever read. I only wish I could spend more time doing grammar.

Please publish more grammar books immediately.

Sincerely,

SIGNATURE

Your Greatest Fan

Abbreviations are typically capitalized when each letter stands for something.

The WHO has expressed concern about the Zika virus and its rapid spread.
Why did NASA cancel the lunar exploration program?
OPEC was founded in 1960 in Baghdad.

Capitalize the first word in every line of traditional poetry.

> "The Elephant"
> by Hilaire Belloc
>
> When people call this beast to mind,
> They marvel more and more
> At such a little tail behind,
> So large a trunk before.

A sentence is a group of words that contains a subject and a predicate. A sentence begins with a capital letter and ends with a punctuation mark.

A statement gives information. A statement always ends with a period.
An exclamation shows sudden or strong feeling. An exclamation always ends with an exclamation point.
A command gives an order or makes a request. A command ends with either a period or an exclamation point.
A question asks something. A question always ends with a question mark.

Look ahead, Rat

Hooray, this is splendid

I wonder which of us had better pack the luncheon-basket

Presently they all sat down to luncheon together

Exercise 121A: Proofreading

Use proofreader's marks to insert the missing capital letters and punctuation marks into the following sentences. They are all taken from mystery novels written by the great English novelist Agatha Christie.

capitalize letter: ≡	make letter lowercase: /
insert period: ⊙	insert exclamation point: ^!
insert comma: ^,	insert question mark: ^?
insert apostrophe: ’v	

If a word or phrase should be italicized, indicate this by underlining.

this is a very pleasant meeting for me miss cynthia

this is my old friend monsieur poirot whom I have not seen for years

no one but i hercule poirot would attempt it

on tuesday the 17th july you went i believe with another guest to visit the dispensary at the red cross hospital in tadminster

The Mysterious Affair at Styles

can i speak to detective inspector hardcastle

a thoroughfare uncompromisingly labelled albany road barred my way

he knew a little about miss pebmarsh, though their paths had never crossed professionally

The Clocks

besides, there was something very cosy and english about old ladies like this old lady and his aunt mildred they could be classed with plum pudding on christmas day and village cricket and open fireplaces with wood fires

then he opened the times and became absorbed in more serious matters

Murder Is Easy

through all gwendas plans and preoccupations the voice of mrs hengrave droned thinly on recounting the details of the late major hengraves last illness

she flinched slightly at the prospect of they walked without feet but supposed she might enjoy it only the point about "significant" plays was that you usually didnt

Sleeping Murder

before god i didnt know what it was sir

indian island had really been bought by miss gabrielle turl the hollywood film star

the train is the 1240 from paddington and you will be met at oakridge station

we were together at bellhaven guest house in august some years ago and we seemed to have so much in common

And Then There Were None

a big scarlet rolls royce had just stopped in front of the local post office

instead he seemed to see a more imposing elizabethan mansion a long sweep of park a more bleak background

m gaston blondin the proprietor of that modish little restaurant chez ma tante was not a man who delighted to honour many of his clientele

dr bessner read sonorously in german from a baedeker pausing every now and then to translate for the benefit of cornelia who walked in a docile manner beside him

the normandie i remember sailed two days after the carmanic

mr fanthorp turned a page of europe from within

Death on the Nile

im american born but ive spent most of my life in england

i must be right therefore this new murder is impossible unless unless oh wait i implore you

Murder on the Links

Exercise 121B: Correct Letter Mechanics

The following text is a letter written by Agatha Christie to an American fan who asked her for an interview. On your own paper (or with your own word processing program), rewrite or retype the text so that it is properly formatted, punctuated, and capitalized. You may choose either letter format from this lesson.

The address of the sender (Agatha Christie) is in England. Churston Ferrers is the town, and South Devon is the county.

Notice that there are no ZIP codes in the address of the recipient, because ZIP codes were only created by the U.S. Post Office in 1963.

The first two sentences in the letter are one paragraph, while the last sentence is its own separate paragraph.

The abbreviation "Esq." follows the name of the recipient, and tells you that the recipient is a lawyer.

When you are finished, compare your letter with the two versions in the Answer Key.

greenway house churston ferrers south devon england may 15 1961 homer hall esq 123 john street de kalb illinois usa dear mr. hall thank you very much for your letter and for sending me the somewhat gruesome photograph i am glad to have it to keep among my mementoes of crime i am so glad you enjoy my stories yours sincerely agatha christie

—LESSON 122—

Commas
Semicolons
Additional Semicolon Rules
Colons
Additional Colon Rules

1. A comma and coordinating conjunction join compound sentences.
2. Commas separate three or more items in a series.
3. Commas separate two or more adjectives that come before a noun (as long as the adjectives can exchange position).
4. A comma precedes the *and* before the last item in a series of three or more (the "Oxford comma").
5. Commas set off terms of direct address.
6. Commas set off non-restrictive adjective clauses.
7. Commas set off parenthetical expressions that are closely related to the sentence.
8. Commas set off most appositives (unless the appositive is only one word and very closely related to the word it renames).
9. Commas may surround or follow interjections.
10. Commas may surround or follow introductory adverbs of affirmation and negation.
11. Commas may set off introductory adverb and adjective phrases.
12. In dates, commas separate the day of the week from the day of the month and the day of the month from the year.
13. In addresses, commas separate the city from the state.
14. Commas follow the greeting and closing of a friendly letter, and the closing of a formal letter.
15. Commas divide large numbers into sets of thousands.
16. A comma follows a dialogue tag or attribution tag that precedes a speech or quote.
17. A comma comes after a speech or quote if a dialogue tag or attribution tag follows.
18. A comma may divide a partial sentence from the block quote it introduces.
19. Commas may be used at any time to prevent misunderstanding and simplify reading.

Exercise 122A: Comma Use

In the blank at the end of each sentence, write the number from the list above that describes the comma use. If more than one number seems to fit equally well, write all suitable numbers.

These sentences are from *The House of Mirth*, by Edith Wharton.

As she entered her bedroom, with its softly-shaded lights, her lace dressing-gown lying across the silken bedspread, her little embroidered slippers before the fire, a vase of carnations filling the air with perfume, and the last novels and magazines lying uncut on a table beside the reading-lamp, she had a vision of Miss Farish's cramped flat, with its cheap conveniences and hideous wall-papers. __________

Oh, Lily, do look at this diamond pendant—it's as big as a dinner-plate! __________

Really, Lily, I don't see why you took the trouble to go to the wedding, if you don't remember what happened or whom you saw there. __________

Gerty hid her face from the light, but it pierced to the crannies of her soul. __________

Here was, after all, something that her charming listless hands could really do; she had no doubt of their capacity for knotting a ribbon or placing a flower to advantage. __________

And of course only these finishing touches would be expected of her: subordinate fingers, blunt, grey, needle-pricked fingers, would prepare the shapes and stitch the linings, while she presided over the charming little front shop—a shop all white panels, mirrors, and moss-green hangings—where her finished creations, hats, wreaths, aigrettes and the rest, perched on their stands like birds just poising for flight. __________

Mr. Bry, a short pale man, with a business face and leisure clothes, met the dilemma hilariously. __________

She rose and handed the hat to Miss Kilroy, who took it with a suppressed smile. __________

No, that's rather out of my line. __________

"I came here because I couldn't bear to be alone," she said. ___________

In her stuffy room at the hotel to which she had gone on landing, Lily Bart that evening reviewed her situation. ___________

On and on it flowed, a current of meaningless sound, on which, startlingly enough, a familiar name now and then floated to the surface. ___________

The row of budding trees, the new brick and limestone house-fronts, the Georgian flat-house with flowerboxes on its balconies, were merged together into the setting of a familiar scene. ___________

The independent clauses of a compound sentence must be joined by a comma and a coordinating conjunction, a semicolon, or a semicolon and a coordinating conjunction. They cannot be joined by a comma alone.

He knew—as the Athenians and Persians did not—exactly when the flooding of the Nile was about to occur, and he managed to hold the combined invasion force off until the waters began to rise rapidly around him.

Thousands of years ago, groups of hunters and gatherers roamed across Asia and Europe, following mammoth herds that fed on the wild grasses. Slowly the ice began to retreat; the patterns of the grass growth changed; the herds wandered north and diminished.

They eat and drink, and thank him for his generosity; but Atrahasis himself, knowing that the feast is a death meal, paces back and forth, ill with grief and guilt.

—Susan Wise Bauer, *The History of the Ancient World*

Block quotes should be introduced by a colon (if preceded by a complete sentence) or a comma (if preceded by a partial sentence).

Piankhe did not try to wipe out his enemies. Instead, he chose to see Egypt as a set of kingdoms, with himself as High King over them:

> Amun of Napata has appointed me governor of this land,

he wrote in another inscription,

> as I might say to someone: "Be king," and he is it, or: "You will not be king," and he is not.

—Susan Wise Bauer, *The History of the Ancient World*

Use a colon after the salutation of a business letter.

The White House
1600 Pennsylvania Ave NW
Washington, DC 20500

Dear Mr. President

Use a colon to separate the hour from minutes in a time.

I went to bed at 11 59 on December 31.

Use a colon to separate the chapter from verse in a Biblical reference.

According to Ecclesiastes 12 12, "much study wearies the body."

If items in a series contain commas within the items, semicolons may separate two or more items in a series.

If semicolons separate items in a series, a colon may set off the series.

> Around the tomb complex, buildings recreated in stone the materials of traditional Egyptian houses: walls of stone, carved to look like reed matting; stone columns shaped into bundles of reeds; even a wooden fence with a partly open gate, chiseled from stone.
>
> Like the Great Pyramid, the Sphinx has attracted its share of nutty theories: it dates from 10,000 B.C. and was built by a disappeared advanced civilization; it was built by Atlanteans (or aliens); it represents a zodiacal sign, or a center of global energy.
>
> Between 4000 and 3000 B.C. is known as the Naqada Period, and was once divided into three phases: the Amratian, which runs from 4000 to 3500 B.C.; the Gerzean, from 3500 to 3200 B.C.; and the Final Predynastic, from 3200 to 3000 B.C.
>
> —Susan Wise Bauer, *The History of the Ancient World*

A colon may introduce a list.

> Stripped of personality, prehistoric peoples too often appear as blocks of shifting color on a map: moving north, moving west, generating a field of cultivated grain, or corralling a herd of newly domesticated animals.
>
> Many thousands of years ago, the Sumerian king Alulim ruled over Eridu: a walled city, a safe space carved out of the unpredictable and harsh river valley that the Romans would later name Mesopotamia.
>
> Plague, drought, and war: these were enough to upset the balance of a civilization that had been built in rocky dry places, close to the edge of survival.
>
> —Susan Wise Bauer, *The History of the Ancient World*

For emphasis, a colon may introduce an item that follows a complete sentence, when that item is closely related to the sentence.

But the historian's task is different: to look for particular human lives that give flesh and spirit to abstract assertions about human behavior.

But the historian's task, to look for particular human lives that give flesh and spirit to abstract assertions about human behavior, is different.

Exercise 122B: Capitalization and Punctuation

Insert all missing punctuation and correct all capitalization into the text that follows. Use these proofreader's marks:

capitalize letter: ≡	make letter lowercase: /
insert period: ⊙	insert exclamation point: ^!
insert comma: ^,	insert question mark: ^?
insert colon: ^:	insert semicolon: ^;
insert dash: (—)	insert quotation marks: ^“
insert hyphen: ^-	

If a word or phrase should be italicized, indicate this by underlining.

122B.1: Sentences

the photograph by herbert mason of st pauls cathedral on december 29 30 1940 expresses an unalterable historical truth and a tragically false prophecy

since september london had been the chief almost the exclusive target of a relentless series of raids by german bombers 27500 high explosive bombs and innumerable incendiaries were dropped on average 160 bombers attacking nightly between september 7 and november 13

the docks were a prime target often in flames the dwellings of the poor who lived nearby were reduced to street after street of smoking rubble

of 147000 serious or fatal casualties caused by bombardment in britain 80000 were in london 29890 killed and 50000 badly injured and 1.5 million homes were destroyed

london: a history, by a n wilson

the battle of britain was over and the attack on coventry wasn't till mid november

what are you doing she shouted over the drone of the bombers

she was exactly where shed told the lab and colin shed be working in a department store on oxford street and sleeping in a tube station that had never been hit

hed set the net so hed come through at 7 pm on september 16 1940

london damaged by bombs the headline read

blackout, by connie willis

she forced the cough back holding her breath and looked up the nave toward the dome and saw flames

they must be blowing in through the shattered stained glass windows from the fires in paternoster row

the sixpenny print of the light of the world caught fire the edges curling up the shut door in the picture burning away to black to ash

all clear, by connie willis

122B.2: Letter Format

The following letters were written by Londoners who lived through the World War II bombing of London by German planes (the Blitz).

The first letter, slightly adapted, is from a mother in London to her six-year-old son, who had been sent away from the city into the country so that he would be safe from the bombing.[1] Roddy is the child's dog, and Bob is his cat. "Anderson" is the brand name of a type of bomb shelter used during the war. "Combinations" were warm underwear that had both pants and a vest.

The second letter is a shortened version of a letter written by Queen Elizabeth The Queen Mother to her mother-in-law, describing a bombing raid on London in 1940.[2] East Ham and West Ham are districts in London.

---

[1] http://www.bbc.co.uk/history/ww2peopleswar/stories/40/a8917040.shtml

[2] https://www.telegraph.co.uk/news/uknews/theroyalfamily/6179312/Queen-Mother-Blitz-letter-in-full.html

59 st. asaph road
brockley london SE4

wednesday, august 23 1944

dear francis

we arrived home safely. the scullery ceiling was down. a bomb had fallen very near the allotment. We now sleep in the public shelter because it is wet in the Anderson It has rained a lot this past few days.

i hope you are well and happy. roddy and bob are all right and the tortoise is still in his box

i have sent two cakes one for you and one for norman and some chocolate, done in two different papers Have one each. they are both the same inside

if you feel cold, put on your combinations

lots of love

mummy

windsor castle

september 13 1940

my darling Mama

i hardly know how to begin to tell you of the horrible attack on buckingham palace this morning. we heard the unmistakable whirr-whirr of a german plane We said ah! a german! and before anything else could be said, there was the noise of aircraft diving at great speed, and then the scream of a bomb It all happened so quickly that we had only time to look foolishly at each other, when the scream hurtled past us, and exploded with a tremendous crash in the quadrangle

i saw a great column of smoke and earth thrown up into the air, and then we all ducked like lightning into the corridor my knees trembled a little bit for a minute or two after the explosions!

luckily at about 130 the all-clear sounded, so we were able to set out on our tour of east and west ham – the damage there is ghastly i really felt as if I was walking in a dead city, when we walked down a little empty street. all the houses evacuated, and yet through the broken windows one saw all the poor little possessions photographs beds just as they were left

at the end of the street is a school which was hit, and collapsed on the top of 500 people waiting to be evacuated – about 20 are still under the ruins it does affect me seeing this terrible and senseless destruction – I think that really i mind it much more than being bombed myself

your loving daughter-in-law
elizabeth

122B.3: Quotes

Bertrand Russell wrote in 1936 that when London was bombed it would be "one vast raving bedlam, the hospitals will be stormed, traffic will cease, the homeless will shriek for help, the city will be a pandemonium

the first Day of the blitz: september 7 1940, by Peter Stansky

So much for the historical truth. the photograph also, by implication, speaks a prophecy that

this england never did, nor never shall,
lie at the proud foot of a conqueror

london: a History, by A. N. Wilson

Bomb disposal teams were taking no chances henry beckingham wrote afterwards

there had been a heavy air raid on the 17th/18th August '43 in the Hull, hedon, and hornsea areas, when a large number of butterfly bombs were dropped, causing havoc For weeks we were still searching in the hedgerows and ditches for these lethal fragmentation bombs

blitz diary: *life Under fire in world war II*, by carol harris

—LESSON 123—

Colons
Dashes
Hyphens
Parentheses
Brackets

But the historian's task is different: to look for particular human lives that give flesh and spirit to abstract assertions about human behavior.

But the historian's task is different—to look for particular human lives that give flesh and spirit to abstract assertions about human behavior.

—Susan Wise Bauer, *The History of the Ancient World*

A colon may introduce an item that follows a complete sentence, when that item is closely related to the sentence.

Dashes — — can enclose words that are not essential to the sentence.
Dashes can also be used singly to separate parts of a sentence.

A dash is twice as long as a hyphen.
When you write a dash, make it a little longer than a hyphen.
When you type a dash, use two hyphens for each dash.

well-educated (hyphen)
Well—that was a mistake. (dash)

Hyphens connect some compound nouns.
self-confidence
wallpaper
air conditioning

Hyphens connect compound adjectives in the attributive position.
self-confident woman
the woman was self confident

Hyphens connect spelled-out numbers between twenty-one and ninety-nine.
seventy-one balloons
he turned seventy-one on Friday

Hyphens divide words between syllables at the end of lines in justified text.
. . . worth inhabiting by reason of its barrenness; and indeed, both for-
saking it because of the prodigious number of tigers, lions, leopards,
and others of the furious creatures which harbour there; so that the . . .

. . . worth inhabiting by reason of its barrenness; and indeed, both
forsaking it because of the prodigious number of tigers, lions, leo-
pards, and others of the furious creatures which harbour there;
so that the . . .

Parentheses ( ) can enclose words that are not essential to the sentence.
Parenthetical expressions often interrupt or are irrelevant to the rest of the sentence.
Punctuation goes inside the parentheses if it applies to the parenthetical material; all other punctuation goes outside the parentheses.
Parenthetical material only begins with a capital letter if it is a complete sentence with ending punctuation.

I had no sooner said so, but I perceived the creature (whatever it was) within two oars' length.

Commas make a parenthetical element a part of the sentence.
Dashes emphasize a parenthetical element.
Parentheses minimize a parenthetical element.

"Particularly," said I, aloud (though to myself), "what should I have done without a gun, without ammunition, without any tools to make anything, or to work with, without clothes, bedding, a tent, or any manner of covering?"

Accordingly, having spent three days in this journey, I came home (so I must now call my tent and my cave); but before I got thither the grapes were spoiled; the richness of the fruit and the weight of the juice having broken them and bruised them, they were good for little or nothing; as to the limes, they were good, but I could bring but a few.

> Well, to take away this discouragement, I resolved to dig into the surface of the earth, and so make a declivity; this I began, and it cost me a prodigious deal of pains (but who grudge pains who have their deliverance in view?); but when this was worked through, and this difficulty managed, it was still much the same, for I could no more stir the canoe than I could the other boat.
>
> I first laid all the planks or boards upon it that I could get, and having considered well what I most wanted, I got three of the seamen's chests, which I had broken open, and emptied, and lowered them down upon my raft; the first of these I filled with provisions—bread, rice, three Dutch cheeses, five pieces of dried goat's flesh (which we lived much upon), and a little remainder of European corn, which had been laid by for some fowls which we brought to sea with us, but the fowls were killed.
>
> —Daniel Defoe, *Robinson Crusoe*

Exercise 123A: Hyphens

Some (but not all) of the following sentences—each taken from an essay in the classic 1914 collection *The Oxford Book of American Essays*—contain words that should be hyphenated. Insert a hyphen into each word that needs one.

At last, the long expected day arrived, preceded by a very restless night.

He is a busy minded personage, who thinks not merely for himself and family, but for all the country round, and is most generously disposed to be everybody's champion.

Though really a good hearted, good tempered old fellow at bottom, yet he is singularly fond of being in the midst of contention.

His family mansion is an old castellated manor house, gray with age, and of a most venerable, though weather beaten appearance.

There are, however, complete suites of rooms apparently deserted and time worn; and towers and turrets that are tottering to decay; so that in high winds there is danger of their tumbling about the ears of the household.

A certain fashion of thought prevailed half a century ago; another is popular today.

We wish to be self sustained.

The civilized nations—Greece, Rome, England—have been sustained by the primitive forests which anciently rotted where they stand.

Such companions befit the season of frosted window panes and crackling fires, when the blast howls through the black ash trees of our avenue, and the drifting snowstorm chokes up the wood paths and fills the highway from stone wall to stone wall.

There is a kind of ludicrous unfitness in the idea of a time stricken and grandfatherly lilac bush.

To judge from your physiognomy, you are now well stricken in years.

The escape of genius from the cloud covered mountain tops of the unknown into human society has not yet been accounted for.

The learned shook their heads at him, for he was a poor half educated varlet, that knew little of Latin, and nothing of Greek, and had been obliged to run the country for deer stealing.

In two respects the absorption of large numbers of immigrants from many nations into the American commonwealth has been of great service to mankind. In the first place, it has demonstrated that people who at home have been subject to every sort of aristocratic or despotic or military oppression become within less than a generation serviceable citizens of a republic; and, in the second place, the United States have thus educated to freedom many millions of men.

Exercise 123B: Parenthetical Elements

The following sentences, also taken from *The Oxford Book of American Essays*, each contain parenthetical elements. Set off each bolded set of words with commas, dashes, or parentheses. Choose the punctuation marks that seem to fit best. Then, compare your answers with the original punctuation in the Answer Key.

My first object as usual was originality.

All possible encouragement therefore should be given to the growth of critics, good or bad.

The blackbirds three species of which consort together are the noisiest of all our feathered citizens.

For all that American literature is in the apt phrase of Mr. Howells "a condition of English literature," nevertheless it is also distinctively American.

There are no richer parterres to my eyes than the dense beds of dwarf andromeda Cassandra calyculata which cover these tender places on the earth's surface.

We were of course very open to satire and attack.

But above all I discovered around me it was near the end of June on the ends of the topmost branches only, a few minute and delicate red cone-like blossoms, the fertile flower of the white pine looking heavenward.

After a few such experiences, I for one have felt as if I were merely one of those horrid things preserved in spirits and very bad spirits, too in a cabinet.

I think that I cannot preserve my health and spirits, unless I spend four hours a day at least and it is commonly more than that sauntering through the woods and over the hills and fields, absolutely free from all worldly engagements.

One sunny morning, he rose from his rug, went into the conservatory he was very thin then, walked around it deliberately, looking at all the plants he knew, and then went to the bay-window in the dining-room, and stood a long time looking out upon the little field, now brown and sere, and toward the garden, where perhaps the happiest hours of his life had been spent.

The neighbors and I am convinced that the advice of neighbors is never good for anything suggested catnip.

Balmy Spring weeks later than we expected, and months later than we longed for her comes at last to revive the moss on the roof and walls of our old mansion.

Popular education is another great field in which public activity should be indefinitely enlarged, not so much through the action of the Federal government though even there a much more effective supervision should be provided than now exists but through the action of states, cities, and towns.

—LESSON 124—

Italics
Quotation Marks
Ellipses
Single Quotation Marks
Apostrophes

In *Around the World in Eighty Days,* Jules Verne describes the arrival of the steamer *Mongolia* at the port of Suez.

Capitalize and italicize the names of ships, trains, and planes.

Italicize the titles of lengthy or major works such as books, newspapers, magazines, major works of art, and long musical compositions.

Use quotation marks for minor or brief works of art and writing or portions of longer works such as short stories, newspaper articles, songs, chapters, and poems.

Watership Down	"The Chief Rabbit"
The Hobbit	"An Unexpected Party"
The New York Times	"In Julia Child's Provençal Kitchen"
National Geographic	
The *Mona Lisa* of Da Vinci	"Saint Jerome in Penitence" by Dürer
The *David* of Michelangelo	
1812 Overture by Tchaikovsky	
The opera *Carmen* by Bizet	"Toreador Song"
	"Scarborough Fair"
	"The Lottery"
The *Odyssey*	"Stopping by Woods on a Snowy Evening"
	"The Raven"

Italicize letters, numbers, and words if they are the subject of discussion. In plural versions, do not italicize the *s*.

The letter *A* begins the alphabet, and a *Z* concludes it.

Most Americans hate the word *moist.*

*A*s and *F*s are hard to write in calligraphy.

Italicize foreign words not adopted into English.

What we call "rapid-eye-movement sleep" the French call *sommeil paradoxal* (paradoxical sleep) because the body is still but the mind is extremely active.
—Pamela Druckerman, *Bringing Up Bébé*

Mark Twain was the nom de plume of Samuel Langhorne Clemens.

English doesn't borrow from other languages. English follows other languages down dark alleys, knocks them over and goes through their pockets for loose grammar.

—Sir Terry Pratchett

Use quotation marks for minor or brief works of art and writing or portions of longer works such as short stories, newspaper articles, songs, chapters, and poems.

Then there crawled from the bushes a dozen more great purple spiders, which saluted the first one and said, "The web is finished, O King, and the strangers are our prisoners."

Dorothy did not like the looks of these spiders at all. They had big heads, sharp claws, small eyes and fuzzy hair all over their purple bodies.

—L. Frank Baum, *Glinda of Oz*

Direct quotations are set off by quotation marks.

Fear of spiders might come in part from children's stories, which often portray spiders as hostile predators. In *Glinda of Oz,* L. Frank Baum writes about a Spider King and his army of "great purple spiders, which . . . said, 'The web is finished, O King, and the strangers are our prisoners.'"

A quote within a quote is surrounded by single quotation marks.

An apostrophe is a punctuation mark that shows possession. It turns a noun into an adjective that tells whose.

Form the possessive of a singular noun by adding an apostrophe and the letter *s*.

spider wand

web sorceress

Form the possessive of a plural noun ending in *-s* by adding an apostrophe only.

spiders troubles

fields lakes

Form the possessive of a plural noun that does not end in *-s* as if it were a singular noun.

sheep hangmen

geese teeth

A contraction is a combination of two words with some of the letters dropped out. An apostrophe shows where the letters have been omitted.

they are ____________________

was not ____________________

were not ____________________

I am ____________________

Exercise 124A: Proofreading Practice

The sentences below have lost most punctuation and capitalization. Insert all missing punctuation marks, and correct all capitalization errors. When you are finished, compare your sentences with the originals.

Use these proofreader's marks:

capitalize letter: ≡	make letter lowercase: /
insert period: ⊙	insert exclamation point: ↑!
insert comma: ^,	insert question mark: ^?
insert colon: ^:	insert semicolon: ^;
insert apostrophe: ∨'	insert quotation marks: ∨"
insert dash: (—)	insert hyphen: ≑

If a word or phrase should be italicized, indicate this by underlining.

the following sentences below are from the trilogy by suzanne collins. the trilogy contains three titles it begins with the hunger games, and then includes two additions to the series *catching fire* and the *mockingjay.* the first book the *hunger games* has three parts the tributes, the games and the victor

prim named him buttercup insisting that his muddy yellow coat matched the bright flowers

effie trinket says as she always does ladies first and crosses to the glass ball with the girls names

i volunteer i gasp i volunteer as tribute

the hunger games

but he did his job more than his job because for the first time in history two tributes were allowed to win i have a problem miss everdeen says president snow a problem that began the moment you pulled out those poisonous berries in the arena

now hes arranging things around my living room clothing fabrics and sketchbooks with designs hes drawn

the rest of the day is a blur of getting to the station bidding everyone good-bye the train pulling out the old team peeta and me effie and haymitch cinna and portia peeta's stylist dining on an indescribably delicious meal i don't remember

the hunger games catching fire

finally plutarch heavensbee the head gamemaker who had organized the rebels in the capitol threw up his hands

music plays them out and then theres a woman reading a list of expected shortages in the capitol fresh fruit solar batteries soap

somewhere in district 13 beetee hits a switch because now its not President Snow but President Coin who's looking at us.

the words traitor liar and enemy bounce off the walls

the hunger games: mockingjay

Exercise 124B: Foreign Phrases That Are Now English Words

The following phrases and words are now part of English and are usually not italicized. Using a dictionary, look up each one. In the blank, write the original language that the word belongs to, the meaning in English, and the meaning in the original language. The first is done for you.

cul-de-sac French, a dead-end street, "bottom of the sack"

glitch ______________________________

kindergarten ______________________________

cafe ______________________________

karaoke ______________________________

klutz ______________________________

guru ______________________________

en masse ______________________________

genre ______________________________

zebra ______________________________

WEEK 34

Advanced Quotations & Dialogue

—LESSON 125—

Dialogue
Additional Rules for Writing Dialogue
Direct Quotations
Additional Rules for Using Direct Quotations

Use dialogue in fiction and to bring other voices into memoir, profiles, and reporting.

> A man was thought to be the painter of "Portrait of an Unknown Lady" when it went on sale in 2014 at an auction in the southern English city of Salisbury. It was bought by Bendor Grosvenor, an art dealer and historian who recognized the work as Carlile's.
>
> In an interview with *The Telegraph*, Mr. Grosvenor said that the artist's style "is quite recognizable if you know what it looks like."
>
> —Roslyn Sulcas, "A 17th-Century Portrait Will Be the Earliest Painting by a Woman at the Tate." The *New York Times,* Sept. 21, 2016

A dialogue tag identifies the person making the speech.

When a dialogue tag comes after a speech, place a comma, exclamation point, or question mark inside the closing quotation marks before the tag.

When a dialogue tag comes before a speech, place a comma after the tag. Put the dialogue's final punctuation mark inside the closing quotation marks.

> "There goes Tommaso the painter," the people would say, watching the big awkward figure passing through the streets on his way to work.

> Diamante said to Filippo, "You have learned well, and it is time now to turn your work to some account."

Speeches do not need to be attached to a dialogue tag as long as the text clearly indicates the speaker.

> The father gave a hopeless sigh and turned away. "So, you will be a painter."

Usually, a new paragraph begins with each new speaker.

> Michelangelo said nothing, but he mounted the scaffolding and pretended to chip away at the nose with his chisel. Meanwhile he let drop some marble chips and dust upon the head of the critic beneath. Then he came down.
>
> "Is that better?" he asked gravely.
>
> "Admirable!" answered the artist. "You have given it life."
>
> "I am growing too old to help you," Leonardo said, but Raphael shook his head. "I will go with you to the ends of the earth," he said.

When a dialogue tag comes in the middle of a speech, follow it with a comma if the following dialogue is an incomplete sentence. Follow it with a period if the following dialogue is a complete sentence.

> "The boy!" said one brother, nudging the other, "has found his brains at last."
>
> The painter's quick eyes examined the work with deep interest. "Send him to me at once," he said. "This is indeed marvellous talent."
>
> —Amy Steedman, *Knights of Art: Stories of the Italian Painters*

RULES FOR USING DIRECT QUOTATIONS

Direct quotations are set off by quotation marks.

Every direct quote must have an attribution tag.

When an attribution tag comes after a direct quote, place a comma, exclamation point, or question mark inside the closing quotation marks.

> "Frederick, is God dead?" asked Sojourner Truth.

When an attribution tag comes before a direct quote, place a comma after the tag. Put the quote's final punctuation mark inside the closing quotation marks.

> The orator paused impressively, and then thundered in a voice that thrilled his audience with prophetic intimations, "No, God is not dead; and therefore it is that slavery must end in blood!"

When an attribution tag comes in the middle of a direct quotation, follow it with a comma if the remaining quote is an incomplete sentence. Follow it with a period if the remaining quote is a complete sentence.

> "A new world had opened up to me," Douglass wrote. "I lived more in one day than in a year of my slave life."
>
> "It was my good fortune," he writes, "to get out of slavery at the right time, to be speedily brought in contact with that circle of highly cultivated men and women, banded together for the overthrow of slavery, of which William Lloyd Garrison was the acknowledged leader."

Direct quotes can be words, phrases, clauses, or sentences, as long as they are set off by quotation marks and form part of a grammatically correct original sentence.

> In his autobiography Douglass commends Mr. Johnson for his "noble-hearted hospitality and manly character."

Ellipses show where something has been cut out of a sentence.

If a direct quotation is longer than three lines, indent the entire quote one inch from the margin in a separate block of text and omit quotation marks.

> In a footnote to the *Life and Times of Garrison* it is stated:
>
> > This enterprise was not regarded with favor by the leading abolitionists, who knew only too well the precarious support which a fifth anti-slavery paper . . . must have . . . As anticipated, it nearly proved the ruin of its projector; but by extraordinary exertions it was kept alive.

If you change or make additions to a direct quotation, use brackets.

> Parker Pillsbury reported that "though it was late in the evening when the young man closed his remarks, none seemed to know or care for the hour. . . . The crowded congregation had been wrought up almost to enchantment during the whole long evening, particularly by some of the utterances of the last speaker [Douglass], as he turned over the terrible apocalypse of his experience in slavery."

A quote within a quote is surrounded by single quotation marks.

ADDITIONAL RULES FOR DIRECT QUOTATIONS

Use direct quotations to provide examples, cite authorities, and emphasize your own points.

An attribution tag may be indirect.

> In the wild songs of the slaves he read, beneath their senseless jargon or their fulsome praise of "old master," the often unconscious note of grief and despair.

A colon may introduce a direct quote.

> Douglass spent a year under Covey's ministrations, and his life there may be summed up in his own words: "The overwork and the brutal chastisements of which I was the victim, combined with that ever-gnawing and soul-destroying thought, 'I am a slave—a slave for life,' rendered me a living embodiment of mental and physical wretchedness."
>
> —Charles W. Chesnutt, *Frederick Douglass*

To quote three or fewer lines of poetry, indicate line breaks by using a slanted line and retain all original punctuation and capitalization.

> Likewise, Paul Laurence Dunbar's 1895 poem "We Wear the Mask" anticipates the "two-ness" of African-American existence expressed most poignantly and poetically by Du Bois nearly a decade later. Dunbar most famously writes: "We wear the mask that grins and lies,/It hides our cheeks and shades our eyes,—/This debt we pay to human guile".
>
> —Rebecka Rutledge Fisher, *Habitations of the Veil*

Four or more lines of poetry should be treated as a block quote.

> In his poem, "We Wear the Mask," Dunbar speaks of a double-consciousness that had been forced on African-Americans:
>
> We wear the mask that grins and lies,
> It hides our cheeks and shades our eyes,—
> This debt we pay to human guile;
> With torn and bleeding hearts we smile,
> And mouth with myriad subtleties.
>
> Dunbar's biographer, Benjamin Brawley, wrote that Dunbar's poetry "soared above race and touched the heart universal."
>
> —Joseph Nazel, *Langston Hughes*

Any poetic citation longer than one line may be treated as a block quote.

Direct quotes should be properly documented.

—LESSON 126—

(Optional)
Documentation

> In *101 Gourmet Cookies for Everyone*, author Wendy Paul claims that her Chocolate Chip Pudding Cookies are "by far the softest chocolate chip cookies" that can be found.[1]
>
> ---
>
> [1]Wendy Paul, *101 Gourmet Cookies for Everyone* (Bonneville Books, 2010), p. 18.

A sentence containing a direct quote should be followed by a citation.

A superscript number may lead to a citation at the bottom of the page (a footnote) or the end of the paper (an endnote).

1. Footnotes and endnotes should follow this format:

   Author name, *Title of Book* (Publisher, year of publication), p. #.

   If there are two authors, list them like this:

   Author name and author name, *Title of Book* (Publisher, year of publication), p. #.

   If your quote comes from more than one page of the book you're quoting, use *pp.* to mean "pages" and put a hyphen between the page numbers.

   Author name, *Title of Book* (Publisher, year of publication), pp. #-#.

   If a book is a second (or third, or fourth, etc.) edition, put that information right after the title.

   Author name, *Title of Book*, 2nd ed. (Publisher, year of publication), p. #.

If no author is listed, simply use the title of the book.

Title of book (Publisher, year of publication), p. #.

All of this information can be found on the copyright page of the book.

2. Footnotes should be placed beneath a dividing line at the bottom of the page. If you are using a word processing program, the font size of the footnotes should be about 2 points smaller than the font size of the main text.

3. Endnotes should be placed at the end of the paper, under a centered heading, like this:

ENDNOTES

[1] Wendy Paul, *101 Gourmet Cookies for Everyone* (Bonneville Books, 2010), p. 18.

[2] Author, *Title of book* (Publisher, year of publication), p. #.

For a short paper (three pages or less), the endnotes can be placed on the last page of the paper itself. A paper that is four or more pages in length should have an entirely separate page for endnotes.

4. The second time you cite a book, your footnote or endnote only needs to contain the following information:

[2] Author last name, p. #.

5. If a paragraph contains several quotes from the same source, a single citation at the end of the entire paragraph can cover all quotations.

Every work mentioned in a footnote or endnote must also appear on a final Works Cited page.

WORKS CITED

Paul, Wendy. *101 Gourmet Cookies for Everyone*. Springville, UT: Bonneville Books, 2010.

1. List sources alphabetically by the author's last name.
2. The format should be: Last name of author, first name. *Title of Book*. City of publication: Publisher, year of publication.
3. If the work has no author, list it by the first word of the title (but ignore the articles *a*, *an*, and *the*).
4. If the city of publication is not a major city (New York, Los Angeles, London, Beijing, New Delhi, Tokyo), include the state (for a U.S. publisher) or country (for an international publisher).
5. For a short paper (three pages or less), the Works Cited section may be at the bottom of the last page. For a paper of four or more pages, attach a separate Works Cited page.

Additional Rules for Citing Sources (Turabian)

1. Magazine articles

   In a footnote or endnote, use the following style:

   [1] Author name, "Name of article." Name of Magazine, Date of publication, page number.

   [2] Jacqueline Harp, "A Breed for Every Yard: Black Welsh Mountain Sheep Break New Ground." *Sheep!*, September/October 2013, p. 27.

   In Works Cited, use the following style:

   Author last name, first name. "Name of article." *Name of Magazine* volume number: issue number (Date of publication), total number of pages article takes up in magazine.

   Harp, Jacqueline. "A Breed for Every Yard: Black Welsh Mountain Sheep Break New Ground." *Sheep!* 34:5 (September/October 2013), pp. 26–28.

2. Websites

   In a footnote or endnote, use the following style:

   [3] Author/editor/sponsoring organization of website, "Name of article," URL (date accessed).

   [4] Mallory Daughtery, "Baa Baa Black and White Sheep Treats," http://www.southernliving.com/home-garden/holidays-occasions/spring-table-settings-centerpieces-00400000041389/page8.html (accessed Sept. 12, 2013).

   In Works Cited, use the following style:

   Author/editor/sponsoring organization of website. "Name of article." URL (date accessed).

   Daughtery, Mallory. "Baa Baa Black and White Sheep Treats." http://www.southernliving.com/home-garden/holidays-occasions/spring-table-settings-centerpieces-00400000041389/page8.html (accessed Sept. 12, 2013).

3. Ebooks with flowing text (no traditional page numbers)

   In a footnote or endnote, use the following style:

   [5] Author name, *Name of book* (Publisher, date), Name of ebook format: Chapter number, any other information given by ebook platform.

   [6] Paul de Kruif, *Microbe Hunters* (Harvest, 1996), Kindle: Ch. 7, Loc. 2134.

   In Works Cited, use the following style:

   Author last name, author first name. *Title of book*. City of publication: Publisher, date. Name of ebook format.

   de Kruif, Paul. *Microbe Hunters*. Fort Washington, PA: Harvest, 1996. Kindle.

In-text citations may be used in scientific or technical writing.

The chemical reactions that take place within Chocolate Chip Pudding Cookies make them "by far the softest chocolate chip cookies" (Paul 2010, 18) that can be found.[1]

About Turabian

The style described in this lesson is the most common one for student papers. It is known as "Turabian," after Kate Turabian, the head secretary for the graduate department at the University of Chicago from 1930 until 1958.

Kate Turabian had to approve the format of every doctoral dissertation and master's thesis submitted to the University of Chicago. These papers were supposed to follow the format of the *University of Chicago Manual of Style*, but the *Manual of Style* is huge and complicated and many students couldn't figure out exactly how to use it. So Kate Turabian wrote a simplified version of the *Manual of Style*, intended just for the use of students writing papers. It was called *A Manual for Writers of Research Papers, Theses, and Dissertations*, and her book has sold over eight million copies.

Alternative Styles for Citation

A. **Turabian** (most common for students)

FOOTNOTE/ENDNOTE

[1] Susan Cooper, *Silver on the Tree* (Atheneum, 1977), p. 52.

IN-TEXT CITATION

(Cooper 1977, 52)

WORKS CITED

Cooper, Susan. *Silver on the Tree.* New York: Atheneum, 1977.

B. **Chicago Manual of Style**

FOOTNOTE/ENDNOTE

[1] Susan Cooper, *Silver on the Tree* (New York: Atheneum 1977), p. 52.

IN-TEXT CITATION

(Cooper 1977, 52)

WORKS CITED

Cooper, Susan. 1977. *Silver on the Tree.* New York: Atheneum, 1977.

C. **APA** (American Psychological Association, the standard for science writing)

FOOTNOTE/ENDNOTE

APA does not recommend the use of footnotes or endnotes.

IN-TEXT CITATION

(Cooper, 1977, p. 52)

WORKS CITED

Cooper, S. (1977). *Silver on the tree.* New York: Atheneum.

D. **MLA** (Modern Language Association, more often used in the arts and humanities)

FOOTNOTE/ENDNOTE

MLA does not recommend the use of footnotes or endnotes for citations. They should only be used to direct the reader to additional books or resources that should be consulted.

IN-TEXT CITATION

(Cooper 52)

WORKS CITED

Cooper, Susan. *Silver on the Tree.* New York, NY, United States: Atheneum, 1977. Print.

—LESSON 127—

Practicing Direct Quotations and Correct Documentation

Your assignment: Write a short essay called "Four Disasters at Sea." It should be at least 250 words, although it will probably need to be longer.

You must quote directly from all four of the sources listed below, footnote each direct quote, and put all four on your Works Cited page.

Your essay must include the following:

a) A brief quote that comes before its attribution tag.
b) A brief quote that comes after its attribution tag.
c) A brief quote divided by its attribution tag.
d) A block quote.
e) A quote that is incorporated into a complete sentence and serves a grammatical function within that sentence.
f) A quote that has been altered with either brackets or ellipses.
g) A second quote from the same source.

One quote can fulfill more than one of these requirements. If you need help, ask your instructor.

Note to Student: There's a challenge below you haven't seen yet—two books by the same author, Logan Marshall!

You've learned that your first reference to a book should be a full listing of author, title, publisher, date, and page number, but that the second time, you can simply list the author's last name and the page number.

If the author has written *two* books that you reference, you have to add a little more information! If Julia Smith wrote *A Guide to Giant Owls* and *Handbook of Pygmy Owls* and you quote both, you still give a full citation for the first time you quote each book, but then the second time you need to specify which book you're citing—so, instead of

Smith, 42

you would write

Smith, *A Guide to Giant Owls*, 42

or

Smith, *Handbook of Pygmy Owls*, 42

Note that you don't have to provide any other information, because that all came in your first citation of each book.

The books below are a little different, though! Tell your instructor what the difference is now. (If you can't figure it out, ask for help!)

Author: Logan Marshall, ed.
Title of Book: *The Sinking of the Titanic and Great Sea Disasters: Thrilling Stories of Survivors*
City of Publication: New York
Publisher: L. T. Myers
Date: 1912

The story begins a short while after the Titanic *hit an iceberg and began to sink.*

41

Once on the deck, many hesitated to enter the swinging life-boats. The glassy sea, the starlit sky, the absence, in the first few moments, of intense excitement, gave them the feeling that there was only some slight mishap; that those who got into the boats would have a chilly half hour below and might, later, be laughed at.

It was such a feeling as this, from all accounts, which caused John Jacob Astor and his wife to refuse the places offered them in the first boat, and to retire to the gymnasium. In the same way H. J. Allison, a Montreal banker, laughed at the warning, and his wife, reassured by him, took her time dressing. They and their daughter did not reach the Carpathia. Their son, less than two years old, was carried into a life-boat by his nurse, and was taken in charge by Major Arthur Peuchen.

42

The admiration felt by the passengers and crew for the matchlessly appointed vessel was translated, in those first few moments, into a confidence which for some proved deadly. The pulsing of the engines had ceased, and the steamship lay just as though she were awaiting the order to go on again after some trifling matter had been adjusted. But in a few minutes the canvas covers were lifted from the life-boats and the crews allotted to each standing by, ready to lower them to the water.

Nearly all the boats that were lowered on the port side of the ship touched the water without capsizing. Four of the others lowered to starboard, including one collapsible, were capsized. All, however, who were in the collapsible boats that practically went to pieces, were rescued by the other boats.

Presently the order was heard: "All men stand back and all women retire to the deck below." That was the smoking-room deck, or the B deck. The men stood away and remained in absolute silence, leaning against the rail or pacing up and down the deck slowly. Many of them lighted cigars or cigarettes and began to smoke.

The boats were swung out and lowered from the A deck above. The women were marshaled quietly in lines along the B deck, and when the boats were lowered down to the level of the latter the women were assisted to climb into them.

As each of the boats was filled with its quota of passengers the word was given and it was carefully lowered down to the dark surface of the water...

64

The captain and officers behaved with superb gallantry, and there was perfect order and discipline among those who were aboard, even after all hope had been abandoned for the salvation of the ship.

65

Many women went down, steerage women who were unable to get to the upper decks where the boats were launched, maids who were overlooked in the confusion, cabin passengers who refused to desert their husbands or who reached the decks after the last of the life-boats was gone and the ship was settling for her final plunge to the bottom of the Atlantic.

Narratives of survivors do not bear out the supposition that the final hours upon the vessel's decks were passed in darkness. They say the electric lighting plant held out until the last, and that even as they watched the ship sink, from their places in the floating life-boats, her lights were gleaming in long rows as she plunged under by the head. Just before she sank, some of the refugees say, the ship broke in two abaft the engine room after the bulkhead explosions had occurred...

67

The bearded admiral of the White Star Line fleet, with every life-saving device launched from the decks, was returning to the deck to perform the sacred office of going down with his ship when a wave dashed over the side and tore him from the ladder.

The Titanic was sinking rapidly by the head, with the twisting sidelong motion that was soon to aim her on her course two miles down. Murdock saw the skipper swept out; but did not move. Captain Smith was but one of a multitude of lost at that moment....

The wave that swept the skipper out bore him almost to the thwart of a crowded lifeboat. Hands reached out, but he wrenched himself away, turned and swam back toward the ship.

Some say that he said, "Good-bye, I'm going back to the ship."

He disappeared for a moment, then reappeared where a rail was slipping under water. Cool and courageous to the end, loyal to his duty under the most difficult circumstances, he showed himself a noble captain, and he died a noble death.

Author/Editor/Sponsoring Organization: Time
Name of Web Article: The Forgotten Maritime Tragedy That Was 6 Times Deadlier Than the Titanic
URL: https://time.com/4198914/wilhelm-gustloff-salt-to-the-sea/
Date of access: Use the date on which you are writing your essay

...the Wilhelm Gustloff, a German ocean liner...was taken down by a Soviet sub on Jan. 30, 1945, killing 9,343 people—most of them war refugees...

The victims of the worst maritime tragedy in history were not only Germans, but also Prussians, Lithuanians, Latvians, Poles, Estonians and Croatians. World War II was drawing to an end, and the Soviet army was advancing. Though it would be months before the final fall of the Nazi regime, it was clear the end was coming—and they were desperate to escape before things came to a head. As a result, 10,582 people were packed onto a cruise ship that was meant to accommodate only about 1,900. Though some on the ship were Nazis themselves, others had been the victims of Nazi aggression. When three torpedoes hit the ship, there weren't nearly enough lifeboats, and many of the those that did exist were frozen to the deck. The majority of the passengers drowned.

Author: Logan Marshall
Title of Book: *The Tragic Story of the Empress of Ireland and Other Great Sea Disasters*
City of Publication: New York
Publisher: L. T. Myers
Date: 1914

The account below tells of the collision of the Canadian ship the Empress of Ireland *and the Norwegian ship* Storstad *on May 28, 1914.*

19

The horrible fact, about which there can be no dispute, is that the *Storstad* crashed bow on into the side of the big Canadian liner, striking it on the starboard side about midway of its length. The steel-sheathed bow of the collier cut through the plates and shell of the *Empress* and penetrated the hull for a distance of about twelve feet, according to the best testimony.

The water didn't flow in. It rushed in. From such stories as could be gathered from survivors and from members of the crew, it appears that Captain Kendall and his officers did all that was humanly possible in the fourteen minutes that the *Empress* hung on the river.

Captain Kendall said that he rang to the engine-room for

20

full speed ahead, with the object of trying to run ashore and save the passengers, but almost immediately after the engines stopped and the ship began to list rapidly...All lights went out almost at once. More than 1,400 persons were fighting for life in the black dark; yet, for the most part the flight was not one of panic, but grim determination to find, if possible, some means of safety.

Wireless operator Bomford and others who managed to win a way to the top deck saw scores leap into the sea. They saw hundreds trying to crawl up decks that were sloping precipitously, lose their balance and fall backward into the rising water. Passengers who couldn't get to the few life-boats in time seized chairs, anything loose they could find, and leaped into the river. Very many persons perished in the cold water while clinging to bits of wreckage and praying for help...

21

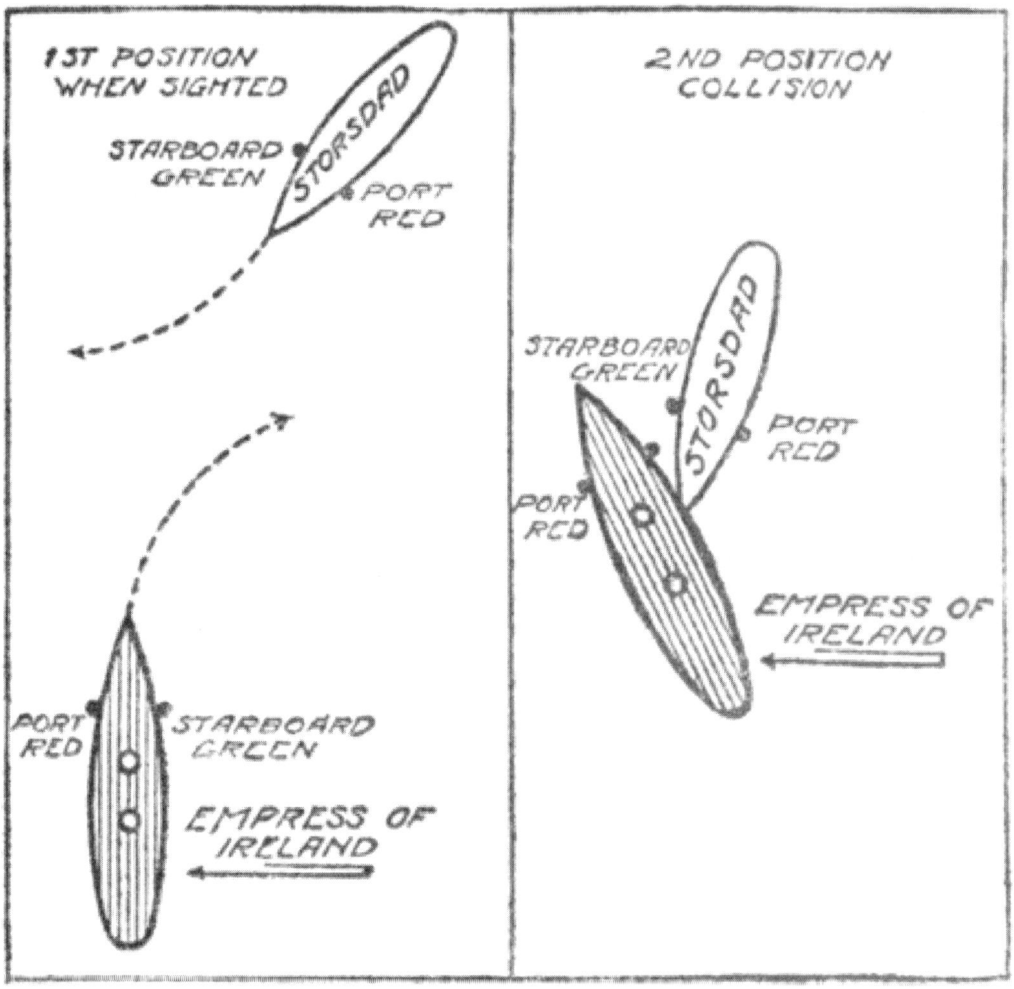

22

In a moment the fate of the *Empress* was known to all. The one smashing blow had done for her and the great bull-nose of the 3,500-ton freighter had crashed through the ribs and bulkheads...The S. O. S. call was ticked out by Edward Bomford, the junior wireless operator...

23

Many steamships picked up the call, but they were hours away. They started for the position given, but long before they had made any progress the *Empress* and two-thirds of her ship's company were under fifteen fathoms of water. Fourteen minutes is too brief a time for much rescue work...

24

The stewards did not have time to rouse the people from their berths. Those who heard the frenzied calls of the officers for the passengers to hurry on deck lost no time in obeying them, rushing up from their cabins in scanty attire. They piled into the boats, which were rapidly lowered, and were rowed away. Many who waited to dress were drowned.

The horror of the interval during which the *Empress of Ireland* was rapidly filling and the frightened throngs on board her were hurrying every effort to escape before she sank was added to by what seemed like an explosion, which quickly followed the ripping and tearing given the liner by the *Storstad*'s bow. As Captain Kendall afterwards explained, this supposed explosion was in reality the pressure of air caused by the in-rushing water. The ship's heavy list as the water pouring in weighted her on the side she was struck, made the work of launching boats increasingly difficult from moment to moment, and when she finally took her plunge to the bottom scores still left on her decks were carried down in the vortex, only a few being able to clear her sides and find support on pieces of wreckage.

Name of Article: Adventures of Men and Ships
Author: James Michener
Magazine: *Life*
Date: December 21, 1962
Volume and issue number: Volume 53, No. 25 Page range of article: 96–98, 111–114

Early in 1942, during World War II, the American ship U.S.S. Houston *was crippled by bombing near Java, and then was trapped by a convoy of Japanese ships.*

113

The U.S. cruiser lay trapped just northwest of Sunda Strait, and the Japanese fleet swarmed in for the kill. Searchlights brilliantly outlined the target. Eight-inch shells were lobbed into her from minimum range. Torpedoes were launched in groups of salvos. At times enemy destroyers came so close that gunners aboard *Houston* fired at them with machine guns.

Miraculously *Houston* withstood this assault for more than an hour. Her skipper, Albert H. Rooks, kept headway and somehow she managed to evade the torpedoes—until after midnight when she took her final blows. The shells that

114

raked her from stem to stern still did not put her out of commission...

Somehow the bridge remained operative most of the time and here Captain Rooks directed the last stages of the defense. That he kept his ship afloat was remarkable enough, but that he could still drive the enemy back with only one remaining turret was astonishing. Every available shell was fired...Finally there was literally nothing left to throw at the enemy. And now no amount of gallantry could prolong the life of the cruiser.

A salvo smashed directly into the bridge, killing Captain Rooks. The captain's Chinese cook sat on the deck beside his body and announced that he, too, would go down with the ship. When *Houston* finally died, the cook went with her.

WEEK 35

Introduction to Sentence Style

The definitions in this lesson use the categories laid out by Thomas Kane in *The New Oxford Guide to Writing*.

—LESSON 128—

Sentence Style: Equal and Subordinating
Sentences with Equal Elements: Segregating, Freight-Train, and Balanced

But, in a larger sense, we cannot dedicate—we cannot consecrate—we cannot hallow this ground.
—Abraham Lincoln, "The Gettysburg Address"

We shall defend our island, whatever the cost may be; we shall fight on the beaches, we shall fight on the landing grounds, we shall fight in the fields and in the streets, we shall fight in the hills; we shall never surrender.
—Winston Churchill, "We Shall Fight on the Beaches"

An equal sentence is made up of a series of independent grammatical elements.

Years and years ago, when I was a boy, when there were wolves in Wales, and birds the color of red-flannel petticoats whisked past the harp-shaped hills, when we sang and wallowed all night and day in caves that smelt like Sunday afternoons in damp front farmhouse parlors, and we chased, with the jawbones of deacons, the English and the bears, before the motor car, before the wheel, before the duchess-faced horse, when we rode the daft and happy hills bareback, it snowed and it snowed.
— Dylan Thomas, *A Child's Christmas in Wales*

Even when pressed by the demands of inner truth, men do not easily assume the task of opposing their government's policy, especially in time of war.
—Martin Luther King, "Beyond Vietnam—A Time to Break Silence"

A subordinating sentence is made up of both independent and dependent elements.

Equal sentences can be segregating, freight train, or balanced.

Segregating sentences express a single idea each, and occur in a series.

The barn was still dark. The sheep lay motionless. Even the goose was quiet.
—E. B. White, *Charlotte's Web*

He hadn't found any doweling that day. He hadn't checked the generator. He hadn't cleaned up the pieces of mirror. He hadn't eaten supper; he'd lost his appetite. That wasn't hard. He lost it most of the time.
—Richard Matheson, *I Am Legend*

They disappear among the poplars. The meadow is empty. The river, the meadow, the cliff and cloud. The princess calls, but there is no one, now, to hear her.
—John Fowles, *The Ebony Tower*

Freight-train sentences link independent clauses together to express a combined idea.

He was energetic and devout; he was polite and handsome; his fame grew in the diocese.
—Lytton Strachey, *Eminent Victorians*

There was much game hanging outside the shops, and the snow powdered in the fur of the foxes and the wind blew their tails.
—Ernest Hemingway, "In Another Country"

I'm very young, I have no real friend here in the barn, it's going to rain all morning and all afternoon, and Fern won't come in such bad weather.
—E. B. White, *Charlotte's Web*

Balanced sentences are made up of two equal parts, separated by a pause.

Darkness is cheap, and Scrooge liked it.
—Charles Dickens, *A Christmas Carol*

It is a far, far better thing that I do, than I have ever done; it is a far, far better rest that I go to than I have ever known.
—Charles Dickens, *A Tale of Two Cities*

But there is something that I must say to my people, who stand on the warm threshold which leads into the palace of justice: In the process of gaining our rightful place, we must not be guilty of wrongful deeds.
—Martin Luther King, "I Have a Dream"

Exercise 128A: Identifying Sentence Types

In the blank that follows each sentence or set of sentences, write *S* for segregating, *FT* for freight-train, or *B* for balanced.

I now quit altogether public affairs, and I lay down my burden.
—Edward VIII, December 11, 1936 ________

And the rain descended, and the flood came, and the winds blew, and they beat on that house, and it did not fall.
—Matthew 7:25 ________

Anne had been too little from home, too little seen. Her spirits were not high. A larger society would improve them. She wanted her to be more known.
—Jane Austen, *Persuasion* ________

The old man leaned the mast with its wrapped sail against the wall and the boy put the box and the other gear beside it.

—Ernest Hemingway, *The Old Man and the Sea* ________

Moon, stars, and street lamps burst back into life. A warm breeze swept the alleyway. Trees rustled in neighbouring gardens and the mundane rumble of cars in Magnolia Crescent filled the air again.

—J. K. Rowling, *Harry Potter and the Order of the Phoenix* ________

The storm had raged for full three hours; the lightning had grown fainter and less frequent; the thunder, from seeming to roll and break above their heads, had gradually died away into a deep hoarse distance; and still the game went on, and still the anxious child was quite forgotten.

—Charles Dickens, *The Old Curiosity Shop* ________

They wanted more land. They wanted our country. Our eyes were opened. Our minds became uneasy. Wars took place.

—Red Jacket of the Seneca People, "Brother, the Great Spirit Has Made Us All" ________

One day when he was out walking, he came to an open place in the middle of the forest, and in the middle of this place was a large oak-tree, and, from the top of the tree, there came a loud buzzing noise.

—A. A. Milne, *Winnie-the-Pooh* ________

We had left the damp fog of the great city behind us, and the night was fairly fine.

—A. Conan Doyle, *The Sign of Four* ________

He was invited to Kellynch Hall; he was talked of and expected all the rest of the year; but he never came.

—Jane Austen, *Persuasion* ________

The robot left with a disconsolate step and Gloria choked back a sob.

—Isaac Asimov, *I, Robot* ________

We've looked and we've looked and we've looked for him, but we can't find him.

—Isaac Asimov, *I, Robot* ________

I think that there is no more to be said; and I suggest that you now disperse quietly to your homes.

—T. S. Eliot, *Murder in the Cathedral* ________

The cellar door opened out of the kitchen. There were five wooden steps leading down. A bacon-rack hung under its ceiling. There was wood in it, and coal.

—E. Nesbit, *The Railway Children* ________

Then the arm of the Station Master was raised, the hand of the Station Master fell on a collar, and there was Peter firmly held by the jacket, with an old carpenter's bag full of coal in his trembling clutch.

—E. Nesbit, *The Railway Children* ________

—LESSON 129—

Subordinating Sentences: Loose, Periodic, Cumulative, Convoluted, and Centered

In a loose sentence, subordinate constructions follow the main clause.

People always think that happiness is a far away thing, something complicated and hard to get.
—Betty Smith, *A Tree Grows in Brooklyn*

He was pacing the room swiftly, eagerly, with his head sunk upon his chest and his hands clasped behind him.
—A. Conan Doyle, "A Scandal in Bohemia"

The spotlight has often been focused on me because I was a late bloomer who turned out to be a prodigy, and perhaps, more than that, because I am a black woman excelling in a white world.
—Misty Copeland, *Life in Motion: An Unlikely Ballerina*

In a periodic sentence, subordinate constructions precede the main clause.

To be, or not to be: that is the question.
—William Shakespeare, *Hamlet*

When Galileo and Newton looked at nature, they saw simplicity.
—Edward Dolnick, *The Clockwork Universe: Isaac Newton, the Royal Society, and the Birth of the Modern World*

Some years ago—never mind how long precisely—having little or no money in my purse, and nothing particular to interest me on shore, I thought I would sail about a little and see the watery part of the world.
—Herman Melville, *Moby Dick*

A cumulative sentence puts multiple subordinate constructions before or after the main clause.

Beyond the obvious facts that he has at some time done manual labour, that he takes snuff, that he is a Freemason, that he has been in China, and that he has done a considerable amount of writing lately, I can deduce nothing else.
—A. Conan Doyle, "The Red-Headed League"

Lastly, she pictured to herself how this same little sister of hers would, in the after-time, be herself a grown woman; and how she would keep, through all her riper years, the simple and loving heart of her childhood; and how she would gather about her other little children, and make their eyes bright and eager with many a strange tale, perhaps even with the dream of Wonderland of long ago; and how she would feel with all their simple sorrows, and find a pleasure in all their simple joys, remembering her own child-life, and the happy summer days.
—Lewis Carroll, *Alice's Adventures in Wonderland*

In a convoluted sentence, subordinate constructions divide the main clause.

The dorm, with two narrow beds to a room, didn't just house dancers studying with ABT.
—Misty Copeland, *Life in Motion: An Unlikely Ballerina*

We, the people of the United States, in order to form a more perfect union, establish justice, insure domestic tranquility, provide for the common defense, promote the general welfare, and secure the blessings of liberty to ourselves and our posterity, do ordain and establish this Constitution for the United States of America.
—The Constitution of the United States

They knew, without my needing to spell it out, every setback or curve in the road: that I had fought for ten years to be recognized, to show that I had the talent and ability to dance in classical ballets.
—Misty Copeland, *Life in Motion: An Unlikely Ballerina*

In a centered sentence, subordinate constructions come on both sides of the main clause.

With an apology for my intrusion, I was about to withdraw when Holmes pulled me abruptly into the room and closed the door behind me.
—A. Conan Doyle, "The Red-Headed League"

And having got rid of this young man who did not know how to behave, she resumed her duties as hostess and continued to listen and watch, ready to help at any point where the conversation might happen to flag.
—Leo Tolstoy, *War and Peace*

Exercise 129A: Identifying Subordinating Sentences

In each sentence, underline the subject(s) of the main clause once and the predicate twice.

Label each sentence in the blank that follows it as *L* for loose, *P* for periodic, *CUMUL* for cumulative, *CONV* for convoluted, or *CENT* for centered. For the purpose of this exercise, any sentence with three or more phrases and dependent clauses before or after the main clause should be considered cumulative. If two or fewer phrases or dependent clauses come before or after the main clause, the sentence should be classified as loose or periodic. Don't worry too much about figuring out exactly how many phrases or clauses are in the sentence—just do your best.

If phrases or clauses come before and after the main clause, the sentence is centered, no matter how many other phrases or clauses there are.

If any phrases or clauses come between the subject, predicate, and any essential parts of the main clause (objects, predicate nominatives, or predicate adjectives), the sentence is convoluted, no matter how many other phrases and clauses there are.

More precision was needed, to define what had caused the outbreak and to find the contaminated food in time to shut the outbreak down. ________

— Maryn McKenna, *Beating Back the Devil: On the Front Lines with the Disease Detectives of the Epidemic Intelligence Service*

But for many reasons—the difficulty of organizing yet another pediatrician's visit for kids already getting many childhood vaccines, the lack of a clear message that children were themselves at risk—the recommendation was not effective. ________

—Maryn McKenna, *Superbug: The Fatal Menace of MRSA*

And then, critically, from time to time they would exchange microbes. ________

—Nathan Wolfe, *The Viral Storm: The Dawn of a New Pandemic Age*

The retrovirus class of viruses begins with RNA genetic code, which is translated into DNA before it can insert itself into the DNA of its host. ________

—Nathan Wolfe, *The Viral Storm: The Dawn of a New Pandemic Age*

On New Year's morning, sometime after breakfast—a cold morning, air temperature in the forties, the grass wet and cold—they drove up the mountain along a muddy track. ________

—Richard Preston, *The Hot Zone*

In 1918, if you heard a neighbour or a relation coughing, or saw them fall down in front of you, you knew there was a good chance that you were already sick yourself. ________

—Laura Spinney, *Pale Rider: The Spanish Flu of 1918 and How It Changed the World*

It is tempting to imagine a single chimpanzee hunter as patient zero—an individual, the first of its species to harbor the novel virus—acquiring these viruses in short order from the monkeys it hunted, possibly on the same day. ________

—Nathan Wolfe, *The Viral Storm: The Dawn of a New Pandemic Age*

While most viruses are ball-shaped particles that look like peppercorns, the thread viruses have been compared to strands of tangled rope, to hair, to worms, to snakes. ________

—Richard Preston, *The Hot Zone*

On the other hand, names the current guidelines would rule out, such as monkey pox, arguably contain useful information about the disease's animal host and hence a potential source of infection. ________

—Laura Spinney, *Pale Rider: The Spanish Flu of 1918 and How It Changed the World*

Perhaps the single most devastating infectious disease that afflicts humans today is malaria. ________

—Nathan Wolfe, *The Viral Storm: The Dawn of a New Pandemic Age*

I was able in my mind's eye to zero in on the little fleshy crevices around Tom's and Jenny's teeth as they ate their meal and to see the turmoil of microbic life there, the spirochetes and vibratos in furious movement, the thicker corkscrewlike spirilla and vibrios gliding back and forth and the more sluggish or quiet chains and clusters and colonies of bacilli and cocci, massed around or boiling between detached epithelial scales and the fibers and debris of cells and food particles. ________

—Theodor Rosebury, *Life on Man*

People who are afflicted with sickle cell have their origins almost exclusively in one of the world's most intensely malaria affected areas—west central Africa. ________

—Nathan Wolfe, *The Viral Storm: The Dawn of a New Pandemic Age*

Ebola virus is named for the Ebola River, which is the headstream of the Mongala River, a tributary of the Congo, or Zaire, River. ________

—Richard Preston, *The Hot Zone*

The smallpox was always present, filling the churchyard with corpses, tormenting with constant fear all whom it had not yet stricken, leaving on those whose lives it spared the hideous traces of its power. _________

—Thomas Babington Macaulay, *History of England*

The Level 4 air lock is a gray area, a place where two worlds meet, where the hot zone touches the normal world. _________

—Richard Preston, *The Hot Zone*

The close relationship we have with dogs, whether as companions, work animals, dinner guests, or a source of food, should not surprise us. _________

—Nathan Wolfe, *The Viral Storm: The Dawn of a New Pandemic Age*

Staph aureus, a spherical bacterium that under a microscope bunches together like clusters of grapes, is everywhere in the environment. _________

— Maryn McKenna, *Beating Back the Devil: On the Front Lines with the Disease Detectives of the Epidemic Intelligence Service*

Cut through the center by a river flowing from a rain forest some hundred or so miles away, it provides a unique microclimate—a well-hydrated strip in an otherwise dry landscape. _________

—Nathan Wolfe, *The Viral Storm: The Dawn of a New Pandemic Age*

The blood culture the doctors had ordered that morning came back positive for methicillin-resistant *Staphylococcus aureus*, MRSA, a bug that could shrug off not only the methicillin family of antibiotics but also a half dozen others. _________

—Jessica Sachs, *Good Germs, Bad Germs: Health and Survival in a Bacterial World*

The holism movement within medicine was never more than a minority voice, and its influence quickly evaporated after World War II, partly because it had been espoused by a number of leading Nazi doctors, and partly because the new range of biologicals and miracle drugs, above all, insulin, penicillin, and cortisone, promised that experimental research might indeed cure all ills. _________

—William Bynum, *The History of Medicine: A Very Short Introduction*

The case of Charles Monet emerges in a cold geometry of clinical fact mixed with flashes of horror so brilliant and disturbing that we draw back and blink, as if we are staring into a discolored alien sun. _________

—Richard Preston, *The Hot Zone*

Dr. Musoke was widely considered to be one of the best young physicians at the hospital, an energetic man with a warm sense of humour, who worked long hours and had a good feel for emergencies. __________

—Richard Preston, *The Hot Zone*

What modern medicine needed, the German pathologist Paul Ehrlich concluded in 1885, was a "magic bullet" that would destroy bacterial cells but leave human cells unscathed. __________

—Jessica Sachs, *Good Germs, Bad Germs: Health and Survival in a Bacterial World*

The quintessential early laboratory, and the one most frequently illustrated, was that of the alchemist, as natural philosophers sought to learn how to turn base metals into gold. __________

—William Bynum, *The History of Medicine: A Very Short Introduction*

In areas where malaria-carrying mosquitoes bite year-round, people develop some immunity to the disease, though the protection takes years to build up and is never absolute. __________

— Maryn McKenna, *Beating Back the Devil: On the Front Lines with the Disease Detectives of the Epidemic Intelligence Service*

Late in the afternoon, near sunset, the clouds thickened and boiled up into an anvil thunderhead that flickered with silent lightning. __________

—Richard Preston, *The Hot Zone*

When a hot virus multiplies in a host, it can saturate the body with virus particles, from the brain to the skin. __________

—Richard Preston, *The Hot Zone*

But that Saturday morning at home, as he laid out his tools and the pieces on an antique clock that needed fixing, he could not stop thinking about the monkeys. __________

—Richard Preston, *The Hot Zone*

But all four children had initially been given the beta-lactam cephalosporin when they were first hospitalized, because it was the first drug on the list for treating childhood infections suspected to be caused by staph. __________

— Maryn McKenna, *Beating Back the Devil: On the Front Lines with the Disease Detectives of the Epidemic Intelligence Service*

Koch and Pasteur's proof that specific microbes cause specific diseases spurred a new generation of medical researchers to launch an all-out war on the world of bacteria with the goal of eradicating them. _________

—Jessica Sachs, *Good Germs, Bad Germs: Health and Survival in a Bacterial World*

Around the hospital and the church stood the beautiful ferocious trees, a complex of camphors and teaks. _________

—Richard Preston, *The Hot Zone*

He liked termites so much that he refrigerated them with his blood samples, to keep the termites fresh all day so that he could snack on them like peanuts with his evening gin as the sun went down over the African plains. _________

—Richard Preston, *The Hot Zone*

The danger lies in the possibility that discovering such infections will set off a call to arms that brings about a historic increase in antibiotic use before we have applied the hard-won lessons of our first Hundred Years War on germs. _________

—Jessica Sachs, *Good Germs, Bad Germs: Health and Survival in a Bacterial World*

The gorge, while not the only one of its kind, is unusual. _________

—Nathan Wolfe, *The Viral Storm: The Dawn of a New Pandemic Age*

Having had centuries of experience with the smallpox virus, the village elders had instituted their own methods for controlling the virus, according to their received wisdom, which was to cut their villages off from the world, to protect their people from a raging plague. _________

—Richard Preston, *The Hot Zone*

—LESSON 130—

Practicing Sentence Style

Choose one of the following assignments:

Exercise 130A: Rewriting

The following list of events, from the very old Norse fairy tale "The Three Billy Goats Gruff," needs to be rewritten as a story.

Think this is an easy task? Just remember that this story must have at least one of each of the following types of sentences:

Segregating (at least three sentences in a row)
Freight-Train
Balanced
Loose
Periodic
Cumulative (with four or more subordinate phrases/clauses; main clause can come either first or last)
Convoluted
Centered

AND the story must be at least 400 words long and make good sense.

So you can't simply write out the story you remember from your childhood picture books—you're going to have to put some brainpower into this assignment!

there were three billy goats (male goats)
they lived at the bottom of a hill
all three of them had the surname "Gruff"
they wanted to go up the hillside
they needed to eat grass and make themselves fat
there was a bridge on the way up the hill
the bridge went over a creek (also called a "burn")
a troll lived under the bridge
the troll had eyes as big as saucers
the troll had a nose as long as a poker
the first billy goat to cross the bridge was the youngest
his hooves went "trip, trap" on the bridge
the troll roared, "who is on my bridge"
the youngest goat said, "it is the tiniest billy goat Gruff"
the youngest goat said, "I am going up to make myself fat"

the youngest goat said this in a small voice
the troll said, "I am coming to gobble you up"
the youngest goat said, "oh, no, don't eat me"
the youngest goat said, "I am too little"
the youngest goat said, "wait for the second billy goat Gruff"
the youngest goat said, "he is much bigger"
the troll told him to go
a little while passed
the second billy goat started to cross the bridge
his hooves went "trip, trap" on the bridge
the troll roared, "who is on my bridge"
the second billy goat said, "it is the second billy goat Gruff"
the second billy goat said," I am going up to make myself fat"
the second billy goat had a louder voice
the troll said, "I am coming to gobble you up"
the second goat said, "oh, no, don't eat me"
the second goat said, "wait for the big billy goat Gruff"
the second goat said, "he is much bigger"
the troll told him to go
just then the biggest billy goat Cruff arrived
his hooves made the sound TRIP TRAP on the bridge
he was large and heavy
the bridge creaked and groaned
the troll roared, "who is on my bridge"
the biggest billy goat said, "it is the biggest billy goat Gruff"
the biggest goat had an ugly loud hoarse voice
the troll said, "I am coming to gobble you up"
the biggest billy goat said, "come along"
he said, "I have two spears"
he said, "I will poke out your eyeballs"
he said, "I've got two curling-stones"
he said, "I will crush you to bits"
the biggest billy goat charged the troll
he poked out the troll's eyes
he crushed the troll to bits
he tossed the troll into the creek
ho went up the hill

all three billy goats got fat
they were so fat they could hardly walk home again
they are still fat now
the end of the tale

Exercise 130B: Original Composition

Write an original composition of at least 400 words, with at least one of each of the following types of sentences:

Segregating (at least three sentences in a row)
Freight-Train
Balanced
Loose
Periodic
Cumulative (with four or more subordinate phrases/clauses; main clause can come either first or last)
Convoluted
Centered

This composition may be one of the following:

a) A plot summary of one of your favorite books or movies,

b) A narrative of some event, happening, trip, or great memory from your past,

c) A scene from a story that you create yourself, or

d) Any other topic you choose.

WEEK 36

—REVIEW 11—

Final Review

Review 11A: Explaining Sentences

Tell your instructor every possible piece of grammatical information about the following sentences. Follow these steps (notice that these are slightly different than the instructions in your previous "explaining" exercise):

1) Identify the sentence type and write it in the left-hand margin.
2) Underline each subordinate clause. Describe the identity and function of each clause and give any other useful information (introductory word, relationship to the rest of the sentence, etc.)
3) Label each preposition as *P* and each object of the preposition as *OP*. Describe the identity and function of each prepositional phrase.
4) Parse, out loud, all verbs acting as predicates.
5) Describe the identity and function of each individual remaining word. Don't worry about the articles and coordinating conjunctions, though.
6) Provide any other useful information that you might be able to think of.

The feeling which beset the child was one of dim uncertain horror.

—Charles Dickens, *The Old Curiosity Shop*

If there's a buzzing-noise, somebody's making a buzzing-noise, and the only reason for making a buzzing-noise that I know of is because you're a bee.

—A. A. Milne, *Winnie-the-Pooh*

So, first of all, let me assert my firm belief that the only thing we have to fear is fear itself — nameless, unreasoning, unjustified terror which paralyses needed efforts to convert retreat into advance.

—Franklin D. Roosevelt, speech given March 4, 1933

When they first went to live at Three Chimneys, the children had talked a great deal about their Father, and had asked a great many questions about him, and what he was doing and where he was and when he would come home.

—E. Nesbit, *The Railway Children*

He whipped out his lens and a tape measure, and hurried about the room on his knees, measuring, comparing, examining, with his long thin nose only a few inches from the planks, and his beady eyes gleaming and deep-set like those of a bird.

—Arthur Conan Doyle, *The Sign of Four*

Had I known it, I would have had the pleasure of talking to him about you.

—Jane Austen, *Persuasion*

Review 11B: Correcting Errors

Rewrite the following sets of sentences on your own paper (or with a word-processing program), inserting all necessary punctuation and capitalization.

Include the citations in your corrections!

ah of course here is a hole in the roof

away is he said holmes in a disappointed voice i am sorry for that for i wanted to speak to mr smith

—arthur conan doyle the sign of four

tecumseh was killed in battle on the thames river near chatham ontario on october 5 1813

—w c vanderwerth and william r carmack eds indian oratory:
famous speeches by noted indian chiefs

lighting her candle she retreated as silently as she had come and gaining her own room once more sat up during the remainder of that long long miserable night

—charles dickens the old curiosity shop

then he climbed a little further and a little further and then just a little further by that time he had thought of another song

its a very funny thought that if bears were bees

theyd build their nests at the bottom of trees

—a a milne winnie-the-pooh

all of harrys spellbooks his wand robes cauldron and top of the line nimbus two thousand broomstick had been locked in a cupboard under the stairs by uncle vern on the instant harry had come home

—j k rowling harry potter and the chamber of secrets

so they all sat down on a great flat grey stone that had pushed itself up out of the grass it was one of many that lay about on the hillside and when mother came out to look for them at eight oclock she found them deeply asleep in a contented sun warmed bunch

—e nesbit the railway children

gloria emerged sulkily You peeked she exclaimed, with gross unfairness besides im tired of playing hide and seek i want a ride

—isaac asimov i, robot

with the exception perhaps of admiral and mrs croft who seemed particularly attached and happy anne could allow no other exceptions even among the married couples there could have been no two hearts so open no tastes so similar no feelings so in unison no countenanccs so beloved

—jane austen persuasion

Review 11C: Fill in the Blank

Each of the following sentences is missing one of the elements listed. Provide the correct required form of a word that seems appropriate to you. When you are finished, compare your sentences with the originals.

__________ a cloth and __________ up the __________ milk helped Bobbie a __________.
present participle — present participle — past participle — adverb

They __________ climbed on to the __________ of the fence, and __________ __________
indefinite adjective — singular noun — adverb — adverb

there was a __________ sound that made them look __________ the line to the right,
present participle — preposition

__________ the __________ mouth of a tunnel __________ __________ in the
subordinating adverb — adjective — past participle — reflexive pronoun

face of a rocky cliff; __________ moment a train __________ out of the tunnel with a
adjective — perfect past, active, indicative, action verb

__________ and a __________, and __________ __________ past them.
singular noun — singular noun — perfect past, active, indicative, action verb — adverb

—E. Nesbit, *The Railway Children*

__________ __________ clouds played __________ in a blue sky, __________ from time
adjective adjective adverb present participle

to time in front of the sun __________ they had come __________ it __________, and
subordinating compound conjunction present active infinitive adverb

then __________ away __________ so that the next __________ his __________.
present participle adverb simple present active, modal action verb singular noun

—A. A. Milne, *Winnie-the-Pooh*

Anne kept her __________; the __________ kept __________, and __________
singular noun plural indefinite pronoun plural possessive pronoun short parenthetical expression

she heard the next __________ that they __________ a __________ __________.
adverbial noun perfect past, active, indicative action verb adjective noun

If he __________ a __________ __________ by such __________, such
simple past, state-of-being, subjunctive verb adverb predicate adjective adjective

__________ __________, who __________?
adjective noun simple present, active, modal action verb

—Jane Austen, *Persuasion*

__________ me __________, __________ me __________, __________ me the
present active imperative action verb plural noun present active imperative action verb singular noun present active imperative action verb

most __________ __________ or the most __________ __________, and I am
adjective singular noun adjective singular noun

__________.
prepositional phrase acting as a predicate adjective

Then came __________ of __________ villas, each with a fronting of __________
plural noun compound adjective adjective

__________, and then again __________ lines of __________ __________ brick
singular noun adjective adjective present participle

buildings— __________.
appositive, containing adjectival clause, renaming the lines of brick buildings

—Arthur Conan Doyle, *The Sign of Four*

His ________ shows ________ that there is ________ chance of ________ that
single noun adverb adjective of negation present participle acting as a noun

this man ________ ever ________ ________ his practice of ________
simple future, active, indicative action verb adverb present participle acting as a noun

force ________ his will. He ________ only ________ by force.
present active infinitive simple present, passive, modal action verb

—Neville Chamberlain, "This country is now at war with Germany," September 3, 1939 (referring to Hitler and his invasion of Poland two days before)

A cheerful fire ________ on the ________, the ________ burnt ________,
progressive present, active, indicative action verb singular noun singular noun adverb

my ________ ________ me with its ________ ________ ________;
singular noun simple past, active, indicative action verb adjective adjective singular noun

________ was quiet, warm and cheering, and in ________ ________ to
indefinite pronoun adjective singular noun

the gloom and darkness ________________.
adjective clause describing gloom and darkness

—Charles Dickens, *The Old Curiosity Shop*

Review 11D: Diagramming

On your own paper, diagram every word of the following sentences.

It was a September evening, and not yet seven o'clock, but the day had been a dreary one, and a dense drizzly fog lay low upon the great city.

There was, to my mind, something eerie and ghost-like in the endless procession of faces which flitted across these narrow bars of light,—sad faces and glad, haggard and merry.

—Arthur Conan Doyle, *The Sign of Four*

King Henry— God bless him— will have to say, for reasons of state, that he never meant this to happen; and there is going to be an awful row; and at the best we shall have to spend the rest of our lives abroad.

—T. S. Eliot, *Murder in the Cathedral*

In the field of world policy I would dedicate this nation to the policy of the good neighbour—the neighbour who resolutely respects himself and, because he does so, respects the rights of others; the neighbour who respects his obligations and respects the sanctity of his agreements in and with a world of neighbors.

—Franklin D. Roosevelt, "The only thing we have to fear is fear itself," March 4, 1933, Washington, DC, USA

You can imagine what a bitter blow it is to me that all my long struggle to win peace has failed, yet I cannot believe that there is anything more, or anything different, that I could have done and that would have been more successful.

—Neville Chamberlain, "This country is now at war with Germany," September 3, 1939

The berries, when they come, are bright scarlet, but if you pick them, they disappoint you by turning black before you get them home.

At the end of the field, among the thin gold spikes of grass and the harebells and Gipsy roses and St. John's Wort, we may just take one last look, over our shoulders, at the white house where neither we nor anyone else is wanted now.

—E. Nesbit, *The Railway Children*

In the summer I often leave home early in the morning, and roam about fields and lanes all day, or even escape for days or weeks together; but, saving in the country, I seldom go out until after dark, though, Heaven be thanked, I love its light and feel the cheerfulness it sheds upon the earth, as much as any creature living.

—Charles Dickens, *The Old Curiosity Shop*

Note to Student: The word *saving* is an archaic preposition meaning *except for.*

There they returned again into the past, more exquisitely happy, perhaps, in their re-union, than when it had been first projected; more tender, more tried, more fixed in a knowledge of each other's character, truth, and attachment; more equal to act, more justified in acting.

—Jane Austen, *Persuasion*

NOTES

NOTES

NOTES